Pro Telerik ASP.NET and Silverlight Controls

Master Telerik Controls for Advanced ASP.NET and Silverlight Projects

José Rolando Guay Paz

Apress®

Pro Telerik ASP.NET and Silverlight Controls: Master Telerik Controls for Advanced ASP.NET and Silverlight Projects

ISBN-13 (pbk): 978-1-4302-2940-7

ISBN-13 (electronic): 978-1-4302-2941-4

Printed and bound in the United States of America 9 8 7 6 5 4 3 2 1

President and Publisher: Paul Manning
Lead Editor: Mark Beckner
Developmental Editor: Ewan Buckingham
Technical Reviewer: Kevin Babcock
Editorial Board: Clay Andres, Steve Anglin, Mark Beckner, Ewan Buckingham, Gary Cornell, Jonathan Gennick, Jonathan Hassell, Michelle Lowman, Matthew Moodie, Duncan Parkes, Jeffrey Pepper, Frank Pohlmann, Douglas Pundick, Ben Renow-Clarke, Dominic Shakeshaft, Matt Wade, Tom Welsh
Coordinating Editor: Kelly Moritz
Copy Editor: Heather Lang
Compositor: Lynn L'Heureux
Indexer: Brenda Miller
Artist: April Milne
Cover Designer: Anna Ishchenko

Distributed to the book trade worldwide by Springer Science+Business Media, LLC., 233 Spring Street, 6th Floor, New York, NY 10013. Phone 1-800-SPRINGER, fax (201) 348-4505, e-mail orders-ny@springer-sbm.com, or visit www.springeronline.com.

For information on translations, please e-mail rights@apress.com, or visit www.apress.com.

Apress and friends of ED books may be purchased in bulk for academic, corporate, or promotional use. eBook versions and licenses are also available for most titles. For more information, reference our Special Bulk Sales–eBook Licensing web page at www.apress.com/info/bulksales.

The source code for this book is available to readers at www.apress.com. You will need to answer questions pertaining to this book in order to successfully download the code.

To God for all the blessings I've received. Thank you Lord.

To my beautiful wife Karina, my wonderful daughter Sara Nicole and our new baby coming soon. Thank you for being with me all the way with this project. I can't thank you enough. I love you. I promise I'll make up the time I stole from you.

To my mother, Nelly, and father, Rolando, for teaching me all I needed. Dad, I know you are not with us anymore but this book is especially for you. I know you would've loved to see it. Thank you both for everything. I love you and miss you.

To my sister Loly, my brothers Juan and Ramon, my nephews and nieces. I love you and miss you all.

Thank you to my family in law for all your support and encouragement through all these years. Thank you.

Special thanks to Aunt Maritza and to Uncle Marco. This never would have happened without them.

Contents at a Glance

Contents

Foreword

When I started writing software, "user experience" was irrelevant. Functionality was king and it was the user's job to figure out how to get the most from an application. But today, user experience is king!

The quality of an application's user experience can make or break the success of an application, especially on the World Wide Web.

One of the real advantages of developing web applications with ASP.NET Web Forms is the rich third party ecosystem of complementary technology accessible to web developers. Though Microsoft provides a fine set of default controls with ASP.NET and Silverlight, many developers choose to enlist the help of third party controls to design and implement their user interface without have to spend many unnecessary person-hours developing UI widgets or controls that a Control ISV (Independent Software Vender) has already created for them.

Telerik is a key contributor to that third party ecosystem and *Pro Telerik ASP.NET and Silverlight Controls* is a unique offering that will guide to you the modern front of web application user interface development.

José Rolando Guay Paz offers a holistic tutorial on building real applications with ASP.NET and Telerik controls by taking you beyond the basics of control usage and including coverage on Layouts, Charting, Reporting, AJAX, MVC, and even OpenAccess ORM.

Though there are many books on general ASP.NET Developer, Web Forms, Silverlight, ASP.NET MVC, etc., this book is unique in that it teaches ASP.NET development form the perspective of combining Microsoft web development technology with Telerik controls.

The combination makes for a powerful web development toolset.

Joe Stagner
Microsoft

About the Author

Originally from Guatemala, Central America, José has a vast experience in the field of software development. He started working in 1995 while still obtaining his Engineering in Computer Science and Systems degree from the University Of San Carlos Of Guatemala. One of his professors recruited him as a developer for a big coffee company to develop internal applications created in Oracle technology with character based terminals. After little over a year and a half he moved to a multinational company dedicated to water systems where he developed most of the internal systems, still in use today, for accounting, sales, production and others, using what was at the time one of the newest and most promising technologies, Oracle Developer/2000. After almost 3 years in that company he then was hired for a much bigger challenge, a job as an Oracle DBA for one of the biggest Oracle installations of its time, the Guatemalan government agency in charge of tax collection.

Finding that position good, but too sedentary, José changed jobs again and went to a completely different environment working for a company developing web software using Microsoft technologies. Microsoft's tools allowed him to leverage his potential and a new era in his professional career was launched. Among the first in Central America to build commercial applications for the .NET Platform, his journey in the web development arena started by developing software for web banking systems in Guatemala, El Salvador and Honduras along with other types of applications for other industries. Since then he has been heavily involved in different activities such as his participation in the creation of the Guatemala .NET Developer User Group (http://guatecommunity.net) and then the creation of the "Comunidad de Desarrolladores .NET de Cobán" in the north of Guatemala (`http://www.dotnetcoban.org`).

José currently holds a position in INETA Latin America as the Delegate for Carebean and Central America. He was a regular speaker at Microsoft's events in Guatemala until 2009 when a job opportunity with CSW Solutions (http://www.cswsolutions.com) moved him to Chicago, IL where he currently lives with his family. He's a Microsoft Certified Developer and a Microsoft Certified SQL Server Specialist. He has been working with Telerik controls for more than two years now and he has developed a well respected reputation for getting the job done applying the best practices for ASP.NET and Telerik implementations.

About the Technical Reviewer

Kevin Babcock is an avid technologist. For the past 12 years he has built software for several small software companies, worked as a Developer Evangelist at Telerik, and served in the U.S. Air Force as a systems administrator. He currently builds web applications for Major League Baseball teams. Though he's worked in a wide range of IT positions his passion has always been software, and more recently the web. He enjoys being involved in the .NET community and can be found speaking at user groups and code camps, working on the occasional open source project, and even writing on his blog once in a while. Kevin is a graduate of Texas A&M University with a degree in Computer Science, and currently lives in Falls Church, VA with his wife and two sons.

Acknowledgments

A lot of people were involved in the process of making this book, and my countless nights and weekends of work would easily been worthless without the help of such a talented team. No doubt, my first big thank you is to Kevin Babcock who was always pointing me into the right direction, making wonderful suggestions, and tackling the errors in the book; Mark Beckner for supporting my idea of this book from the beginning; Ewan Buckingham for his valuable feedback during all the writing and revision processes; Kelly Moritz for her great patience with my continuous delays; and last but not least Heather Lang for her work with the copy edits. Thank you all.

José Rolando Guay Paz

Introduction

ASP.NET and Silverlight are powerful platforms that allow developers to build rich and sophisticated web systems. One of the most important features is extensibility. While it provides, out of the box, a whole set of controls that enables developers to create web applications, they are very basic controls. This is where Telerik comes in. Telerik is a company that provides a set of controls targeting ASP.NET and Silverlight which empower the developer with the richness of their features, allowing them to take the web applications to the next level.

You will find in this book a clear and complete explanation of the main features of each control in Telerik's RadControls for ASP.NET AJAX and Telerik RadControls for Silverlight suites of controls, along with sample code on implementing them and also integrating with each other. The book covers the whole set of controls for the ASP.NET platform. This includes not only the Webforms platform but also ASP.NET MVC through the use of the Telerik Extensions for ASP.NET MVC. It also covers the Silverlight suite of controls which targets Silverlight 3 and 4.

This book also includes Telerik Reporting to help you build from simple to complex reports; additionaly the book includes a full chapter about Telerik Open Access, the ORM product for all data access.

Why Telerik RadControls?

Over the course of the last few years the complexity of business models have pushed technology to limits so far unknown to many software developers. Companies like Telerik understand that this complexity exists and their products are designed to help these developers in creating software that delivers high performance, are great from the usability point of view and increase the developer's productivity. Telerik is the first company to provide native Silverlight controls which make them the leaders in the area. The controls not only look good but they are very flexible and implement some unique features.

Who is This Book For

This book is aimed at .NET developers working with ASP.NET Webforms and MVC and Silverlight who want to take advantage of the prewritten controls that Telerik provides when developing their software. No prior knowledge of Telerik controls is required, but a working knowledge of ASP.NET Webforms and MVC as well as Silverlight is assumed.

What Do You Need to Use This Book

In order to create web applications using Telerik RadControls (and open the projects included in this book) you need the following tools:

- All the projects use the following tools
    - Visual Studio 2010 (any edition)
    - Microsof SQL Server 2008 (download a trial or free edition at `http://bit.ly/mssqltrials`)
- For the ASP.NET Webforms project
    - Telerik RadControls for ASP.NET AJAX (download a trial at `http://bit.ly/teleriktrialaspnetajax`)
- For the ASP.NET MVC project
    - Telerik Extensions for ASP.NET MVC (download for free at `http://bit.ly/teleriktrialaspnetmvc`)
- For the Silverlight project
    - Microsoft Silverlight 4 Tools for Visual Studio 2010 (free download at `http://bit.ly/Silverlight4ToolsForVS2010`)
    - Telerik RadControls for Silverlight (download a trial at `http://bit.ly/teleriktrialsilverlight`)
- For the Telerik Reporting projects
    - Telerik Reporting (download a trial at `http://bit.ly/teleriktrialreporting`)
- For the Telerik OpenAccess ORM project
    - Telerik OpenAccess ORM (download a trial at `http://bit.ly/teleriktrialopenaccess`)

Let's get started building web applications.

CHAPTER 1

Introducing ASP.NET and Telerik

The Internet can be seen as a huge collection of information and services, but it has evolved in such a magnificent way that now it is virtually impossible to conceive of our lives without it. And present-day requirements for sophisticated applications mean developers need to find the right tools to deliver those applications.

Microsoft understood this need and, despite entering the Internet arena a bit late, did a wonderful job of creating the .NET Framework—a platform that is not only robust enough for the most demanding applications but also is secure, easy to adopt, and highly extensible.

Almost at the same time, Telerik was founded and produced one of the first suites of controls enabling developers to build rich and powerful applications not just for the Web but for the Windows platform too.

This chapter will briefly explain ASP.NET, the part of Microsoft's .NET Framework that allows you to build web applications, as well as some of the features that make the environment great. I will also introduce Telerik and RadControls, its great suite of components for developing Windows and web applications.

ASP.NET

According to Microsoft's documentation at `http://msdn.microsoft.com/en-us/library/4w3ex9c2.aspx`, "ASP.NET is a unified Web development model that includes the services necessary for you to build enterprise-class web applications with a minimum of coding. ASP.NET is part of the .NET Framework, and when coding ASP.NET applications, you have access to classes in the .NET Framework. You can code your applications in any language compatible with the Common Language Runtime (CLR), including Microsoft Visual Basic, C#, JScript .NET, and J#. These languages enable you to develop ASP.NET applications that benefit from the common language runtime, type safety, inheritance, and so on."

ASP.NET includes the following:

- A page and controls framework
- The ASP.NET compiler
- Security infrastructure
- State-management facilities
- Application configuration
- Health monitoring and performance features
- Debugging support

- An XML web services framework
- Extensible hosting environment and application life cycle management
- An extensible designer environment

In ASP.NET, you have a rich and powerful environment in which you can build web applications using your language of choice. And the best part? It's free.

In this framework, you can build applications with a tool as simple as Notepad, but a more sophisticated tool would increase your productivity by doing a lot of work for you—yes, I'm talking about Microsoft Visual Studio. Several versions of Visual Studio are available, and if money is a problem, you can use the free Visual Web Developer Express.

One of the major benefits of ASP.NET was the change to compiled code from interpreted code, which was used for classic ASP (the programming model before ASP.NET), and this change offered web applications better performance. When code in the application is first compiled by the high-level language (C#, VB.NET, etc.) compiler, that compiler generates MSIL code (MSIL is an assembly language supercharged with lots of vitamins and minerals), and later, the MSIL code generates native machine code by the just-in-time compiler.

Web applications created with ASP.NET technology are hosted and executed by the .NET Framework, not the operating system. This allows applications to have access to all the .NET Framework libraries, and most importantly, ASP.NET applications are type safe, take advantage of automatic memory garbage collection, have structured error handling and multithreading support, and contain information about classes and members. In general, all ASP.NET code is stored as metadata in the assemblies generated at compile time, so obviously, deployment of web applications is fairly simple. Since the .NET Framework is already installed on the server, all you need to do is copy the files to the server to make the application work. Of course, we still need to set up Internet Information Services (IIS), but typically, an administrator will likely handle that trivial task.

It is important to note that ASP.NET is fully object oriented (OO), meaning that not only the code we write but also the code supporting ASP.NET is OO. Your code will have full access to all objects in the .NET Framework, and you can implement all the goodies of an OO environment (inheritance, polymorphism, and encapsulation).

ASP.NET also takes care of the problem of multibrowser and multidevice support by providing a set of rich web server controls that render the appropriate markup for any supported type of device and browser.

ASP.NET and the .NET Framework have come a long way since their first releases. Each release has added more and more functionality on top of previous versions, and the latest release, version 4.0, is no exception.

Now, there are three technologies related to web applications in ASP.NET:

- ASP.NET web forms
- ASP.NET Model View Controller (MVC)
- Silverlight

ASP.NET Web Forms

In general, ASP.NET pages are better known as *web forms*. This is the original programming model that was released when the .NET Framework was first introduced in 2002.

Web forms allow you to create web applications in the same way you would create a WinForms application. This means that you have a control-based interface and a split view of a page; on one view there is markup where you design how your page will look and which controls it will use (this is a file with extension ASPX), and the other view is the code that handles events and interactions of all the objects in the page; this could be on the same ASPX page or in a separate file called code-behind file, which has an extension associated with the programming language, it could be CS for C# or VB for VB.NET.

Whenever ASP.NET processes a page it passes through several stages and different events are raised to handle the processing of the page and its controls. You write code to handle these events and thus respond to various actions related to the processing of a page. For example, you might wish to write code that gets called when a page is first loaded to determine if the user is requesting the page or posting back to the server. When a page is first requested, you often have to initialize data and controls. However, when it posts back, you don't need to run this code.

A *postback* happens when a control on the page raises an event that must be handled by the server. It is very important to understand the page events and how they are processed to effectively work with web forms. Table 1-1 lists the page events and the effect they have on the page and its controls.

Table 1-1. *Page Life Cycle Events (from the MCTS Self-Paced Training Kit (Exam 70-562): Microsoft® .NET Framework 3.5 ASP.NET Application Development. – Chapter 2, Page 47)*

Event	Description
`PreInit`	This is the first real event you might handle for a page. You typically use this event only if you need to dynamically (from code) set values such as master page or theme. This event is also useful when you are working with dynamically created controls for a page. You want to create the controls inside this event.
`Init`	This event fires after each control has been initialized. You can use this event to change initialization values for controls.
`InitComplete`	It is raised once all initializations of the page and its controls have been completed.
`PreLoad`	This event fires before view state has been loaded for the page and its controls and before PostBack processing. This event is useful when you need to write code after the page is initialized but before the view state has been wired back up to the controls.
`Load`	The page is stable at this time; it has been initialized and its state has been reconstructed. Code inside the page load event typically checks for PostBack and then sets control properties appropriately. The page's load event is called first. Then, the load event for each child control is called in turn (and their child controls, if any). This is important to know if you are writing your own user or custom controls.
`Control` (`PostBack`) event(s)	ASP.NET now calls any events on the page or its controls that caused the PostBack to occur. This might be a button's click event, for example.
`LoadComplete`	At this point all controls are loaded. If you need to do additional processing at this time you can do so here.
`PreRender`	Allows final changes to the page or its control. This event takes place after all regular PostBack events have taken place. This event takes place before saving ViewState, so any changes made here are saved.

Table 1-1. *Continued*

`SaveStateComplete`	Prior to this event the view state for the page and its controls is set. Any changes to the page's controls at this point or beyond are ignored. This is useful if you need to write processing that requires the view state to be set.
`Render`	This is a method of the page object and its controls (and not an event). At this point, ASP.NET calls this method on each of the page's controls to get its output. The Render method generates the client-side HTML, Dynamic Hypertext Markup Language (DHTML), and script that are necessary to properly display a control at the browser. This method is useful if you are writing your own custom control. You override this method to control output for the control.
`UnLoad`	This event is used for cleanup code. You use it to release any managed resources in this stage. Managed resources are resources that are handled by the runtime, such as instances of classes created by the .NET common language runtime.

The view state is the information about the page controls status. After each postback, the page view state is modified with the new statuses of all the controls in the page. As a default, the view state is stored in a hidden field inside each page, and its scope and lifetime are limited to the page it belongs to (see Figure 1-1).

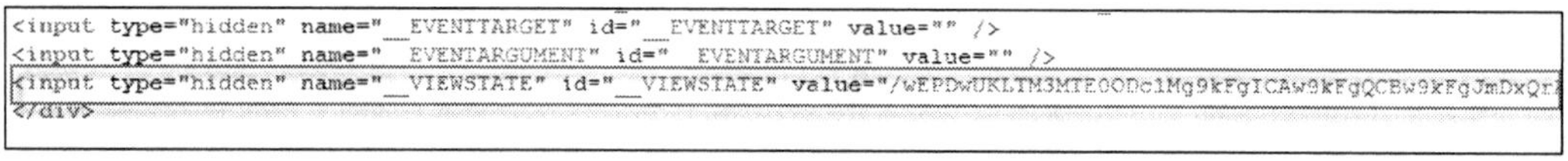

```
<input type="hidden" name="__EVENTTARGET" id="__EVENTTARGET" value="" />
<input type="hidden" name="__EVENTARGUMENT" id="__EVENTARGUMENT" value="" />
<input type="hidden" name="__VIEWSTATE" id="__VIEWSTATE" value="/wEPDwUKLTM3MTE0ODc1Mg9kFgICAw9kFgQCBw9kFgJmDxQr
</div>
```

Figure 1-1. *The view state's hidden field*

An ASP.NET web application contains several types of files, and each type serves a specific purpose within the application. See Table 1-2 for a list of the most important files in an application.

Table 1-2. *ASP.NET File Types*

File Type	Description
`.aspx` file	This ASP.NET web forms file contains the markup (or user interface code) of the file and optionally the underlying application code.
`.cs` or `.vb` files	These are the code-behind files. If the page has indicated so, the underlying application code will be created here. This is the default setting.
`web.config`	This is the application's general configuration file. It is an XML-based file that contains all settings for customizing the connection strings, application settings, security, external assemblies, memory, state management, and so on.
`global.ascx`	In this file, you can add code for event handlers at the application level. Events are those for when the application starts or ends or when an error is thrown.

Table 1-2. *Continued*

`.ascx` files	These are user control files. In these files, you can create small pieces of functionality the same way as with a full ASPX page, but the difference is that they can not be accessed directly and must be hosted inside ASPX pages. You can reuse these user controls in any page of your application.
`.asmx` or `.svc` files	ASMX files are ASP.NET web services. These files provide services for pages in your application or any other program that can access them. ASMX web services are being slowly replaced by Windows Communication Foundation (WCF) services, which have the extension .svc and offer improved security and scalability features.
`.master` files	Master pages are like ASPX pages with the difference that they are used as templates for other pages, sharing the look and feel and base functionality. Master pages inside other master pages are called *nested master pages.*

We can create two types of web applications in Visual Studio: ASP.NET web applications and ASP.NET web sites. While you can work with either one, in this book, we'll primarily be creating web applications for the benefits they provide, such as compilation to one DLL file, memory and performance profiling capabilities, smooth integration with other projects, and so forth. See Figures 1-2 and 1-3.

Another important choice to make is the type of controls you'll have in our application. You can choose HTML or Web server controls or both. Consider using HTML server controls when any of the following conditions exist:

- You are migrating existing, classic ASP pages over to ASP.NET.
- The control needs to have custom client-side JavaScript attached to the control's events.
- The web page has lots of client-side JavaScript that is referencing the control.

In nearly all other cases, you should consider using the more powerful web server controls.

Web server controls follow a programming model and naming standard that's similar to Windows forms. In addition, they do not map to a single HTML tag. Instead, they can generate multiple lines (or tags) of HTML and JavaScript as their rendered output. These controls also have other benefits, such as multibrowser rendering support, a powerful programming model, layout control, and theme support.

■ **Note** For more information about the differences between HTML server controls and web server controls, visit `http://msdn.microsoft.com/en-us/zsyt68f1.aspx`.

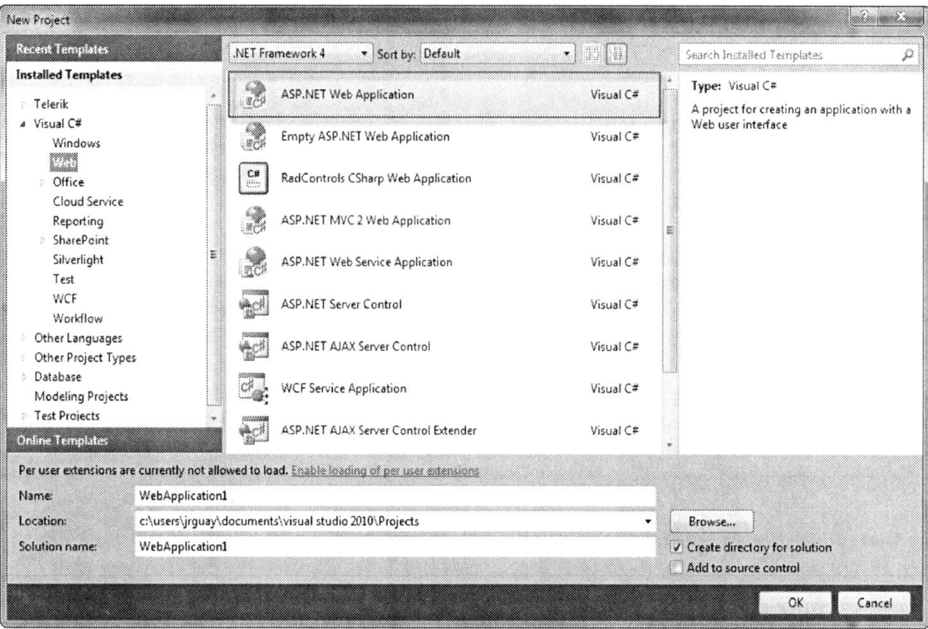

Figure 1-2. *A new Visual Studio 2010 ASP.NET web application project*

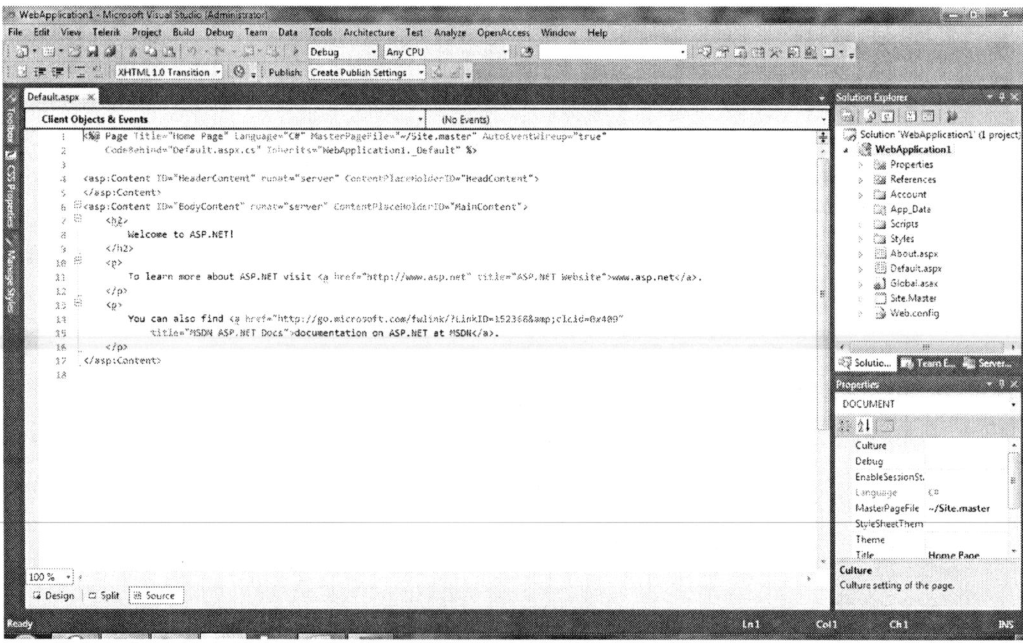

Figure 1-3. *A new ASP.NET web application's file structure*

The default template for a new web application offers a ready-to-use web site with a master page and includes integrated security through the use of the ASP.NET Membership System and jQuery (a JavaScript library for client-side support).

Note For more information about jQuery, visit `http://jquery.com`.

Once the web application is constructed, you simply deploy it to the final location where it will serve its users. Visual Studio provides an easy way to do this; you just right-click the project name and select the Publish option. The window shown in Figure 1-4 will open and offer different choices for the configuration, method of deployment, location of the service, and security credentials.

For an improved deployment experience, the Publish option allows you to create different deployment profiles, so you can have different configurations for various environments (staging, production, quality, etc.).

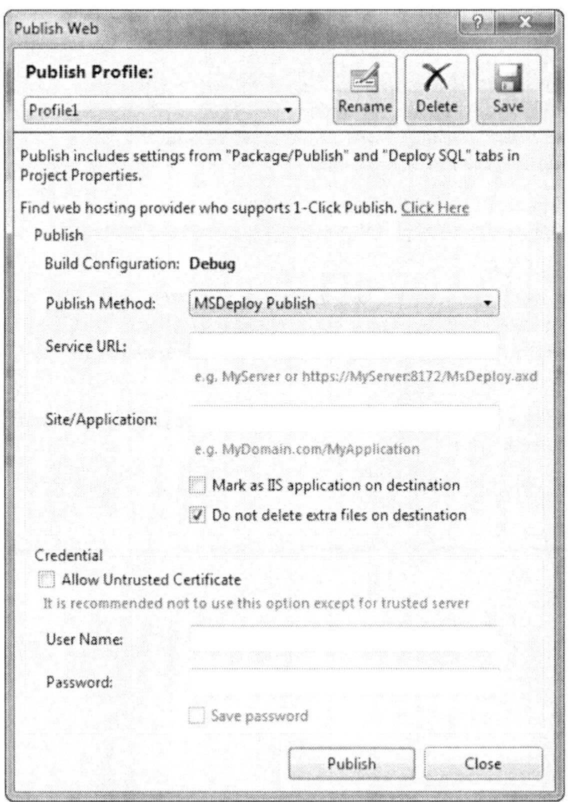

Figure 1-4. *The Publish Web window*

ASP.NET MVC

ASP.NET MVC is a free and fully supported Microsoft framework for building web applications that use a Model View Controller (MVC) pattern. Like ASP.NET web forms, ASP.NET MVC is built on the ASP.NET Framework.

ASP.NET MVC provides the following benefits:

- Complete control over your HTML markup
- Rich AJAX integration
- Intuitive web site URLs
- Clear separation of concerns, which results in web applications that are easier to maintain and extend over time
- Testability, including support for test-driven development

In the ASP.NET MVC world, many improvements to ASP.NET have been taken care of by default. The main purpose of this design pattern is to isolate business logic from the user interface to focus on better maintainability and testability and a cleaner structure to the application.

Each part of the MVC pattern plays an important role that needs to be understood prior to start programming:

- The model in the MVC pattern represents the parts of the application that implement the data domain logic. The operation of the model might come from the generation of classes representing objects in a data store such as a database like Entity Framework and NHibernate are examples of technologies used to create the model.
- Views are the visible elements in the application. By "visible," I mean they are the components that typically show users data from the model. Depending on user selections, the view can be editable or not.
- The controllers are components that collect the user actions, work with the model, and ultimately select a view to render the appropriate user interface (UI). Unlike in other models, in MVC applications, a view only displays information; the controller responds to user input and interaction.

Figure 1-5 illustrates a simple implementation of the MVC pattern. The straight lines indicate direct associations, and the curved ones show indirect associations.

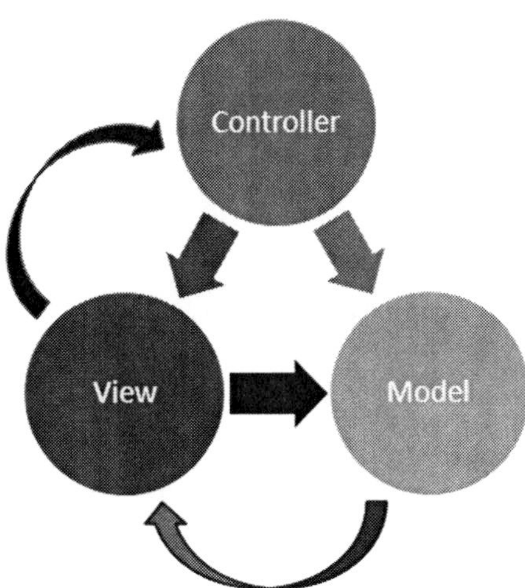

Figure 1-5. *MVC implementation*

In a standard ASP.NET web site, URLs typically map to physical files on the server (most of the time, these are ASPX files). The files contain the markup and code that will be executed to produce the resulting HTML for rendering to the user's browser at each request.

This is not the case in ASP.NET MVC, where URLs map to specific actions within the controllers. As the controllers handle requests made by users, they execute the appropriate application and data logic then calling a view to display the appropriate HTML response.

The ASP.NET MVC framework uses the powerful ASP.NET routing engine, which provides flexible mappings of URLs to controllers. The routing engine is also capable of parsing variables defined in the URL and can pass these variables to the controller as parameter arguments. You define the rules by which the routing engine works at design time.

■ **Note** For more information about ASP.NET routing, visit `http://msdn.microsoft.com/en-us/library/cc668201(VS.100).aspx`.

The ASP.NET MVC framework does not use the web forms postback model for interactions with the server. All user interactions are routed to a controller. As a result, the page life cycle events and view state are not integrated with MVC-based views. This separation allows for greater testability of the business logic in the controllers and data domain processing in the model.

Figure 1-6 shows the New Project creation window in Visual Studio, with a new ASP.NET MVC 2 Web Application selected. Figure 1-7 shows the Create Unit Test Project window, the second in the process of creating an MVC application. By default, the Visual Studio Unit Test Framework is selected, but you can use any framework you want, including NUnit, MBUnit, and XUnit. Figure 1-8 shows the resulting file structure for the newly created ASP.NET MVC 2 application.

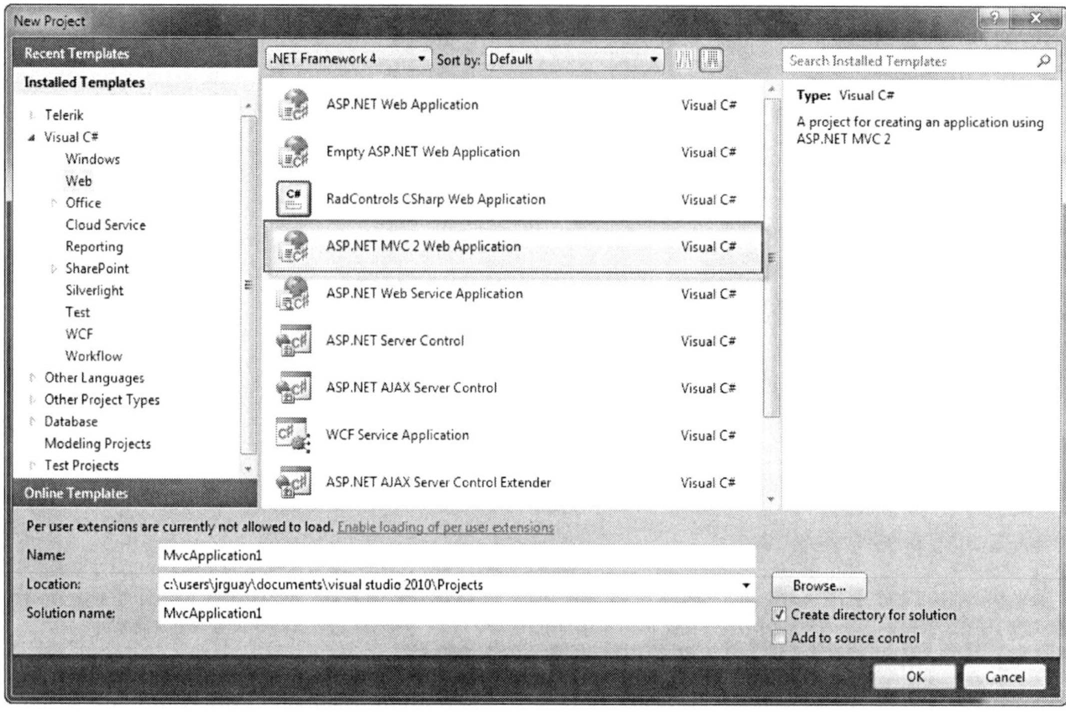

Figure 1-6. *Beginning to create a new Visual Studio 2010 ASP.NET MVC 2 project*

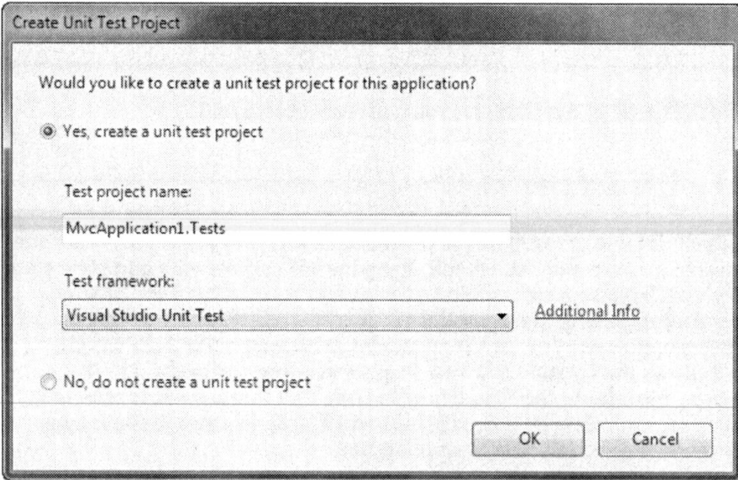

Figure 1-7. *Selecting to create a unit test project and the test framework*

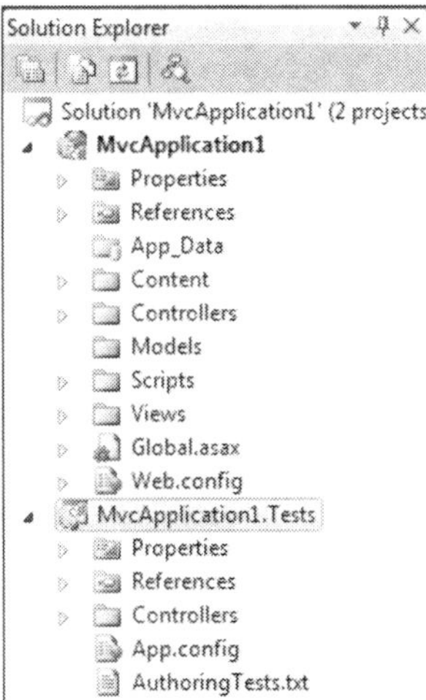

Figure 1-8. *Visual Studio 2010's default ASP.NET MVC 2 project template in Solution Explorer*

The execution of an ASP.NET MVC application is, as you would expect, different from web forms. Table 1-3 lists the stages of execution of an ASP.NET MVC application.

1. Receive first request for the application: In the `Global.asax` file, `Route` objects are added to the `RouteTable` object.
2. Perform routing: The `UrlRoutingModule` module uses the first matching `Route` object in the `RouteTable` collection to create the `RouteData` object, which it then uses to create a `RequestContext` object.
3. Create MVC request handler: The `MvcRouteHandler` object creates an instance of the `MvcHandler` class and passes the `RequestContext` instance to the handler.
4. Create controller: The `MvcHandler` object uses the `RequestContext` instance to identify the `IControllerFactory` object (typically an instance of the `DefaultControllerFactory` class) to create the controller instance with.
5. Execute controller: The `MvcHandler` instance calls the controller's controller's `Execute` method.
6. Invoke action: For controllers that inherit from the `ControllerBase` class, the `ControllerActionInvoker` object that is associated with the controller determines which action method of the controller class to call and then calls that method.
7. Execute result: The action method receives user input, prepares the appropriate response data, and then executes the result by returning a result type. The built-in result types that can be executed include the following: `ViewResult` (which renders a view and is the most-often used result type), `RedirectToRouteResult`, `RedirectResult`, `ContentResult`, `JsonResult`, `FileResult`, and `EmptyResult`.

The ASP.NET MVC framework provides the following features:

- It provides separation of application tasks (input logic, business logic, and UI logic), testability, and test-driven development (TDD). All core contracts in the MVC framework are interface-based and can be tested by using mock objects, which are simulated objects that imitate the behavior of actual objects in the application. You can unit test the application without having to run the controllers in an ASP.NET process, which makes unit testing fast and flexible. You can use any unit testing framework that is compatible with the .NET Framework.
- It's an extensible and pluggable framework. The components of the ASP.NET MVC framework are designed so that they can be easily replaced or customized. You can plug in your own view engine, URL routing policy, action-method parameter serialization, and other components. The ASP.NET MVC framework also supports the use of dependency injection (DI) and inversion of control (IOC) container models. DI enables you to inject objects into a class, instead of relying on the class to create the object itself. IOC specifies that if an object requires another object, the first objects should get the second object from an outside source such as a configuration file. These features makes testing easier.
- Extensive support is included for ASP.NET routing, which is a powerful URL-mapping component that lets you build applications that have comprehensible and searchable URLs. URLs do not have to include file-name extensions and are designed to support URL naming patterns that work well for search engine optimization (SEO) and representational state transfer (REST) addressing.
- There's support for using the markup in existing ASP.NET pages (`.aspx` files), user control pages (`.ascx` files), and master page (`.master` files) markup files as view templates. You can use existing ASP.NET features with the ASP.NET MVC framework, such as nested master pages, in-line expressions, declarative server controls, templates, data-binding, localization, and so on.
- Existing ASP.NET features are supported. ASP.NET MVC lets you use features such as forms and Windows authentication, URL authorization, membership and roles, output and data caching, session and profile state management, health monitoring, the configuration system, and the provider architecture.

The ASP.NET MVC framework offers the following advantages:

- It makes managing complexity easier by dividing an application into the model, view, and controller.
- It does not use view state or server-based forms. This makes the MVC framework ideal for developers who want full control over the behavior of an application.
- It uses a Front Controller pattern that processes web application requests through a single controller. This enables you to design an application that supports a rich routing infrastructure.
- It provides better support for TDD.
- It works well for web applications that are supported by large teams of developers and for web designers who need a high degree of control over the application behavior.

■ **Note** For more information about ASP.NET MVC, visit `http://www.asp.net/mvc/` and `http://msdn.microsoft.com/en-us/library/dd394709(VS.100).aspx`.

Telerik's RadControls Suite of Components

Telerik was founded in 2002; its headquarters are located in Sofia, Bulgaria, with other offices in Germany and the United States.

According to the Telerik web site, the company "is a leading vendor of User Interface (UI) components for Microsoft .NET technologies (ASP.NET AJAX, ASP.NET MVC, WinForms, Windows Presentation Foundation, and Silverlight), as well as tools for .NET Reporting, ORM, TFS, and web content management."

Telerik offers a full set of controls and tools targeting a specific need:

- *RadControls for ASP.NET AJAX*: The set of controls designed for the web forms platform
- *RadControls for WinForms*: Designed for the Windows platform
- *RadControls for Silverlight*: Designed specifically designed for Silverlight (including Silverlight 4).
- *RadControls for WPF*: Offers the controls for programming in the Windows Presentation Foundation (WPF) platform
- *Extensions for ASP.NET MVC*: Provides helper extensions for creating sophisticated controls in the ASP.NET MVC platform

Despite being a relative newcomer, Telerik is one of the top software vendors for UI components in the world and offers high-quality products and support. The community web site offers numerous tools to get your job done, including community-driven forums, blogs from Telerik engineers, and code samples. Because Telerik believes developers are the heart of its business, it offers them the following key features:

- All purchased licenses of RadControls for ASP.NET AJAX and Telerik Extensions for ASP.NET MVC come with full source code, updates for up to one year, unlilmited deployments and full distribution rights
- Licenses can be purchased with standard support (responses within 48 hours) and priority support (within 24 hours).
- Platform-specific components for ASP.NET AJAX, Silverlight, Windows Forms, and WPF. Other products include Telerik OpenAccess ORM, Telerik Reporting, and WebUI Test Studio. The Telerik Premium Collection for .NET package includes all components.
- Telerik also offers free tools including WebAii Testing Framework, Telerik Extensions for ASP.NET MVC, Team Foundation Server (TFS) Tools, RadEditor Lite and RadFormDecorator for ASP.NET AJAX, and Telerik OpenAccess ORM Express.
- Access to special web sites, like Telerik Labs, Code Library, and Code Converter, is available to allow you to download test and beta content.
- And if you are all about helping your peers, the Telerik MVP Program recognizes those who put extra effort into helping other developers in the community forums, writing code samples, and other activities.

■ **Note** For more information about Telerik visit `http://www.telerik.com/`, `http://www.telerik.com/community.aspx`, and `http://www.telerik.com/company.aspx`.

Summary

ASP.NET is the platform for building web applications for Microsoft's .NET Framework, and it supports both ASP.NET web forms and ASP.NET MVC. A web form contains a well-defined object model for building web applications that include a control-based interface, a postback model, view states, and event-driven objects. ASP.NET MVC is the implementation of the Model View Controller pattern for the .NET Framework in web applications. It allows you to fully control the generated markup and separation of concerns, which yields superior testability, a powerful routing engine, and integration with existing ASP.NET features such as user controls and master pages.

Telerik is one of the top software vendors of UI components for ASP.NET for both web forms and MVC. It offers a complete set of controls for all platforms and a full support package developers. The set of controls contains RadControls for ASP.NET AJAX, Extensions for ASP.NET MVC, RadControls for Silverlight, RadControls for WinForms, and RadControls for WPF. Other tools are Telerik Reporting, OpenAccess ORM, and WebAii Testing Framework.

CHAPTER 2

■ ■ ■

Getting Started With Telerik RadControls

One of the most important tasks you have to take care of while working with Telerik RadControls is the actual setup and configuration of the development machine. Fortunately, with every new release of the RadControls, this task has become less and less cumbersome.

Installing the controls is a very simple procedure, and with the help of the new Visual Studio Extensions add-in (included in the installation of RadControls for ASP.NET AJAX), setting up an application has become also a trivial one.

In this chapter, I will show you how to set up the development machine by installing all the tools we'll use throughout this book, specifically Telerik RadControls for ASP.NET AJAX and Silverlight, the WebAii Testing Framework, Telerik Extensions for ASP.NET MVC, Telerik Reporting, and Telerik OpenAccess ORM.

Once installation is complete, I will show you how to set up your application, so you can use the controls and the testing framework, reporting and ORM tools.

Installing the Controls and Tools

The installation of Telerik's RadControls and tools in a development machine is a click-next process in which the installer does all the work. The steps to installation and configuration are as follows:

1. Verify your development machine meets the system requirements.
2. Log in to your account on Telerik's web site (`www.telerik.com`).
3. Go to the Downloads section, and download the installers.
4. Execute the installer, and follow the instructions on screen.

The first step is to check the system requirements for your development machine. You will need the following:

- Any of the following operating system and Internet Information Services (IIS):

  Microsoft Windows 2000 Server or Pro with IIS 5.x

  Microsoft Windows XP Pro or Home with IIS 5.x

  Microsoft Windows Server 2003 with IIS 5.x

  Microsoft Windows Vista or Windows 7 with IIS 7.x

  Microsoft Windows Server 2008 with IIS 7.x

- Microsoft .NET Framework 2.0, 3.5, or 4.0
- SUSE Linux Enterprise and Mono 2.4+
- Microsoft ASP.NET MVC Framework (only if you are running Telerik Extensions for ASP.NET MVC)
- Any of the following development environments:
    - Microsoft Visual Studio 2005, 2008, or 2010
    - Microsoft Visual Web Developer Express 2005, 2008, or 2010
    - Microsoft FrontPage
    - Borland Delphi 2005
    - Microsoft Office SharePoint Server (MOSS)
    - DotNetNuke
- Any of the browsers listed in Table 2-1.

Table 2-1. *Browser Support Matrix*

Browser	Windows	Mac OS	Linux
Internet Explorer	6.0+	--	--
Firefox	1.5+	1.5+	1.5+
Google Chrome	0.2+	--	--
Opera	9.0+	9.0+	--
Safari	3.0+	3.0+	--
Netscape	9.0+	9.0+	9.0+

Note Browsers in beta stages are not supported. Internet Explorer for Mac is not supported anymore either because of Microsoft's decision to stop its development.

Downloading the Installers

Next, you have to log in to your account in the Telerik's web site. Figure 2-1 shows Telerik's home page; the Login button in the top-right corner will take you to the login page where you can to identify yourself.

Figure 2-1. *Telerik's home page with the Login button in the top-right corner*

Once in your account page, click the Downloads link to go the page where you can download all the installers for the licensed software you have purchased (see Figure 2-2). Telerik normally releases three major upgrades each year and names the files and product versions with the quarter and year of the release. For example, the version of the release for the first quarter of 2010 is named Q1 2010.

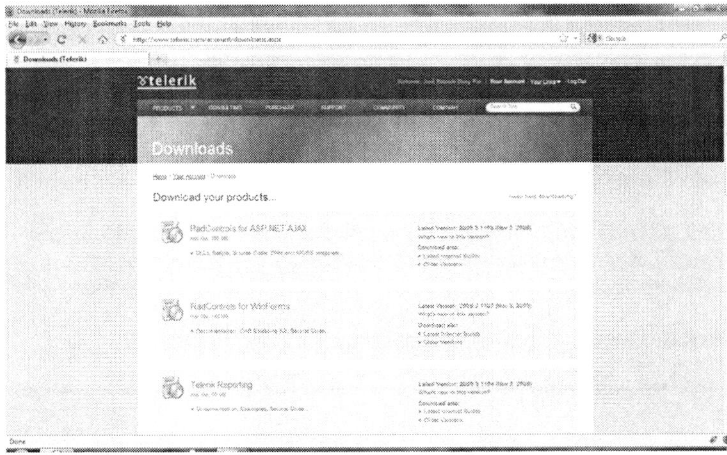

Figure 2-2. *The Downloads page*

The installers you can download will vary depending on the product version and whether you purchased a single product or a subscription. Figure 2-3 shows the installers from the Telerik Premium Collection for the Q1 2010 release. We will not be using all of the installers in this book, only those for Telerik RadControls for ASP.NET AJAX, RadControls for Silverlight, Telerik Reporting, OpenAccess ORM, and Extensions for ASP.NET MVC.

Name	Date modified	Type	Size
JustCodeBeta_2010.1.212_Dev.msi	2/14/2010 11:37 PM	Windows Installer ...	8,528 KB
RadControls_for_ASP.NET_AJAX_2009_3_1314_dev.msi	1/27/2010 8:49 PM	Windows Installer ...	169,023 KB
RadControls_for_Silverlight_2009_3_1314_DEV.msi	1/27/2010 8:54 PM	Windows Installer ...	169,312 KB
RadControls_for_WPF_2009_3_1314_DEV.msi	2/14/2010 11:15 PM	Windows Installer ...	135,812 KB
RadControls_WinForms_2009_3_1203_dev.exe	2/14/2010 11:09 PM	Application	153,449 KB
Telerik_Extensions_for_ASPNET_MVC_2009_3_1320_dev.zip	1/27/2010 8:51 PM	WinRAR ZIP archive	8,833 KB
Telerik_OpenAccess_ORM_2009_3_1119_dev.zip	2/14/2010 11:35 PM	WinRAR ZIP archive	83,160 KB
Telerik_Reporting_2009_3_1211_dev.msi	2/14/2010 11:21 PM	Windows Installer ...	53,247 KB
WebAii_Testing_Framework_for_RadControls_2009_3_1314.msi	1/27/2010 9:12 PM	Windows Installer ...	22,743 KB

Figure 2-3. *Installers*

Installing the Suites

Installing Telerik RadControls for ASP.NET AJAX, RadControls for Silverlight, and WebAii Testing Framework is a very simple process. Executing the installer for the RadControls for ASP.NET AJAX suite will bring up the welcome screen shown in **Figure 2-4.** The rest of the procedure is simple:

1. On the welcome screen, click Next to start the installation.
2. Accept the license agreement by clicking in the appropriate box, and then click Next.
3. Select if you want a complete or customized installation. Click Next.
4. If you selected a customized installation, choose what you want to install (see Figure 2-5). Click Next.
5. Verify the choices you selected in the summary, and if everything is fine, click Next.

The installation of Telerik RadControls for ASP.NET AJAX will automatically install Telerik Visual Studio Extensions (VSX), which is an add-in for Visual Studio. This add-in provides functionality for configuring your web applications and allows you to create new pages based on templates that include Telerik controls.

The installation procedure for RadControls for Silverlight is exactly the same as the RadControls for ASP.NET AJAX. When installing Telerik Reporting, if you selected to install the examples, an additional step allows you to enter the login information for a SQL Server database to set up the sample reports.

Telerik OpenAccess ORM installation follows a similar pattern than Telerik Reporting.

Figure 2-4. *Welcome screen*

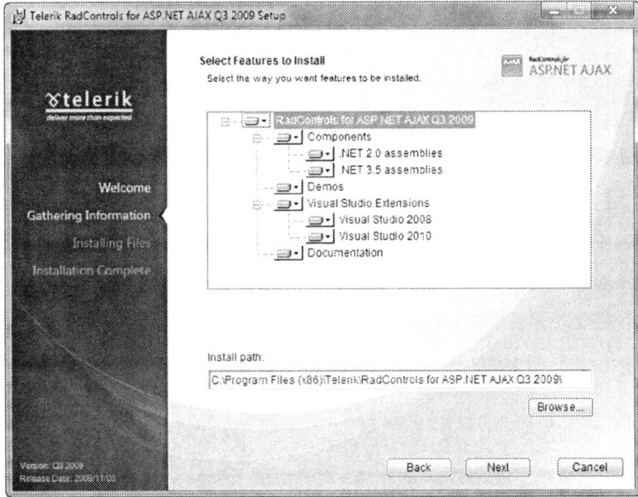

Figure 2-5. *Selecting custom features to install*

Note When installing the .NET 2.0 assemblies (for projects in .NET 2.0 or 3.0), you need to first install ASP.NET AJAX Extensions 1.0. If you are using Visual Studio 2008, you won't see any Telerik tools in the toolbox; because the installer doesn't register them automatically, you will have to do it manually. For more details, you can read the article at `http://www.telerik.com/help/aspnet-ajax/using-radcontrols-net20-30-35-projects-vs2008.html`.

Once the components and selected features are installed, the option to install the Telerik WebAii Testing Framework pops up. You can launch the installer from this screen or download a separate installer to install it at later time. To run the installer from this screen, click the Install Now button. Because the installation procedure for this framework and the rest of the tools in this chapter is nearly same as the one you just finished, I'm not going to repeat it again completely. I'll just point out the differences in the various tools as we go.

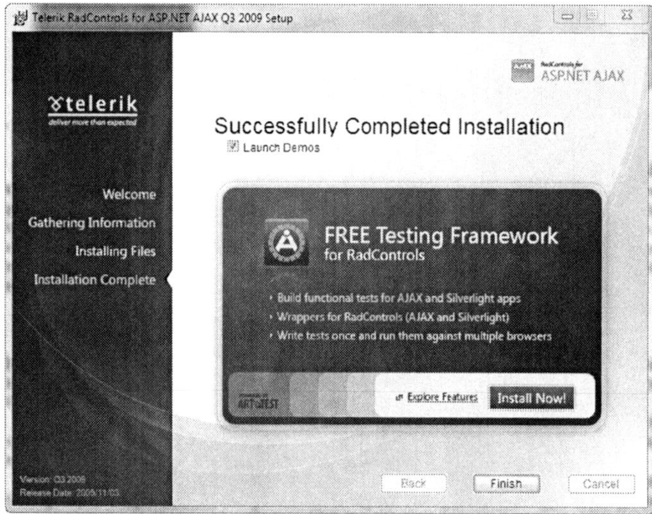

Figure 2-6. *Once the controls and features are installed, you have the option to install the WebAii Testing Framework.*

■ **Note** If you installed the testing framework right after the installation of RadControls for ASP.NET AJAX, you do not need to install it again after the Silverlight controls are installed.

Installing Telerik Extensions for ASP.NET MVC

The installation of Telerik Extensions for ASP.NET MVC, starting with the Q1 2010 release, is the same as the one for RadControls for ASP.NET AJAX. After the installation process is finished, you will have a structure composed of the following folders (see Figure 2-7):

- `Binaries`: Contains the assemblies
- `Content`: Contains the themes, which are Cascading Style Sheets (CSS) files and images
- `Examples`: Contains the sample applications
- `Help`: Contains this manual in compiled HTML format (`.chm` files)
- `Scripts`: Contains the JavaScript files required by the components
- `Source`: Contains the full source code of Telerik Extensions for ASP.NET MVC

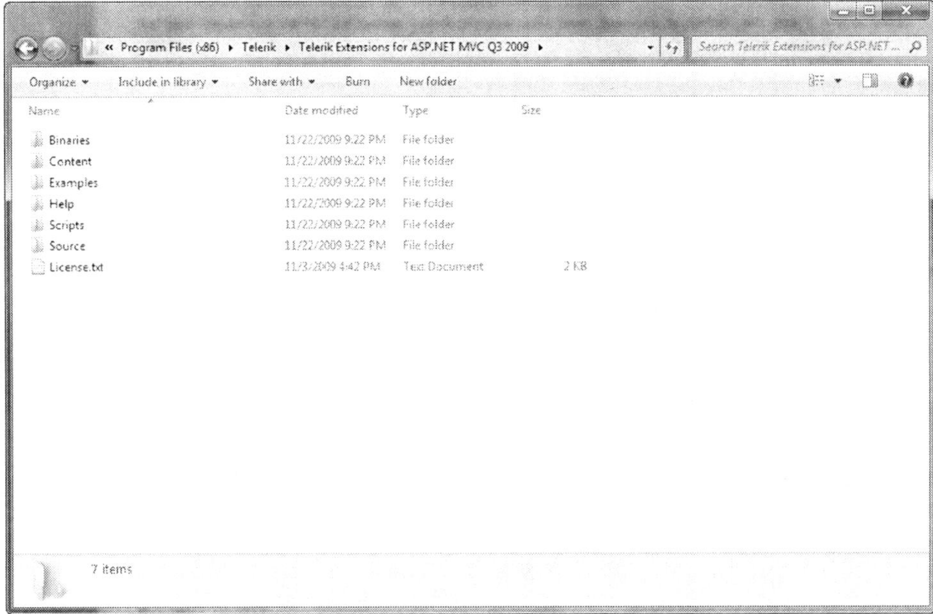

Figure 2-7. *Files and folders for Telerik ASP.NET MVC Extensions*

Installing and Updating Controls Manually

You can install or update your controls and tools manually. For this, you need either a zip file with the installation files or the package file with all the DLLs and script files.

To manually install controls, extract the assembly files from the `Binaries` folder in the zip file, and add the ones you need to your projects. The process is outlined as follows:

1. If the upgrade is major (e.g., from version Q3 2009 to Q1 2010), please review the Changes and Backward Compatibility section of Telerik's web site for breaking changes and specific version instructions.
2. Back up your application. This step is *very important*!
3. Close Visual Studio or the development environment you use, which may lock the old assembly.
4. From the newly downloaded and unzipped files, copy the new DLL (located in the `bin` folder) to your web application's `bin` folder, replacing the old DLL.
5. If you are using Visual Studio, update the control's reference in your project to point to the new DLL.
6. Recompile your project.
7. If you have added the control in the Global Assembly Cache (GAC), run a `gacUtil` command to remove the old copy, and then add the new one.
8. Run the project.

Sometimes, you might run into problems with the update. One common issue is to get the old version of Telerik RadControls for ASP.NET AJAX even after you update. Sometimes, the .NET Framework wrongly caches the Telerik RadControls for ASP.NET AJAX framework's DLL, so the update may seem to have failed. Try the following to ensure that this is not the case:

1. Shut down IIS, or terminate the `aspnet_wp.exe` process from the Windows Task Manager.
2. Open a Windows Explorer window, and navigate to `C:\Windows(WINNT)\Microsoft.NET\Framework\v[YOUR_VERSION]\Temporary ASP.NET Files`.
3. Delete all folders with names corresponding to your Telerik projects, for example, `RadControls for ASP.NET AJAX`.
4. Delete any Visual Studio web project caches, which should be located in `C:\Documents and Settings\[YOUR USER]\VSWebCache`.
5. Delete your browser cache by selecting Tools ➤ Internet Options ➤ Delete Files.

The other most common issue is to get a message stating that the product is still a trial product. If you have purchased the control, you may still have installed the trial version. Make sure you have downloaded and installed the proper version of the products. You will recognize the installer file by the `Dev` abbreviation in the file name.

Setting Up Your Application to Use Telerik RadControls

You can set up your web applications to use Telerik RadControls in several ways. Which option you choose will depend mostly on whether or not your application is new. If the application is new, you can create it using a predefined Visual Studio template for a Telerik RadControls Web Application (using C# or VB.NET), or you can create a new ASP.NET web application and configure it to use Telerik RadControls.

If your application already exists, you only need to enable it to use Telerik RadControls. To enable the web application's use of RadControls, you must configure several files manually or using Telerik Visual Studio Extensions add-in. I strongly encourage you to use Telerik Visual Studio Extensions, since the add-in takes care of all the tasks you need on your web application, including the following:

- Create a new Telerik web project.
- Upgrade a web project to a new version of Telerik RadControls.
- Modify the configuration of an existing Telerik web project.
- Add new web forms based on Telerik RadControls templates, such as RadGrid or RadScheduler.

Figure 2-8 shows how to launch Telerik Visual Studio Extensions. Visual Studio Extensions enhances your productivity with ready-to-use templates and configuration tools. These templates are also available by selecting File ➤ New Project(see Figure 2-9).

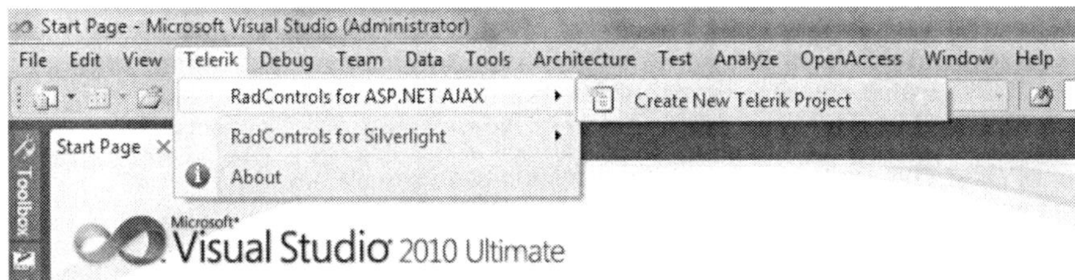

Figure 2-8. *Launching the Create New Telerik Project from Telerik Visual Studio Extensions*

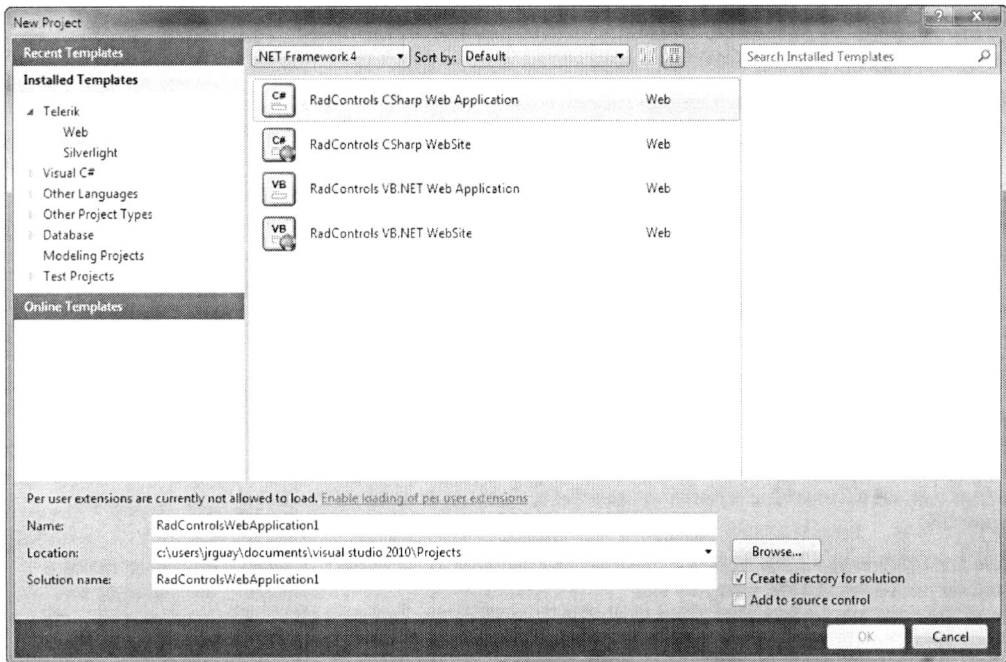

Figure 2-9. *Telerik project templates*

Creating a new web application using Visual Studio Extensions will ensure that the configuration will be correct from the beginning; you'll create a project with everything you need to start using the Telerik RadControls.

Figure 2-10 shows the project configuration wizard, which offers the following options and will help you perform the configuration for the newly created project:

- *Currently Used Telerik.Web.UI Version*: The configuration wizard will examine what versions are available in your development machine, and you can choose the version you want to work with. I encourage you to work with the latest version, since it will provide the best security, reliability, and capabilities.

- *Skin*: Telerik RadControls uses the skinning features of ASP.NET, so you can choose one of the built-in skins to apply to the controls and establish a standard look and feel across your entire application. You can also create your own skins manually or using Telerik Visual Style Builder, an online tool to modify an existing skin or create a new one from scratch.
- *Max Request Length (kB)*: This is the maximum length each request can handle. You can modify the default value of 4096KB up to the maximum of 2GB (this is particularly useful if your application will accept file uploads).
- *Execution Timeout (seconds)*: Here, you can configure the maximum allowed execution time for your pages. If you are uploading files, you should increase the default value.
- *Enable Compression Module*: This option will register the Telerik RadCompression `HttpModule` in `web.config`, causing all AJAX and web service responses to be compressed before being sent to the client. The result for the end users will be faster data transfers and improved page performance. The compression process is completely transparent to your client-side (JavaScript or Silverlight) and server-side code.
- *Enable RadUploadModule*: This option will register the RadUploadModule in `web.config` so the RadUpload control can work and accept uploads in your application. Leaving it unchecked does not prohibit future use of `RadUploadModule`.
- *Use Ajaxified Templates*: This option will add a RadAjaxManager to the `Default.aspx` page. Leaving it unchecked does not prohibit future use of the `RadAjax` controls.
- *Use jQuery Support*: jQuery is available, since it ships with Telerik RadControls for ASP.NET AJAX. By selecting this option, Visual Studio Extensions adds two entries in the `RadScriptManager`, making the jQuery library available to that page and all pages created based on the templates from Visual Studio Extensions. This allows you to reuse the jQuery library that ships with the Telerik assembly. If RadControls are used on a page, the jQuery library file is probably already downloaded and cached on the client; otherwise the script references added to `RadScriptManager` will ensure it gets downloaded on pages where it is needed. If you elect to keep the jQuery library file in a separate script folder and reference it in pages already using the RadControls, you will end up forcing users to download the script twice. In the end, it's better to use the script that is already included with the Telerik controls.
- *Use ScriptManager CDN and Use Style Sheet Manager CDN*: With options to enable content delivery network (CDN) support you allow `RadScriptManager` and `RadStyleSheetManager` to load the controls scripts and skins from the Telerik CDN. Telerik's CDN is hosted on the Amazon CloudFront service, which is a global content delivery service with locations in the United States, Europe, and Asia. Using the CDN has a number of advantages:

  Reduced latency: Requests will be automatically redirected to the nearest server.

  Compressed output: The JavaScript files are already compressed so they are in minimum size.

  Caching: Each resource only needs to be downloaded once.

  Reduced hosting expenses: Telerik hosts the resources for you so you can pay less.

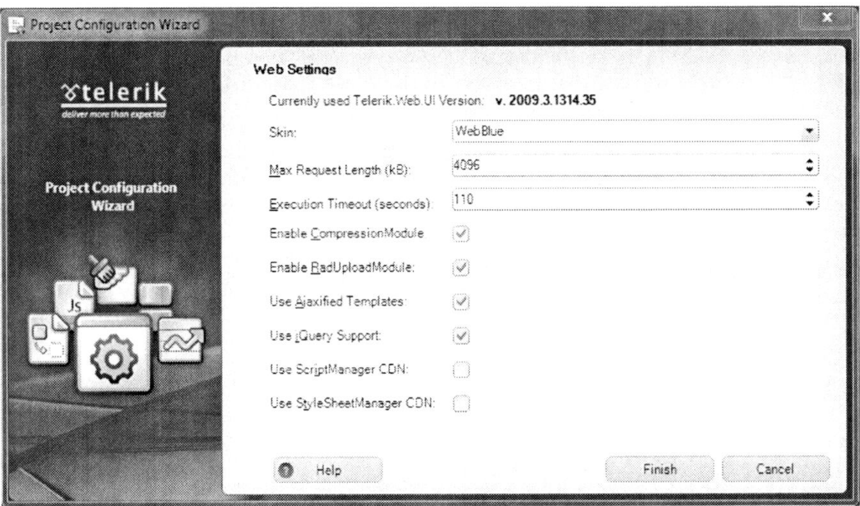

Figure 2-10. *The Project Configuration Wizard*

Now, you know how to create a new web application with the necessary configuration to use Telerik RadControls by default, but what if you already have an application that you wish to enable for usage of RadControls? You can use the Convert to Telerik Web Application Wizard within Visual Studio Extensions; Figure 2-11 shows how to open the wizard.

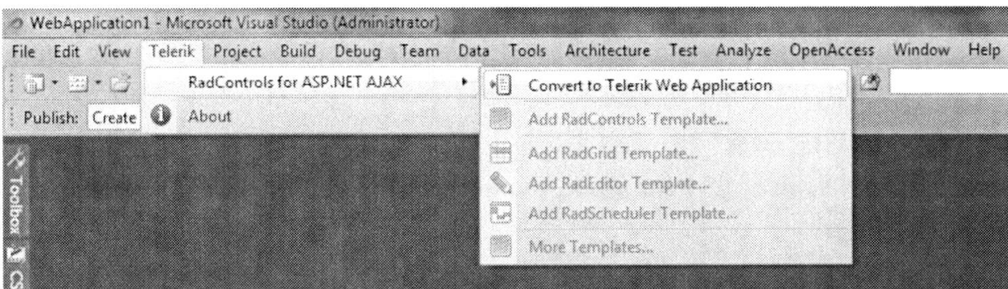

Figure 2-11. *Selecing the Convert to Telerik Web Application option*

This option will open the Project Configuration Wizard shown in **Figure 2-10.** All the enabled settings in the project configuration wizard will help the wizard to configure the existing web application; it will add the necessary assembly references, `web.config` settings, additional files, and so forth. Once the wizard finishes, you will have an application ready to use Telerik RadControls.

If you want to manually configure your application you can do so by following these steps:

1. Add a reference to the assembly `Telerik.Web.UI.dll` to your project. If your application is configured for .NET 3.5, you should use the assembly in the `Bin35` folder from the Telerik RadControls for ASP.NET AJAX installation folder. For .NET 2.0 or 3.0, you should use the one in the `Bin` folder.

2. If you are using the RadEditor control, you will need the files for the dictionaries located in `App_Data\RadSpell` folder. Copy the `RadSpell` folder and its content to the `App_Data` folder in your application.

3. You need to add the following HTTP handlers to the `web.config` file:

```
<add path="Telerik.Web.UI.DialogHandler.aspx"
             type="Telerik.Web.UI.DialogHandler"
             verb="*"
             validate="false" />

<add path="Telerik.Web.UI.WebResource.axd"
             type="Telerik.Web.UI.WebResource"
             verb="*"
             validate="false" />
```

4. To support charts, also add the following handler:

```
<add path="ChartImage.axd"
             type="Telerik.Web.UI.ChartHttpHandler"
             verb="*"
             validate="false" />
```

5. And to support spell checking, add this one:

```
<add path="Telerik.Web.UI.SpellCheckHandler.axd"
             type="Telerik.Web.UI.SpellCheckHandler"
             verb="*"
             validate="false" />
```

6. If your application will run on IIS 7 and above, you will need to add the following handlers:

```
<system.webServer>
<handlers>
    <add name="ChartImage_axd"
         path="ChartImage.axd"
         type="Telerik.Web.UI.ChartHttpHandler"
         verb="*"
         preCondition="integratedMode,runtimeVersionv2.0" />

    <add name="Telerik_Web_UI_SpellCheckHandler_axd"
         path="Telerik.Web.UI.SpellCheckHandler.axd"
         type="Telerik.Web.UI.SpellCheckHandler"
         verb="*"
         preCondition="integratedMode,runtimeVersionv2.0" />
```

```
        <add name="Telerik_Web_UI_DialogHandler_aspx"
             path="Telerik.Web.UI.DialogHandler.aspx"
             type="Telerik.Web.UI.DialogHandler" verb="*"
             preCondition="integratedMode,runtimeVersionv2.0" />

        <add name="Telerik_Web_UI_WebResource_axd"
             path="Telerik.Web.UI.WebResource.axd"
             type="Telerik.Web.UI.WebResource"
             verb="*"
             preCondition="integratedMode,runtimeVersionv2.0" />
    </handlers>
    </system.webServer>
```

7. If you want to set up a global skin for your application, you can do so by adding the `Telerik.Skin` key in the `AppSettings` section of the `web.config` file and setting its value to the name of the skin you want:

```
<appSettings>
  <add key="Telerik.Skin" value="Forest" />
</appSettings>
```

Configuring Telerik RadCompression

During the launch of version Q3 2008 SP2 of the RadControls for ASP.NET AJAX, Telerik released the first version of the RadCompression `HttpModule` designed to compress the response of AJAX and web services calls.

The RadCompression module works by intercepting the information being sent from the server to the browser and compressing it before sending it to the client application. Once the information reaches the client, it is decompressed and delivered to the user as part of the browser communication process.

Telerik RadCompression works very well in compressing AJAX and web services responses, so think of it as a complement to, rather than a replacement for, other compression tools such the IIS 7 Compression Module that doesn't have that feature. That being said, I must be clear in saying what Telerik RadCompression actually will compress. It will analyze the HTTP headers and identify the following content types for compression:

- `application/x-www-form-urlencode`
- `application/json`
- `application/xml`
- `application/atom+xml`

These content types are generally associated to AJAX web services, ADO.NET data services, and AJAX `UpdatePanels`, `RadAjaxManager`, or `RadAjaxPanel` requests. With the exception of Internet Explorer 6 (which doesn't support compression very well), most modern browsers will have no problems working with Telerik RadCompression. Requests sent from Internet Explorer 6 will just be ignored, and content will be delivered uncompressed.

Now is time for the big question—how do you enable Telerik RadCompression? Just open your `web.config` file, and add the following definition to the `httpModules` section:

```
<system.web>
  <httpModules>
      <add name="RadCompression" type="Telerik.Web.UI.RadCompression" />
  </httpModules>
</system.web>
```

If you are working with IIS7, you must add the following configuration too:

```
<system.webServer>
   <modules>
    <add name="RadCompression" type="Telerik.Web.UI.RadCompression" />
   </modules>
</system.webServer>
```

You could also enable RadCompression using Telerik Visual Studio Extensions Project Configuration Wizard (see Figure 2-10), which will add the configuration lines to the web.config file for you.

■ **Note** A detailed report on Telerik RadCompression is in Todd Anglin's (Telerik's chief evangelist) blog Telerikwatch.com at http://telerikwatch.com/2009/01/optimization-tips-radcompression-module.html.

Configuring Telerik RadUpload

Telerik RadUpload enables your applications to upload files. Configuration is very simple, because all you need to do is register the module in the web.config file the same way we did with Telerik RadCompression.

There are actually three options to enable RadUpload in your application. First, you can manually enable it by adding the module to the httpModules section in the web.config file as follows:

```
<system.web>
  <httpModules>
          <add name="RadUploadModule"
               type="Telerik.Web.UI.RadUploadHttpModule, Telerik.Web.UI" />
  </httpModules>
   <HttpHandlers>
          <add path="Telerik.RadUploadProgressHandler.ashx"
               type="Telerik.Web.UI.RadUploadProgressHandler, Telerik.Web.UI"
               validate="false"
               verb="*"  />
   </HttpHandlers>
</system.web>
```

If you are running your application in IIS 7, you will also need this:

```
<system.webServer>
 <modules>
     <add name="RadUploadModule"
          type="Telerik.Web.UI.RadUploadHttpModule, Telerik.Web.UI"
          preCondition="integratedMode"/>

 </modules>

 <handlers>
     <add name="Telerik_RadUploadProgressHandler_ashx"
          path="Telerik.RadUploadProgressHandler.ashx"
          verb="*"
          type="Telerik.Web.UI.Upload.RadUploadProgressHandler, Telerik.Web.UI"
          preCondition="integratedMode"/>

 </handlers>

</system.webServer>
```

The second option for configuring RadUpload is using Telerik Visual Studio Extensions Project Configuration Wizard (see Figure 2-10), which will write the configuration to the `web.config` file for you.

The final option for configuring RadUpload is using the SmartTag of the `RadProgressManager` control. This control is needed for the operation of RadUpload; therefore, it must be present whenever RadUpload is used. To create a `RadProgressManager` control, drag it from the toolbox onto the page where you will allow uploads, and open its SmartTag, as shown in **Figure 2-12.** Next, click both options highlighted by the red box to add the `HttpModule` to the `web.config` file.

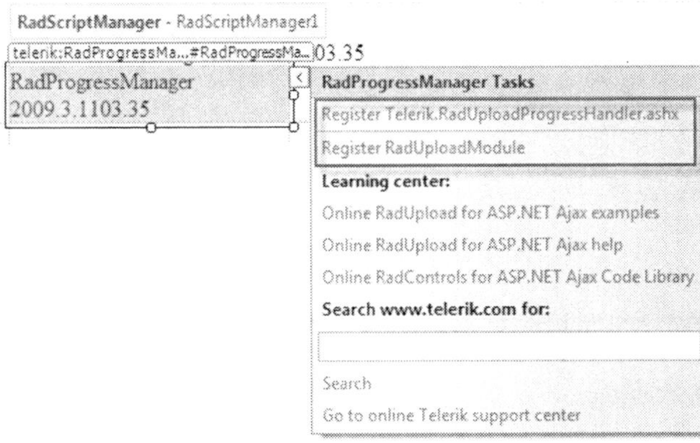

Figure 2-12. *Enable RadUpload with the RadProgressManager SmartTag.*

Enabling RadScriptManager and RadStyleSheetManager

Each control in the RadControls suite has its own set of JavaScript and CSS files that allows it to work properly in client-side browsers. Every time a page is loaded, a separate request is made for each of these JavaScript and CSS files, thus increasing traffic and slowing down the load time of the page. This slowdown is a known problem that can be solved by gathering all these resources to minimize the number of requests the browser has to make.

`RadScriptManager` enables this functionality for all JavaScript resources. For all the RadControls in a page, the `RadScriptManager` will create a single request and load all the necessary JavaScript files to support such controls. In much the same way, the `RadStyleSheetManager` control enables the single request functionality for resources of type CSS files.

All you need to do to enable these controls is drop them onto the pages where the RadControls are being used.

Both of these controls need to be configured in the `web.config` file, and for that purpose, both of them have the "Register the Telerik.Web.UI.WebResource.axd module" option among their SmartTags, as shown in **Figure 2-13.**

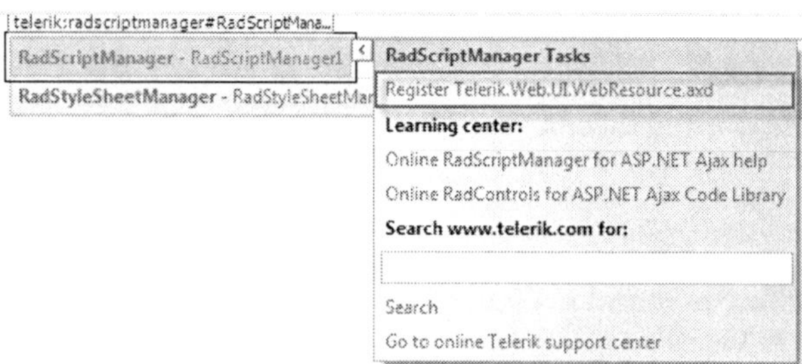

Figure 2-13. *Enabing RadScriptManager and RadStyleSheetManager with the SmartTag*

You can also configure the controls manually by adding the following setting to the `web.config` file:

```
<system.web>
  <httpHandlers>
    <add path="Telerik.Web.UI.WebResource.axd"
         type="Telerik.Web.UI.WebResource"
         verb="*"
         validate="false" />
  </httpHandlers>
</system.web>
```

If you are using IIS7, you have to add the following too:

```
<system.webServer>
  <handlers>
    <add name="Telerik_Web_UI_WebResource_axd"
             path="Telerik.Web.UI.WebResource.axd"
             type="Telerik.Web.UI.WebResource"
             verb="*"
             preCondition="integratedMode" />
  </handlers>
</system.webServer>
```

Summary

The procedures for installing and configuring Telerik RadControls have been kept simple, so you can focus on building your application. The installation programs must be downloaded from your account page in Telerik's web site, and all of them require minimal user interaction.

To prevent possible typographical and other errors in configuration, you are strongly advised to use the automated tools, such as Telerik Visual Studio Extensions and RadControls SmartTags. They will also help you by making the configuration tasks go faster.

The RadCompression module can help you compress AJAX and web services responses by examining their HTTP headers. With minimal configuration, you can gain all the benefits of compressing such responses, thus improving the performance of your application by reducing the traffic in the network.

RadUpload enables your application to accept uploaded files and takes only a couple of steps to configure. `RadScriptManager` and `RadStyleSheetManager` help you organize JavaScript and CSS resource files by combining them and minimizing requests of those files to the server.

CHAPTER 3

Input RadControls

The first controls that we will examine are the text controls. They are probably the most basic controls in the sense that, in most applications, you typically allow users to enter and modify text such as words to search, names of products, quantities in stock, or even prices from different countries and cultures.

The primary RadControls text control set is called RadInput, and it is accompanied by RadEditor with RadSpell. You will see how powerful these controls are, and even though they perform simple tasks, they can be extended to work the way we need them to beyond the default behavior.

Introducing RadInput

The RadInput set contains five controls. Four controls—`RadTextBox`, `RadMaskedTextBox`, `RadNumericTextBox`, and `RadDateInput`—each allow users to enter a particular type of value and automatically restricts the values users can enter to that type. The fifth control, `RadInputManager`, provides RadInput functionality to ASP.NET text boxes. They all automatically handle parsing of values that the user enters and formatting those values for display.

Although the controls differ, they share some common functionality and features, such as keyboard and mouse wheel support, skinning, empty message support (also known as *watermarking*), labels and buttons, rich client- and server-side APIs, and much more.

Note More information on RadInput features can be found at `http://www.telerik.com/help/aspnet-ajax/inputoverview.html`.

Understanding Common Properties and Events

All of the RadControls input controls share common properties and events; the most important of them are listed in Table 3-1.

Table 3-2 lists the style properties; each is actually a set of subproperties that determine specific style elements for an input control based on its current state. Every style property has the following subproperties: `BackColor`, `BorderColor`, `BorderWidth`, `CssClass`, `Font`, `ForeColor`, `Height`, `HorizontalAlign`, `LetterSpacing`, `PaddingBottom`, `PaddingLeft`, `PaddingRight`, `PaddingTop`, and `Width`.

In Table 3-3, I list the shared client-side events for all input controls.

Sample skins for the RadInput controls can be found at `http://www.telerik.com/help/aspnet-ajax/input_appearanceskins.html`.

Table 3-1. *RadInput's Most Important Common Properties*

Property	Description
`ButtonCssClass`	This property is the CSS class to be used for the text box button.
`ButtonContainer`	This one gets the control that contains the button of RadInput.
`ButtonsPosition`	This position setting indicates if the button is to appear to the right or to the left of the actual text box. The value can be `Right` (the default) or `Left`.
`EmptyMessage`	This message will show in an empty text box (if no data has been entered yet). When `EmptyMessage` is displayed, the style of the control is determined by the `EmptyMessageStyle` property.
`EnableViewState`	When this is set to `False`, the control won't save its state for use in postback scenarios. The default is `True`.
`InvalidStyleDuration`	This is the time, in milliseconds, that an invalid style will be displayed, and it must be a positive integer.
`Label`	This property sets the text of the associated label for the input control.
`LabelCssClass`	This CSS class is applied to the label of the control.
`RegisterWithScriptManager`	When this property is set to `False`, the control will not register itself with the `ScriptManager` control in the page. The default value is `True`.
`SelectionOnFocus`	Use this property to specify whether the text in the control will be selected once the control has focus and the mode of the selection. The value can be `None` (the default), `CaretToBeggining`, `CaretToEnd`, and `SelectAll`.
`ShowButton`	When this property is set to `True`, the control will display a button next to the input control. The default image for the control is a small bent arrow. You control the appearance of the button with the `ButtonCssClass` property.
`Skin`	Indicate the skin to be use by the control for style and appearance with this property.
`Text`	This property sets the text of the control, which can be defined programmatically or declaratively.

Table 3-2. *Common Style Properties*

Property	Application
DisabledStyle	For the disabled input control
EmptyMessageStyle	When the value is not set and the input control does not have focus
EnabledStyle	For the enabled input control
FocusedStyle	When the input control has focus
HoveredStyle	When the mouse hovers over the input control
InvalidStyle	When the value of the input control is invalid
ReadOnlyStyle	When the ReadOnly property of the input control is set to True.
NegativeStyle	When the value of the input control is negative (only used in RadNumericTextBox controls)

Table 3-3. *Client-Side Events*

Event	Occurs When. . .
OnBlur	The control loses focus.
OnButtonClick	The user clicks on the button that is associated with the input control.
OnDisable	The control is disabled.
OnEnable	The control is enabled.
OnEnumerationChanged	The value of an enumeration part of a mask is set.
OnError	The user enters an invalid value.
OnFocus	The control gets focus.
OnKeyPress	The user presses a key to enter a value.
OnLoad	The control is loaded on the client.
OnMouseOut	The mouse leaves the input area.
OnMouseOver	The mouse enters the input area.

Table 3-3. *Continued*

OnMouseDown	The user decreases the value of an enumeration or numeric range mask part.
OnMoveUp	The user increases the value of an enumeration or numeric range mask part.
OnValuechanged	A new value has been assigned when the control loses focus.
OnValueChanging	The control loses focus after the user has changed its value and before the new value is assigned (Does not apply to the RadMaskedTextBox control)

■ **Note** All RadInput controls provide the TextChanged server event, which is raised when the AutoPostBack property is set to True.

Using RadTextBox

The RadTextBox control allows users to enter any alphanumeric value (letters, numbers, and symbols). As with the regular ASP.NET TextBox, you can set the maximum length of characters allowed and the input mode (password, single-line, or multiline).

This control features some special characteristics that can be set through its properties. Listing 3-1 shows how the EmptyMessage, Label, and ToolTip properties work, and Figure 3-1 shows the code in action. The property EmptyMessage will provide a message to the user whenever the control doesn't have a value (this is also known as watermark).

Listing 3-1. *Basic Properties for a Declarative RadTextBox*

```
<telerik:RadTextBox ID="RadTextBox1" Runat=server
                    ClientIDMode="Static"
                    EmptyMessage="Please enter something..."
                    Label="RadTextBox Label"
                    ToolTip="this is the tooltip"
                    Width="336px"
</telerik:RadTextBox>
```

RadTextBox Label | Please enter something...

this is the tooltip

Figure 3-1. *Our declarative RadTextBox*

■ **Note** The Width property for the RadInput control indicates the width for the HTML container element that surrounds the entire control, including any label, button, or text box. If you specify a width and make the label very large, the actual text box may end up being too small.

Getting and Setting RadTextBox Values

RadTextBox has the familiar property Text that can be used in server-side code to handle get and set operations of the control's value. On the client-side, however, the task is not as intuitive as working with a single property; you have to use the get_value() and set_value() methods in order to do the same tasks as in server-side code. Listing 3-2 and Figure 3-2 illustrate the use of these methods.

■ **Note** One important thing to know when working with client-side code is that, in order to have access to the control itself, you must use the $find function and pass its assigned client ID. The result is a reference to the control object. If you use the $get function, the difference is that it will return a reference to the DOM object associated with the control and that won't give you access to the full range of client-side methods, properties, and events the controls have.

When using the ClientIDMode in ASP.NET 4.0 with a value of Static, you use the same string in the ID property to find the control. Otherwise, you have to first find the client ID of the control to call the $find method. You can find the client ID using the ClientID property like this: `var id = '<%= RadTextBox1.ClientID %>'`.

Listing 3-2. *Getting and Setting a Value for RadTextBox on the Client Side*

ASPX Page

```
<telerik:RadTextBox ID="RadTextBox2" Runat="server"
                    ClientIDMode="Static"
                    Width="336px">
</telerik:RadTextBox>

<input type="button" value="Get Value" onclick="getValue();" />
<input type="button" value="Set Value" onclick="setValue();" />

<script type="text/javascript">
    function setValue() {
        var txtObj = $find("RadTextBox1");
        txtObj.set_value("value set from client code");
    }

    function getValue() {
        var txtObj = $find("RadTextBox1");
        var value = txtObj.get_value();
        alert(value);
    }
</script>
```

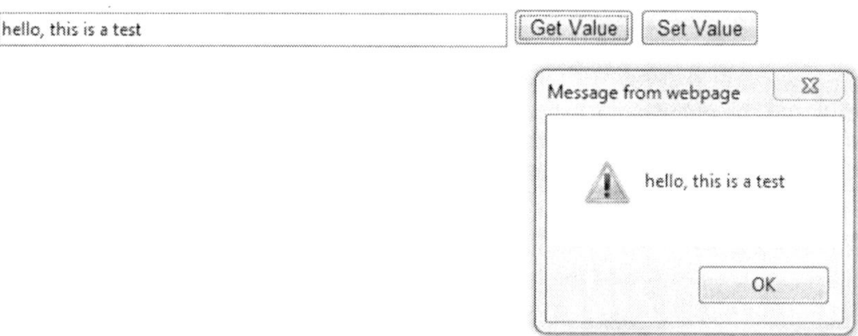

Figure 3-2. *The value of our RadTextBox*

Working with Buttons

You can add a two type of buttons to a RadInput control. The first one is a simple button that is shown as a small image to the left or right of the control (managed by the `ButtonsPosition` property). The second type of button is the spin button that applies to `RadNumericTextBox`. This buttons provide visual elements to allow the user to increment or decrement the value of the control. These buttons doesn't cause a postback and instead execute on the client.

Listing 3-3 shows how the default control button works. Figure 3-3 shows the result of the code execution. Listing 3-4 illustrates how, with a little CSS magic, we can make the button appear inside the text box area (this doesn't work correctly in Internet Explorer 6 because of its limited CSS support). Figure 3-4 shows how the resulting control looks.

Listing 3-3. *Working with the Default Control Button*

ASPX Page

```
<telerik:RadTextBox ID="RadTextBox3" Runat="server"
                        ClientIDMode="Static"
                        ShowButton="true"
                        ButtonsPosition="Right">
        <ClientEvents OnButtonClick="GetValueByButton" />
</telerik:RadTextBox>

<script type="text/javascript">
        function GetValueByButton() {
            var txtObj = $find("RadTextBox3");
            var value = txtObj.get_value();
            alert(value);
        }
</script>
```

Figure 3-3. *Our default control button*

Listing 3-4. *Placing a Button Inside the Text Area*

ASPX Page

```
<style type="text/css">
    .MyButtonClass
    {
        position: relative;
        left: -20px;
    }
</style>

<telerik:RadTextBox ID="RadTextBox3" Runat="server"
                        ClientIDMode="Static"
                        ShowButton="true"
                        ButtonsPosition="Right"
                        ButtonCssClass="MyButtonclass">
        <ClientEvents OnButtonClick="GetValueByButton" />
</telerik:RadTextBox>
```

Figure 3-4. *Our button inside the text area*

Using RadNumericTextBox

The RadNumericTextBox control is designed to handle numeric input. It can be configured to allow general numeric, currency (culture-specific or inherited), and percentage input. Some of its features include the ability to limit input to valid numeric ranges and to automatically correct invalid entries to meet those ranges.

Setting Minimum and Maximum Values

The use of the properties MinValue and MaxValue enables you to limit the range of allowed values inside a RadNumericTextBox control. The example in Listing 3-5 shows how these properties are implemented. Figure 3-5 shows the result.

Listing 3-5. *Setting RadNumericTextBox MaxValue and MinValue for Spin Buttons*

ASPX Page

```
<telerik:RadNumericTextBox ID="RadNumericTextBox1" runat="server"
                        Type="Percent"
                        Culture="en-US"
                        MaxValue="100"
                        MinValue="1"
                        ShowSpinButtons="True">
</telerik:RadNumericTextBox>
```

3.00 %

Figure 3-5. *RadNumericTextBox MaxValue and MinValue settings showing the spin buttons*

■ **Note** The `RadNumericTextBox` does not support maximum and minimum values with a magnitude greater than 2^{46}. Setting the `MaxValue` property to more than 2^{46} or the `MinValue` property to less than -2^{46} can cause abnormalities in the `RadNumericTextBox` behavior.

Setting the Type of Numeric Values

The type of values the control accepts depends on the `Type` property that can be set to `Number`, `Currency`, or `Percent`. With each of these types, certain attributes are enabled. For example, when setting the control to accept currency values, the `Culture` property can be set to specify currency symbol and its position when displayed. If the `Percent` option is set, then the percent symbol (%) is displayed.
Listing 3-6 shows how to configure RadNumericTextBox to use British currency, and the result is shown in Figure 3-6.

Listing 3-6. *Configuring RadNumericTextBox for British Currency*

ASPX Page

```
<telerik:RadNumericTextBox ID="RadNumericTextBox2"
                           runat="server"
                           Culture="en-GB"
                           Type="Currency">
</telerik:RadNumericTextBox>
```

£3.00

Figure 3-6. *RadNumericTextBox settings for British currency*

Using RadDateInput

The `RadDateInput` control is designed to let users enter values that will be converted to dates and times according to the specifications in the `DateFormat` and `DisplayedDateFormat` properties. The procedure is simple: If the value entered can be converted, it will be formatted. If not, the `InvalidStyle` property will be applied.

`RadDateInput` uses the standard ASP.NET date format strings to format its value. The `DateFormat` property sets the format when the date is being edited (the control has focus) and the `DisplayDateFormat` property when it doesn't have focus.

Formatting Dates

RadDateInput works by using standard format strings. Table 3-4 lists the format characters. When you set the DateFormat or DisplayDateFormat property to one of these format characters, the RadDateInput control automatically expands it into a format string built of the patterns listed in the table.

If this is the case, changes to the Culture property after setting the DateFormat or DisplayDateFormat property to one of these format characters will not change the overall pattern, but only the interpretation of symbols within the pattern.

Table 3-4. *Format Characters*

Format Character	Pattern Description
d	Short date
D	Long date
f	Full date and time (long date and short time)
F	Full date and time (long date and long time)
g	General (short date and short time)
G	General (short date and long time)
m, M	Month and day
r, R	RFC1123 standard–compliant format
s	Sortable date time (based on ISO 8601) using local time
t	Short time
T	Long time
y	Month and year

Table 3-5 shows a list of format characters that can be combined to create custom patterns. The patterns are case sensitive; for example, MM is recognized, but mm is not. If the custom pattern contains white-space characters or characters enclosed in single quotation marks, the output string will also contain those characters. Characters not defined as part of a format pattern or as format characters are reproduced literally.

Listing 3-7 shows how to format dates with RadDateInput, and the results of the listing are show in Figure 3-7.

Table 3-5. *Format Patterns*

Format Patterns	Description
d	If this pattern is used in the context of a longer pattern, it specifies the day of the month. Single-digit days have no leading zero. (d on its own represents the short date pattern.)
dd	This signifies the day of the month. Single-digit days have a leading zero.
ddd	This is the abbreviated name of the day of the week.
dddd	This is the full name of the day of the week.
M	This is the numeric month if used in the context of a longer pattern (a single M on its own represents the month and day pattern.) Single-digit months have no leading zero.
MM	This pattern indicates the numeric month. Single-digit months have a leading zero.
MMM	This is the abbreviated name of the month.
MMMM	This is the full name of the month.
y	This one displays the year without the century and displays no leading zero if the year without the century is less than 10. This pattern works only in the context of a longer pattern. (y on its own represents the month and year pattern.)
yy	This pattern also displays the year without the century, but here, if that year is less than 10, a leading zero is displayed.
yyy	This displays the four-digit year, including the century.
gg	This pattern specifies the period or era (e.g., A.D.) and is ignored if the date to be formatted does not have an associated period or era.
h	This shows the hour using a 12-hour clock such that single-digit hours have no leading zero.
hh	In this 12-hour clock display, single-digit hours have a leading zero.
H	This shows the hour using a 24-hour clock such that single-digit hours have no leading zero.
HH	In this 24-hour clock display, single-digit hours have a leading zero.
m	This pattern specifies minutes if used in the context of a longer pattern (m on its own represents the month and day pattern). Single-digit minutes have no leading zero.

Table 3-5. *Continued*

Mm	In this minute pattern, single-digit minutes have a leading zero.
s	This pattern specifies second if used in the context of a longer pattern (s on its own represents the month and day pattern). Single-digit seconds have no leading zero.
ss	This also displays seconds, but single-digit seconds have a leading zero.
t	This pattern, if used in the context of a longer one, displays the first character in the AM/PM designator (t on its own represents the short time pattern).
tt	This is the AM/PM designator.

Listing 3-7. *Formatting with RadDateInput*

ASPX Page

```
<telerik:RadDateInput ID="RadDateInput1" runat="server"
                DateFormat="MM/dd/yyyy"
                DisplayDateFormat="yyyy/MM/dd">
</telerik:RadDateInput>
```


Figure 3-7. *RadDateInput formatting style based on focus.*

Validating Dates

With RadDateInput, you can be certain that the date entered is valid through various mechanisms such as setting the MaxDate and MinDate for date range validation (see Listing 3-8, which is illustrated in Figure 3-8). Any date outside the range will be invalid, and InvalidStyle will be applied to the control. Also, you can set only one of those properties to enable an open range, from a valid date or up to a valid date.

Listing 3-8. *Using RadDateInput to Specify a Valid Range of Dates*

ASPX Page

```
<telerik:RadDateInput ID="RadDateInput2" runat="server"
                MinDate="01/01/2010"
                MaxDate="01/31/2010">
</telerik:RadDateInput>
```

Figure 3-8. *RadDateInput validating the allowed range of dates*

Parsing Dates

Since the `RadDateInput` control will try to recognize and convert its value into a valid date, some processing is done following the values of the properties, and some assumptions are made based on the user input.

The value can contain date and time parts. It is always parsed from left to right, and the date matching is always attempted before the time matching.

A date is a complex piece of data composed of several different parts, so a complex process is needed to make an accurate conversion. The first step in the parsing process is to decompose the value in different blocks of data so that each represents a part of the date. The control can recognize the following:

- *Numbers*: These are integer values that are interpreted as decimal numbers.
- *Month names*: Both normal and abbreviated month names are recognized. The names will be different for each culture.
- *Weekday names*: Both normal and abbreviated names are again recognized, and these, too, are culture specific.
- *Time separators*: This is a culture-specific setting (for example, a colon symbol is used for the American English culture).
- *AM/PM designator*: This is also a culture-specific setting.

Date parts can be combinations of the following:

- *A month/day/year triplet*: A month can be either a numeric value or a month name. The order of the parts in the triplet is culture specific.
- *A month/day or day/year pair*: Again, months can be specified with a number or a name, and the order is culture specific.
- *A single entry*: This can be a day, weekday, month, or year.

The time part is less complex, as it is always one to three numbers and an AM/PM component. The separator symbol for the numbers is culture specific.

■ **Note** `RadDateInput` has two modes of operation when determine the end of the date part and the start of the time part. They are `DateTime` and `TimeOnly`, and the one used is based on the `DateFormat` property. More information can be found at `http://www.telerik.com/help/aspnet-ajax/input_raddateinputparsing.html`.

The final step is to actually convert the value to a real date. Some rules apply to this process:

- When a date is incomplete, the current date is taken as the base date to make the completion. For example, "November 15" will be interpreted as "November 15 of this year".
- Any number greater than 31 will be evaluated as a year (when possible). The values of `MinDate` and `MaxDate` will be used.
- In a two-digit–year parsing, the two digits are matched to the `ShortDateCenturyStart` and `ShortDateCenturyEnd` properties.

- When a weekday name is provided, the value of the day is selected based on the next weekday that matches the name. If you type **Friday**, the value will be the one of the next Friday (except if the current day is Friday, in which case it will be the same day).
- Weekday names are ignored when a fully specified date is already entered. A fully specified date is one that already has a date composed of its three parts (month, day, and year).
- When you're using month names, the other parts of the date are matched to the current date. For example, if you enter **November** and the current date is September 15, the parsed date will be November 15.

Finally, `RadDateInput` can interpret entries without separators. If you enter a six- or eight-digit date (for example `MMddyy` or `MMddyyyy`), the control will try to evaluate the date with the format of the culture specified in the `Culture` property. In this case, correctly setting the `Culture` property is absolutely necessary to avoid erroneous entries.

Using RadMaskedTextBox

The fourth input control is `RadMaskedTextBox`. It enables you, as a developer, to provide users with a means to enter data with a predefined mask. The masking capabilities are not limited to those set by the `Mask` property; you can also define `MaskParts`, which is a collection of strings that define each part of the mask so you have complete control of how the mask is constructed.

Setting the RadMaskedTextBox Mask

You can define the mask of the control by using one of three different options:

- Set the mask through the `Mask` property using the properties pane. This method is very easy but has no design-time support.
- Use the control's smart tag, and select the `Mask` option. This option opens a dialog window that allows you to select one of the predefined masks, such as telephone number or ZIP code, or you can define your custom mask if you need to. The window will give you a preview of how the mask will look and work in the control. See **Figure 3-9.**
- Using the `MaskParts` property in the properties pane will open the `MaskPart` collection editor. This option will let you build your mask bit by bit by entering each part of the mask. When you use this option, the `Mask` property is automatically updated to match the mask you build. See **Figure 3-9.**

Regardless of the method you choose, you need to understand the different elements that can be used to create the mask, and these are listed in **Table 3-6.** Figure 3-10 shows the input mask dialog where you can add, modify or delete masks.

Table 3-6. *RadMaskedTextBox Masks*

<table>
<tr><th>Mask Element</th><th>MaskPartClass</th><th>Description</th></tr>
<tr><td>#</td><td>DigitMaskPart</td><td>Digit or space (optional), rendered as a prompt character if this position is blank in the mask</td></tr>
<tr><td>L</td><td>UpperMaskPart</td><td>Uppercase letter (required), restricts input to the ASCII letters A–Z</td></tr>
<tr><td>l</td><td>LowerMaskPart</td><td>Lowercase letter (required), restricts input to the ASCII letters a–z</td></tr>
<tr><td>a</td><td>FreeMaskPart</td><td>Accepts any character, rendered as a prompt character if this position is blank in the mask</td></tr>
<tr><td><n..m></td><td>NumericRangeMaskPart</td><td>Restricts the user to an integer in the declared numeric range (Numeric range mask parts can occupy multiple positions._</td></tr>
<tr><td><option1|option2|option3></td><td>EnumerationPart</td><td>Restricts the user to one of a fixed set of options and pipe characters (|) serve as separators between the option values</td></tr>
<tr><td>\</td><td>N/A</td><td>Escape character, allowing the following character to act as literal text. For example \a is the character "a" . \\ is the literal back slash character.</td></tr>
<tr><td>Any other character</td><td>LiteralPart</td><td>All nonmask elements appear as themselves. Literals always occupy a static position in the mask at run time and cannot be moved or deleted by the user.</td></tr>
</table>

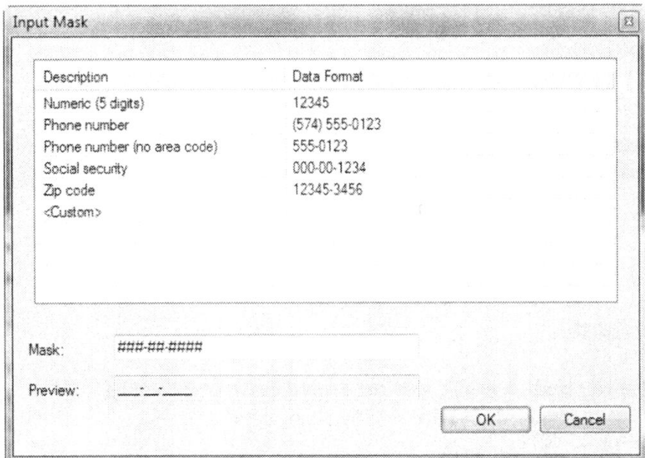

Figure 3-9. *Setting the mask from the smart tag using the Input Mask Dialog*

Figure 3-10 shows the MaskPart Collection Editor. Here, you can define the individual parts that compose a mask.

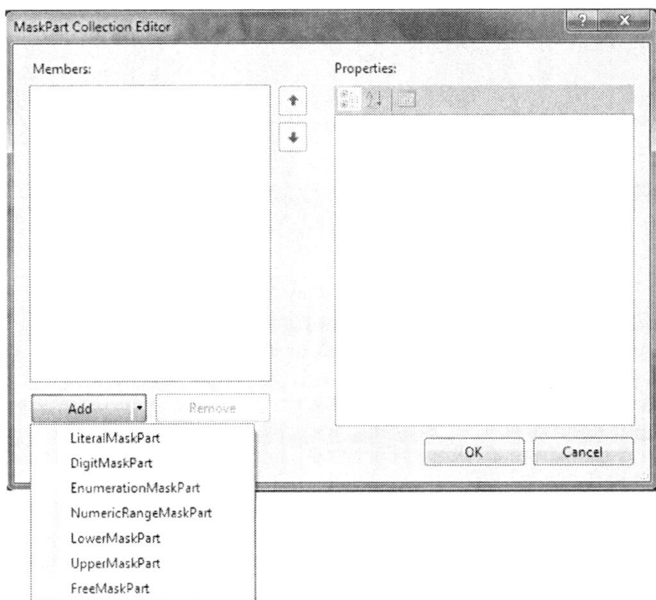

Figure 3-10. *MaskPart Collection Editor*

The example in Listing 3-9 shows how to declaratively add a mask to a `RadMaskedTextBox` control. Figure 3-11 shows what get's produced with the example.

Listing 3-9. *Setting a Mask for a RadMaskedTextBox*

```
ASPX Page

<telerik:RadMaskedTextBox ID="RadMaskedTextBox1" runat="server"
                          Mask="(###) ###-####">
</telerik:RadMaskedTextBox>
```

(___) ___-____

Figure 3-11. *Setting a mask for a RadMaskedTextBox*

After using the MaskPart Collection Editor to create a mask, the generated code is shown in Listing 3-10. Figure 3-12 shows how it works when the code is run.

Listing 3-10. *Setting a mask with the MaskPart Editor*

```
ASPX Page

<telerik:RadMaskedTextBox ID="RadMaskedTextBox1" runat="server"
                          Mask="&lt;Q1|Q2|Q3|Q4&gt;"
                          Text="Q1"
                          TextWithLiterals="Q1">
</telerik:RadMaskedTextBox>
```

Q1|

Figure 3-12. *RadMaskedTextBox with a mask generated with the MaskPart Collection Editor*

Using RadInputManager

An additional control called RadInputManager enables some RadInput capabilities in regular ASP.NET text boxes. This control is useful in scenarios where you are migrating an older versions of your application and don't want to spend time changing ASP.NET TextBox controls just to add certain functionality. But the biggest benefit is the reduction in the number of client scripts when your page has a lot of input controls. Input controls all need their own scripts, buttons, and other shared capabilities, therefore having an input manager means they can share all that code, which, in turn, means increased performance.

You can enable text boxes to accept and validate input just as a RadInput control would do without the hassle of changing everything in your application. Listing 3-11 shows how to enable a text box to accept only numeric values between 1 and 10. As a side-effect of applying RadInput capabilities, the text box also will be skinnable.

Listing 3-11. *Using RadInputManager*

```
<asp:TextBox ID="TextBox1" runat="server">
</asp:TextBox>
```

```
<telerik:RadInputManager ID="RadInputManager1" runat="server">
    <telerik:NumericTextBoxSetting
                MaxValue="10"
                MinValue="1">
        <TargetControls>
            <telerik:TargetInput ControlID="TextBox1" />
        </TargetControls>
    </telerik:NumericTextBoxSetting>
</telerik:RadInputManager>
```

Introducing RadEditor

RadEditor is a powerful text editor with unique features and sophisticated capabilities that will make your applications professional-looking and easy to use. Some of its features are true cross-browser support, multilevel undo and redo capabilities with action trails, and AJAX-based browser dialogs. It has keyboard support for enhanced accesibility. It's also a super-fast and uses very small scripts.

RadEditor offer a security model that will enable you to define roles so you control who can insert, update, or delete resources such as images, Flash content, Windows Media files, and documents. It also has a powerful engine that allows you to paste content from Word and format that content in several different ways, including cleaning fonts and sizes, pasting as HTML, and even saving Word content to a clipboard.

A new algoritm to handle CSS styles has been introduced, so styles are applied without overlaping tags. You can also make use of content filters, which are code snippets executed in sequence whenever the mode (HTML, design, or preview) is changed or the page is submited. Table 3-7 lists the filters in the `EditorFilters` enumeration.

You can also insert portions of HTML obtained from external templates (for example, preformatted tables signatures). Template files can be in any format that your server will allow you to read (HTML, text files, etc.) Templates are similar to code snippets except they are obtained from individual files that the user can browse, upload, delete, and so on.

Then too, HTML mode has been enhanced to display nicely indented code by default, so code is easier to read and modify.

Table 3-7. *RadEditor Content Filters*

Filter	Description
`None`	Use no filters.
`RemoveScripts`	Delete the script tags to reduce the possibility of cross-site scripting and other script-related problems.
`EncodeScripts`	Encode all script tags from the content.
`MakeUrlsAbsolute`	Make all `src` and `href` attributes in the editor content have absolute URLs.
`FixUlBoldItalic`	Remove deprecated `U` tags and replace them with CSS styles.
`FixEnclosingP`	Remove a paragraph indicator if all of the content is inside it.

Table 3-7. *Continued*

Filter	Description
IECleanAnchors	Remove the current page href from all anchor (#) links.
MozEmStrong	Change b, strong, i, and em in Mozilla browsers.
ConvertFontToSpan	Change the deprecated font tags to compliant span tags.
ConvertToXhtml	Convert HTML from the editor content area to valid XHTML.
IndentHTMLContent	Indent HTML content so it is more readable when you view the code.
DefaultFilters	Enable all of the default filters.

RadEditor can import content such as images or Flash files, but to perform the upload operation, it must have enabled the FileBrowser dialogs. You can enable the dialogs either from the control smart tag by choosing the Enable RadEditor Dialogs option or manually by registering the handlers for them in the web.config file.

If you are using the manual option, you have to add to the web.config file the handlers specified in Listing 3-12. Table 3-8 list the properties related to the RadEditor dialogs.

The FileBrowser dialogs consist of a FileBrowser object, an object previewer or property manager, and a file uploader tab. The FileBrowser object provides the ability to browse directories and locate a file item. Selected file items are loaded into the previewer.

Listing 3-12. *web.config Handlers to Enable RadEditor Dialogs*

```
<httpHandlers>
        <add path="Telerik.Web.UI.DialogHandler.aspx"
             verb="*"
             type="Telerik.Web.UI.DialogHandler"
             validate="false" />
</httpHandlers>
```

If you are hosting your application in IIS 7, you will need also the following configuration.

```
<system.webServer>
   <handlers>
     <add name="Telerik_Web_UI_DialogHandler_aspx"
          verb="*"
          preCondition="integratedMode"
          path="Telerik.Web.UI.DialogHandler.aspx"
          type="Telerik.Web.UI.DialogHandler" />
   </handlers>
</system.webServer>
```

Table 3-8. *RadEditor Properties Related to FileBrowser Dialogs*

Property	Description
`DialogHandlerUrl`	URL to make the AJAX call when a dialog is to be open
`DialogOpener`	Actually a set of properties that manage how the dialogs are open
`DialogsCssFile`	CSS files associated with the dialogs
`DialogsScriptFile`	Script files associated with the dialogs
`DocumentManager`	Set of properties to handle general purpose documents. The subproperties are as follows: `ContentProviderTypeName` is the name of the custom provider class to handle documents. DeletePaths lists server directories where the users will have access to delete documents. `MaxUploadFileSize` is the maximun size for a document when being uploaded. SearchPatterns lists file extensions that will be shown in the document manager dialog. UploadPaths lists server directories where the users will upload documents. ViewPaths lists server directories where the users will have access to view documents.
`ExternalDialogsPath`	Path to the folder where the editor dialogs (web user controls files) reside when you are working with custom dialogs that either modify the original dialogs or are brand new ones
`FlashManager`	Set of properties to handle Flash files. The subproperties are as follows: `ContentProviderTypeName` is the name of the custom provider class to handle Flash files. DeletePaths lists server directories where the users will have access to delete Flash files. MaxUploadFileSize is the maximun size for a Flash file when being uploaded. SearchPatterns lists file extensions that will be shown in the document manager dialog. UploadPaths lists server directories where the users will upload Flash files. ViewPaths lists server directories where the users will have access to view Flash files.
`ImageManager`	Set of properties to handle image files. The subproperties are as follows: ContentProviderTypeName is the name of the custom provider class to handle image files. DeletePaths lists server directories where users will have access to delete image files. EnableImageEditor specifies hether the Image Editor Button will be enabled; the default is `true`. EnableThumbnailLinking enables thumbnail linking. ImageEditorFileSufix is the string to append to the file name when saving changes in the Image Editor. MaxUploadFileSize is the maximun size for an image file when being uploaded. SearchPatterns lists file extensions that will be shown in the image files manager dialog. UploadPaths lists server directories where users will upload image files. ViewPaths lists server directories where users will have access to view image files.
`MediaManager`	Set of properties to handle Windows Media files. The subproperties are the same as the DocumentManager property.
`SilverlightManager`	Set of properties to handle Silverlight files. The subproperties are the same as the `DocumentManager` property.
`TemplateManager`	Set of properties to handle templates. The subproperties are the same as the `DocumentManager` property.

Creating a Custom FileBrowser

If your application needs support for a custom implementation, such as integration with a third-party content management system (CMS), you can add that support by following these steps:

1. Create a class that implements the abstract class `FileBrowserContentProvider`.
2. Include the namespace `Telerik.Web.UI.Widget`.
3. In the class file, add a constructor with the following signature. The constructor provides basic dialog and path information. The context parameter allows you to access the current HTTP state, including the HTTP `Request` object.

```
public MyFileBrowserContentProvider(HttpContext context,
                                    string[] searchPatterns,
                                    string[] viewPaths,
                                    string[] uploadPaths,
                                    string[] deletePaths,
                                    string selectedUrl,
                                    string selectedItemTag) :
base(context, searchPatterns, viewPaths, uploadPaths,
        deletePaths, selectedUrl, selectedItemTag)
{

}
```

4. You need to implement all required methods from the abstract class. Use Visual Studio's refactor mechanism (or your favorite refactoring tool) by right-clicking the abstract class name and selecting the option Implement Abstract Class, so Visual Studio automatically adds all the methods to be implemented.
5. Once all methods are implemented, save and compile the class.
6. Set the dialog's `ContentProviderTypeName` property to the value of the newly created class in the form of the fully qualified assembly name (for example, `namespace.class.name, Assembly.name`). If the assembly where the class is defined will be located in the Global Assembly Cache (GAC), you should include the full assembly name, version, public key token, and so on.

■ **Note** There are some important elements to notice when creating your own custom `FileBrowser` content provider. Please visit `http://www.telerik.com/help/aspnet-ajax/customfilebrowsercontentprovider.html` to get more information.

Customizing the Appearance and Tools

You can customize the appearance and functionality of the RadEditor control using the `skin` and `Tools` properties.

The `skin` property as with all controls in the suite enables the usage of predefined skins or custom skins to match your web site's look and feel.

The `Tools` property is in charge of the definition of the buttons and toolbars available to the user to perform operations such as formatting and importing external content.

To work with the Tools property, you need to understand a few concepts. *Groups* are the abstraction of RadEditor for toolbars; they contain several items normaly related or with similar functionality. ToolStrips are special tools that contain other tools; they group tools to prevent toolbar clutter and look like buttons with drop-down arrows.

There are three ways of defining the tools a RadEditor control will use: declaratively in the HTML declaration of the control, through code behind (C# or VB.NET for example), and the using an XML file with a specific format. While the first option provides full design-time support, it causes a maintanability problem, as does the code option. The suggested option is to use XML files (you can use one file configuring all of the RadEditors in your application, or you can have as many files as you need).

The general structure of the Tools file is in Listing 3-13 and a sample one is in Listing 3-14. Figure 3-13 shows how RadEditor looks with the sample tools file.

Listing 3-13. *General Structure of the XML Tools File*

```
<root>
    <modules>
            <module />
            <module />
    </modules>
    <tools>
            <tool />
            <tool />
            ...
   </tools>
   <tools>
            <tool />
            ...
   </tools>
    ...
   <links>
           <link />
           <link />
   </links>
   <colors>
           <color />
           <color />
   </colors>
</root>
```

Listing 3-14. *A Sample XML Tools File*

ASPX Page

```
<telerik:RadEditor ID="RadEditor1" Runat="server"
                   ToolsFile="~/App_Data/SampleTools.xml">
</telerik:RadEditor>
```

SampleTools.xml

```
<root>

        <tools name="MainToolbar" dockable="true" enabled="true">
                <tool name="FindAndReplace" />
                <tool separator="true"/>
                <tool name="Undo" />
                <tool name="Redo" />
                <tool separator="true"/>
                <tool name="Cut" />
                <tool name="Copy" />
                <tool name="Paste" shortcut="CTRL+!"/>
        </tools>

        <tools name="Formatting" enabled="true" dockable="true">
                <tool name="Bold" />
                <tool name="Italic" />
                <tool name="Underline" />
                <tool separator="true"/>
                <tool name="ForeColor" />
                <tool name="BackColor"/>
                <tool separator="true"/>
                <tool name="FontName"/>
                <tool name="RealFontSize"/>
        </tools>

        <colors>
            <color value="#FFFFFF" />
            <color value="#000000" />
        </colors>
</root>
```

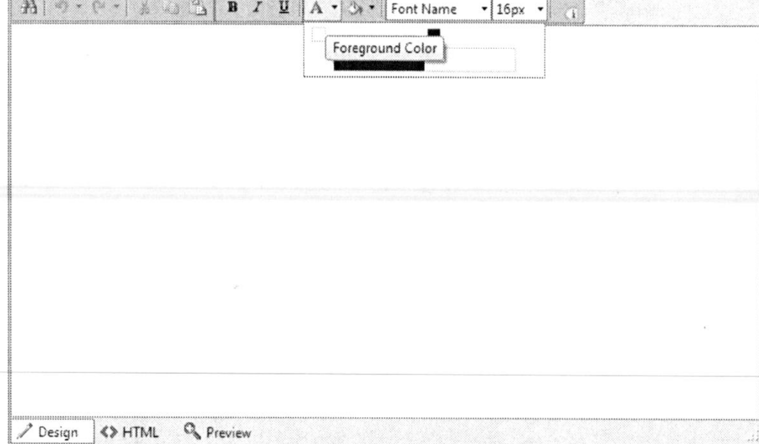

Figure 3-13. *RadEditor configured using an XML tools file.*

Localizing RadEditor

RadEditor is fully localizable, and localization can be set using one of three methods: global resources, the `Localization` property, and the `Text` property.

When using global resources, you need to create the `App_GlobalResources` folder in the root of your application and create the `.resx` files within it. The RadControls installation contains resource files for three languages (English, French, and German), so you can copy the files into the folder and start using them. Once you have copied the files, how do you tell RadEditor to use them? Easy—use the `Language` property to set the language you want to use, and the control will look for the resource file automatically.

The example in Listing 3-15 shows how to set up the RadEditor control to use the French language. See Figure 3-14 for the result.

Listing 3-15. *RadEditor Localization in French*

ASPX Page

```
<telerik:RadEditor ID="RadEditor1" Runat="server"
                   Language="fr-FR">
</telerik:RadEditor>
```

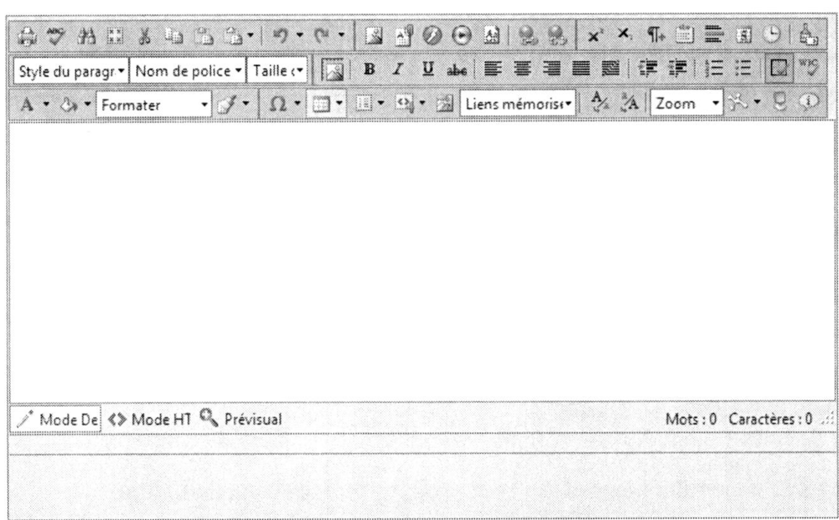

Figure 3-14. *RadEditor in French*

But wait; what if your application needs to run in other languages such as Spanish, Italian, or Hebrew? Well, there are no files for those languages, so you will need to create the resource files yourself. Simply copy one of the existing language files, and replace the values with those in your desired language. Just remember to rename your files as appropriate, so you don't accidentally overwrite the default language files.

There are four different language resource files, and if you are creating a new language, you will need to make translations for all four of them:

- `RadEditor.Dialogs.resx`
- `RadEditor.Main.resx`
- `RadEditor.Modules.resx`
- `RadEditor.Tools.resx`

When creating the new language, you will have to name the files as follows:

- `RadEditor.Dialogs.<your language>.resx`
- `RadEditor.Main.<your language>.resx`
- `RadEditor.Modules.<your language>.resx`
- `RadEditor.Tools.<your language>.resx`

■ **Note** The Telerik Developer Community has helped developed a lot of localization packages that are freely available to download at `http://www.telerik.com/community/forums/aspnet-ajax/editor/radeditor-for-asp-net-ajax-localizations.aspx`. If you help with building one, you will get a nice reward from Telerik.

Listing 3-16 shows how to localize using the `Localization` property using code as well as the `Text` property.

Listing 3-16. *Localizing RadEditor for Spanish Using the Localization property*

```
Code Behind

protected void Page_Load(object sender, EventArgs e)
{
   if (Page.IsPostBack) return;
   RadEditor1.Localization.Tools.Copy = "Copiar";
}
```

The example in Listing 3-17 shows the usage of the `Text` property for localizing RadEditor.

Listing 3-17. *Localizaing RadEditor for Spanish Using the Text Property*

```
Code Behind

protected void Page_Load(object sender, EventArgs e)
{
   if (Page.IsPostBack) return;
   Telerik.Web.UI.EditorTool tool = RadEditor1.FindTool("Copy");
       if (tool != null)
       {
           tool.Text = "Copiar";
       }
```

```
}
```

Checking Spelling

RadEditor supports spell-checking with the help of the RadSpell control. RadSpell is enabled by simply copying the dictionaries and registering RadSpell.

First, if you haven't done so, add the `App_Data` folder to your application, and inside it, create a folder called `RadSpell`. Within that folder, copy the three dictionaries already provided with your installation of RadControls for ASP.NET AJAX (see Figure 3-15).

Once you've copied the files, all you need to do is register the RadSpell `HttpHandler` in the `web.config` file, so the application is aware of the dictionaries and that you want to use RadSpell. See Listing 3-18 for the configuration.

Listing 3-18. *Configuration Changes to use RadSpell.*

```
Web.Config File

<httpHandlers>
      <add path="Telerik.Web.UI.SpellCheckHandler.axd"
           type="Telerik.Web.UI.SpellCheckHandler"
           verb="*"
           validate="false" />
</httpHandlers>
```

If you are hosting your application in IIS 7 you will need also the following configuration.

```
<handlers>
      <add name="Telerik_Web_UI_SpellCheckHandler_axd"
           path="Telerik.Web.UI.SpellCheckHandler.axd"
           type="Telerik.Web.UI.SpellCheckHandler"
           verb="*"
           preCondition="integratedMode,runtimeVersionv2.0" />
</handlers>
```

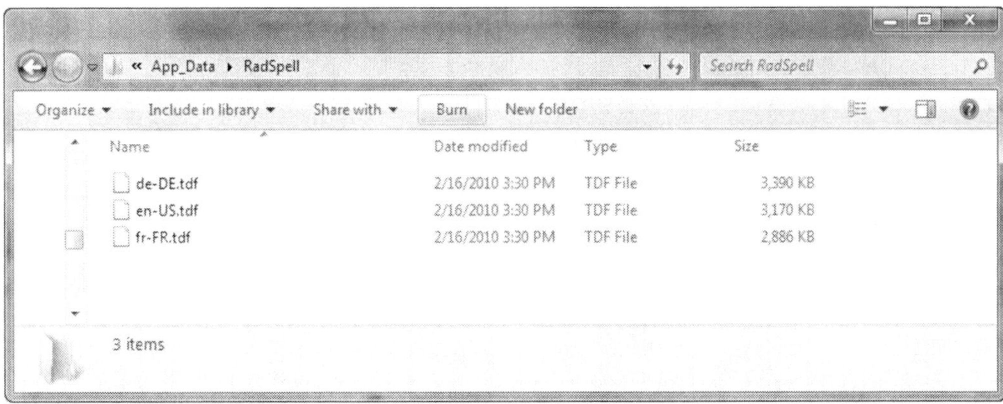

Figure 3-15. *The dictionaries for RadSpell*

And you are all set! Now, all you need to do is instruct RadEditor in which language you want to perform the spell check. You do so using the `Language` property (U.S. English by default) or the `Languages` property (see Listing 3-19).

Listing 3-19. *Using RadSpell with RadEditor*

ASPX File

```
<telerik:RadEditor ID="RadEditor1" Runat="server" Skin="Simple">
    <Languages>
        <telerik:SpellCheckerLanguage Code="fr-FR" Title="French" />
    </Languages>
</telerik:RadEditor>
```

Creating Your Own Dictionary

If you need a new dictionary, you should check the following ready-to-use RadSpell dictionaries page before creating your own: `http://www.telerik.com/community/forums/aspnet-ajax/spell/147971-radspell-dictionaries.aspx`.

If the one you need isn't there, you can also check the OpenOffice Dictionaries web site at `http://wiki.services.openoffice.org/wiki/Dictionaries`, which contains a huge collection of dictionary files you can download.

If the language you need is not in either place, you can create your own dictionary file by following the one-word-per-line rule and avoiding special characters such slashes, dots, colons, and so forth.

Once you have your dictionary file, follow these steps to create a RadSpell-compatible dictionary:

1. Save the text file (or downloaded file) with the Unicode (UTF-8 with signature) encoding.
2. Change the file extension from `.dic` or `.txt` to `.tdf`.
3. Convert the file using the Dictionary Configurator tool that can be obtained from the community project page at `http://www.telerik.com/community/code-library/aspnet-ajax/spell/dictionary-configuration.aspx`. Place the new dictionary in the `\RadControls\Spell\TDF` folder of the Dictionary Configuration project, and then test and verify that the spellchecker works properly with it.
4. If the dictionary language is incompatible with the phonetic spell check provider, set the spellchecker to use `EditDistanceProvider (SpellCheckProvider="EditDistanceProvider")`.

Using System Modules

System modules are special tools that work within the RadEditor control. They look like toolbars but, instead of holding buttons, they are used for a specific purpose like counting the words and letters in the document.

Several out-of-the-box modules are available for use:

- *Statistics*: This module displays general text statistics, specifically the number of words and number of characters (including spaces).
- *DOM/Tag inspector*: This module displays the DOM path of the current tag. It allows you to easily select a given tag in the hierarchy and remove it using the Remove Element button.

- *Node inspector*: This powerful module displays relevant properties of the currently selected tag. As a result, the user can quickly configure the element (e.g., set the cell width, shading, and image alignment) without the need to open dialogs. To conserve space, only important and frequently used properties are displayed.
- *HTML inspector*: This module displays a pane with the HTML code of the content. The HTML is updated in real time and kept in sync with the WYSIWYG content pane.

Creating Your Own Module

Listing 3-20 shows how you can create and implement custom modules, and Figure 3-16 shows how it works.

Listing 3-20. *Creating Custom Modules*

```
ASPX Page

<telerik:radeditor runat="server" ID="RadEditor1" >
   <Modules>
       <telerik:EditorModule Name="MyModule"
                        Enabled="true"
                        Visible="true" />
       <telerik:EditorModule Name="RadEditorStatistics"
                        Enabled="true"
                        Visible="true" />
   </Modules>
</telerik:radeditor>

<script type="text/javascript">

MyModule = function(element) {
   MyModule.initializeBase(this, [element]);
}

MyModule.prototype = {
   initialize : function() {
       MyModule.callBaseMethod(this, 'initialize');
       var selfPointer = this;
       this.get_editor().add_selectionChange(function (){ selfPointer.doSomething(); });
       this.doSomething();
   },
```

```
    // A method that does the actual work - it is usually
    // attached to the "selection changed" editor event
    doSomething : function(){
         var span = document.createElement("SPAN");
         span.innerHTML = this.get_editor().get_html();
         var liCount = span.getElementsByTagName("LI").length;
         var element = this.get_element();
         element.innerHTML = "<b>CUSTOM MODULE: Number of Bullets: " + liCount  + "</b>";
         element.style.border = "1px solid navy";
         element.style.backgroundColor = "#c6d9f0";
         element.style.color = "#e36c09";    }
    };

MyModule.registerClass('MyModule', Telerik.Web.UI.Editor.Modules.ModuleBase);

</script>
```

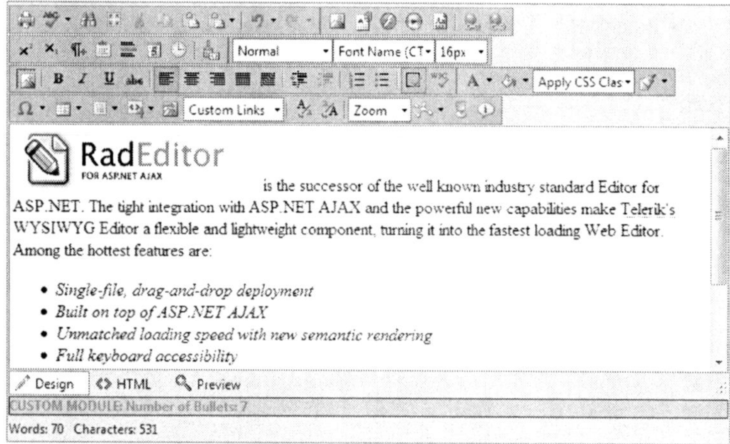

Figure 3-16. *Our custom modules in action*

Summary

There are five basic input controls, each targeting specific needs such as general text, numeric values, and date values. RadTextBox is a general-purpose text input control that can handle any alphanumeric value entered. RadNumericTextBox is the control to use to handle input of numeric values such as currency and percentage values. RadDateInput enables automatic date parsing for user input. RadMaskedTextBox enables you to define masks to validate user input of pieces of information such as telephone numbers or ZIP codes. With the help of RadInputManager, you can add RadInput technology to basic ASP.NET TextBox and reduce the size of the script and resources downloaded to the client when many input controls are necessary.

RadEditor is a powerful ASP.NET editor capable of localization, and it can even be enhanced with custom file browser providers. You can use RadEditor to allow users enter different types of content, including HTML, images, and Flash files. Also, it includes multiple options to paste content from Microsoft Word and clean up the formatting.

CHAPTER 4

Navigation RadControls

Now, we will examine the navigation controls, which allow your users to perform actions such as navigating to another page, showing different information, or updating other controls. The controls are RadMenu, RadToolBar, RadTreeView, RadSiteMap, and RadPanelBar, and in this chapter, you will see how powerful they are when used with custom templates to bind all kinds of elements and how easy it is to get them to work for your application.

Using RadMenu and RadToolBar

RadMenu is a flexible navigation component to use in ASP.NET applications. It is composed of two similar controls that enable you to create traditional and context menus. The first control is the RadMenu itself, and the other one is `RadContextMenu`. While they share the same base functionality, they differ in that `RadContextMenu` will activate only on context menu events, such as a mouse right-click.

On the other hand, RadToolBar is a component targeted to build toolbars with commands (traditionally buttons), much like the toolbars in traditional Windows applications.

RadMenu and RadToolBar complement each other, providing various means to achieve the same commands and to create web forms that resemble their desktop counterparts. The components also provide some common functionality such as powerful data binding, design time and keyboard support, server and client APIs, custom attributes, different item types, cross-page postbacks, support for ASP.NET validation, many options for controlling appearance, minimal markup generation (but not for tables), and so on.

RadMenu is basically structured on sets of `RadMenuItem` controls in a hierarchical manner. At the top of the hierarchy are root items available in server-side code through the `RadMenu.Items` collection. All root items may have, nested within them, a set of child items known as level 1 items. The children of level 1 items are known as level 2 items, and so forth.

RadToolBar is based on tool bar buttons that can be of type `RadToolBarButton`, `RadToolBarDropDown`, or `RadToolBarSplitButton`. A `RadToolBarButton` button can reside within a RadToolBar and can perform an operation when clicked. A `RadToolBarDropDown` does not perform any operation; it's simply a container for other `RadToolBarButtons` and displays itself as a drop-down list. The `RadToolBarSplitButton` combines the features of toolbar and drop-down buttons; a user can click the button part of the split button to perform the associated action and can click the drop-down arrow to select a new button to perform its action. After that, the latest selection remains for the user to keep using it.

Figure 4-1 shows the design-time support for the RadMenu control. Here, you can define all the items in your menu and their properties. This design-time support window is also available for RadContextMenu.

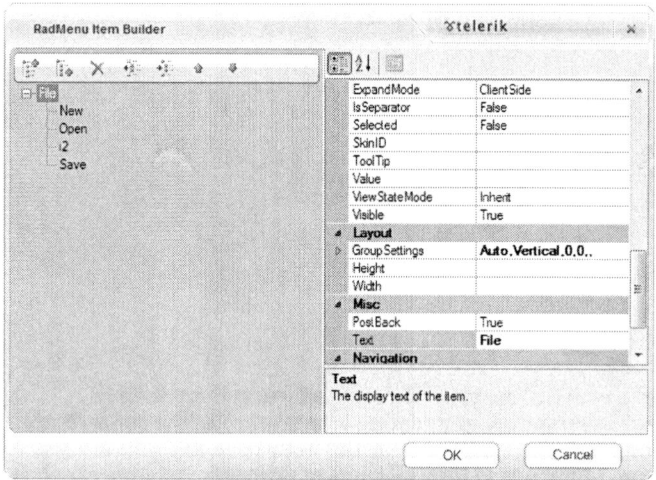

Figure 4-1. *The design-time support window for RadMenu*

Listing 4-1 shows the generated markup for the RadMenu shown in Figure 4-1.

Listing 4-1. *RadMenu Markup*

ASPX Page

```
<telerik:RadMenu ID="RadMenu1" runat="server" Skin="Sunset">
    <Items>
        <telerik:RadMenuItem runat="server" Text="File">
            <Items>
                <telerik:RadMenuItem runat="server"
                        Text="New"
                        ImageUrl="~/Images/icons/file.png">
                </telerik:RadMenuItem>
                <telerik:RadMenuItem runat="server"
                        Text="Open"
                        ImageUrl="~/Images/icons/folder_open.png">
                </telerik:RadMenuItem>
                <telerik:RadMenuItem runat="server"
                        IsSeparator="true">
                </telerik:RadMenuItem>
                <telerik:RadMenuItem runat="server"
                        Text="Save"
                        ImageUrl="~/Images/icons/save.png">
                </telerik:RadMenuItem>
            </Items>
        </telerik:RadMenuItem>
    </Items>
</telerik:RadMenu>
```

Design-time support is also provided for RadToolBar. The window, shown in Figure 4-2, is slightly different from RadMenu's, but the functionality is pretty much the same, and you have the ability to add toolbar buttons and define properties. The generated markup for the RadToolBar shown in Figure 4-2 is in Listing 4-2. Figure 4-3 shows the different button types of RadToolBar.

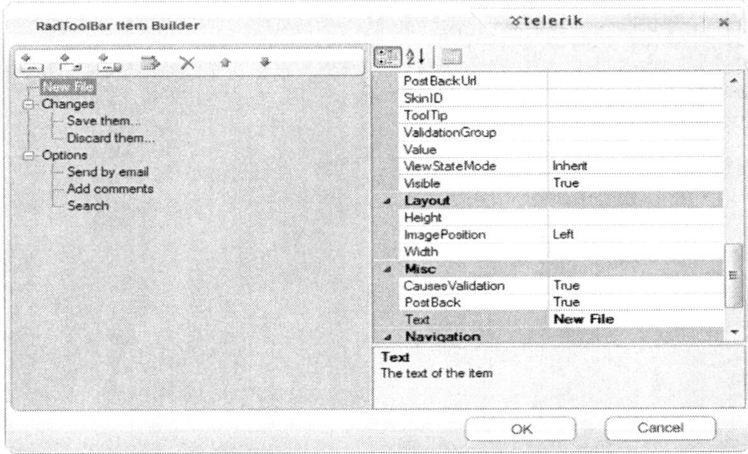

Figure 4-2. *The design-time support window for RadToolBar*

Listing 4-2. *RadToolBar Markup*

ASPX Page

```
<telerik:RadToolBar ID="RadToolBar1" Runat="server" Skin="Windows7">
    <Items>
        <telerik:RadToolBarButton runat="server"
                ImageUrl="~/Images/icons/file.png"
                Text="New File">
        </telerik:RadToolBarButton>
        <telerik:RadToolBarDropDown runat="server"
                        Text="Changes">
            <Buttons>
                <telerik:RadToolBarButton runat="server"
                        ImageUrl="~/Images/icons/action_check.png"
                        Text="Save them...">
                </telerik:RadToolBarButton>
                <telerik:RadToolBarButton runat="server"
                        ImageUrl="~/Images/icons/action_delete.png"
                        Text="Discard them...">
                </telerik:RadToolBarButton>
            </Buttons>
        </telerik:RadToolBarDropDown>
        <telerik:RadToolBarSplitButton runat="server" Text="Options">
            <Buttons>
                <telerik:RadToolBarButton runat="server"
                        ImageUrl="~/Images/icons/letter.png"
                        Text="Send by email">
                </telerik:RadToolBarButton>
```

```
                <telerik:RadToolBarButton runat="server"
                        ImageUrl="~/Images/icons/comments.png"
                        Text="Add comments">
                </telerik:RadToolBarButton>
                <telerik:RadToolBarButton runat="server"
                        ImageUrl="~/Images/icons/search.png"
                        Text="Search">
                </telerik:RadToolBarButton>
            </Buttons>
        </telerik:RadToolBarSplitButton>
    </Items>
</telerik:RadToolBar>
```

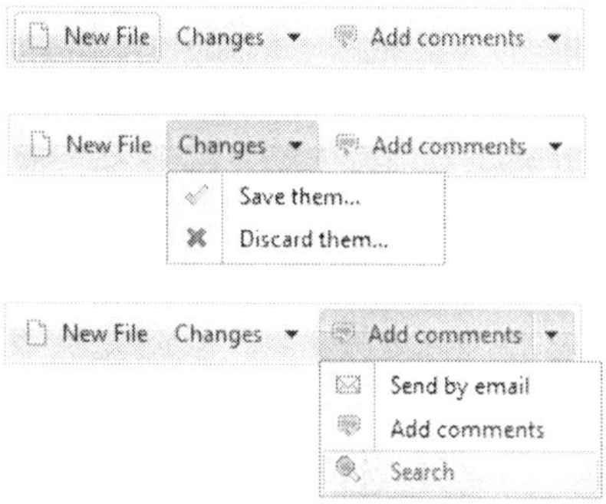

Figure 4-3. *Different types of RadToolBar buttons*

Binding RadMenu to a Datasource

When binding RadMenu to a datasource, you have to keep in mind that a specific structure is needed for the bind to work. Since RadMenu presents hierarchical data, the source must provide all the hierarchy information for the menu to be constructed, thus some properties must be correctly filled in order for the menu construction to work. Table 4-1 lists all of these properties.

The `DataFieldID`, `DataFieldParentID`, and the parent of an item can be of any type, and RadMenu will convert them to strings. Listing 4-3 shows an how to bind RadMenu to a database and Figure 4-4 shows how it looks when the example is run.

Table 4-1. *RadMenu Properties for Data Binding*

Property	Description
`DataSourceID`	The control ID of a datasource control (`ISourceControl`) that will be used as the datasource for the control; required for the binding operation
`DataMember`	The member within the datasource control to be used for binding
`DataFieldID`	Field name from the datasource containing the ID of each item; required for the binding operation

Table 4-1. *Continued*

`DataFieldParentID`	Field name from the datasource containing the parent ID of each item; required for the binding operation
`DataTextField`	Field name from the datasource where the string for the `Text` property of each item; required for the binding operation
`DataValueField`	Field name from the datasource where the string for the `Value` property of each item is
`DataNavigateUrlField`	Field name from the datasource for the string for the `NavigateUrl` property of each item

Listing 4-3. *RadMenu with Database Binding*

ASPX Page

```
<telerik:RadMenu ID="RadMenu1" runat="server"
        DataFieldID="EmployeeID"
        DataFieldParentID="ReportsTo"
        DataSourceID="SqlDataSource1"
        DataTextField="Name"
        DataValueField="EmployeeID"
        Skin="Windows7">
</telerik:RadMenu>

<asp:SqlDataSource ID="SqlDataSource1" runat="server"
    ConnectionString="<%$ ConnectionStrings:NorthwindConnectionString %>"
    SelectCommand="SELECT [EmployeeID],
                          [LastName] + ', ' + [FirstName] AS [Name],
                          [ReportsTo]
                     FROM [Employees]">
</asp:SqlDataSource>
```

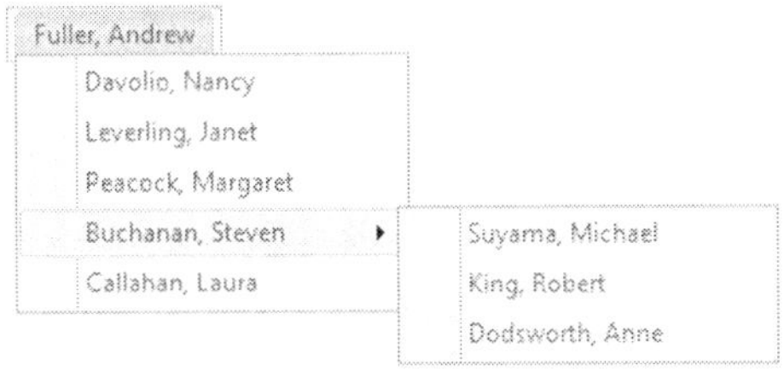

Figure 4-4. *A RadMenu example with database binding*

Showing Items in Multiple Columns

One of the great new additions to the RadMenu control is the ability to show items in multiple columns. This feature is particularly useful when you have too many items to show under one menu option and can't do anything about it; maybe because they come from a datasource as in Listing 4-4. Figure 4-5 shows the menu created in the listing.

Listing 4-4. *Multicolumn RadMenu*

ASPX Page

```
<telerik:RadMenu ID="RadMenu2" runat="server"
        DataFieldID="ID"
        DataFieldParentID="parentID"
        DataSourceID="SqlDataSource2"
        DataTextField="Name"
        DataValueField="ID"
        Skin="Windows7">
    <DefaultGroupSettings
        RepeatColumns="2"
        RepeatDirection="Horizontal" />
</telerik:RadMenu>

<asp:SqlDataSource ID="SqlDataSource2" runat="server"
    ConnectionString="<%$ ConnectionStrings:NorthwindConnectionString %>"
    SelectCommand="select ProductID as ID, ProductName as Name, CategoryID+1000 as parentID
                   from Products p
                   union all
                   select CategoryID+1000 as ID, CategoryName as Name, null as parentID
                   from Categories">
</asp:SqlDataSource>
```

Figure 4-5. *RadMenu with enabled multiple columns*

Navigating with RadMenu

Among of the possible uses for RadMenu are site and data navigation. You can determine exactly which item was selected and, in turn, execute an action that in this case will be to navigate to some page on the web site or another section of data by either opening a new page or executing a page method.

You can identify the selected item in client- or server-side code, depending on the event you are handling. In server-side code, you normally handle the OnItemClick event. The event handler has a parameter of type RadMenuEventArgs, which has a property named Item that represents the RadMenuItem that was clicked.

When working in client-side code, you handle the OnClientItemClicked event. This event has two parameters: the RadMenu object that raised the event and an argument parameter that has a method called get_item() to return the clicked RadMenuItem. The RadMenuItem object on the client side has two methods called get_text() and get_value() that return the displayed text and value of the item, respectively.

Listing 4-5 shows a sample of handling the server-side event, and Listing 4-6 shows the client-side version. Figure 4-6 shows what happens when you run Listing 4-5, and Figure 4-7 shows Listing 4-6 in action.

Listing 4-5. *Using the Server-Side Event ItemClick*

```
ASPX Page

<telerik:RadMenu ID="RadMenu2" runat="server"
        DataFieldID="ID"
        DataFieldParentID="parentID"
        DataSourceID="SqlDataSource2"
        DataTextField="Name"
        DataValueField="ID"
        Skin="Windows7"
        OnItemClick="RadMenu2_ItemClick">
    <DefaultGroupSettings
        RepeatColumns="2"
        RepeatDirection="Horizontal" />
</telerik:RadMenu>

<br /><br />
<asp:Label ID="lblMenuItem" runat="server"></asp:Label>

<asp:SqlDataSource ID="SqlDataSource2" runat="server"
    ConnectionString="<%$ ConnectionStrings:NorthwindConnectionString %>"
    SelectCommand="select ProductID as ID, ProductName as Name, CategoryID+1000 as parentID
                   from Products p
                   union all
                   select CategoryID+1000 as ID, CategoryName as Name, null as parentID
                   from Categories">
</asp:SqlDataSource>

Code Behind

protected void RadMenu2_ItemClick(object sender, RadMenuEventArgs e)
{
    lblMenuItem.Text = string.Format("The selected item was: {0}", e.Item.Text);
}
```

Figure 4-6. *Our RadMenu ItemClick event*

Listing 4-6. *RadMenu ClientItemClicked Event*

ASPX Page

```
<telerik:RadMenu ID="RadMenu2" runat="server"
        DataFieldID="ID"
        DataFieldParentID="parentID"
        DataSourceID="SqlDataSource2"
        DataTextField="Name"
        DataValueField="ID" Skin="Windows7"
        OnClientItemClicked="RadMenu2_ClientItemClicked"
    <DefaultGroupSettings
        RepeatColumns="2"
        RepeatDirection="Horizontal" />
</telerik:RadMenu>

<br /><br />

<asp:Label ID="lblMenuItem" runat="server"></asp:Label>

<asp:SqlDataSource ID="SqlDataSource2" runat="server"
    ConnectionString="<%$ ConnectionStrings:NorthwindConnectionString %>"
    SelectCommand="select ProductID as ID, ProductName as Name, CategoryID+1000 as parentID
                    from Products p
                    union all
                    select CategoryID+1000 as ID, CategoryName as Name, null as parentID
                    from Categories">
</asp:SqlDataSource>

<script type="text/javascript" language="javascript">
    function RadMenu2_ClientItemClicked(sender, args) {
        var item = args.get_item();
        var text = item.get_text();
        alert(text);
    }
</script>
```

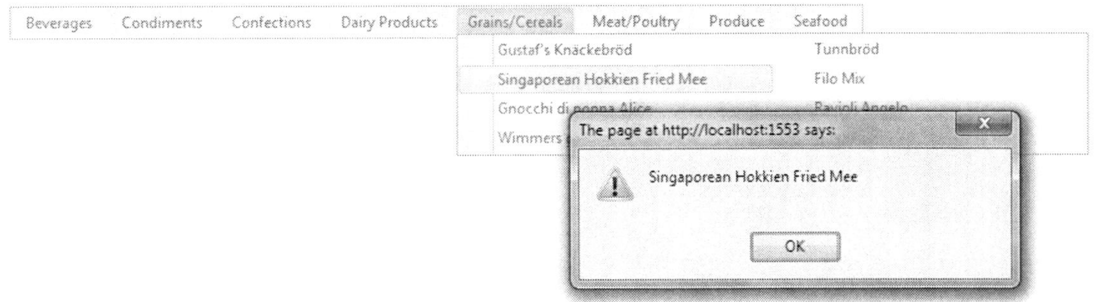

Figure 4-7. *Our RadMenu ClientItemClicked event*

Using RadMenu Templates

One of the most powerful features of RadMenu is its ability to be customized using templates. Customization in this way will not only affect how the items render but enrich the user experience by providing a means to add text, images, and a whole world of controls and markup to each item.

Let's say, for example, you need a menu item to be a check box so a user can enable or disable an option. Better yet, how about having a `RadGrid` control inside a `RadMenuItem`? (We'll examine `RadGrid` in detail in Chapter 6). The point is that, basically, anything can serve as an `Item` template.

RadMenu supports two types of item templates:

- The global `RadMenuItem` template affects the appearance of all items in the menu.
- Individual `Item` templates affect the appearance of a single menu item, overriding the global `RadMenuItem` template if it is set

In addition to the item templates, RadMenu also supports a Loading Status template, which acts as a placeholder for a child group that is loaded from a Web service while a request for items is being serviced.

Listing 4-7 shows an implementation of a menu with templates, and Figure 4-8 shows how the template looks at runtime.

Listing 4-7. *RadMenu Templates*

ASPX Page

```
<telerik:RadMenu ID="RadMenu3" runat="server"
         DataFieldID="ID"
         DataFieldParentID="parentID"
         DataSourceID="SqlDataSource2"
         OnItemDataBound="RadMenu3_ItemDataBound"
         DataTextField="Name"
         DataValueField="ID"
         Skin="Windows7">
<ItemTemplate>
<asp:CheckBox ID="chkProduct" runat="server"
Visible='<%# int.Parse(DataBinder.Eval(Container.DataItem, "ID").ToString()) < 1000 %>' />
    <asp:Label ID="lblProduct" runat="server"
Text='<%# DataBinder.Eval(Container.DataItem, "Name") %>' />
</ItemTemplate>
</telerik:RadMenu>
```

```
<asp:SqlDataSource ID="SqlDataSource2" runat="server"
    ConnectionString="<%$ ConnectionStrings:NorthwindConnectionString %>"
    SelectCommand="select ProductID as ID, ProductName as Name, CategoryID+1000 as parentID
                    from Products p
                    union all
                    select CategoryID+1000 as ID, CategoryName as Name, null as parentID
                    from Categories">
</asp:SqlDataSource>
```

Figure 4-8. *The RadMenu template from Listing 4-7*

Setting RadMenuItem Custom Attributes

`RadMenuItem` has the ability to define custom attributes (actually, all RadControls with the exception of `RadSiteMap` have the ability to define custom attributes). These attributes can be defined inline, in server-side code through the `Attributes` collection, and in client-side code using the `getAttribute()` and `setAttribute()` methods.

Custom attributes are important, because they offer the possibility of adding more information to the menu items that we can access later. A common scenario would be to prevent additional requests to the database. If you load all the information when binding RadMenu, the additional information can be added to these attributes avoiding future requests to the database thus improving performance. Listing 4-8 shows an example of setting the custom attributes in server-side code and loading them in client-side code, and their usage are illustrated in Figure 4-9.

Listing 4-8. *RadMenuItem Custom Attributes*

ASPX Page

```
<telerik:RadMenu ID="RadMenu4" runat="server"
                DataFieldID="ID"
                DataFieldParentID="parentID"
                DataSourceID="SqlDataSource2"
                OnItemDataBound="RadMenu4_ItemDataBound"
                OnClientItemClicked="RadMenu4_ClientItemClicked"
                DataTextField="Name"
                DataValueField="ID"
                Skin="Windows7">
</telerik:RadMenu>
```

```
<asp:SqlDataSource ID="SqlDataSource2" runat="server"
    ConnectionString="<%$ ConnectionStrings:NorthwindConnectionString %>"
    SelectCommand="select ProductID as ID, ProductName as Name, UnitPrice,
                          CategoryID+1000 as parentID
                   from Products p
                   union all
                   select CategoryID+1000 as ID, CategoryName as Name, 0 as UnitPrice,
                          null as parentID
                   from Categories">
</asp:SqlDataSource>

<script type="text/javascript" language="javascript">
    function RadMenu4_ClientItemClicked(sender, args) {
        var item = args.get_item();
        var id = item.get_value();
        if (id < 1000) {
                var attributes = item.get_attributes();
                var price = attributes.getAttribute("UnitPrice");
                alert("Unit Price: " + price);
        }
    }
</script>
```

Code Behind

```
protected void RadMenu4_ItemDataBound(object sender, RadMenuEventArgs e)
{
    // If it is a category then don't add the custom attribute
    int id = Convert.ToInt32(e.Item.Value);
    if (id > 1000)
        return;

    // If it is a product add the custom attribute
    DataRowView dataRow = e.Item.DataItem as DataRowView;
    If (dataRow != null)
    {
        e.Item.Attributes["UnitPrice"] = string.Format("{0:c}", dataRow["UnitPrice"]);
    }
}
```

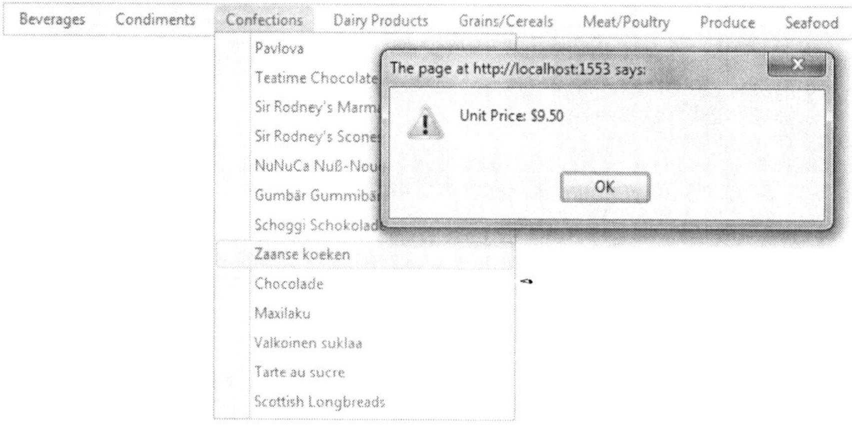

Figure 4-9. *A custom attribute is used to show the products unit price.*

Creating a Two-State RadToolBarButton

You can create two-state `RadToolBarButton` objects with the `CheckOnClick` property. A two-state button (also known as a toggle button) is one that remains checked (turned on) after releasing the mouse button. This type of button also supports mutually exclusivity when creating a group of buttons, meaning that only one button in the group can be checked (just like the alignment buttons in the Microsoft Word toolbar). Listing 4-9 shows a sample of a two-state `RadToolBarButton`, which is illustrated in Figure 4-10.

Listing 4-9. *A Two-State RadToolBarButton*

ASPX Page

```
<telerik:RadToolBar ID="RadToolBar2" Runat="server"
        Skin="Windows7">
        <Items>
                <telerik:RadToolBarButton runat="server"
                        ImageUrl="~/Images/icons/file.png"
                        Text="Enable New Items"
                        CheckOnClick="true"
                        AllowSelfUnCheck="true">
                </telerik:RadToolBarButton>

                <telerik:RadToolBarButton IsSeparator="true" />

                <telerik:RadToolBarButton
                        ImageUrl="~/Images/left2.gif"
                        Text="Left"
                        Group="Align"
                        CheckOnClick="true">
                </telerik:RadToolBarButton>
```

```
            <telerik:RadToolBarButton
                    ImageUrl="~/Images/center.gif"
                    Text="Center"
                    Group="Align"
                    CheckOnClick="true"
                    Checked="true">
            </telerik:RadToolBarButton>
            <telerik:RadToolBarButton
                    ImageUrl="~/Images/right2.gif"
                    Text="Right"
                    Group="Align"
                    CheckOnClick="true">
            </telerik:RadToolBarButton>
        </Items>
</telerik:RadToolBar>
```

Figure 4-10. *The Left, Center, and Right buttons are grouped so only one can be selected at a time and have enabled the CheckOnClick property for the two-state behavior.*

Using RadTreeView

The RadTreeView control is easy to use but powerful, and it supports capabilities such as loading on demand, templates, data binding, enhanced drag-and-drop functionality, built-in context menus, animations, multinode selection, check box support, and full-featured client-side and server-side APIs.

Performing Simple Navigation

Navigation with a RadTreeView is very easy with the use of the `NavigateUrl` property of the `RadTreeNode` object, which is shown in Listing 4-10.

Listing 4-10. *RadTreeView Navigation*

ASPX Page

```
<telerik:RadTreeView ID="RadTreeView11" runat="server"
        Skin="Web20">
        <Nodes>
                <telerik:RadTreeNode
                        Text="Products"
                        NavigateUrl="Products/Default.aspx">
                        <Nodes>
                                <telerik:RadTreeNode
                                        Text="Bread"
                                        NavigateUrl="Products/Bread.aspx">
                                </telerik:RadTreeNode>
```

```
                        <telerik:RadTreeNode
                                Text="Butter"
                                NavigateUrl="Products/Butter.aspx">
                        </telerik:RadTreeNode>
                        <telerik:RadTreeNode
                                Text="Milk"
                                NavigateUrl="Products/Milk.aspx">
                        </telerik:RadTreeNode>
                        <telerik:RadTreeNode
                                Text="Ham"
                                NavigateUrl="Products/Ham.aspx">
                        </telerik:RadTreeNode>
                </Nodes>
        </telerik:RadTreeNode>
        <telerik:RadTreeNode
                Text="Stores"
                NavigateUrl="Stores/Default.aspx">
                <Nodes>
                        <telerik:RadTreeNode
                                Text="HQ"
                                NavigateUrl="Stores/hq.aspx">
                        </telerik:RadTreeNode>
                        <telerik:RadTreeNode
                                Text="North"
                                NavigateUrl="Stores/North.aspx">
                        </telerik:RadTreeNode>
                        <telerik:RadTreeNode
                                Text="South"
                                NavigateUrl="Stores/South.aspx">
                        </telerik:RadTreeNode>
                </Nodes>
        </telerik:RadTreeNode>
    </Nodes>
</telerik:RadTreeView>
```

Implementing Drag-and-Drop Functionality

The drag-and-drop functionality can be used on client-side or server-side code; you should choose which mechanism to use based on the complexity of the operation you need to perform. RadTreeView supports dragging and dropping between nodes in the same tree and different trees and between different objects such as grids or HTML controls.

Listing 4-11 shows you how to perform the drag and drop between nodes in the same tree, and Listing 4-12 shows you another example where the node is dropped onto a simple ASP.NET list box control.

Listing 4-11. *Using RadTreeView to Drag and Drop Beetween Nodes in the Same Tree*

ASPX Page

```
<telerik:RadTreeView ID="RadTreeView1" runat="server"
        Skin="Web20"
        EnableDragAndDrop="true"
        EnableDragAndDropBetweenNodes="true"
```

```
        DataSourceID="SqlDataSource1"
        OnNodeDrop="RadTreeView1_NodeDrop"
        DataFieldID="ID"
        DataFieldParentID="parentID"
        DataTextField="Name"
        DataValueField="ID">
</telerik:RadTreeView>

<asp:SqlDataSource ID="SqlDataSource1" runat="server"
ConnectionString="<%$ ConnectionStrings:NorthwindConnectionString %>"
SelectCommand="select ProductID as ID, ProductName as Name, CategoryID+1000 as parentID
                from Products p
                union all
                select CategoryID+1000 as ID, CategoryName as Name, null as parentID
                from Categories">
</asp:SqlDataSource>
```

Code Behind

```
protected void RadTreeView1_NodeDrop(object sender, RadTreeNodeDragDropEventArgs e)
{
    RadTreeNode sourceNode = e.SourceDragNode;
    RadTreeNode destNode = e.DestDragNode;
    int destinationNodeValue = Convert.ToInt32(destNode.Value);
    int sourceNodeValue = Convert.ToInt32(sourceNode.Value);
    int parentNodeValue = destNode.ParentNode == null
                ? destinationNodeValue
                : Convert.ToInt32(destNode.ParentNode.Value);
    int nodeValue = destinationNodeValue > 1000
                        ? destinationNodeValue
                        : parentNodeValue;
    int categoryID = nodeValue - 1000;

    RadTreeWebService.UpdateProductCategory(sourceNodeValue, categoryID);

    // Move the node in the tree to visually see the drop operation
    if (sourceNode.TreeView.SelectedNodes.Count <= 1)
    {
        if (!sourceNode.IsAncestorOf(destNode))
        {
            sourceNode.Owner.Nodes.Remove(sourceNode);
            if (destinationNodeValue > 1000)
            {
                destNode.Nodes.Add(sourceNode);
            }
            else
            {
                destNode.ParentNode.Nodes.Add(sourceNode);
            }
        }
    }
```

```
    else
    {
        if (sourceNode.TreeView.SelectedNodes.Count > 1)
        {
            RadTreeView1.SelectedNodes
                        .Where(node => !node.IsAncestorOf(destNode))
                        .ToList()
                        .ForEach(node =>
                        {
                            node.Owner.Nodes.Remove(node);
                            if (destinationNodeValue > 1000)
                            {
                                destNode.Nodes.Add(node);
                            }
                            else
                            {
                                destNode.ParentNode.Nodes.Add(sourceNode);
                            }
                        });
        }
    }}
```

RadTreeWebService.asmx

```
public static void UpdateProductCategory(int ID, int catid)
{
        string connectionString = ConfigurationManager
                                        .ConnectionStrings["NorthwindConnectionString"]
                                        .ConnectionString;
        string sql = "UPDATE Products ";
        sql += string.Format("SET CategoryID = '{0}' ", categoryID);
        sql += string.Format("WHERE ProductID = {1}", ID);

        using (SqlConnection connection = new SqlConnection(connectionString))
        {
                using (SqlCommand command = new SqlCommand(sql, connection))
                {
                        try
                        {
                                connection.Open();
                                command.ExecuteNonQuery();
                        }
                        catch (Exception ex)
                        {
                                // Error handling logic
                        }
                }
        }
}
```

Listing 4-12. *Using RadTreeView to Drag and Drop to HTML Controls*

ASPX Page

```
<telerik:RadTreeView ID="RadTreeView6" runat="server"
        Skin="Web20"
        EnableDragAndDrop="true"
        EnableDragAndDropBetweenNodes="false"
        ataSourceID="SqlDataSource1"
        OnNodeDrop="RadTreeView6_NodeDrop"
        DataFieldID="ID"
        DataFieldParentID="parentID"
        DataTextField="Name"
        DataValueField="ID">
</telerik:RadTreeView>

<asp:ListBox ID="listProducts" runat="server"
        Width="200px"
        Height="100px">
</asp:ListBox>
```

Code Behind

```
protected void RadTreeView6_NodeDrop(object sender, RadTreeNodeDragDropEventArgs e)
{
        RadTreeNode sourceNode = e.SourceDragNode;
        ListBox htmlList = Page.FindControlRecursive(this, e.HtmlElementID) as ListBox;
        if (htmlList != null)
        {
                htmlList.Items.Add(sourceNode.Text);
        }
}

protected Control FindControlRecursive(Control root, string id)
{
        if (root.ID == id)
        {
                return root;
        }

        foreach (Control c in root.Controls)
        {
                Control t = FindControlRecursive(c, id);
                if (t != null)
                {
                        return t;
                }
        }

        return null;
}
```

Supporting Check Boxes

RadTreeView supports the use of check boxes for nodes; this allows you to more clearly provide a user with multinode selection and even triple-state check boxes. Triple-state check boxes are those that have a third state named `Indeterminate` by the effect of not having all child nodes checked. The possible states of the check box node follow:

- *Checked*: The check boxes of all child nodes are checked.
- *Unchecked*: The check boxes of all child nodes are unchecked.
- *Indeterminate*: There are checked and unchecked child node check boxes.

The example in Listing 4-13 shows how to work with check boxes, and Figure 4-11 shows the example in action.

Listing 4-13. *Using RadTreeView for Triple-State Check Boxes*

ASPX Page

```
<telerik:RadTreeView ID="RadTreeView21" runat="server"
        Skin="Web20" CheckBoxes="true"
        DataFieldID="ID"
        DataFieldParentID="parentID"
        DataSourceID="SqlDataSource1"
        DataTextField="Name"
        DataValueField="ID"
        TriStateCheckBoxes="true">
</telerik:RadTreeView>

<asp:SqlDataSource ID="SqlDataSource1" runat="server"
    ConnectionString="<%$ ConnectionStrings:NorthwindConnectionString %>"
    SelectCommand="SELECT ProductID AS ID, ProductName AS Name,
                          CategoryID + 1000 AS parentID
                   FROM Products p
                   UNION ALL
                   SELECT CategoryID + 1000 AS ID, CategoryName AS Name, null AS parentID
                   FROM Categories">
</asp:SqlDataSource>
```

Figure 4-11. *Triple-State RadTreeView check boxes*

The example in Listing 4-14 is a modification of the previous example in which I hide the check box for the parent nodes. Figure 4-12 shows the end result.

Listing 4-14. *Using RadTreeView to Hide Check Boxes for Parent Nodes*

ASPX Page

```
<telerik:RadTreeView ID="RadTreeView2" runat="server"
        Skin="Web20" CheckBoxes="true"
        DataFieldID="ID"
        DataFieldParentID="parentID"
        DataSourceID="SqlDataSource1"
        DataTextField="Name"
        DataValueField="ID">
        <DataBindings>
                <telerik:RadTreeNodeBinding
                        Depth="0"
                        Checkable="false" />
        </DataBindings>
</telerik:RadTreeView>

<asp:SqlDataSource ID="SqlDataSource1" runat="server"
    ConnectionString="<%$ ConnectionStrings:NorthwindConnectionString %>"
    SelectCommand="SELECT ProductID AS ID, ProductName AS Name,
                          CategoryID + 1000 AS parentID
                   FROM Products p
                   UNION ALL
                   SELECT CategoryID + 1000 AS ID, CategoryName AS Name, null AS parentID
                   FROM Categories">
</asp:SqlDataSource>
```

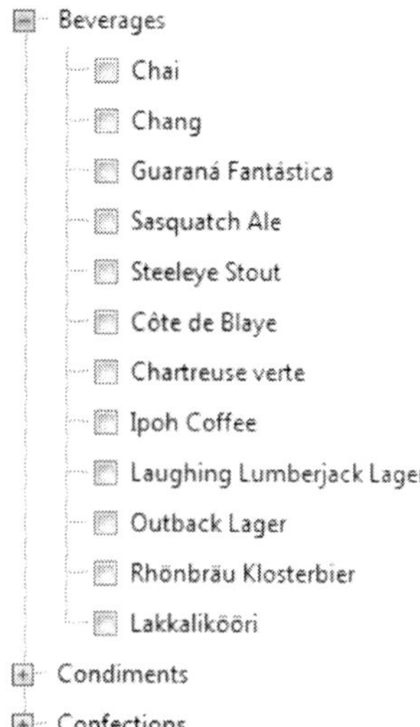

Figure 4-12. *RadTreeView has hidden the check boxes for parent nodes.*

Loading Nodes on Demand

RadTreeView supports loading nodes on demand, which improves the initial load time by not completely filling the tree view from the beginning. You can load nodes on demand using various technologies such as web services and client- and server-side events.

The example in Listing 4-15 shows you how to load nodes on demand using a web service. The tree root items are loaded using the `SlqDataSource`; and when they are expanded, an event is raised in the node calling the web service method to load the child nodes.

Listing 4-15. *Using RadTreeView to Load on Demand with a Web Service*

ASPX Page

```
<telerik:RadTreeView ID="RadTreeView3" runat="server"
        Skin="Web20"
        DataFieldID="CategoryID"
        DataSourceID="SqlDataSource2"
        DataTextField="CategoryName"
        DataValueField="CategoryID">
        <DataBindings>
                <telerik:RadTreeNodeBinding
                        Depth="0"
                        ExpandMode="WebService" />
        </DataBindings>
        <WebServiceSettings
                Path="RadTreeWebService.asmx"
                Method="GetProducts" />
</telerik:RadTreeView>
```

```
<asp:SqlDataSource ID="SqlDataSource2" runat="server"
        ConnectionString="<%$ ConnectionStrings:NorthwindConnectionString %>"
        SelectCommand="select CategoryID, CategoryName from Categories">
</asp:SqlDataSource>
```

RadTreeWebSerivce.asmx

```
[WebMethod]
public RadTreeNodeData[] GetProducts(RadTreeNodeData node, object context)
{
    string connectionString = ConfigurationManager
                              .ConnectionStrings["NorthwindConnectionString"]
                              .ConnectionString;
    string sql = "SELECT ProductID, ProductName ";
           sql += " FROM Products ";
           sql += string.Format("WHERE CategoryID = {0}", node.Value);
    DataTable products = new DataTable();
    using (SqlConnection connection = new SqlConnection(connectionString))
    using (SqlCommand command = new SqlCommand(sql, connection))
    using (SqlDataAdapter adapter = new SqlDataAdapter(command))
    {
        try
        {
            adapter.Fill(products);
        }
        catch (Exception ex)
        {
            // Error handling logic
        }
    }

    int count = products.Rows.Count;
    RadTreeNodeData[] result = new RadTreeNodeData[count];
    for (int i = 0; i < count; i++)
    {
        RadTreeNodeData itemData = new RadTreeNodeData
        {
            Text = products.Rows[i]["ProductName"].ToString(),
            Value = products.Rows[i]["ProductID"].ToString()
        };
        result[i] = itemData;
    }

    return result;
}
```

Modifying Node Text

One common scenario for using the RadTreeView control is to present data loaded from a source such as a database. In this scenario, one of the most common tasks is to enable the user to change the text of the information represented in each of the nodes. This task is very simple with the use of the

AllowNodeEditing property and the OnNodeEdit server-side event. When editing mode is enabled, users can press F12 on the keyboard or click the node a second time.

Listing 4-16 shows this functionality by enabling the user to change the node text and modifying the database to reflect the change. In Figure 4-13 you can see the editing mode enabled.

Listing 4-16. *Using the property AllowNodeEditing in RadTreeView to allow users to modify the node's text*

ASPX Page

```
<telerik:RadTreeView ID="RadTreeView4" runat="server"
        Skin="Web20"
        DataFieldID="ID"
        DataFieldParentID="parentID"
        DataSourceID="SqlDataSource1"
        DataTextField="Name"
        DataValueField="ID"
        AllowNodeEditing="true"
        OnNodeEdit="RadTreeView4_NodeEdit">
</telerik:RadTreeView>
```

Code Behind

```
protected void RadTreeView4_NodeEdit(object sender, RadTreeNodeEditEventArgs e)
{
    int id = Convert.ToInt32(e.Node.Value);

    if (id > 1000)
        RadTreeWebService.UpdateCategoryName(id - 1000, e.Text);
    else
        RadTreeWebService.UpdateProductName(id, e.Text);

    e.Node.Text = e.Text;
}
```

RadTreeWebSerivce.asmx

```
public static void UpdateProductName(int ID, string name)
{
    string connectionString = ConfigurationManager
                                  .ConnectionStrings["NorthwindConnectionString"]
                                  .ConnectionString;
    string sql = "UPDATE Products ";
           sql += string.Format("SET ProductName = '{0}' ", name);
           sql += string.Format("WHERE ProductID = {1}", ID);

    using (SqlConnection connection = new SqlConnection(connectionString))
    using (SqlCommand command = new SqlCommand(sql, connection))
    {
        try
        {
            connection.Open();
            command.ExecuteNonQuery();
        }
```

```
        catch (Exception ex)
        {
            // Error handling logic
        }
    }
}

public static void UpdateCategoryName(int ID, string name)
{
    string connectionString = ConfigurationManager
                              .ConnectionStrings["NorthwindConnectionString"]
                              .ConnectionString;
    string sql = "UPDATE Categories ";
           sql += string.Format("SET CategoryName = '{0}' ", name);
           sql += string.Format("WHERE CategoryID = {1}", ID);
    using (SqlConnection connection = new SqlConnection(connectionString))
    using (SqlCommand command = new SqlCommand(sql, connection))
    {
        try
        {
            connection.Open();
            command.ExecuteNonQuery();
        }
        catch (Exception ex)
        {
            // Error handling logic
        }
    }
}
```

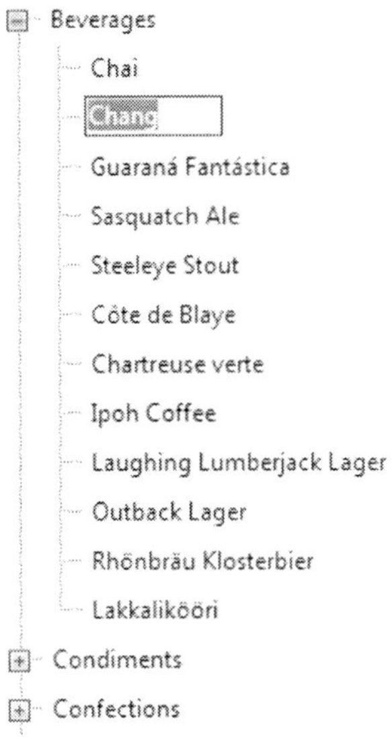

Figure 4-13. *RadTreeView with editing mode enabled*

Using Node Templates

RadTreeView also supports node templates. With node templates, you can alter the default rendering of the nodes by adding any type of styling or information to tree nodes. Listing 4-17 shows the creation of node templates, and Figure 4-14 shows how the nodes look.

Listing 4-17. *Creating RadTreeView Node Templates*

ASPX Page

```
<style type="text/css">
    .category-node,
    .product-node
    {
        border: 1px solid navy;
        background-color:#36f;
        color:#fff;
        height:20px;
        width:200px
    }

    .product-node
    {
        background-color:#339;
        height:40px;
    }
</style>

<telerik:RadTreeView ID="RadTreeView5" runat="server"
        Skin="Web20"
        DataFieldID="ID"
        DataFieldParentID="parentID"
        DataSourceID="SqlDataSource1"
        DataTextField="Name"
        DataValueField="ID"
        OnNodeDataBound="RadTreeView5_NodeDataBound">
        <NodeTemplate>
                <div id="divElement" runat="server">
                        <asp:Label ID="lblNodeText" runat="server"></asp:Label>
                        <asp:Label ID="lblPrice" runat="server"></asp:Label>
                </div>
        </NodeTemplate>
</telerik:RadTreeView>
```

Code Behind

```
protected void RadTreeView5_NodeDataBound(object sender, RadTreeNodeEventArgs e)
{
    DataRowView dataRow = e.Node.DataItem as DataRowView;
    HtmlGenericControl divNode = e.Node.FindControl("node") as HtmlGenericControl;
    Label lblName = e.Node.FindControl("lblNodeText") as Label;
    Label lblPrice = e.Node.FindControl("lblPrice") as Label;
```

```
    if (dataRow != null && divNode != null && lblName != null && lblPrice != null)
    {
        int id = Convert.ToInt32(dataRow["ID"]);
        if (id > 1000)
        {
            divNode.Attributes["class"] = "category-node";
            lblName.Text = String.Format("Category: {0}", dataRow["Name"]);
        }
        else
        {
            divNode.Attributes["class"] = "product-node";
            lblName.Text = String.Format("Product: {0}", dataRow["Name"]);
            lblPrice.Text = string.Format("<br />Unit Price: {0:c}", dataRow["UnitPrice"]);
        }
    }
}
```

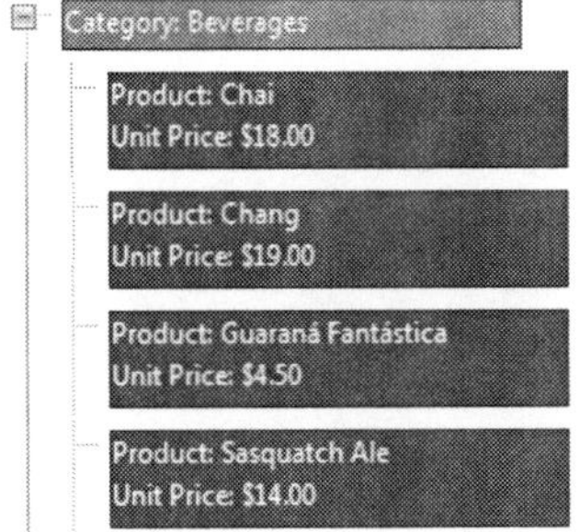

Figure 4-14. *RadTreeView node templates*

Using RadSiteMap

The RadSiteMap control will allow you to create lightweight and highly customizable sitemaps for your web site. With its efficient semantic rendering, RadSiteMap gives you a lightning-fast solution and highly optimized HTML output. You can organize and list the pages on your web site, customize the layout, choose from a variety of appearance options and templates, and if that's not enough, add value to your web site by optimizing it for crawlers and search engines with no extra development effort.

Basically, the control will read your sitemap file and build the list of pages with the layout defined. The layout created is semantic HTML, meaning it does not rely on tables.

Another approach is to bind the control to a datasource, so you can create, for example, a map for your products pages navigating through the categories of products.

Working with the Layout

RadSiteMap has several properties to control the final layout. Listing 4-18 shows the usage of the `Layout` property, and Listing 4-19 shows how to work with the `ShowNoLines` property. Figure 4-15 illustrates the sample in Listing 4-18, and Figure 4-16 illustrates the sample in Listing 4-19. You will find that you can customize the appearance of the generated links at any level, meaning that you can control how each of the different levels in the page hierarchy will render.

Listing 4-18. *The RadSiteMap Layout Property*

```
Web.sitemap file

<?xml version="1.0" encoding="utf-8" ?>
<siteMap xmlns="http://schemas.microsoft.com/AspNet/SiteMap-File-1.0" >
    <siteMapNode url="" title="Root"  description="">
        <siteMapNode url=""
                title="Services"
                description="Our range of services is so complete you will
                                end up hiring us">
        <siteMapNode url=""
                title="Web Development"
                description="Need a custom development? We are here for you." />
        <siteMapNode url=""
                title="Web Hosting"
                description="For all your hosting needs we provide the most
                                reliable and full featured plans" />
        <siteMapNode url=""
                title="SEO"
                description="Our SEO services will garantee your website
                                will ve visible to the whole world" />
        </siteMapNode>
        <siteMapNode url=""
                title="Products"
                description="Products created thinking of you">
        <siteMapNode url=""
                title="CRM"
                description="Our CRM tool is what you need to keep and
                                ehance your client relations" />
        <siteMapNode url=""
                title="Portal"
                description="The portal solution that will integrate all
                                of your company departments in one place" />
        <siteMapNode url=""
                title="UI Components"
                description="UI components to aid in the development
                                of new solutions" />
        </siteMapNode>
        <siteMapNode url="" title="About Us" description="Want to know about us?">
        <siteMapNode url="" title="Company History"  description="How we came to be." />
        <siteMapNode url="" title="Our Team"  description="Want to mee us?" />
        <siteMapNode url="" title="Carrers"  description="Want to join us?" />
        <siteMapNode url="" title="Contact"  description="Want to contact us?" />
      </siteMapNode>
    </siteMapNode>
</siteMap>
```

ASPX Page

```
<telerik:RadSiteMap ID="RadSiteMap1" runat="server"
        DataSourceID="RadSiteMapDataSource1"
        Skin="Forest">
        <LevelSettings>
                <telerik:SiteMapLevelSetting
                        Level="0"
                        Layout="List">
                        <ListLayout
                                RepeatColumns="3"
                                RepeatDirection="Horizontal" />
                </telerik:SiteMapLevelSetting>
                <telerik:SiteMapLevelSetting
                        Level="1"
                        Layout="Flow">
                </telerik:SiteMapLevelSetting>
        </LevelSettings>
</telerik:RadSiteMap>

<telerik:RadSiteMapDataSource ID="RadSiteMapDataSource1" runat="server"
        SiteMapFile="~/Web.sitemap"
        ShowStartingNode="False" />
```

Services	Products	About Us
Web Development | Web Hosting | SEO	CRM | Portal | UI Components	Company History | Our Team | Carrers | Contact

Figure 4-15. *The RadSiteMap Layout property in action*

Listing 4-19. *The RadSiteMap ShowNodeLines Property*

ASPX Page

```
<telerik:RadSiteMap ID="RadSiteMap1" runat="server"
        ShowNodeLines="true"
        DataSourceID="RadSiteMapDataSource1"
        Skin="Forest">
        <LevelSettings>
                <telerik:SiteMapLevelSetting
                        Level="0"
                        Layout="List">
                        <ListLayout
                                RepeatColumns="3"
                                RepeatDirection="Horizontal" />
                </telerik:SiteMapLevelSetting>
```

```
                <telerik:SiteMapLevelSetting
                        Level="1"
                        Layout="List">
                </telerik:SiteMapLevelSetting>
        </LevelSettings>
</telerik:RadSiteMap>

<telerik:RadSiteMapDataSource ID="RadSiteMapDataSource1" runat="server"
        SiteMapFile="~/Web.sitemap"
        ShowStartingNode="False" />
```

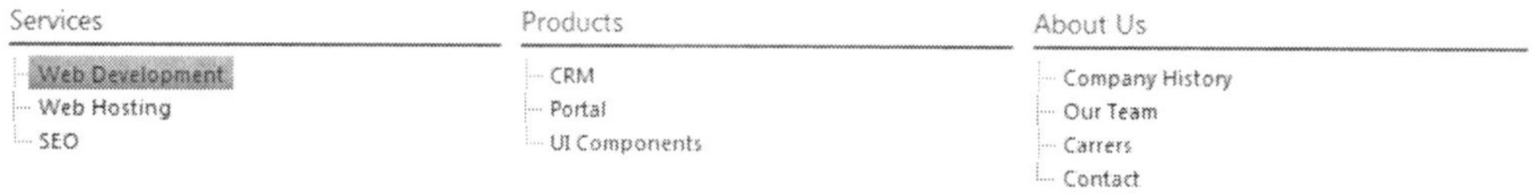

Services	Products	About Us
Web Development	CRM	Company History
Web Hosting	Portal	Our Team
SEO	UI Components	Carrers
		Contact

Figure 4-16. *RadSiteMap's ShowNodeLines in action*

Working with Templates

You can define templates at different levels: globally, per level, and per node. As with the other control templates you have seen, you can pretty much define anything inside the template. See in Listing 4-20 how to apply templates to RadSiteMap. Figure 4-17 shows how the template looks.

Listing 4-20. *Creating a Node Template for RadSiteMap*

ASPX Page

```
<telerik:RadSiteMap ID="RadSiteMap3" runat="server"
        ShowNodeLines="true"
        DataSourceID="RadSiteMapDataSource1"
        Skin="Forest">
        <LevelSettings>
                <telerik:SiteMapLevelSetting
                        Level="0"
                        Layout="List">
                        <ListLayout
                                RepeatColumns="3"
                                RepeatDirection="Horizontal" />
                        <NodeTemplate>
                                <h1>
                                        <%# DataBinder.Eval(Container.DataItem, "title") %>
                                </h1>
                                <p>
                                <%# DataBinder.Eval(Container.DataItem, "description") %>
                                </p>
                        </NodeTemplate>
                </telerik:SiteMapLevelSetting>
```

```
                <telerik:SiteMapLevelSetting
                        Level="1"
                        Layout="List">
                </telerik:SiteMapLevelSetting>
        </LevelSettings>
</telerik:RadSiteMap>

<telerik:RadSiteMapDataSource ID="RadSiteMapDataSource1" runat="server"
        SiteMapFile="~/Web.sitemap"
        ShowStartingNode="False" />
```

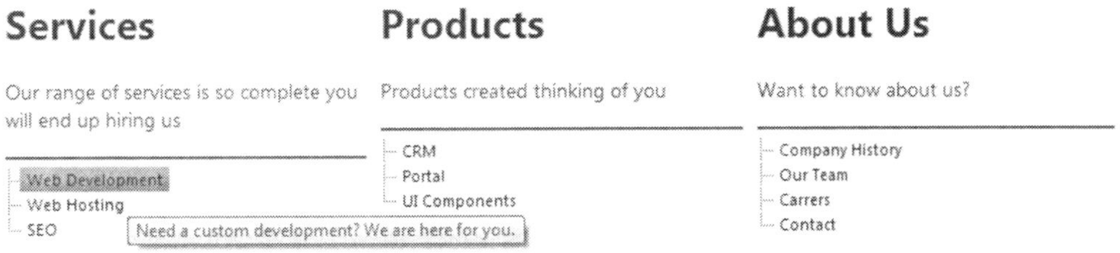

Figure 4-17. *The node template in RadSiteMap for the first level nodes*

Binding RadSiteMap to a Datasource

When binding RadSiteMap to a datasource, it is important to correctly define the properties listed in Table 4-1. In this case, they will apply to nodes in the map structure instead of menu items and tree nodes (see Figure 4-18), but they are defined in the same way.

Listing 4-21. *RadSiteMap Data Binding*

ASPX Page

```
<telerik:RadSiteMap ID="RadSiteMap4" runat="server"
        ShowNodeLines="true"
        DataSourceID="SqlDataSource1"
        Skin="Forest"
        DataFieldID="ID"
        DataFieldParentID="parentID"
        DataTextField="Name"
        DataValueField="ID">
        <LevelSettings>
                <telerik:SiteMapLevelSetting
                        Level="0"
                        Layout="List">
                        <ListLayout
                                AlignRows="true"
                                RepeatColumns="3"
                                RepeatDirection="Horizontal" />
                </telerik:SiteMapLevelSetting>
```

```
                <telerik:SiteMapLevelSetting
                    Level="1"
                    Layout="List">
                </telerik:SiteMapLevelSetting>
        </LevelSettings>
</telerik:RadSiteMap>

<asp:SqlDataSource ID="SqlDataSource1" runat="server"
    ConnectionString="<%$ ConnectionStrings:NorthwindConnectionString %>"
    SelectCommand="select ProductID as ID, ProductName as Name, CategoryID+1000 as parentID
                from Products p
                union all
                select CategoryID+1000 as ID, CategoryName as Name, null as parentID
                from Categories">
</asp:SqlDataSource>
```

Beverages

- Chai
- Chang
- Guaraná Fantástica
- Sasquatch Ale
- Steeleye Stout
- Côte de Blaye
- Chartreuse verte
- Ipoh Coffee
- Laughing Lumberjack Lager
- Outback Lager
- Rhönbräu Klosterbier
- Lakkalikööri

Condiments

- Aniseed Syrup
- Chef Anton's Cajun Seasoning
- Chef Anton's Gumbo Mix
- Grandma's Boysenberry Spread
- Northwoods Cranberry Sauce
- Genen Shouyu
- Gula Malacca
- Sirop d'érable
- Vegie-spread
- Louisiana Fiery Hot Pepper Sauce
- Louisiana Hot Spiced Okra
- Original Frankfurter grüne Soße

Confections

- Pavlova
- Teatime Chocolate Biscuits
- Sir Rodney's Marmalade
- Sir Rodney's Scones
- NuNuCa Nuß-Nougat-Creme
- Gumbär Gummibärchen
- Schoggi Schokolade
- Zaanse koeken
- Chocolade
- Maxilaku
- Valkoinen suklaa
- Tarte au sucre
- Scottish Longbreads

Dairy Products

- Queso Cabrales
- Queso Manchego La Pastora
- Gorgonzola Telino
- Mascarpone Fabioli
- Geitost
- Raclette Courdavault
- Camembert Pierrot
- Gudbrandsdalsost
- Flotemysost
- Mozzarella di Giovanni

Grains/Cereals

- Gustaf's Knäckebröd
- Tunnbröd
- Singaporean Hokkien Fried Mee
- Filo Mix
- Gnocchi di nonna Alice
- Ravioli Angelo
- Wimmers gute Semmelknödel

Meat/Poultry

- Mishi Kobe Niku
- Alice Mutton
- Thüringer Rostbratwurst
- Perth Pasties
- Tourtière
- Pâté chinois

Produce

- Uncle Bob's Organic Dried Pears
- Tofu
- Rössle Sauerkraut
- Manjimup Dried Apples
- Longlife Tofu

Seafood

- Ikura
- Konbu
- Carnarvon Tigers
- Nord-Ost Matjeshering
- Inlagd Sill

Figure 4-18. *This RadSiteMap shows the structure of the products and its categories*

Using RadPanelBar

RadPanelBar is a component for building collapsible panels much like Microsoft Outlook's side panels. It is basically a multiple-panel container that has the ability to behave as a side menu or tool bar as well as a container for other items through the use of templates. It can be bound to a datasource and can be configured to have icons and animations and supports CSS and keyboard navigation. Its lightweight semantic rendering (no HTML tables) minimizes the impact on performance.

Navigating with RadPanelBar

Navigation with RadPanelBar is achieved using the `NavigateUrl` property for each item in the control. The field can be filled manually for each item or assigned through the `DataNavigateUrlField` property when bound to a datasource.

In Listing 4-22, you will find how the control is bound to a sitemap file and automatically filled with the values provided in the file. Figure 4-19 illustrates the results of running the code.

Listing 4-22. *RadPanelBar Navigation*

ASPX Page

```
<telerik:RadPanelBar ID="RadPanelBar1" runat="server"
        DataSourceID="RadSiteMapDataSource1"
        DataFieldID="Title"
        DataNavigateUrlField="Url"
        DataTextField="Title"
        DataValueField="Title"
        ExpandMode="SingleExpandedItem">
</telerik:RadPanelBar>

<telerik:RadSiteMapDataSource ID="RadSiteMapDataSource1" runat="server"
        SiteMapFile="Web.Sitemap"
        ShowStartingNode="false" />
```

Figure 4-19. *Our RadPanelBar navigation*

Binding to a Database

Binding to a database is very easy. You can use any of the datasource controls, such as `SqlDataSource` or `XmlDataSource`. You need to remember to set the properties in Table 4-1. `RadPanelBar` will automatically recognize the root-level items, as well as items at any other level, and build the interface for you.

You can further customize the appearance of the items with the use of the DataBindings collection where you can define specific properties such as CSS classes, enable or disable images, and so forth for each of the levels in the hierarchy.

Listing 4-23 shows how to bind RadPanelBar to a database, and Figure 4-20 shows the code in action.

Listing 4-23. *RadPanelBar Data Binding*

ASPX Page

```
<telerik:RadPanelBar ID="RadPanelBar2" runat="server"
        DataSourceID="SqlDataSource1"
        DataFieldID="ID"
        DataFieldParentID="parentID"
        DataTextField="Name"
        DataValueField="ID"
        ExpandMode="SingleExpandedItem">
</telerik:RadPanelBar>
<asp:SqlDataSource ID="SqlDataSource1" runat="server"
        ConnectionString="<%$ ConnectionStrings:NorthwindConnectionString %>"
        SelectCommand="select ProductID as ID, ProductName as Name,
                              CategoryID+1000 as parentID
                       from Products p
                       union all
                       select CategoryID+1000 as ID, CategoryName as Name, null as parentID
                       from Categories">
</asp:SqlDataSource>
```

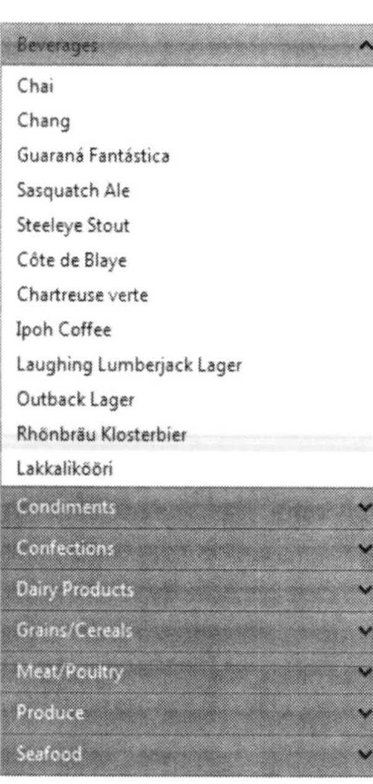

Figure 4-20. *A RadPanelBar with bound data*

Creating an Automatic Hierarchy

As explained before, RadPanelBar will create the hierarchy in the data when the control is bound to a datasource; it does so with the help of the `DataFieldID` and `DataFieldParentID` properties. The previous example showed a simple hierarchy with only two levels, and Listing 4-24 shows you more levels (see Figure 4-21 for an illustration of the listing code running).

Listing 4-24. *RadPanelBar's Automatic Hierarchy*

ASPX Page

```
<telerik:RadPanelBar ID="RadPanelBar3" runat="server"
        DataSourceID="SqlDataSource2"
        DataFieldID="ID"
        DataFieldParentID="ParentID"
        DataTextField="Name"
        DataValueField="ID">
</telerik:RadPanelBar>

<asp:SqlDataSource ID="SqlDataSource2" runat="server"
    ConnectionString="<%$ ConnectionStrings:NorthwindConnectionString %>"
    SelectCommand="SELECT [EmployeeID] AS ID, [LastName] + ',' + [FirstName] as Name,
                        NULL AS ParentID
                    FROM [Employees]
                   WHERE ReportsTo = 2
                   UNION ALL
                   SELECT o.OrderID AS ID,
                       'Order: ' + CAST(o.OrderID AS VARCHAR) + ' - Date: ' +
                               CONVERT(VARCHAR, o.OrderDate, 101) AS NAME,
                       CAST(o.EmployeeID AS BIGINT) AS ParentID
                   FROM dbo.Orders o
                   WHERE o.EmployeeID IN
                               (SELECT [EmployeeID] FROM [Employees] WHERE ReportsTo=2)
                   UNION ALL
                   SELECT ROW_NUMBER()
                               OVER (ORDER BY d.OrderID, d.ProductID) + 20000 AS ID,
                       'Product: ' + d.ProductName,
                       CAST(d.OrderID AS BIGINT) AS ParentID
                   FROM dbo.[Order Details Extended] d
                   WHERE d.OrderID IN (SELECT o.OrderID FROM dbo.Orders o
                   WHERE o.EmployeeID IN (SELECT [EmployeeID] FROM [Employees]
                                                WHERE ReportsTo=2))">
</asp:SqlDataSource>
```

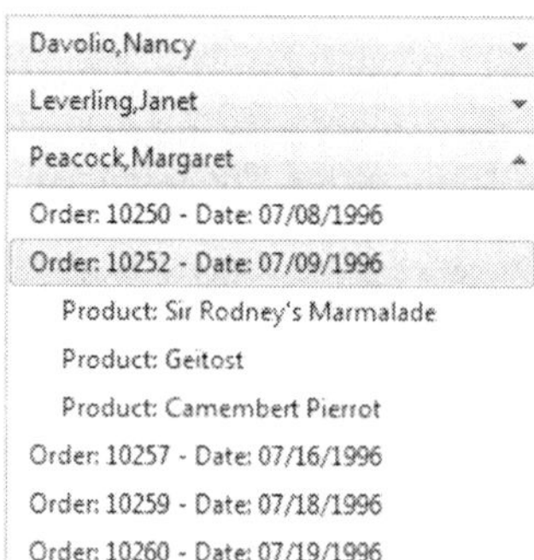

Figure 4-21. *You can see how the hierarchy was automatically created showing the customer's orders and the items for each order.*

Defining Templates

Like with other controls, you can define templates to be used in items for RadPanelBar. You can have any type of control, style, or resource inside those templates. Item templates can be defined globally for or per item. If they are defined globally, all the items will use the template except for those that have a specific (per item) template.

Listing 4-25 shows how to create item templates, and Figure 4-22 illustrates the sample code.

Listing 4-25. *Creating RadPanelBar Item Templates*

ASPX Page

```
<style type="text/css">
    .web-sites .search-engines td,
    .web-sites .software-companies td
    {
        width:100px;
        text-align:center;
        vertical-align:bottom
    }

    .web-sites .search-engines img,
    .web-sites .software-companies img
    {
        display: block;
    }

    .web-sites .software-companies td
    {
        width: 120px;
    }
</style>
```

```
<telerik:RadPanelBar ID="RadPanelBar4" runat="server"
    CssClass="web-sites"
    Width="500px">
    <Items>
        <telerik:RadPanelItem
            Text="Search Engines"
            Expanded="true">
            <Items>
                <telerik:RadPanelItem>
                    <ItemTemplate>
                        <table class="search-engines">
                            <tr>
                               <td>
                                 <img src="http://is.gd/8y3RD" width="50px" alt="Bing" />
                                 <a href="http://www.bing.com/" target="_blank">Bing</a>
                               </td>
                               <td>
                                 <img src="http://is.gd/8y3Xf" width="50px" alt="Google" />
                                 <a href="http://www.google.com/" target="_blank">Google</a>
                               </td>
                               <td>
                                 <img src="http://is.gd/8y3Z8" width="50px" alt="Yahoo!" />
                                 <a href="http://www.yahoo.com/" target="_blank">Yahoo!</a>
                               </td>
                            </tr>
                        </table>
                    </ItemTemplate>
                </telerik:RadPanelItem>
            </Items>
        </telerik:RadPanelItem>
        <telerik:RadPanelItem Text="Software Companies">
            <Items>
                <telerik:RadPanelItem>
                    <ItemTemplate>
                        <table class="software-companies">
                            <tr>
                                <td>
                                    <img src="http://is.gd/8y41b" alt="Telerik" />
                                    <a href="http://www.telerik.com/"
                                                target="_blank">Telerik</a>
                                </td>
                                <td>
                                    <img src="http://is.gd/8y42L" width="100px"
                                        alt="Microsoft" />
                                    <a href="http://www.microsoft.com/"
                                        target="_blank">Microsoft</a>
                                </td>
                                <td>
                                    <img src="http://is.gd/8y44m" alt="CSW Solutions" />
                                    <a href="http://www.cswsolutions.com/"
                                        target="_blank">CSW Solutions</a>
                                </td>
                            </tr>
                        </table>
```

```
                    </ItemTemplate>
                </telerik:RadPanelItem>
            </Items>
        </telerik:RadPanelItem>
    </Items>
</telerik:RadPanelBar>
```

Figure 4-22. *RadPanelBar templates in action*

Summary

Navigation controls allow users to easily navigate through web sites and data. They provide functionality such as data binding, custom attributes, and a rich client-side API.

With RadMenu, you can create for your applications navigation menus that can be created declaratively or by data binding. The `RadContextMenu` control allows you to create context menus as well. Your menus can have multiple columns, and you can use templates go beyond traditional text and images in your menus.

RadToolBar provides the functionality to create buttons that act very much like the toolbars in Windows Forms applications. Buttons in a toolbar can be regular, two-state, drop-down, and split. Regular buttons perform an action when they are clicked, but two-state buttons stay selected when they are clicked. Drop-down and split buttons both display drop-downs with more buttons, but split buttons keep the last selected button so users can click it again without having to expand the drop-down.

RadTreeView is an advanced tree control that supports capabilities such as loading nodes on demand, using node templates, and dragging and dropping. It natively supports data binding the same way as RadMenu; it will infer the hierarchy based on the information from the datasource using the `DataFieldID` and `DataFieldParentID` properties. RadTreeView items support node text changes, and you can implement custom logic by handling an event raised after the node text changed. Items also support check boxes.

RadSiteMap is a control designed to create graphical representations or maps from a sitemap file or with data binding. You can define how you want to render the sitemap, and you can control how this rendering is performed for each depth level with the `LevelSettings` property.

RadPanelBar is a component for building collapsible panels with the ability to behave as side menus or tool bars, as well as a container for other items through the use of templates. The control can be bound to a datasource and support different levels of hierarchy.

CHAPTER 5

Date, Time, and Scheduling RadControls

Applications frequently have to provide users with an easy and intuitive way to manage dates, times, and scheduling information. For that purpose, Telerik has built an incredible set of components that will allow you to deliver great applications with interfaces like those found in desktop applications such as Microsoft Outlook.

In this chapter, we will dive into the RadCalendar set of controls. Like RadInput, RadCalendar is composed of several different controls targeted to a specific type of date and time management. For example, the `RadCalendar` control itself is a calendar control that you can use to enable the user to see a particular month or multiple months in a single view. There is also the `RadDatePicker` control, which has a text area and a drop-down button to display a calendar for selecting dates. Another control is `RadTimePicker` with similar functionality as `RadDatePicker`, but this one is for selecting times from a collection. And of course, the `RadDateTimePicker` control is a combination of both previous controls and allows users to select a date and time in the same control. RadScheduler is probably one of the most complex controls in the suite, but the functionality it provides is amazing. You can have a calendar with appointment management that you can customize to meet the needs of your application.

Using the RadCalendar Control

Using the `RadCalendar` control, users can select one date or multiple dates depending on how you've configured the control. It is possible also to show a multiple-month view, and the highly configurable template structure means you can make the calendar look like part of your own environment. Some of the features include special dates, templates, localization, globalization, and rich server-side and client-side APIs.

Choosing a Month View

`RadCalendar` can be configured to show a single-month or multiple-month view. The default view is single-month (see Figure 5-1), so for that, you don't need to configure anything. Just add a `RadCalendar` instance, as shown in Listing 5-1.

Listing 5-1. *RadCalendar Single-Month View*

ASPX Page

```
<telerik:RadCalendar ID="RadCalendar1" runat="server">
</telerik:RadCalendar>
```

Figure 5-1. *The single-month RadCalendar*

To display a multiple-month view calendar, you need to configure the MultipleViewColumns and MultipleViewRows properties with the number of months to display in a grid format (rows and columns), as in Listing 5-2. The calendar view is shown in Figure 5-2.

Listing 5-2. *RadCalendar Multiple-Month View*

ASPX Page

```
<telerik:RadCalendar ID="RadCalendar2"  runat="server"
        MultiViewColumns="3"
        MultiViewRows="2"
        AutoPostBack="True"
        EnableMultiSelect="False">
</telerik:RadCalendar>
```

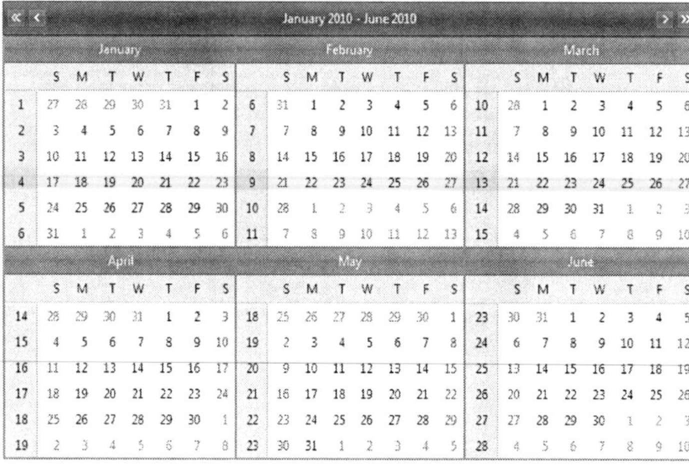

Figure 5-2. *A multiple-month RadCalendar*

Adding Special Dates and Day Templates

RadCalendar supports a special collection of dates called SpecialDates. Items in this collection have certain attributes that allow a high level of granularity in configuring how the control should treat dates. For example, you could have in the collection a set of dates that are disabled (in your application, these dates could be holidays or blackout dates).

If you have dates or events with special meanings, for example, doctor appointments, you can use the DayTemplates collection to give those dates a specific look and feel.

You also have to configure the Repeatable property to instruct the control how the special date will be repeated across months. Repeatable takes one of the values from the Telerik.Web.UI.Calendar.RecurringEvents enumeration. These values represent rules for recurrences that will be used by the calendar to property represent the special dates.

For example, in the enumeration the value DayAndMonth tells the control to show the special date matching the day and the month and repeat it every year after; the value DayInMonth means to match only the day in the month, so it will repeat every month on the day specified.

Listing 5-3 shows how to use the special date's collection and the day templates. You can see in Figure 5-3 what the calendar looks like.

Listing 5-3. *RadCalendar Special Dates and Day Templates*

ASPX Page

```
<telerik:RadCalendar ID="RadCalendar3" runat="server"
        AutoPostBack="true">
        <SpecialDays>
                <telerik:RadCalendarDay
                        IsToday="true"
                        Repeatable="Today">
                        <ItemStyle
                                BorderColor="Red"
                                BorderStyle="Solid"
                                Font-Bold="true
                ...
                ...
        </SpecialDays>
        <CalendarDayTemplates>
        ...
        </CalendarDayTemplates>
</telerik:RadCalendar>
<CalendarDayTemplates>
                <telerik:DayTemplate ID="VisitDoctor" runat="server">
                        <Content>
                                <div>D</div>
                        </Content>
                </telerik:DayTemplate>
</CalendarDayTemplates>
</telerik:RadCalendar>
```

```
CSS Style

<style type="text/css">
.disabled_date
{
        background-image: url('../Images/disabled.png');
        background-repeat: no-repeat;
        background-position: center center;
}
</style>
```

Figure 5-3. *RadCalendar displays the special dates with the appropiate styles*

Configuring Localization and Globalization

The `RadCalendar` control is fully localizable out of the box; just set the `Culture` property to the value representing the language and region you need it to work with.

Listing 5-4 shows two examples of localization, one for the French language and one for Hebrew, and the two calendars are shown in Figure 5-4.

Listing 5-4. *RadCalendar Localization*

```
ASPX Page

    <telerik:RadCalendar ID="RadCalendar4" runat="server"
        CultureInfo="fr-FR">
    </telerik:RadCalendar>

    <telerik:RadCalendar ID="RadCalendar41" runat="server"
        CultureInfo="he-IL">
    </telerik:RadCalendar>
```

Figure 5-4. *Two RadCalendars showing the French and Hebrew languages*

Controlling the Appearance of the Day with the DayRender Event

`RadCalendar` exposes the `DayRender` server and client event that enables you to modify the appearance of the days as they are being rendered.

The `DayRender` server event handler has a `DayRenderEventArgs` parameter, which is a member of the `Telerik.Web.UI.Calendar.DayRenderEventArgs` namespace and not the `System.Web.UI.WebControls` namespace. Listing 5-5 shows how to work with this event on the server, and Figure 5-5 shows the end result.

Listing 5-5. *Declaring the RadCalendar DayRender server event*

ASPX Page

```
<telerik:RadCalendar ID="RadCalendar5" runat="server"
        AutoPostBack="true"
        OnDayRender="RadCalendar5_DayRender">
</telerik:RadCalendar>
```

Code Behind

```
protected void RadCalendar5_DayRender(object sender, DayRenderEventArgs e)
{
    if (e.Day.Date.Day != 1) return;
    e.Cell.Style["background-color"] = "Yellow";
    e.Cell.Style["border-style"] = "solid";
    e.Cell.Style["border-width"] = "1px";
    e.Cell.Style["border-color"] = "Red";
    e.Cell.Style["color"] = "White";
}
```

Figure 5-5. *RadCalendar showing a modified date based on the DayRender server event*

When using the client-side version of the DayRender event, you need to understand that it will work in response to client-side operations, such as month navigation. When the client-side event occurs, it will force the calendar to render again and therefore raise the event. This explains why you won't see the event handler working when the calendar initially loads.

It is also important to note here that the client-side method signature is similar to its server-side counterpart; it has the object that raised the event and an arguments parameter. Through the use of the arguments parameter, we can call the get_renderDay() method that will return an array of three values containing the year, month, and day respectively. Listing 5-6 demonstrates how to use the DayRender client event.

Listing 5-6. *RadCalendar DayRender Client-Side Event*

ASPX Page

```
<telerik:RadCalendar ID="RadCalendar6" runat="server">
        <ClientEvents OnDayRender="ClientDayRender" />
</telerik:RadCalendar>

<script type="text/javascript">
    function ClientDayRender(sender, eventArgs) {
        var cell = eventArgs.get_cell();
        var day = eventArgs.get_renderDay();
        if (day) {
            /* Check if this is the 1st of the month */
            if (eventArgs.get_date()[2] == 1) {
                cell.style.backgroundColor = "Yellow";
                cell.style.borderColor = "Red";
                cell.style.borderStyle = "solid";
                cell.style.borderWidth = "1px";
            }
        }
    }
</script>
```

Setting the RadDatePicker Allowed Date Rage

RadDatePicker is one of the controls in the RadCalendar set. It has a text box where users can type a date and a drop-down button that displays a calendar to graphically select a date. Most importantly, it provides a quick and intuitive way to select a date. It has the ability to define the range of available dates for the end user to pick from. For that purpose, you must set the MinDate and MaxDate properties as shown in Listing 5-7. Note in Figure 5-6 how other dates outside the specified range are shown but disabled.

Listing 5-7. *RadDatePicker with a Restricted Date Range*

ASPX Page

```
<telerik:RadDatePicker ID="RadDatePicker1" runat="server"
        MinDate="2010/01/15"
        MaxDate="2010/01/31">
</telerik:RadDatePicker>
```

Figure 5-6. *In the calendar, only the dates within the specified date range are available for selection and the other dates are shown but disabled.*

Using RadDatePicker Shared Calendars

When your application requires multiple date pickers in a single page, the amount of HTML required to render the controls can be minimized by using a shared calendar. Sharing a calendar means that all the date pickers will render only the necessary HTML to work. However, they won't need to render any HTML for the calendar, because they all will use the same calendar object that is already rendered in the page.

Sharing calendars will increase the performance of the page because of the reduced size of the HTML required for all the controls to work, but most importantly, it reduces the number of client scripts needed for all of the date pickers to operate because only a single client-side object is required.

In Listing 5-8, I'm using two RadDatePickers that will share one RadCalendar. Note in Figure 5-7 that even known I haven't set any visibility property for the shared calendar, it is hidden because the controls are smart enough to understand that the calendar will be used for the date pickers. It will be shown only when called from the RadDatePicker's toggle button.

Listing 5-8. *RadDatePicker Shared Calendars*

ASPX Page

```
<telerik:RadDatePicker ID="RadDatePicker2" runat="server"
    SharedCalendarID="RadCalendar1">
</telerik:RadDatePicker>

<telerik:RadDatePicker ID="RadDatePicker3" runat="server"
    SharedCalendarID="RadCalendar1">
</telerik:RadDatePicker>
```

Figure 5-7. *Two RadDatePickers sharing a calendar*

Intercepting the Selected Date

`RadDatePicker` exposes the `OnSelectedDateChanged` server event and `OnDateSelected` client event to recognize that a new date has been selected (see Listing 5-9), and it exposes methods and properties to read the new and old values. Figure 5-8 shows the `OnSelectedDateChanged` in action.

Listing 5-9. *RadDatePicker Intercepting the Selected Date*

ASPX Page

```
<telerik:RadDatePicker ID="RadDatePicker4" runat="server"
        AutoPostBack="true"
        OnSelectedDateChanged="RadDatePicker4_SelectedDateChanged">
</telerik:RadDatePicker>

<asp:Label ID="lblSelectedDate" runat="server" />

<telerik:RadDatePicker ID="RadDatePicker5" runat="server">
        <ClientEvents OnDateSelected="ClientDateSelected" />
</telerik:RadDatePicker>

<asp:Label ID="lblClientSelectedDate" runat="server" />

<script language="javascript" type="text/javascript">
    function ClientDateSelected(sender, eventArgs) {
        var newDate = eventArgs.get_newDate();
        var html = String.format("You selected '{0}/{1}/{2}' from the client",
            newDate.getMonth() + 1, // month values are 0-based
            newDate.getDate(),
            newDate.getFullYear());
        $get("<%= lblClientSelectedDate.ClientID %>").innerHTML = html;
    }
</script>
```

Code Behind

```
protected void RadDatePicker4_SelectedDateChanged(
                        object sender,
                        SelectedDateChangedEventArgs e)
{
    if (e.NewDate.HasValue)
        lblSelectedDate.Text = string.Format("You selected '{0}' from the server",
                                e.NewDate.Value.ToShortDateString());
}
```

1/21/2010
You selected '1/21/2010' from the server
1/22/2010
You selected '01/22/2010' from the client

Figure 5-8. *RadDatePicker intercepts the selected dates*

Using RadTimePicker and RadDateTimePicker

The last controls are a logical derivation of the previous two controls: `RadTimePicker` is for selecting times from a list, and `RadDateTimePicker` for selecting a date and a time in a single control.

`RadTimePicker` enables users to not only select a time from a list of hours but also type in the hour they want. `RadDateTimePicker` also lets a user type the date and time, and using the client API, the drop-down button can be toggled to show and hide the hour's list or the calendar. You use the `showPopup()` and `hidePopup()` methods to show and hide the date calendar and the `showTimePopup()` and `hideTimePopup()` methods to show and hide the time list.

Listing 5-10 shows how to declaratively create these controls and Figure 5-9 shows how they look like.

Listing 5-10. *Declaratively Creating a RadTimePicker and a RadDateTimePicker*

ASPX Page

```
<telerik:RadTimePicker ID="RadTimePicker1" runat="server">
</telerik:RadTimePicker>

<telerik:RadDateTimePicker ID="RadDateTimePicker1" runat="server">
</telerik:RadDateTimePicker>
```

Time Picker		
12:00 AM	1:00 AM	2:00 AM
3:00 AM	4:00 AM	5:00 AM
6:00 AM	7:00 AM	8:00 AM
9:00 AM	10:00 AM	11:00 AM
12:00 PM	1:00 PM	2:00 PM
3:00 PM	4:00 PM	5:00 PM
6:00 PM	7:00 PM	8:00 PM
9:00 PM	10:00 PM	11:00 PM

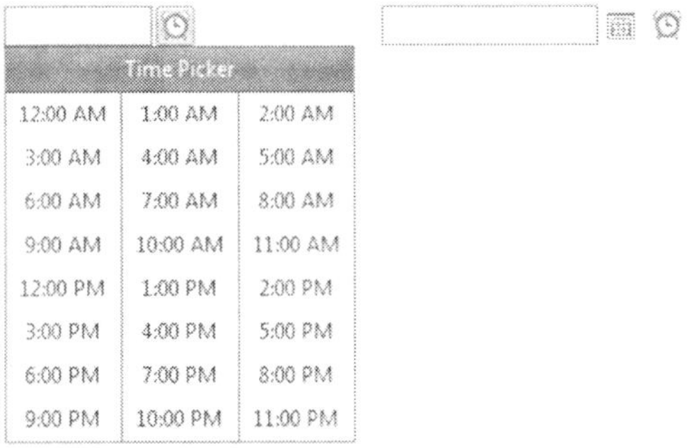

Figure 5-9. *RadTimePicker and RadDateTimePicker*

Creating Custom Hours Collection

`RadTimePicker` and `RadDateTimePicker` support custom hours collections. This is a feature that enables you to define your own set of hours (see Listing 5-11). This collection is particularly useful and very easy to configure; basically, all you need to do is bind the control to a list of hours, and that's it (OK, yes, if you want to get fancy, you can bind the control to a list of dates, an array of dates, a `DateTime` array, or an array of objects). Note in Figure 5-10 how the list of hours is completely different from the default list.

Listing 5-11. *Creating a Custom Hours Collection for RadTimePicker and RadDateTimePicker*

ASPX Page

```
<telerik:RadTimePicker ID="RadTimePicker2" runat="server">
</telerik:RadTimePicker>

<telerik:RadDateTimePicker ID="RadDateTimePicker2" runat="server">
</telerik:RadDateTimePicker>
```

Code Behind

```
protected void Page_Load(object sender, EventArgs e)
{
    if (Page.IsPostBack) return;
    List<DateTime> hoursList = new List<DateTime>();
    hoursList.Add(new DateTime(2010,04,07,3,8,9));
    hoursList.Add(new DateTime(2010,04,07,4,8,9));
    hoursList.Add(new DateTime(2010,04,07,5,8,9));
    hoursList.Add(new DateTime(2010,04,07,6,8,9));
    hoursList.Add(new DateTime(2010,04,07,7,8,9));
    hoursList.Add(new DateTime(2010,04,07,8,8,9));
    RadTimePicker2.TimeView.DataList.DataSource = hoursList;
    RadTimePicker2.TimeView.DataList.DataBind();
    RadDateTimePicker2.TimeView.DataList.DataSource = hoursList;
    RadDateTimePicker2.TimeView.DataList.DataBind();
}
```

Figure 5-10. *RadTimePicker and RadDateTimePicker showing a list of custom hours*

Using RadScheduler

RadScheduler is a comprehensive scheduling component that enables customer to manage appointments (or tasks) from a calendar. This component resembles Microsoft Outlook's calendar, in which you can schedule, move, modify, categorize, and delete appointments, set recurrence rules, and much more.

RadScheduler can be configured to work against several data sources, such as XML files, databases, and web services. It can work with different data providers, such as Entity Framework and LINQ, and you also can define custom data providers to work with custom data sources.

The control also supports the concept of *resources*, which group appointments so that RadScheduler can display the appointments grouped by resource.

With RadScheduler's fully supported templating structure, you can configure the look and feel of the appointments as well as the forms to insert and edit appointment. Then too, you have access to the skinning architecture of all the RadControls for a fully customizable appearance experience.

Declarative Data Binding to a Database

One of the most important capabilities of RadScheduler is the possibility to bind it to any ASP.NET data source control. However, the control needs to be defined, at the minimum, with information for the `DataKeyField`, `DataStartField`, `DataEndField`, and `DataSubjectField` properties. You can optionally define the `DataDescriptionField`, `DataRecurrenceField`, and `DataRecurrenceParentKeyField` properties to enrich the appointment's capabilities.

The `DataKeyField` in an appointment is an identifier RadScheduler uses to correctly and uniquely identify each appointment, and the identifier doesn't have to be a numeric value, since the property is of type `string` and therefore can for example be GUIDs.

`DataStartField` and `DataEndField` represent the start and end dates and times for each appointment. These properties are of type `DateTime`.

`DataSubjectField` is a string that represents the subject of each appointment, and `DataDescriptionField` is a string containing a more descriptive explanation of the appointment.

The `DataRecurrenceField` property is used for the recurrence rule for the appointment. `DataRecurrenceParentKeyField` is used when a particular occurrence of a recurrent appointment is modified; a new appointment record is created based on the recurrent appointment. Individual pieces of information can be modified to affecting only one particular occurrence of the appointment, but this property is set to the ID of the original recurrent appointment so RadScheduler can keep track of all appointments and their individual changes.

Storing Appointments

Appointments can be stored by defining only the required properties for RadScheduler. However, the appointment structure offers some more information. In addition to the described properties, you can also add fields to be used as resources and other, custom fields.

The following is a SQL Server definition of a table that stores appointments that include recurrence rules. Note that I'm using an automatically incremented integer for the ID of appointments, but remember that I'm doing so only for my convenience so I don't have to worry about how the IDs are generated. Please don't take the use of an integer to be a rule. You can also opt to use `VARCHAR` fields instead of the `NVARCHAR` ones that I used.

```
CREATE TABLE [dbo].[Appointments]
(
   [ID]                    INT IDENTITY(1,1)   NOT NULL,
   [Subject]               nvarchar(255)       NOT NULL,
   [Description]           nvarchar(1024)      NULL,
   [Start]                 datetime            NOT NULL,
   [End]                   datetime            NOT NULL,
   [RecurrenceRule]        nvarchar(1024)      NULL,
   [RecurrenceParentID]    INT                 NULL,
   [Annotations]           nvarchar(50)        NULL,

   CONSTRAINT [PK_Appointments] PRIMARY KEY CLUSTERED
      ([ID]),

   CONSTRAINT [FK_Appointments_ParentAppointments] FOREIGN KEY
      ([RecurrenceParentID])
   REFERENCES
      [dbo].[Appointments] ([ID])
)
GO
```

Listing 5-12 shows how to create a RadScheduler control bound declaratively to a `SqlDataSource` that uses the previous appointments table and Figure 5-11 shows the RadScheduler working with bound data.

Listing 5-12. *RadScheduler Declaratively Data Binding to Database*

ASPX Page

```
<telerik:RadScheduler ID="RadScheduler1" runat="server"
        DataKeyField="ID"
        DataSubjectField="Subject"
        DataStartField="Start"
        DataEndField="End"
        DataDescriptionField="Description"
        DataRecurrenceField="RecurrenceRule"
        DataRecurrenceParentKeyField="RecurrenceParentID"
        DataSourceID="SqlDataSource1">
</telerik:RadScheduler>

<asp:SqlDataSource ID="SqlDataSource1" runat="server"
    ConnectionString="<%$ ConnectionStrings:SchedulerConnectionString %>"
    DeleteCommand="DELETE FROM [Appointments] WHERE [ID] = @ID"
    InsertCommand="INSERT INTO [Appointments] (
                        [Subject],
                        [Description],
                        [Start],
                        [End],
                        [RecurrenceRule],
                        [RecurrenceParentID],
                        [Annotations]
                    ) VALUES (
                        @Subject,
                        @Description,
                        @Start,
                        @End,
                        @RecurrenceRule,
                        @RecurrenceParentID,
                        @Annotations)"
    OldValuesParameterFormatString="{0}"
    SelectCommand="SELECT * FROM [Appointments]"
    UpdateCommand="UPDATE [Appointments]
                   SET [Subject] = @Subject,
                       [Description] = @Description,
                       [Start] = @Start,
                       [End] = @End,
                       [RecurrenceRule] = @RecurrenceRule,
                       [RecurrenceParentID] = @RecurrenceParentID,
                       [Annotations] = @Annotations
                   WHERE [ID] = @ID">
    <DeleteParameters>
        <asp:Parameter Name="ID" Type="Int32" />
    </DeleteParameters>
```

```
    <InsertParameters>
        <asp:Parameter Name="Subject" Type="String" />
        <asp:Parameter Name="Description" Type="String" />
        <asp:Parameter Name="Start" Type="DateTime" />
        <asp:Parameter Name="End" Type="DateTime" />
        <asp:Parameter Name="RecurrenceRule" Type="String" />
        <asp:Parameter Name="RecurrenceParentID" Type="Int32" />
        <asp:Parameter Name="Annotations" Type="String" />
    </InsertParameters>
    <UpdateParameters>
        <asp:Parameter Name="Subject" Type="String" />
        <asp:Parameter Name="Description" Type="String" />
        <asp:Parameter Name="Start" Type="DateTime" />
        <asp:Parameter Name="End" Type="DateTime" />
        <asp:Parameter Name="RecurrenceRule" Type="String" />
        <asp:Parameter Name="RecurrenceParentID" Type="Int32" />
        <asp:Parameter Name="Annotations" Type="String" />
        <asp:Parameter Name="ID" Type="Int32" />
    </UpdateParameters>
</asp:SqlDataSource>
```

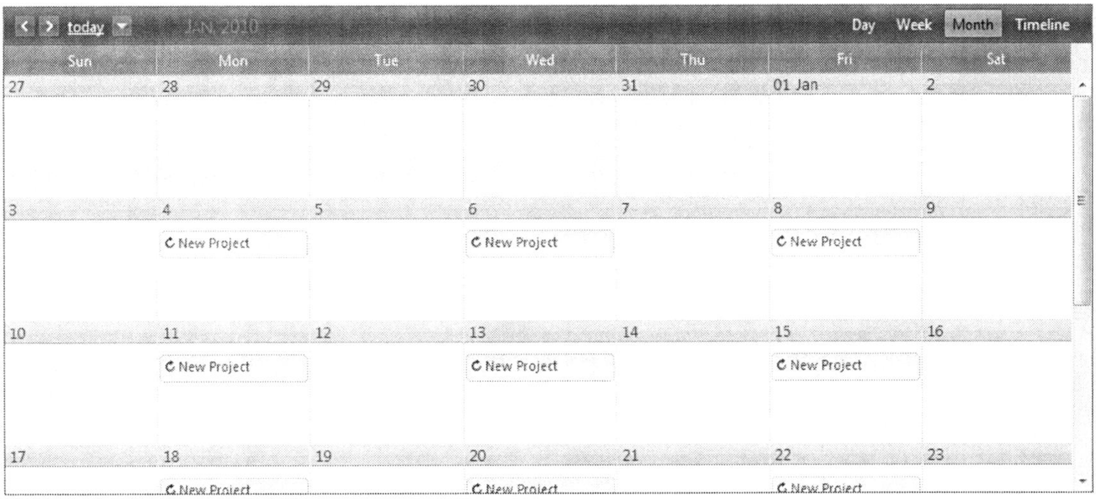

Figure 5-11. *RadScheduler displaying bound database data*

To create an appointment, just double-click an empty time slot in the scheduler to open the screen shown in Figure 5-12. To edit an appointment, double-click the appointment.

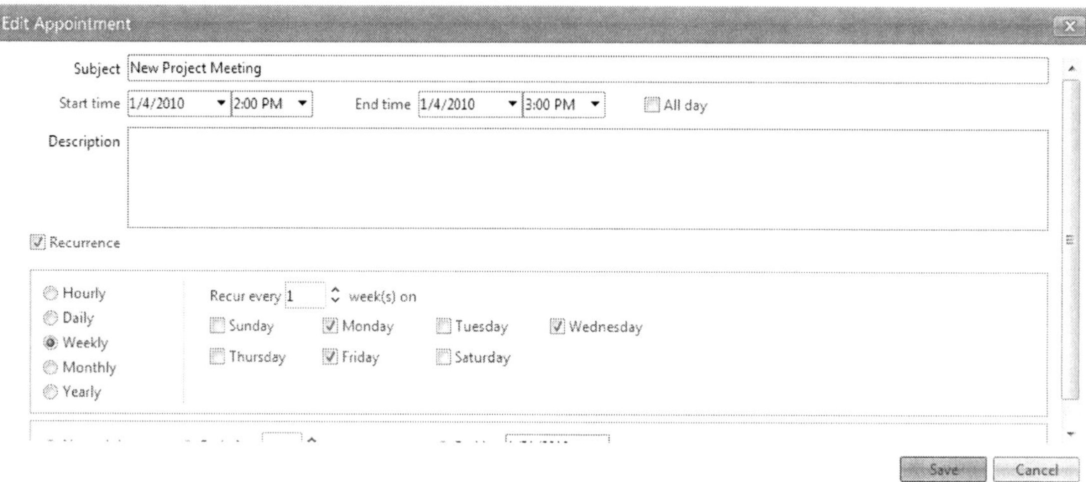

Figure 5-12. ***The*** *RadScheduler default appointment edit form*

Data Binding to a Web Service

To improve performance, you can bind RadScheduler to a web service. An advantage of this approach is that the HTML rendered is minimized and no postbacks occur, but as a trade off, grouped views are not fully supported.

Using the web service data binding requires the implementation of a data provider. This is a great way to conveniently wrap up the communication with the real data storage that can be anywhere and of any type exposing only what's needed to manipulate appointments.

Implementing the Data Provider

Let's implement an example data provider for a SQL Server database. This data provider can be easily ported to be any database (Oracle for example) or data source, but for the sake of simplicity, we'll keep it in SQL Server.

First, you need to create a class that derives from `SchedulerProviderBase`, which is shown in Listing 5-13. This class implements the following methods:

- `IEnumerable<Appointment> GetAppointments(RadScheduler owner)`
- `void Insert(RadScheduler owner, Appointment appointmentToInsert)`
- `void Update(RadScheduler owner, Appointment appointmentToUpdate)`
- `void Delete(RadScheduler owner, Appointment appointmentToDelete)` `IEnumerable<ResourceType> GetResourceTypes(RadScheduler owner)`
- `IEnumerable<Resource> GetResourcesByType(RadScheduler owner, string resourceType)`

Listing 5-13. *The RadSchedulerDatabaseProvider.cs Class*

```
public class RadSchedulerDatabaseProvider : SchedulerProviderBase
{
    private static readonly string connectionString = WebConfigurationManager
                    .ConnectionStrings["SchedulerConnectionString"]
                    .ConnectionString;

    public override IEnumerable<Appointment> GetAppointments(RadScheduler owner)
    {
        var appointmentsList = new List<Appointment>();
        using (var connection = new SqlConnection(connectionString))
        {
            connection.Open();
                var sql = @"SELECT *
                             FROM Appointments
                            WHERE [Start] >= @start
                              AND [End] <= @end";
                var start = owner.VisibleRangeStart;
                var end = owner.VisibleRangeEnd;
                using( var command = new SqlCommand(sql, connection))
                {
                    command.Parameters.AddWithValue("start", start);
                    command.Parameters.AddWithValue("end", end);
                    using (var reader = command.ExecuteReader())
                    {
                       try
                       {
                         while (reader.Read())
                         {
                            Appointment appointment = new Appointment();
                            appointment.ID = reader.GetInt32(0);
                            appointment.Subject = reader.GetString(1);
                            appointment.Description = reader.IsDBNull(2)
                                                      ? null
                                                      : reader.GetString(2);
                            appointment.Start = reader.GetDateTime(3);
                            appointment.End = reader.GetDateTime(4);
                            appointment.RecurrenceRule = reader.IsDBNull(5)
                                                      ? null
                                                      : reader.GetString(5);
                            appointment.RecurrenceParentID = reader.IsDBNull(6)
                                                      ? null
                                                      : reader.GetValue(6);
                            appointmentsList.Add(appointment);
                         }
                      }
```

```
                    catch (Exception)
                    {
                        // Error handling logic
                    }
                }
            }
        }

        return appointmentsList;
    }

    public override void Insert(RadScheduler owner, Appointment appointmentToInsert)
    {
            var recurrentParentId = appointmentToInsert.RecurrenceParentID ?? DBNull.Value;

            string sql = @"INSERT INTO Appointments (
                                    [Subject],
                                    [Description],
                                    [Start],
                                    [End],
                                    [RecurrenceRule],
                                    [RecurrenceParentID])
                                VALUES (
                                    @subject,
                                    @description,
                                    @start,
                                    @end,
                                    @recurrenceRule,
                                    @recurrenceParentID)";

            using (var connection = new SqlConnection(connectionString))
            using (var command = new SqlCommand(sql, connection))
            {
                try
                {
                    command.Parameters.AddWithValue("subject", appointmentToInsert.Subject);
                    command.Parameters.AddWithValue("description",
                                                    appointmentToInsert.Description);
                    command.Parameters.AddWithValue("start", appointmentToInsert.Start);
                    command.Parameters.AddWithValue("end", appointmentToInsert.End);
                    command.Parameters.AddWithValue("recurrenceRule",
                                                    appointmentToInsert.RecurrenceRule);
                    command.Parameters.AddWithValue("recurrenceParentID",
                                                    recurrentParentId);
                    connection.Open();
                    command.ExecuteNonQuery();
                }
                catch (Exception)
                {
                    // Error handling logic
                }
            }
    }
```

```
public override void Update(RadScheduler owner, Appointment appointmentToUpdate)
{
        var recurrentParentId = appointmentToUpdate.RecurrenceParentID ?? DBNull.Value;

        string sql = @"UPDATE Appointments
                              SET [Subject] = @subject,
                                [Description] = @description,
                                [Start] = @start,
                                [End] = @end,
                                [RecurrenceRule] = @recurrenceRule,
                                [RecurrenceParentID] = @recurrenceParentID
                              WHERE [ID] = @id";

        using (var connection = new SqlConnection(connectionString))
        using (var command = new SqlCommand(sql, connection))
        {
            try
            {
                command.Parameters.AddWithValue("id", appointmentToUpdate.ID);
                command.Parameters.AddWithValue("subject", appointmentToUpdate.Subject);
                command.Parameters.AddWithValue("description",
                                            appointmentToUpdate.Description);
                command.Parameters.AddWithValue("start", appointmentToUpdate.Start);
                command.Parameters.AddWithValue("end", appointmentToUpdate.End);
                command.Parameters.AddWithValue("recurrenceRule",
                                            appointmentToUpdate.RecurrenceRule);
                command.Parameters.AddWithValue("recurrenceParentID",
                                            recurrentParentId);
                connection.Open();
                command.ExecuteNonQuery();
            }
            catch (Exception)
            {
                // Error handling logic
            }
        }
}

public override void Delete(RadScheduler owner, Appointment appointmentToDelete)
{
    string sql = "DELETE FROM Appointments WHERE [ID] = @id";

    using (var connection = new SqlConnection(connectionString))
    using (var command = new SqlCommand(sql, connection))
    {
        try
        {
            command.Parameters.AddWithValue("id", appointmentToDelete.ID);
            connection.Open();
            command.ExecuteNonQuery();
        }
```

```
            catch (Exception)
            {
                // Error handling logic
            }
        }
    }

    public override IEnumerable<ResourceType> GetResourceTypes(RadScheduler owner)
    {
        var resourcesList = new List<ResourceType>();
        return resourcesList;
    }

    public override IEnumerable<Resource> GetResourcesByType(
                                            RadScheduler owner,
                                            string resourceType)
    {
        var resourcesList = new List<Resource>();
        return resourcesList;
    }
```

Now, it's time to create the web service as shown in Listing 5-14. It is a good idea to create a separate web service with the single purpose of serving the RadScheduler through the use of the newly created scheduler provider.

Listing 5-14. *SchedulerWebService.asmx*

```
namespace WebApplication1
{
    /// <summary>
    /// Summary description for SchedulerWebService
    /// </summary>
    [WebService(Namespace = "http://tempuri.org/")]
    [WebServiceBinding(ConformsTo = WsiProfiles.BasicProfile1_1)]
    [System.ComponentModel.ToolboxItem(false)]
    [ScriptService]
    public class SchedulerWebService : WebService
    {

        private WebServiceAppointmentController controller;

        private WebServiceAppointmentController Controller
        {
            get
            {
                this.controller =
                        this.controller ??
                        new WebServiceAppointmentController("RadSchedulerDatabaseProvider");
                return this.controller;
            }
        }
```

```
[WebMethod]
public IEnumerable<AppointmentData> GetAppointments(SchedulerInfo schedulerInfo)
{
    return Controller.GetAppointments(schedulerInfo);
}

[WebMethod]
public IEnumerable<AppointmentData> InsertAppointment(
    SchedulerInfo schedulerInfo,
    AppointmentData appointmentData)
{
    return Controller.InsertAppointment(schedulerInfo, appointmentData);
}

[WebMethod]
public IEnumerable<AppointmentData> UpdateAppointment(
    SchedulerInfo schedulerInfo,
    AppointmentData appointmentData)
{
    return Controller.UpdateAppointment(schedulerInfo, appointmentData);
}

[WebMethod]
public IEnumerable<AppointmentData> CreateRecurrenceException(
    SchedulerInfo schedulerInfo,
    AppointmentData recurrenceExceptionData)
{
    return Controller
             .CreateRecurrenceException(schedulerInfo, recurrenceExceptionData);
}

[WebMethod]
public IEnumerable<AppointmentData> RemoveRecurrenceExceptions(
    SchedulerInfo schedulerInfo,
    AppointmentData masterAppointmentData)
{
    return Controller
             .RemoveRecurrenceExceptions(schedulerInfo, masterAppointmentData);
}
[WebMethod]
public IEnumerable<AppointmentData> DeleteAppointment(
    SchedulerInfo schedulerInfo,
    AppointmentData appointmentData,
    bool deleteSeries)
{
    return Controller
             .DeleteAppointment(schedulerInfo, appointmentData, deleteSeries);
}
```

```
        [WebMethod]
        public IEnumerable<ResourceData> GetResources(SchedulerInfo schedulerInfo)
        {
            return Controller.GetResources(schedulerInfo);
        }
    }
}
```

Now that we have created the provider and web service, we need to made our application aware of the provider so it can be used. For this, we need update the application's `web.config` file as shown in Listing 5-15.

Listing 5-15. *web.config file modifications for the Scheduler Data Provider*

```
<configSections>
    <sectionGroup name="telerik.web.ui">
      <section name="radScheduler"
               type="Telerik.Web.UI.RadSchedulerConfigurationSection,
                     Telerik.Web.UI, PublicKeyToken=121fae78165ba3d4"
               allowDefinition="MachineToApplication" />
    </sectionGroup>
</configSections>

…

<telerik.web.ui>
  <radScheduler defaultAppointmentProvider="Integrated">
    <appointmentProviders>
      <add name="RadSchedulerDatabaseProvider"
           type="RadSchedulerDatabaseProvider"
           persistChanges="true"/>
    </appointmentProviders>
  </radScheduler>
</telerik.web.ui>
```

Now, we define the binding in the definition of RadScheduler in our page as shown in Listing 5-16.

Listing 5-16. *Declaration of RadScheduler with Web Service Binding*

```
<telerik:RadScheduler ID="RadScheduler2" runat="server"
        DataDescriptionField="Description"
        DataEndField="End"
        DataKeyField="ID"
        DataRecurrenceField="RecurrenceRule"
        DataRecurrenceParentKeyField="RecurrenceParentID"
        DataStartField="Start"
        DataSubjectField="Subject">
        <WebServiceSettings Path="SchedulerWebService.asmx" />
</telerik:RadScheduler>
```

Once you run your application, you will see that RadScheduler runs a lot faster, and no postbacks happens between operations such as inserting or editing appointments or changing the scheduler view. Figure 5-13 shows how our RadScheduler runs in Firefox, but the important part here is at the bottom— note the time the page took to complete the loading of RadScheduler and see that the data that was transmitted is minimal.

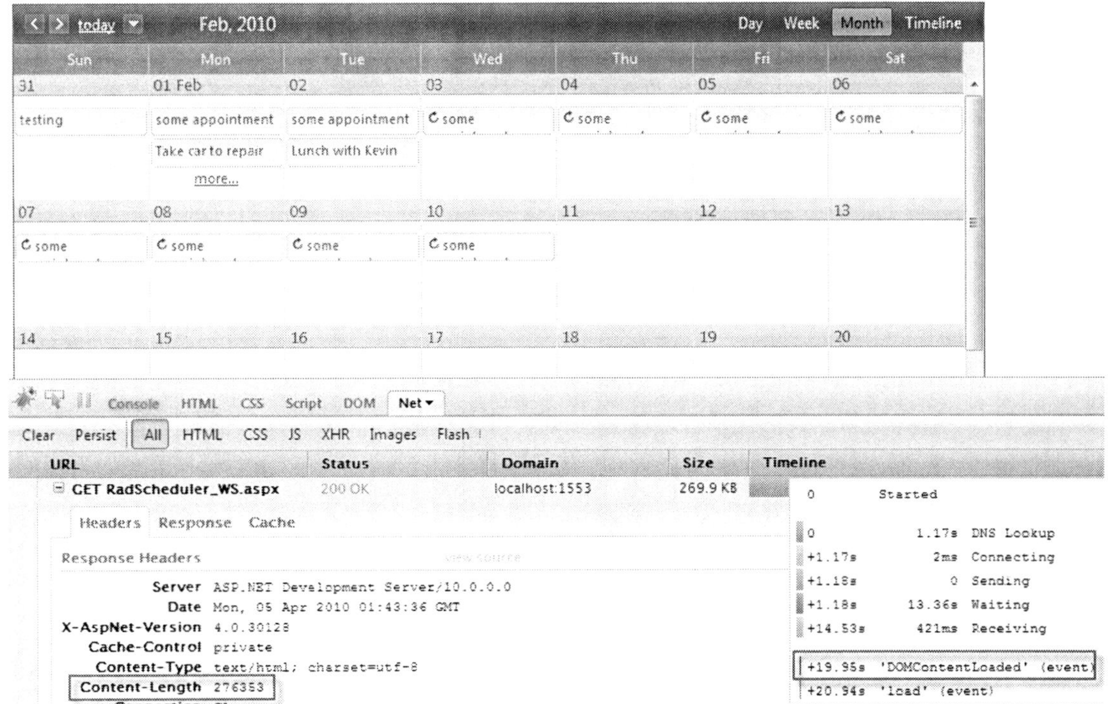

Figure 5-13. *RadScheduler with web service binding execution*

Localizing and Globalizing

RadScheduler fully supports localization and globalization either manually or using global resource files.

You can manually change the strings and date and time formats to match the language needs by using the `Localization` properties for the control, as shown in Figure 5-14. This is an easy solution but is not scalable and can only support one language change.

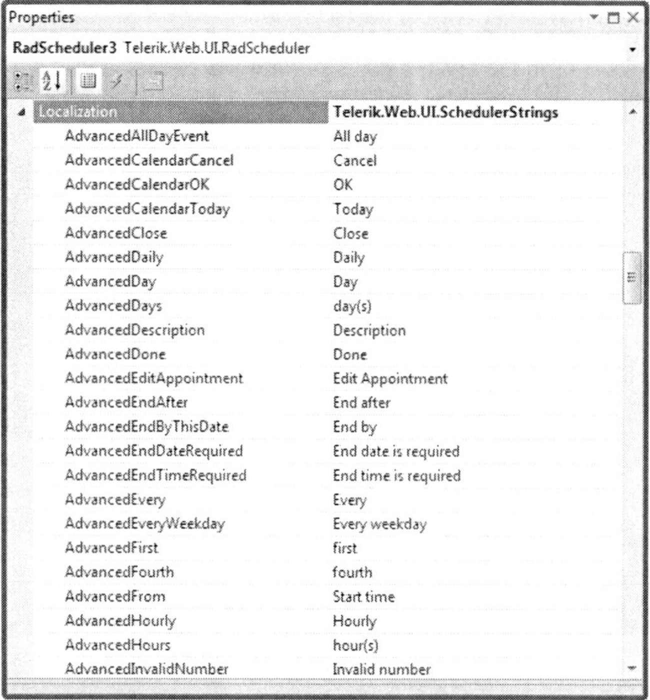

Figure 5-14. *RadScheduler Localization strings*

You can declaratively define these strings in the `<Localization />` section of RadScheduler:

```
<telerik:RadScheduler ID="RadScheduler3" runat="server"
    DataDescriptionField="Description"
    DataEndField="End" DataKeyField="ID"
    DataRecurrenceField="RecurrenceRule"
    Culture="es-GT"
    DataRecurrenceParentKeyField="RecurrenceParentID"
    DataStartField="Start"
    DataSubjectField="Subject">
    <WebServiceSettings Path="SchedulerWebService.asmx" />
     <Localization AdvancedAllDayEvent="All Day"
                   AdvancedCalendarCancel="Cancel"
                   AdvancedCalendarOK="OK"
                   AdvancedCalendarToday="Today"
                   ... />
</telerik:RadScheduler>
```

The preferred method is using global resources. All you need to do is copy the `RadScheduler.Main.resx` file that ships with the installation of RadControls into the `~/App_GlobalResources` folder of your application and add the culture-specific information to the name (`RadScheduler.Main.es.resx` for Spanish for example). Next, translate the strings in the `.resx` file; the date and time format will render according to the culture specification (see Figure 5-15).

■ **Note** When binding RadScheduler to a web service, you need to take extra steps for globalization to work properly. You need to add `EnableScriptGlobalization="true"` to the script manager definition, and you need to add `Culture="es-GT"` to the page definition or `<globalization culture="es-GT"/>` to the `web.config` file (in this case, we're adding Spanish). More information on adding globalization configuration to the `web.config` file can be found at `http://msdn.microsoft.com/en-us/library/hy4kkhe0.aspx`.

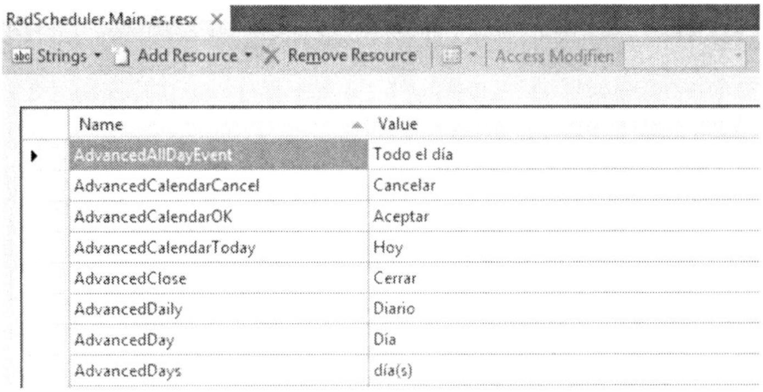

RadScheduler.Main.es.resx ×

Strings ▾ Add Resource ▾ × Remove Resource | Access Modifier:

Name	Value
AdvancedAllDayEvent	Todo el día
AdvancedCalendarCancel	Cancelar
AdvancedCalendarOK	Aceptar
AdvancedCalendarToday	Hoy
AdvancedClose	Cerrar
AdvancedDaily	Diario
AdvancedDay	Día
AdvancedDays	día(s)

Figure 5-15. *The RadScheduler global resource file for translation to Spanish*

Listing 5-17 makes usage of the global resource to display RadScheduler in Spanish. Note in Figure 5-16 that the look and feel are the same, but all the labels are in Spanish.

Listing 5-17. *RadScheduler localized for Spanish*

ASPX Page

```
<%@ Page Title="" Language="C#" Culture="es-GT" ... %>

<telerik:RadScriptManager ID="RadScriptManager1" runat="server"
        EnableScriptGlobalization="true">
</telerik:RadScriptManager>

<telerik:RadScheduler ID="RadScheduler3" runat="server"
    DataDescriptionField="Description"
    DataEndField="End"
    DataKeyField="ID"
    DataRecurrenceField="RecurrenceRule"
    Culture="es-gt"
    DataRecurrenceParentKeyField="RecurrenceParentID"
    DataStartField="Start"
    DataSubjectField="Subject">
    <WebServiceSettings Path="SchedulerWebService.asmx" />
</telerik:RadScheduler>
```

Figure 5-16. *RadScheduler in Spanish*

Adding Context Menus

RadScheduler supports out-of-the-box context menus for handling operations in the control; they are called default context menus, and they are enabled in the `AppointmentContextMenuSettings` property as shown in Listing 5-18. Note in Figures 5-17 and 5-18 how the default context menus are displayed for empty time slots and appointments. Context menus are defined for appointments and time slots, and yes, you can have your own customized context menus to handle your own interactions with the control (see Listing 5-19).

Listing 5-18. *RadScheduler Default Context Menus*

ASPX Page

```
<telerik:RadScheduler ID="RadScheduler4" runat="server"
    DataDescriptionField="Description"
    DataEndField="End"
    DataKeyField="ID"
    DataRecurrenceField="RecurrenceRule"
    DataRecurrenceParentKeyField="RecurrenceParentID"
    DataStartField="Start"
    DataSubjectField="Subject">
    <WebServiceSettings Path="SchedulerWebService.asmx" />
    <AppointmentContextMenuSettings EnableDefault="true" />
    <TimeSlotContextMenuSettings EnableDefault="true" />
</telerik:RadScheduler>
```

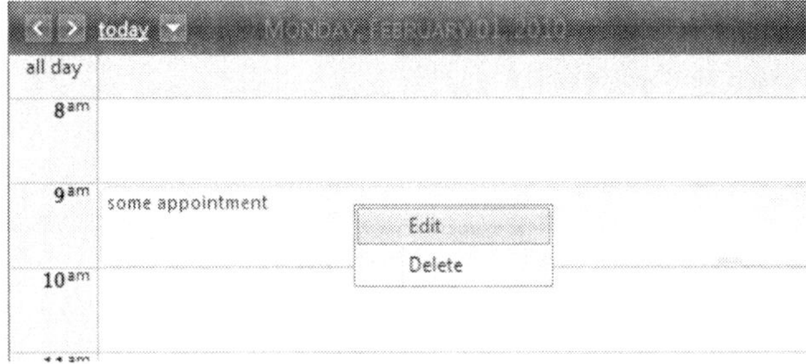

Figure 5-17. *RadScheduler default context menus for appointments*

Figure 5-18. *RadScheduler default context menus for time slots*

Context menus can also be customized. Listing 5-19 shows how to create custom context menus with client-side event handlers. Figure 5-19 shows the custom context menus.

Listing 5-19. *RadScheduler Custom Context Menus*

```
ASPX Page
<telerik:RadScheduler ID="RadScheduler1" runat="server"
    DataDescriptionField="Description"
    DataEndField="End"
    DataKeyField="ID"
    DataRecurrenceField="RecurrenceRule"
    DataRecurrenceParentKeyField="RecurrenceParentID"
    DataStartField="Start"
    DataSubjectField="Subject"
    OnClientAppointmentContextMenuItemClicked="RadSchedulerContextMenuItemClicked">
    <WebServiceSettings Path="SchedulerWebService.asmx" />
   <AppointmentContextMenus>
       <telerik:RadSchedulerContextMenu runat="server" ID="ContextMenu1">
           <Items>
               <telerik:RadMenuItem Text="Edit" Value="CommandEdit" />
               <telerik:RadMenuItem Text="Move 1 hour ahead" Value="MoveAhead" />
               <telerik:RadMenuItem Text="Move 1 hour behind" Value="MoveBehind" />
               <telerik:RadMenuItem IsSeparator="True" />
               <telerik:RadMenuItem Text="Delete" Value="CommandDelete" />
           </Items>
       </telerik:RadSchedulerContextMenu>
   </AppointmentContextMenus>
</telerik:RadScheduler>
```

```
<script type="text/javascript">
    function RadSchedulerContextMenuItemClicked(sender, eventArgs) {
        // get the objects (appointment, menu item clicked and scheduler)
        var appt = eventArgs.get_appointment();
        var item = eventArgs.get_item();
        var scheduler = $find('<%= RadScheduler1.ClientID %>');

        // get the current start and end dates
        var start = appt.get_start();
        var end = appt.get_end();

        // if the item is the one to move the appointment 1 hour ahead then do it
        if (item.get_value() == 'MoveAhead') {
            // move the start and end 1 hour ahead
            start.setHours(start.getHours() + 1);
            end.setHours(end.getHours() + 1);
        }
        // if the item is the one to move the appointment 1 hour behind then do it
        else if (item.get_value() == 'MoveBehind') {
            // move the start and end 1 hour ahead
            start.setHours(start.getHours() - 1);
            end.setHours(end.getHours() - 1);
        }

        // update the appointment
        appt.set_start(start);
        appt.set_end(end);

        // update the scheduler
        scheduler.updateAppointment(appt, false);
    }
</script>
```

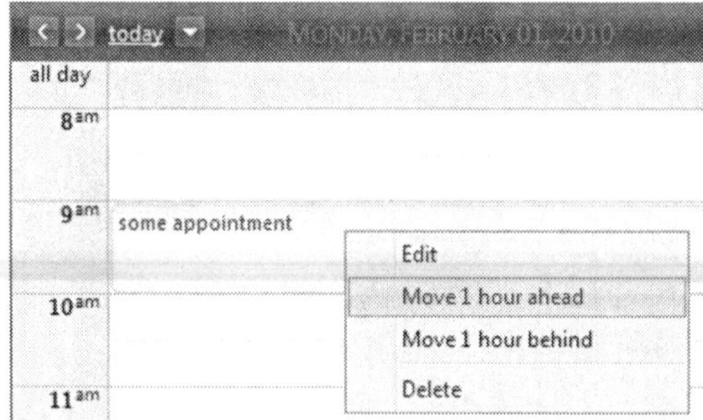

Figure 5-19. *Custom context menus for appointments*

Working with Templates

Templates in RadScheduler provide you with a rich environment for formatting appointments. You can add any type of content in a template—ASP.NET controls, other Telerik controls, HTML content, and so forth. See Listing 5-20 for an example of implementing appointment templates and Figure 5-10 for the end result.

RadScheduler supports five types of templates:

- `AppointmentTemplate`: Determines how appointments are rendered within the scheduler's view
- `InlineInsertTemplate`: Determines how the in-line editor appears for inserting a new appointment
- `InlineEditTemplate`: Determines how the in-line editor appears for editing an existing appointment
- `AdvancedInsertTemplate`: Determines how the advanced edit form appears for inserting a new appointment.
- `AdvancedEditTemplate`: Determines how the advanced edit form appears for editing an existing appointment.

Listing 5-20. *RadScheduler AppointmentTemplate*

ASPX Page

```
<telerik:RadScheduler ID="RadScheduler6" runat="server"
    DataDescriptionField="Description"
    DataEndField="End"
    DataKeyField="ID"
    DataRecurrenceField="RecurrenceRule"
    EnableDescriptionField="true"
    DataRecurrenceParentKeyField="RecurrenceParentID"
    DataSourceID="SqlDataSource1"
    DataStartField="Start"
    DataSubjectField="Subject">
    <AppointmentTemplate>
        <div class="rsAptSubject">
            <%# Eval("Subject") %>
        </div>
        <hr />
        <div style="font-style:italic; background-color:Lime"><%# Eval("Description") %></div>
     </AppointmentTemplate>
</telerik:RadScheduler>
```

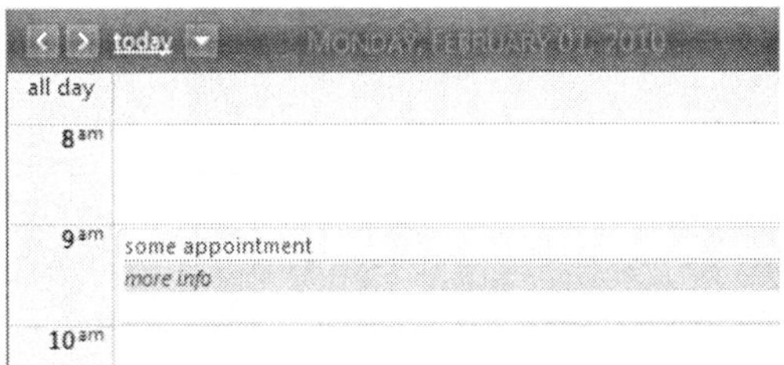

Figure 5-20. *Note how the appointment appearance was modified using the appointment template*

Exporting to iCal Format

iCal is a calendar file format designed to transport calendar tasks or meetings from one computer to another in an easy and lightweight way. It is supported by several major calendars, such as Microsoft Outlook and Apple's iCal.

Here's an example of what an iCal file looks like:

```
BEGIN:VCALENDAR
VERSION:2.0
PRODID:-//hacksw/handcal//NONSGML v1.0//EN
BEGIN:VEVENT
UID:uid1@example.com
DTSTAMP:20100407T170000Z
ORGANIZER;CN=Jose Guay:MAILTO:jose.guay@hotmail.com
DTSTART:20100407T170000Z
DTEND:20100407T035959Z
SUMMARY:Jose's Birthday
END:VEVENT
END:VCALENDAR
```

Many times, you need to let users export appointments to local calendars either on their desktop computers or mobile devices. RadScheduler enables you to export the information of the appointments to iCal format, as shown in Listing 5-21, so it can then be imported in any calendar program that supports that format. You can export individual appointments or the whole calendar. Figure 5-21 shows a file downloaded with all the appointment information in iCal format. Figure 5-22 shows the appointment once it was imported into Microsoft Outlook.

Listing 5-21. *RadScheduler Exporting to iCal*

ASPX Page

```
<telerik:RadAjaxManager ID="RadAjaxManager1" runat="server">
</telerik:RadAjaxManager>

<asp:Button ID="btnExportCalendar" runat="server"
    Text="Export All Calendar to iCal"
    OnClick="btnExportCalendar_Click" />

<telerik:RadScheduler ID="RadScheduler1" runat="server"
    DataDescriptionField="Description"
    DataEndField="End"
    DataKeyField="ID"
    DataRecurrenceField="RecurrenceRule"
    EnableDescriptionField="true"
    DataRecurrenceParentKeyField="RecurrenceParentID"
    DataSourceID="SqlDataSource1"
    DataStartField="Start"
    DataSubjectField="Subject"
    OnAppointmentCommand="RadScheduler1_AppointmentCommand">
    <AppointmentTemplate>
        <div class="rsAptSubject">
            <%# Eval("Subject") %>
        </div>
```

```
        <hr />
        <asp:Button ID="btnExport" runat="server"
            Text="Export to iCal"
            CommandName="Export"
            OnClientClick="Export(this, event); return false;" />
    </AppointmentTemplate>
</telerik:RadScheduler>

<telerik:RadCodeBlock ID="RadCodeBlock1" runat="server">
    <script type="text/javascript">
        function Export(sender, e) {
            var ajaxManager = $find('<%= RadAjaxManager1.ClientID %>')
            ajaxManager.set_enableAJAX(false);
            ajaxManager.ajaxRequestWithTarget(sender.name, '');
        }
    </script>
</telerik:RadCodeBlock>
```

Code Behind

```
private void WriteCalendar(string data)
{
    HttpResponse response = Page.Response;
    response.Clear();
    response.Buffer = true;
    response.ContentType = "text/calendar";
    response.ContentEncoding = Encoding.UTF8;
    response.Charset = "utf-8";
    response.AddHeader("Content-Disposition", "attachment;filename=\"Appointment.ics\"");
    response.Write(data);
    response.End();
}

protected void RadScheduler1_AppointmentCommand(
                        object sender,
                        AppointmentCommandEventArgs e)
{
    if (e.CommandName == "Export")
    {
        string iCal = RadScheduler.ExportToICalendar(e.Container.Appointment);
        this.WriteCalendar(iCal);
    }
}

protected void btnExportCalendar_Click(object sender, EventArgs e)
{
    string iCal = RadScheduler.ExportToICalendar(RadScheduler1.Appointments);
    this.WriteCalendar(iCal);
}
```

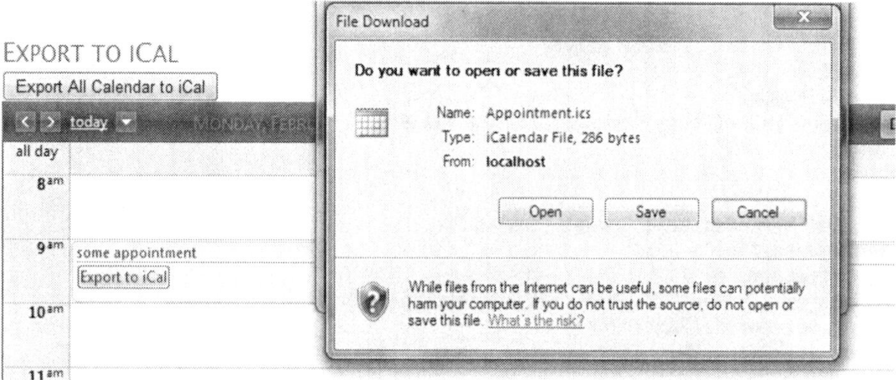

Figure 5-21. *RadScheduler export to iCal*

Figure 5-22. *Imported calendar from RadScheduler to Microsoft Outlook*

Using Resources

Resources are basically a categorization of appointments. What this means is that you can relate your appointments to resources and then have RadScheduler show them grouped by resource, so they are more easily understood.

To work with resources, you need to define a set of resources that your appointments are aware of. For example, if you scheduler control shows tasks to be accomplished by users, you can add a user field in the appointment and have the scheduler show appointments grouped by user.

In the example in Listing 5-22, I added a new field called `UserID` to the `Appointments` table; `UserID` relates to a new table called `Users`. Once the relation is in place you group appointments by `UserID`. Note how they are presented in Figure 5-23.

Listing 5-22. *RadScheduler Resources*

```
New Table

CREATE TABLE [Users]
(
   [ID]        INT                 NOT NULL,
   [UserName]  nvarchar(255)       NOT NULL,
   CONSTRAINT [PK_Users] PRIMARY KEY CLUSTERED  ([ID])
)
GO
ALTER TABLE [Appointments]
ADD UserID INT
GO

Add Users

INSERT INTO [Users] VALUES (1, 'Jose')
INSERT INTO [Users] Values (2, 'Kevin')


ASPX Page

<telerik:RadScheduler ID="RadScheduler1" runat="server"
    GroupBy="User"
    DataDescriptionField="Description"
    DataEndField="End"
    DataKeyField="ID"
    DataRecurrenceField="RecurrenceRule"
    EnableDescriptionField="true"
    DataRecurrenceParentKeyField="RecurrenceParentID"
    DataSourceID="SqlDataSource1"
    DataStartField="Start"
    DataSubjectField="Subject"
    SelectedView="WeekView">
    <ResourceTypes>
        <telerik:ResourceType
            KeyField="ID"
            Name="User"
            TextField="UserName"
            ForeignKeyField="UserID"
            DataSourceID="UsersDataSource" />
    </ResourceTypes>
</telerik:RadScheduler>
```

```
<asp:SqlDataSource ID="UsersDataSource" runat="server"
    ConnectionString="<%$ ConnectionStrings:NorthwindConnectionString %>"
    SelectCommand="SELECT * FROM [Users]" >
</asp:SqlDataSource>
```

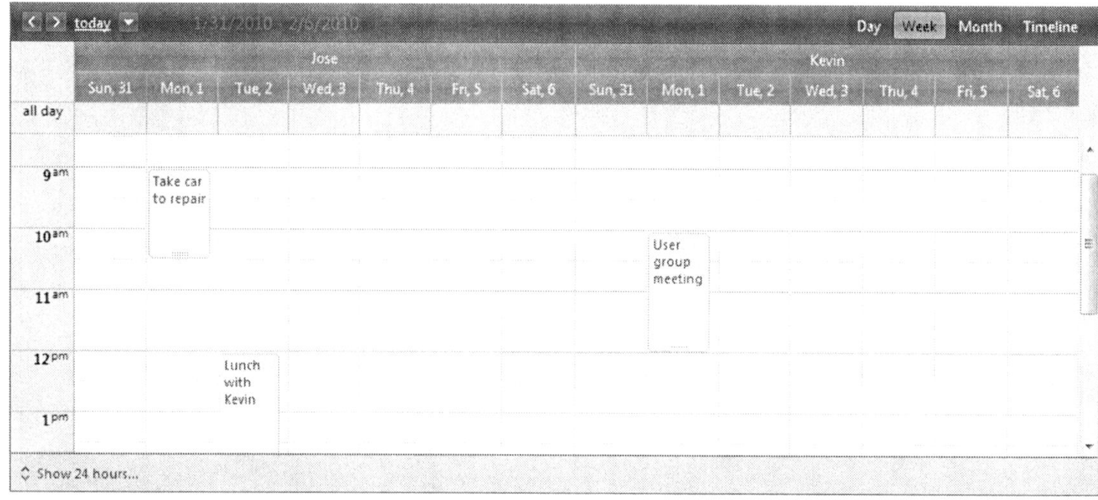

Figure 5-23. *Appointments grouped by User*

When inserting or editing appointments, RadScheduler is smart enough to know that resources are defined, and it populates the corresponding fields in the default editors, so your appointments are never filled incomplete.

One thing to remember is that, once you define resources for your appointments, you can't avoid them; the resources are mandatory fields to fill in (see Figure 5-24).

Edit Appointment
Subject Take car to repair
Start time 2/1/2010 9:00 AM End time 2/1/2010 10:30 AM All day
User: Jose
Description needs brake check
Recurrence

Figure 5-24. *Resources in appointment edit form*

Summary

In this chapter, you've seen how powerful the date and time controls are. RadCalendar provides a lot of functionality for displaying calendars in your applications and enables you to have input-like controls called pickers for date, time, and date/time values. The pickers are very easy to implement and use, and they minimize the HTML rendered for improved performance. You're also provided a rich API to work with them.

RadCalendar can be displayed using single-month and multiple-month views to meet the specific needs of your application and exposes a collection of special days, so you can define sets of days to have a particular behavior. You can also restrict which dates are allowed for events.

RadScheduler is a very complex component that exposes a huge collection of features. You can modify the appearance of the appointments through the use of templates as well as localize controls to work with languages other than English. Data binding is another rich feature enabling binding to services, databases, and XML files.

Out of the box, RadScheduler supports context menus for appointments and time slots, but you can always define your own custom menus. Also, it is possible to group appointments using resources. Then too, the default editors for inserting and editing appointments support automatic population of each resource type, so your appointments are always filled properly. You're also able to export information in iCal format.

CHAPTER 6

Data RadControls, Part 1

The Data RadControls are probably the most widely used controls of the entire suite. They provide the means to load data from data sources, present it for interaction with users, and then update it again.

Since these controls require in-depth coverage, I will split their explanation across two chapters. The controls we'll cover in this chapter are `RadComboBox` and `RadGrid`. In the next chapter, we will look at the complimentary `RadFilter`, `RadListBox`, and `RadListView` controls to provide complete coverage.

`RadComboBox` is a drop-down control that has features for loading data from different data sources either all at once or on demand. Also, you can configure it to display the data using the standard items or customized templates.

`RadGrid` is an incredible, advanced grid component designed to provide rich functionality without impacting the performance and responsiveness of the application.

RadComboBox

`RadComboBox` is an advanced drop-down control that can perform sophisticated operations such as loading on demand and template-based binding. The features include the following:

- A powerful client-side API to perform operations from JavaScript
- Data binding with web services, XML, and others datasources
- Loading on demand with callbacks
- Automatic completion functionality
- Filtering and sorting of elements
- Multiple columns (with column headers)
- End user restrictions
- Customizable items and custom template support
- Animations
- Validation and right-to-left support
- Keyboard support and compliance with the XHTML 1.1 and Section 508 for software standards for accessibility, as well as Level AAA with the W3C guidelines
- A full set of server- and client-side events for easy manipulation
- Overlay support and screen boundary detection.

RadComboBox has a structure composed of an input area, a drop-down toggle, a drop-down list, and a set of items. For each item, you can configure different settings such as fonts, sizes, images, and so forth. All of these elements are accessible on the server side and, with a few exceptions, on the client side.

Binding RadComboBox

The basic use of the RadComboBox is to present a collection of items in a user-friendly way, while maintaining item values for easy retrieval during user interactions. For this control to function properly, you must bind it to a data source and respond to user interactions.

RadComboBox can be bound declaratively or programmatically to datasource controls. It supports binding to DataTable, DataSet, Dataview, Array, and ArrayList, as well as to ASP.NET DataSource components such as SqlDataSource, LinqDataSource, EntityDataSource, and XML.

Listing 6-1 shows how to declaratively bind a RadComboBox to a database table, and Figure 6-1 shows how RadComboBox looks when the example runs.

Listing 6-1. *Binding a RadComboBox to a Database Table Declaratively*

ASPX Page

```
<telerik:RadComboBox ID="RadComboBox1" Runat="server"
        DataSourceID="SqlDataSource1"
        DataTextField="CategoryName"
        DataValueField="CategoryID">
</telerik:RadComboBox>

<asp:SqlDataSource ID="SqlDataSource1" runat="server"
    ConnectionString="<%$ ConnectionStrings:NorthwindConnectionString %>"
    SelectCommand="SELECT [CategoryID], [CategoryName] FROM [Categories">
</asp:SqlDataSource>
```

Figure 6-1. *RadComboBox presents a collection of items from the datasource.*

Another important aspect of the RadComboBox is its built-in ability to automatically consume and bind to XML files, and the powerful client-side API allows you to add and remove items client-side to improve performance. In Listing 6-2, a RadComboBox is bound to an XML file using the LoadContentFile() method. When the LoadContentFile() method is invoked, it reads the file and matches the Items node to the Items property and then matches the Item nodes to RadComboBoxItem elements along with the Text and Value properties. Properties in the node that don't have a corresponding property in RadComboBoxItem are mapped to Custom properties.

Listing 6-2. *Adding Items from an XML File*

App_Data/Planets.xml

```
<Items>
 <Item Text="Mercury" Value="1" />
 <Item Text="Venus" Value="2" />
 <Item Text="Earth" Value="3" Selected="true" />
 <Item Text="Mars" Value="4" />
 <Item Text="Jupiter" Value="5" />
 <Item Text="Saturn" Value="6" />
 <Item Text="Uranus" Value="7" />
 <Item Text="Neptune" Value="8" />
</Items>
```

Code Behind

```
protected void Page_Load(object sender, EventArgs e)
{
    if (Page.IsPostBack) return;
    RadComboBox1.LoadContentFile("~/App_Data/Planets.xml");
}
```

The same result can be achieved when binding RadComboBox to an XML string. The process works in the same way when binding to an XML file, as shown in Listing 6-3. The difference is that the method LoadXml() is used instead of LoadContentFile().

Listing 6-3. *Adding Items from an XML String*

```
StringBuilder sb = new StringBuilder();
sb.Append("<Items>");
sb.Append(" <Item Text='Mercury' />");
sb.Append(" <Item Text='Venus' />");
sb.Append(" <Item Text='Earth' />");
sb.Append("</Items>");

protected void Page_Load(object sender, EventArgs e)
{
        string xmlString = sb.ToString();
        RadComboBox1.LoadXml(xmlString);
}
```

Implementing Client Operations

RadComboBox provides a rich client-side API that enables you to perform operations on the client like adding, removing, disabling, and enabling items.

The process starts with getting access to the RadComboBox object in using the $find() method. Then, you have access to the methods that perform the operations.

As shown in Listing 6-4, adding a new item starts with creating a new object of type Telerik.Web.UI.RadComboBoxItem(). After the object is created, set the at least the Text property using the item's set_text() method and add the item to the box's list of items using the get_items().add() method.

To remove an item, you need to get access to the RadComboBoxItem you want to remove and then invoke the remove() method of the RadComboBox's items collection with the desired RadComboBoxItem as a parameter.

You can enable and disable items using the enable() and disable() methods of the RadComboBoxItem object.

Listing 6-4. *Implmenting RadComboBox Client Operations*

ASPX Page

```
<input type="button" value="Add Item" onclick="javascript:AddNewItem();" />
<input type="button" value="Remove Item" onclick="javascript:RemoveItem();" />
<input type="button" value="Disable Item" onclick="javascript:DisableItem();" />
<input type="button" value="Enable Item" onclick="javascript:EnableItem();" />

<telerik:RadComboBox ID="RadComboBox2" Runat="server" >
<Items>
    <telerik:RadComboBoxItem Text="Item1" Value="Item1"></telerik:RadComboBoxItem>
    <telerik:RadComboBoxItem Text="Item2" Value="Item2"></telerik:RadComboBoxItem>
    <telerik:RadComboBoxItem Text="Item3" Value="Item3"></telerik:RadComboBoxItem>
    <telerik:RadComboBoxItem Text="Item4" Value="Item4"></telerik:RadComboBoxItem>
    <telerik:RadComboBoxItem Text="Item5" Value="Item5"></telerik:RadComboBoxItem>
</Items>
</telerik:RadComboBox>

<script type="text/javascript" language="javascript">
    function AddNewItem() {
        var combo = $find("<%= RadComboBox2.ClientID %>");
        var index = combo.get_items().get_count() + 1;
        var comboItem = new Telerik.Web.UI.RadComboBoxItem();
        comboItem.set_text("Item" + index);
        combo.get_items().add(comboItem);
        comboItem.select();
    }

    function RemoveItem() {
        var combo = $find("<%= RadComboBox2.ClientID %>");
        var comboItem = combo.get_selectedItem();
        if (comboItem) {
            combo.get_items().remove(comboItem);
        }
    }

    function DisableItem() {
        var combo = $find("<%= RadComboBox2.ClientID %>");
        var comboItem = combo.get_selectedItem();
        if (comboItem) {
            comboItem.disable();
        }
    }
```

```
    function EnableItem() {
        var combo = $find("<%= RadComboBox2.ClientID %>");
        var comboItem = combo.get_selectedItem();
        if (comboItem && !comboItem.get_enabled()) {
            comboItem.enable();
        }
    }
</script>
```

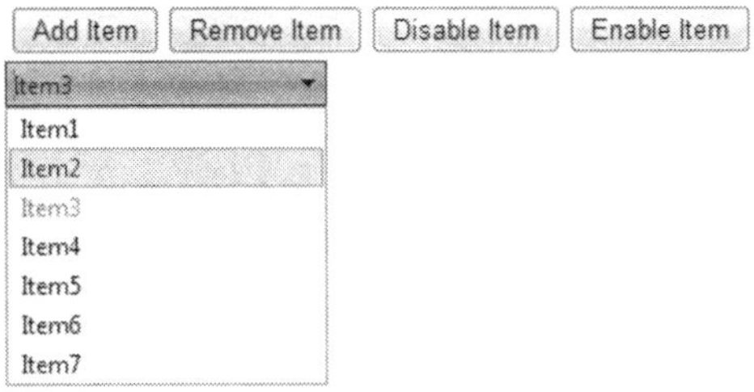

Figure 6-2. *Item 3 in the RadComboBox was disabled on the client side.*

Accessing Client Changes in the Code Behind

In Web Forms, changes made on the client via JavaScript are not automatically persisted to the server on postback. `RadComboBox` overcomes this problem with the help of the `trackChanges()` and `commitChanges()` methods.

To access to client-side changes in server-side code, you need to start the client operations with a call to the `trackChanges()` method. Once all changes have been made, you call `commitChanges()` to save them. In the code behind, you access these changes iterating through the `RadComboBox`'s `ClientChanges` collection.

During a postback, all changes are persisted and can be accessed via the `ClientChanges` collection. Each item in the collection has a `Type` property exposing a `ClientOperationType` enumeration. This value indicates which operation was performed to make the change on the client.

The example in Listing 6-5 shows you how to put all of these concepts into action. Note in Figure 6-3 how the client changes were accessible to the server on postback.

Listing 6-5. *Accesing Client Changes in The Code Behind*

ASPX Page

```
<input type="button" value="Add Item" onclick="javascript:AddNewItem2();" />
<input type="button" value="Remove Item" onclick="javascript:RemoveItem2();" />
<input type="button" value="Disable Item" onclick="javascript:DisableItem2();" />
<input type="button" value="Enable Item" onclick="javascript:EnableItem2();" />

<asp:Button ID="btnPostBack" runat="server"
                Text="Do PostBack"
                OnClick="btnPostBack_Click" />

<telerik:RadComboBox ID="RadComboBox3" Runat="server" >
<Items>
    <telerik:RadComboBoxItem Text="Item1" Value="Item1"></telerik:RadComboBoxItem>
    <telerik:RadComboBoxItem Text="Item2" Value="Item2"></telerik:RadComboBoxItem>
```

```
    <telerik:RadComboBoxItem Text="Item3" Value="Item3"></telerik:RadComboBoxItem>
    <telerik:RadComboBoxItem Text="Item4" Value="Item4"></telerik:RadComboBoxItem>
    <telerik:RadComboBoxItem Text="Item5" Value="Item5"></telerik:RadComboBoxItem>
</Items>
</telerik:RadComboBox>

<asp:ListBox ID="listChanges" runat="server" Width="400px" Height="100px">
</asp:ListBox>

<script type="text/javascript" language="javascript">
    function AddNewItem2() {
        var combo = $find("<%= RadComboBox3.ClientID %>");
        var index = combo.get_items().get_count() + 1;
        var comboItem = new Telerik.Web.UI.RadComboBoxItem();
        comboItem.set_text("Item" + index);
        combo.trackChanges();
        combo.get_items().add(comboItem);
        combo.commitChanges();
        comboItem.select();
    }

    function RemoveItem2() {
        var combo = $find("<%= RadComboBox3.ClientID %>");
        var comboItem = combo.get_selectedItem();
        if (comboItem) {
            combo.trackChanges();
            combo.get_items().remove(comboItem);
            combo.commitChanges();
        }
    }

    function DisableItem2() {
        var combo = $find("<%= RadComboBox3.ClientID %>");
        var comboItem = combo.get_selectedItem();
        if (comboItem) {
            combo.trackChanges();
            comboItem.disable();
            combo.commitChanges();
        }
    }

    function EnableItem2() {
        var combo = $find("<%= RadComboBox3.ClientID %>");
        var comboItem = combo.get_selectedItem();
        if (comboItem && !comboItem.get_enabled()) {
            combo.trackChanges();
            comboItem.enable();
            combo.commitChanges();
        }
    }
</script>
```

Code Behind

```
protected void btnPostBack_Click(object sender, EventArgs e)
{
    foreach (var operation in RadComboBox3.ClientChanges)
    {
        var item = operation.Item;
        var message = "";

        switch (operation.Type)
        {
            case ClientOperationType.Insert:
                message = "Added item: \"" + item.Text + "\"";
                break;
            case ClientOperationType.Remove:
                message = "Removed item: \"" + item.Text + "\"";
                break;
            case ClientOperationType.Update:
                var update = operation as UpdateClientOperation<RadComboBoxItem>;
                if (update != null)
                    message = "Updated item: \"" + item.Text + "\". Property updated: "
                                        + update.PropertyName;
                break;
        }

        listChanges.Items.Add(message);
    }
}
```

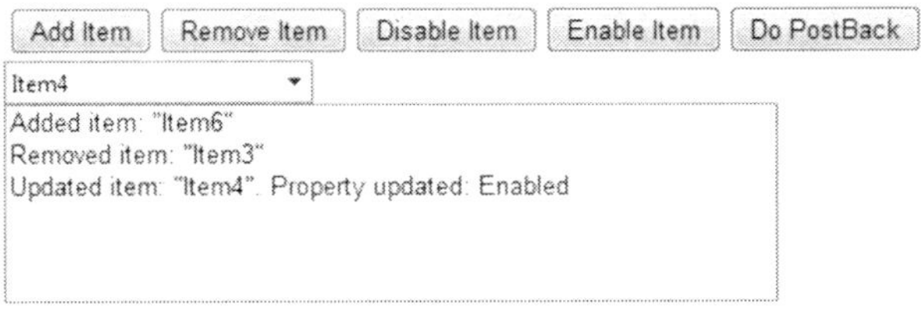

Add Item | Remove Item | Disable Item | Enable Item | Do PostBack

Item4

Added item: "Item6"
Removed item: "Item3"
Updated item: "Item4". Property updated: Enabled

Figure 6-3. *Client changes in the code behind*

Loading Items on Demand

One important feature of RadComboBox is its ability to load items on demand. On-demand control items are not available until the user types hints of what items are needed or expands the control to see what items are available. This feature works great for scenarios where the items to be added to the control are too numerous to load when the control is created and loading them on demand will filter the items to improve performance.

There used to be basically two methods for loading items on demand—in a special event handler during a server-side postback and with a call to a web service—but with the launch of WCF, Telerik added the ability to load items on demand from a WCF service. There is no functionality that distinguishes between ASMX and WCF; basically, they both work the same way.

You need to choose a method for building the load-on-demand mechanism and enable the load-on-demand feature in the RadComboBox by setting the property EnableLoadOnDemand to True.

Listing 6-6 shows how to enable load on demand using the server-side mechanism. For this to work, you need to handle the `ItemsRequested` server-side event to create the new list of items. This event is raised whenever the control needs to update its list of items. Figures 6-4 and 6-5 illustrate the states of the `RadComboBox` when no critiera has been typed and when one criterion has been typed, respectively.

Listing 6-6. *Load-on-Demand Using the Server-Side Mechanism*

ASPX Page

```
<telerik:RadComboBox ID="RadComboBox4" Runat="server"
                EnableLoadOnDemand="True"
                MaxHeight="300px"
                DropDownWidth="250px"
                OnItemsRequested="RadComboBox4_ItemsRequested">
</telerik:RadComboBox>
```

Code Behind

```
protected void RadComboBox4_ItemsRequested(object o, RadComboBoxItemsRequestedEventArgs e)
{
    var combo = (RadComboBox)o;
    var sql = "SELECT * from Products WHERE ProductName LIKE '" + e.Text + "%'";
    var data = new DataTable();

    using (SqlConnection cnn = new
                    SqlConnection(ConfigurationManager
                            .ConnectionStrings["NorthwindConnectionString"]
                            .ConnectionString))
    {
        using (SqlDataAdapter adapter = new SqlDataAdapter(sql, cnn))
        {
            try
            {
                cnn.Open();
                adapter.Fill(data);
            }
            catch (Exception ex)
            {
                // write error handling logic here
            }
        }
    }

    try
    {
        const int itemsPerRequest = 20;
        int itemOffset = e.NumberOfItems;
        int endOffset = itemOffset + itemsPerRequest;
        if (endOffset > data.Rows.Count)
        {
            endOffset = data.Rows.Count;
        }
```

```
        for (int i = itemOffset; i < endOffset; i++)
        {
            string productName = data.Rows[i]["ProductName"].ToString();
            RadComboBoxItem comboItem = new RadComboBoxItem(productName);
            combo.Items.Add(comboItem);
        }
        e.Message = data.Rows.Count > 0 ?
                String.Format("Items <b>1</b>-<b>{0}</b> out of <b>{1}</b>",
                                endOffset, data.Rows.Count)
                : "No matches";
    }
    catch
    {
        e.Message = "No matches";
    }
}
```

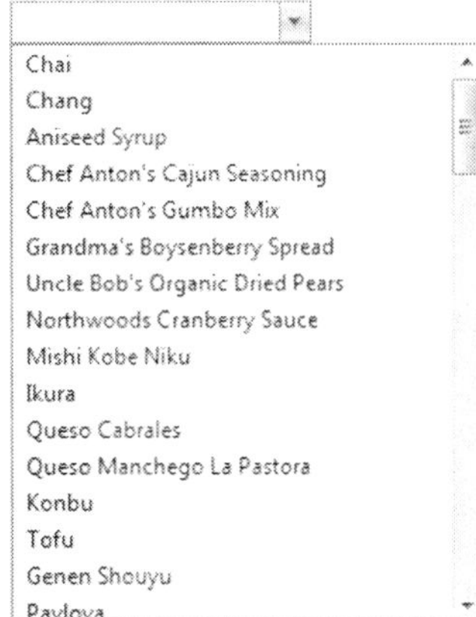

Figure 6-4. *No search criteria has been typed, so all items are loaded in RadComboBox.*

Figure 6-5. *When a criterion is typed, the ItemsRequested event handler searches for those items that mach what the user typed.*

Listing 6-7 will show how to work with a web service. It is a similar procedure; instead of using the `ItemsRequested` event, you have to use the `OnClientItemsRequesting` client-side event, which is raised just before the call to the web method in the web service, and it will be used to store the context information (what the user typed in the input field of the `RadComboBox`). Once the context is saved, it is available to the web service, and the web method can perform the search of the items.

Listing 6-7. *Load-on-Demand Using the Web Service Mechanism*

MyComboBoxItemData.cs

```
namespace WebApplication1
{
    public class MyComboBoxItemData
    {
        public string Text { get; set; }
        public string Value { get; set; }
    }
}
```

RadComboBox_Products.asmx

```
    [WebService(Namespace = "http://tempuri.org/")]
    [WebServiceBinding(ConformsTo = WsiProfiles.BasicProfile1_1)]
    [System.ComponentModel.ToolboxItem(false)]
    [ScriptService]
    public class RadComboBox_Products : WebService
    {

        [WebMethod]
        public MyComboBoxItemData[] GetProducts(object context)
        {
            // create the dictionary object to hold the context information that
            // comes from the RadComboBox
            IDictionary<string, object> contextDictionary =
                                (IDictionary<string, object>)context;

            // get the items from database
            string filterString = ((string)contextDictionary["FilterString"]).ToLower();
            string sql = "SELECT ProductName from Products WHERE ProductName LIKE '" +
                                                        filterString + "%'";
            DataTable products = new DataTable();
            using (SqlConnection connection = new
                SqlConnection(ConfigurationManager
                                .ConnectionStrings["NorthwindConnectionString"]
                                .ConnectionString))
            {
                using (SqlCommand selectCommand = new SqlCommand(sql, connection))
                {
                    using (SqlDataAdapter adapter = new SqlDataAdapter(selectCommand))
                    {
                        try
                        {
                            adapter.Fill(products);
                        }
```

```
                    catch (Exception ex)
                    {
                        // error handling logic here
                    }
                }

            }
        }

        // build the list of items
        List<MyComboBoxItemData> result = new
                            List<MyComboBoxItemData>(products.Rows.Count);
        foreach (DataRow row in products.Rows)
        {
            MyComboBoxItemData itemData = new MyComboBoxItemData();
            itemData.Text = row["ProductName"].ToString();
            itemData.Value = row["ProductName"].ToString();
            result.Add(itemData);
        }
        return result.ToArray();
}
    }
```

ASPX Page

```
<telerik:RadComboBox ID="RadComboBox5" runat="server"
    EnableLoadOnDemand="True"
    MaxHeight="300px"
    OnClientItemsRequesting="OnClientItemsRequesting"
    DropDownWidth="250px">
    <WebServiceSettings
        Method="GetProducts"
        Path="~/WebServices/RadComboBox_Products.asmx" />
</telerik:RadComboBox>

<script type="text/javascript">
    function OnClientItemsRequesting(sender, eventArgs) {
        var context = eventArgs.get_context();
        context["FilterString"] = eventArgs.get_text();
    }
</script>
```

Implementing RadComboBox Caching

RadComboBox has the ability to cache items on the client in a load on demand scenario. This feature will save roundtrips to the server by caching the requests made by the user, so if the user types something that is already in the cache, the control will re-create the list of items from the cache thus improving performance. To enable caching, you need to enable load on demand and then set the value of the property EnableItemCaching to True.

Now, loading items from a WCF service is a very straightforward process. Just create an AJAX-enabled WCF service, and Visual Studio will create all the configuration for you. You can also use any

WCF service, but you would need to set the attribute AspNetCompatibilityRequirementsMode to Allowed. Listing 6-8 will show you a working sample.

Listing 6-8. *Load-on-Demand with Caching*

RadComboBox_WCFProductsService.svc

```
[ServiceContract(Namespace = "")]
[AspNetCompatibilityRequirements(RequirementsMode =
                            AspNetCompatibilityRequirementsMode.Allowed)]
public class RadComboBox_WCFProductsService
{
    [OperationContract]
    public RadComboBoxData GetProducts(RadComboBoxContext context)
    {
        RadComboBoxData result = new RadComboBoxData();
        // create the dictionary object to hold the context information that
        // comes from the RadComboBox
        IDictionary<string, object> contextDictionary =
                                (IDictionary<string, object>)context;

        // get the items from database
        string filterString = ((string)contextDictionary["FilterString"]).ToLower();
        string sql = "SELECT ProductName from Products WHERE ProductName LIKE '" +
                                                  filterString + "%'";
        DataTable products = new DataTable();
        using (SqlConnection connection = new
                    SqlConnection(ConfigurationManager
                                .ConnectionStrings["NorthwindConnectionString"]
                                .ConnectionString))
        {
            using (SqlCommand selectCommand = new SqlCommand(sql, connection))
            {
                using (SqlDataAdapter adapter = new SqlDataAdapter(selectCommand))
                {
                    try
                    {
                        adapter.Fill(products);
                    }
                    catch (Exception ex)
                    {
                        // error handling logic here
                    }
                }

            }
        }
```

```
            // build the list of items
            List<RadComboBoxItemData> items = new List<RadComboBoxItemData>();
            foreach (DataRow row in products.Rows)
            {
                RadComboBoxItemData itemData = new RadComboBoxItemData();
                itemData.Text = row["ProductName"].ToString();
                itemData.Value = row["ProductName"].ToString();
                items.Add(itemData);
            }
            result.Items = items.ToArray();
            return result;
        }

    }
```

ASPX Page

```
<telerik:RadComboBox ID="RadComboBox6" Runat="server"
                     EnableLoadOnDemand="True"
                     MaxHeight="300px"
                     OnClientItemsRequesting="OnClientItemsRequesting"
                     DropDownWidth="250px"
                     EnableItemCaching="true">
    <WebServiceSettings Method="GetProducts"
                        Path="RadComboBox_WCFProductsService.svc"  />
</telerik:RadComboBox>

<script type="text/javascript">
    function OnClientItemsRequesting(sender, eventArgs) {
        var context = eventArgs.get_context();
        context["FilterString"] = eventArgs.get_text();
    }
</script>
```

Web.Config File

```
<system.serviceModel>
        <behaviors>
                <endpointBehaviors>
                        <behavior name="WebApplication1.WCFService1AspNetAjaxBehavior">
                                <enableWebScript/>
                        </behavior>
                </endpointBehaviors>
        </behaviors>
        <serviceHostingEnvironment aspNetCompatibilityEnabled="true"/>
        <services>
   <service name="WebApplication1.RadComboBox_WCFProductsService">
    <endpoint address="" behaviorConfiguration="WebApplication1➥
.WCFService1AspNetAjaxBehavior"
     binding="webHttpBinding" contract="WebApplication1.RadComboBox_WCFProductsService" />
   </service>
  </services>
</system.serviceModel>
```

Using ShowMoreResultsBox and EnableVirtualScrolling Properties

Another option for loading on demand is the use of the ShowMoreResultsBox and EnableVirtualScrolling properties. These properties allow you to poll results in batches, so if the user's filter results in too many records, the data will be returned piecemeal. To use these properties, you need to handle the ItemsRequested server-side event and calculate the next set of items to load.

The RadComboBoxItemsRequestedEventArgs object passed to the event handler has two important properties, NumberOfItems and Message; these indicate the number of items already loaded to the control and the message displayed in the ShowMoreResults box, respectively. The following example shows how to enable this functionality.

Items added in the ItemsRequested event handler are cleared when the next ItemsRequested event fires. However, if you use the ShowMoreResultsBox or EnableVirtualScrolling properties, the items will not be cleared upon clicking the ShowMoreResultsBox arrow or scrolling down. The EnableLoadOnDemand property allows the user to enter text in the input area, regardless of the value of the AllowCustomText property, because the load on demand mechanism requires the user to be able to enter text. Listing 6-9 implements this load-on-demand mechanism, and Figure 6-6 illustrates the main differences in the behavior of RadComboBox.

Listing 6-9. *Loading on Demand Using the ShowMoreResultsBox and EnableVirtualScrolling Properties*

ASPX Page

```
<telerik:RadComboBox ID="RadComboBox7" Runat="server"
                     EnableLoadOnDemand="True"
                     MaxHeight="300px"
                     OnItemsRequested="RadComboBox7_ItemsRequested"
                     DropDownWidth="250px"
                     ShowMoreResultsBox="true"
                     EnableVirtualScrolling="true" >
</telerik:RadComboBox>
```

Code Behind

```
protected void RadComboBox7_ItemsRequested(object o, RadComboBoxItemsRequestedEventArgs e)
{
    var combo = (RadComboBox)o;
    var sql = "SELECT * from Products WHERE ProductName LIKE '" + e.Text + "%'";
    var data = new DataTable();

    using (SqlConnection cnn = new
            SqlConnection(ConfigurationManager
                    .ConnectionStrings["NorthwindConnectionString"]
                    .ConnectionString))
    {
        using (SqlDataAdapter adapter = new SqlDataAdapter(sql, cnn))
        {
            try
            {
                cnn.Open();
                adapter.Fill(data);
            }
```

```
                catch (Exception ex)
                {
                    // write error handling logic here
                }
            }
        }

        try
        {
            const int itemsPerRequest = 20;
            int itemOffset = e.NumberOfItems;
            int endOffset = itemOffset + itemsPerRequest;
            if (endOffset > data.Rows.Count)
            {
                endOffset = data.Rows.Count;
            }
            for (int i = itemOffset; i < endOffset; i++)
            {
                string productName = data.Rows[i]["ProductName"].ToString();
                RadComboBoxItem comboItem = new RadComboBoxItem(productName);
                combo.Items.Add(comboItem);
            }
            e.Message = data.Rows.Count > 0 ?
                            String.Format("Items <b>1</b>-<b>{0}</b> out of <b>{1}</b>",
                                                        endOffset, data.Rows.Count)
                            : "No matches";
        }
        catch
        {
            e.Message = "No matches";
        }
    }
```

Figure 6-6. *Note the summary description in the footer of RadComboBox with the ShowMore button.*

Implementing Automatic Loading On Demand

RadComboBox also includes the feature of automatic load-on-demand (or codeless load-on-demand). This feature enables you to add load on demand to RadComboBox by just configuring the property EnableAutomaticLoadOnDemand instead of EnableLoadOnDemand, and it will configure the server-side load-on-demand functionality for you. You can also use the ItemsPerRequest property to specify how many items to load on each request.

Listing 6-10 illustrates how to configure automatic load-on-demand functionality with a declarative datasource.

Listing 6-10. *Automatically Loading on Demand*

ASPX Page

```
<telerik:RadComboBox ID="RadComboBox9" Runat="server"
                     MaxHeight="300px"
                     DropDownWidth="250px"
                     DataSourceID="SqlDataSource3"
                     DataTextField="ProductName"
                     DataValueField="ProductID"
                     EnableAutomaticLoadOnDemand="true"
                     ItemsPerRequest="10"
                     ShowMoreResultsBox="true"
                     EnableVirtualScrolling="true" >
</telerik:RadComboBox>

<asp:SqlDataSource ID="SqlDataSource3" runat="server"
    ConnectionString="<%$ ConnectionStrings:NorthwindConnectionString %>"
    SelectCommand="SELECT [ProductID], [ProductName] FROM [Products]">
</asp:SqlDataSource>
```

This example works very well, but how about the scenario when you define the datasource using code? Well, it works exactly the same, but you need to define the DataSource property of RadComboBox on every request to ensure it knows where to load the data every time.

The example in Listing 6-11 creates a list of products (or FakeProducts to differentiate from the Products table in the database). Then, on every request it configures the DataSource property of RadComboBox.

Listing 6-11. *Automatically Loading on Demand with DataSource Configured in the Code Behind*

ASPX Page

```
<telerik:RadComboBox ID="RadComboBox9" Runat="server"
                     MaxHeight="300px"
                     DropDownWidth="250px"
                     DataTextField="ProductName"
                     DataValueField="ProductID"
                     EnableAutomaticLoadOnDemand="true"
                     ItemsPerRequest="10"
                     ShowMoreResultsBox="true"
                     EnableVirtualScrolling="true" >
</telerik:RadComboBox>
```

Code Behind

```
public class FakeProduct
{
    public FakeProduct(int id, string name)
    {
        ProductID = id;
        ProductName = name;
    }
    public int ProductID { get; set; }
    public string ProductName { get; set; }
}

protected void Page_Load(object sender, EventArgs e)
{
    RadComboBox9.DataSource = LoadFakeProducts();
    if (Page.IsPostBack) return;

    // the initial load logic here
}

private List<FakeProduct> LoadFakeProducts()
{
    List<FakeProduct> listOfProducts = new List<FakeProduct>();
    for (int i = 0; i < 1000; i++)
    {
        FakeProduct fp = new FakeProduct(i, string.Format("Product{0}",i));
        listOfProducts.Add(fp);
    }
    return listOfProducts;
}
```

One important thing to mention about automatically loading on demand is that even though it works "automatically," the ItemsRequested event still fires on every request, and you can use it to alter the normal flow of items by modifying the Message property. In this way, you can add or remove items or even stop the next requests by setting the EndOfItems event argument.

Creating Item Templates

RadComboBox exposes a flexible templating architecture that enables you to alter the default behavior of the drop-down area. You have three different templates: Header, Item, and Footer. They are accesible at design time from the control's smart tag or in markup.

Templates expand the possibilities for programming by providing a means for richer functionality. Not only will you have a control that does all you need in selecting items from a collection but you're also able to create an enhanced experience for the end user.

Listing 6-12 shows a RadComboBox with all three templates defined and a mechanism for selecting multiple items using check boxes instead of regular Items.

Listing 6-12. *RadComboBox with Templates*

ASPX Page

```
<telerik:RadComboBox ID="RadComboBox8" Runat="server"
                     EnableLoadOnDemand="True"
                     MaxHeight="300px"
                     DropDownWidth="300px"
                     DataSourceID="SqlDataSource2"
                     HighlightTemplatedItems="True"
                     DataTextField="ProductName"
                     DataValueField="ProductID" >
  <HeaderTemplate>
      <table style="width: 250px; text-align: left">
        <tr>
           <td style="width: 250px;">Product Name</td>
        </tr>
      </table>
    </HeaderTemplate>
    <ItemTemplate>
        <asp:CheckBox ID="chkProduct" runat="server"
                      onclick="ProductClick(this)"
                      Text='<%# DataBinder.Eval(Container.DataItem, "ProductName") %>' />
    </ItemTemplate>
    <FooterTemplate>
      <table style="width: 250px; text-align: left">
        <tr>
           <td style="width: 250px;">
                <asp:Label ID="lblFooter" runat="server"></asp:Label>
           </td>
        </tr>
      </table>
    </FooterTemplate>
</telerik:RadComboBox>

<asp:SqlDataSource ID="SqlDataSource2" runat="server"
    ConnectionString="<%$ ConnectionStrings:NorthwindConnectionString %>"
    SelectCommand="SELECT [ProductID], [ProductName] FROM [Products] ➥
ORDER BY [ProductName]">
</asp:SqlDataSource>

<script type="text/javascript" language="javascript">
    function ProductClick(chk) {
        var combo = $find("<%= RadComboBox8.ClientID %>");
        var text = "";
        var items = combo.get_items();

        for (var i = 0; i < items.get_count(); i++) {
            var item = items.getItem(i);
            //get the checkbox element of the current item
            var chk1 = $get(combo.get_id() + "_i" + i + "_chkProduct");
            if (chk1.checked)
                text += item.get_text() + ",";
```

```
        }
        text = text.replace(/,$/, "");

        if (text.length > 0)
            combo.set_text(text);
        else
            combo.set_text("");
    }

</script>
```

Code Behind

```
protected void Page_Load(object sender, EventArgs e)
{
    if (Page.IsPostBack) return;
    RadComboBox8.DataBind();
    Label lbl = (Label) RadComboBox8.Footer.FindControl("lblFooter");
    lbl.Text = string.Format("{0} Products", RadComboBox8.Items.Count);
}
```

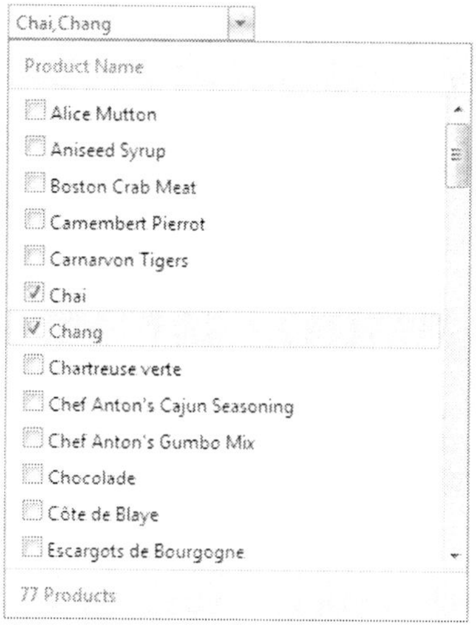

Figure 6-7. *The templates in RadComboBox allow customization, such as inlcuding check boxes instead of just text as items and enabling users to select multiple items.*

RadGrid

`RadGrid` is Telerik's grid control, which has tons of features for both client- and server-side programming. You can bind it to ASP.NET 2.0+ data components like `SqlDataSource`, `LinqDataSource`, `EntityDataSource`, and `AccessDataSource` and to business objects, and with the client mechanisms, you can bind it to web services and page methods.

RadGrid possesses a vast client-side API that enables you to have rich interactions with the grid without making a roundtrip to the server. This gives you a lot of control and allows you to provide your users with a more responsive application.

This control has integrated filtering capabilities for all its different types of columns, and with its great extensibility, you can create your own column type and add the functionality you need. On top of that, you are not restricted to a flat table representation; you can create hierarchical grids (or nested grids) in which you show related data in a single view.

The layout of RadGrid can be easily customized to adjust to your application needs, and it supports all built-in and custom skins, so you can make it match your application design. With the help of templates, you can change the default presentation from tabular to other formats, such as business cards or RadListView (which we'll examine later in this chapter).

What about huge datasources? With features such as client data binding, LINQ queries, and expressions and load modes, RadGrid is capable of handling hundreds of thousands and even millions of rows of information.

RadGrid has lots of additional functionality like built-in column grouping, paging, scrolling, and automatic insert, update, and delete operations. Let's explore those now.

Understanding the Structure of RadGrid

The structure of RadGrid looks somewhat complex but basically is composed of rows and columns grouped in the form of a table. There are different types of columns and different types of grids, so let's dive into all the elements that compose a RadGrid.

Understanding the Types of Grids

There are two types of RadGrids, flat and hierarchical. A flat RadGrid displays one level of data from the datasource. A hierarchical RadGrid displays several levels of data, linking each level with a parent-child relation definition (this is actually an object of type ParentTableRelation). It's worth mentioning that when working with hierarchical RadGrids, you have one top level grid and several lower level grids, and in the lower levels, you can have more than one grid in the same level.

Regardless of the type of RadGrid, there is always one property named MasterTableView, which represents the table of data at the top level (sometimes called the topmost table) and is of type GridTableView. If the RadGrid is a hierarchical one, there are also one or more child tables of data (each one of type GridTableView) in the DetailTables property; these represent the other levels of data (the DetailTables property is of type GridTableViewCollection).

Before going any further, you need to understand the relationship between RadGrid, MasterTableView, and DetailTables. Basically, when you configure properties at the RadGrid level, they apply to the whole set of GridTableView items in the grid (MasterTableView and DetailTables). Now, contrary to what you might be thinking, properties set at the MasterTableView level apply only to the MasterTableView and are not inherited by the child tables in the DetailTables collection, but properties set on the MasterTableView and GridTableViews in DetailTables override the defaults set by RadGrid.

Working with RadGrid Columns

RadGrid columns are composed of a header, a set of items, and footer. The header allows users to perform certain operations such as sorting (when the property AllowSorting is set to true), grouping (when the property ShowGroupPanel is set to true), reorder columns (if the property ClientSettings.AllowColumnsReorder is set to true), resize columns (if the property ClientSettings.Resizing.AllowColumnResize is set to true) and display the built-in context menu (if the property EnableHeaderContextMenu is set to true).

Column Items are the regular data cells that look and behave according to their type and definition. column Footer is displayed at the bottom of the RadGrid and cannot perform the same operations as the header; instead, it is used for displaying information such as aggregate functions results. For aggregate function to work, you need to define, for each column, an aggregate operation the Aggregate property with the name of the operation you want to perform (Sum, Min, Max, Last, First, Count, Avg, or Custom). When you're using a custom aggregate, RadGrid raises the OnCustomAggregate event, so you can make the calculations you need on the server side and assign the results to the Result property of the event arguments parameter.

RadGrid has two types of columns: data and structure. Data columns hold actual data from the datasource, and structure columns are created to facilitate RadGrid features such as grouping and resizing.

There are three structure columns: GridRowIndicatorColumn is automatically added when row resizing is enabled by setting the property ClientSettings.Resizing.AllowRowResize to True. This column appears immediately before the first data column. GridGroupSplitterColumn appears when grouping is enabled (setting the property AllowGrouping to True). It contains controls that allow users to expand and collapse groups of rows; this column always appears first. GridExpandColumn appears when the RadGrid is hierarchical and lets the user expand and collapse detail tables in the grid. The GridExpandColumn is always placed in front of all other grid content columns unless the grouping is enabled, and in that case, this column is after GridGroupSplitterColumn.

Data columns display data from the datasource and alternatively can contain controls that operate on the data. Normally, they are automatically generated, but if you need (or want) more control over their behavior and data representation, you can create them at design time using the RadGrid Property Builder, which will generate the definition markup to the RadGrid declaration, or you can add them to the Columns property dynamically at runtime.

Automatically generated columns are added at runtime when the AutoGenerateColumns property of the table view is set to True, as it is by default. They are easy to implement, and the best part is that they are aware of the data type of the field they represent. Also, a column is added for every field of the data source to which the table view is bound, and these columns can be accessed using the AutoGeneratedColumns property collection.

Why is knowing the data type of the field in the data source important? Regardless of whether or not the column is automatically generated, RadGrid needs to implement the correct column type to support the correct editor for insert, update, and filter operations.

A column can have several properties depending on its type. However, they share some important common properties such as Display and Visible. If you set the display property to false, the column is rendered, but a style of display:none is added to its definition. On the other hand, if you set Visible to false, the column is not even rendered on the page. If the column is editable (meaning it implements the IGridEditableColumn interface), it has a ReadOnly property that determines if the column editor will be shown in the edit form.

To bind a grid column to a field in the datasource, you only need to specify the DataField property. Identifying the data type using the DataType property forces a validation of the data type from the datasource field. The UniqueName property is, by default, set to the same DataField if it is not specified, but in general, this property defines a name for the column that is unique among the whole set of grid columns. DataField refers to the name of the field in the datasource that the column will represent, and DataType is the data type of that field. UniqueName is a string that is unique in the Columns collection and will be used to reference that column in server or client code.

If sorting is enabled, the DataField property is used to create the sorting expression, but if you need to define a specific sorting expression, you can use the SortExpression property. The HeaderText property defines the text that will appear in the header of the column.

The following list contains all the columns currently supported in RadGrid and the most important properties you need to configure to make them work property; keep in mind that Telerik is constantly improving its controls and this list might change in future versions:

- GridBoundColumn displays a table view column bound to a field in the datasource, is editable, and by default, it implements a GridTextBoxColumnEditor to allow editing the text in the cell. It also exposes the HtmlEncode property, which specifies if the text will be automatically encoded and the EmptyDataText property for the text that will be displayed when the field value is empty or null.
- GridButtonColumn displays a button for each entry in the column. It can be of type PushButton, LinkButton, or ImageButton, and you can define the CommandName and CommandArgument properties for command operations. There are two predefined commands: select and delete. When the button implements the select command and the button is clicked, the entire row is selected. When the button implements the delete command, and the button is clicked the entire row is deleted. This column is not editable.
- GridEditCommandColumn initially displays an edit button. Once that button is clicked, if RadGrid is configured for in-line editing it displays two buttons to Update or Cancel the changes made. The same as with GridButtonColumn, the button can be configured to be a PushButton, LinkButton, or ImageButton.
- GridHyperLinkColumn renders the column as a hyperlink. You can use the Text property to display a static text for the hyperlink or use the DataTextField property to define the field whose value will be used for the link's text. The actual target of the hyperlink (href property) is set with the DataNavigateUrlFields property that holds the collection of field names to be used in the composition of the URL and DataNavigateUrlFormatString property, which will construct the actual URL.
- GridImageColumn renders an image. You use either the ImageUrl property for a fixed image location or the DataImageUrlFields and DataImageUrlFormatString properties. The DataAlternateTextField property is set to a field that will render the Alt property for the image.
- GridBinaryImageColumn basically does the same thing as GridImageColumn, but the source of the image is binary data from a field that you must specify in the DataField property. You can additionally set the DataAlternateTextField for the Alt property of the image, the ImageHeight and ImageWidth for specific dimensions and the ResizeMode property to any of Fit (the image will be resized to fit the given dimensions), Crop (the image will be trimmed) or None (the default).
- GridCheckBoxColumn displays a check box to represent a Boolean value. This column type is useful for bit (or Boolean) fields from database. Use the DataField property to specify the Boolean field from the datasource. This column is editable and displays a GridCheckBoxListColumnEditor for editing items.
- GridClientSelectColumn also displays a check box in the column, but it is used for a different purpose—selecting or deselecting the row. For this column to function property, you need to set the ClientSettings.Selecting.AllowRowSelect property to true. Also, if you enable multiple row selection with the AllowMultiRowSelection property, it adds a check box in the header for selecting or deselecting all rows in the current page of the RadGrid control.

- GridDropDownColumn looks and behaves much like a GridBoundColumn, but when switching to edit mode, it displays a drop-down control for each editable cell in the column. You need to provide the column with its own datasource and bind it for displaying its possible values. For binding use the properties DataSourceID, ListTextField and ListValueField in the same way as for a RadComboBox. Also set the DataField property to the field in the RadGrid data source that will be used for the SelectedValue property in the dropdown control. You can also use the DropDownControlType property to determine the type of control it will render (RadComboBox or DropDownList). Another common scenario is when the value is empty or null; therefore there is no match for any item in the list of items of the drop down column. To enable this scenario you need to configure the EnableEmptyListItem property to true, EmptyListItemText to a string to display and EmptyListItemValue to a default value that represents an empty entry.
- GridDateTimeColumn looks and behaves like a GridBoundColumn but in the edit form it renders a RadDateInput, RadDatePicker, RadTimePicker or RadDateTimePicker depending on the setting of the PickerType property (to display a RadDateInput set the value of the PickerType property to None).
- GridNumericColumn looks and behaves like a GridBoundColumn but in the edit form it displays a RadNumericTextBox. The DataField property must identify a valid numeric field from the data source or an error will be thrown. Also use the NumericType property to further identify the numeric data as a Currency, Percent, or Numeric value.
- GridMaskedColumn looks and behaves like a GridBoundColumn, but in the edit form, it displays a RadMaskedTextBox control. Use the Mask property to specify the edit mask to be used by the control.
- GridHTMLEditorColumn is designed for columns whose value is a string with HTML. In the edit form, it renders a RadEditor control for WYSIWYG editing of the HTML value.
- GridCalculatedColumn displays a value that is calculated based on the values of the fields defined in the DataFields property (a comma-separated list), and the operations specified in the Expression property. Valid operations are addition, subtraction, multiplication and division (+, -, *, and /).
- GridTemplateColumn each cell in the column in accordance with a specified template. This lets you provide custom controls in the column. There are four templates you can use: ItemTemplate, EditItemTemplate, HeaderTemplate, and FooterTemplate. And you access these either declaratively in the HTML editor or graphically from the Edit Templates link in the smart tag of a RadGrid control. Note that even if you don't need anything in the ItemTemplate, you need to define an empty one because RadGrid needs its definition for internal operations. When binding controls inside templates, you need to specify a binding expression with either Bind or Eval.

- GridAttachmentColumn enables you to have a way to upload and download content—documents or images—right from the datasource. When in normal mode, the column will render a download button, and when in edit mode, it will render a RadUpload control so you can upload content. This column works with is own datasource for the binary data stream; therefore, you need to define the DataSourceID, AttachmentKeyFields, and AttachmentDataFields properties at the minimum for it to work. The AttachmentKeyFields specifies the field names from RadGrid's datasource that are used to populate the attachment datasource select parameters, and AttachmentDataFields specifies the field from GridAttachmentColumn's datasource where the attachment is stored as binary data. Other properties that can be configured are FileName (specifies the file name of the downloaded attachment), FileNameTextField (specifies the name of the field from RadGrid's datasource, the values of which will be used as file names of the downloaded attachments), FileNameTextFormatString (specifies the format string used to format the value of the field specified by the FileNameTextField property), Text (specifies the text of the download button), DataTextField (specifies the data field from parent GridTableView's datasource, the values of which will be used for the download button text), DataTextFormatString (specifies the format string used to format the value of the field specified by DataTextField), AllowedFileExtensions (specifies the allowed file extensions), and MaxFileSize (specifies the maximum allowed file size in bytes).
- GridRatingColumn displays a RadRating control. You can use it to give your users rating functionality and to load and store the ratings in a numeric field from the datasource specified in the DataField property. You can configure properties such as ItemCount to instruct the rating control how many items to show, SelectionMode to determine how to RadRating will select the rating (Single or Continuous), Precision for selecting an exact portion (half or whole item), and IsDirectionReversed to set the direction of rating. Of particular importance is AllowRatingInViewMode, which determines if users can rate when RadGrid is in view mode (if set to false it will make RadRating read-only in view mode).

Working with RadGrid Rows

Each row of data in RadGrid is located in the GridTableview.Items property, which is a collection of GridDataItem objects. Each GridDataItem in the Items collection has a type represented by the ItemType property, which can be useful for styling purposes. For example, you can apply a style to all odd rows and a different one for even rows. All odd items are of type GridItemType.Item, and all even items are of type GridItemType.AlternatingItem.

Rows can be divided into two basic groups: static and dynamic. Static rows are always present in each RadGrid regardless of its visibility; under this category fall the header and footer rows, command item, status bar, and pager rows. On the other hand, dynamic rows may or may not be present, because they represent the actual data rows from the datasource.

The Pager is a row that contains the paging navigation controls and will be visible only when the grid's AllowPaging property is set to True. The CommandItem is a placeholder for commands that can perform some action on the items in the grid, which in turn, can be processed on the selected items or on all items in the grid. The GridStatusBarItem appears below all other items in the grid and displays the information about the current RadGrid status. This item is intended primarily for use when RadGrid is used with RadAjaxManager (which we'll examine in Chapter 10) to indicate when RadGrid is performing asynchronous AJAX requests. To show the status bar item, set the ShowStatusBar property to True.

Accessing Rows and Cells

To access the data in RadGrid, you first obtain a reference to the specific row (or set of rows) you want and then get the column cell where the data is. In the code behind, you access the GridTableView.Items collection of the RadGrid object. GridTableView represents either the MasterTableView or any child table view in a hierarchical RadGrid. Each item in the collection is of type GridDataItem or GridEditFormItem, depending on the state of the control. In turn, each GridDataItem (and GridEditFormItem) has a property called ItemIndex that is the index of the item in the collection.

Once you have the GridDataItem object, you access the row columns by using the UniqueName property of each column. You can use the index of the columns, but depending on the reordering and grouping configuration, the index might change—and that can give you headaches. Therefore, the UniqueName property method is preferred. The example in Listing 6-13 illustrates what I just explained.

Listing 6-13. *Accesing Rows and Cells in the Code Behind*

```
foreach (var item in RadGrid1.Items)
{
   if (item is GridDataItem)
   {
      GridDataItem dataItem = item as GridDataItem; // found the row (GridDataItem)
      TableCell cell = dataItem[“ProductID”];  // found the cell (TableCell)
      String cellValue = cell.Text;    // found the cell value (string)
   }
   else
      if (item is GridEditFormItem)
      {
         GridEditFormItem editItem = item as GridEditFormItem; // found the row
         TableCell cell = editedItem["ColumnUniqueName"];   // found the cell
         TextBox txt = cell.Controls[0] as TextBox; // found the control
         string itemValue = txt.Text; // found the control’s value
      }
}
```

The code in Listing 6-14 works for all types of columns except for GridTemplateColumns , where you must first find (using the FindControl method) the control in the template to then get its value.

Now, let’s look at how we can do the same thing but on the client side; see Listing 6-15 for the code.

Listing 6-14. *Accesing Rows and Cells on the Client Side*

```
<script type="text/javascript" language="javascript">
    function LoadValues() {
        var grid = $find("<%=RadGrid1.ClientID %>");
        var masterTable = grid.get_masterTableView();
        // get all rows in the grid
        selectedRows = masterTable.get_dataItems();
        for (var i = 0; i < selectedRows.length; i++) {
            var row = selectedRows[i];     // found the row
            var cell = MasterTable.getCellByColumnUniqueName(row, "ProductID") // cell
            var cellValue = cell.innerHTML;  // value
        }
    }
</script>
```

Suppose you're working with hierarchical RadGrids and need to access the values of the cells. To do so, you have a property for each item in the GridTableView.Items collection called ChildItem that is of type GridNestedViewItem. Each ChildItem, in turn, has a NestedTableView property that is a collection of GridTableView objects that hold all the child tables for that item. Listing 6-15 shows how to access rows in a hierarchical RadGrid using the code behind.

Listing 6-15. *Accesing Rows and Cells in a Hierarchical RadGrid in the Code Behind*

```
foreach (GridDataItem item in RadGrid1.Items) {
    foreach (GridTableView detTable in item.ChildItem.NestedTableViews) {
        foreach (GridDataItem detTableItem in detTable.Items) {
            TableCell cell = detTableItem["ProductID"];
            string cellValue = cell.Text;
        }
    }
}
```

In Listing 6-16, I do the same navigation of a hierarchical RadGrid to access rows, but this time, the implementation is using the client-side API.

Listing 6-16. *Accesing Rows and Cells in a Hierarchical RadGrid in Client Side Code.*

```
<script type="text/javascript" language="javascript">
    function LoadValues() {
        var grid = $find("<%=RadGrid1.ClientID %>");
        var masterTable = grid.get_masterTableView();
        // get all rows in the grid
        selectedRows = masterTable.get_dataItems();
        for (var i = 0; i < selectedRows.length; i++) {
            var row = selectedRows[i]; // found the row
            for (var j = 0; j < row.get_nestedViews().length; j++) {
                var detTable = row.get_nestedViews()[j]; // found the child table
                var childRows = detTable.get_dataItems();
                for (var k = 0; k < childRows.length; k++) {
                    var cRow = childRows[k];
                    var cell = cRow.getCellByColumnUniqueName(row, "ProductID")
                    var cellValue = cell.innerHTML;
                }
            }
        }
    }
</script>
```

Making Use of the Design Time Support

RadGrid has a great design time support—you can build the entire RadGrid declaration with graphical tools. Using the smart tag and selecting property builder will open the configuration window where you can define all the properties for your RadGrid. Figures 6-8 and 6-9 show how this window looks.

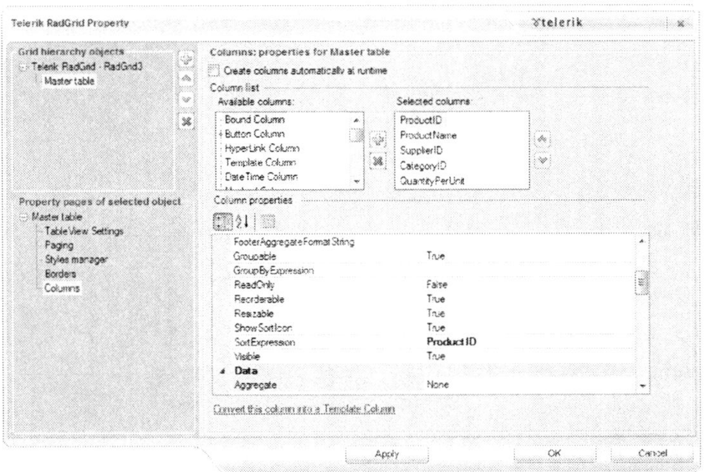

Figure 6-8. *The Columns section in the property builder window*

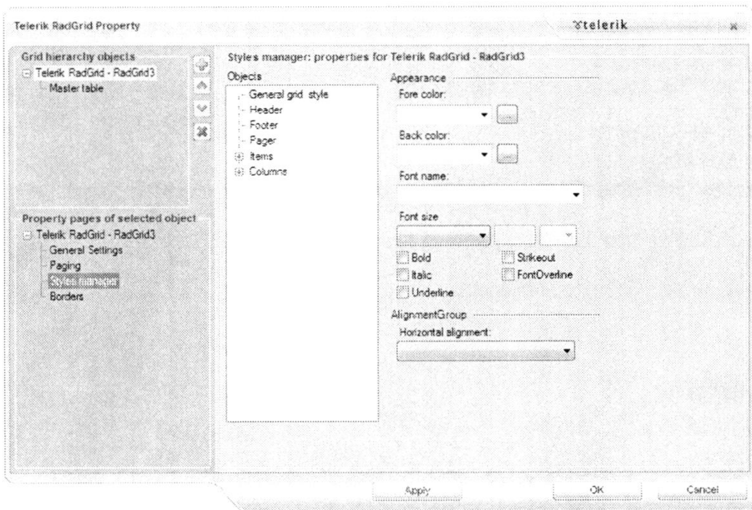

Figure 6-9. *The "Style manager" section of the property builder window*

Implementing Simple DataBinding

Simple binding occurs when you set up your `RadGrid` to use the `DataSource` property and `DataBind()` method for a datasource through code (programmatic data binding).

While this method is quite simple, it is not recommended for complex operations such as grouping, hierarchy, filtering, sorting, paging, and insert, update, and delete operations using user web controls or form templates. For these scenarios, it is better to use declarative data binding or advanced data binding by handling the `NeedDataSource` event.

Listing 6-17 shows you how to do simple data binding, and Figure 6-10 shows how `RadGrid` looks after the binding operation.

Listing 6-17. *RadGrid Simple Data Binding*

```
ASPX Page

<telerik:RadGrid ID="RadGrid0" runat="server"
                     GridLines="None"
                     Skin="Vista">
</telerik:RadGrid>

Code Behind

protected void Page_Load(object sender, EventArgs e)
{
    if (Page.IsPostBack) return;
    RadGrid0.DataSource = GetProductsDataTable();
    RadGrid0.DataBind();
}

public DataTable GetProductsDataTable()
{
    string ConnString = ConfigurationManager
                .ConnectionStrings["NorthwindConnectionString"]
                .ConnectionString;
    string query = "SELECT * FROM Products";
    DataTable myDataTable = new DataTable();
    using (SqlConnection conn = new SqlConnection(ConnString))
    {
        using (SqlDataAdapter adapter = new SqlDataAdapter())
        {
            adapter.SelectCommand = new SqlCommand(query, conn);
            try
            {
                conn.Open();
                adapter.Fill(myDataTable);
            }
            finally
            {
                conn.Close();
            }
        }
    }
    return myDataTable;
}
```

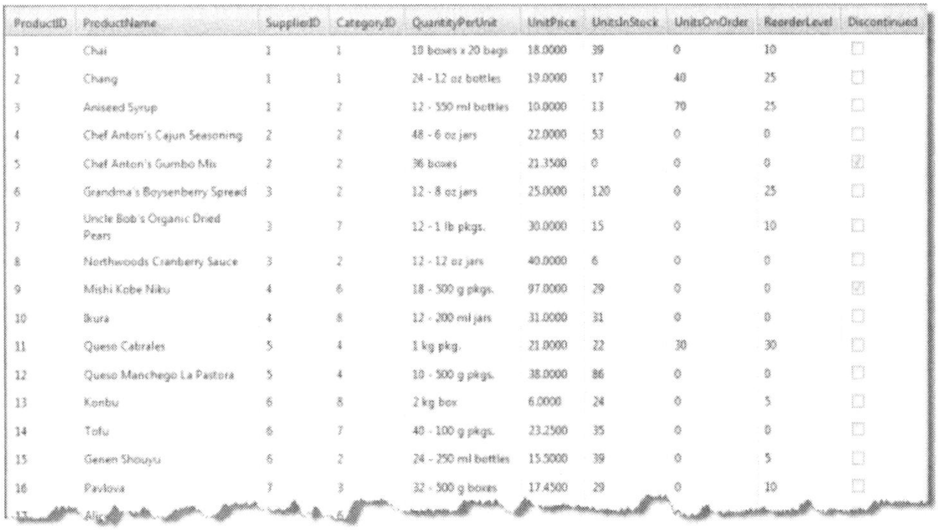

ProductID	ProductName	SupplierID	CategoryID	QuantityPerUnit	UnitPrice	UnitsInStock	UnitsOnOrder	ReorderLevel	Discontinued
1	Chai	1	1	10 boxes x 20 bags	18.0000	39	0	10	☐
2	Chang	1	1	24 - 12 oz bottles	19.0000	17	40	25	☐
3	Aniseed Syrup	1	2	12 - 550 ml bottles	10.0000	13	70	25	☐
4	Chef Anton's Cajun Seasoning	2	2	48 - 6 oz jars	22.0000	53	0	0	☐
5	Chef Anton's Gumbo Mix	2	2	36 boxes	21.3500	0	0	0	☑
6	Grandma's Boysenberry Spread	3	2	12 - 8 oz jars	25.0000	120	0	25	☐
7	Uncle Bob's Organic Dried Pears	3	7	12 - 1 lb pkgs.	30.0000	15	0	10	☐
8	Northwoods Cranberry Sauce	3	2	12 - 12 oz jars	40.0000	6	0	0	☐
9	Mishi Kobe Niku	4	6	18 - 500 g pkgs.	97.0000	29	0	0	☑
10	Ikura	4	8	12 - 200 ml jars	31.0000	31	0	0	☐
11	Queso Cabrales	5	4	1 kg pkg.	21.0000	22	30	30	☐
12	Queso Manchego La Pastora	5	4	10 - 500 g pkgs.	38.0000	86	0	0	☐
13	Konbu	6	8	2 kg box	6.0000	24	0	5	☐
14	Tofu	6	7	40 - 100 g pkgs.	23.2500	35	0	0	☐
15	Genen Shouyu	6	2	24 - 250 ml bottles	15.5000	39	0	5	☐
16	Pavlova	7	3	32 - 500 g boxes	17.4500	29	0	10	☐

Figure 6-10. *RadGrid showing information from a datasource using simple data binding*

Implementing Declarative Data Binding

Use the DataSourceID property for a datasource component declared in the page. The datasource can be any of those included in ASP.NET 2.0+ (SqlDataSource, AccessDataSource, LinqDataSource, XmlDataSource, etc.).

In Listing 6-18, a LinqDataSource is created declaratively, and RadGrid paging and sorting are enabled. There is no need for any code behind in this example. See how the RadGrid looks in Figure 6-11.

Listing 6-18. *RadGrid Declarative Data Binding with a LinqDataSource*

ASPX Page

```
<asp:UpdatePanel ID="UpdatePanel1" runat="server">
<ContentTemplate>
    <telerik:RadGrid ID="RadGrid1" runat="server"
                     AllowPaging="True"
                     AllowSorting="True"
                     DataSourceID="ProductsDataSource"
                     GridLines="None"
                     Skin="Vista">
        <ClientSettings>
            <Scrolling AllowScroll="True" UseStaticHeaders="True" />
        </ClientSettings>
        <MasterTableView DataKeyNames="ProductID"
                    DataSourceID="ProductsDataSource">
        <RowIndicatorColumn>
        <HeaderStyle Width="20px"></HeaderStyle>
        </RowIndicatorColumn>
```

```
        <ExpandCollapseColumn>
        <HeaderStyle Width="20px"></HeaderStyle>
        </ExpandCollapseColumn>

        </MasterTableView>
    </telerik:RadGrid>
    <asp:LinqDataSource ID="ProductsDataSource" runat="server"
        ContextTypeName="WebApplication1.NorthwindDataContext"
        EntityTypeName=""
        TableName="Products">
    </asp:LinqDataSource>
</ContentTemplate>
</asp:UpdatePanel>
```

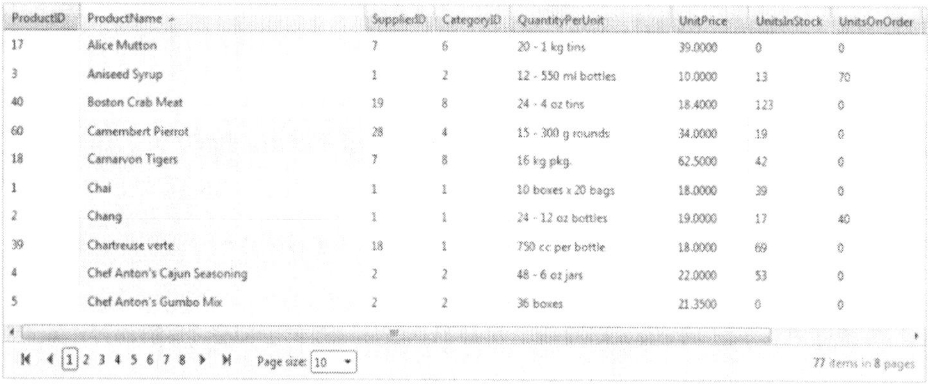

ProductID	ProductName	SupplierID	CategoryID	QuantityPerUnit	UnitPrice	UnitsInStock	UnitsOnOrder
17	Alice Mutton	7	6	20 - 1 kg tins	39.0000	0	0
3	Aniseed Syrup	1	2	12 - 550 ml bottles	10.0000	13	70
40	Boston Crab Meat	19	8	24 - 4 oz tins	18.4000	123	0
60	Camembert Pierrot	28	4	15 - 300 g rounds	34.0000	19	0
18	Carnarvon Tigers	7	8	16 kg pkg.	62.5000	42	0
1	Chai	1	1	10 boxes x 20 bags	18.0000	39	0
2	Chang	1	1	24 - 12 oz bottles	19.0000	17	40
39	Chartreuse verte	18	1	750 cc per bottle	18.0000	69	0
4	Chef Anton's Cajun Seasoning	2	2	48 - 6 oz jars	22.0000	53	0
5	Chef Anton's Gumbo Mix	2	2	36 boxes	21.3500	0	0

1 2 3 4 5 6 7 8 Page size: 10 77 items in 8 pages

Figure 6-11. *Paging and sorting are enabled in a RadGrid control showing information from the LinqDataSource*

Implementing Advanced DataBinding

To work with advanced data binding in `RadGrid`, you have to do the following:

- Remove any declaration you might have for the property `DataSourceID` in the `RadGrid` declaration, `MasterTableView` declaration, and any of the child tables in `DetailTables` collection.
- Remove all calls to the RadGrid's `DataBind()` method in your code.
- Add a handler to the `NeedDataSource` event that is fired whenever `RadGrid` "needs" to load data and use the `DataSource` property within that event handler to load the data into the RadGrid.

Basically, you perform all data binding in the `NeedDataSource` event handler you define, and let the `RadGrid` figure out when and how the `NeedDataSource` event is raised. The signature of the event handler is

```
protected void NeedDataSource(object source,
                          Telerik.Web.UI.GridNeedDataSourceEventArgs e)
{
}
```

The handler uses a source object to know which RadGrid raises the event and a GridNeedDataSourceEventArgs parameter that has two properties that interest us. The first one is IsFromDetailTable, which pretty much explains itself. It has a value of true if the event is raised when binding to a child table in the DetailTables collection and false if the event is raised when binding to the MasterTableView table. The second property is RebindReason, which is of type GridRebindReason. The enumeration GridRebindReason can be of the type DetailTableBinding, ExplicitRebind, InitialLoad, NotSpecified, PostBackEvent, or PostbackViewStateNotPersisted.

RadGrid knows exactly when it needs to load data, so it just made sense to name the event actually that, NeedDataSource. The control will raise the NeedDataSource event when any of the data-related operations needs to be performed, for example, when the page loads; when paging, sorting, grouping, CRUD operations; when calls are made to the Rebind() method; when filtering, and so forth. Fortunately, the programmers at Telerik decided to wrap all of these into one single event, so we would not have to worry about handling each operation individually.

The Rebind() method causes the NeedDataSource event to be raised with a GridRebindReason.ExplicitRebind value in the GridNeedDataSourceEventArgs parameter. Also, if you call Rebind() but the DataSource property holds a reference to data (i.e., it is not null), you must set DataSource to null or the NeedDataSource event will *not* be raised.

■ **Note** When working with advanced data binding you should never call the Rebind() or DataBind() methods inside the NeedDataSource event handler. This is because Rebind() will cause the NeedDataSoruce event to be raised again, and a DataBind() call is done internally.

Understanding the RadGrid Event Life Cycle

It is also important to understand what happens when working with RadGrid and advanced binding, because several events are raised during the interaction with the page and the control itself. On top of that, there is a slightly different set of events raised when ViewState is turned off.

When the page is first loaded the events happen like this:

1. The Page.Load event is raised.
2. Then, the RadGrid.NeedDataSource event is raised (for each of the RadGrid instances declared in the page).
3. After that, for each row of data loaded the ItemCreated and ItemDataBound events are raised (in that order);
4. Finally, the Page.PreRender event is raised, and the page will continue its own event life cycle.

When a postback is initiated by a control outside RadGrid, the events are as follows:

1. For each row in the RadGrid, the ItemCreated event is raised.
2. Next, the Page.Load event is raised.

3. Then, the postback event occurs.
4. Finally, the Page.PreRender event is raised.

If the postback was initiated by a control inside the RadGrid, this is the process:

1. First, the Page.Load event is raised.
2. The next event raised is ItemCommand.
3. If a row (or group of rows) is selected, the SelectedIndexChanged is raised, but if an edit, update, delete, or insert operation is triggered, the EditCommand, UpdateCommand, or InsertCommand events are raised depending on the action.
4. If the paging, sorting, grouping, or filtering operations are triggered, the PageIndexChanged, SortCommand, GroupsChanging, or ItemCommand events are raised; plus the NeedDataSource event is raised.
5. Finally, the ItemCreated and ItemDataBound events for the newly created set of rows are raised.

When ViewState is turned off, the events are different when a postback occurs. In this scenario, if the postback is initiated by a control outside RadGrid, the following occurs:

1. ItemDataBound is also raised after the ItemCreated event.
2. Next, the Page.Load event is raised.
3. After that, the RadGrid.NeedDataSource is raised.
4. If a server selection is performed, the RadGrid.NeedDataSource event is also raised.
5. With the other operations after the Page.Load event, the RadGrid.NeedDataSource is raised for RadGrid along with the ItemCreated and ItemDataBound for each item before the other specific events for the operation.

■ **Note** For full details on RadGrid life cycle, please see the resources in Telerik's RadGrid documentation in the "The control lifecycle" section at http://www.telerik.com/help/aspnet-ajax/grdcontrollifecycle.html.

Let's get to an example now on how to implement advanced data binding (see Listing 6-19). Here, the NeedDataSource event handler is used to load information from a SQL Server database and generates a DataTable that is then set as the DataSource for RadGrid. Also note in the code that I'm not using the DataBind() method like I did with simple data binding, and yet you are able to use sorting and paging.

Listing 6-19. *Implementing Advanced Data Binding in RadGrid*

ASPX Page

```
<asp:UpdatePanel ID="UpdatePanel2" runat="server">
<ContentTemplate>
    <telerik:RadGrid ID="RadGrid2" runat="server"
                     AllowPaging="True"
                     AllowSorting="True"
                     GridLines="None"
```

```
                Skin="Vista"
                OnNeedDataSource="RadGrid2_NeedDataSource">
        <ClientSettings>
            <Scrolling AllowScroll="True" UseStaticHeaders="True" />
        </ClientSettings>
        <MasterTableView DataKeyNames="OrderID, ProductID">
        <RowIndicatorColumn>
        <HeaderStyle Width="20px"></HeaderStyle>
        </RowIndicatorColumn>

        <ExpandCollapseColumn>
        <HeaderStyle Width="20px"></HeaderStyle>
        </ExpandCollapseColumn>

        </MasterTableView>
    </telerik:RadGrid>
</ContentTemplate>
</asp:UpdatePanel>

Code Behind

protected void RadGrid2_NeedDataSource(object source, GridNeedDataSourceEventArgs e)
{
    RadGrid2.DataSource = GetOrdersDetails();
}

private DataTable GetOrdersDetails()
{
    string ConnString = ConfigurationManager
            .ConnectionStrings["NorthwindConnectionString"]
            .ConnectionString;
    string query = "SELECT * FROM [Order Details]";
    DataTable myDataTable = new DataTable();
    using (SqlConnection conn = new SqlConnection(ConnString))
    {
        using (SqlDataAdapter adapter = new SqlDataAdapter())
        {
            adapter.SelectCommand = new SqlCommand(query, conn);

            conn.Open();
            try
            {
                adapter.Fill(myDataTable);
            }
            finally
            {
                conn.Close();
            }
        }
    }
    return myDataTable;
}
```

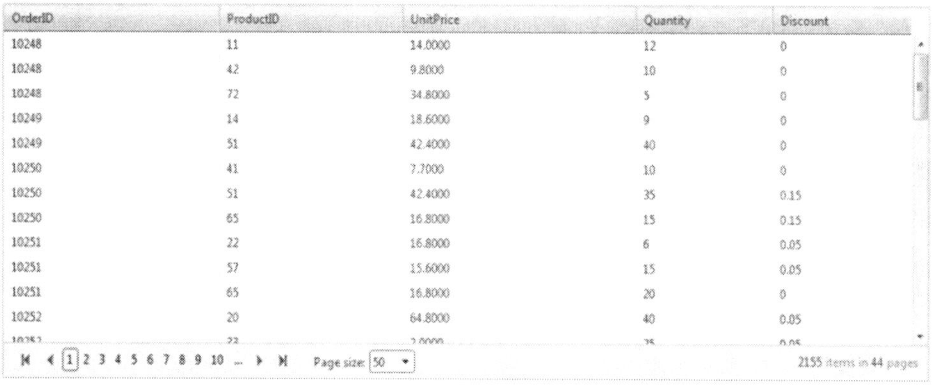

OrderID	ProductID	UnitPrice	Quantity	Discount
10248	11	14.0000	12	0
10248	42	9.8000	10	0
10248	72	34.8000	5	0
10249	14	18.6000	9	0
10249	51	42.4000	40	0
10250	41	7.7000	10	0
10250	51	42.4000	35	0.15
10250	65	16.8000	15	0.15
10251	22	16.8000	6	0.05
10251	57	15.6000	15	0.05
10251	65	16.8000	20	0
10252	20	64.8000	40	0.05

1 2 3 4 5 6 7 8 9 10 ... Page size: 50 2155 items in 44 pages

Figure 6-12. *RadGrid advanced data binding*

Binding RadGrid on the Client Side

It's time to review the client-side data binding capabilities of `RadGrid`. The `RadGrid` offers two approaches to client-side data binding: declarative and programmatic. Each approach will require a source of data that can be accessed on the client side such as a web service or `PageMethod`. `RadGrid` declarative client-side data binding is very similar to `ObjectDataSource` data binding. You need to specify `SelectMethod` and `SelectCountMethod` (if needed) along with `Location` property, and the control will automatically invoke the specified method as `PageMethod` or web service method. Use the `ClientSettings.DataBinding` section of the `RadGrid` definition to declare these methods.

The web method used in the `SelectMethod` property must return an `IEnumerable`. Optionally, if the `RadGrid` will support other options like paging, sorting, and filtering, you send the information as parameters, for example:

```
public List<MyBusinessObject> GetData(int startRowIndex,
                                      int maximumRows,
                                      List<GridSortExpression> sortExpression,
                                      List<GridFilterExpression> filterExpression)
{
}
```

Here, `MyBusinessObject` is a class with the representation of the data you want to present in your `RadGrid`. The two parameters `startRowIndex` and `maximumRows` are used for paging operations; the collection `sortExpression` is used for sorting, and `filterExpression` is for filtering. The `SelectCount` method takes no arguments but returns an numeric value.

When a `RadGrid` is implemented, it makes two calls: one is to obtain the data using the method specified in the `SelectMethod` property, and the second one is for the record count in the method specified in the `SelectCount` property.

To improve performance, you can define a single method that returns the data and the count at the same time. In this scenario, you could implement a `Dictionary` or `Class` to contain both the data and the count, and in the `RadGrid.ClientSettings.DataBind` section (either declaratively or in code), you define the values for the `CountPropertyName` and `DataPropertyName` properties to the appropriate class fields or key/value pair in the dictionary returned by the method in the `SelectMethod` property.

The example in Listing 6-20 implements a `RadGrid` with declarative client-side data binding and a web service with a method that will return the data and the count of records.

Listing 6-20. *RadGrid Declarative Client-Side Data Binding*

ASPX Page

```
<telerik:RadGrid ID="RadGrid3" runat="server"
                 AutoGenerateColumns="false"
                 AllowPaging="True"
                 AllowSorting="True"
                 AllowFilteringByColumn="true"
                 GridLines="None"
                 Skin="Vista" >
    <MasterTableView DataKeyNames="ProductID">
    <Columns>
        <telerik:GridBoundColumn DataField="ProductID"
                                 HeaderText="ProductID"
                                 SortExpression="ProductID"
                                 UniqueName="ProductID"
                                 DataType="System.Int32">
        </telerik:GridBoundColumn>
        <telerik:GridBoundColumn DataField="ProductName"
                                 HeaderText="ProductName"
                                 SortExpression="ProductName"
                                 UniqueName="ProductName"
                                 DataType="System.String">
        </telerik:GridBoundColumn>
        <telerik:GridBoundColumn DataField="SupplierID"
                                 HeaderText="SupplierID"
                                 SortExpression="SupplierID"
                                 UniqueName="SupplierID"
                                 DataType="System.Int32">
        </telerik:GridBoundColumn>
        <telerik:GridBoundColumn DataField="CategoryID"
                                 HeaderText="CategoryID"
                                 SortExpression="CategoryID"
                                 UniqueName="CategoryID"
                                 DataType="System.Int32">
        </telerik:GridBoundColumn>
        <telerik:GridBoundColumn DataField="QuantityPerUnit"
                                 HeaderText="QuantityPerUnit"
                                 SortExpression="QuantityPerUnit"
                                 UniqueName="QuantityPerUnit"
                                 DataType="System.String">
        </telerik:GridBoundColumn>
    </Columns>
    </MasterTableView>
    <ClientSettings>
        <DataBinding Location="RadGrid_Products.asmx" SelectMethod="GetData" />
    </ClientSettings>
</telerik:RadGrid>
```

MyProduct.cs

```
// Class used as the business object to be returned
public class MyProduct
```

```
{
    public int ProductID { get; set; }
    public string ProductName { get; set; }
    public int? SupplierID { get; set; }
    public int? CategoryID { get; set; }
    public string QuantityPerUnit { get; set; }
    public decimal? UnitPrice { get; set; }
    public short? UnitsInStock { get; set; }
    public short? UnitsOnOrder { get; set; }
    public short? ReorderLevel { get; set; }
    public bool Discontinued { get; set; }
}
```

RadGrid_Products.asmx.cs

```
    [WebService(Namespace = "http://tempuri.org/")]
    [WebServiceBinding(ConformsTo = WsiProfiles.BasicProfile1_1)]
    [System.ComponentModel.ToolboxItem(false)]
    [ScriptService]
    public class RadGrid_Products : WebService
    {

        [WebMethod(EnableSession = true)]
        public ResultData GetData(int startRowIndex,
                                  int maximumRows,
                                  List<GridSortExpression> sortExpression,
                                  List<GridFilterExpression> filterExpression)
        {
            List<MyProduct> productsList = new List<MyProduct>();
            int rowCount;
            string where = string.Empty;

            if (filterExpression.Count > 0)
            {
                foreach (var gridFilterExpression in filterExpression)
                {
                    // Check that the filter is EqualTo or NotEqualTo
                    // other filters are not implemented
                    if (gridFilterExpression.FilterFunction != "EqualTo"
                        && gridFilterExpression.FilterFunction != "NotEqualTo")
                        continue;
                    where += string.IsNullOrEmpty(where)
                                 ? Filter(gridFilterExpression)
                                 : " AND " + Filter(gridFilterExpression);
                }
            }

                string sql = "DECLARE @startRowIndex int ";
                sql += "DECLARE @maximumRows int ";
                sql += String.Format("SET @startRowIndex = {0} ", startRowIndex);
                sql += String.Format("SET @maximumRows = {0} ", maximumRows);
                sql += "DECLARE @first_id int, @startRow int ";
                sql += "DECLARE @sIndex INT ";
                sql += "SET @sIndex = @startRowIndex + 1 ";
```

```
        sql += "SET ROWCOUNT 0 ";
        sql += string.Format("SELECT *, ROW_NUMBER() OVER (ORDER BY {0}) [RowNum]",
                        (sortExpression.Count > 0
                               ? sortExpression[0].ToString()
                               : "ProductID"));
       sql += "INTO #TempProducts ";
        sql += "FROM Products ";
        if (!string.IsNullOrEmpty(where))
            sql += string.Format("WHERE {0}", where);
        sql += string.Format("ORDER BY {0}",
                            (sortExpression.Count > 0
                                   ? sortExpression[0].ToString()
                                   : "ProductID"));
        sql += "SET ROWCOUNT @sIndex ";
        sql += "SELECT @first_id = RowNum ";
        sql += "FROM #TempProducts ";
        sql += "ORDER BY RowNum ";
        sql += "SET ROWCOUNT @maximumRows ";
        sql += "SELECT p.* ";
        sql += "  FROM #TempProducts p ";
        sql += " WHERE RowNum >= @first_id ";
        if (!string.IsNullOrEmpty(where))
            sql += string.Format(" AND {0}", where);
        sql += string.Format("ORDER BY {0}",
                    (sortExpression.Count > 0
                           ? sortExpression[0].ToString()
                           : "ProductID"));
        sql += "DROP TABLE #TempProdudcts ";

    string countSql = "SELECT COUNT(*) FROM Products ";
    if (!string.IsNullOrEmpty(where))
        countSql += string.Format("WHERE {0}", where);

    using (SqlConnection connection = new
        SqlConnection(ConfigurationManager
                        .ConnectionStrings["NorthwindConnectionString"]
                        .ConnectionString))
    {
        connection.Open();
        using (SqlCommand countCommand = new SqlCommand(countSql,connection))
        {
            rowCount = int.Parse(countCommand.ExecuteScalar().ToString());
        }
        using (SqlCommand selectCommand = new SqlCommand(sql, connection))
        {
            using (SqlDataReader rd = selectCommand.ExecuteReader())
            {
                try
                {
                    while (rd.Read())
                    {
                        MyProduct pd = new MyProduct();
                        pd.ProductID = int.Parse(rd[0].ToString());
                        pd.ProductName = rd[1].ToString();
```

```
                        if (string.IsNullOrEmpty(rd[2].ToString()))
                            pd.SupplierID = null;
                        else
                            pd.SupplierID = int.Parse(rd[2].ToString());
                        if (string.IsNullOrEmpty(rd[3].ToString()))
                            pd.CategoryID = null;
                        else
                            pd.CategoryID = int.Parse(rd[3].ToString());

                        pd.QuantityPerUnit = rd[4].ToString();
                        if (string.IsNullOrEmpty(rd[5].ToString()))
                            pd.UnitPrice = null;
                        else
                            pd.UnitPrice = decimal.Parse(rd[5].ToString());
                        if (string.IsNullOrEmpty(rd[6].ToString()))
                            pd.UnitsInStock = null;
                        else
                            pd.UnitsInStock = short.Parse(rd[6].ToString());
                        if (string.IsNullOrEmpty(rd[7].ToString()))
                            pd.UnitsOnOrder = null;
                        else
                            pd.UnitsOnOrder = short.Parse(rd[7].ToString());
                        if (string.IsNullOrEmpty(rd[8].ToString()))
                            pd.ReorderLevel = null;
                        else
                            pd.ReorderLevel = short.Parse(rd[8].ToString());

                        pd.Discontinued = bool.Parse(rd[9].ToString());

                        productsList.Add(pd);
                    }
                }
                catch (Exception ex)
                {
                    // error handling logic here
                }
            }

        }
    }
    ResultData results = new ResultData();
    results.Data = productsList;
    results.Count = rowCount;
    return results;
}

public string Filter(GridFilterExpression filterExpression)
{
    var filter = string.Empty;
    switch (filterExpression.DataTypeName)
    {
        case "System.Int16":
        case "System.Int32":
```

```
                case "System.Int64":
                case "System.Short":
                    filter = string.Format("{0} {1} {2}", filterExpression.FieldName,
                                            GetFilterOperator(filterExpression.➥
FilterFunction),
                                            filterExpression.FieldValue);
                    break;
                case "System.String":
                    filter = string.Format("{0} {1} '{2}'", filterExpression.FieldName,
                                            GetFilterOperator(filterExpression.➥
FilterFunction),
                                            filterExpression.FieldValue);
                    break;
            }

            return filter;
        }

        private string GetFilterOperator(string filterFunction)
        {
            // This has been implemented only
            // for EqualTo and NotEqualTo
            var op = string.Empty;
            switch (filterFunction)
            {
                case "EqualTo":
                    op = "=";
                    break;
                case "NotEqualTo":
                    op = "<>";
                    break;
            }
            return op;
        }
    }

    public class ResultData
    {
        public int Count { get; set; }
        public List<MyProduct> Data { get; set; }
    }
}
```

The example in Listing 6-21 shows how to programatically bind a RadGrid to a datasource in client-side code. I will use PageMethods this time to illustrate a different type of binding. Remember that in order to use PageMethods, you need to configure the ScriptManager.EnablePageMethods property to true, and your methods must be static.

To use this type of binding, you need to know that all actions on the client-side raise the OnCommand client event, so in ClientSettings.ClientEvents, we need to add a handler for that event. This is mandatory when implementing programmatic client-side data binding. RadGrid checks whether or not this event is defined before rendering the grid. If it is not defined and there is no data for the RadGrid to bind on the server (which will be the case when using client-side data binding), the MasterTableView client-side markup and JavaScript object will not be rendered and therefore trying to access it (and bind data to it) will result in a JavaScript exception. If the OnCommand event is defined and there is no data to bind on the server, the RadGrid will still render the MasterTableView with *n* number of empty rows.

Additionally, I will add a handler for the pageLoad client event to handle the initial load.

Listing 6-21. *RadGrid Client-Side Data Binding*

ASPX Page

```
<telerik:RadGrid ID="RadGrid8" runat="server"
                 AutoGenerateColumns="false"
                 AllowPaging="True"
                 AllowSorting="True"
                 AllowFilteringByColumn="true"
                 GridLines="None"
                 Skin="Vista" >
    <MasterTableView DataKeyNames="ProductID">
    <Columns>
        <telerik:GridBoundColumn DataField="ProductID"
                                 HeaderText="ProductID"
                                 SortExpression="ProductID"
                                 UniqueName="ProductID"
                                 DataType="System.Int32">
        </telerik:GridBoundColumn>
        <telerik:GridBoundColumn DataField="ProductName"
                                 HeaderText="ProductName"
                                 SortExpression="ProductName"
                                 UniqueName="ProductName"
                                 DataType="System.String">
        </telerik:GridBoundColumn>
        <telerik:GridBoundColumn DataField="SupplierID"
                                 HeaderText="SupplierID"
                                 SortExpression="SupplierID"
                                 UniqueName="SupplierID"
                                 DataType="System.Int32">
        </telerik:GridBoundColumn>
        <telerik:GridBoundColumn DataField="CategoryID"
                                 HeaderText="CategoryID"
                                 SortExpression="CategoryID"
                                 UniqueName="CategoryID"
                                 DataType="System.Int32">
        </telerik:GridBoundColumn>
        <telerik:GridBoundColumn DataField="QuantityPerUnit"
                                 HeaderText="QuantityPerUnit"
                                 SortExpression="QuantityPerUnit"
                                 UniqueName="QuantityPerUnit"
                                 DataType="System.String">
        </telerik:GridBoundColumn>
    </Columns>
    </MasterTableView>
    <ClientSettings>
        <ClientEvents OnCommand="RadGrid8_Command" />
    </ClientSettings>
</telerik:RadGrid>
```

```
<telerik:RadCodeBlock ID="RadCodeBlock1" runat="server">
<script type="text/javascript">
    function pageLoad(sender, eventArgs) {
        var tableView = $find("<%= RadGrid8.ClientID %>").get_masterTableView();
        var pageSize = tableView.get_pageSize();
        var sortExpression = tableView.get_sortExpressions().toString();
        var filterExpression = tableView.get_filterExpressions().toString();

        PageMethods.GetProducts(0,
                                pageSize,
                                sortExpression,
                                filterExpression,
                                BindGrid);

        PageMethods.GetCount(filterExpression, updateVirtualItemCount);
    }

    function RadGrid8_Command(sender, args) {
        args.set_cancel(true);

        var tableView = $find("<%= RadGrid8.ClientID %>").get_masterTableView();
        var pageSize = tableView.get_pageSize();
        var sortExpression = tableView.get_sortExpressions().toString();
        var filterExpression = tableView.get_filterExpressions().toString();
        var currentPageIndex = sender.get_masterTableView().get_currentPageIndex();

        if (args.get_commandName() == "Filter")
            currentPageIndex = 0;

        PageMethods.GetProducts(currentPageIndex * pageSize,
                                pageSize,
                                sortExpression,
                                filterExpression,
                                BindGrid);

        // we only need to count the items again if the filter changed
        if (args.get_commandName() == "Filter") {
            PageMethods.GetCount(filterExpression, updateVirtualItemCount);
        }
    }

    function BindGrid(result) {
        var tableView = $find("<%= RadGrid8.ClientID %>").get_masterTableView();
        tableView.set_dataSource(result);
        tableView.dataBind();
    }

    function updateVirtualItemCount(result) {
        var tableView = $find("<%= RadGrid8.ClientID %>").get_masterTableView();
        tableView.set_virtualItemCount(result);
    }

</script>
</telerik:RadCodeBlock>
```

```
Code Behind

[WebMethod]
public static List<MyProduct> GetProducts(int startRowIndex,
                                         int maximumRows,
                                         string sortExpression,
                                         string filterExpression)
{
    List<MyProduct> productsList = new List<MyProduct>();
    string where = string.Empty;

    if (!string.IsNullOrEmpty(filterExpression))
    {
        where += filterExpression;
    }

    string sql = "DECLARE @startRowIndex int ";
    sql += "DECLARE @maximumRows int ";
    sql += String.Format("SET @startRowIndex = {0} ", startRowIndex);
    sql += String.Format("SET @maximumRows = {0} ", maximumRows);
    sql += "DECLARE @first_id int, @startRow int ";
    sql += "DECLARE @sIndex INT ";
    sql += "SET @sIndex = @startRowIndex + 1 ";
    sql += "SET ROWCOUNT 0 ";
    sql += string.Format("SELECT *, ROW_NUMBER() OVER (ORDER BY {0}) [RowNum]",
            (sortExpression.Count > 0
                    ? sortExpression[0].ToString()
                    : "ProductID"));
    sql += "INTO #TempProducts ";
    sql += "FROM Products ";
    if (!string.IsNullOrEmpty(where))
        sql += string.Format("WHERE {0}", where);
    sql += string.Format("ORDER BY {0}",
        (sortExpression.Count > 0
                ? sortExpression[0].ToString()
                : "ProductID"));
    sql += "SET ROWCOUNT @sIndex ";
    sql += "SELECT @first_id = RowNum ";
    sql += "FROM #TempProducts ";
    sql += "ORDER BY RowNum ";
    sql += "SET ROWCOUNT @maximumRows ";
    sql += "SELECT p.* ";
    sql += "  FROM #TempProducts p ";
    sql += " WHERE RowNum >= @first_id ";
    if (!string.IsNullOrEmpty(where))
        sql += string.Format(" AND {0}", where);
    sql += string.Format("ORDER BY {0}",
        (sortExpression.Count > 0
                ? sortExpression[0].ToString()
                : "ProductID"));
    sql += "DROP TABLE #TempProdudcts ";
```

```
using (SqlConnection connection = new
    SqlConnection(ConfigurationManager
                .ConnectionStrings["NorthwindConnectionString"]
                .ConnectionString))
{
    connection.Open();
    using (SqlCommand selectCommand = new SqlCommand(sql, connection))
    {
        using (SqlDataReader rd = selectCommand.ExecuteReader())
        {
            try
            {
                while (rd.Read())
                {
                    var pd = new MyProduct();
                    pd.ProductID = int.Parse(rd[0].ToString());
                    pd.ProductName = rd[1].ToString();

                    if (string.IsNullOrEmpty(rd[2].ToString()))
                        pd.SupplierID = null;
                    else
                        pd.SupplierID = int.Parse(rd[2].ToString());
                    if (string.IsNullOrEmpty(rd[3].ToString()))
                        pd.CategoryID = null;
                    else
                        pd.CategoryID = int.Parse(rd[3].ToString());

                    pd.QuantityPerUnit = rd[4].ToString();
                    if (string.IsNullOrEmpty(rd[5].ToString()))
                        pd.UnitPrice = null;
                    else
                        pd.UnitPrice = decimal.Parse(rd[5].ToString());
                    if (string.IsNullOrEmpty(rd[6].ToString()))
                        pd.UnitsInStock = null;
                    else
                        pd.UnitsInStock = short.Parse(rd[6].ToString());
                    if (string.IsNullOrEmpty(rd[7].ToString()))
                        pd.UnitsOnOrder = null;
                    else
                        pd.UnitsOnOrder = short.Parse(rd[7].ToString());
                    if (string.IsNullOrEmpty(rd[8].ToString()))
                        pd.ReorderLevel = null;
                    else
                        pd.ReorderLevel = short.Parse(rd[8].ToString());

                    pd.Discontinued = bool.Parse(rd[9].ToString());

                    productsList.Add(pd);
                }
            }
```

```
                catch (Exception ex)
                {
                    // error handling logic here
                }
            }

        }
    }
    return productsList;
}

[WebMethod]
public static int GetCount(string filterExpressions)
{
    string sql = string.Format("SELECT COUNT(*) from Products {0}",
                           (string.IsNullOrEmpty(filterExpressions)
                                ? ""
                                : string.Format(" WHERE {0}", filterExpressions)));
    int recordCount;

    using (SqlConnection connection = new
        SqlConnection(ConfigurationManager
                .ConnectionStrings["NorthwindConnectionString"]
                .ConnectionString))
    {
        connection.Open();
        using (SqlCommand selectCommand = new SqlCommand(sql, connection))
        {
            recordCount = int.Parse(selectCommand.ExecuteScalar().ToString());
        }
    }

    return recordCount;
}
```

Implementing RadGrid Data Manipulation Operations

Well, it's time now to examine the operations we can do in RadGrid to manipulate the data we are now seeing. RadGrid operations are sorting, filtering, scrolling, paging, and grouping. The data manipulation operations allow you to insert, edit, or delete records.

Sorting

Every table present in a RadGrid—be it the MasterTableView or a child table in DetailTables—is represented by a GridTableView class that has a property called SortExpressions, which is a collection of GridSortExpression objects. GridSortExpression has properties with all the information needed to build the sort expression to pass to the datasource.

The properties are FieldName, which stores the name of the field in the data source for which a sort is requested, and SortOrder, which indicates if the sort is ascending or descending or none.

Whenever a column in a RadGrid is sorted, a new sort expression object is added to the table's SortExpression collection. Also RadGrid supports multicolumn sorting, and that's when the having a sort expression collection makes more sense.

RadGrid also supports what is called a natural sort—basically allowing a field to be unsorted. To do this, you need to set the AllowNaturalSort property to true.

For RadGrid to sort a column, it needs the column to have specified the field for which to sort in the SortExpression property, including in GridTemplateColumn columns.

Another important aspect of sorting is that you can modify how sorting is made through the SortCommand event handler. When you capture this event, you can change the sorting behavior. For example, instead of sorting alphabetically, you could do it by the length of the field content.

The example in Listing 6-22 shows how to apply different sorting operations to a RadGrid. You can see that the two check boxes enable or disable the multicolumn sorting feature and the natural sort feature through the use of the RadGrid.MasterTableView.AllowMultiColumnSorting and RadGrid.MasterTableView.AllowNaturalSort properties.

Listing 6-22. *Implementing RadGrid Multicolumn and Natural Sorting*

```
ASPX Page

<asp:CheckBox ID="chkMultiColumn" runat="server"
              AutoPostBack="true"
              OnCheckedChanged="chkMultiColumn_CheckedChanged">
</asp:CheckBox>

<asp:CheckBox ID="chkNatural" runat="server"
              AutoPostBack="true"
              OnCheckedChanged="chkNatural_CheckedChanged">
</asp:CheckBox>

<telerik:RadGrid ID="RadGrid4" runat="server"
                 AllowPaging="True"
                 AllowSorting="True"
                 DataSourceID="ProductsDataSource2"
                 GridLines="None"
                 Skin="Vista">
    <ClientSettings>
        <Scrolling AllowScroll="True" UseStaticHeaders="True" />
    </ClientSettings>
    <MasterTableView DataKeyNames="ProductID"
              DataSourceID="ProductsDataSource" AutoGenerateColumns="False">
    <RowIndicatorColumn>
    <HeaderStyle Width="20px"></HeaderStyle>
    </RowIndicatorColumn>

    <ExpandCollapseColumn>
    <HeaderStyle Width="20px"></HeaderStyle>
    </ExpandCollapseColumn>
        <Columns>
            <telerik:GridBoundColumn DataField="ProductID"
                                     DataType="System.Int32"
                                     HeaderText="ProductID"
                                     ReadOnly="True"
```

```
                                SortExpression="ProductID"
                                UniqueName="ProductID">
        </telerik:GridBoundColumn>
        <telerik:GridBoundColumn DataField="ProductName"
                                HeaderText="ProductName"
                                SortExpression="ProductName"
                                UniqueName="ProductName">
        </telerik:GridBoundColumn>
        <telerik:GridBoundColumn DataField="SupplierID"
                                DataType="System.Int32"
                                HeaderText="SupplierID"
                                SortExpression="SupplierID"
                                UniqueName="SupplierID">
        </telerik:GridBoundColumn>
        <telerik:GridBoundColumn DataField="CategoryID"
                                DataType="System.Int32"
                                HeaderText="CategoryID"
                                SortExpression="CategoryID"
                                UniqueName="CategoryID">
        </telerik:GridBoundColumn>
        <telerik:GridBoundColumn DataField="QuantityPerUnit"
                                HeaderText="QuantityPerUnit"
                                SortExpression="QuantityPerUnit"
                                UniqueName="QuantityPerUnit">
        </telerik:GridBoundColumn>
        <telerik:GridBoundColumn DataField="UnitPrice"
                                DataType="System.Decimal"
                                HeaderText="UnitPrice"
                                SortExpression="UnitPrice"
                                UniqueName="UnitPrice">
        </telerik:GridBoundColumn>
        <telerik:GridBoundColumn DataField="UnitsInStock"
                                DataType="System.Int16"
                                HeaderText="UnitsInStock"
                                SortExpression="UnitsInStock"
                                UniqueName="UnitsInStock">
        </telerik:GridBoundColumn>
        <telerik:GridBoundColumn DataField="UnitsOnOrder"
                                DataType="System.Int16"
                                HeaderText="UnitsOnOrder"
                                SortExpression="UnitsOnOrder"
                                UniqueName="UnitsOnOrder">
        </telerik:GridBoundColumn>
        <telerik:GridBoundColumn DataField="ReorderLevel"
                                DataType="System.Int16"
                                HeaderText="ReorderLevel"
                                SortExpression="ReorderLevel"
                                UniqueName="ReorderLevel">
        </telerik:GridBoundColumn>
        <telerik:GridTemplateColumn HeaderText="Discontinued"
                                SortExpression="Discontinued">
```

```
                <ItemTemplate>
                    <asp:CheckBox ID="chkDiscontinued" runat="server"
                              Checked='<%#Eval("Discontinued") %>' />
                </ItemTemplate>
            </telerik:GridTemplateColumn>
        </Columns>

    </MasterTableView>
</telerik:RadGrid>
<asp:SqlDataSource ID="ProductsDataSource2" runat="server"
    ConnectionString="<%$ ConnectionStrings:NorthwindConnectionString %>"
    SelectCommand="SELECT * FROM [Products]">
</asp:SqlDataSource>
```

Code Behind

```
protected void chkMultiColumn_CheckedChanged(object sender, EventArgs e)
{
    RadGrid4.MasterTableView.AllowMultiColumnSorting = chkMultiColumn.Checked;
}

protected void chkNatural_CheckedChanged(object sender, EventArgs e)
{
    RadGrid4.MasterTableView.AllowNaturalSort = chkNatural.Checked;
}
```

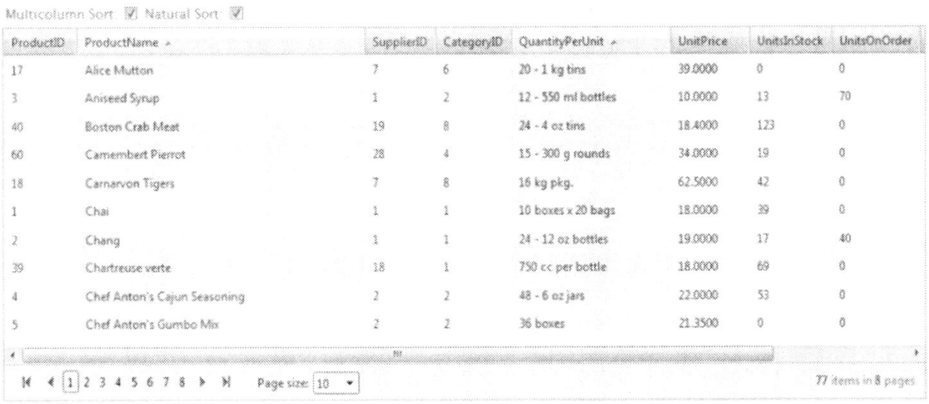

Multicolumn Sort ☑ Natural Sort ☑

ProductID	ProductName	SupplierID	CategoryID	QuantityPerUnit	UnitPrice	UnitsInStock	UnitsOnOrder
17	Alice Mutton	7	6	20 - 1 kg tins	39.0000	0	0
3	Aniseed Syrup	1	2	12 - 550 ml bottles	10.0000	13	70
40	Boston Crab Meat	19	8	24 - 4 oz tins	18.4000	123	0
60	Camembert Pierrot	28	4	15 - 300 g rounds	34.0000	19	0
18	Carnarvon Tigers	7	8	16 kg pkg.	62.5000	42	0
1	Chai	1	1	10 boxes x 20 bags	18.0000	39	0
2	Chang	1	1	24 - 12 oz bottles	19.0000	17	40
39	Chartreuse verte	18	1	750 cc per bottle	18.0000	69	0
4	Chef Anton's Cajun Seasoning	2	2	48 - 6 oz jars	22.0000	53	0
5	Chef Anton's Gumbo Mix	2	2	36 boxes	21.3500	0	0

1 2 3 4 5 6 7 8 Page size: 10 — 77 items in 8 pages

Figure 6-13. *RadGrid with multicolumn and natural sorting enabled*

Paging

`RadGrid` support for paging enables users to view data in sets of specific sizes that can be configured as a fixed amount of rows, or you can let users specify the size of the dataset at runtime.

Paging is accessed and controlled by a `GridPagerItem`, which can be displayed at the top or bottom of `RadGrid` (or both) with the `PagerStyle.Position` property. The pager item can be also configured to display different modes of paging with the `PagerStyle.Mode` property; the possible options are `NextPrev`, `NumericPages`, `NextPrevAndNumeric`, `Advanced`, `NextPrevNumericAndAdvanced`, or `Slider` (the example in

Listing 6-23 will show you all this options in action). NextPrev will only show arrows to navigate forward and backward through RadGrid pages and to navigate to the first and last pages. NextPrevAndNumeric will additionally show a numeric list of pages to easily navigate to a specific page and an option to change the page size. NumericPages will only show the numeric list. Advanced shows text boxes for the user to change the page size and enter the page number to navigate to. NextPrevNumericAndAdvanced shows all the options. When Slider is selected, the pager shows a slider to change pages. Figure 6-14 illustrates the pager styles.

The pager can also be modified to present any type of content with the PagerTemplate, which can be configured to have more content than the default pager or to be styled in a different way.

When dealing with large amounts of data in a RadGrid, it is a good idea to query only the set of records that are currently viewable, instead of loading the whole set. However, querying only a limited dataset affects the automatic calculations for paging operations, meaning that the total number of pages cannot be determined, since only the current page is loaded. For this purpose, you can configure RadGrid to work with custom paging by setting the property AllowCustomPaging property to true and, in the NeedDataSource event, setting the VirtualItemCount property to the total number of records the grid will have so it can correctly create the pager buttons.

■ **Note** RadGrid also supports SEO-friendly paging. You can find more information about this feature in the documentation at http://www.telerik.com/help/aspnet-ajax/grdseopaging.html and a working sample at http://demos.telerik.com/aspnet-ajax/grid/examples/programming/seopaging/defaultcs.aspx.

Listing 6-23. *RadGrid Paging*

ASPX Page

```
<telerik:RadComboBox ID="rcbPagerPosition" runat="server"
                     AutoPostBack="true"
                     OnSelectedIndexChanged="rcbPagerPosition_SelectedIndexChanged">
</telerik:RadComboBox>

<telerik:RadComboBox ID="rcbPagerMode" runat="server"
                     AutoPostBack="true"
                     DropDownWidth="150px"
                     OnSelectedIndexChanged="rcbPagerMode_SelectedIndexChanged">
</telerik:RadComboBox>

<telerik:RadGrid ID="RadGrid5" runat="server"
                 AllowPaging="True"
                 DataSourceID="ProductsDataSource3"
                 GridLines="None"
                 Skin="Vista">
    <ClientSettings>
        <Scrolling AllowScroll="True" UseStaticHeaders="True" />
    </ClientSettings>
    <MasterTableView DataKeyNames="ProductID"
                DataSourceID="ProductsDataSource"
                AutoGenerateColumns="False">
    <RowIndicatorColumn>
    <HeaderStyle Width="20px"></HeaderStyle>
    </RowIndicatorColumn>
```

```
<ExpandCollapseColumn>
<HeaderStyle Width="20px"></HeaderStyle>
</ExpandCollapseColumn>
    <Columns>
        <telerik:GridBoundColumn DataField="ProductID"
                                 DataType="System.Int32"
                                 HeaderText="ProductID"
                                 ReadOnly="True"
                                 SortExpression="ProductID"
                                 UniqueName="ProductID">
        </telerik:GridBoundColumn>
        <telerik:GridBoundColumn DataField="ProductName"
                                 HeaderText="ProductName"
                                 SortExpression="ProductName"
                                 UniqueName="ProductName">
        </telerik:GridBoundColumn>
        <telerik:GridBoundColumn DataField="SupplierID"
                                 DataType="System.Int32"
                                 HeaderText="SupplierID"
                                 SortExpression="SupplierID"
                                 UniqueName="SupplierID">
        </telerik:GridBoundColumn>
        <telerik:GridBoundColumn DataField="CategoryID"
                                 DataType="System.Int32"
                                 HeaderText="CategoryID"
                                 SortExpression="CategoryID"
                                 UniqueName="CategoryID">
        </telerik:GridBoundColumn>
        <telerik:GridBoundColumn DataField="QuantityPerUnit"
                                 HeaderText="QuantityPerUnit"
                                 SortExpression="QuantityPerUnit"
                                 UniqueName="QuantityPerUnit">
        </telerik:GridBoundColumn>
        <telerik:GridBoundColumn DataField="UnitPrice"
                                 DataType="System.Decimal"
                                 HeaderText="UnitPrice"
                                 SortExpression="UnitPrice"
                                 UniqueName="UnitPrice">
        </telerik:GridBoundColumn>
        <telerik:GridBoundColumn DataField="UnitsInStock"
                                 DataType="System.Int16"
                                 HeaderText="UnitsInStock"
                                 SortExpression="UnitsInStock"
                                 UniqueName="UnitsInStock">
        </telerik:GridBoundColumn>
        <telerik:GridBoundColumn DataField="UnitsOnOrder"
                                 DataType="System.Int16"
                                 HeaderText="UnitsOnOrder"
                                 SortExpression="UnitsOnOrder"
                                 UniqueName="UnitsOnOrder">
        </telerik:GridBoundColumn>
```

```
            <telerik:GridBoundColumn DataField="ReorderLevel"
                                     DataType="System.Int16"
                                     HeaderText="ReorderLevel"
                                     SortExpression="ReorderLevel"
                                     UniqueName="ReorderLevel">
            </telerik:GridBoundColumn>
            <telerik:GridTemplateColumn HeaderText="Discontinued"
                                     SortExpression="Discontinued">
                <ItemTemplate>
                    <asp:CheckBox ID="chkDiscontinued" runat="server"
                              Checked='<%#Eval("Discontinued") %>' />
                </ItemTemplate>
            </telerik:GridTemplateColumn>
        </Columns>

    </MasterTableView>
</telerik:RadGrid>

<asp:SqlDataSource ID="ProductsDataSource3" runat="server"
    ConnectionString="<%$ ConnectionStrings:NorthwindConnectionString %>"
    SelectCommand="SELECT * FROM [Products]">
</asp:SqlDataSource>

Code Behind

protected void rcbPagerPosition_SelectedIndexChanged(
                                object o,
                                RadComboBoxSelectedIndexChangedEventArgs e)
{
    GridPagerPosition position;
    if (Enum.TryParse(e.Text, true, out position))
        RadGrid5.PagerStyle.Position = position;
}

protected void rcbPagerMode_SelectedIndexChanged(
                                object o,
                                RadComboBoxSelectedIndexChangedEventArgs e)
{
    GridPagerMode mode;
    if (Enum.TryParse(e.Text, true, out mode))
        RadGrid5.PagerStyle.Mode = mode;
}
```

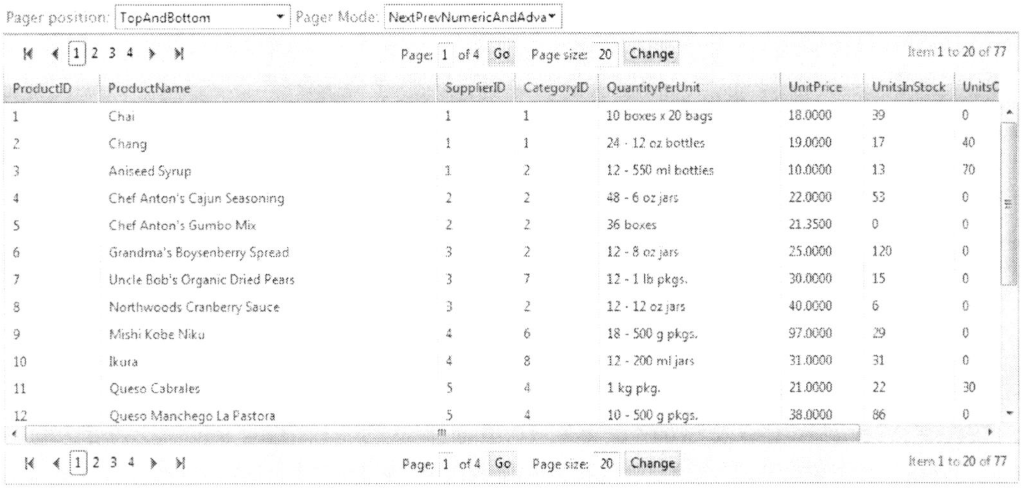

Pager position: TopAndBottom Pager Mode: NextPrevNumericAndAdva

1 2 3 4 Page: 1 of 4 Go Page size: 20 Change Item 1 to 20 of 77

ProductID	ProductName	SupplierID	CategoryID	QuantityPerUnit	UnitPrice	UnitsInStock	UnitsC
1	Chai	1	1	10 boxes x 20 bags	18.0000	39	0
2	Chang	1	1	24 - 12 oz bottles	19.0000	17	40
3	Aniseed Syrup	1	2	12 - 550 ml bottles	10.0000	13	70
4	Chef Anton's Cajun Seasoning	2	2	48 - 6 oz jars	22.0000	53	0
5	Chef Anton's Gumbo Mix	2	2	36 boxes	21.3500	0	0
6	Grandma's Boysenberry Spread	3	2	12 - 8 oz jars	25.0000	120	0
7	Uncle Bob's Organic Dried Pears	3	7	12 - 1 lb pkgs.	30.0000	15	0
8	Northwoods Cranberry Sauce	3	2	12 - 12 oz jars	40.0000	6	0
9	Mishi Kobe Niku	4	6	18 - 500 g pkgs.	97.0000	29	0
10	Ikura	4	8	12 - 200 ml jars	31.0000	31	0
11	Queso Cabrales	5	4	1 kg pkg.	21.0000	22	30
12	Queso Manchego La Pastora	5	4	10 - 500 g pkgs.	38.0000	86	0

1 2 3 4 Page: 1 of 4 Go Page size: 20 Change Item 1 to 20 of 77

Figure 6-14. *RadGrid paging configured to show the pager at the top and bottom of RadGrid in NextPrevNumericAndAdvanced mode*

Scrolling

RadGrid supports vertical and horizontal scrolling when the property `ClientSettings.Scrolling.AllowScroll` is set to `true`. This is useful in scenarios where the available space in the page for the `RadGrid` is small. The actual (true) size of the area defined for scrolling is defined in the property `ClientSettings.Scrolling.ScrollHeight` that is set to a numeric value defined in pixels. The default value is 300 pixels.

The property `ClientSettings.Scrolling.ScrollHeight` is different from `RadGrid.Height`, since the latter includes all elements of `RadGrid` (header, footer, pager, etc.), while the former refers only to the actual scrolling area.

The property `ClientSettings.Scrolling.UseStaticHeaders` determines whether the vertical scroll bar will or will not include the headers when scrolling. When set to `true`, the header remains visible and provides a better experience for the user by preserving the context of the information that is there.

Sometimes, it is also desirable to keep columns always visible, and for that purpose, `RadGrid` includes the property `ClientSettings.Scrolling.FrozenColumnsCount`, which indicates how many columns (starting from the left to the right) will always be visible.

In scenarios with large datasources, you can enable what is called *virtual scrolling*. With virtual scrolling, the scrolling bar can be used to navigate through the available pages. To enable virtual scrolling, you need to set the property `ClientSettings.Scrolling.EnableVirtualScrollPaging` to `true`.

Listing 6-24 is an example that implements the scrolling features in `RadGrid`. In it, you can see how to enable or disable scrolling, use static headers, enable or disable virtual scrolling, and freeze columns. Figure 6-15 shows the example running.

Listing 6-24. *RadGrid Scrolling*

ASPX Page

```
<asp:CheckBox ID="chkScroll" runat="server"
                Checked="true"
                AutoPostBack="true"
                OnCheckedChanged="chkScroll_CheckedChanged" />

<asp:CheckBox ID="chkVirtualScroll" runat="server"
                Checked="true"
                AutoPostBack="true"
                OnCheckedChanged="chkVirtualScroll_CheckedChanged" />

<asp:CheckBox ID="chkStaticHeaders" runat="server"
                Checked="true"
                AutoPostBack="true"
                OnCheckedChanged="chkStaticHeaders_CheckedChanged" />

<asp:CheckBox ID="chkFreeze" runat="server"
                AutoPostBack="true"
                OnCheckedChanged="chkFreeze_CheckedChanged" />

<telerik:RadGrid ID="RadGrid6" runat="server"
                 AllowPaging="True"
                 DataSourceID="ProductsDataSource4"
                 GridLines="None"
                 PageSize="20"
                 Width="450px"
                 Skin="Vista">
    <ClientSettings>
        <Scrolling AllowScroll="True"
                   UseStaticHeaders="True"
                   EnableVirtualScrollPaging="true" />
    </ClientSettings>
    <MasterTableView DataKeyNames="ProductID"
                DataSourceID="ProductsDataSource4" AutoGenerateColumns="False">
    <RowIndicatorColumn>
    <HeaderStyle Width="20px"></HeaderStyle>
    </RowIndicatorColumn>

    <ExpandCollapseColumn>
    <HeaderStyle Width="20px"></HeaderStyle>
    </ExpandCollapseColumn>
```

```
<Columns>
    <telerik:GridBoundColumn DataField="ProductID"
                         DataType="System.Int32"
                         HeaderText="ProductID"
                         ReadOnly="True"
                         SortExpression="Product ID"
                         UniqueName="ProductID">
        <ItemStyle Width="80px" />
        <HeaderStyle Width="80px" />
    </telerik:GridBoundColumn>
    <telerik:GridBoundColumn DataField="ProductName"
                         HeaderText="Product Name"
                         SortExpression="ProductName"
                         UniqueName="ProductName">
        <ItemStyle Width="200px" />
        <HeaderStyle Width="200px" />
    </telerik:GridBoundColumn>
    <telerik:GridBoundColumn DataField="SupplierName"
                         HeaderText="Supplier Name"
                         SortExpression="SupplierName"
                         UniqueName="SupplierName">
        <ItemStyle Width="200px" />
        <HeaderStyle Width="200px" />
    </telerik:GridBoundColumn>
    <telerik:GridBoundColumn DataField="CategoryName"
                         HeaderText="Category Name"
                         SortExpression="CategoryName"
                         UniqueName="CategoryName">
        <ItemStyle Width="200px" />
        <HeaderStyle Width="200px" />
    </telerik:GridBoundColumn>
    <telerik:GridBoundColumn DataField="QuantityPerUnit"
                         HeaderText="Quantity Per Unit"
                         SortExpression="QuantityPerUnit"
                         UniqueName="QuantityPerUnit">
        <ItemStyle Width="150px" />
        <HeaderStyle Width="150px" />
    </telerik:GridBoundColumn>
    <telerik:GridBoundColumn DataField="UnitPrice"
                         DataType="System.Decimal"
                         HeaderText="Unit Price"
                         SortExpression="UnitPrice"
                         UniqueName="UnitPrice"
                         DataFormatString="{0:c}">
        <ItemStyle Width="80px" />
        <HeaderStyle Width="80px" />
    </telerik:GridBoundColumn>
```

```
            <telerik:GridBoundColumn DataField="UnitsInStock"
                                     DataType="System.Int16"
                                     HeaderText="Units In Stock"
                                     SortExpression="UnitsInStock"
                                     UniqueName="UnitsInStock">
                <ItemStyle Width="80px" />
                <HeaderStyle Width="80px" />
            </telerik:GridBoundColumn>
            <telerik:GridBoundColumn DataField="UnitsOnOrder"
                                     DataType="System.Int16"
                                     HeaderText="Units On Order"
                                     SortExpression="UnitsOnOrder"
                                     UniqueName="UnitsOnOrder">
                <ItemStyle Width="80px" />
                <HeaderStyle Width="80px" />
            </telerik:GridBoundColumn>
            <telerik:GridBoundColumn DataField="ReorderLevel"
                                     DataType="System.Int16"
                                     HeaderText="Reorder Level"
                                     SortExpression="ReorderLevel"
                                     UniqueName="ReorderLevel">
                <ItemStyle Width="80px" />
                <HeaderStyle Width="80px" />
            </telerik:GridBoundColumn>
        </Columns>

    </MasterTableView>
</telerik:RadGrid>

<asp:SqlDataSource ID="ProductsDataSource4" runat="server"
    ConnectionString="<%$ ConnectionStrings:NorthwindConnectionString %>"
    SelectCommand="SELECT p.ProductID, p.ProductName, s.CompanyName SupplierName,
                      c.CategoryName, p.QuantityPerUnit, p.UnitPrice, p.UnitsInStock,
                      p.UnitsOnOrder, p.ReorderLevel, p.Discontinued
                    FROM dbo.Products p INNER JOIN dbo.Suppliers s
                    ON p.SupplierID = s.SupplierID INNER JOIN dbo.Categories c
                    ON p.CategoryID = c.CategoryID">
</asp:SqlDataSource>
```

Code Behind

```
protected void chkScroll_CheckedChanged(object sender, EventArgs e)
{
    RadGrid6.ClientSettings.Scrolling.AllowScroll = chkScroll.Checked;
}


protected void chkStaticHeaders_CheckedChanged(object sender, EventArgs e)
{
    RadGrid6.ClientSettings.Scrolling.UseStaticHeaders = chkStaticHeaders.Checked;
}
```

```
protected void chkFreeze_CheckedChanged(object sender, EventArgs e)
{
    RadGrid6.ClientSettings.Scrolling.FrozenColumnsCount = chkFreeze.Checked ? 2 : 0;
}

protected void chkVirtualScroll_CheckedChanged(object sender, EventArgs e)
{
    RadGrid6.ClientSettings.Scrolling.EnableVirtualScrollPaging = chkVirtualScroll.Checked;
}
```

Enable Scroll: ☑
Enable Virtual Scroll: ☑
Use Statick Headers: ☑
Freeze ProductID and ProductName: ☑

ProductID	Product Name	Unit Price	Units In Stock
21	Sir Rodney's Scones	$10.00	3
22	Gustaf's Knäckebröd	$21.00	104
23	Tunnbröd	$9.00	61
24	Guaraná Fantástica	$4.50	20
25	NuNuCa Nuß-Nougat-Creme	$14.00	76
26	Gumbär Gummibärchen	$31.23	15
27	Schoggi Schokolade	$43.90	49
28	Rössle Sauerkraut	$45.60	26
29	Thüringer Rostbratwurst	$123.79	0
30	Nord-Ost Matjeshering	$25.89	10
31	Gorgonzola Telino	$12.50	0
32	Mascarpone Fabioli	$32.00	9

1 2 3 4 Page size: 20 77 items in 4 pages

Figure 6-15. *RadGrid with all the scrolling features enabled*

Grouping

You can group rows, in the same way you would group e-mails in Microsoft Outlook, using the grouping functionality in RadGrid.

To group the data, specify the grouping criteria by setting the GroupByExpressions property of a GridTableView in the grid. You can set the GroupByExpressions declaratively at design time or programmatically in the code behind.

The first thing you need to do to enable the grouping functionality is to turn it on by setting the RadGrid.ShowGroupPanel property to true. This will make the GridGroupPanel area to appear on top of the header. In this area, you drop the columns for which the grouping will be performed. To enable users to drop columns in the GroupPanel, you also need to switch the ClientSettings.AllowDragToGroup property to true. You can manipulate this area with the GroupPanel property and modify the styling with the GroupPanel.PanelStyle and GroupPanel.PanelItemsStyle properties. Additionally, you can enable the ungroup button for the columns in this area by setting the GroupingSettings.ShowUnGroupButton property to true.

When you have defined your groups, the GridGroupSplitterColumn appears and in that column there is a button to expand or collapse the group. The expand operation can be performed in the server or in the client. By default this is set to be done in the server and every time a group is expanded a postback occurs; now, to improve performance you can do it on the client if no other operation needs to be done at expand time. To change where the expand operation will be done you need to change the property GroupLoadMode to either Server or Client; however, if you set it to Client you also need to set the ClientSettings.AllowGroupExpandCollapse property to true.

Grouping is often enabled to present data in that displays not only the items in a grouped form but also to have information such as group totals. For this functionality you first need to define what aggregate function needs to be done in each column for the field it represents. Aggregate functions can be Sum, Min, Max, Last, First, Count, Avg, Custom, and None. If you define a Custom aggregate then the CustomAggregate event is raised so you can perform the operation needed and then assign the final result to the Result property of the argument parameter. Then you need to define where to show this group totals and the most common area to do this is in the footer item of each group. To show the group footer, you need to set the ShowGroupFooter property to true, and the control will automatically show all the totals defined in the Aggregate property of each column.

Grouping is defined through the GroupByExpressions property, which is a collection of GroupByExpression objects. In turn, GroupByExpression contains two other collections that define the behavior of the groups; they are SelectFields and GroupByFields, and they determine the fields that will be displayed in the header and fields that will be used to group the data, respectively. Both collections have items that are of type GridGroupByField.

■ **Note** You can also create groups by passing a group expression string that is then parsed to build the GridGroupByExpression object. You can find more information in the online documentation here http://www.telerik.com/help/aspnet-ajax/grdgroupbydeclarativedefinition.html.

The example in Listing 6-25 shows you how to enable grouping declaratively. Note in Figure 6-16 how the products in the RadGrid are grouped by the Category column.

Listing 6-25. *RadGrid Declarative Grouping*

ASPX Page

```
<telerik:RadGrid ID="RadGrid9" runat="server"
                 AllowPaging="True"
                 ShowGroupPanel="true"
                 DataSourceID="ProductsDataSource6"
                 GridLines="None"
                 PageSize="20"
                 Skin="Vista">
    <ClientSettings AllowDragToGroup="true">
        <Scrolling AllowScroll="True" UseStaticHeaders="True" />
    </ClientSettings>

    <GroupingSettings ShowUnGroupButton="true"
                      RetainGroupFootersVisibility="true" />
```

```
<MasterTableView DataKeyNames="ProductID"
                    GroupLoadMode="Client"
                    ShowGroupFooter="true"
                    DataSourceID="ProductsDataSource6"
                    AutoGenerateColumns="False">
<GroupByExpressions>
     <telerik:GridGroupByExpression>
       <SelectFields>
         <telerik:GridGroupByField
           FieldAlias="Category"
           FieldName="CategoryName" />
       </SelectFields>
       <GroupByFields>
         <telerik:GridGroupByField
           FieldAlias="Category"
           FieldName="CategoryName" />
       </GroupByFields>
    </telerik:GridGroupByExpression>
</GroupByExpressions>
<RowIndicatorColumn>
<HeaderStyle Width="20px"></HeaderStyle>
</RowIndicatorColumn>

<ExpandCollapseColumn>
<HeaderStyle Width="20px"></HeaderStyle>
</ExpandCollapseColumn>
    <Columns>
        <telerik:GridBoundColumn DataField="ProductID"
                                 DataType="System.Int32"
                                 HeaderText="ProductID"
                                 ReadOnly="True"
                                 SortExpression="Product ID"
                                 UniqueName="ProductID">
            <ItemStyle Width="80px" />
            <HeaderStyle Width="80px" />
        </telerik:GridBoundColumn>
        <telerik:GridBoundColumn DataField="ProductName"
                                 HeaderText="Product Name"
                                 SortExpression="ProductName"
                                 UniqueName="ProductName"
                                 Aggregate="Count">
            <ItemStyle Width="200px" />
            <HeaderStyle Width="200px" />
        </telerik:GridBoundColumn>
        <telerik:GridBoundColumn DataField="SupplierName"
                                 HeaderText="Supplier Name"
                                 SortExpression="SupplierName"
                                 UniqueName="SupplierName">
            <ItemStyle Width="200px" />
            <HeaderStyle Width="200px" />
        </telerik:GridBoundColumn>
```

```
<telerik:GridBoundColumn DataField="CategoryName"
                         HeaderText="Category Name"
                         SortExpression="CategoryName"
                         UniqueName="CategoryName">
    <ItemStyle Width="200px" />
    <HeaderStyle Width="200px" />
</telerik:GridBoundColumn>
<telerik:GridBoundColumn DataField="QuantityPerUnit"
                         HeaderText="Quantity Per Unit"
                         SortExpression="QuantityPerUnit"
                         UniqueName="QuantityPerUnit">
    <ItemStyle Width="150px" />
    <HeaderStyle Width="150px" />
</telerik:GridBoundColumn>
<telerik:GridBoundColumn DataField="UnitPrice"
                         DataType="System.Decimal"
                         HeaderText="Unit Price"
                         SortExpression="UnitPrice"
                         UniqueName="UnitPrice"
                         DataFormatString="{0:c}"
                         Aggregate="Avg"
                         FooterAggregateFormatString="Avg {0:c}">
    <ItemStyle Width="80px" />
    <HeaderStyle Width="80px" />
</telerik:GridBoundColumn>
<telerik:GridBoundColumn DataField="UnitsInStock"
                         DataType="System.Int16"
                         HeaderText="Units In Stock"
                         SortExpression="UnitsInStock"
                         UniqueName="UnitsInStock">
    <ItemStyle Width="80px" />
    <HeaderStyle Width="80px" />
</telerik:GridBoundColumn>
<telerik:GridBoundColumn DataField="UnitsOnOrder"
                         DataType="System.Int16"
                         HeaderText="Units On Order"
                         SortExpression="UnitsOnOrder"
                         UniqueName="UnitsOnOrder">
    <ItemStyle Width="80px" />
    <HeaderStyle Width="80px" />
</telerik:GridBoundColumn>
<telerik:GridBoundColumn DataField="ReorderLevel"
                         DataType="System.Int16"
                         HeaderText="Reorder Level"
                         SortExpression="ReorderLevel"
                         UniqueName="ReorderLevel">
    <ItemStyle Width="80px" />
    <HeaderStyle Width="80px" />
</telerik:GridBoundColumn>
</Columns>

    </MasterTableView>
</telerik:RadGrid>
```

```
<asp:SqlDataSource ID="ProductsDataSource6" runat="server"
    ConnectionString="<%$ ConnectionStrings:NorthwindConnectionString %>"
    SelectCommand="SELECT p.ProductID, p.ProductName, s.CompanyName SupplierName,
                          c.CategoryName, p.QuantityPerUnit, p.UnitPrice,
                          p.UnitsInStock, p.UnitsOnOrder, p.ReorderLevel,
                          p.Discontinued
                     FROM dbo.Products p INNER JOIN dbo.Suppliers s
                        ON p.SupplierID = s.SupplierID INNER JOIN dbo.Categories c
                        ON p.CategoryID = c.CategoryID">
</asp:SqlDataSource>
```

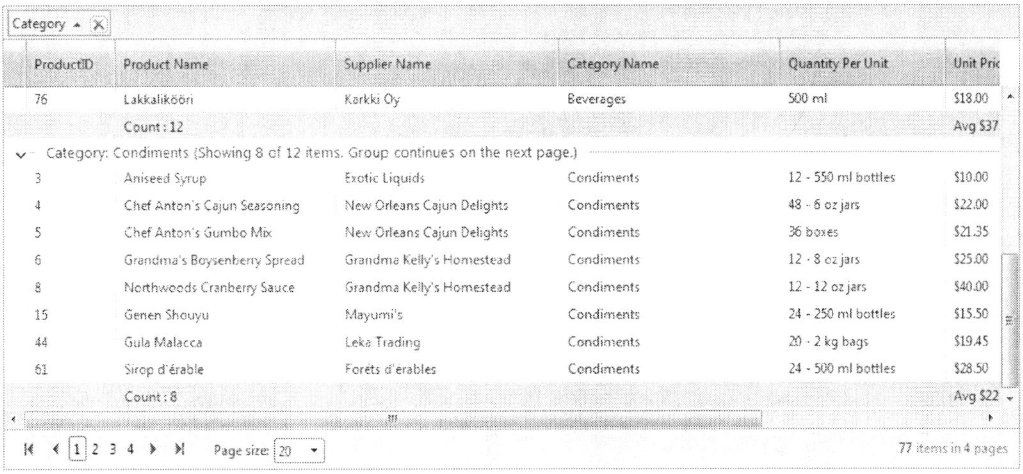

Figure 6-16. *RadGrid declarative grouping*

In Listing 6-26, the grouping expressions are created programmatically. The end result is shown in Figure 6-17.

Listing 6-26. *RadGrid Programmatic Grouping*

ASPX Page

```
<asp:CheckBox ID="chkGrouping" runat="server"
              AutoPostBack="true"
              OnCheckedChanged="chkGrouping_CheckedChanged" />

<asp:CheckBox ID="chkClientGroupLoad" runat="server"
              AutoPostBack="true"
              OnCheckedChanged="chkClientGroupLoad_CheckedChanged" />

<asp:CheckBox ID="chkGroupFooter" runat="server"
              AutoPostBack="true"
              OnCheckedChanged="chkGroupFooter_CheckedChanged" />

<asp:CheckBox ID="chkGroupBySupplier" runat="server"
              AutoPostBack="true"
              OnCheckedChanged="chkGroupBySupplier_CheckedChanged" />
```

```
<telerik:RadGrid ID="RadGrid7" runat="server"
                AllowPaging="True"
                DataSourceID="ProductsDataSource5"
                GridLines="None"
                Skin="Vista">
    <ClientSettings>
        <Scrolling AllowScroll="True" UseStaticHeaders="True" />
    </ClientSettings>
    <GroupingSettings ShowUnGroupButton="true" />
    <MasterTableView DataKeyNames="ProductID"
                     GroupLoadMode="Client"
                     DataSourceID="ProductsDataSource5"
                     AutoGenerateColumns="False">
    <RowIndicatorColumn>
    <HeaderStyle Width="20px"></HeaderStyle>
    </RowIndicatorColumn>

    <ExpandCollapseColumn>
    <HeaderStyle Width="20px"></HeaderStyle>
    </ExpandCollapseColumn>
        <Columns>
            <telerik:GridBoundColumn DataField="ProductID"
                                     DataType="System.Int32"
                                     HeaderText="ProductID"
                                     ReadOnly="True"
                                     SortExpression="Product ID"
                                     UniqueName="ProductID">
                <ItemStyle Width="80px" />
                <HeaderStyle Width="80px" />
            </telerik:GridBoundColumn>
            <telerik:GridBoundColumn DataField="ProductName"
                                     HeaderText="Product Name"
                                     SortExpression="ProductName"
                                     UniqueName="ProductName"
                                     Aggregate="Count">
                <ItemStyle Width="200px" />
                <HeaderStyle Width="200px" />
            </telerik:GridBoundColumn>
            <telerik:GridBoundColumn DataField="SupplierName"
                                     HeaderText="Supplier Name"
                                     SortExpression="SupplierName"
                                     UniqueName="SupplierName">
                <ItemStyle Width="200px" />
                <HeaderStyle Width="200px" />
            </telerik:GridBoundColumn>
            <telerik:GridBoundColumn DataField="CategoryName"
                                     HeaderText="Category Name"
                                     SortExpression="CategoryName"
                                     UniqueName="CategoryName">
                <ItemStyle Width="200px" />
                <HeaderStyle Width="200px" />
            </telerik:GridBoundColumn>
```

```
        <telerik:GridBoundColumn DataField="QuantityPerUnit"
                                 HeaderText="Quantity Per Unit"
                                 SortExpression="QuantityPerUnit"
                                 UniqueName="QuantityPerUnit">
            <ItemStyle Width="150px" />
            <HeaderStyle Width="150px" />
        </telerik:GridBoundColumn>
        <telerik:GridBoundColumn DataField="UnitPrice"
                                 DataType="System.Decimal"
                                 HeaderText="Unit Price"
                                 SortExpression="UnitPrice"
                                 niqueName="UnitPrice"
                                 DataFormatString="{0:c}"
                                 Aggregate="Avg"
                                 FooterAggregateFormatString="Avg {0:c}">
            <ItemStyle Width="80px" />
            <HeaderStyle Width="80px" />
        </telerik:GridBoundColumn>
        <telerik:GridBoundColumn DataField="UnitsInStock"
                                 DataType="System.Int16"
                                 HeaderText="Units In Stock"
                                 SortExpression="UnitsInStock"
                                 UniqueName="UnitsInStock">
            <ItemStyle Width="80px" />
            <HeaderStyle Width="80px" />
        </telerik:GridBoundColumn>
        <telerik:GridBoundColumn DataField="UnitsOnOrder"
                                 DataType="System.Int16"
                                 HeaderText="Units On Order"
                                 SortExpression="UnitsOnOrder"
                                 UniqueName="UnitsOnOrder">
            <ItemStyle Width="80px" />
            <HeaderStyle Width="80px" />
        </telerik:GridBoundColumn>
        <telerik:GridBoundColumn DataField="ReorderLevel"
                                 DataType="System.Int16"
                                 HeaderText="Reorder Level"
                                 SortExpression="ReorderLevel"
                                 UniqueName="ReorderLevel">
            <ItemStyle Width="80px" />
            <HeaderStyle Width="80px" />
        </telerik:GridBoundColumn>
    </Columns>

  </MasterTableView>
</telerik:RadGrid>
<asp:SqlDataSource ID="ProductsDataSource5" runat="server"
    ConnectionString="<%$ ConnectionStrings:NorthwindConnectionString %>"
    SelectCommand="SELECT p.ProductID, p.ProductName, s.CompanyName SupplierName,
                          c.CategoryName, p.QuantityPerUnit, p.UnitPrice,
                          p.UnitsInStock, p.UnitsOnOrder, p.ReorderLevel,
                          p.Discontinued
```

```
                        FROM dbo.Products p INNER JOIN dbo.Suppliers s
                           ON p.SupplierID = s.SupplierID INNER JOIN dbo.Categories c
                           ON p.CategoryID = c.CategoryID">
</asp:SqlDataSource>
```

Code Behind

```
protected void chkGrouping_CheckedChanged(object sender, EventArgs e)
{
    RadGrid7.ShowGroupPanel = chkGrouping.Checked;
    RadGrid7.ClientSettings.AllowDragToGroup = chkGrouping.Checked;
}

protected void chkClientGroupLoad_CheckedChanged(object sender, EventArgs e)
{
    RadGrid7.MasterTableView.GroupLoadMode = chkClientGroupLoad.Checked
                                             ? GridGroupLoadMode.Client
                                             : GridGroupLoadMode.Server;
    If (chkClientGroupLoad.Checked)
       RadGrid7.ClientSettings.AllowGroupExpandCollapse = true;
}

protected void chkGroupFooter_CheckedChanged(object sender, EventArgs e)
{
    RadGrid7.MasterTableView.ShowGroupFooter = chkGroupFooter.Checked;
    RadGrid7.GroupingSettings.RetainGroupFootersVisibility = chkGroupFooter.Checked;
}

protected void chkGroupBySupplier_CheckedChanged(object sender, EventArgs e)
{
    chkGrouping.Checked = true;
    RadGrid7.ShowGroupPanel = true;
    RadGrid7.ClientSettings.AllowDragToGroup = true;

    GridGroupByExpression groupExpression = new GridGroupByExpression();
    GridGroupByField gridSelectField = new GridGroupByField();
    GridGroupByField gridGroupByField = new GridGroupByField();
    gridSelectField = new GridGroupByField();
    gridSelectField.FieldName = "SupplierName";
    gridSelectField.FieldAlias = "Supplier";
    gridSelectField.HeaderText = "Supplier";
    gridSelectField.HeaderValueSeparator = " for current group: ";
    gridSelectField.FormatString = "<strong>{0}</strong>";
    groupExpression.SelectFields.Add(gridSelectField);

    gridGroupByField = new GridGroupByField();
    gridGroupByField.FieldName = "SupplierName";
    gridGroupByField.FieldAlias = "Supplier";
    groupExpression.GroupByFields.Add(gridGroupByField);

    RadGrid7.MasterTableView.GroupByExpressions.Add(groupExpression);
}
```

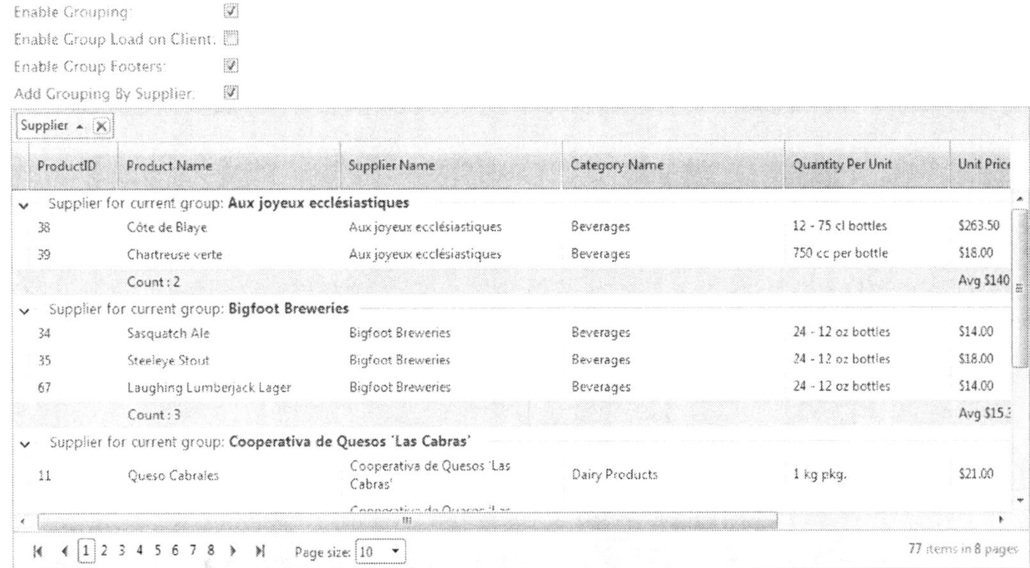

Figure 6-17. *RadGrid implementing grouping expressions created programmatically with group footers*

Filtering

RadGrid natively supports filtering based on values of its columns on any table. You enable filtering by setting the property AllowFilteringByColumn to true. This enables the GridFilteringItem to appear right below the header item. For all the columns that have filtering enabled, users will see a box to enter values and a filter type menu that is activated by a button with a filter icon.

The filtering menu is independent for each column in RadGrid, and its available options are created based on the data column's data type. However, this behavior can be overridden by the FilterListOptions property that accepts one of the following options:

- VaryByDataType: This is the default option, and it populates the filtering options based on the column data type.
- VaryByDataTypeAllowCustom: This option is the same as VarybyDataType, but it shows an additional Custom option that, when selected, is treated by RadGrid by taking the value in the filter box and passed as the whole filter expression. In other words, the option will assume that the column selected contains the field, operator, and value to filter.
- AllowAllFilters: This list all filters regardless of the column's data type.

Keep in mind that whenever a user clicks the filter button, the ItemCommand event is raised, and the command name in this case is Filter. Thus, by handling this event in the code behind, you are able to modify the default behavior of the filter being applied.

You can also configure columns to do a postback whenever a user enters a value in the filter box and then presses the Enter key. In this case, RadGrid assumes the value entered will be compared using the EqualTo operator for numeric columns and Contains for strings.

RadGrid also supports templates for filtering. This option is available in GridBoundColumns and GridTemplateColumns, so you can create a different type of filter for a specific column; for example, you can add a RadComboBox instead of a text box.

■ **Note** The engineers at Telerik also have created a very interesting implementation of a Google-like filtering demonstration that not only illustrates how to build custom filters but also shows how to extend the current columns by creating a new custom column that will be included in the `RadGrid`. You can find the documentation of this demonstration at `http://www.telerik.com/help/aspnet-ajax/grdgooglelikefiltering.html` and the working demonstration at `http://demos.telerik.com/aspnet-ajax/controls/examples/integration/gridandcombo/defaultvb.aspx?product=grid`.

Listing 6-27 shows how to implement filtering in `RadGrid`, and Figure 6-18 shows how `RadGrid` looks when filtering is enabled.

Listing 6-27. *RadGrid Filtering*

ASPX Page

```
<telerik:RadGrid ID="RadGrid10" runat="server"
                 AllowPaging="True"
                 AllowFilteringByColumn="true"
                 DataSourceID="ProductsDataSource7"
                 GridLines="None"
                 PageSize="20">
    <ClientSettings>
        <Scrolling AllowScroll="True" UseStaticHeaders="True" />
    </ClientSettings>

    <MasterTableView DataKeyNames="ProductID"
                DataSourceID="ProductsDataSource7"
                AutoGenerateColumns="False">
    <RowIndicatorColumn>
    <HeaderStyle Width="20px"></HeaderStyle>
    </RowIndicatorColumn>

    <ExpandCollapseColumn>
    <HeaderStyle Width="20px"></HeaderStyle>
    </ExpandCollapseColumn>
        <Columns>
            <telerik:GridBoundColumn DataField="ProductID"
                                     DataType="System.Int32"
                                     HeaderText="ProductID"
                                     ReadOnly="True"
                                     SortExpression="Product ID"
                                     UniqueName="ProductID">
                <ItemStyle Width="80px" />
                <HeaderStyle Width="80px" />
            </telerik:GridBoundColumn>
            <telerik:GridBoundColumn DataField="ProductName"
                                     HeaderText="Product Name"
                                     SortExpression="ProductName"
                                     UniqueName="ProductName"
                                     Aggregate="Count">
```

```
        <ItemStyle Width="200px" />
        <HeaderStyle Width="200px" />
    </telerik:GridBoundColumn>
    <telerik:GridBoundColumn DataField="SupplierName"
                        HeaderText="Supplier Name"
                        SortExpression="SupplierName"
                        UniqueName="SupplierName">
        <ItemStyle Width="200px" />
        <HeaderStyle Width="200px" />
    </telerik:GridBoundColumn>
    <telerik:GridBoundColumn DataField="CategoryName"
                        HeaderText="Category Name"
                        SortExpression="CategoryName"
                        UniqueName="CategoryName">
        <ItemStyle Width="200px" />
        <HeaderStyle Width="200px" />
    </telerik:GridBoundColumn>
    <telerik:GridBoundColumn DataField="QuantityPerUnit"
                        HeaderText="Quantity Per Unit"
                        SortExpression="QuantityPerUnit"
                        UniqueName="QuantityPerUnit">
        <ItemStyle Width="150px" />
        <HeaderStyle Width="150px" />
    </telerik:GridBoundColumn>
    <telerik:GridBoundColumn DataField="UnitPrice"
                        DataType="System.Decimal"
                        HeaderText="Unit Price"
                        SortExpression="UnitPrice"
                        UniqueName="UnitPrice"
                        DataFormatString="{0:c}"
                        Aggregate="Avg"
                        FooterAggregateFormatString="Avg {0:c}">
        <ItemStyle Width="80px" />
        <HeaderStyle Width="80px" />
    </telerik:GridBoundColumn>
    <telerik:GridBoundColumn DataField="UnitsInStock"
                        DataType="System.Int16"
                        HeaderText="Units In Stock"
                        SortExpression="UnitsInStock"
                        UniqueName="UnitsInStock">
        <ItemStyle Width="80px" />
        <HeaderStyle Width="80px" />
    </telerik:GridBoundColumn>
    <telerik:GridBoundColumn DataField="UnitsOnOrder"
                        DataType="System.Int16"
                        HeaderText="Units On Order"
                        SortExpression="UnitsOnOrder"
                        UniqueName="UnitsOnOrder">
        <ItemStyle Width="80px" />
        <HeaderStyle Width="80px" />
    </telerik:GridBoundColumn>
```

```
            <telerik:GridBoundColumn DataField="ReorderLevel"
                                     DataType="System.Int16"
                                     HeaderText="Reorder Level"
                                     SortExpression="ReorderLevel"
                                     UniqueName="ReorderLevel">
                <ItemStyle Width="80px" />
                <HeaderStyle Width="80px" />
            </telerik:GridBoundColumn>
        </Columns>

    </MasterTableView>
</telerik:RadGrid>

<asp:SqlDataSource ID="ProductsDataSource7" runat="server"
    ConnectionString="<%$ ConnectionStrings:NorthwindConnectionString %>"
    SelectCommand="SELECT p.ProductID, p.ProductName, s.CompanyName SupplierName,
                          c.CategoryName, p.QuantityPerUnit, p.UnitPrice,
                          p.UnitsInStock, p.UnitsOnOrder, p.ReorderLevel,
                          p.Discontinued
                     FROM dbo.Products p INNER JOIN dbo.Suppliers s
                        ON p.SupplierID = s.SupplierID INNER JOIN dbo.Categories c
                        ON p.CategoryID = c.CategoryID">
</asp:SqlDataSource>
```

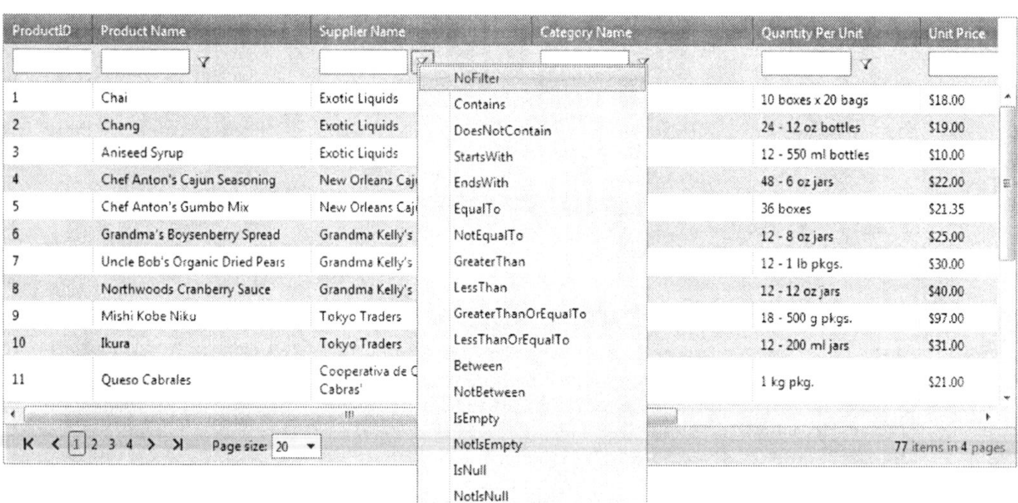

Figure 6-18. *In this example of RadGrid with filtering enabled, the filter menu is displayed with the available filters for the selected column.*

Inserting, Updating, and Deleting Records

RadGrid has built-in support for inserting, updating, and deleting records from its datasource. These capabilities are implemented through the use of column editors that can be automatically created for you, or you can create your own custom editor.

There are several different editors and their usage is based on the type of column for a field in RadGrid. For example, a GridBoundColumn will use by default a GridTextBoxColumnEditor for editing operations; a GridDateTimeColumn will use by default a GridDateTimeColumnEditor and so on. Not all types of columns are editable though, only those that implement or are derived from a class that implements the IGridEditableColumn interface. They are as follows:

- GridBoundColumn
- GridDropDownColumn
- GridCheckBoxColumn
- GridDateTimeColumn
- GridNumericColumn
- GridMaskedColumn
- GridHTMLEditorColumn
- GridTemplateColumn
- GridBinaryImageColumn
- GridAttachmentColumn

You have three options for implementing editors. The first one is using one of the built-in columns that generate the desired editor. This is codeless and requires minimum effort, and these editors are called *auto-generated editors*. Another option is to add one of the built-in editors to the page, implement the properties as desired, and then bind it to the column in RadGrid. These are *declarative custom editors*. Finally, you can create your own class that implements the IGridColumnEditor interface to build a column editor from the ground up or inherit from one of the built-in editor classes, such as GridDropDownEditor. This technique is the most complicated and should be used with caution because it could cause unexpected side effects in RadGrid if is not properly implemented.

RadGrid has four different edit modes to determine how users will interact with its editors. The current mode is accessed and manipulated from the MasterTableView.EditMode property. The four modes follow:

- InPlace: This will show the editors within the line of each row of data, keeping the layout and structure of the RadGrid intact.
- EditForms: This mode generates a form-like area below the row of data with all the editors for the columns that are editable.
- PopUp: This mode creates a pop-up window with the same generated form as in EditForms.
- Custom: When in EditForms or PopUp mode, RadGrid examines the EditFormSettings property to further customize the edit form. This property has a subproperty called EditFormType that can have one of the following values:

  AutoGenerated: It will use the columns definition and generate the edit form based on the default editors.

  WebUserControl: It will use the web user control specified in the UserControl property as the edit form.

  Template: You can use the Template section of the EditFormSettings property.

> With the WebUserControl and Template options, you are free to use any type of editors for your values, but you are also responsible for correctly binding the controls to the fields in the datasource. Between these two, I'm personally in favor of a WebUserControl implementation because not only is the markup not within RadGrid but it will allow you to modify your user control separately; you could change its behavior with minimal impact to the rest of the RadGrid implementation.

To allow RadGrid to perform insert, update, and delete operations, you must enable them by using the properties AllowAutomaticInsert, AllowAutomaticUpdate, and AllowAutomaticDelete. You set these properties on the RadGrid instance, or separately for each GridTableView (MasterTableView or DetailTables).

You need to use declarative or advanced data binding to enable any type of editing capabilities. Simple data binding can't be used.

One of the nice features of RadGrid is the CommandItem. This special item is a panel that can be shown on top or bottom of RadGrid (or both) and is basically a container for buttons that perform certain actions such as creating new records, refreshing records, exporting, or you can create custom buttons.

The example in Listing 6-28 show you how to implement inline editors with a datasource from a table in SQL Server with automatic insert, delete, and update capabilities. The resulting editors are shown in Figure 6-19.

Listing 6-28. *RadGrid with Automatically Generated Inline Editors*

ASPX Page

```
<telerik:RadGrid ID="RadGrid11" runat="server"
                 AllowAutomaticDeletes="True"
                 AllowAutomaticInserts="True"
                 AllowAutomaticUpdates="True"
                 AutoGenerateColumns="False"
                 AutoGenerateDeleteColumn="True"
                 AutoGenerateEditColumn="True"
                 DataSourceID="SqlDataSource1"
                 GridLines="None">
    <MasterTableView CommandItemDisplay="Top"
                     DataKeyNames="CategoryID"
                     DataSourceID="SqlDataSource1"
                     EditMode="InPlace">
    <RowIndicatorColumn>
    <HeaderStyle Width="20px"></HeaderStyle>
    </RowIndicatorColumn>

    <ExpandCollapseColumn>
    <HeaderStyle Width="20px"></HeaderStyle>
    </ExpandCollapseColumn>
        <Columns>
            <telerik:GridBoundColumn DataField="CategoryID"
                                     DataType="System.Int32"
                                     HeaderText="CategoryID"
                                     ReadOnly="True"
                                     SortExpression="CategoryID"
                                     UniqueName="CategoryID">
            </telerik:GridBoundColumn>
```

```
            <telerik:GridBoundColumn DataField="CategoryName"
                                     HeaderText="CategoryName"
                                     SortExpression="CategoryName"
                                     UniqueName="CategoryName"
                                     DataType="System.String">
            </telerik:GridBoundColumn>
            <telerik:GridBoundColumn DataField="Description"
                                     HeaderText="Description"
                                     SortExpression="Description"
                                     UniqueName="Description"
                                     DataType="System.String">
            </telerik:GridBoundColumn>
        </Columns>
        <EditFormSettings CaptionDataField="ID"
                          CaptionFormatString="Category {0}">
        </EditFormSettings>
    </MasterTableView>
</telerik:RadGrid>

<asp:SqlDataSource ID="SqlDataSource1" runat="server"
    ConnectionString="<%$ ConnectionStrings:NorthwindConnectionString %>"
    DeleteCommand="DELETE FROM [Categories] WHERE [CategoryID] = @original_CategoryID"
    InsertCommand="INSERT INTO [Categories] ([CategoryName], [Description])
                    VALUES (@CategoryName, @Description)"
    OldValuesParameterFormatString="original_{0}"
    SelectCommand="SELECT [CategoryID], [CategoryName], [Description] FROM [Categories]"
    UpdateCommand="UPDATE [Categories]
                  SET [CategoryName] = @CategoryName,
                      [Description] = @Description
                WHERE [CategoryID] = @original_CategoryID">
    <DeleteParameters>
        <asp:Parameter Name="original_CategoryID" Type="Int32" />
    </DeleteParameters>
    <InsertParameters>
        <asp:Parameter Name="CategoryName" Type="String" />
        <asp:Parameter Name="Description" Type="String" />
    </InsertParameters>
    <UpdateParameters>
        <asp:Parameter Name="CategoryName" Type="String" />
        <asp:Parameter Name="Description" Type="String" />
        <asp:Parameter Name="original_CategoryID" Type="Int32" />
    </UpdateParameters>
</asp:SqlDataSource>
```

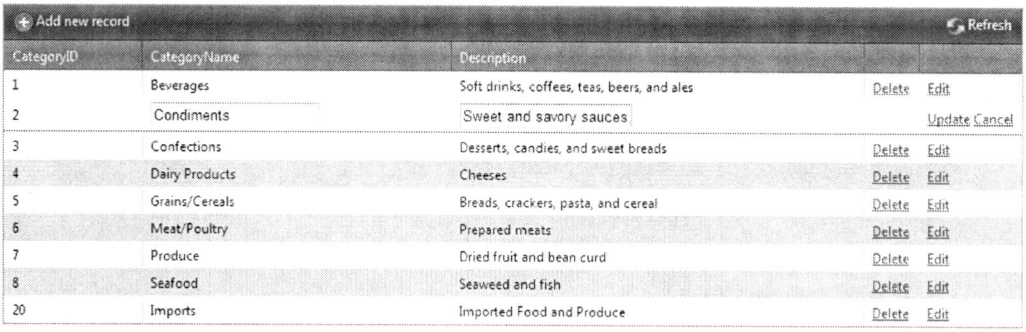

Add new record Refresh

CategoryID	CategoryName	Description		
1	Beverages	Soft drinks, coffees, teas, beers, and ales	Delete	Edit
2	Condiments	Sweet and savory sauces		Update Cancel
3	Confections	Desserts, candies, and sweet breads	Delete	Edit
4	Dairy Products	Cheeses	Delete	Edit
5	Grains/Cereals	Breads, crackers, pasta, and cereal	Delete	Edit
6	Meat/Poultry	Prepared meats	Delete	Edit
7	Produce	Dried fruit and bean curd	Delete	Edit
8	Seafood	Seaweed and fish	Delete	Edit
20	Imports	Imported Food and Produce	Delete	Edit

Figure 6-19. *RadGrid creates automatic editors so data can be easily manipulated.*

The example in Listing 6-29 shows how to implement a web user control, instead of the default editors, as an editor of `RadGrid`. This is useful when custom logic needs to be implemented to manipulate data. Figure 6-20 illustrates the web user control used as an editor.

Listing 6-29. *A RadGrid Web User Control Edit Form*

ASPX Page

```
<telerik:RadGrid ID="RadGrid12" runat="server"
             AutoGenerateColumns="False"
             AutoGenerateDeleteColumn="True"
             AutoGenerateEditColumn="True"
             GridLines="None"
             OnNeedDataSource="RadGrid12_NeedDataSource"
             OnInsertCommand="RadGrid12_InsertCommand"
             OnUpdateCommand="RadGrid12_UpdateCommand"
             OnDeleteCommand="RadGrid12_DeleteCommand">
        <MasterTableView CommandItemDisplay="Top"
                         DataKeyNames="CategoryID"
                         EditMode="PopUp">
        <RowIndicatorColumn>
        <HeaderStyle Width="20px"></HeaderStyle>
        </RowIndicatorColumn>

        <ExpandCollapseColumn>
        <HeaderStyle Width="20px"></HeaderStyle>
        </ExpandCollapseColumn>
            <Columns>
                <telerik:GridBoundColumn DataField="CategoryID"
                                DataType="System.Int32"
                                HeaderText="CategoryID"
                                ReadOnly="True"
                                SortExpression="CategoryID"
                                UniqueName="CategoryID">
                </telerik:GridBoundColumn>
```

```
            <telerik:GridBoundColumn DataField="CategoryName"
                        HeaderText="CategoryName"
                        SortExpression="CategoryName"
                        UniqueName="CategoryName"
                        DataType="System.String">
            </telerik:GridBoundColumn>
            <telerik:GridBoundColumn DataField="Description"
                        HeaderText="Description"
                        SortExpression="Description"
                        UniqueName="Description"
                        DataType="System.String">
            </telerik:GridBoundColumn>
        </Columns>
        <EditFormSettings EditFormType="WebUserControl"
                UserControlName="MyCategory_RadGridCustomFormEditor.ascx">
        </EditFormSettings>
    </MasterTableView>
</telerik:RadGrid>
```

Code Behind

```
    private List<MyCategory> ListOfCategories
    {
        get
        {
            List<MyCategory> categories;
            if (Session["ListOfCategories"] == null)
            {
                categories = MyCategoryController.GetAll();
                Session["ListOfCategories"] = categories;
            }
            else
                categories = (List<MyCategory>) Session["ListOfCategories"];

            return categories;
        }
        set
        {
            Session["ListOfCategories"] = value;
        }
    }

    protected void RadGrid12_NeedDataSource(object source, GridNeedDataSourceEventArgs e)
    {
        RadGrid12.DataSource = ListOfCategories;
    }

    protected void RadGrid12_InsertCommand(object source, GridCommandEventArgs e)
    {
        GridEditableItem editedItem = e.Item as GridEditableItem;
        UserControl userControl =
                (UserControl)e.Item.FindControl(GridEditFormItem.EditFormUserControlID);
        List<MyCategory> categories = ListOfCategories;
```

```
        //Create new row in the DataSource
        MyCategory newCategory = new MyCategory();

        //Insert new values
        Hashtable newValues = new Hashtable();
        newValues["CategoryName"] =
                        (userControl.FindControl("txtName") as TextBox).Text;
        newValues["Description"] =
                        (userControl.FindControl("txtDescription") as TextBox).Text;

        try
       {
            newCategory.CategoryName = newValues["CategoryName"].ToString();
            newCategory.Description = newValues["Description"].ToString();
            newCategory.Insert();
            categories.Add(newCategory);
            ListOfCategories = categories;
        }
        catch (Exception ex)
        {
            Label lblError = new Label();
            lblError.Text = "Unable to insert category. Reason: " + ex.Message;
            lblError.ForeColor = System.Drawing.Color.Red;
            RadGrid12.Controls.Add(lblError);

            e.Canceled = true;
        }
    }

    rotected void RadGrid12_UpdateCommand(object source, GridCommandEventArgs e)
    {
        GridEditableItem editedItem = e.Item as GridEditableItem;
        UserControl userControl =
                (UserControl)e.Item.FindControl(GridEditFormItem.EditFormUserControlID);
        List<MyCategory> categories = ListOfCategories;
        //Prepare new row to add it in the DataSource
        string Id = editedItem.OwnerTableView
                        .DataKeyValues[editedItem.ItemIndex]["CategoryID"].ToString();
        IEnumerable<MyCategory> changedCategories =
                        categories.Where(c => c.CategoryID == int.Parse(Id));

        if (changedCategories.Count() != 1)
        {
            RadGrid1.Controls
                .Add(new LiteralControl("Unable to locate the category for updating."));
            e.Canceled = true;
            return;
        }
```

```
        //Update new values
        Hashtable newValues = new Hashtable();
       newValues["CategoryName"] =
                        (userControl.FindControl("txtName") as TextBox).Text;
        newValues["Description"] =
                        (userControl.FindControl("txtDescription") as TextBox).Text;

        try
        {
            MyCategory cat =
                        changedCategories.SingleOrDefault(c => c.CategoryID ==➥
 int.Parse(Id));
            cat.CategoryName = newValues["CategoryName"].ToString();
            cat.Description = newValues["Description"].ToString();
            cat.Update();
            ListOfCategories = categories;
        }
        catch (Exception ex)
        {
            Label lblError = new Label();
            lblError.Text = "Unable to update category. Reason: " + ex.Message;
            lblError.ForeColor = System.Drawing.Color.Red;
            RadGrid12.Controls.Add(lblError);

            e.Canceled = true;
        }
    }

    protected void RadGrid12_DeleteCommand(object source, GridCommandEventArgs e)
    {
        string Id = (e.Item as
                GridDataItem).OwnerTableView.DataKeyValues[e.Item.ItemIndex]["CategoryID"]
                            .ToString();
        List<MyCategory> categories = ListOfCategories;
        MyCategory cat = categories.SingleOrDefault(c => c.CategoryID == int.Parse(Id));
        if (cat != null)
        {
            cat.Delete();
           categories.Remove(cat);
        }
        ListOfCategories = categories;
}
```

MyCategory.cs

```
public class MyCategory
{
        public int CategoryID { get; set; }
        public string CategoryName { get; set; }
        public string Description { get; set; }
```

```
public void Insert ()
{
    string sqlInsert = "INSERT INTO [Categories] ([CategoryName], [Description])
                        VALUES (@CategoryName, @Description);
                        SELECT SCOPE_IDENTITY();";
    using (SqlConnection cnn = new SqlConnection(WebConfigurationManager
                .ConnectionStrings["NorthwindConnectionString"]
                .ConnectionString))
    {
        using (SqlCommand cmd = new SqlCommand(sqlInsert, cnn))
        {
            cmd.Parameters.Add(new SqlParameter("CategoryName", CategoryName));
            cmd.Parameters.Add(new SqlParameter("Description", Description));
            try
            {
                cnn.Open();
                CategoryID = int.Parse(cmd.ExecuteScalar().ToString());
            }
            catch (Exception ex)
            {

            }
        }
    }
}

public void Update ()
{
    string sqlInsert = "UPDATE [Categories]
                           SET [CategoryName] = @CategoryName,
                               [Description] = @Description
                         WHERE [CategoryID] = @original_CategoryID";
    using (SqlConnection cnn = new SqlConnection(WebConfigurationManager
                        .ConnectionStrings["NorthwindConnectionString"]
                        .ConnectionString))
    {
        using (SqlCommand cmd = new SqlCommand(sqlInsert, cnn))
        {
            cmd.Parameters.Add(new SqlParameter("original_CategoryID", CategoryID));
            cmd.Parameters.Add(new SqlParameter("CategoryName", CategoryName));
            cmd.Parameters.Add(new SqlParameter("Description", Description));
            try
            {
                cnn.Open();
                cmd.ExecuteNonQuery();
            }
            catch (Exception ex)
            {

            }
        }
    }
}
```

```
        public void Delete ()
        {
            string sqlInsert = "DELETE FROM [Categories]
                                WHERE [CategoryID] = @original_CategoryID";
            using (SqlConnection cnn = new SqlConnection(WebConfigurationManager
                                .ConnectionStrings["NorthwindConnectionString"]
                                .ConnectionString))
            {
                using (SqlCommand cmd = new SqlCommand(sqlInsert, cnn))
                {
                    cmd.Parameters.Add(new SqlParameter("original_CategoryID", CategoryID));
                    try
                    {
                        cnn.Open();
                        cmd.ExecuteNonQuery();
                    }
                    catch (Exception ex)
                    {

                    }
                }
            }
        }
    }
}
```

MyCategoryController.cs

```
public static class MyCategoryController
{
        public static List<MyCategory> GetAll()
        {
            List<MyCategory> categories = new List<MyCategory>();
            string sqlInsert = "SELECT [CategoryID], [CategoryName], [Description]
                                FROM [Categories]";
            using (SqlConnection cnn = new SqlConnection(WebConfigurationManager
                                .ConnectionStrings["NorthwindConnectionString"]
                                .ConnectionString))
            {
                using (SqlCommand cmd = new SqlCommand(sqlInsert, cnn))
                {
                    try
                    {
                        cnn.Open();
                        using (SqlDataReader rd = cmd.ExecuteReader())
                        {
                            if (rd != null)
                                while (rd.Read())
                                {
                                    MyCategory cat = new MyCategory();
                                    cat.CategoryID = int.Parse(rd["CategoryID"].ToString());
                                    cat.CategoryName = rd["CategoryName"].ToString();
                                    cat.Description = rd["Description"].ToString();
                                    categories.Add(cat);
```

```
                                }
                            }
                        }
                        catch (Exception ex)
                        {

                        }
                    }
                }
                return categories;
            }
}
```

MyCategory_RadGridCustomFormEditor.ascx

```
<%@ Control Language="C#" AutoEventWireup="true"
            CodeBehind="MyCategory_RadGridCustomFormEditor.ascx.cs"
            Inherits="WebApplication1.MyCategory_RadGridCustomFormEditor" %>
<table>
    <tr>
        <th colspan="2">Category Details</th>
    </tr>
    <tr>
        <td>Name:</td>
        <td>
            <asp:TextBox ID="txtName" runat="server"
                         Text='<%# DataBinder.Eval( Container, "DataItem.CategoryName" ) %>'
                         MaxLength="15">
            </asp:TextBox>
        </td>
    </tr>
    <tr>
        <td>Name:</td>
        <td>
            <asp:TextBox ID="txtDescription" runat="server"
                         Text='<%# DataBinder.Eval( Container, "DataItem.Description" ) %>'
                         Columns="35"
                         Rows="7"
                         TextMode="MultiLine">
            </asp:TextBox>
        </td>
    </tr>
    <tr>
        <td colspan="2"> </td>
    </tr>
    <tr>
        <td colspan="2">
                <asp:button id="btnUpdate" runat="server"
                        text="Update"
                        CommandName="Update"
                        Visible='<%# !(DataItem is Telerik.Web.UI.GridInsertionObject) %>'>
                </asp:button>
```

```
                <asp:button id="btnInsert" runat="server"
                        text="Insert"
                        CommandName="PerformInsert"
                        Visible='<%# DataItem is Telerik.Web.UI.GridInsertionObject %>'>
                </asp:button>
                         
                <asp:button id="btnCancel" runat="server"
                        text="Cancel"
                        causesvalidation="False"
                        commandname="Cancel">
                </asp:button>
        </td>
    </tr>
</table>

MyCategory_RadGridCustomFormEditor.ascx.cs

public partial class MyCategory_RadGridCustomFormEditor : UserControl
{
        private object _dataItem;

        public object DataItem
        {
            get
            {
                return _dataItem;
            }
            set
            {
                _dataItem = value;
            }
        }

        protected void Page_Load(object sender, EventArgs e)
        {

        }
}
```

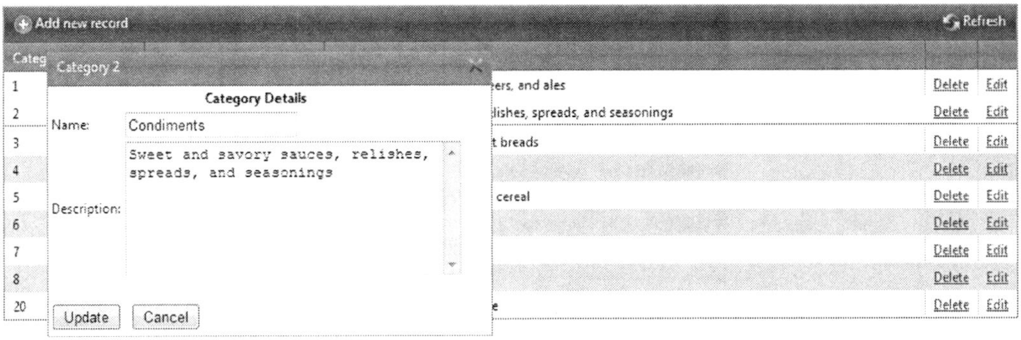

Figure 6-20. *The RadGrid web user control edit editor created in Listing 6-29*

In Listing 6-30, I create a custom editor for one of the columns. The example uses a class that derives from GridDropDownColumnEditor and implements a custom RadComboBox that is automatically bound to a database table. Then, the editor is assigned to the category column in code. Figure 6-21 shows the custom editor in action.

Listing 6-30. *Implementing a Custom Editor*

ASPX Page

```
<telerik:RadGrid ID="RadGrid13" runat="server"
            AutoGenerateColumns="False"
            AutoGenerateDeleteColumn="True"
            AllowPaging="True"
            DataSourceID="ProductsDataSource13"
            AllowAutomaticDeletes="True"
            AllowAutomaticInserts="True"
            AllowAutomaticUpdates="True"
            AutoGenerateEditColumn="True"
            GridLines="None"
            OnCreateColumnEditor="RadGrid13_CreateColumnEditor">
    <MasterTableView CommandItemDisplay="Top"
                     DataKeyNames="ProductID"
                     EditMode="PopUp">
    <RowIndicatorColumn>
    <HeaderStyle Width="20px"></HeaderStyle>
    </RowIndicatorColumn>

    <ExpandCollapseColumn>
    <HeaderStyle Width="20px"></HeaderStyle>
    </ExpandCollapseColumn>
        <Columns>
            <telerik:GridBoundColumn DataField="ProductID"
                                     DataType="System.Int32"
                                     HeaderText="ProductID"
                        ReadOnly="True"
                        SortExpression="ProductID"
                                     UniqueName="ProductID">
            </telerik:GridBoundColumn>
            <telerik:GridBoundColumn DataField="ProductName"
                                     HeaderText="ProductName"
                                     SortExpression="ProductName"
                                     UniqueName="ProductName">
            </telerik:GridBoundColumn>
            <telerik:GridDropDownColumn DataField="SupplierID"
                                     DataType="System.Int32"
                                     HeaderText="Supplier"
                                     SortExpression="SupplierID"
                                     UniqueName="SupplierID"
                                     DataSourceID="SuppliersDataSource"
                                     ListTextField="CompanyName"
                                     ListValueField="SupplierID">
            </telerik:GridDropDownColumn>
```

```
            <telerik:GridDropDownColumn DataField="CategoryID"
                                        DataType="System.Int32"
                                        HeaderText="CategoryID"
                                        SortExpression="CategoryID"
                                        UniqueName="CategoryID">
            </telerik:GridDropDownColumn>
            <telerik:GridBoundColumn DataField="QuantityPerUnit"
                                        HeaderText="QuantityPerUnit"
                                        SortExpression="QuantityPerUnit"
                                        UniqueName="QuantityPerUnit">
            </telerik:GridBoundColumn>
            <telerik:GridBoundColumn DataField="UnitPrice"
                                        DataType="System.Decimal"
                                        HeaderText="UnitPrice"
                                        SortExpression="UnitPrice"
                                        UniqueName="UnitPrice">
            </telerik:GridBoundColumn>
            <telerik:GridBoundColumn DataField="UnitsInStock"
                                        DataType="System.Int16"
                                        HeaderText="UnitsInStock"
                                        SortExpression="UnitsInStock"
                                        UniqueName="UnitsInStock">
            </telerik:GridBoundColumn>
            <telerik:GridBoundColumn DataField="UnitsOnOrder"
                                        DataType="System.Int16"
                                        HeaderText="UnitsOnOrder"
                                        SortExpression="UnitsOnOrder"
                                        UniqueName="UnitsOnOrder">
            </telerik:GridBoundColumn>
            <telerik:GridBoundColumn DataField="ReorderLevel"
                                        DataType="System.Int16"
                                        HeaderText="ReorderLevel"
                                        SortExpression="ReorderLevel"
                                        ColumnEditorID="GridTextBoxColumnEditor1"
                                        UniqueName="ReorderLevel">
            </telerik:GridBoundColumn>
            <telerik:GridCheckBoxColumn DataField="Discontinued"
                                        DataType="System.Boolean"
                                        HeaderText="Discontinued"
                                        SortExpression="Discontinued"
                                        UniqueName="Discontinued">
            </telerik:GridCheckBoxColumn>
        </Columns>
    </MasterTableView>
    <ClientSettings>
        <Scrolling AllowScroll="true" UseStaticHeaders="true" />
    </ClientSettings>
</telerik:RadGrid>
```

```
    <telerik:GridTextBoxColumnEditor ID="GridTextBoxColumnEditor1" runat="server">
        <TextBoxStyle   Font-Bold="true"
                        Font-Italic="true"
                        BackColor="Yellow"
                        ForeColor="Red" />
    </telerik:GridTextBoxColumnEditor>

<asp:SqlDataSource ID="SuppliersDataSource" runat="server"
    ConnectionString="<%$ ConnectionStrings:NorthwindConnectionString %>"
    SelectCommand="SELECT SupplierID, CompanyName FROM [Suppliers]" >
</asp:SqlDataSource>

<asp:SqlDataSource ID="ProductsDataSource13" runat="server"
    ConnectionString="<%$ ConnectionStrings:NorthwindConnectionString %>"
    SelectCommand="SELECT * FROM [Products]"
    DeleteCommand="DELETE FROM [Products] WHERE [ProductID] = @ProductID"
    InsertCommand="INSERT INTO [Products] ([ProductName], [SupplierID],
                                [CategoryID], [QuantityPerUnit], [UnitPrice],
                                [UnitsInStock], [UnitsOnOrder], [ReorderLevel],
                                [Discontinued])
                        VALUES (@ProductName, @SupplierID, @CategoryID,
                                @QuantityPerUnit, @UnitPrice, @UnitsInStock,
                                @UnitsOnOrder, @ReorderLevel, @Discontinued)"
    UpdateCommand="UPDATE [Products]
                      SET [ProductName] = @ProductName,
                          [SupplierID] = @SupplierID,
                          [CategoryID] = @CategoryID,
                          [QuantityPerUnit] = @QuantityPerUnit,
                          [UnitPrice] = @UnitPrice,
                          [UnitsInStock] = @UnitsInStock,
                          [UnitsOnOrder] = @UnitsOnOrder,
                          [ReorderLevel] = @ReorderLevel,
                          [Discontinued] = @Discontinued
                    WHERE [ProductID] = @ProductID">
    <DeleteParameters>
        <asp:Parameter Name="ProductID" Type="Int32" />
    </DeleteParameters>
    <InsertParameters>
        <asp:Parameter Name="ProductName" Type="String" />
        <asp:Parameter Name="SupplierID" Type="Int32" />
        <asp:Parameter Name="CategoryID" Type="Int32" />
        <asp:Parameter Name="QuantityPerUnit" Type="String" />
        <asp:Parameter Name="UnitPrice" Type="Decimal" />
        <asp:Parameter Name="UnitsInStock" Type="Int16" />
        <asp:Parameter Name="UnitsOnOrder" Type="Int16" />
        <asp:Parameter Name="ReorderLevel" Type="Int16" />
        <asp:Parameter Name="Discontinued" Type="Boolean" />
    </InsertParameters>
    <UpdateParameters>
        <asp:Parameter Name="ProductName" Type="String" />
        <asp:Parameter Name="SupplierID" Type="Int32" />
        <asp:Parameter Name="CategoryID" Type="Int32" />
        <asp:Parameter Name="QuantityPerUnit" Type="String" />
        <asp:Parameter Name="UnitPrice" Type="Decimal" />
```

```
        <asp:Parameter Name="UnitsInStock" Type="Int16" />
        <asp:Parameter Name="UnitsOnOrder" Type="Int16" />
        <asp:Parameter Name="ReorderLevel" Type="Int16" />
        <asp:Parameter Name="Discontinued" Type="Boolean" />
        <asp:Parameter Name="ProductID" Type="Int32" />
    </UpdateParameters>
</asp:SqlDataSource>
```

Code Behind

```
protected void RadGrid13_CreateColumnEditor(object sender,➥
 GridCreateColumnEditorEventArgs e)
{
    if (!(e.Column is GridDropDownColumn)) return;
    if (((GridDropDownColumn) e.Column).DataField == "CategoryID")
    {
        e.ColumnEditor = new CategoryColumnEditor();
    }
}
```

CategoryColumnEditor.cs

```
public class CategoryColumnEditor : GridDropDownColumnEditor
{
        private RadComboBox rcb = new RadComboBox();
        protected override void AddControlsToContainer()
        {
            RadComboBox combo = new RadComboBox();
            combo.DataTextField = "CategoryName";
            combo.DataValueField = "CategoryID";
            combo.DataSource = LoadCategories();
            combo.DropDownWidth = Unit.Pixel(200);
            ContainerControl.Controls.Add(combo);
        }

        private DataTable LoadCategories()
        {
            string ConnString = ConfigurationManager
                                .ConnectionStrings["NorthwindConnectionString"]
                                .ConnectionString;
            string query = "SELECT CategoryID, CategoryName FROM Categories";
            DataTable myDataTable = new DataTable();
            using (SqlConnection conn = new SqlConnection(ConnString))
            {
                using (SqlDataAdapter adapter = new SqlDataAdapter())
                {
                    adapter.SelectCommand = new SqlCommand(query, conn);

                    conn.Open();
                    try
                    {
                        adapter.Fill(myDataTable);
                    }
```

```
                finally
                {
                    conn.Close();
                }
            }
        }
        return myDataTable;
    }

    protected override void LoadControlsFromContainer()
    {
        rcb = ContainerControl.Controls[0] as RadComboBox;
    }

    public override void DataBind()
    {

    }

    public override int SelectedIndex
    {
        get { return rcb.SelectedIndex; }
        set { rcb.SelectedIndex = value; }
    }

    public override string SelectedValue
    {
        get { return rcb.SelectedValue; }
        set { rcb.SelectedValue = value; }
    }

    public override string SelectedText
    {
        get { return rcb.SelectedItem.Text; }
        set { rcb.SelectedItem.Text = value; }
    }
}
```

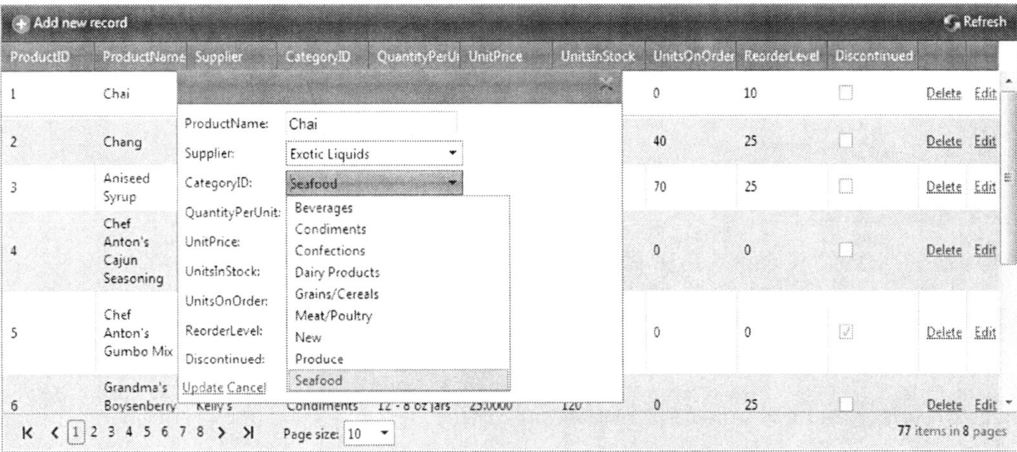

Figure 6-21. *In this RadGrid, a custom editor is being used for the CategoryID column.*

Implementing Client-Side API

The client-side API exposed by `RadGrid` is by far one of the most extensive ones you will find in a single control. There is not much you can't do with the `RadGrid` on the client side, and using the API is easy and straightforward.

There are four client-side objects: `RadGrid`, `GridTableView`, `GridDataItem`, and `GridColumn`. And you perform operations with the methods exposed by these objects.

To work with the client-side API, you must obtain a reference to the `RadGrid` client object. This will give you access to the `GridTableView` objects and each of their `GridDataItem` and `GridColumn` objects.

The best way to show you how to work with it is with an example. I have implemented a `RadGrid` in this section's example, and all the operations are done entirely on the client side (except for three `PageMethods` that perform the actual insert, update, and delete operations on the database).

I have added a few modifications to our `MyCategory` class in order to provide better support for the insert, update, and delete operations.

The next example is an implementation of `RadGrid`'s Client API. I have split the code into several sections, so I can explain what is being done. Listings 6-31 to 6-35 must be combined for the example to run. The `RadGrid` in the example is bound on the client side using a web service, and I'm using a modified version of the `MyCategory` business object shown before. First, we'll examine how the business object was modified to support the client operations. In Figure 6-22, you can see the how the application looks when all the listings are implemented.

Listing 6-31 shows the modifications made to the `MyCategory` class. The class is nearly the same as the one shown in Listing 6-30; the difference is that I have added a default constructor to support the creation of a new category and a constructor that accepts a category ID that loads the specified category from the database.

Listing 6-31. *MyCategory.cs Business Object Class Modifications*

```
public MyCategory()
{

}

public MyCategory(int id)
{
    string sql = "SELECT [CategoryID], [CategoryName], [Description] ";
          sql += " FROM [Categories] WHERE [CategoryID] = @CategoryID";
    using (SqlConnection cnn = new SqlConnection(WebConfigurationManager
                                .ConnectionStrings["NorthwindConnectionString"]
                                .ConnectionString))
    {
        using (SqlCommand cmd = new SqlCommand(sql, cnn))
        {
            try
            {
                cnn.Open();
                cmd.Parameters.Add(new SqlParameter("CategoryID", id));
                using (SqlDataReader rd = cmd.ExecuteReader())
                {
                    if (rd != null)
                        while (rd.Read())
                        {
                            CategoryID = id;
                            CategoryName = rd["CategoryName"].ToString();
                            Description = rd["Description"].ToString();
                        }
                }
            }
            catch (Exception ex)
            {
                CategoryID = 0;
            }
        }
    }
}
```

The next step is to create a new web form that will be used by the user to create a new category and modify an existing one. Listing 6-32 shows the web form, which uses a query string parameter to determine if it must load the information of an existing category from the database or present an empty form. The web form is opened in a RadWindow, and once the information is saved, the RadWindow is closed and the typed information is returned to the caller window so it can perform the appropriate action (insert or update).

Listing 6-32. *A Web Form to Enter Information for a New Category or Edit an Existing One*

```
radgrid_editform.aspx
<%@ Page Language="C#"
        AutoEventWireup="true"
        CodeBehind="radgrid_editform.aspx.cs"
        Inherits="WebApplication1.radgrid_editform" %>
```

```
<!DOCTYPE html PUBLIC "-//W3C//DTD XHTML 1.0 Transitional//EN"
        "http://www.w3.org/TR/xhtml1/DTD/xhtml1-transitional.dtd">

<html xmlns="http://www.w3.org/1999/xhtml">
<head runat="server">
    <title></title>
</head>
<body>
    <form id="form1" runat="server">
    <table>
        <tr>
            <th colspan="2">Category Details</th>
        </tr>
        <tr>
            <td>Name:</td>
            <td>
                <asp:TextBox ID="txtName" runat="server"
                             MaxLength="15">
                </asp:TextBox>
                <asp:RequiredFieldValidator ID="RequiredFieldValidator1" runat="server"
                                            ErrorMessage="*"
                                            ControlToValidate="txtName"
                                            Display="Dynamic">
                </asp:RequiredFieldValidator>
            </td>
        </tr>
        <tr>
            <td>Description:</td>
            <td>
                <asp:TextBox ID="txtDescription" runat="server"
                             Columns="35"
                             Rows="7"
                             TextMode="MultiLine">
                </asp:TextBox>
                <asp:RequiredFieldValidator ID="RequiredFieldValidator2" runat="server"
                                            ErrorMessage="*"
                                            ControlToValidate="txtDescription"
                                            Display="Dynamic">
                </asp:RequiredFieldValidator>
            </td>
        </tr>
        <tr>
            <td colspan="2"> </td>
        </tr>
        <tr>
            <td colspan="2">
                        <asp:button id="btnUpdate" runat="server"
                            text="Save"
                            OnClientClick="javascript:Save();return false;">
                </asp:button>
                         
                        <asp:button id="btnCancel" runat="server"
                            text="Cancel"
```

```
                        causesvalidation="False"
                        OnClientClick="javascript:Cancel();return false;">
                </asp:button>
            </td>
        </tr>
    </table>
    <script language="javascript" type="text/javascript">
        function GetRadWindow() {
            var oWindow = null;
            if (window.radWindow) oWindow = window.radWindow;
            else if (window.frameElement.radWindow) oWindow = window.frameElement.radWindow;
            return oWindow;
        }

        function Save() {
                // create the argument parameter to return with the
                // new/updated information
            var arg = new Object();
                // find the textboxes
            var txtn = document.getElementById("txtName");
            var txtd = document.getElementById("txtDescription");
            arg.id = '<%=Request.QueryString["id"] %>';
                // load the data
            arg.Name = txtn.value;
            arg.Description = txtd.value;
                // close the window and pass the argument parameter
            var wnd = GetRadWindow();
            wnd.close(arg);
        }

        function Cancel() {
                // if the user clicked on cancel, then just close the window.
                // no argument parameter.
            var wnd = GetRadWindow();
            wnd.close();
        }

    </script>
    </form>
</body>
</html>
```

radgrid_editform.aspx.cs

```
public partial class radgrid_editform : Page
{
        protected void Page_Load(object sender, EventArgs e)
        {
            if (Page.IsPostBack) return;
            string id = Request.QueryString["id"];
            if (!string.IsNullOrEmpty(id))
                LoadData(id);
        }
```

```
        private void LoadData(string id)
        {
            string ConnString =
                        ConfigurationManager
                                .ConnectionStrings["NorthwindConnectionString"]
                                .ConnectionString;
            string query = "SELECT * FROM Categories WHERE CategoryID = @categoryID";
            using (SqlConnection conn = new SqlConnection(ConnString))
            {
                SqlCommand cmd = new SqlCommand(query, conn);
                cmd.Parameters.Add(new SqlParameter("categoryID", id));
                conn.Open();
                using (SqlDataReader rd = cmd.ExecuteReader())
                {
                    if (rd != null)
                        if (rd.Read())
                        {
                            txtName.Text = rd["CategoryName"].ToString();
                            txtDescription.Text = rd["Description"].ToString();
                        }
                }
                conn.Close();
            }

        }
}
```

The code in Listings 6-31 and 6-32, as mentioned before, is only part of the complete code needed to complete the interaction with the database and user in certain actions. Now, let's examine the RadGrid definition in Listing 6-33. This RadGrid supports grouping, paging, and sorting denoted by the AllowFilteringbyColumn, AllowPaging, and AllowSorting properties.

An important part here is the MasterTableView.ClientDataKeyNames property. This property is used to define what columns in RadGrid.MasterTableView can be accessed by the getDataKeyValue() method. This is a key element when identifying the rows in RadGrid for which an action must be taken.

Next, we have a CommandItemTemplate that modifies the default CommandItem bar. In the template are the definitions of three buttons aimed to trigger the insert, update, and delete operations.

The third part to pay attention to is the ClientSetting.ClientEvents section. Here, I have handled the OnCommand and OnRowDblClick events. The OnCommand event handler will be used to cancel the default RadGrid commands, because our code will be used to perform them. The OnRowDblClick will be used to trigger the update operation of a specific row in RadGrid.

Additionally, there is the definition of a RadWindowManager object to handle the RadWindows.

Listing 6-33. *RadGrid Working with the Client API*

ASPX Page

```
<telerik:RadGrid ID="RadGrid14" runat="server"
                 AutoGenerateColumns="false"
                 AllowPaging="True"
                 AllowSorting="True"
                 AllowFilteringByColumn="true"
                 GridLines="None">
```

```
    <MasterTableView DataKeyNames="CategoryID"
                     ClientDataKeyNames="CategoryID"
                     CommandItemDisplay="Top">
    <CommandItemTemplate>
           <asp:Button ID="btnAddNew" runat="server"
                       Text="Add New"
                       OnClientClick="javascript:AddNew();return false;" />
            
           <asp:Button ID="btnEdit" runat="server"
                       Text="Edit Selected"
                       OnClientClick="javascript:Edit();return false;" />
            
           <asp:Button ID="btnDelete" runat="server"
                       Text="Delete Selected"
                       OnClientClick="javascript:Delete();return false;" />
    </CommandItemTemplate>
    <Columns>
        <telerik:GridBoundColumn DataField="CategoryID"
                                HeaderText="CategoryID"
                                SortExpression="CategoryID"
                                UniqueName="CategoryID"
                                DataType="System.Int32">
        </telerik:GridBoundColumn>
        <telerik:GridBoundColumn DataField="CategoryName"
                                HeaderText="CategoryName"
                                SortExpression="CategoryName"
                                UniqueName="CategoryName"
                                DataType="System.String">
        </telerik:GridBoundColumn>
        <telerik:GridBoundColumn DataField="Description"
                                HeaderText="Description"
                                SortExpression="Description"
                                UniqueName="Description"
                                DataType="System.String">
        </telerik:GridBoundColumn>
    </Columns>
    </MasterTableView>
    <ClientSettings>
        <Selecting AllowRowSelect="true" />
        <ClientEvents OnCommand="RadGrid14_Command"
                OnRowDblClick="RadGrid14_RowDblClick" />
    </ClientSettings>
</telerik:RadGrid>

<telerik:RadWindowManager ID="RadWindowManager1" runat="server"
                       DestroyOnClose="false"
                       VisibleStatusbar="false"
                       Modal="true"
                       Behaviors="Close"
                       ShowContentDuringLoad="false"
                       ReloadOnShow="true"
                       style="z-index:20000">
</telerik:RadWindowManager>
```

Listing 6-34 shows the implementation of the client event handlers to support the client operations we need to perform. The supporting page methods will be in Listing 6-35. The pageLoad() method is called when the page has finished rendering and is ready to execute client code.

The initial loading is performed by a call to a page method with the callback function BindGrid(), which will perform the data binding. The callback function BindGrid() invokes the set_dataSource()method in the RadGrid and the dataBind() method. A second page method call is performed to gather the record count information, so RadGrid can create the paging structure properly.

The function RadGrid14_RowDblClick(sender, eventArgs) is the event handler for the OnRowDblClick. It's only purpose is to trigger the update operation, which is also triggered by the Update button in the CommandItem.

The Edit() function handles the identification of the row to be updated. First, we find the grid client object then using the RadGrid.get_masterTableView().get_selectedItems() collection and verify that a row was actually selected to perform the update. If no row was selected, an error is thrown with a radalert(). If a row was selected, we find it by taking the first row in the collection, because the RadGrid in this example doesn't support multiple row selection—the collection only has one item.

Once the selected row has been identified, we use the getDataKeyValue() method to get the ID of the category we want to edit. This step is crucial, because this ID will be passed in the query string of the edit form created in Listing 6-32.

The final step is to open the RadWindow by calling the edit form that will be used to capture the new data for the category. An important aspect here is the add_close() method that creates a callback when the RadWindow is closed. The callback function is named grid_update in this case, and grid_update identifies whether an actual update is to be made. If an update is needed, a call to a page method is performed. If the update is successful, RadGrid reloads the data in the current page again with a call to the Reload() callback method. On the other hand, if the page method throws an error, a call to the GetError() callback method is performed to inform the user about the error.

The AddNew() function works the same as the Edit() function only the reference to an existing category is not passed in the query string to the edit web form, thus empty text boxes are shown.

The Delete() function works nearly the same as Edit(), but it doesn't open a RadWindow to perform the delete and includes a call to radconfirm() to ask the user for confirmation before executing the page method that will delete the category.

The function RadGrid14_RowDblClick(sender, eventArgs) is the event handler for the OnCommand event. Since the program is handling the operations, we don't need to have RadGrid do that too, so the main purpose of the handler is to cancel RadGrid's commands in favor of our handlers.

Listing 6-34. *Client Event Handlers*

```
<telerik:RadCodeBlock ID="RadCodeBlock2" runat="server">

<script type="text/javascript">

    function pageLoad(sender, eventArgs) {
        var tableView = $find("<%= RadGrid14.ClientID %>").get_masterTableView();
        var pageSize = tableView.get_pageSize();
        var sortExpression = tableView.get_sortExpressions().toString();
        var filterExpression = tableView.get_filterExpressions().toString();

        PageMethods.GetCategories(0,
                              pageSize,
                              sortExpression,
                              filterExpression,
                              BindGrid);
```

```
        PageMethods.GetCatCount(filterExpression, updateVirtualItemCount);
    }

    function BindGrid(result) {
        // find the grid
        var grid = $find("<%= RadGrid14.ClientID %>");
        // find the master table view
        var tableView = grid.get_masterTableView();
        // bind the data gathered to the grid
        tableView.set_dataSource(result);
        tableView.dataBind();

        // clear the selected items just in case
        grid.clearSelectedItems();
    }

    function updateVirtualItemCount(result) {
        // find the grid
        var grid = $find("<%= RadGrid14.ClientID %>");
        // find the master table view
        var tableView = grid.get_masterTableView();
        // update the VirtualItemCount property
        tableView.set_virtualItemCount(result);
        // clear the selected items just in case
        grid.clearSelectedItems();
    }

    function RadGrid14_RowDblClick(sender, eventArgs) {
        // when an item is double clicked this event is raised
        Edit();
    }

    function Edit() {
        // find the grid
        var grid = $find("<%=RadGrid14.ClientID %>");
        // verify if there were selected items. If not can't edit.
        if (grid.get_masterTableView().get_selectedItems().length == 0) {
            radalert("You must select a row to edit.");
            return;
        }
        // get the selected item
        var selected = grid.get_masterTableView().get_selectedItems()[0];
        // now get the key value of the item so we know which item
        // to edit.
        var id = selected.getDataKeyValue("CategoryID");
        // open the editor window and pass the key value as parameter
        window.setTimeout(function () {
            var manager = GetRadWindowManager();
            var oWnd2 = manager.open("radgrid_editform.aspx?id=" + id, "RadWindow1");
            oWnd2.setSize(500, 400);
            oWnd2.center();
```

```
        oWnd2.set_title("Edit Category");
        oWnd2.set_modal(true);
            // When editing is done, handle the new values in the close event.
        oWnd2.add_close(grid_update);
    }, 0)
}

function grid_update(sender, eventArgs) {
    // verify that the user actually clicked "Save"
    var arg = eventArgs.get_argument();
    if (arg) {
            // save the updated information
        PageMethods.UpdateCategory(arg.id, arg.Name, arg.Description, Reload, GetError);
    }
}

function AddNew() {
    window.setTimeout(function () {
            // find the RadWindowManager and open the custom editor
            // to enter data
        var manager = GetRadWindowManager();
        var oWnd2 = manager.open("radgrid_editform.aspx", "RadWindow1");
        oWnd2.setSize(500, 400);
        oWnd2.center();
        oWnd2.set_title("Add New Category");
        oWnd2.set_modal(true);
            // Attach the handler for the client side closed event of the window.
            // When the window is closed this event will be rised to handle the
            // the data collected in the editor window.
        oWnd2.add_close(grid_add);
    }, 0)
}

function grid_add(sender, eventArgs) {
    // verify that the user actually clicked "Save"
    var arg = eventArgs.get_argument();
    if (arg) {
            // If he/she did, then add the new category
        PageMethods.AddCategory(arg.Name, arg.Description, Reload, GetError);
    }
}

function GetError(result) {
    // if PageMethods returned an error then show what happened.
    alert(result.get_message());
}

function Reload(result) {
    // verify that the PageMethods operation went good. If not then don't do anything.
    if (result != "OK") return;
    // find the grid
    var grid = $find("<%= RadGrid14.ClientID %>");
    // find the master table view
    var tableView = grid.get_masterTableView();
```

```
    // get the current page size (paging)
    var pageSize = tableView.get_pageSize();
    // get the sort expressions list (sorting)
    var sortExpression = tableView.get_sortExpressions().toString();
    // get the filter expressions list (filtering)
    var filterExpression = tableView.get_filterExpressions().toString();
    // where are we? Get the page.
    var currentPageIndex = tableView.get_currentPageIndex();
    // do the render of the records again to load the changes.
    // I'm not using the client side methods insert, update, delete
    // because I'm not use in place editors.
    PageMethods.GetCategories(currentPageIndex * pageSize,
                              pageSize,
                              sortExpression,
                              filterExpression,
                              BindGrid2);

    // count the items again
    PageMethods.GetCatCount(filterExpression, updateVirtualItemCount2);

    // clear the selected items
    grid.clearSelectedItems();
}

function Delete() {
    // find the grid
    var grid = $find("<%=RadGrid14.ClientID %>");
    // verify that an actual item was selected to delete
    if (grid.get_masterTableView().get_selectedItems().length == 0) {
        radalert("You must select a category to delete.");
        return;
    }
    // let's confirm that the user actually want's to delete the record
    radconfirm("Are you sure you want to delete the category?", ConfirmDelete);
}

function ConfirmDelete(arg) {
    if (arg) {
            // if the user really want's to delete the record then do it.
            // find the grid
        var grid = $find("<%=RadGrid14.ClientID %>");
            // find the selected item
        var selected = grid.get_masterTableView().get_selectedItems()[0];
            // get the key value
        var id = selected.getDataKeyValue("CategoryID");
            // perform the delete operation
        PageMethods.DeleteCategory(id, Reload);
    }
}

function RadGrid14_Command(sender, args) {
    // cancel commands from RadGrid (we'll handle them on our own)
    args.set_cancel(true);
```

```
        // find the master table view
        var tableView = $find("<%= RadGrid14.ClientID %>").get_masterTableView();
        // get the current page size (paging)
        var pageSize = tableView.get_pageSize();
        // get the sort expressions list (sorting)
        var sortExpression = tableView.get_sortExpressions().toString();
        // get the filter expressions list (filtering)
        var filterExpression = tableView.get_filterExpressions().toString();
        // where are we? Get the page.
        var currentPageIndex = sender.get_masterTableView().get_currentPageIndex();

        // if the user was filtering records then reset the current page index.
        if (args.get_commandName() == "Filter")
            currentPageIndex = 0;

        // reload the data
        PageMethods.GetCategories(currentPageIndex * pageSize,
                                  pageSize,
                                  sortExpression,
                                  filterExpression,
                                  BindGrid);

        // we only need to count the items again if the filter changed
        if (args.get_commandName() == "Filter") {
            PageMethods.GetCatCount(filterExpression, updateVirtualItemCount);
        }
    }

</script>

</telerik:RadCodeBlock>
```

Listing 6-35 shows the implementation of the static methods in the code behind file that are decorated with the WebMethod property that will be called from the client code using the PageMethods collection in the script manager. Remember that, to enable this type of call, you need to set the script manager's EnablePageMethods property to true. The methods perform the real operations against the datasource, which in this case is a database table.

Listing 6-35. *Code Behind File with the Declaration of the Methods to Be Called from Client Code*

```
[WebMethod]
public static List<MyCategory> GetCategories(int startRowIndex,
                                             int maximumRows,
                                             string sortExpression,
                                             string filterExpression)
{
    List<MyCategory> categoriesList = new List<MyCategory>();

    string where = string.Empty;
    if (!string.IsNullOrEmpty(filterExpression))
    {
        where += filterExpression;
    }
```

```
StringBuilder sqlBuilder = new StringBuilder();
sqlBuilder.AppendLine("DECLARE @startRowIndex int");
sqlBuilder.AppendLine("DECLARE @maximumRows int");
sqlBuilder.AppendLine(String.Format("SET @startRowIndex = {0}", startRowIndex));
sqlBuilder.AppendLine(String.Format("SET @maximumRows = {0}", maximumRows));
sqlBuilder.AppendLine("DECLARE @first_id int, @startRow int ");
sqlBuilder.AppendLine("DECLARE @sIndex INT");
sqlBuilder.AppendLine("SET @sIndex = @startRowIndex + 1");
sqlBuilder.AppendLine("SET ROWCOUNT 0");
sqlBuilder.AppendLine(string.Format("SELECT CategoryID, CategoryName,
                      Description, ROW_NUMBER() OVER (ORDER BY {0}) [RowNum]",
                      (!string.IsNullOrEmpty(sortExpression) ? sortExpression :
                      "CategoryID")));
sqlBuilder.AppendLine("INTO #TempCategories");
sqlBuilder.AppendLine("FROM Categories");
if (!string.IsNullOrEmpty(where))
    sqlBuilder.AppendLine(string.Format("WHERE {0}", where));
sqlBuilder.AppendLine(string.Format("ORDER BY {0}",
                      (!string.IsNullOrEmpty(sortExpression) ?
                              sortExpression
                              : "CategoryID")));
sqlBuilder.AppendLine("SET ROWCOUNT @sIndex");
sqlBuilder.AppendLine("SELECT @first_id = RowNum");
sqlBuilder.AppendLine("FROM #TempCategories ");
sqlBuilder.AppendLine("ORDER BY RowNum");
sqlBuilder.AppendLine("SET ROWCOUNT @maximumRows");
sqlBuilder.AppendLine("SELECT c.*");
sqlBuilder.AppendLine("FROM #TempCategories c");
sqlBuilder.AppendLine("WHERE RowNum >= @first_id");
if (!string.IsNullOrEmpty(where))
    sqlBuilder.AppendLine(string.Format(" AND {0}", where));
sqlBuilder.AppendLine(string.Format("ORDER BY {0}",
                      (!string.IsNullOrEmpty(sortExpression) ?
                              sortExpression
                              : "CategoryID")));
sqlBuilder.AppendLine("DROP TABLE #TempCategories");

string sql = sqlBuilder.ToString();
using (SqlConnection connection = new
    SqlConnection(ConfigurationManager
                  .ConnectionStrings["NorthwindConnectionString"]
                  .ConnectionString))
{
    connection.Open();
    using (SqlCommand selectCommand = new SqlCommand(sql, connection))
    {
        using (SqlDataReader rd = selectCommand.ExecuteReader())
        {
            try
            {
                while (rd.Read())
                {
                    var cat = new MyCategory();
                    cat.CategoryID = int.Parse(rd[0].ToString());
```

```
                    cat.CategoryName = rd[1].ToString();
                    cat.Description = rd[2].ToString();
                    categoriesList.Add(cat);
                }
            }
            catch (Exception ex)
            {
                // error handling logic here
            }
        }

    }
}
return categoriesList;
}

[WebMethod]
public static int GetCatCount(string filterExpressions)
{
    string sql = string.Format("SELECT COUNT(*) from Categories {0}",
                               (string.IsNullOrEmpty(filterExpressions)
                                    ? ""
                                    : string.Format(" WHERE {0}", filterExpressions)));
    int recordCount;

    using (SqlConnection connection = new
        SqlConnection(ConfigurationManager
                        .ConnectionStrings["NorthwindConnectionString"]
                        .ConnectionString))
    {
        connection.Open();
        using (SqlCommand selectCommand = new SqlCommand(sql, connection))
        {
            recordCount = int.Parse(selectCommand.ExecuteScalar().ToString());
        }
    }

    return recordCount;
}

[WebMethod]
public static string AddCategory(string name, string description)
{
    string result = "OK";

    try
    {
        MyCategory cat = new MyCategory();
        cat.CategoryName = name;
        cat.Description = description;
        cat.Insert();
    }
```

```
    catch (Exception ex)
    {
        result = ex.Message;
    }

    return result;
}

[WebMethod]
public static string UpdateCategory(string id, string name, string description)
{
    string result = "OK";

    try
    {
        MyCategory cat = new MyCategory(int.Parse(id));
        cat.CategoryName = name;
        cat.Description = description;
        cat.Update();
    }
    catch (Exception ex)
    {
        result = ex.Message;
    }

    return result;
}

[WebMethod]
public static string DeleteCategory(string id)
{
    string result = "OK";

    try
    {
        MyCategory cat = new MyCategory(int.Parse(id));
        cat.Delete();
    }
    catch (Exception ex)
    {
        result = ex.Message;
    }

    return result;
}
```

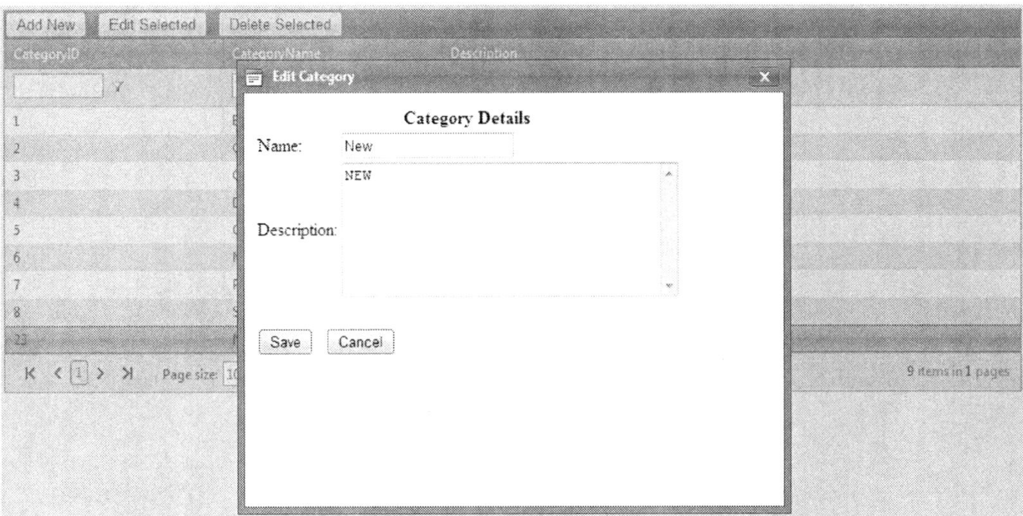

Figure 6-22. *RadGrid displaying a RadWindow to perform operations using the client side API*

Summary

In this chapter, we have begun examining the Data RadControls and the most important capabilities they expose for the purpose of manipulating data. Specifically, we have looked at the `RadComboBox` and `RadGrid`.

`RadComboBox` is an advanced drop-down control that can be configured to load all items initially or particular items on demand. It supports different binding mechanisms including ASP.NET 2.0+ data sources, web services, and in-memory collections. It also supports item templates to enhance the usability of the control and present a lot of more information and functionality in a drop-down manner. The client-side API allows you to modify the control and its items by providing methods and properties to enable, disable, add, or remove items on the client and make them available on the server. It supports caching and automatic (or codeless) loading on demand.

`RadGrid` is a powerful grid component that has a vast amount of functionality. It supports simple, declarative, and advanced server-side data binding as well as client-side binding, which greatly improves performance and responsiveness of the application. You can configure `RadGrid` to allow data operations such as sorting, paging, scrolling, grouping, filtering, and more to provide a rich experience to the end user.

`RadGrid` natively supports inserting, updating, and deleting records in the datasource. You can configure the control to use the built-in column editors or build your own. Also, you can use inline editing and insert forms, or you can use a web user control for the job if you need complex operations or calculations.

In the next chapter, we will complete our coverage of the Data RadControls with a look at the `RadFilter`, `RadListView`, and `RadListBox` controls.

CHAPTER 7

■ ■ ■

Data RadControls, Part 2

This chapter completes the coverage of the RadControls begun in Chapter 6. Here, we will discuss the `RadFilter`, `RadListBox`, and `RadListView` controls.

`RadFilter` is a brand-new control built from the ground up to enable you to create complex filtering expressions based on the data type of the source files. It can be integrated within other controls, such as `RadGrid` and `RadListView`. `RadListBox` is a control designed to display a list items that can be sorted, reordered, and transferred to or from other `RadListBox` controls. `RadListView` is an enhanced version of the ASP.NET `ListView` control, with integrated editing, paging, sorting, grouping, and other capabilities. It allows you customize the layout of the items displayed.

RadFilter

The `RadFilter` control is intended to help users build complex, strongly typed filters for data-bound controls such as `RadListView` and `RadGrid`. The control is capable of loading the structure of the bound control's datasource to which it is linked.

You can also build the list of field editors declaratively at design time. All you need to do is define the field name and data type for each field editor in the list.

When `RadFilter` is linked to a data-bound control, you use the `FilterContainerID` property to indicate the ID of the control. `RadFilter` will automatically build the list of field editors to create the filter expression. When you use the `FilterContainerID` property, if you have defined field editors declaratively, they will be overwriten with those created from the data-bound control. Normally, you will have different `RadFilter` instances for different purposes, and you won't mix declarative with automatically created field editors.

`RadFilter` is built on the provider model, so it uses query providers to understand and correctly apply the filter expressions to the controls or to create string expressions to use manually. As of this writing, five built-in providers are available for building and evaluating query expressions:

- `RadFilterSqlQueryProvider`
- `RadFilterDynamicLinqQueryProvider`
- `RadFilterOqlQueryProvider`
- `RadFilterEntitySqlQueryProvider`
- `RadFilterListViewQueryProvider`

While the built-in providers cover almost all scenarios, you can also create your own provider to support your application's particular needs.

The example in Listing 7-1 demonstrates how to create a `RadFilter` control with declaratively defined field editors, handle the `OnApply` server-side event, and generate a string representation built on the selected provider. Figure 7-1 shows how `RadFilter` looks when a filter expression is built.

Listing 7-1. *RadFilter with Declaratively Defined Field Editors, Using the SQL Query Provider*

ASPX Page

```
<telerik:RadFilter ID="RadFilter1" runat="server"
        OnApplyExpressions="RadFilter1_ApplyExpressions">
    <FieldEditors>
        <telerik:RadFilterTextFieldEditor FieldName="City" />
        <telerik:RadFilterTextFieldEditor FieldName="State" />
        <telerik:RadFilterNumericFieldEditor FieldName="Price" />
        <telerik:RadFilterBooleanFieldEditor DataType="System.Boolean"
                                            FieldName="IsActive" />
        <telerik:RadFilterDateFieldEditor DataType="System.DateTime"
                                         FieldName="ActivationDate" />
    </FieldEditors>
</telerik:RadFilter>

<asp:Label ID="lblExpression" runat="server"></asp:Label>
```

Code Behind

```
protected void RadFilter1_ApplyExpressions(object sender, EventArgs e)
{
    RadFilterSqlQueryProvider provider = new RadFilterSqlQueryProvider();
    provider.ProcessGroup(RadFilter1.RootGroup);
    lblExpression.Text = provider.Result;
}
```

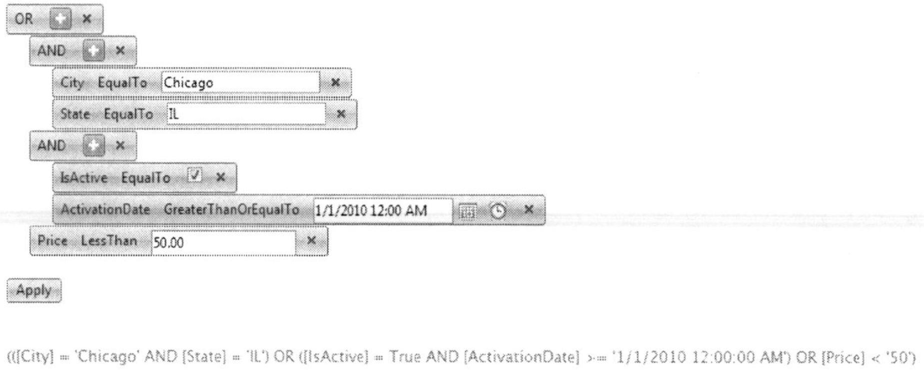

Figure 7-1. *RadFilter provides a highly intuitive interface for creating filtering expressions.*

If you need to add filter expressions manually, you can do so by adding items to the `RootGroup` property with the `AddExpression` method, as shown in Listing 7-2. Figure 7-2 shows how `RadFilter` looks with the manually added filter expression.

Listing 7-2. *Manually Adding a Filter Expression*

```
RadFilterEqualToFilterExpression<int> expression = new
                        RadFilterEqualToFilterExpression<int>("Price");
RadFilter1.RootGroup.AddExpression(expression);
expression.Value = 50;
```

Figure 7-2. *RadFilter with a manually added expression*

The example in Listing 7-3 shows how to integrate `RadFilter` with `RadListView` to create an interactive query system for your users. You integrate the controls by defining `RadFilter`'s `FilterContainerID` property with the name of the `RadListView` you want to communicate with. When working in this mode, `RadFilter`'s Apply button works automatically to apply the filter to `RadListView`, so no extra code is needed. Figure 7-3 shows the integrated controls.

Listing 7-3. *Integrating RadFilter with RadListView*

```
ASPX Page

<telerik:RadFilter ID="RadFilter3" runat="server"
                   FilterContainerID="RadListView1">
</telerik:RadFilter>

<telerik:RadListView ID="RadListView1" runat="server"
                     AllowPaging="True"
                     DataKeyNames="EmployeeID"
                     DataSourceID="SqlDataSource1"
                     Skin="WebBlue">
    <LayoutTemplate>
         <div class="RadListView RadListViewFloated RadListView_Default">
            <div class="rlvFloated">
                <div ID="itemPlaceholder" runat="server">
                </div>
            </div>
        </div>
    </LayoutTemplate>
    <ItemTemplate>
        <div class="idcard">
            <div class="companyName">
                My Company
            </div>
```

```
                <div class="picture">
                     <asp:Image ID="employeePhoto" Width="150"
                          Height="200"
                          ImageAlign="Middle"
                          runat="server"
                          ImageUrl='<%# "Images/employees/"
                                    + Eval("EmployeeID")
                                    + ".jpg" %>' />
               </div>
                <div class="employeeInfo">
                    <div class="employeeName">
                    <asp:Label ID="lblName" runat="server"
                            Text='<%# Eval("LastName") + ", " + Eval("FirstName") %>'>
                    </asp:Label>
                    </div>
                    <div class="employeeTitle">
                    <asp:Label ID="lblTitle" runat="server"
                            Text='<%# Eval("Title") %>'>
                    </asp:Label>
                    </div>
                    <div class="employeeOffice">
                    Works in our office located on:
                    <asp:Label ID="lblOffice" runat="server"
                            Text='<%# Eval("City") + ", " + Eval("Country") %>'>
                    </asp:Label>
                    </div>
                </div>
            </div>
        </ItemTemplate>
        <AlternatingItemTemplate>
            <div class="idcard">
                <div class="companyName">
                    My Company
                </div>
                <div class="picture">
                     <asp:Image ID="employeePhoto" Width="150"
                          Height="200"
                          ImageAlign="Middle"
                          runat="server"
                          ImageUrl='<%# "Images/employees/"
                                    + Eval("EmployeeID")
                                    + ".jpg" %>' />
                </div>
                <div class="employeeInfo">
                    <div class="employeeName">
                    <asp:Label ID="lblName" runat="server"
                            Text='<%# Eval("LastName") + ", " + Eval("FirstName") %>'>
                    </asp:Label>
                    </div>
                    <div class="employeeTitle">
                    <asp:Label ID="lblTitle" runat="server"
                            Text='<%# Eval("Title") %>'>
                    </asp:Label>
                    </div>
```

```
                <div class="employeeOffice">
                Works in our office located on:
                <asp:Label ID="lblOffice" runat="server"
                        Text='<%# Eval("City") + ", " + Eval("Country") %>'>
                </asp:Label>
                </div>
            </div>
        </div>
    </AlternatingItemTemplate>
</telerik:RadListView>
<asp:SqlDataSource ID="SqlDataSource1" runat="server"
    ConnectionString="<%$ ConnectionStrings:NorthwindConnectionString %>"
    SelectCommand="SELECT [EmployeeID], [LastName], [FirstName],
                          [Title], [HireDate], [ReportsTo], [City],
                          [Country], [Extension]
                     FROM [Employees]">
</asp:SqlDataSource>
</ContentTemplate>
</asp:UpdatePanel>
```

Figure 7-3. *RadFilter displays the filter expression applied to RadListView.*

RadListView

Telerik RadListView is an advanced data control that is similar to the original ASP.NET ListView control. RadListView includes many useful features, such as integration with predefined layouts, a client-side API, and different modes for data binding. It can also support paging, sorting, filtering, selecting, and other functionality.

You work with RadListView by specifying the datasource (either declaratively or programmatically) and the layout templates that will contain the necessary controls for the user to interact with the data.

Implementing Data Binding for RadListView

RadListView supports binding to the same sources as other data controls in the suite. You can bind it to ASP.NET 2.0+ datasource components when using declarative or simple data binding, and to any datasource when implementing advanced data binding. For a RadListView to support functionality such as inserting, updating, deleting, paging, sorting, and so forth, you must use the declarative or advanced data-binding method.

Listing 7-4 demonstrates a RadListView control that implements the declarative binding method. Notice the use of the RadDataPager control to provide paging capabilities. RadDataPager has a property called PagedControlID, which maps to the control to which it will provide the paging—in this case, RadListView1. Figure 7-4 shows the resulting RadListView.

Listing 7-4. *RadListView Declarative Data Binding*

ASPX Page

```
<telerik:RadListView ID="RadListView1" runat="server"
                     DataKeyNames="ProductID"
                     DataSourceID="ProductsDataSource"
                     ItemPlaceholderID="itemsContainer"
                     AllowPaging="true"
                     PageSize="10">
    <LayoutTemplate>
        <table border="1" cellpadding="3" cellspacing="1">
            <thead>
                <tr>
                    <th>ID</th>
                    <th>Name</th>
                    <th>Category</th>
                    <th>Qty Per Unit</th>
                </tr>
            </thead>
            <tbody>
                <asp:Literal id="itemsContainer" runat="server">

                </asp:Literal>
            </tbody>
```

```
                <tfoot>
                    <tr>
                        <td colspan="4">
                            <telerik:RadDataPager ID="RadDataPager1" runat="server"
                                                PagedControlID="RadListView1">
                                <Fields>
                                    <telerik:RadDataPagerButtonField FieldType="First" />
                                    <telerik:RadDataPagerButtonField FieldType="Prev" />
                                    <telerik:RadDataPagerButtonField FieldType="Numeric" />
                                    <telerik:RadDataPagerButtonField FieldType="Next" />
                                    <telerik:RadDataPagerButtonField FieldType="Last" />
                                </Fields>
                            </telerik:RadDataPager>
                        </td>
                    </tr>
                </tfoot>
            </table>
        </LayoutTemplate>
        <AlternatingItemTemplate>
            <tr style="background-color:Teal; color:White">
                <td><%# Eval("ProductID")%></td>
                <td><%# Eval("ProductName") %></td>
                <td><%# Eval("CategoryName") %></td>
                <td><%# Eval("QuantityPerUnit")%></td>
            </tr>
        </AlternatingItemTemplate>
        <ItemTemplate>
            <tr style="color:Teal">
                <td><%# Eval("ProductID")%></td>
                <td><%# Eval("ProductName") %></td>
                <td><%# Eval("CategoryName") %></td>
                <td><%# Eval("QuantityPerUnit")%></td>
            </tr>
        </ItemTemplate>
</telerik:RadListView>

<asp:SqlDataSource ID="ProductsDataSource" runat="server"
        ConnectionString="<%$ ConnectionStrings:NorthwindConnectionString %>"
        SelectCommand="SELECT [ProductID], [ProductName], [QuantityPerUnit], [CategoryName]
                        FROM [Products] INNER JOIN [Categories]
                             ON [Products].[CategoryID] = [Categories].[CategoryID]">
</asp:SqlDataSource>
```

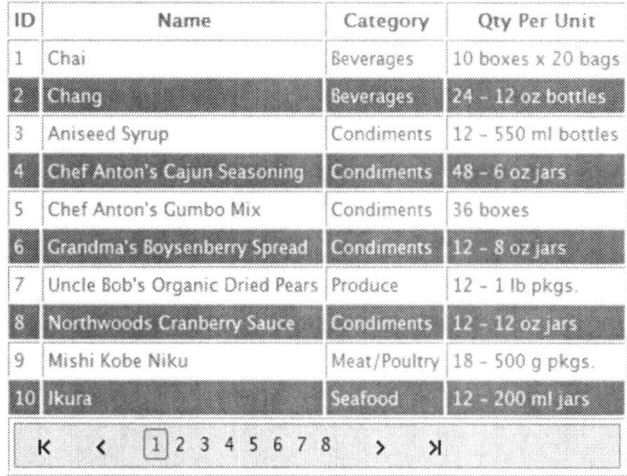
ID	Name	Category	Qty Per Unit
1	Chai	Beverages	10 boxes x 20 bags
2	Chang	Beverages	24 - 12 oz bottles
3	Aniseed Syrup	Condiments	12 - 550 ml bottles
4	Chef Anton's Cajun Seasoning	Condiments	48 - 6 oz jars
5	Chef Anton's Gumbo Mix	Condiments	36 boxes
6	Grandma's Boysenberry Spread	Condiments	12 - 8 oz jars
7	Uncle Bob's Organic Dried Pears	Produce	12 - 1 lb pkgs.
8	Northwoods Cranberry Sauce	Condiments	12 - 12 oz jars
9	Mishi Kobe Niku	Meat/Poultry	18 - 500 g pkgs.
10	Ikura	Seafood	12 - 200 ml jars

Figure 7-4. *With declarative data binding, RadListView can implement operations such as paging.*

Listing 7-5 shows how RadListView is implemented using simple data binding. This type of data binding is done with the DataSource property with a call to the DataBind() method. In the example, the datasource is a DataTable presenting information from the Categories table in the database. Figure 7-5 shows the result.

Listing 7-5. *RadListView Simple Data Binding*

ASPX Page

```
<telerik:RadListView ID="RadListView2" runat="server"
                     DataKeyNames="CategoryID"
                     ItemPlaceholderID="itemsContainer">
    <LayoutTemplate>
        <table border="1" cellpadding="3" cellspacing="1">
            <thead>
                <tr>
                    <th>ID</th>
                    <th>Name</th>
                </tr>
            </thead>
            <tbody>
                <asp:Literal id="itemsContainer" runat="server">

                </asp:Literal>
            </tbody>
        </table>
    </LayoutTemplate>
    <AlternatingItemTemplate>
        <tr style="background-color:Teal; color:White">
            <td><%# Eval("CategoryID")%></td>
            <td><%# Eval("CategoryName") %></td>
        </tr>
    </AlternatingItemTemplate>
```

```
    <ItemTemplate>
        <tr style="color:Teal">
            <td><%# Eval("CategoryID")%></td>
            <td><%# Eval("CategoryName") %></td>
        </tr>
    </ItemTemplate>
</telerik:RadListView>

Code Behind

protected void Page_Load(object sender, EventArgs e)
{
    if (Page.IsPostBack) return;
    LoadDataForSimpleDatabind();
}

private void LoadDataForSimpleDatabind()
{
    RadListView2.DataSource = GetCategoriesDataTable();
    RadListView2.DataBind();
}

private DataTable GetCategoriesDataTable()
{
    string ConnString = ConfigurationManager
                        .ConnectionStrings["NorthwindConnectionString"]
                        .ConnectionString;
    string query = "SELECT [CategoryID], [CategoryName]";
    query += "       FROM [Categories]";
    DataTable myDataTable = new DataTable();
    using (SqlConnection conn = new SqlConnection(ConnString))
    {
        using (SqlDataAdapter adapter = new SqlDataAdapter())
        {
            adapter.SelectCommand = new SqlCommand(query, conn);

            try
            {
                conn.Open();
                adapter.Fill(myDataTable);
            }
            catch (Exception ex)
            {
            }
            finally
            {
                conn.Close();
            }
        }
    }
    return myDataTable;
}
```

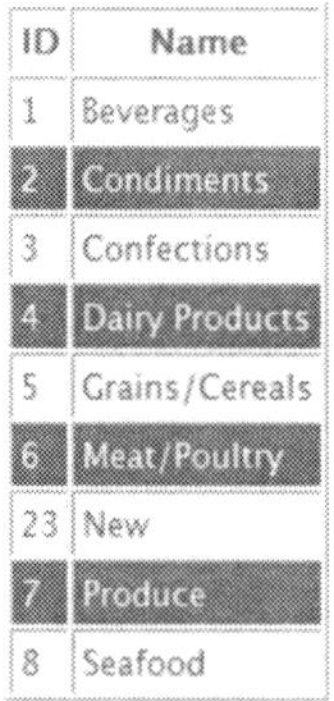

ID	Name
1	Beverages
2	Condiments
3	Confections
4	Dairy Products
5	Grains/Cereals
6	Meat/Poultry
23	New
7	Produce
8	Seafood

Figure 7-5. *RadListView displays only the items when implemented with simple data binding.*

Finally, Listing 7-6 shows RadListView implemented using advanced data binding. The binding operation is done in the OnNeedDataSource event. This event works the same as with RadGrid, It fires whenever RadListView needs the data from the source, so you don't need to worry about implementing data-loading methods in different events. Remember not to call neither Rebind() or DataBind() inside the OnNeedDataSource event handler. Figure 7-6 shows how RadListView looks with advanced data binding.

Listing 7-6. *RadListView Advanced Data Binding*

ASPX Page

```
<telerik:RadListView ID="RadListView3" runat="server"
                     DataKeyNames="ProductID"
                     ItemPlaceholderID="itemsContainer"
                     AllowPaging="true"
                     PageSize="10"
                     OnNeedDataSource="RadListView_NeedDataSource">
    <LayoutTemplate>
        <table border="1" cellpadding="3" cellspacing="1">
            <thead>
                <tr>
                    <th>ID</th>
                    <th>Name</th>
                    <th>Category</th>
                    <th>Qty Per Unit</th>
                </tr>
            </thead>
            <tbody>
                <asp:Literal id="itemsContainer" runat="server">

                </asp:Literal>
            </tbody>
```

```
                <tfoot>
                    <tr>
                        <td colspan="4">
                            <telerik:RadDataPager ID="RadDataPager1" runat="server"
                                        PagedControlID="RadListView3">
                                <Fields>
                                    <telerik:RadDataPagerButtonField FieldType="First" />
                                    <telerik:RadDataPagerButtonField FieldType="Prev" />
                                    <telerik:RadDataPagerButtonField FieldType="Numeric" />
                                    <telerik:RadDataPagerButtonField FieldType="Next" />
                                    <telerik:RadDataPagerButtonField FieldType="Last" />
                                </Fields>
                            </telerik:RadDataPager>
                        </td>
                    </tr>
                </tfoot>
            </table>
        </LayoutTemplate>
        <AlternatingItemTemplate>
            <tr style="background-color:Teal; color:White">
                <td><%# Eval("ProductID")%></td>
                <td><%# Eval("ProductName") %></td>
                <td><%# Eval("CategoryName") %></td>
                <td><%# Eval("QuantityPerUnit")%></td>
            </tr>
        </AlternatingItemTemplate>
        <ItemTemplate>
            <tr style="color:Teal">
                <td><%# Eval("ProductID")%></td>
                <td><%# Eval("ProductName") %></td>
                <td><%# Eval("CategoryName") %></td>
                <td><%# Eval("QuantityPerUnit")%></td>
            </tr>
        </ItemTemplate>
</telerik:RadListView>
```

Code Behind

```
protected void RadListView_NeedDataSource(object sender, EventArgs e)
{
    RadListView listView = (RadListView) sender;
    listView.DataSource = GetProductsDataTable();
}

private DataTable GetProductsDataTable()
{
    string ConnString = ConfigurationManager
                            .ConnectionStrings["NorthwindConnectionString"]
                            .ConnectionString;
    string query = "SELECT [ProductID], [ProductName], [QuantityPerUnit], [CategoryName],";
    query += "                [Products].[CategoryID], [Products].[Discontinued]";
    query += "         FROM [Products] INNER JOIN [Categories]";
    query += "           ON [Products].[CategoryID] = [Categories].[CategoryID]";
    DataTable myDataTable = new DataTable();
```

```
    using (SqlConnection conn = new SqlConnection(ConnString))
    {
        using (SqlDataAdapter adapter = new SqlDataAdapter())
        {
            adapter.SelectCommand = new SqlCommand(query, conn);

            try
            {
                conn.Open();
                adapter.Fill(myDataTable);
            }
            catch (Exception ex)
            {
            }
            finally
            {
                conn.Close();
            }
        }
    }
    return myDataTable;
}
```

ID	Name	Category	Qty Per Unit
1	Chai	Beverages	10 boxes x 20 bags
2	Chang	Beverages	24 - 12 oz bottles
3	Aniseed Syrup	Condiments	12 - 550 ml bottles
4	Chef Anton's Cajun Seasoning	Condiments	48 - 6 oz jars
5	Chef Anton's Gumbo Mix	Condiments	36 boxes
6	Grandma's Boysenberry Spread	Condiments	12 - 8 oz jars
7	Uncle Bob's Organic Dried Pears	Produce	12 - 1 lb pkgs.
8	Northwoods Cranberry Sauce	Condiments	12 - 12 oz jars
9	Mishi Kobe Niku	Meat/Poultry	18 - 500 g pkgs.
10	Ikura	Seafood	12 - 200 ml jars

K < 1 2 3 4 5 6 7 8 > >|

Figure 7-6. *RadListView implementing advanced data binding*

Handling RadListView Editing Operations

To support insert, update, and delete operations, `RadListView` implements a simple mechanism to handle the `OnItemCommand` event. The event signature includes a `RadListViewCommandEventArgs` parameter that has a `ListViewItem` property that gives you access to the item being accesed in the list of items. If you define one or more column names with the `DataKeyNames` property, you can use the `GetDataKeyValue()` method to get the identifier for the item being updated or deleted.

You can have `RadListView` handle the editing operations automatically or manually. When done automatically, you normally use declarative data binding with a datasource that handles these operations. If you want to do it manually, you need to handle the OnItemCommand event; in the event handler, you recognize the operation and perform the action as requested.

The EditItemTemplate and InsertItemTemplate are also created to provide the data-entry form where users can modify and insert new items, respectively. The OnItemCommand event handler is in charge of recognizing the command being sent, along with the information to perform the editing operations. All interactions with the database are implemented using parameterized queries.

The example in Listing 7-7 demonstrates the manual approach to handling editing operations. RadListView handles the OnNeedDataSource and OnItemCommand events to perform the binding and editing operations, respectively. Figure 7-7 shows the result.

Listing 7-7. *Implementing Manual Editing Operations in RadListView Against a SQL Server Database*

ASPX Page

```
<telerik:RadListView ID="RadListView4" runat="server"
                     DataKeyNames="ProductID, CategoryID"
                     ItemPlaceholderID="itemsContainer"
                     AllowPaging="true"
                     PageSize="10"
                     OnNeedDataSource="RadListView_NeedDataSource"
                     OnItemCommand="RadListView4_ItemCommand">
    <LayoutTemplate>
                <table border="1">
                <thead>
                <tr>
                    <th>ID</th>
                    <th>Name</th>
                    <th>Category</th>
                    <th>Qty Per Unit</th>
                    <th>Discontinued</th>
                    <th><asp:Button ID="btnInsert" runat="server"
                                    Text="Insert"
                                    OnClick="btnInsert_Click" />
                    </th>
                </tr>
                </thead>
                <tbody>
                    <asp:Literal id="itemsContainer" runat="server">

                    </asp:Literal>
                </tbody>
                <tfoot>
                    <tr>
                        <td colspan="6">
                            <telerik:RadDataPager ID="RadDataPager1" runat="server"
                                          PagedControlID="RadListView4">
                                <Fields>
                                   <telerik:RadDataPagerButtonField FieldType="First" />
                                   <telerik:RadDataPagerButtonField FieldType="Prev" />
                                   <telerik:RadDataPagerButtonField FieldType="Numeric" />
```

```
                                        <telerik:RadDataPagerButtonField FieldType="Next" />
                                        <telerik:RadDataPagerButtonField FieldType="Last" />
                                    </Fields>
                                </telerik:RadDataPager>
                            </td>
                        </tr>
                    </tfoot>
                    </table>
        </LayoutTemplate>
        <AlternatingItemTemplate>
                <tr style="background-color:Teal; color:White">
                    <td><%# Eval("ProductID")%></td>
                    <td><%# Eval("ProductName") %></td>
                    <td><%# Eval("CategoryName") %></td>
                    <td><%# Eval("QuantityPerUnit")%></td>
                    <td><asp:CheckBox ID="chkDiscontinued" runat="server"
                                    Enabled="false"
                                    Checked='<%# Bind("Discontinued")%>' />
                    </td>
                    <td>
                        <asp:Button ID="btnEdit" runat="server"
                                    Text="Edit"
                                    CommandName="Edit" />
                        <asp:Button ID="btnDelete" runat="server"
                                Text="Delete"
                                OnClientClick="javascript:return ConfirmDelete(this);"
                                CommandName="Delete" />
                    </td>
                </tr>
        </AlternatingItemTemplate>
        <ItemTemplate>
                <tr style="color:Teal">
                    <td><%# Eval("ProductID")%></td>
                    <td><%# Eval("ProductName") %></td>
                    <td><%# Eval("CategoryName") %></td>
                    <td><%# Eval("QuantityPerUnit")%></td>
                    <td><asp:CheckBox ID="chkDiscontinued" runat="server"
                                    Enabled="false"
                                    Checked='<%# Bind("Discontinued")%>' />
                    </td>
                    <td>
                        <asp:Button ID="btnEdit" runat="server"
                                Text="Edit"
                                CommandName="Edit" />
                        <asp:Button ID="btnDelete" runat="server"
                                Text="Delete"
                                OnClientClick="javascript:return ConfirmDelete(this);"
                                CommandName="Delete" />
                    </td>
                </tr>
        </ItemTemplate>
```

```
<EditItemTemplate>
        <tr>
            <td><asp:Label ID="lblID" runat="server"
                            Text='<%# Eval("ProductID")%>'>
                </asp:Label>
            </td>
            <td><telerik:RadTextBox ID="txtName" runat="server"
                            Text='<%# Bind("ProductName") %>'>
                </telerik:RadTextBox>
            </td>
            <td><telerik:RadComboBox ID="rcbCategory" runat="server"
                            DataSourceID="CategoriesDataSource"
                            DataTextField="CategoryName"
                            DataValueField="CategoryID"
                            SelectedValue='<%# Bind("CategoryID") %>'>
                </telerik:RadComboBox>
            </td>
            <td><telerik:RadTextBox ID="txtQuantity" runat="server"
                            Text='<%# Bind("QuantityPerUnit")%>'>
                </telerik:RadTextBox>
            </td>
            <td><asp:CheckBox ID="chkDiscontinued" runat="server"
                            Enabled="true"
                            Checked='<%# Bind("Discontinued")%>' />
            </td>
            <td>
                <asp:Button ID="btnUpdate" runat="server"
                        Text="Update"
                        CommandName="Update" />
                <asp:Button ID="btnCancel" runat="server"
                        Text="Cancel"
                        CommandName="Cancel" />
            </td>
        </tr>
</EditItemTemplate>
<InsertItemTemplate>
        <tr>
            <td><asp:Label ID="lblID" runat="server"
                        Text='<%# Eval("ProductID")%>'>
                </asp:Label>
            </td>
            <td><telerik:RadTextBox ID="txtName" runat="server"
                        Text='<%# Bind("ProductName") %>'>
                </telerik:RadTextBox>
            </td>
            <td><telerik:RadComboBox ID="rcbCategory" runat="server"
                        DataSourceID="CategoriesDataSource"
                        DataTextField="CategoryName"
                        DataValueField="CategoryID"
                        SelectedValue='<%# Bind("CategoryID") %>'>
                </telerik:RadComboBox>
            </td>
```

```
                    <td><telerik:RadTextBox ID="txtQuantity" runat="server"
                                Text='<%# Bind("QuantityPerUnit")%>'>
                        </telerik:RadTextBox>
                    </td>
                    <td><asp:CheckBox ID="chkDiscontinued" runat="server"
                                Enabled="true"
                                Checked='<%# Bind("Discontinued")%>' />
                    </td>
                    <td>
                        <asp:Button ID="btnPerformInsert" runat="server"
                                Text="Insert"
                                CommandName="PerformInsert" />
                        <asp:Button ID="btnCancel" runat="server"
                                Text="Cancel"
                                CommandName="Cancel" />
                    </td>
                </tr>
        </InsertItemTemplate>
</telerik:RadListView>

<asp:SqlDataSource ID="CategoriesDataSource" runat="server"
        ConnectionString="<%$ ConnectionStrings:NorthwindConnectionString %>"
        SelectCommand="SELECT * FROM Categories">
</asp:SqlDataSource>

<telerik:RadWindowManager ID="RadWindowManager1" runat="server">
</telerik:RadWindowManager>

<script type="text/javascript">
     function ConfirmDelete(sender) {
            var callBackFn = function (args) {
                return args;
            }
            radconfirm('Are you sure you want to delete this item?', callBackFn);
        }
</script>
```

Code Behind

```
protected void RadListView4_ItemCommand(object sender, RadListViewCommandEventArgs e)
{
    SqlCommand cmd = new SqlCommand();
    string sql = string.Empty;
    switch (e.CommandName)
    {
        case RadListView.UpdateCommandName:
            {
                RadListViewEditableItem editedItem =➥
 (RadListViewEditableItem)e.ListViewItem;
                Hashtable newValues = new Hashtable();
                editedItem.ExtractValues(newValues);
                string productId = editedItem.GetDataKeyValue("ProductID").ToString();
                sql = "UPDATE Products ";
                sql += "  SET [ProductName] = @name, ";
```

```
                sql += "      [CategoryID] = @category, ";
                sql += "      [QuantityPerUnit] = @qty, ";
                sql += "      [Discontinued] = @discontinued ";
                sql += "WHERE [ProductID] = @productId ";
                cmd.Parameters.Add(new SqlParameter("name", newValues["ProductName"]));
                cmd.Parameters.Add(new SqlParameter("category", newValues["CategoryID"]));
                cmd.Parameters.Add(new SqlParameter("qty", newValues["QuantityPerUnit"]));
                cmd.Parameters.Add(new
                                SqlParameter("discontinued", newValues["Discontinued"]));
                cmd.Parameters.Add(new SqlParameter("productId", productId));
                cmd.CommandText = sql;
                ExecuteCommand(cmd);
            }
            break;
        case RadListView.PerformInsertCommandName:
            {
                RadListViewEditableItem insertedItem =
                                        (RadListViewEditableItem)e.ListViewItem;
                Hashtable newValues = new Hashtable();
                insertedItem.ExtractValues(newValues);
                sql = "INSERT INTO Products (ProductName, CategoryID, ";
                sql += "                    QuantityPerUnit, Discontinued) ";
                sql += " VALUES(@name, @category, @qty, @discontinued) ";
                cmd.Parameters.Add(new SqlParameter("name", newValues["ProductName"]));
                cmd.Parameters.Add(new SqlParameter("category", newValues["CategoryID"]));
                cmd.Parameters.Add(new SqlParameter("qty", newValues["QuantityPerUnit"]));
                cmd.Parameters.Add(new
                                SqlParameter("discontinued", newValues["Discontinued"]));
                cmd.CommandText = sql;
                ExecuteCommand(cmd);
                RadListView4.FindControl("btnInsert").Visible = true;
            }
            break;
        case RadListView.DeleteCommandName:
            {
                RadListViewDataItem insertedItem = (RadListViewDataItem)e.ListViewItem;
                Hashtable newValues = new Hashtable();
                insertedItem.ExtractValues(newValues);
                string productId = insertedItem.GetDataKeyValue("ProductID").ToString();
                sql = "DELETE FROM Products ";
                sql += "WHERE [ProductID] = @productId ";
                cmd.Parameters.Add(new SqlParameter("productId", productId));
                cmd.CommandText = sql;
                ExecuteCommand(cmd);
            }
            break;
        case RadListView.CancelCommandName:
            RadListView4.InsertItemPosition = RadListViewInsertItemPosition.None;
            RadListView4.FindControl("btnInsert").Visible = true;
            break;
    }
}
```

```
private void ExecuteCommand(SqlCommand cmd)
{

    string ConnString = ConfigurationManager
                              .ConnectionStrings["NorthwindConnectionString"]
                              .ConnectionString;
    using (SqlConnection conn = new SqlConnection(ConnString))
    {
        try
        {
            conn.Open();
            cmd.Connection = conn;
            cmd.ExecuteNonQuery();
        }
        finally
        {
            conn.Close();
        }
    }
}

protected void btnInsert_Click(object sender, EventArgs e)
{
    RadListView4.InsertItemPosition = RadListViewInsertItemPosition.FirstItem;
    RadListView4.Rebind();
    (sender as Button).Visible = false;
}
```

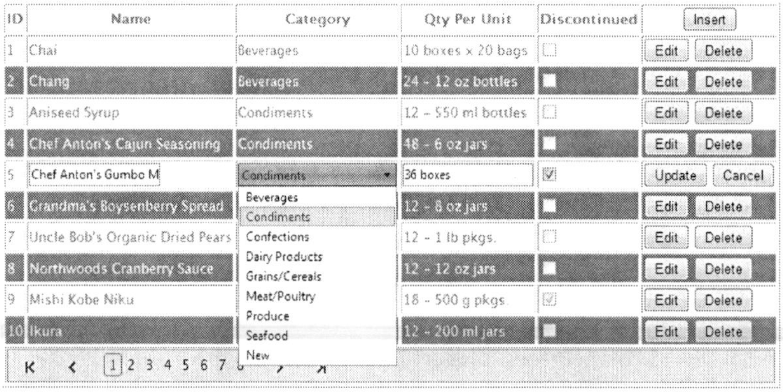

ID	Name	Category	Qty Per Unit	Discontinued	Insert
1	Chai	Beverages	10 boxes x 20 bags	☐	Edit Delete
2	Chang	Beverages	24 - 12 oz bottles	■	Edit Delete
3	Aniseed Syrup	Condiments	12 - 550 ml bottles	☐	Edit Delete
4	Chef Anton's Cajun Seasoning	Condiments	48 - 6 oz jars	■	Edit Delete
5	Chef Anton's Gumbo M	Condiments	36 boxes	☑	Update Cancel
6	Grandma's Boysenberry Spread	Beverages	12 - 8 oz jars	■	Edit Delete
7	Uncle Bob's Organic Dried Pears	Condiments Confections	12 - 1 lb pkgs.	☐	Edit Delete
8	Northwoods Cranberry Sauce	Dairy Products Grains/Cereals	12 - 12 oz jars	■	Edit Delete
9	Mishi Kobe Niku	Meat/Poultry Produce	18 - 500 g pkgs.	☑	Edit Delete
10	Ikura	Seafood	12 - 200 ml jars	■	Edit Delete

K < 1 2 3 4 5 6 7 8 New > >|

Figure 7-7. *Updating an item in RadListView with manual editing operations*

The example in Listing 7-8 works similarly to the one in Listing 7-7, but this `RadListView` works with automatic editing operations. A `LinqDataSource` object with automatic insert, update, and delete operations is used for interaction with the database table. `RadListView` will send the editing transactions to the `LinqDataSource` so they are resolved there. Notice that neither the `OnItemCommand` event nor the `OnNeedDataSource` event is handled here; instead, the `DataSourceID` property is used. The controls in the `InsertItemTemplate` and `EditItemTemplate` are bound to the datasource fields. Figure 7-8 shows the result.

Listing 7-8. *Implementing Automatic Editing Operations in RadListView*

ASPX Page

```
<telerik:RadListView ID="RadListView5" runat="server"
                     DataKeyNames="ProductID, CategoryID"
                     ItemPlaceholderID="itemsContainer"
                     AllowPaging="true"
                     PageSize="10"
                     DataSourceID="LinqDataSource1">
        <LayoutTemplate>
                   <table border="1">
                   <thead>
                   <tr>
                       <th>ID</th>
                       <th>Name</th>
                       <th>Category</th>
                       <th>Qty Per Unit</th>
                       <th>Discontinued</th>
                       <th><asp:Button ID="btnInsert1" runat="server"
                                       Text="Insert"
                                       OnClick="btnInsert1_Click" />
                       </th>
                   </tr>
                   </thead>
                   <tbody>
                       <asp:Literal id="itemsContainer" runat="server">
                       </asp:Literal>
                   </tbody>
                   <tfoot>
                       <tr>
                           <td colspan="6">
                               <telerik:RadDataPager ID="RadDataPager1" runat="server"
                                                     PagedControlID="RadListView5">
                                   <Fields>
                                      <telerik:RadDataPagerButtonField FieldType="First" />
                                      <telerik:RadDataPagerButtonField FieldType="Prev" />
                                      <telerik:RadDataPagerButtonField FieldType="Numeric" />
                                      <telerik:RadDataPagerButtonField FieldType="Next" />
                                      <telerik:RadDataPagerButtonField FieldType="Last" />
                                   </Fields>
                               </telerik:RadDataPager>
                           </td>
                       </tr>
                   </tfoot>
                   </table>
        </LayoutTemplate>
```

```
        <AlternatingItemTemplate>
                <tr style="background-color:Teal; color:White">
                    <td><%# Eval("ProductID")%></td>
                    <td><%# Eval("ProductName") %></td>
                    <td><%# Eval("CategoryID") %></td>
                    <td><%# Eval("QuantityPerUnit")%></td>
                    <td><asp:CheckBox ID="chkDiscontinued" runat="server"
                                    Enabled="false"
                                    Checked='<%# Bind("Discontinued")%>' />
                    </td>
                    <td>
                        <asp:Button ID="btnEdit" runat="server"
                                    Text="Edit"
                                    CommandName="Edit" />
                        <asp:Button ID="btnDelete" runat="server"
                                    Text="Delete"
                                    OnClientClick="javascript:return ➥
ConfirmDelete(this);"
                                    CommandName="Delete" />
                    </td>
                </tr>
        </AlternatingItemTemplate>
        <ItemTemplate>
                <tr style="color:Teal">
                    <td><%# Eval("ProductID")%></td>
                    <td><%# Eval("ProductName") %></td>
                    <td><%# Eval("CategoryID") %></td>
                    <td><%# Eval("QuantityPerUnit")%></td>
                    <td><asp:CheckBox ID="chkDiscontinued" runat="server"
                                    Enabled="false"
                                    Checked='<%# Bind("Discontinued")%>' />
                    </td>
                    <td>
                        <asp:Button ID="btnEdit" runat="server"
                                    Text="Edit"
                                    CommandName="Edit" />
                        <asp:Button ID="btnDelete" runat="server"
                                    Text="Delete"
                                    OnClientClick="javascript:return ➥
ConfirmDelete(this);"
                                    CommandName="Delete" />
                    </td>
                </tr>
        </ItemTemplate>
        <EditItemTemplate>
                <tr>
                    <td><asp:Label ID="lblID" runat="server"
                                    Text='<%# Eval("ProductID")%>'>
                        </asp:Label>
                    </td>
                    <td><telerik:RadTextBox ID="txtName" runat="server"
                                    Text='<%# Bind("ProductName") %>'>
                        </telerik:RadTextBox>
                    </td>
```

```
            <td><telerik:RadComboBox ID="rcbCategory" runat="server"
                              DataSourceID="CategoriesDataSource"
                              DataTextField="CategoryName"
                              DataValueField="CategoryID"
                              SelectedValue='<%# Bind("CategoryID") %>'>
                </telerik:RadComboBox>
            </td>
            <td><telerik:RadTextBox ID="txtQuantity" runat="server"
                              Text='<%# Bind("QuantityPerUnit")%>'>
                </telerik:RadTextBox>
            </td>
            <td><asp:CheckBox ID="chkDiscontinued" runat="server"
                              Enabled="true"
                              Checked='<%# Bind("Discontinued")%>' />
            </td>
            <td>
                <asp:Button ID="btnUpdate" runat="server"
                        Text="Update"
                        CommandName="Update" />
                <asp:Button ID="btnCancel" runat="server"
                        Text="Cancel"
                        CommandName="Cancel" />
            </td>
        </tr>
</EditItemTemplate>
<InsertItemTemplate>
        <tr>
            <td><asp:Label ID="lblID" runat="server"
                              Text='<%# Eval("ProductID")%>'>
                </asp:Label>
            </td>
            <td><telerik:RadTextBox ID="txtName" runat="server"
                              Text='<%# Bind("ProductName") %>'>
                </telerik:RadTextBox>
            </td>
            <td><telerik:RadComboBox ID="rcbCategory" runat="server"
                              DataSourceID="CategoriesDataSource"
                              DataTextField="CategoryName"
                              DataValueField="CategoryID"
                              SelectedValue='<%# Bind("CategoryID") %>'>
                </telerik:RadComboBox>
            </td>
            <td><telerik:RadTextBox ID="txtQuantity" runat="server"
                              Text='<%# Bind("QuantityPerUnit")%>'>
                </telerik:RadTextBox>
            </td>
            <td><asp:CheckBox ID="chkDiscontinued" runat="server"
                              Enabled="true"
                              Checked='<%# Bind("Discontinued")%>' />
            </td>
```

```
                    <td>
                        <asp:Button ID="btnUpdate" runat="server"
                                Text="Insert"
                                CommandName="PerformInsert" />
                        <asp:Button ID="btnCancel" runat="server"
                                Text="Cancel"
                                CommandName="Cancel" />
                    </td>
                </tr>
        </InsertItemTemplate>
</telerik:RadListView>

    <asp:LinqDataSource ID="LinqDataSource1" runat="server"
                ContextTypeName="WebApplication1.NorthwindDataContext"
                EnableDelete="True"
                EnableInsert="True"
                EnableUpdate="True"
                EntityTypeName=""
                TableName="Products">
    </asp:LinqDataSource>
```

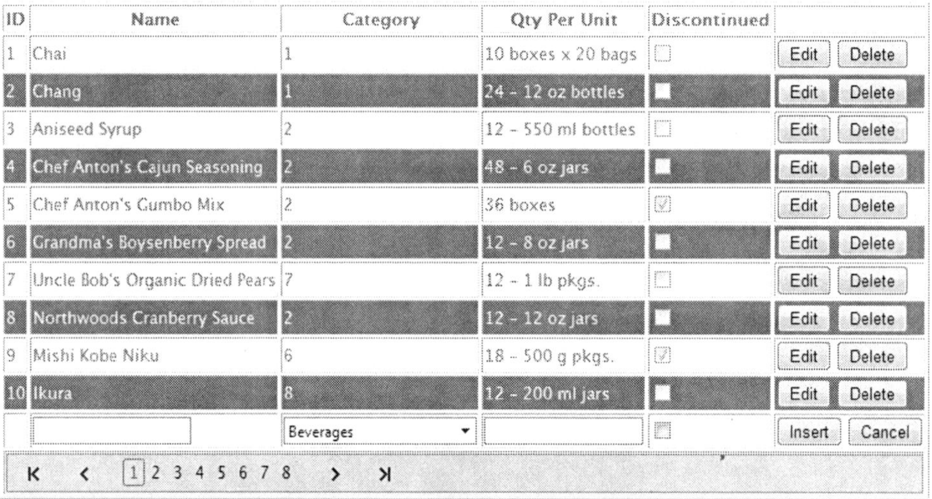

ID	Name	Category	Qty Per Unit	Discontinued	
1	Chai	1	10 boxes x 20 bags	☐	Edit Delete
2	Chang	1	24 - 12 oz bottles	☐	Edit Delete
3	Aniseed Syrup	2	12 - 550 ml bottles	☐	Edit Delete
4	Chef Anton's Cajun Seasoning	2	48 - 6 oz jars	☐	Edit Delete
5	Chef Anton's Gumbo Mix	2	36 boxes	☑	Edit Delete
6	Grandma's Boysenberry Spread	2	12 - 8 oz jars	☐	Edit Delete
7	Uncle Bob's Organic Dried Pears	7	12 - 1 lb pkgs.	☐	Edit Delete
8	Northwoods Cranberry Sauce	2	12 - 12 oz jars	☐	Edit Delete
9	Mishi Kobe Niku	6	18 - 500 g pkgs.	☑	Edit Delete
10	Ikura	8	12 - 200 ml jars	☐	Edit Delete
		Beverages		☐	Insert Cancel

K < 1 2 3 4 5 6 7 8 > >|

Figure 7-8. *Automatic editing operations implemented in RadListView against a LINQ datasource*

Working with RadListView Templates

Unlike RadGrid or RadComboBox, RadListView doesn't have a predefined layout; instead, you must define the layout yourself. RadListView provides the following templates for you to build your layout:

- LayoutTemplate: This is a mandatory template that defines the overall layout. Here, you define the header, footer, and paging elements. It must contain an element designated as the item placeholder, meaning you must define an ASP.NET PlaceHolder element, a Literal, or any element with the runat="server" attribute. The ID of the element must be defined in RadListView's ItemPlaceholderID property or its ID must be exactly "itemPlaceholder".
- ItemTemplate: This a mandatory template that defines the layout of each data-bound item when RadListView is not in edit mode. This template is also known as a data template.
- AlternatingItemTemplate: This template acts the same as ItemTemplate, but is defined to handle a different appearance for odd items (ItemTemplate is used for even items). If you don't specify this template, all items will use the layout in ItemTemplate.
- EmptyDataTemplate: This template is used when RadListView's datasource doesn't return any rows of data.
- EmptyItemTemplate: This template is when there are no more data items to display in the last row of the current data page.
- ItemSeparatorTemplate: This template defines the style for a separator item (if needed).
- EditItemTemplate: This template is used for rendering the edit form that will contain all the controls to capture data modifications to existing rows of data in the datasource.
- InsertItemTemplate: This template is used for rendering the form that will contain all the controls to capture data for new rows in the datasource.
- SelectItemTemplate: This template is used for the layout of the selected rows in the control.
- GroupTemplate: This template is used when grouping is enabled. It will render the layout for the group items.
- GroupSeparatorTemplate: This template is for the layout of the separator item in the group items.

Building your layouts through templates has the advantage of letting you define whatever you need for your bound items. However, this freedom comes with a price: You must build all the templates, including the edit and insert templates, because RadListView doesn't come with integrated editors as RadGrid does.

To help you out with the definition of templates, RadListView includes predefined layouts that give you a starting point to build your layout. To use a predefined layout, use the SmartTag and select Open Layout Editor, as shown in Figure 7-9.

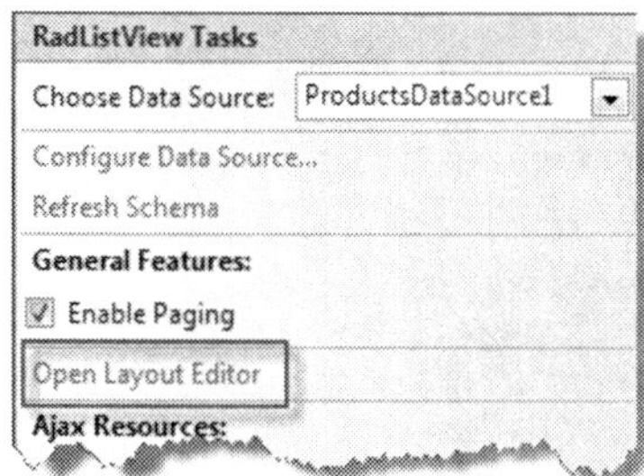

Figure 7-9. *RadListView Open Layout Editor option in the SmartTag*

As shown in Figure 7-10, the layout editor lets you define one of six possible layouts for your `RadListView` and the skin to be applied. You can decide to include everything necessary to support editing operations, as well as enable selection and paging.

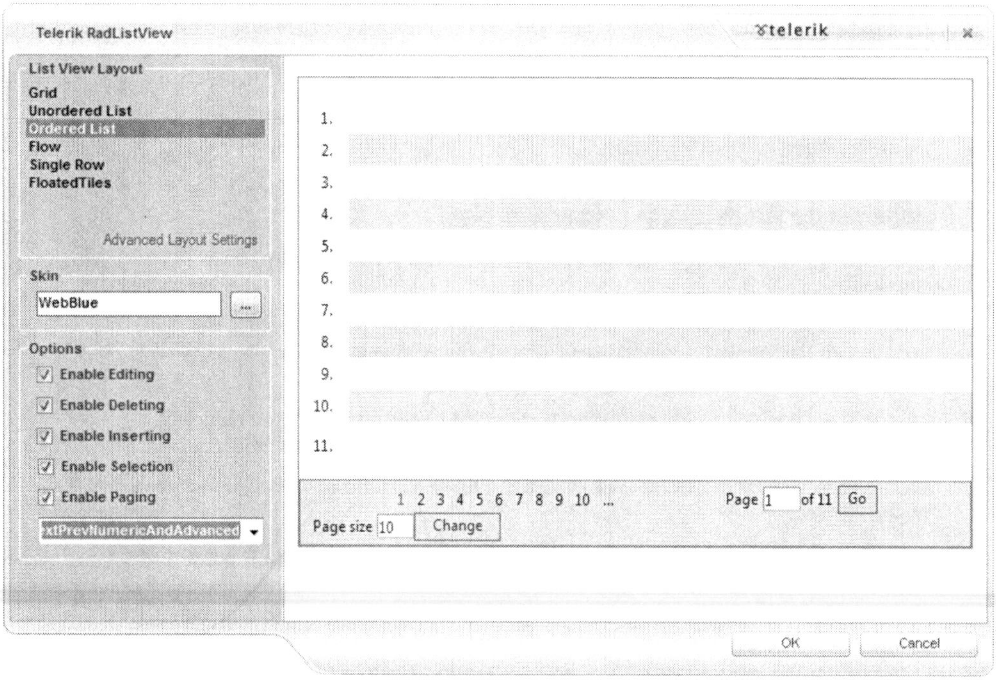

Figure 7-10. *RadListView layout editor*

The layout editor creates basic templates that define styling. As of this writing, the layout editor does not generate the field binding from the datasource; therefore, it won't add to the layout the field definition nor the controls for the editing operations in the `EditItemTemplate` and `InsertItemTemplate`, because as mentioned earlier, `RadListView` doesn't include field editors.

The previous `RadListView` examples used templates that I created. Listing 7-9 was generated using the layout editor. Notice that the markup is a little different than in previous examples. The example implements a `RadGrid`-like layout, as shown in Figure 7-11.

Listing 7-9. *Using a RadListView Predefined Layout*

ASPX Page

```
<telerik:RadListView ID="RadListView6" runat="server"
                    DataKeyNames="ProductID"
                    DataSourceID="ProductsDataSource1"
                    AllowPaging="True"
                    InsertItemPosition="LastItem"
                    Skin="WebBlue">
    <LayoutTemplate>
        <div class="RadListView RadListView_WebBlue">
            <table cellspacing="0" style="width:100%;">
                <thead>
                    <tr class="rlvHeader">
                        <th> </th>
                        <th>ID</th>
                        <th>Name</th>
                        <th>Supplier</th>
                        <th>Category</th>
                        <th>Quantity Per Unit</th>
                        <th>Discontinued</th>
                    </tr>
                </thead>
                <tfoot>
                    <tr>
                        <td colspan="7">
                            <telerik:RadDataPager ID="RadDataPager1" runat="server"
                                                  Skin="WebBlue"
                                                  PagedControlID="RadListView6">
                                <Fields>
                                    <telerik:RadDataPagerButtonField FieldType=➥
"FirstPrev" />
                                    <telerik:RadDataPagerButtonField FieldType="Numeric" />
                                    <telerik:RadDataPagerButtonField FieldType="NextLast" />
                                    <telerik:RadDataPagerGoToPageField />
                                    <telerik:RadDataPagerNumericPageSizeField />
                                </Fields>
                            </telerik:RadDataPager>
                        </td>
                    </tr>
                </tfoot>
                <tbody>
                    <tr ID="itemPlaceholder" runat="server">
                    </tr>
                </tbody>
            </table>
        </div>
    </LayoutTemplate>
```

```
<ItemTemplate>
    <tr class="rlvI">
        <td>
            <asp:Button ID="SelectButton" runat="server"
                    CommandName="Select"
                    CssClass="rlvBSel"
                    Text=" " />
            <asp:Button ID="DeleteButton" runat="server"
                    CommandName="Delete"
                    CssClass="rlvBDel"
                    Text=" " />
            <asp:Button ID="EditButton" runat="server"
                    CommandName="Edit" CssClass="rlvBEdit"
                    Text=" " />
        </td>
        <td><%# Eval("ProductID")%></td>
        <td><%# Eval("ProductName") %></td>
        <td><%# Eval("SupplierID") %></td>
        <td><%# Eval("CategoryID") %></td>
        <td><%# Eval("QuantityPerUnit")%></td>
        <td><asp:CheckBox ID="chkDiscontinued" runat="server"
                        Enabled="false"
                        Checked='<%# Bind("Discontinued")%>' />
        </td>
    </tr>
</ItemTemplate>
<AlternatingItemTemplate>
    <tr class="rlvA">
        <td>
            <asp:Button ID="SelectButton" runat="server"
                    CommandName="Select"
                    CssClass="rlvBSel"
                    Text=" " />
            <asp:Button ID="DeleteButton" runat="server"
                    CommandName="Delete"
                    CssClass="rlvBDel"
                    Text=" " />
            <asp:Button ID="EditButton" runat="server"
                    CommandName="Edit" CssClass="rlvBEdit"
                    Text=" " />
        </td>
        <td><%# Eval("ProductID")%></td>
        <td><%# Eval("ProductName") %></td>
        <td><%# Eval("SupplierID") %></td>
        <td><%# Eval("CategoryID") %></td>
        <td><%# Eval("QuantityPerUnit")%></td>
        <td><asp:CheckBox ID="chkDiscontinued" runat="server"
                        Enabled="false"
                        Checked='<%# Bind("Discontinued")%>' />
        </td>
    </tr>
</AlternatingItemTemplate>
```

```
<EditItemTemplate>
    <tr class="rlvIEdit">
        <td>
            <table cellspacing="0" class="rlvEditTable">
                <tr>
                    <td colspan="2">
                        <asp:Button ID="UpdateButton" runat="server"
                                    CommandName="Update"
                                    CssClass="rlvBUpdate"
                                    Text=" " />
                        <asp:Button ID="CancelButton" runat="server"
                                    CausesValidation="False"
                                    CommandName="Cancel"
                                    CssClass="rlvBCancel"
                                    Text=" " />
                    </td>
                </tr>
            </table>
        </td>
        <td><asp:Label ID="lblID" runat="server"
                    Text='<%# Eval("ProductID")%>'>
            </asp:Label>
        </td>
        <td><telerik:RadTextBox ID="txtName" runat="server"
                    Text='<%# Bind("ProductName") %>'>
            </telerik:RadTextBox>
        </td>
        <td><telerik:RadComboBox ID="rcbCategory" runat="server"
                    DataSourceID="CategoriesDataSource"
                    DataTextField="CategoryName"
                    DataValueField="CategoryID"
                    SelectedValue='<%# Bind("CategoryID") %>'>
            </telerik:RadComboBox>
        </td>
        <td><telerik:RadComboBox ID="rcbSupplier" runat="server"
                    DataSourceID="SuppliersDataSource"
                    DataTextField="CompanyName"
                    DataValueField="SupplierID"
                    SelectedValue='<%# Bind("SupplierID") %>'>
            </telerik:RadComboBox>
        </td>
        <td><telerik:RadTextBox ID="txtQuantity" runat="server"
                    Text='<%# Bind("QuantityPerUnit")%>'>
            </telerik:RadTextBox>
        </td>
        <td><asp:CheckBox ID="chkDiscontinued" runat="server"
                    Enabled="true"
                    Checked='<%# Bind("Discontinued")%>' />
       </td>
    </tr>
</EditItemTemplate>
```

```
<InsertItemTemplate>
    <tr class="rlvIEdit">
        <td>
            <table cellspacing="0" class="rlvEditTable">
                <tr>
                    <td colspan="2">
                        <asp:Button ID="PerformInsertButton" runat="server"
                                    CommandName="PerformInsert"
                                    CssClass="rlvBAdd"
                                    Text=" " />
                        <asp:Button ID="CancelButton" runat="server"
                                    CausesValidation="False"
                                    CommandName="Cancel"
                                    CssClass="rlvBCancel"
                                    Text=" " />
                    </td>
                </tr>
            </table>
        </td>
        <td><asp:Label ID="lblID" runat="server"
                    Text='<%# Eval("ProductID")%>'>
            </asp:Label>
        </td>
        <td><telerik:RadTextBox ID="txtName" runat="server"
                    Text='<%# Bind("ProductName") %>'>
            </telerik:RadTextBox>
        </td>
        <td><telerik:RadComboBox ID="rcbCategory" runat="server"
                    DataSourceID="CategoriesDataSource"
                    DataTextField="CategoryName"
                    DataValueField="CategoryID"
                    SelectedValue='<%# Bind("CategoryID") %>'>
            </telerik:RadComboBox>
        </td>
        <td><telerik:RadComboBox ID="rcbSupplier" runat="server"
                    DataSourceID="SuppliersDataSource"
                    DataTextField="CompanyName"
                    DataValueField="SupplierID"
                    SelectedValue='<%# Bind("SupplierID") %>'>
            </telerik:RadComboBox>
        </td>
        <td><telerik:RadTextBox ID="txtQuantity" runat="server"
                    Text='<%# Bind("QuantityPerUnit")%>'>
            </telerik:RadTextBox>
        </td>
        <td><asp:CheckBox ID="chkDiscontinued" runat="server"
                    Enabled="true"
                    Checked='<%# Bind("Discontinued")%>' />
       </td>
    </tr>
</InsertItemTemplate>
```

```
    <EmptyDataTemplate>
        <div class="RadListView RadListView_WebBlue">
            <div class="rlvEmpty">
                There are no items to be displayed.</div>
        </div>
    </EmptyDataTemplate>
    <SelectedItemTemplate>
        <tr class="rlvISel">
            <td>
                <asp:Button ID="DeselectButton" runat="server"
                        CommandName="Deselect"
                        CssClass="rlvBSel"
                        Text=" " />
                <asp:Button ID="DeleteButton" runat="server"
                        CommandName="Delete"
                        CssClass="rlvBDel"
                        Text=" " />
                <asp:Button ID="EditButton" runat="server"
                        CommandName="Edit"
                        CssClass="rlvBEdit"
                        Text=" " />
            </td>
            <td><%# Eval("ProductID")%></td>
            <td><%# Eval("ProductName") %></td>
            <td><%# Eval("SupplierID") %></td>
            <td><%# Eval("CategoryID") %></td>
            <td><%# Eval("QuantityPerUnit")%></td>
            <td><asp:CheckBox ID="chkDiscontinued" runat="server"
                        Enabled="false"
                        Checked='<%# Bind("Discontinued")%>' />
            </td>
        </tr>
    </SelectedItemTemplate>
</telerik:RadListView>

<asp:SqlDataSource ID="ProductsDataSource1" runat="server"
    ConnectionString="<%$ ConnectionStrings:NorthwindConnectionString %>"
    SelectCommand="SELECT * FROM Products">
</asp:SqlDataSource>

<asp:SqlDataSource ID="SuppliersDataSource" runat="server"
    ConnectionString="<%$ ConnectionStrings:NorthwindConnectionString %>"
    SelectCommand="SELECT * FROM Suppliers">
</asp:SqlDataSource>
```

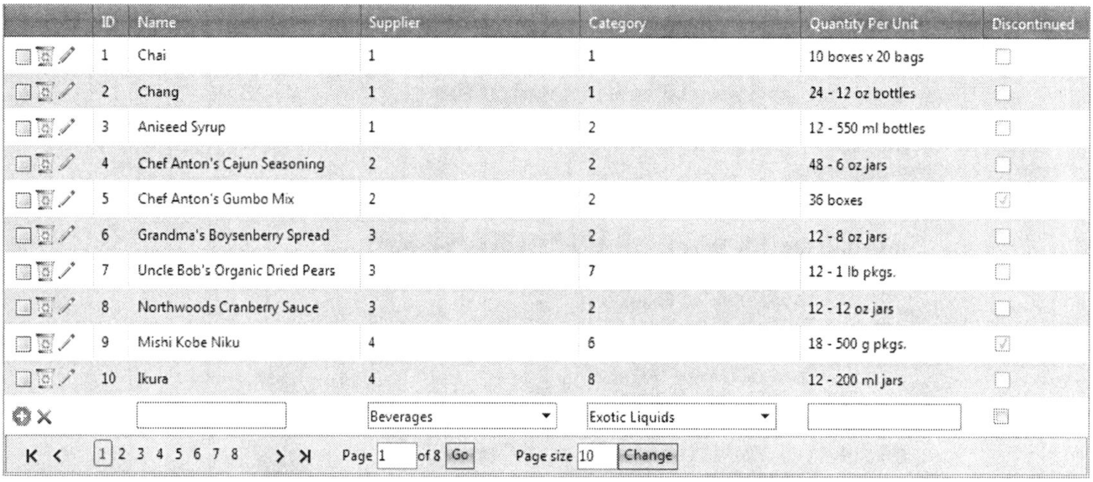

	ID	Name	Supplier	Category	Quantity Per Unit	Discontinued
	1	Chai	1	1	10 boxes x 20 bags	
	2	Chang	1	1	24 - 12 oz bottles	
	3	Aniseed Syrup	1	2	12 - 550 ml bottles	
	4	Chef Anton's Cajun Seasoning	2	2	48 - 6 oz jars	
	5	Chef Anton's Gumbo Mix	2	2	36 boxes	
	6	Grandma's Boysenberry Spread	3	2	12 - 8 oz jars	
	7	Uncle Bob's Organic Dried Pears	3	7	12 - 1 lb pkgs.	
	8	Northwoods Cranberry Sauce	3	2	12 - 12 oz jars	
	9	Mishi Kobe Niku	4	6	18 - 500 g pkgs.	
	10	Ikura	4	8	12 - 200 ml jars	
			Beverages	Exotic Liquids		

K < 1 2 3 4 5 6 7 8 > >| Page 1 of 8 Go Page size 10 Change

Figure 7-11. *RadListView layout created with the layout editor*

Selecting Items in RadListView

RadListView supports item selection in the same way as RadGrid does. The selected items are accessible through the SelectedItems collection, which consists of RadListViewDataItem elements.

There are several methods to select items:

- Have a button with the CommandName property set to "Select".
- Add the item index to the SelectedIndexes collection.
- Set the Selected property of the RadListViewDataItem to true.
- Select items in the client side by using the selectItem() method of the RadListView object and passing the item index as a parameter.

Also, you can enable multiple-row selection by setting the property AllowMultipleItemSelection to true.

To deselect an item, you can use the following methods:

- Use the Deselect command.
- Set the RadListViewDataItem's Selected property to false.
- Remove the item index from the SelectedIndexes collection.
- In the client side, use the deselectItem() method of the RadListView object.

In the previous example in Listing 7-9, notice the usage of buttons that fire the Select/Deselect command in the ItemTemplate and AlternatingItemTemplate. Figure 7-12 shows the result of adding AllowMultipleItemSelection="true" in the RadListView definition.

	ID	Name	Supplier	Category	Quantity Per Unit	Discontinued
	1	Chai	1	1	10 boxes x 20 bags	
	2	Chang	1	1	24 - 12 oz bottles	
	3	Aniseed Syrup	1	2	12 - 550 ml bottles	
	4	Chef Anton's Cajun Seasoning	2	2	48 - 6 oz jars	
	5	Chef Anton's Gumbo Mix	2	2	36 boxes	
	6	Grandma's Boysenberry Spread	3	2	12 - 8 oz jars	
	7	Uncle Bob's Organic Dried Pears	3	7	12 - 1 lb pkgs.	
	8	Northwoods Cranberry Sauce	3	2	12 - 12 oz jars	
	9	Mishi Kobe Niku	4	6	18 - 500 g pkgs.	
	10	Ikura	4	8	12 - 200 ml jars	
			Beverages	Exotic Liquids		

1 2 3 4 5 6 7 8 Page 1 of 8 Go Page size 10 Change

Figure 7-12. *RadListView with multiple-item selection*

Implementing Paging in RadListView

As you probably have noticed, `RadListView` supports paging natively. In fact, it supports paging in three different ways:

- Integrated paging is enabled by setting the property `AllowPaging` to `true` (by default, it is set to `false`). This type of paging works best with a reasonable amount of items, because it relies on the default loading mechanism that reads the entire datasource to know the items in the page that need to be rendered.
- To support large amounts of data, use custom paging by setting the property `AllowCustomPaging` to `true` and querying only the data in the current page in the `NeedDataSource` event. This type of paging uses the `VirtualItemCount` property to know how many items are in the datasource and to build the pager accordingly.
- Use the `RadDataPager` control and link it to `RadListView`. Having an external control manage your paging operations gives you more control over the pager's look and feel and positioning. You can use the following `RadDataPager` elements in your pager control:

    `RadDataPagerButtonField`

    `RadDataPagerPageSizeField`

    `RadDataPagerSliderField`

    `RadDataPagerGoToPageField`

    `RadDataPagerTemplatePageField`

When `RadDataPager` has `RadDataPagerTemplatePageField`, you can define a custom layout and appearance for the pager field. Here, you can reference the `RadDataPager` control by using the `Container.Owner` property, and you can access any public property of the `RadDataPager` control, including the starting row index, the page size, and the total number of rows currently bound to the `RadListView` control. The previous examples in this chapter use the `RadDataPager` control for paging.

Listing 7-10 shows an implementation of custom paging with buttons to handle the page navigation (it does not use RadDataPager). It reuses the example in Listing 7-9, but the definition of RadListView and the layouttemplate are a little different, so I have removed the rest of the templates for clarity. The key changes happen in the code behind. First, only the items in the current page are loaded from the database, as you can see in the definition of the OnNeedDataSource event handler, which queries only the items in the page. The second key element is that since there is no integrated pager and no RadDataPager, a set of buttons is implemented to handle the next, previous, first, and last page navigation with the help of the OnPageIndexChanged event. Whenever a new page of data is needed, the OnPageIndexChanged event is raised and a new set of items is loaded in RadListView. Figure 7-13 shows the result.

Listing 7-10. *RadListView Custom Paging*

ASPX Page

```
<telerik:RadListView ID="RadListView7" runat="server"
        DataKeyNames="ProductID"
        AllowPaging="True"
        AllowCustomPaging="true"
        InsertItemPosition="LastItem"
        Skin="WebBlue"
        OnNeedDataSource="RadListView7_NeedDataSource"
        OnPageIndexChanged="RadListView7_PageIndexChanged">
    <LayoutTemplate>
        <div class="RadListView RadListView_WebBlue">
            <table cellspacing="0" style="width:100%;">
                <thead>
                    <tr class="rlvHeader">
                        <th> </th>
                        <th>ID</th>
                        <th>Name</th>
                        <th>Supplier</th>
                        <th>Category</th>
                        <th>Quantity Per Unit</th>
                        <th>Discontinued</th>
                    </tr>
                </thead>
                <tfoot>
                    <tr>
                        <td colspan="7">
                            <asp:Button ID="btnFirst" runat="server"
                                        Text="<< First"
                                        CommandName="Page"
                                        CommandArgument="First" />
                            <asp:Button ID="btnPrev" runat="server"
                                        Text="< Prev"
                                        CommandName="Page"
                                        CommandArgument="Prev" />
                            <asp:Button ID="btnNext" runat="server"
                                        Text="Next >"
                                        CommandName="Page"
                                        CommandArgument="Next" />
```

```
                    <asp:Button ID="btnLast" runat="server"
                                Text="Last >>"
                                CommandName="Page"
                                CommandArgument="Last" />
                </td>
            </tr>
        </tfoot>
        <tbody>
            <tr ID="itemPlaceholder" runat="server">
            </tr>
        </tbody>
    </table>
  </div>
</LayoutTemplate>
...
// the other templates should be here
...
</telerik:RadListView>

<asp:SqlDataSource ID="SuppliersDataSource3" runat="server"
    ConnectionString="<%$ ConnectionStrings:NorthwindConnectionString %>"
    SelectCommand="SELECT * FROM Suppliers">
</asp:SqlDataSource>
<asp:SqlDataSource ID="CategoriesDataSource3" runat="server"
    ConnectionString="<%$ ConnectionStrings:NorthwindConnectionString %>"
    SelectCommand="SELECT * FROM Categories">
</asp:SqlDataSource>
```

Code Behind

```
protected void RadListView7_PageIndexChanged(object sender, ➥
RadListViewPageChangedEventArgs e)
{
    RadListView listView = (RadListView)sender;
    listView.VirtualItemCount = GetCount("");
    decimal pageSize = Convert.ToDecimal(listView.PageSize);
    int pageCount = Convert.ToInt32(Math.Ceiling(listView.VirtualItemCount/pageSize));
    if (Session["NewPageIndex"] == null) Session["NewPageIndex"] = 0;
    switch (e.CommandArgument.ToString())
    {
        case "First":
            Session["NewPageIndex"] = 0;
            break;
        case "Prev":
            if (int.Parse(Session["NewPageIndex"].ToString()) > 0)
                Session["NewPageIndex"] = int.Parse(Session["NewPageIndex"].ToString()) - 1;
            break;
        case "Next":
            if (int.Parse(Session["NewPageIndex"].ToString()) < pageCount - 1)
                Session["NewPageIndex"] = int.Parse(Session["NewPageIndex"].ToString()) + 1;
            break;
```

```
            case "Last":
                Session["NewPageIndex"] = pageCount - 1;
                break;
        }
        int startIndex = int.Parse(Session["NewPageIndex"].ToString()) * listView.PageSize;
        listView.DataSource = GetProducts(startIndex, listView.PageSize, "", "");
    }

    protected void RadListView7_NeedDataSource(object sender, EventArgs e)
    {
        RadListView listView = (RadListView)sender;
        listView.DataSource = GetProducts(0, listView.PageSize, "", "");

    }

    public static int GetCount(string filterExpressions)
    {
        string sql = string.Format("SELECT COUNT(*) from Products {0}",
                                (string.IsNullOrEmpty(filterExpressions)
                                    ? ""
                                    : string.Format(" WHERE {0}", filterExpressions)));
        int recordCount;

        using (SqlConnection connection = new
            SqlConnection(ConfigurationManager
                            .ConnectionStrings["NorthwindConnectionString"]
                            .ConnectionString))
        {
            connection.Open();
            using (SqlCommand selectCommand = new SqlCommand(sql, connection))
            {
                recordCount = int.Parse(selectCommand.ExecuteScalar().ToString());
            }
        }

        return recordCount;
    }

    public static List<MyProduct> GetProducts(int startRowIndex,
                                              int maximumRows,
                                              string sortExpression,
                                              string filterExpression)
    {
        List<MyProduct> productsList = new List<MyProduct>();

        string where = string.Empty;
        if (!string.IsNullOrEmpty(filterExpression))
        {
            where += filterExpression;
        }

        StringBuilder sqlBuilder = new StringBuilder();
        sqlBuilder.AppendLine("DECLARE @startRowIndex int");
        sqlBuilder.AppendLine("DECLARE @maximumRows int");
```

```
    sqlBuilder.AppendLine(String.Format("SET @startRowIndex = {0}", startRowIndex));
    sqlBuilder.AppendLine(String.Format("SET @maximumRows = {0}", maximumRows));
    sqlBuilder.AppendLine("DECLARE @first_id int, @startRow int ");
    sqlBuilder.AppendLine("DECLARE @sIndex INT");
    sqlBuilder.AppendLine("SET @sIndex = @startRowIndex + 1");
    sqlBuilder.AppendLine("SET ROWCOUNT 0");
    sqlBuilder.AppendLine(string.Format("SELECT *, ROW_NUMBER() OVER (ORDER BY {0}) ➥
[RowNum]",
                                (!string.IsNullOrEmpty(sortExpression) ?
                                        sortExpression
                                        : "ProductID")));
    sqlBuilder.AppendLine("INTO #TempProducts");
    sqlBuilder.AppendLine("FROM Products");
    if (!string.IsNullOrEmpty(where))
        sqlBuilder.AppendLine(string.Format("WHERE {0}", where));
    sqlBuilder.AppendLine(string.Format("ORDER BY {0}",
                                (!string.IsNullOrEmpty(sortExpression) ?
                                        sortExpression
                                        : "ProductID")));
    sqlBuilder.AppendLine("SET ROWCOUNT @sIndex");
    sqlBuilder.AppendLine("SELECT @first_id = RowNum");
    sqlBuilder.AppendLine("FROM #TempProducts ");
    sqlBuilder.AppendLine("ORDER BY RowNum");
    sqlBuilder.AppendLine("SET ROWCOUNT @maximumRows");
    sqlBuilder.AppendLine("SELECT p.*");
    sqlBuilder.AppendLine("FROM #TempProducts p");
    sqlBuilder.AppendLine("WHERE RowNum >= @first_id");
    if (!string.IsNullOrEmpty(where))
        sqlBuilder.AppendLine(string.Format(" AND {0}", where));
    sqlBuilder.AppendLine(string.Format("ORDER BY {0}",
                                (!string.IsNullOrEmpty(sortExpression) ?
                                        sortExpression
                                        : "ProductID")));
    sqlBuilder.AppendLine("DROP TABLE #TempProducts");

    string sql = sqlBuilder.ToString();
    using (SqlConnection connection = new
        SqlConnection(ConfigurationManager
                        .ConnectionStrings["NorthwindConnectionString"]
                        .ConnectionString))
    {
        connection.Open();
        using (SqlCommand selectCommand = new SqlCommand(sql, connection))
        {
            using (SqlDataReader rd = selectCommand.ExecuteReader())
            {
                try
                {
                    while (rd.Read())
                    {
                        var pd = new MyProduct();
                        pd.ProductID = int.Parse(rd[0].ToString());
                        pd.ProductName = rd[1].ToString();
```

```
                        if (string.IsNullOrEmpty(rd[2].ToString()))
                            pd.SupplierID = null;
                        else
                            pd.SupplierID = int.Parse(rd[2].ToString());
                        if (string.IsNullOrEmpty(rd[3].ToString()))
                            pd.CategoryID = null;
                        else
                            pd.CategoryID = int.Parse(rd[3].ToString());

                        pd.QuantityPerUnit = rd[4].ToString();
                        if (string.IsNullOrEmpty(rd[5].ToString()))
                            pd.UnitPrice = null;
                        else
                            pd.UnitPrice = decimal.Parse(rd[5].ToString());
                        if (string.IsNullOrEmpty(rd[6].ToString()))
                            pd.UnitsInStock = null;
                        else
                            pd.UnitsInStock = short.Parse(rd[6].ToString());
                        if (string.IsNullOrEmpty(rd[7].ToString()))
                            pd.UnitsOnOrder = null;
                        else
                            pd.UnitsOnOrder = short.Parse(rd[7].ToString());
                        if (string.IsNullOrEmpty(rd[8].ToString()))
                            pd.ReorderLevel = null;
                        else
                            pd.ReorderLevel = short.Parse(rd[8].ToString());

                        pd.Discontinued = bool.Parse(rd[9].ToString());

                        productsList.Add(pd);
                    }
                }
                catch (Exception ex)
                {
                    // error handling logic here
                }
            }

        }
    }
    return productsList;
}
```

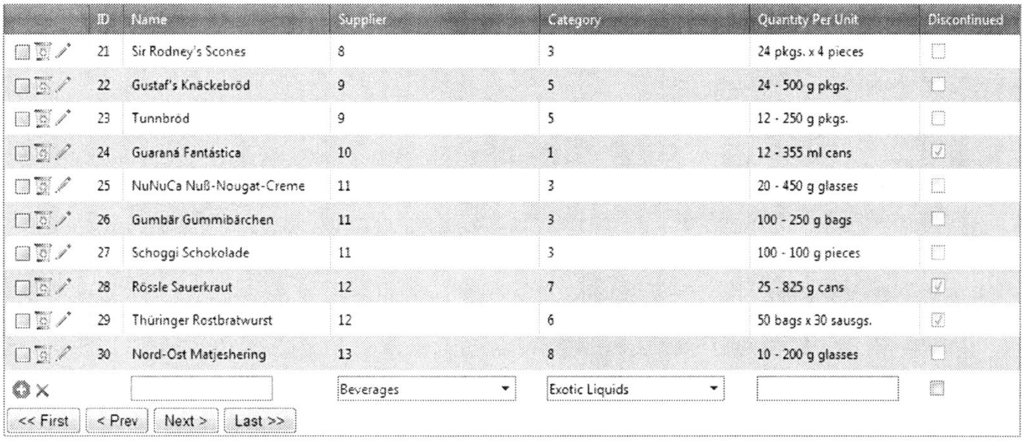

	ID	Name	Supplier	Category	Quantity Per Unit	Discontinued
	21	Sir Rodney's Scones	8	3	24 pkgs. x 4 pieces	
	22	Gustaf's Knäckebröd	9	5	24 - 500 g pkgs.	
	23	Tunnbröd	9	5	12 - 250 g pkgs.	
	24	Guaraná Fantástica	10	1	12 - 355 ml cans	✓
	25	NuNuCa Nuß-Nougat-Creme	11	3	20 - 450 g glasses	
	26	Gumbär Gummibärchen	11	3	100 - 250 g bags	
	27	Schoggi Schokolade	11	3	100 - 100 g pieces	
	28	Rössle Sauerkraut	12	7	25 - 825 g cans	✓
	29	Thüringer Rostbratwurst	12	6	50 bags x 30 sausgs.	✓
	30	Nord-Ost Matjeshering	13	8	10 - 200 g glasses	
			Beverages	Exotic Liquids		

<< First < Prev Next > Last >>

Figure 7-13. *Custom paging implemented in RadListView (notice the buttons in the pager area)*

Grouping in RadListView

RadListView supports basic grouping. The grouping functionality in RadListView is handled by counting the number of items that must be included in each group. This is different from how it is handled by other bound controls like RadGrid, which perform grouping based on fields. So, RadListView doesn't group items by fields, but only by number of items.

You need to set the property GroupItemCount to the number of items you want to display in each group. Then set the GroupPlaceHolderID property to the ID of a placeholder in the LayoutTemplate. Finally, place the item placeholder element in the GroupTemplate. Optionally, you can define a separator layout for each group with the GroupSeparatorTemplate.

The example in Listing 7-11 shows how to implement RadListView basic grouping. Notice the differences between RadListView grouping and RadGrid grouping in Figure 7-14.

Listing 7-11. *RadListView Basic Grouping*

ASPX Page

```
<telerik:RadListView ID="RadListView8" runat="server"
    DataKeyNames="ProductID"
    DataSourceID="ProductsDataSource1"
    AllowMultiItemSelection="True"
    GroupPlaceholderID="GroupPlaceHolder"
    GroupItemCount="4"
    ItemPlaceholderID="ProductsPlaceholder"
    Skin="WebBlue">
    <GroupTemplate>
        <div class="RadListView RadListView_WebBlue">
            <div ID="ProductsPlaceholder" runat="server">
            </div>
        </div>
    </GroupTemplate>
```

```
    <GroupSeparatorTemplate>
        <div style="height:20px"> </div>
    </GroupSeparatorTemplate>
    <LayoutTemplate>
        <asp:PlaceHolder ID="GroupPlaceHolder" runat="server" />
    </LayoutTemplate>
    <ItemTemplate>
        <div class="rlvI">
            <div><%# Eval("ProductName") %></div>
        </div>
    </ItemTemplate>
    <AlternatingItemTemplate>
        <div class="rlvA">
            <div><%# Eval("ProductName") %></div>
        </div>
    </AlternatingItemTemplate>
    <EmptyDataTemplate>
        <div class="RadListView RadListView_WebBlue">
            <div class="rlvEmpty">
                There are no items to be displayed.</div>
        </div>
    </EmptyDataTemplate>
</telerik:RadListView>
```

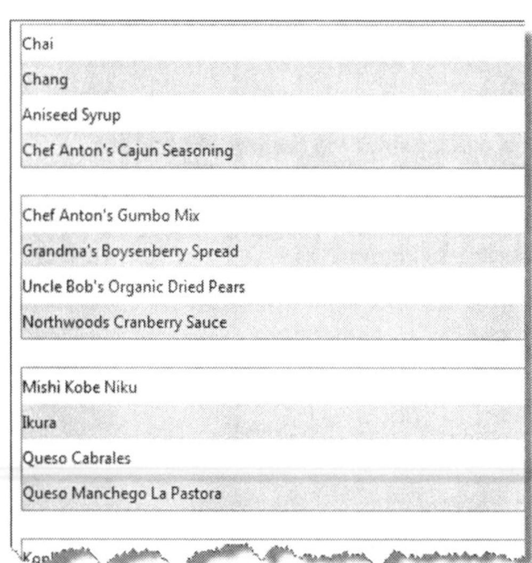

Figure 7-14. *Grouping in RadListView is based on the number of items, not a particular field.*

Implementing Filtering and Sorting in RadListView

RadListView supports filtering through integration with RadFilter, as you saw earlier in this chapter. However, in general, filtering is implemented in RadListView using filter expressions. You can use the FilterExpressions property programmatically to add or remove filters as needed.

The FilterExpressions property is a collection of RadListViewFilterExpression objects, which support several filtering capabilities. The filter expressions can be added in several ways:

- Create instances of the new filter expressions and add them to the FilterExpressions collection:

```
RadListView1.FilterExpressions.Add(
       new RadListViewGreaterThanFilterExpression("CategoryID")
                      {CurrentValue = 3}
);

RadListView1.FilterExpressions.Add(
       new RadListViewContainsFilterExpression("ProductName")
                      {CurrentValue = "Queso"}
);
```

- Use the fluent expression builder object. With this approach, it is necessary call to the Build() method:

```
RadListView1.FilterExpressions.BuildExpression()
        .GreaterThan("CategoryID", 3)
        .Or()
        .Contains("ProductName", "Queso")
        .Build();
```

- Use an overload of the FilterExpressions.BuildExpression property that takes in an action delegate:

```
RadListView1.FilterExpressions.BuildExpression(ex => ex
        .GreaterThan("CategoryID", 3)
        .Or()
        .Contains("OrderID", "Queso")));
```

Implementing sorting is as straightforward as implementing filtering. You use the SortExpressions property, which is a collection of objects of type SortExpression. Each sort expression needs the field name and sort order to complete the sorting criteria. Finally, you just rebind the list view.

The example in Listing 7-12 applies a filter to a RadListView based on the category ID or the product name fields. It uses the FilterExpressions.BuildExpression property to build the filter expression. It can also sort by any of the fields in the datasource. Notice that it uses the method SortExpressions.AddSortExpression to add the new sort expression. Figure 7-15 shows the filtering portion of the example, and Figure 7-16 shows the sorting part.

Listing 7-12. *Implementing Filtering and Sorting in RadListView*

ASPX Page

```
<table>
    <tr>
        <td>Filter By</td>
        <td>
            <telerik:RadComboBox ID="rcbFilterBy" runat="server"
                OnClientSelectedIndexChanged="rcbFilterBy_ClientSelectedIndexChanged">
                <Items>
                    <telerik:RadComboBoxItem Text="CategoryID" Value="CategoryID" />
```

```
                    <telerik:RadComboBoxItem Text="ProductName" Value="ProductName" />
                </Items>
            </telerik:RadComboBox>
        </td>
        <td> </td>
        <td>
            <div id="numericFilter">
            <telerik:RadComboBox ID="rcbNumericFilter" runat="server">
                <Items>
                    <telerik:RadComboBoxItem Text="EqualTo" Value="EqualTo"/>
                    <telerik:RadComboBoxItem Text="NotEqualTo" Value="NotEqualTo"/>
                    <telerik:RadComboBoxItem Text="GreaterThan" Value="GreaterThan"/>
                    <telerik:RadComboBoxItem Text="LessThan" Value="LessThan"/>
                    <telerik:RadComboBoxItem Text="GreaterThanOrEqualTo"
                                        Value="GreaterThanOrEqualTo"/>
                    <telerik:RadComboBoxItem Text="LessThanOrEqualTo"
                                        Value="LessThanOrEqualTo"/>
                </Items>
            </telerik:RadComboBox>
            </div>
            <div id="stringFilter" style="display:none">
                <telerik:RadComboBox ID="rcbStringFilter" runat="server">
                    <Items>
                        <telerik:RadComboBoxItem Text="EqualTo" Value="EqualTo"/>
                        <telerik:RadComboBoxItem Text="Contains" Value="Contains"/>
                    </Items>
                </telerik:RadComboBox>
            </div>
        </td>
        <td> </td>
        <td>
            <telerik:RadTextBox ID="txtFilterValue" runat="server"></telerik:RadTextBox>
        </td>
        <td>
            <asp:Button ID="btnApplyFilter" runat="server"
                        Text="Apply Filter"
                        OnClick="btnApplyFilter_Click" />
        </td>
    </tr>
        <tr>
            <td>Sort By</td>
            <td>
                <telerik:RadComboBox ID="rcbSortBy" runat="server">
                    <Items>
                        <telerik:RadComboBoxItem Text="ProductID" Value="ProductID" />
                        <telerik:RadComboBoxItem Text="ProductName" Value="ProductName" />
                        <telerik:RadComboBoxItem Text="SupplierID" Value="SupplierID" />
                        <telerik:RadComboBoxItem Text="CategoryID" Value="CategoryID" />
                        <telerik:RadComboBoxItem Text="QuantityPerUnit"
                                            Value="QuantityPerUnit" />
                        <telerik:RadComboBoxItem Text="Discontinued" Value="Discontinued" />
                    </Items>
                </telerik:RadComboBox>
            </td>
```

```
            <td> </td>
            <td>
                <telerik:RadComboBox ID="rcbSortOrder" runat="server">
                    <Items>
                        <telerik:RadComboBoxItem Text="Ascending" Value="Asc"/>
                        <telerik:RadComboBoxItem Text="Descending" Value="Desc"/>
                        <telerik:RadComboBoxItem Text="None" Value="None" />
                    </Items>
                </telerik:RadComboBox>
            </td>
            <td colspan="3">
                <asp:Button ID="btnApplySort" runat="server"
                                Text="Apply Sort"
                                OnClick="btnApplySort_Click" />
            </td>
        </tr>
</table>

<telerik:RadCodeBlock ID="RadCodeBlock1" runat="server">
<script type="text/javascript">
    function rcbFilterBy_ClientSelectedIndexChanged(sender, eventArgs) {
        var divStringFilter = $get("stringFilter");
        var divNumericFilter = $get("numericFilter");
        var item = eventArgs.get_item();
        var value = item.get_value();
        if (value == "CategoryID") {
            divStringFilter.style.display = "none";
            divNumericFilter.style.display = "block";
        }
        else {
            divStringFilter.style.display = "block";
            divNumericFilter.style.display = "none";
        }
    }
</script>
</telerik:RadCodeBlock>

<telerik:RadListView ID="RadListView9" runat="server"
    DataKeyNames="ProductID"
    DataSourceID="ProductsDataSource1"
    AllowMultiItemSelection="true"
    AllowPaging="True"
    InsertItemPosition="LastItem"
    Skin="WebBlue">
    <LayoutTemplate>
        <div class="RadListView RadListView_WebBlue">
            <table cellspacing="0" style="width:100%;">
                <thead>
                    <tr class="rlvHeader">
                        <th>ID</th>
                        <th>Name</th>
                        <th>Supplier</th>
                        <th>Category</th>
```

```
                    <th>Quantity Per Unit</th>
                    <th>Discontinued</th>
                </tr>
            </thead>
            <tfoot>
                <tr>
                    <td colspan="6">
                        <telerik:RadDataPager ID="RadDataPager1" runat="server"
                                              Skin="WebBlue">
                <Fields>
                    <telerik:RadDataPagerButtonField
                             FieldType="FirstPrev" />
                    <telerik:RadDataPagerButtonField
                             FieldType="Numeric" />
                    <telerik:RadDataPagerButtonField
                             FieldType="NextLast" />
                    <telerik:RadDataPagerGoToPageField />
                    <telerik:RadDataPagerNumericPageSizeField />
                </Fields>
                        </telerik:RadDataPager>
                  </td>
                </tr>
            </tfoot>
            <tbody>
                <tr ID="itemPlaceholder" runat="server">
                </tr>
            </tbody>
        </table>
    </div>
</LayoutTemplate>
<ItemTemplate>
    <tr class="rlvI">
        <td><%# Eval("ProductID")%></td>
        <td><%# Eval("ProductName") %></td>
        <td><%# Eval("SupplierID") %></td>
        <td><%# Eval("CategoryID") %></td>
        <td><%# Eval("QuantityPerUnit")%></td>
        <td><asp:CheckBox ID="chkDiscontinued" runat="server"
                          Enabled="false"
                          Checked='<%# Bind("Discontinued")%>' />
        </td>
    </tr>
</ItemTemplate>
<AlternatingItemTemplate>
    <tr class="rlvA">
        <td><%# Eval("ProductID")%></td>
        <td><%# Eval("ProductName") %></td>
        <td><%# Eval("SupplierID") %></td>
        <td><%# Eval("CategoryID") %></td>
        <td><%# Eval("QuantityPerUnit")%></td>
        <td><asp:CheckBox ID="chkDiscontinued" runat="server"
                          Enabled="false"
                          Checked='<%# Bind("Discontinued")%>' />
        </td>
```

```
        </tr>
    </AlternatingItemTemplate>
    <EmptyDataTemplate>
        <div class="RadListView RadListView_WebBlue">
            <div class="rlvEmpty">
                There are no items to be displayed.</div>
        </div>
    </EmptyDataTemplate>
</telerik:RadListView>
```

Code Behind

```
protected void btnApplyFilter_Click(object sender, EventArgs e)
{
    if (string.IsNullOrEmpty(txtFilterValue.Text)) return;
    RadListView9.FilterExpressions.Clear();
    switch (rcbFilterBy.SelectedValue)
    {
        case "CategoryID":
            int category = int.Parse(txtFilterValue.Text);
            switch (rcbNumericFilter.SelectedValue)
            {
                case "EqualTo":
                    RadListView9.FilterExpressions.BuildExpression(ex => ex
                        .EqualTo("CategoryID", category)
                        .Build());
                    break;
                case "NotEqualTo":
                    RadListView9.FilterExpressions.BuildExpression(ex => ex
                        .NotEqualTo("CategoryID", category)
                        .Build());
                    break;
                case "GreaterThan":
                    RadListView9.FilterExpressions.BuildExpression(ex => ex
                        .GreaterThan("CategoryID", category)
                        .Build());
                    break;
                case "LessThan":
                    RadListView9.FilterExpressions.BuildExpression(ex => ex
                        .LessThan("CategoryID", category)
                        .Build());
                    break;
                case "GreaterThanOrEqualTo":
                    RadListView9.FilterExpressions.BuildExpression(ex => ex
                        .GreaterThanOrEqualTo("CategoryID", category)
                        .Build());
                    break;
                case "LessThanOrEqualTo":
                    RadListView9.FilterExpressions.BuildExpression(ex => ex
                        .LessThanOrEqualTo("CategoryID", category)
                        .Build());
                    break;
            }
            break;
```

```
        case "ProductName":
            switch (rcbStringFilter.SelectedValue)
            {
                case "EqualTo":
                    RadListView9.FilterExpressions.BuildExpression(ex => ex
                        .EqualTo("ProductName", txtFilterValue.Text)
                        .Build());
                    break;
                case "Contains":
                    RadListView9.FilterExpressions.BuildExpression(ex => ex
                        .Contains("ProductName", txtFilterValue.Text)
                        .Build());
                    break;
            }
            break;
    }
    RadListView9.Rebind();
}

protected void btnApplySort_Click(object sender, EventArgs e)
{
    RadListViewSortExpression sortExpression = new RadListViewSortExpression();
    sortExpression.FieldName = rcbSortBy.SelectedValue;
    switch (rcbSortOrder.SelectedValue)
    {
        case "Asc":
            sortExpression.SortOrder = RadListViewSortOrder.Ascending;
            break;
        case "Desc":
            sortExpression.SortOrder = RadListViewSortOrder.Descending;
            break;
        default:
            sortExpression.SortOrder = RadListViewSortOrder.None;
            break;
    }
    RadListView9.SortExpressions.AddSortExpression(sortExpression);
    RadListView9.Rebind();
}
```

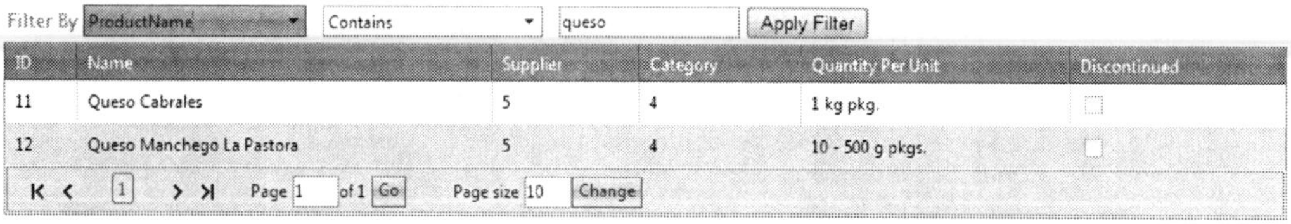

Filter By ProductName | Contains | queso | Apply Filter

ID	Name	Supplier	Category	Quantity Per Unit	Discontinued
11	Queso Cabrales	5	4	1 kg pkg.	☐
12	Queso Manchego La Pastora	5	4	10 - 500 g pkgs.	☐

K < 1 > >I Page 1 of 1 Go Page size 10 Change

Figure 7-15. *RadListView filtering*

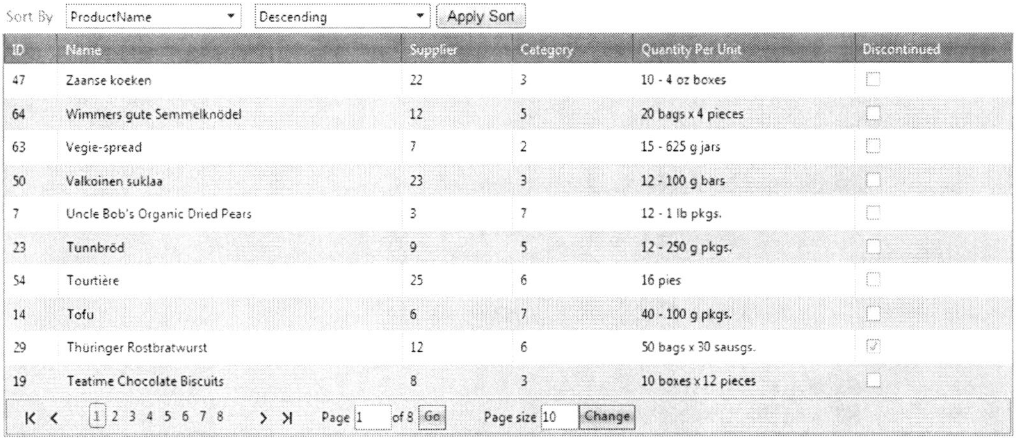

Sort By ProductName ▾ Descending ▾ Apply Sort

ID	Name	Supplier	Category	Quantity Per Unit	Discontinued
47	Zaanse koeken	22	3	10 - 4 oz boxes	☐
64	Wimmers gute Semmelknödel	12	5	20 bags x 4 pieces	☐
63	Vegie-spread	7	2	15 - 625 g jars	☐
50	Valkoinen suklaa	23	3	12 - 100 g bars	☐
7	Uncle Bob's Organic Dried Pears	3	7	12 - 1 lb pkgs.	☐
23	Tunnbröd	9	5	12 - 250 g pkgs.	☐
54	Tourtière	25	6	16 pies	☐
14	Tofu	6	7	40 - 100 g pkgs.	☐
29	Thüringer Rostbratwurst	12	6	50 bags x 30 sausgs.	☑
19	Teatime Chocolate Biscuits	8	3	10 boxes x 12 pieces	☐

1 2 3 4 5 6 7 8 Page 1 of 8 Go Page size 10 Change

Figure 7-16. *RadListView sorting*

RadListBox

Our final control in the data controls category is RadListBox, a powerful ASP.NET AJAX control. RadListBox supports various operations that make it one of the best solutions for working with lists of items. You can select multiple items, reorder the items, and move items between RadListBox controls (either with buttons or double-clicking). RadListBox displays buttons automatically to perform the operations and supports item templates. The items support icons and check boxes, and you can control the appearance of items by applying different layouts.

Another attractive feature of RadListBox is its ability to perform automatic updates of the datasource (if the datasource supports automatic updates). This functionality is quite useful in scenarios where you allow users to change the order of appearance of items, such as the order of products inside a category in an e-commerce web site.

Implementing Data Binding for RadListBox

RadListBox can be bound to any ASP.NET 2.0+ datasource components, either declaratively or programmatically. It can also be bound to datasets, data tables, arrays, array lists, and generic lists. However, it doesn't support client-side data binding.

To bind RadListBox to an ASP.NET datasource, all you need to do is configure the DataSource or DataSourceID for declarative binding to the source of the data, and set the DataValueField and DataTextField properties for the key/value pair's items.

The example in Listing 7-13 uses a LinqDataSource object to bind the RadListBox control declaratively using the DataSourceID property. In the example, the DataValueField maps to the ProductID field in the datasource, and the DataTextField maps to the ProductName field, which is the text shown for each item in RadListBox. Figure 7-17 shows the result.

Listing 7-13. *Implementing RadListBox Data Binding to a LinqDataSource Object*

ASPX Page

```
<telerik:RadListBox ID="RadListBox1" runat="server"
                    DataKeyField="ProductID"
                    DataSourceID="ProductsLinqDataSource"
                    DataTextField="ProductName"
                    DataValueField="ProductID">
</telerik:RadListBox>

<asp:LinqDataSource ID="ProductsLinqDataSource" runat="server"
        ContextTypeName="WebApplication1.NorthwindDataContext"
        EntityTypeName=""
        OrderBy="ProductName"
        Select="new (ProductID, ProductName)"
        TableName="Products">
</asp:LinqDataSource>
```

Figure 7-17. *RadListBox declarative data binding*

Reordering Items in RadListBox

You can reorder the `RadListBox` control's items in a codeless manner by setting the `AllowReorder` property to `true`. This functionality also supports the automatic update of the datasource—whenever you move an item to a new position, it updates the datasource for you.

To use the automatic update feature, the datasource must support automatic updates. Also, `RadListBox` must be using a declarative defined datasource with its `UpdateCommand` and/or `DeleteCommand` configured.

For automatic updates to work, you need to set the `AllowAutomaticUpdates` property to `true`, enable automatic postbacks by setting the `AutoPostBackOnReorder` property to `true`, and define the field in the datasource that will be updated with the `DataSortField` property.

The example in Listing 7-14 implements the reordering feature of `RadListBox`. Notice in Figure 7-18 that the control automatically implemented two buttons to move the items up and down.

Listing 7-14. *Implementing the Reordering Feature in RadListBox*

ASPX Page

```
<telerik:RadListBox ID="RadListBox2" runat="server"
    DataKeyField="CategoryID"
    DataSourceID="CategoriesSqlDataSource"
    DataTextField="CategoryName"
```

```
    DataValueField="CategoryID"
    AllowReorder="True"
    AllowAutomaticUpdates="True"
    AutoPostBackOnReorder="True"
    DataSortField="DisplayOrder">
</telerik:RadListBox>

<asp:SqlDataSource ID="CategoriesSqlDataSource" runat="server"
    ConnectionString="<%$ ConnectionStrings:NorthwindConnectionString %>"
    DeleteCommand="DELETE FROM [Categories] WHERE [CategoryID] = @CategoryID"
    InsertCommand="INSERT INTO [Categories] ([CategoryName], [DisplayOrder])
                   VALUES (@CategoryName, @DisplayOrder)"
    SelectCommand="SELECT [CategoryID], [CategoryName], [DisplayOrder]
                FROM [Categories]
               ORDER BY [DisplayOrder]"
    UpdateCommand="UPDATE [Categories]
                 SET [CategoryName] = @CategoryName,
                     [DisplayOrder] = @DisplayOrder
               WHERE [CategoryID] = @CategoryID">
    <DeleteParameters>
        <asp:Parameter Name="CategoryID" Type="Int32" />
    </DeleteParameters>
    <InsertParameters>
        <asp:Parameter Name="CategoryName" Type="String" />
        <asp:Parameter Name="DisplayOrder" Type="Int32" />
    </InsertParameters>
    <UpdateParameters>
        <asp:Parameter Name="CategoryName" Type="String" />
        <asp:Parameter Name="DisplayOrder" Type="Int32" />
        <asp:Parameter Name="CategoryID" Type="Int32" />
    </UpdateParameters>
</asp:SqlDataSource>
```

Beverages
Condiments
Dairy Products
Confections
Grains/Cereals
Meat/Poultry

Figure 7-18. *RadListBox with reordering capabilities*

Transferring Items Between RadListBoxes

You can transfer items between `RadListBox` controls automatically. As with reordering, this feature can also support automatic updating of the datasource.

For this feature to work, you need two `RadListBox` controls: one to serve as the source of items and the other to serve as the destination. Then you relate the first list box with the second one using the `TransferToID` property, in which you define the ID of the destination list box. Finally, you need to enable transfers by setting the `AllowTransfer` property to `true`.

With the TransferMode property, you are able to modify the transfer behavior. If you set the property to Copy instead of Move, RadListBox will copy the item to the destination list box and leave the original item in the source list box.

As explained in the previous section, if you want to perform automatic updates to the datasource, set the AutoPostBackOnTransfer and AllowAutomaticUpdates properties to true. For this to work, the datasources must implement automatic insert, update, and delete operations.

Listing 7-15 implements item transfer between RadListBox controls. Figure 7-19 shows the result.

Listing 7-15. *RadListBox Transfer with Buttons and Double-Click*

ASPX Page

```
<telerik:RadListBox ID="RadListBox3" runat="server"
        DataKeyField="CategoryID"
        DataSourceID="CategoriesLinqDataSource"
        DataTextField="CategoryName"
        DataValueField="CategoryID"
        AllowTransfer="true"
        AllowTransferOnDoubleClick="true"
        TransferToID="RadListBox4">
</telerik:RadListBox>
<telerik:RadListBox ID="RadListBox4" runat="server">
</telerik:RadListBox>
<asp:LinqDataSource ID="CategoriesLinqDataSource" runat="server"
        ContextTypeName="WebApplication1.NorthwindDataContext"
        EntityTypeName=""
        OrderBy="CategoryName"
        Select="new (CategoryID, CategoryName)"
        TableName="Categories">
</asp:LinqDataSource>
```

Figure 7-19. *RadListBox with item transfer capabilities*

Adding Images and Check Boxes to RadListBox Items

Items in RadListBox can be configured to have a check box and an image. To enable check boxes, just set the property Checkboxes to true. If you need to hide the check box for a particular item (or items), set the Checkable property of the item (or items) to false. In the code behind, use the property Checked to know if the item is checked. (Note that selecting an item won't automatically check its check box.)

To add images to the items, use the item's ImageUrl property to point to the image file for the item.

Listing 7-16 shows how to use both features. Figure 7-20 shows the result.

Listing 7-16. *RadListBox with Check Boxes and Images*

ASPX Page

```
<telerik:RadListBox ID="RadListBox5" runat="server"
                    CheckBoxes="True" >
    <Items>
        <telerik:RadListBoxItem runat="server"
                    ImageUrl="~/Images/icons/action_add.png"
                    ListBox="RadListBox5"
                    Text="Add" />
        <telerik:RadListBoxItem runat="server"
                    Checkable="False"
                    ImageUrl="~/Images/icons/action_check.png"
                    ListBox="RadListBox5"
                    Text="Check" />
        <telerik:RadListBoxItem runat="server"
                    ImageUrl="~/Images/icons/action_delete.png"
                    ListBox="RadListBox5"
                    Text="Delete" />
        <telerik:RadListBoxItem runat="server"
                    ImageUrl="~/Images/icons/application.png"
                    ListBox="RadListBox5"
                    Text="Application" />
        <telerik:RadListBoxItem runat="server"
                    ImageUrl="~/Images/icons/arrow_back.png"
                    ListBox="RadListBox5"
                    Text="Back" />
        <telerik:RadListBoxItem runat="server"
                    ImageUrl="~/Images/icons/question.gif"
                    ListBox="RadListBox5"
                    Text="Question" />
    </Items>
</telerik:RadListBox>
```

Figure 7-20. *Items in RadListBox with check boxes and images*

Working with RadListBox Item Templates

The RadListBoxItems in a RadListBox control support templates, so you can configure them to host multiple controls and customize their appearance. You use the templates in a similar manner as with other ASP.NET controls.

The example in Listing 7-17 shows how to create an `ItemTemplate` and bind the controls contained within the template to fields in the datasource. Notice in Figure 7-21 how the items now look a lot different (and better).

Listing 7-17. *RadListBox Item Templates*

ASPX Page

```
<telerik:RadListBox ID="RadListBox6" runat="server"
    DataKeyField="EmployeeID"
    DataSourceID="EmployeesDataSource"
    DataTextField="EmployeeID"
    DataValueField="EmployeeID"
    Width="600px" Height="400px">
    <ItemTemplate>
        <table>
            <tr>
                <td>
                    <asp:Image ID="employeePic" runat="server"
                         ImageUrl='<%# "~/images/employees/"
                                   + Eval("EmployeeID")
                                   + ".jpg" %>'
                         width="100px">
                    </asp:Image>
                    <br />
                    Rate me
                    <telerik:RadRating ID="EmployeeRating" runat="server" Precision="Half">
                    </telerik:RadRating>
                </td>
                <td>
                    <asp:Label ID="lblEmployeeName" runat="server"
                              Font-Bold="true" Font-Size="14px"
                              Text='<%# Eval("FirstName") + " " + Eval("LastName") %>'>
                    </asp:Label>
                    <br />
                    <asp:Label ID="lblTitle" runat="server"
                              Text='<%# Eval("Title") %>'>
                    </asp:Label>
                    <hr />
                    <asp:Label ID="lblNotes" runat="server"
                              Text='<%# Eval("Notes") %>'>
                    </asp:Label>
                </td>
            </tr>
        </table>
    </ItemTemplate>
</telerik:RadListBox>

<asp:LinqDataSource ID="EmployeesDataSource" runat="server"
        ContextTypeName="WebApplication1.NorthwindDataContext"
        EntityTypeName=""
        TableName="Employees">
</asp:LinqDataSource>
```

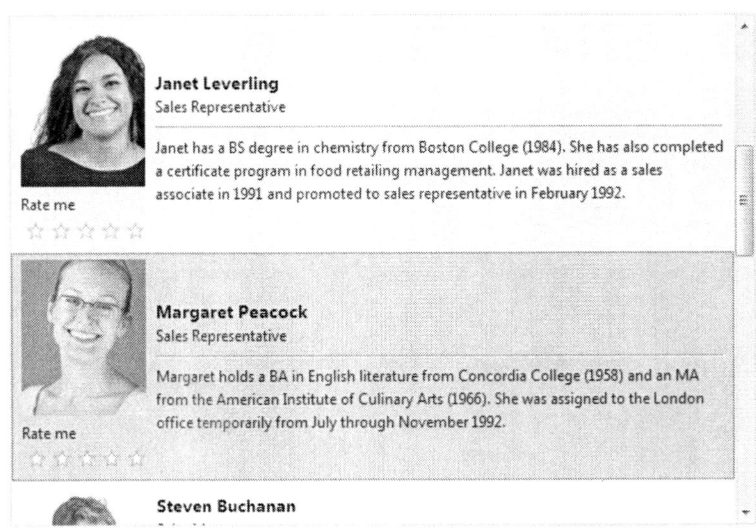

Figure 7-21. *Item templates in RadListBox make items look a lot better.*

Summary

In this chapter, we have completed our examination of the data RadControls and the most important capabilities they expose for manipulating data. We have considered `RadFilter`, `RadListView`, and `RadListBox`.

`RadFilter` is a control that builds filter expressions that can be passed to controls such as `RadListView` and `RadGrid`. The advantage of using this control is empowering end users to write their own filters so they can have full control of the data they need to see.

`RadListView` is an enhanced version of the ASP.NET `ListView` control. It also supports simple, declarative, and advanced data binding for all your needs. With the predefined templates, you can quickly build attractive list views that match your overall web application styles. `RadListView` supports editing operations automatically or manually. You can also implement paging, sorting, filtering, and selecting to provide additional functionality.

`RadListBox` is a control for displaying a list of items. It allows for multiple selection of items, reordering, and transferring between two `RadListBox` controls. You can easily control the `RadListBox`'s appearance by arranging the buttons in different layouts or changing their text. Icons and check boxes are supported within `RadListBox` items.

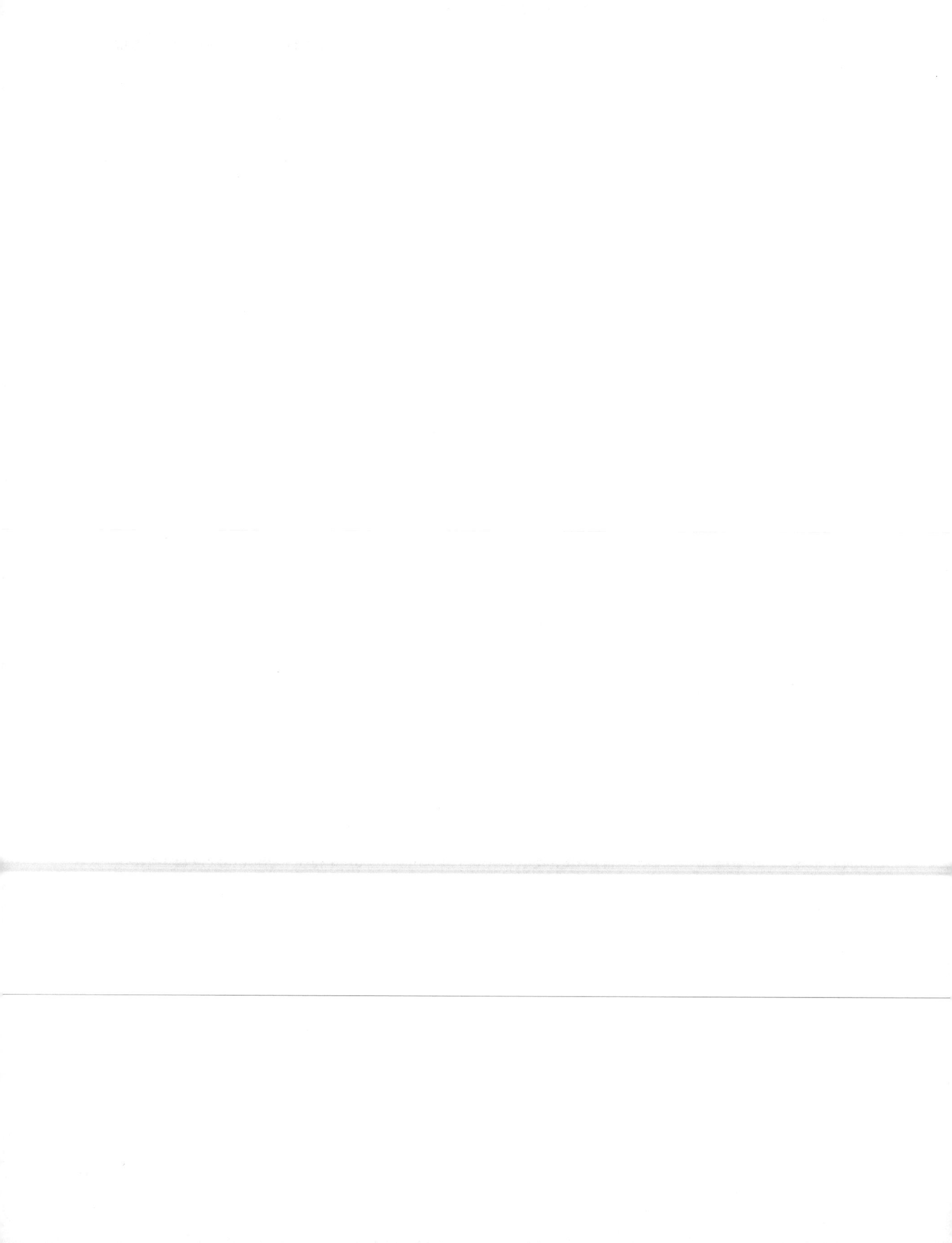

CHAPTER 8

Layout RadControls

One of the most important and sometimes complicated tasks for developers is the layout of the user interface. On one hand, they must meet the functionality requirements for the application, but on the other hand, they have to create interfaces that not only comply with the functionality requirements but also comply with the easy-of-use and look-and-feel requirements of a great UI.

Toward that end, Telerik has several controls that allow you to manipulate and organize your application's UI. The controls are `RadTabStrip`, `RadMultiPage`, `RadWindow`, `RadWindowManager`, `RadSplitter`, `RadDock`, and `RadRotator`.

Using RadTabStrip and RadMultiPage

`RadTabStrip` is a component that provides a tabular interface for web applications. At first, it might look like a navigation control, but although you can use it for that purpose, the main feature is the organization of the information and control on the page.

The control has several interesting abilities, and integration with `RadMultiPage` certainly turns it into a very powerful platform for organizing the contents of web applications.

One of the nice features of `RadTabStrip` is that it can span several rows or have scrolling buttons if you have more tabs than can fit in the horizontal display area. Another feature is the ability to place the tabs on the top, bottom, left, or right of the content, so you can leverage your imagination for visually appealing applications.

`RadTabStrip` and `RadMultiPage` include full-featured server and client APIs, and the versatile template model enables you to create complex structures very easily and with little programming effort. The enhanced rendering engine provides minimum HTML and support for modern standards (no more HTML tables).

Listing 8-1 illustrates how you can configure `RadTabStrip` for simple navigation (we'll get that out of the way so we can move on to the most interesting stuff). You can achieve navigation in two ways: using the `NavigateUrl` property or using client- or server-side code. For the purpose of this scenario, we create an `iframe` that will be hosting the page to which we should navigate. The URL will be assigned to the `iframe` on the client side based on the selected tab, since we have stored it in the `Value` property. Figure 8-1 shows the `RadTabStrip`.

Listing 8-1. *Simple RadTabStrip Navigation*

ASPX Page

```
<telerik:RadTabStrip ID="RadTabStrip1" runat="server"
        OnClientTabSelected="RadTabStrip1_ClientTabSelected">
        <Tabs>
                <telerik:RadTab Text="Telerik" Value="http://www.telerik.com">
                </telerik:RadTab>
                <telerik:RadTab Text="Google" Value="http://www.google.com">
                </telerik:RadTab>
                <telerik:RadTab Text="CSW Solutions" Value="http://www.cswsolutions.com">
                </telerik:RadTab>
        </Tabs>
</telerik:RadTabStrip>

<iframe id="tabFrame" width="800px" height="300px">
</iframe>

<script type="text/javascript">
    function RadTabStrip1_ClientTabSelected(sender, eventArgs) {
        var tab = eventArgs.get_tab();
        var frame = $get("tabFrame");
        frame.src = tab.get_value();
    }
</script>
```

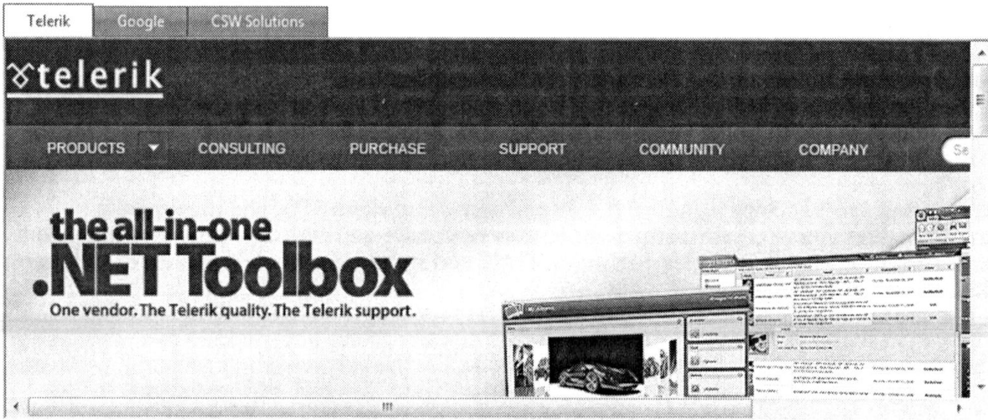

Figure 8-1. *Using RadTabStrip to navigate to different pages*

Creating a Hierarchical RadTabStrip

RadTabStrip can work as a hierarchical structure with different levels of depth. The same as with RadTreeView, we can know the level we are and the hierarchy is automatically created for us when bound to a datasource with hierarchical data.

The example in Listing 8-2 is created with a datasource from our `web.sitemap` file. Note how the correct property settings enable with minimum effort the creation of the hierarchy and how the tabs are generated for us. Figure 8-2 illustrates the example.

Listing 8-2. *Creating a Hierarchical RadTabStrip Using RadSiteMapDataSource*

ASPX Page

```
<telerik:RadTabStrip ID="RadTabStrip2" runat="server"
        OnClientTabSelected="RadTabStrip2_ClientTabSelected"
        DataSourceID="RadSiteMapDataSource1">
</telerik:RadTabStrip>

<telerik:RadSiteMapDataSource ID="RadSiteMapDataSource1" runat="server"
        ShowStartingNode="false"
        SiteMapFile="Web.sitemap" />

<asp:Label ID="lblSelectedTab" runat="server"></asp:Label>

<script type="text/javascript" language="javascript">
    function RadTabStrip2_ClientTabSelected(sender, eventArgs) {
        var tab = eventArgs.get_tab();
        var label = $get("<%=lblSelectedTab.ClientID %>");
        label.innerHTML = "You selected the tab: " + tab.get_text() +
                        " on level " + tab.get_level();
    }
</script>
```


Figure 8-2. *RadTabStrip with multiple hierarchical levels*

Binding to a Database

`RadTabStrip` supports data binding to standard ASP.NET datasources including `EntityDataSource`, `LinqDataSource`, and `XmlDataSource`. It can also be bound to any .NET collection type, such as those that implement the `IEnumerable` and `IList` interfaces.

The example in Listing 8-3 shows how to bind to data retrieved from a SQL Server database, using the `SqlDataSource` control and how to use some of the client-side API functions to get information about the current tab. The example uses the `Orientation` property to show the tabs on the left side and not on the top, which more common (see Figure 8-3).

Listing 8-3. *RadTabStrip Database Binding*

ASPX Page

```
<telerik:RadTabStrip ID="RadTabStrip3" runat="server"
        DataFieldID="EmployeeID"
        DataSourceID="SqlDataSource1"
        DataTextField="Name"
        DataValueField="EmployeeID"
        OnClientTabSelected="RadTabStrip3_ClientTabSelected"
        Orientation="VerticalLeft">
</telerik:RadTabStrip>

<img id="employeePic" runat="server" alt="" src="" />

<asp:SqlDataSource ID="SqlDataSource1" runat="server"
    ConnectionString="<%$ ConnectionStrings:NorthwindConnectionString %>"
    SelectCommand="SELECT [EmployeeID], [LastName] + ',' + [FirstName] AS [Name]
                    FROM [Employees]
               ORDER BY [LastName], [FirstName]">
</asp:SqlDataSource>

<script type="text/javascript">
    function RadTabStrip3_ClientTabSelected(sender, eventArgs) {
        var tab = eventArgs.get_tab();
        var img = $get("<%=employeePic.ClientID %>");
        img.src = "images/employees/" + tab.get_value() + ".jpg";
    }
</script>
```

Figure 8-3. *RadTabStrip retrieves information from the bound datasource*

Working with Templates and Scrolling

A template is a powerful tool for enhancing how items in a control are rendered in `RadTabStrip`, and Listing 8-4 shows how to create a `RadTabStrip` with templated tabs. In this example, we access a control inside the template and use data binding for the nested controls.

Scrolling is a feature that enables the control to span the boundaries of the page (or container of the control) by showing only part of the available tabs and buttons to navigate to the rest of them. Figure 8-4 illustrates both features.

Listing 8-4. *Defining Templates and Enabling Scrolling for RadTabStrip*

ASPX Page

```
<telerik:RadTabStrip ID="RadTabStrip4" runat="server"
        DataFieldID="CategoryID"
        DataSourceID="SqlDataSource2"
        DataTextField="CategoryName"
        DataValueField="CategoryID"
        ScrollButtonsPosition="Right"
        ScrollChildren="true"
        PerTabScrolling="true"
        OnTabClick="RadTabStrip4_TabClick"
        OnTabDataBound="RadTabStrip4_ItemDataBound">
    <TabTemplate>
        <%# Eval("CategoryName") %>
        <telerik:RadComboBox ID="comboProducts" runat="server"
                                DropDownWidth="250px"
                                DataTextField="ProductName"
                                DataValueField="ProductID"
                                AutoPostBack="true"
                                OnSelectedIndexChanged="comboProducts_SelectedIndexChanged">
        </telerik:RadComboBox>
        <asp:SqlDataSource ID="SqlDataSource3" runat="server"
            ConnectionString="<%$ ConnectionStrings:NorthwindConnectionString %>"
            SelectCommand="SELECT [ProductID], [ProductName]
                            FROM [Products]
                            WHERE ([CategoryID] = @CategoryID)">
            <SelectParameters>
                <asp:Parameter Name="CategoryID" Type="Int32" />
            </SelectParameters>
        </asp:SqlDataSource>
    </TabTemplate>
</telerik:RadTabStrip>
<asp:Label ID="lblCatProd" runat="server"></asp:Label>
<asp:SqlDataSource ID="SqlDataSource2" runat="server"
    ConnectionString="<%$ ConnectionStrings:NorthwindConnectionString %>"
    SelectCommand="SELECT [CategoryID], [CategoryName] FROM [Categories]">
</asp:SqlDataSource>
```

Code Behind

```
protected void RadTabStrip4_ItemDataBound(object sender, RadTabStripEventArgs e)
{
    RadComboBox combo = (RadComboBox)e.Tab.FindControl("comboProducts");
    SqlDataSource sqlds = (SqlDataSource) e.Tab.FindControl("SqlDataSource3");
    sqlds.SelectParameters[0].DefaultValue = e.Tab.Value;
    combo.DataSource = sqlds;
    combo.DataBind();
}
```

```
protected void RadTabStrip4_TabClick(object sender, RadTabStripEventArgs e)
{
    RadComboBox combo = (RadComboBox)e.Tab.FindControl("comboProducts");
    lblCatProd.Text = string.Format("Category: {0} - Product: {1}",
                                    e.Tab.Text,
                                    combo.SelectedItem.Text);
}

protected void comboProducts_SelectedIndexChanged(
                        object o,
                        RadComboBoxSelectedIndexChangedEventArgs e)
{
    RadComboBox combo = (RadComboBox) o;
    RadTab tab = (RadTab) combo.Parent;
    tab.Selected = true;
    lblCatProd.Text = string.Format("Category: {0} - Product: {1}",
                                    tab.Text,
                                    e.Text);
}
```

Figure 8-4. *Note that each tab in the sample RadTabStrip is now much more than just text.*

Combining RadTabStrip and RadMultiPage

RadMultiPage is a container control that expands the possibilities of RadTabStrip by enabling communication between both controls, so any kind of content can be accessible with your tabs.

RadMultiPage is analogous to the traditional ASP.NET MultiView control. It is based on a collection of RadPageView objects for holding web content in the same way as MultiView's View controls.

RadTabStrip provides the mechanism to navigate through the content, and RadMultiPage provides the containers for the content.

Here's how they work together: At the TabStrip level, you assign the MultiPageID property to the ID of the RadMultiPage control; this connects both controls. Then, for each tab you want to handle content from the RadMultiPage control, you set the PageViewID property to the ID of the RadPageView control inside the RadMultiPage.

This configuration may seem complicated, but frankly, it's not. Let's take a look at the example in Listing 8-5, and you'll see what I mean. Figure 8-5 shows the example running.

Listing 8-5. *RadTabStrip and RadMultiPage Working Together*

ASPX Page

```
<telerik:RadTabStrip ID="RadTabStrip5" runat="server"
    MultiPageID="RadMultiPage1"
    SelectedIndex="0">
```

```
    <Tabs>
        <telerik:RadTab runat="server" Text="RadEditor" PageViewID="RadPageView1"
            Selected="True">
        </telerik:RadTab>
        <telerik:RadTab runat="server" Text="RadTreeView" PageViewID="RadPageView2">
        </telerik:RadTab>
        <telerik:RadTab runat="server" Text="RadScheduler" PageViewID="RadPageView3">
        </telerik:RadTab>
    </Tabs>
</telerik:RadTabStrip>

<telerik:RadMultiPage ID="RadMultiPage1" runat="server"
        SelectedIndex="0">
    <telerik:RadPageView ID="RadPageView1" runat="server">
        <telerik:RadEditor ID="RadEditor1" runat="server">
        </telerik:RadEditor>
        <asp:SqlDataSource ID="SqlDataSource3" runat="server"
            ConnectionString="<%$ ConnectionStrings:NorthwindConnectionString %>"
            SelectCommand="SELECT [EmployeeID], [LastName], [FirstName], [Photo]
                            FROM [Employees]">
        </asp:SqlDataSource>
    </telerik:RadPageView>
    <telerik:RadPageView ID="RadPageView2" runat="server">
        <telerik:RadTreeView ID="RadTreeView1" runat="server"
                DataValueField="ID"
                DataSourceID="SqlDataSource4"
                DataFieldID="ID"
                DataFieldParentID="parentID"
                DataTextField="Name" >
        </telerik:RadTreeView>
        <asp:SqlDataSource ID="SqlDataSource4" runat="server"
        ConnectionString="<%$ ConnectionStrings:NorthwindConnectionString %>"
        SelectCommand="select ProductID as ID, ProductName as Name,
                                UnitPrice, CategoryID+1000 as parentID
                        from Products p
                        union all
                        select CategoryID+1000 as ID, CategoryName as Name,
                                0 as UnitPrice, null as parentID
                        from Categories">
        </asp:SqlDataSource>
    </telerik:RadPageView>
    <telerik:RadPageView ID="RadPageView3" runat="server">
        <telerik:RadScheduler ID="RadScheduler1" runat="server"
                DataDescriptionField="Description"
                DataEndField="End" DataKeyField="ID"
                DataRecurrenceField="RecurrenceRule"
                DataRecurrenceParentKeyField="RecurrenceParentID"
                DataSourceID="SqlDataSource5"
                DataStartField="Start"
                DataSubjectField="Subject">
        </telerik:RadScheduler>
```

```
        <asp:SqlDataSource ID="SqlDataSource5" runat="server"
            ConnectionString="<%$ ConnectionStrings:NorthwindConnectionString %>"
            DeleteCommand="DELETE FROM [Appointments] WHERE [ID] = @original_ID"
            InsertCommand="INSERT INTO [Appointments]
                                        ([Subject], [Description], [Start],
                                        [End], [RoomID], [UserID],
                                        [RecurrenceRule],
                                        [RecurrenceParentID],
                                        [Annotations])
                                VALUES (@Subject, @Description, @Start, @End,
                                        @RoomID, @UserID,
                                        @RecurrenceRule,
                                        @RecurrenceParentID,
                                        @Annotations)"
            OldValuesParameterFormatString="original_{0}"
            SelectCommand="SELECT * FROM [Appointments]"
            UpdateCommand="UPDATE [Appointments] SET [Subject] = @Subject,
                                [Description] = @Description, [Start] = @Start,
                                [End] = @End, [RoomID] = @RoomID, [UserID] = @UserID,
                                [RecurrenceRule] = @RecurrenceRule,
                                [RecurrenceParentID] = @RecurrenceParentID,
                                [Annotations] = @Annotations
                        WHERE [ID] = @original_ID">
            <DeleteParameters>
                <asp:Parameter Name="original_ID" Type="Int32" />
            </DeleteParameters>
            <InsertParameters>
                <asp:Parameter Name="Subject" Type="String" />
                <asp:Parameter Name="Description" Type="String" />
                <asp:Parameter Name="Start" Type="DateTime" />
                <asp:Parameter Name="End" Type="DateTime" />
                <asp:Parameter Name="RoomID" Type="Int32" />
                <asp:Parameter Name="UserID" Type="Int32" />
                <asp:Parameter Name="RecurrenceRule" Type="String" />
                <asp:Parameter Name="RecurrenceParentID" Type="Int32" />
                <asp:Parameter Name="Annotations" Type="String" />
            </InsertParameters>
            <UpdateParameters>
                <asp:Parameter Name="Subject" Type="String" />
                <asp:Parameter Name="Description" Type="String" />
                <asp:Parameter Name="Start" Type="DateTime" />
                <asp:Parameter Name="End" Type="DateTime" />
                <asp:Parameter Name="RoomID" Type="Int32" />
                <asp:Parameter Name="UserID" Type="Int32" />
                <asp:Parameter Name="RecurrenceRule" Type="String" />
                <asp:Parameter Name="RecurrenceParentID" Type="Int32" />
                <asp:Parameter Name="Annotations" Type="String" />
                <asp:Parameter Name="original_ID" Type="Int32" />
            </UpdateParameters>
        </asp:SqlDataSource>
    </telerik:RadPageView>
</telerik:RadMultiPage>
```

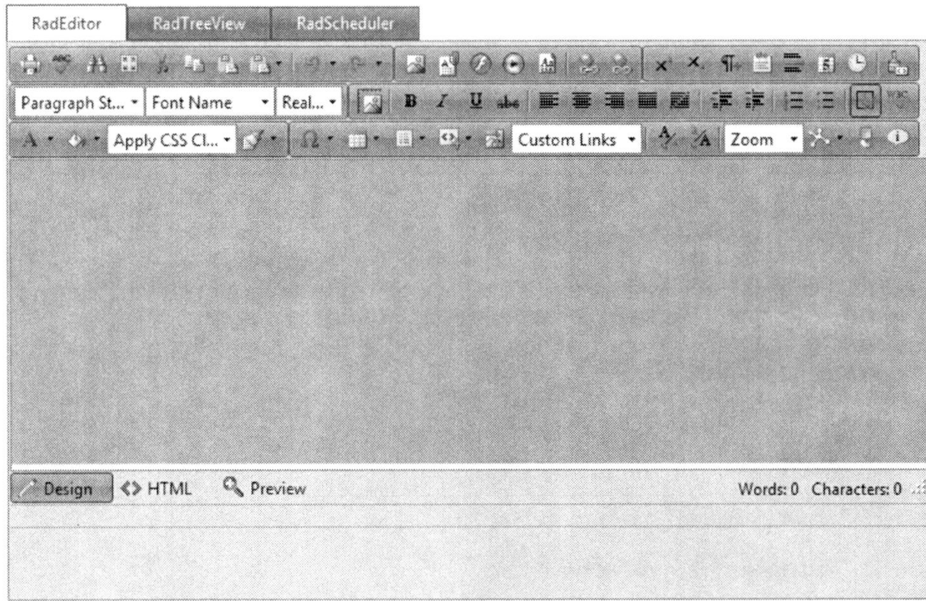

Figure 8-5. *RadTabStrip, with the help of RadMultiPage, is capable of displaying diverse content.*

Using RadWindow and RadWindowManager

The next couple of components provide functionality to create windowed applications. The `RadWindow` component creates window objects that may host external or application-based content (from a database for example) for the user to take action, interact with the object, or it can just to present information regarding the current state of the work in the application. With the help of `Behaviors`, you can customize how the `RadWindow` is displayed and the level of interaction for users (you can restrict the resizing, moving, closing, minimizing, and so on).

`RadWindowManager` is a component designed to set common properties shared by all `RadWindows` in your page. You also don't have to create separate `RadWindows` in the page; for this purpose, you use the `RadWindowManager.Windows` collection to define specific properties when needed.

One of the great features of `RadWindowManager` is the replacement for browser dialogs. You won't have to use the ugly alert, confirm, and prompt dialogs from the browser any longer. Now, you can create nice-looking and less-intrusive `RadAlert`, `RadConfirm`, and `RadPrompt` dialogs; these have the same functionality as their ancestors—only better looking.

You can communicate between a `RadWindow` and its parent; you can even call functions in opened `RadWindows`. `RadWindows` can be cached, and most importantly, they won't be blocked by pop-up blockers, because they don't actually open new browser windows when called (they open `iframe` objects styled as windows).

Also, you can define minimized zones where your minimized windows rest, thus creating an effect similar to the taskbar in Windows.

■ **Note** `RadWindow` and `RadWindowManager` expose almost all of their functionality through their client-side APIs; therefore you can't open or manipulate a `RadWindow` using server-side code. The only things you can do on the server side are declare `RadWindow` objects, modify their properties, and register client-side scripts to run `RadWindow` commands.

Creating and Opening RadWindows

The example in Listing 8-6 implements a window that is opened when the user clicks a button. The window will open an external link and render its contents (see Figure 8-6).

Listing 8-6. *RadWindow with External Content*

ASPX Page

```
<asp:Button ID="btnOpenRadWindow1" runat="server"
        Text="Open a RadWindow"
        OnClientClick="ShowRadWindow1();return false;" />

<telerik:RadWindow ID="RadWindow1" runat="server"
        Width="600px"
        Height="450px"
        style="z-index:20000">
</telerik:RadWindow>
<script language="javascript" type="text/javascript">
    function ShowRadWindow1() {
        var wnd = $find("<%=RadWindow1.ClientID %>");
        wnd.setUrl("http://www.cswsolutions.com");
        wnd.show();
    }
</script>
```

Figure 8-6. *Opening external pages with RadWindow*

Adding RadWindow Behaviors

Behaviors are the actions a user can take with a `RadWindow`, for example, move, maximize, minimize, or resize a window. Figure 8-7 shows the available behaviors for a `RadWindow`.

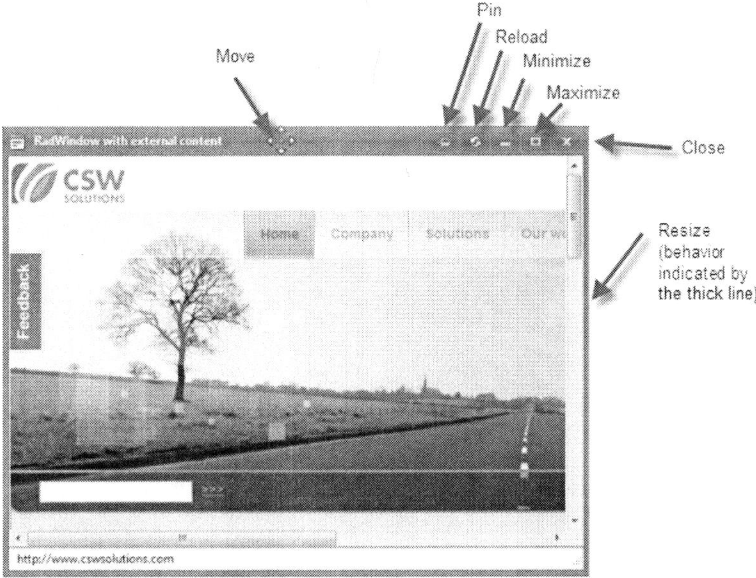

Figure 8-7. *Behaviors of a RadWindow*

The behaviors are defined through the `Behaviors` property used declaratively, in server-side code, or in client-side code via the `set_behaviors()` method passing the behaviors in the `Telerik.Web.UI.WindowBehavior` enumeration. It is a comma-separated value with all the actions we want the user to be able to do. The possible values follow:

- *Minimize*: Allows the window to be minimized
- *Close*: Allows the window to be closed
- *Pin*: Allows the window to be pinned in its current position
- *Maximize*: Allows the window to be maximized
- *Move*: Allows the window to be moved from its current location
- *Resize*: Allows the window to be resized
- *Reload*: Reloads the content of the window

The example in Listing 8-7 will demonstrate how to set up behaviors for `RadWindow`. You can see in Figure 8-8 how `RadWindow` was modified and the behaviors were removed.

Listing 8-7. *Defining RadWindow Behaviors Declaratively*

ASPX Page

```
<asp:Button ID="btnOpenRadWindow2" runat="server"
                Text="Open a RadWindow that can only be moved and closed"
                OnClientClick="ShowRadWindow2();return false;" />

<telerik:RadWindow ID="RadWindow2" runat="server"
                Width="600px"
                Height="450px"
                Behaviors="Close, Move"
                style="z-index:20000">
</telerik:RadWindow>

<script language="javascript" type="text/javascript">
    function ShowRadWindow2() {
        var wnd = $find("<%=RadWindow2.ClientID %>");
        wnd.setUrl("http://www.cswsolutions.com");
        wnd.show();
    }
</script>
```

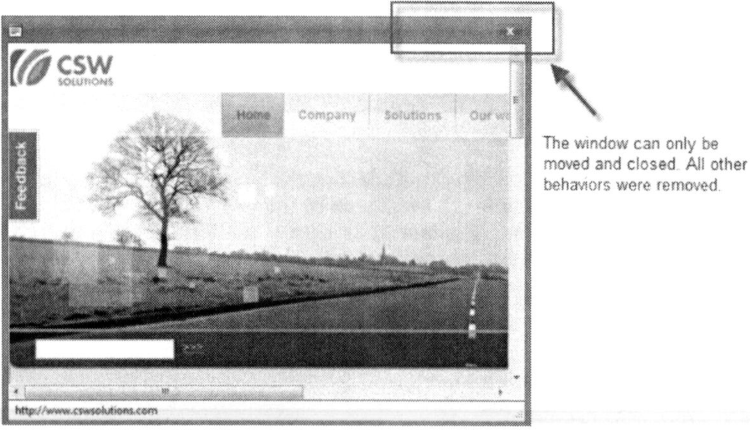

Figure 8-8. *Note, in the opened RadWindow, that users can only move and close the window.*

Creating a Modal RadWindow

An important feature for pop-up windows in web applications is to behave as a modal window. A *modal window* is a window that has the focus in the application and won't allow the user to work in any other part of the application until it's been closed.

RadWindow can behave as a modal window too. You can set the modal property to true or use the client-side method set_modal() with the parameter true to enable the modal behavior. Listing 8-8 defines the modal behavior shown in Figure 8-9. Note that the window is on top of the page and the page is grayed out and unavailable.

Listing 8-8. *Creating a Modal RadWindow*

ASPX Page

```
<asp:Button ID="btnOpenRadWindow3" runat="server"
            Text="Open a Modal RadWindow"
            OnClientClick="ShowModalRadWindow();return false;" />

<telerik:RadWindow ID="RadWindow3" runat="server"
            Width="600px"
            Height="450px"
            style="z-index:20000">
</telerik:RadWindow>

<script type="text/javascript">
    function ShowModalRadWindow() {
        var wnd = $find("<%=RadWindow3.ClientID %>");
        wnd.setUrl("http://www.cswsolutions.com");
        wnd.set_modal(true);
        wnd.show();
    }
</script>
```

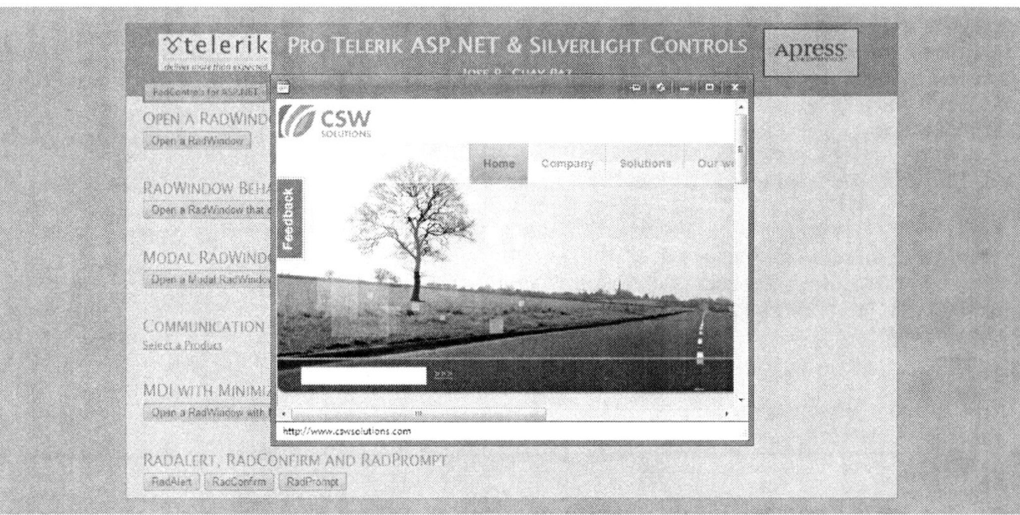

Figure 8-9. *Modal RadWindow*

Communicating Between RadWindows

RadWindows can exchange information with the use of the argument object that is passed between calls. By obtaining a reference to the RadWindow and calling the method get_argument(), you get access to the argument object, which, in turn, can have any number of properties with values set by the called window.

The technique is simple. You first open a RadWindow that has defined a handler for the OnClientClose event, which is fired once the called RadWindow is closed by the user after its work is done. When closing the RadWindow, you use JavaScript to create an object, set the necessary properties with the values you want to return, and pass the object as a parameter of the Close() method.

Finally, in the OnClientClose event handler, you call the get_argument() method to retrieve the argument object created in the RadWindow at closing time. If the argument object is valid (not null), you can access the values of the properties.

Listing 8-9 shows how to implement this mechanism. It first load a RadWindow where you are supposed to select a product from a list, but to populate the list of products, you need to select a category. For that purpose, you need to open a second RadWindow where you select the category. Once you select from and close the categories window, a JavaScript object is created for the selected category (see Figure 8-10). When the control is returned to the products window, it populates the list of products based on the selected category. Now, you are ready to select a product, and when you close the products window, your selection is passed to the calling page (see Figure 8-11).

The example also shows how to open a RadWindow from another RadWindow and have a complete communication channel between both of them and the parent page. Another interesting feature of this example is the use of a regular HTML hyperlink to open the products RadWindow.

Listing 8-9. *Communication Between RadWindows*

ASPX Main Page

```
<a href=" OpenProductsRadWindow();">Select a Product</a>
<telerik:RadWindow ID="ProductsRadWindow" runat="server"
        Width="600px"
        Height="450px"
        OnClientClose="ProductSelected"
        style="z-index:20000"
        Title="Products">
</telerik:RadWindow>

<asp:Label ID="lblProductSelected" runat="server"></asp:Label>

<script type="text/javascript">
    function OpenProductsRadWindow() {
        var wnd = $find("<%=ProductsRadWindow.ClientID %>");
        wnd.setUrl("radwindow_Products.aspx");
        wnd.show();
    }

    function ProductSelected(sender, eventArgs) {
        var arg = eventArgs.get_argument();

        if (arg) {
            var lbl = $get("<%=lblProductSelected.ClientID %>");
            lbl.innerHTML = "You selected the product: " + arg.ProductName;
        }
    }
</script>
```

radwindow_Products.aspx Page

```
<div>
    <asp:ScriptManager ID="ScriptManager1" runat="server">
    </asp:ScriptManager>
    <asp:Button ID="btnCategories" runat="server"
                OnClientClick="OpenCategoriesWindow();return false;"
                Text="Load products from category" />
    <br />
    <asp:Label ID="lblCategory" runat="server"></asp:Label><br />
    <asp:ListBox ID="lstProducts" runat="server"
                Height="200px"
                Width="300px">
    </asp:ListBox>
    <telerik:RadWindow ID="CategoriesRadWindow" runat="server"
                Width="300px"
                Height="300px"
                Title="Categories"
                OnClientClose="CategorySelected"
                Modal="true">
    </telerik:RadWindow>
    <asp:Button ID="btnClose" runat="server"
                OnClientClick="CloseWindow();return false;"
                Text="Close" />
</div>

<script type="text/javascript">
    function GetRadWindow() {
        var oWindow = null;
        if (window.radWindow)
                oWindow = window.radWindow;
        else
                if (window.frameElement.radWindow)
                        oWindow = window.frameElement.radWindow;
        return oWindow;
     }

     function CloseWindow() {
         var arg = new Object();
         var lst = document.getElementById("<%=lstProducts.ClientID %>");
         arg.ProductName = lst.options[lst.selectedIndex].text;
         var wnd = GetRadWindow();
         wnd.close(arg);
     }

     function OpenCategoriesWindow() {
         var wnd = $find("<%=CategoriesRadWindow.ClientID %>");
         wnd.setUrl("radwindow_Categories.aspx");
         wnd.show();
     }

     function CategorySelected(sender, eventArgs) {
         var arg = eventArgs.get_argument();
```

```
        if (arg) {
            $get("<%=lblCategory.ClientID %>").innerHTML =
                                  "Select products from category: " + arg.CategoryName;
            window.location = "radwindow_Products.aspx?cat=" + arg.CategoryID;
        }
    }
</script>
```

radwindow_Products.aspx Code Behind

```
protected void Page_Load(object sender, EventArgs e)
{
    if (Page.IsPostBack) return;
    if (!string.IsNullOrEmpty(Request.QueryString["cat"]))
        LoadProducts(Request.QueryString["cat"]);
}


private void LoadProducts(string cat)
{
    lstProducts.Items.Clear();
    using (var cnn = new SqlConnection(WebConfigurationManager
                                    .ConnectionStrings["NorthwindConnectionString"]
                                    .ConnectionString))
    {
        cnn.Open();
        string sSql = string.Format(@"SELECT CategoryName
                                    FROM Categories
                                   WHERE CategoryID = {0}", cat);
        SqlCommand cmd = new SqlCommand(sSql, cnn);
        string result = cmd.ExecuteScalar().ToString();
        lblCategory.Text = string.Format("Select products from category: {0}", result);
        sSql = string.Format(@"SELECT ProductName
                             FROM Products
                            WHERE CategoryID = {0}", cat);
        cmd = new SqlCommand(sSql, cnn);
        using (var rd = cmd.ExecuteReader())
        {
            if (rd != null)
                while (rd.Read())
                {
                    lstProducts.Items.Add(rd["ProductName"].ToString());
                }
            lstProducts.DataBind();
        }
        cnn.Close();
    }
}
```

radwindow_Categories.aspx

```
<asp:ListBox ID="lstCategories" runat="server"
        DataSourceID="SqlDataSource1"
        DataTextField="CategoryName"
        DataValueField="CategoryID"
        Height="150px"
        Width="250px">
</asp:ListBox>

<asp:SqlDataSource ID="SqlDataSource1" runat="server"
    ConnectionString="<%$ ConnectionStrings:NorthwindConnectionString %>"
    SelectCommand="SELECT [CategoryID], [CategoryName] FROM [Categories]">
</asp:SqlDataSource>

<asp:Button ID="btnClose" runat="server"
        OnClientClick="CloseWindow();return false;"
Text="Close" />

<script language="javascript" type="text/javascript">
    function GetRadWindow() {
        var oWindow = null;
        if (window.radWindow)
                oWindow = window.radWindow;
        else
                if (window.frameElement.radWindow)
                        oWindow = window.frameElement.radWindow;
        return oWindow;
    }

    function CloseWindow() {
        var arg = new Object();
        var lst = document.getElementById("<%=lstCategories.ClientID %>");
        arg.CategoryID = lst.options[lst.selectedIndex].value;
        arg.CategoryName = lst.options[lst.selectedIndex].text;
        var wnd = GetRadWindow();
        wnd.close(arg);
    }
</script>
```

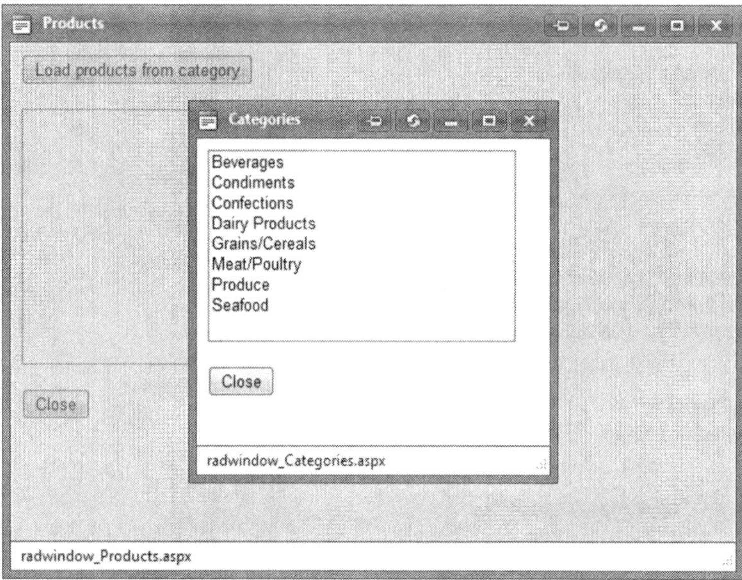

Figure 8-10. *Opening a RadWindow from another RadWindow and return a value*

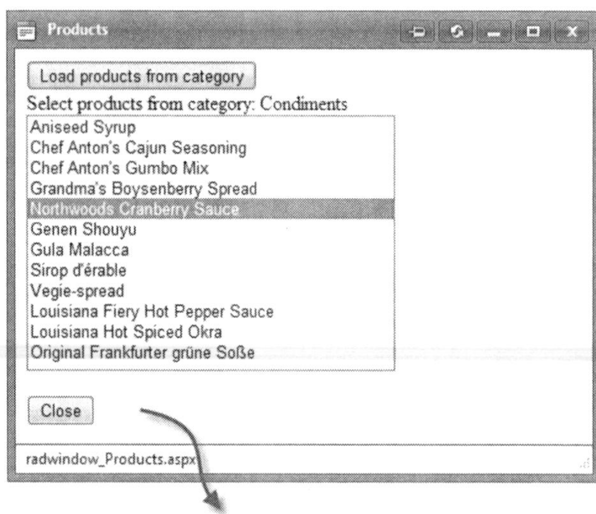

Select a Product You selected the product: Northwoods Cranberry Sauce

Figure 8-11. *Selecting a value in a RadWindow to pass to the calling page*

Implementing MDI and Minimized Zones

RadWindow can act as a multiple document interface (MDI) container for other RadWindows. Basically, the functionality is ready out of the box by just creating a RadWindow that loads a page that contains a RadWindowManager. Then, you open new RadWindows using the RadWindowManager.Open() method, so all RadWindows are kept inside the boundaries of the main RadWindow.

In Listing 8-10, I create an MDI container that holds a page with an ASP.NET panel that acts as a minimized zone. A *minimized zone* is an area (a panel or div) that resembles the functionality of Windows taskbar. When a RadWindow is minimized, it is shown in that area; otherwise, the minimized RadWindow would be minimized in its current location. Figure 8-12 shows the example running.

Listing 8-10. *MDI Implementation and Minimized Zones*

ASPX Main Page

```
<asp:Button ID="btnMinimizedZone" runat="server"
            Text="Open a RadWindow with Minimized Zones"
            OnClientClick="ShowRadWindowM();return false;" />
<telerik:RadWindow ID="RadWindow4" runat="server"
                Width="600px"
                Height="450px"
                style="z-index:20000">
</telerik:RadWindow>
<script type="text/javascript">
    function ShowRadWindowM() {
        var wnd = $find("<%=RadWindow4.ClientID %>");
        wnd.setUrl("radwindow_MinimizeZone.aspx");
        wnd.show();
        wnd.maximize();
    }
</script>
```

radwindow_MinimizeZone.aspx

```
<asp:Panel id="panelMinimizedZone" runat="server"
           style="width:100%; height:30px; border: 1px solid #000000">
</asp:Panel>

<telerik:RadScriptManager ID="RadScriptManager1" runat="server">
</telerik:RadScriptManager>
<telerik:RadWindowManager ID="RadWindowManager1" runat="server">
    <Windows>
        <telerik:RadWindow ID="windowGoogle" runat="server"
                        Width="600px"
                        Height="450px"
                        Title="Google"
                        MinimizeZoneID="panelMinimizedZone">
        </telerik:RadWindow>
```

```
        <telerik:RadWindow ID="windowMicrosoft" runat="server"
                           Width="600px"
                           Height="450px"
                           Title="Microsoft"
                           MinimizeZoneID="panelMinimizedZone">
        </telerik:RadWindow>
        <telerik:RadWindow ID="windowTelerik" runat="server"
                           Width="600px"
                           Height="450px"
                           Title="Telerik"
                           MinimizeZoneID="panelMinimizedZone">
        </telerik:RadWindow>
    </Windows>
</telerik:RadWindowManager>
<telerik:RadCodeBlock ID="RadCodeBlock1" runat="server">
    <script language="javascript" type="text/javascript">
        function pageLoad() {
            window.setTimeout(function () {
                var manager = $find("<%=RadWindowManager1.ClientID %>");
                manager.open("http://www.google.com", "windowGoogle");
                manager.open("http://www.microsoft.com", "windowMicrosoft");
                manager.open("http://www.telerik.com", "windowTelerik");
                manager.cascade();
            }, 0);
        }
    </script>
</telerik:RadCodeBlock>
```

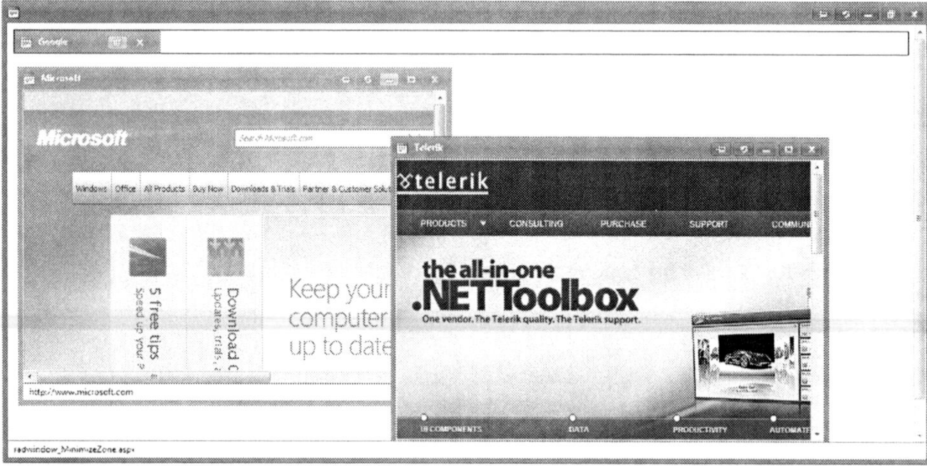

Figure 8-12. *Note the minimized zone at the top of the page, and note that all of the windows are inside the main window.*

Replacements for Browser Dialogs

As mentioned before, RadWindow provides functionality to replace the default browser dialogs. You have a high degree of control with the RadAlert, RadConfirm, and RadPrompt dialogs. Note that, for the dialogs to work, you need a RadWindowManager control in the page, and all dialogs will render based on the properties set up in the control.

RadAlert has five parameters: the message to display, the width, the height, a reference to the caller object, and the title of the dialog window that gets opened.

RadConfirm has six parameters: the message to display, the name of the callback function that is called once the user makes a selection or closes the dialog window, the width, the height, a reference to the caller object, and the title of the dialog window.

RadPrompt has seven parameters: those from RadConfirm plus the default text for the text area where users will type.

Listing 8-11 shows how to implement these replacement dialogs. RadAlert is shown in Figure 8-13, RadConfirm in Figure 8-14, and RadPrompt in Figure 8-15.

Listing 8-11. *Implementing the Replacement Browser Dialogs*

ASPX Page

```
<asp:Button ID="btnRadAlert" runat="server"
                Text="RadAlert"
                OnClientClick=" ShowRadAlert();return false;" />

<asp:Button ID="btnRadConfirm" runat="server"
                Text="RadConfirm"
                OnClientClick="ShowRadConfirm();return false;" />

<asp:Button ID="btnRadPrompt" runat="server"
                Text="RadPrompt"
                OnClientClick="ShowRadPrompt();return false;" />

<asp:Label ID="lblResponse" runat="server"></asp:Label>

<script type="text/javascript">
    function ShowRadAlert() {
        radalert('This is an alert! <br /><br />
                See how I can add <b>a lot</b> of content here.<br /><br />
                <i>Nice! Isn\'t it?</i>',
                350,
                250,
                null,
                'RadAlert');
    }
    function ShowRadConfirm() {
        radconfirm('Do you like it?',
                RadConfirmCallBack,
                300,
                100,
                null,
                'RadConfirm');
    }
```

```
    function RadConfirmCallBack(args) {
        $get("<%=lblResponse.ClientID %>").innerHTML =
                            "You clicked on: " + (args ? "OK" : "Cancel");
    }

    function ShowRadPrompt() {
        radprompt('Enter some text',
                  RadPromptCallBack,
                  300,
                  200,
                  null,
                  'RadPrompt',
                  'text');
    }

    function RadPromptCallBack(args) {
        $get("<%=lblResponse.ClientID %>").innerHTML = "You entered: " + args;
    }
</script>
```

Figure 8-13. *RadAlert*

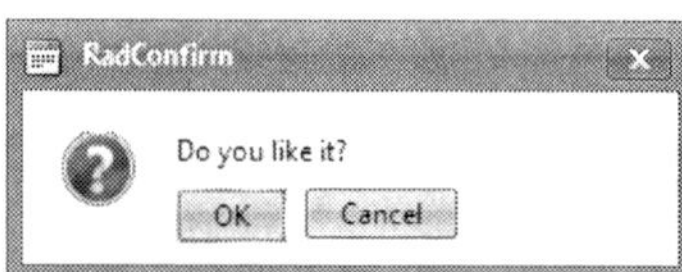

Figure 8-14. *RadConfirm*

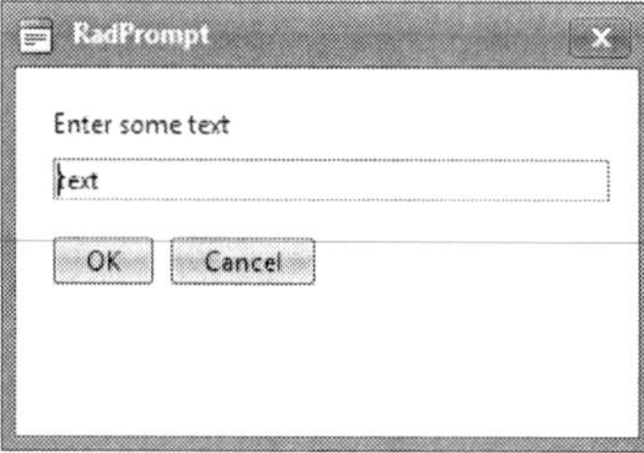

Figure 8-15. *RadPrompt*

Using RadSplitter

Our next component provides special page layout management. RadSplitter allows the logical division of a page in different areas called *panes* that are represented by objects of type RadPane. The panes can be separated by RadSplitBar objects that provide the ability to resize the panes in different ways, so you can, for example, make one pane bigger than another. You can also create collapsible panes, so users can maximize one pane by hiding the others.

RadSplitter also enables you to have sliding panes. These types of panes are represented by objects of type RadSlidingPane and work inside areas of type RadSlidingZone. Sliding panes can be extended, pinned, or hidden the same way as the side panels in Visual Studio.

This control exposes a rich client- and server-side API, but just like RadWindow, it is declared on the server, and its behavior is initialized and managed on the client.

Dividing Page Content with RadSplitter

Listing 8-12 shows how to work with RadSplitter in its most basic form. It uses one main splitter that divides the page horizontally. In the top pane is another RadSplitter that splits the pane vertically. Scroll bars are automatically included whenever the content is larger than the available space, but they can be configured to show only the vertical scrollbar, only the horizontal scrollbar, or both scrollbars. Figure 8-16 displays the splitters working.

Listing 8-12. *Implementing RadSplitter*

ASPX Page

```
<telerik:RadSplitter ID="RadSplitter1" runat="server"
        Width="100%"
        Height="300px"
        Orientation="Horizontal">
        <telerik:RadPane ID="RadPane1" Runat="server"
                Width="100%"
                Height="50%">
                <telerik:RadSplitter ID="RadSplitter2" runat="server"
                        Orientation="Vertical"
                        Width="100%"
                        Height="100%">
                        <telerik:RadPane ID="RadPane3" runat="server"
                                Width="50%"
                                Height="100%"
                                ContentUrl="http://www.telerik.com">
                        </telerik:RadPane>
                        <telerik:RadSplitBar ID="RadSplitBar2" runat="server" />
                        <telerik:RadPane ID="RadPane4" runat="server"
                                Width="50%"
                                Height="100%"
                                ContentUrl="http://www.microsoft.com">
                        </telerik:RadPane>
                </telerik:RadSplitter>
        </telerik:RadPane>
        <telerik:RadSplitBar ID="RadSplitBar1" Runat="server"
                Width="100%"
                EnableResize="true" />
```

```
        <telerik:RadPane ID="RadPane2" Runat="server"
                Width="100%"
                Height="50%"
                ContentUrl="http://www.cswsolutions.com">
        </telerik:RadPane>
</telerik:RadSplitter>
```

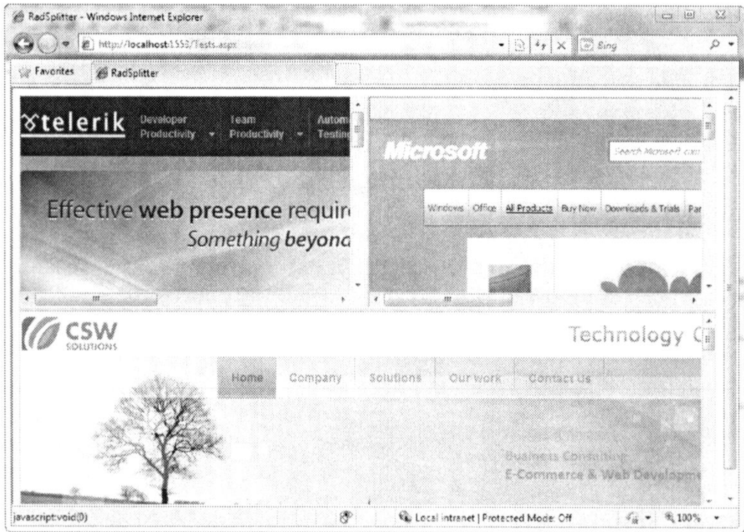

Figure 8-16. *Showing different content using RadSplitter. The screen is split into three different areas, each with its own content. Scrollbars are shown because the content is bigger than the display area.*

Implementing Collapsible Panes

You get the collapsible panes functionality by setting the `CollapseMode` property of the `RadSplitBar` object. The possible values of the property follow:

- *None*: Collapsing is disabled.
- *Forward*: The pane at the left (top) position of the split bar will be collapsed. This is the default value.
- *Backward*: The pane at the right (bottom) position of the split bar will be collapsed.
- *Both*: Panes can be collapsed in both directions.

One of the interesting features of RadSplitBar is that it can have both collapse/expand and resize behaviors. You only need to set the property `EnableResize` to `true` along with some of the values of `CollapseMode`. Listing 8-13 shows how to implement the collapsible panes, and you can see how they look in Figure 8-17.

Listing 8-13. *Collapsible Panes*

ASPX Page

```
<telerik:RadSplitter ID="RadSplitter3" runat="server"
                Width="100%"
                Height="300px"
                Orientation="Horizontal">
    <telerik:RadPane ID="RadPane5" Runat="server"
                        Width="100%"
                        Height="50%">
        <telerik:RadSplitter ID="RadSplitter4" runat="server"
                                Orientation="Vertical"
                                Width="100%"
                                Height="100%">
            <telerik:RadPane ID="RadPane6" runat="server"
                                        Width="33%"
                                        Height="100%"
                                        ContentUrl="http://www.telerik.com">
            </telerik:RadPane>
            <telerik:RadSplitBar ID="RadSplitBar3" runat="server"
                                        CollapseMode="Backward" />
            <telerik:RadPane ID="RadPane7" runat="server"
                                        Width="34%"
                                        Height="100%"
                                        ContentUrl="http://www.microsoft.com">
            </telerik:RadPane>
            <telerik:RadSplitBar ID="RadSplitBar5" runat="server"
                                        CollapseMode="Forward" />
            <telerik:RadPane ID="RadPane9" runat="server" Width="33%"
                                        Height="100%"
                                        ContentUrl="http://www.google.com">
            </telerik:RadPane>
        </telerik:RadSplitter>
    </telerik:RadPane>
    <telerik:RadSplitBar ID="RadSplitBar4" Runat="server"
                                Width="100%"
                                EnableResize="true"
                                CollapseMode="Both" />
    <telerik:RadPane ID="RadPane8" Runat="server"
                        Width="100%"
                        Height="50%"
                        ContentUrl="http://www.cswsolutions.com">
    </telerik:RadPane>
</telerik:RadSplitter>
```

Figure 8-17. *The circles show handles to collapse and expand panes.*

Resizing to Fill a Window

One common scenario when building web applications is having content that must completely fill a window, meaning the content will occupy 100 percent of the available width and height of the window and must resize itself if the window is resized.

RadSplitter can offer that behavior with a little help from CSS to control the width and height of the page. Listing 8-14 shows you how to achieve such functionality, and Figure 8-18 shows the example running.

Listing 8-14. *Full Window Resizing*

ASPX Page

```
<asp:Button ID="btnResizeWindow" runat="server"
            Text="Open Window"
            OnClientClick="ShowRadWindow1();return false;" />

<telerik:RadWindow ID="RadWindow1" runat="server"
            Title="RadSplitter in RadWindow"
            Width="600px"
            Height="450px"
            style="z-index:20000">
</telerik:RadWindow>
```

```
<script type="text/javascript">
    function ShowRadWindow1() {
        var wnd = $find("<%=RadWindow1.ClientID %>");
        wnd.setUrl("radsplitter_FullWindow.aspx");
        wnd.show();
    }
</script>
```

radsplitter_FullWindow.aspx

```
<!DOCTYPE html PUBLIC
        "-//W3C//DTD XHTML 1.0 Transitional//EN"
        "http://www.w3.org/TR/xhtml1/DTD/xhtml1-transitional.dtd">

<html xmlns="http://www.w3.org/1999/xhtml">
<head runat="server">
    <title></title>
    <style type="text/css">
    html, body, form
    {
        height: 100%;
        margin: 0px;
        padding: 0px;
        overflow: hidden;
    }
    </style>
</head>
<body>
    <form id="form1" runat="server">
        <telerik:RadScriptManager ID="RadScriptManager1" runat="server">
        </telerik:RadScriptManager>
        <telerik:RadSplitter ID="RadSplitter1" runat="server"
                Width="100%"
                Height="100%"
                FullScreenMode="True"
                SplitBarsSize="">
                <telerik:RadPane ID="RadPane3" runat="server"
                        Width="100%"
                        Height="100%"
                        ContentUrl="http://www.telerik.com">
                </telerik:RadPane>
                <telerik:RadSplitBar ID="RadSplitBar2" runat="server" />
                <telerik:RadPane ID="RadPane4" runat="server"
                        Width="100%"
                        Height="100%"
                        ContentUrl="http://www.microsoft.com">
                </telerik:RadPane>
        </telerik:RadSplitter>
    </form>
</body>
</html>
```

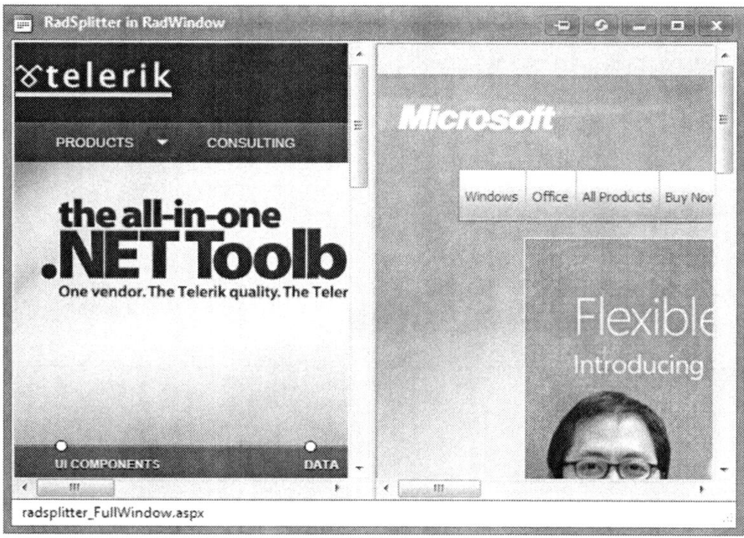

Figure 8-18. *RadSplitter is ocupying the full window.*

Creating Sliding Panes

Sliding panes are a great way to save space on a page and present users an interface that enables them to focus on their main areas. Panes are available on either mouse click or hover and can be docked.

To implement sliding panes, you need at least one `RadSlidingZone` object, which will contain all the sliding panes and can be configured to appear at any edge of the splitter control.

The sliding pane tab can be configured to show text, an icon, or both. All you need to do is define that in the `TabView` property to any of the valid values—`TextAndImage`, `TextOnly`, or `ImageOnly`—and set the `IconUrl` and `Title` properties accordingly.

■ **Note** The state of the `RadSplitter` and its objects are automatically persisted on postbacks, so you don't need to re-create the view of the controls. More information on this subject can be found in the documentation online at `http://www.telerik.com/help/aspnet-ajax/splitter_panespersisting.html`. If you do need to manually persist the state of the `RadSplitter` control, you can check the example at `http://demos.telerik.com/aspnet-ajax/splitter/examples/saveloadstateonserver/defaultcs.aspx`.

The example in Listing 8-15 shows a `RadSplitter` with four `RadSlidingZones`, each of which contains a `RadSlidingPane` and is attached to one of the edges. The contents of a `RadSlidingPane` can be anything, but for our example, the panes contain a button that will load information in the central pane. Figure 8-19 shows the sliding panes in action.

Listing 8-15. *Sliding Panes*

ASPX Page

```
<asp:UpdatePanel ID="UpdatePanel1" runat="server">
<ContentTemplate>
    <telerik:RadSplitter ID="RadSplitter5" runat="server"
        Width="700"
        Height="500">
        <telerik:RadPane ID="LeftPane" runat="server"
                Width="22px"
                Scrolling="none">
                <telerik:RadSlidingZone ID="SlidingZone1" runat="server"
                        Width="22px"
                        SlideDirection="Right">
                        <telerik:RadSlidingPane ID="RadSlidingPane1"
                                Title="Employees"
                                runat="server"
                                Width="250px">
                                <asp:Button ID="Button1" runat="server"
                                        Text="Load Employees"
                                        OnCommand="btnLoadData_Command"
                                        CommandName="Employees" />
                        </telerik:RadSlidingPane>
                </telerik:RadSlidingZone>
        </telerik:RadPane>
        <telerik:RadSplitBar ID="Radsplitbar6" runat="server"
                        EnableResize="false">
        </telerik:RadSplitBar>
        <telerik:RadPane ID="MiddlePane1" runat="server"
                Scrolling="None">
                <telerik:RadSplitter ID="RadSplitter6" runat="server"
                        Orientation="Horizontal">
                        <telerik:RadPane ID="RadPane10" runat="server"
                                Height="22px">
                                <telerik:RadSlidingZone ID="RadSlidingZone2" runat="server"
                                        Height="22px"
                                        Width="100%"
                                        SlideDirection="Bottom">
                                        <telerik:RadSlidingPane ID="Radslidingpane3"
                                                Title="Products"
                                                runat="server"
                                                Width="250px">
                                                <asp:Button ID="Button3" runat="server"
                                                        Text="Load Products"
                                                        OnCommand="btnLoadData_Command"
                                                        CommandName="Products" />
                                        </telerik:RadSlidingPane>
                                </telerik:RadSlidingZone>
                        </telerik:RadPane>
                <telerik:RadSplitBar ID="Radsplitbar9" runat="server"
                        EnableResize="false">
                </telerik:RadSplitBar>
                <telerik:RadPane ID="RadPane11" runat="server"
```

```
                        Width="100%">
                        <telerik:RadGrid ID="RadGrid1" runat="server">
                                <ClientSettings>
                                        <Scrolling UseStaticHeaders="true" />
                                </ClientSettings>
                        </telerik:RadGrid>
                </telerik:RadPane>
                <telerik:RadSplitBar ID="Radsplitbar8" runat="server"
                        EnableResize="false">
                </telerik:RadSplitBar>
                <telerik:RadPane ID="RadPane12" runat="server" Height="22px">
                        <telerik:RadSlidingZone ID="RadSlidingZone3" runat="server"
                                Height="22px"
                                Width="100%"
                                SlideDirection="Top">
                                <telerik:RadSlidingPane ID="Radslidingpane4"
                                        Title="Categories"
                                        runat="server"
                                        Width="250px">
                                        <asp:Button ID="Button4" runat="server"
                                                Text="Load Categories"
                                                OnCommand="btnLoadData_Command"
                                                CommandName="Categories" />
                                </telerik:RadSlidingPane>
                        </telerik:RadSlidingZone>
                </telerik:RadPane>
        </telerik:RadSplitter>
        </telerik:RadPane>
        <telerik:RadSplitBar ID="Radsplitbar7" runat="server"
                EnableResize="false">
        </telerik:RadSplitBar>
        <telerik:RadPane ID="RightPane" runat="server"
                Width="22px"
                Scrolling="None">
                <telerik:RadSlidingZone ID="RadSlidingZone1" runat="server"
                        Width="22px"
                        SlideDirection="Left">
                        <telerik:RadSlidingPane ID="Radslidingpane2" runat="server"
                                Title="Customers"
                                Width="250px">
                                <asp:Button ID="Button2" runat="server"
                                        Text="Load Customers"
                                        OnCommand="btnLoadData_Command"
                                        CommandName="Customers" />
                        </telerik:RadSlidingPane>
                </telerik:RadSlidingZone>
        </telerik:RadPane>
</telerik:RadSplitter>
</ContentTemplate>
</asp:UpdatePanel>
```

Code Behind

```
protected void btnLoadData_Command(object sender, CommandEventArgs e)
{
    using (var cnn = new SqlConnection(WebConfigurationManager
                                    .ConnectionStrings["NorthwindConnectionString"]
                                    .ConnectionString))
    {
        cnn.Open();
        string sSql = "";
        switch (e.CommandName)
        {
            case "Employees":
                sSql = string.Format(@"SELECT [EmployeeID],
                                          [FirstName] + ' ' + [LastName] as [Name]
                                    FROM [Employees]");
                break;
            case "Customers":
                sSql = string.Format(@"SELECT [CustomerID], [CompanyName], [ContactName]
                                    FROM [Customers]");
                break;
            case "Products":
                sSql = string.Format(@"SELECT [ProductID], [ProductName]
                                    FROM [Products]");
                break;
            case "Categories":
                sSql = string.Format(@"SELECT [CategoryID], [CategoryName]
                                    FROM [Categories]");
                break;
        }
        var cmd = new SqlCommand(sSql, cnn);
        RadGrid1.DataSource = cmd.ExecuteReader();
        RadGrid1.DataBind();
        cnn.Close();
    }
}
```

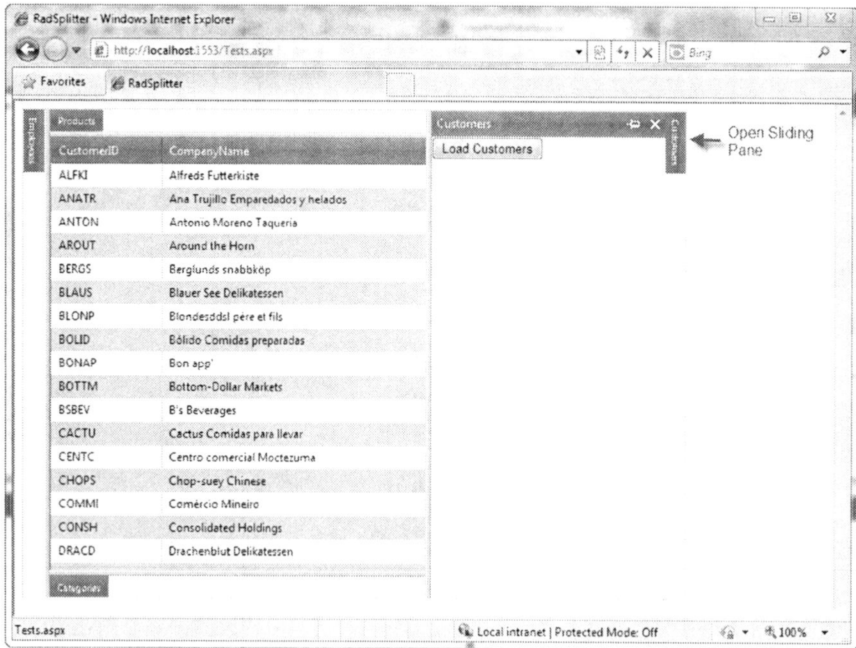

Figure 8-19. *Note that the right sliding pane is open, while others are closed. Once the mouse no longer hovers over the pane, it will close again.*

Using RadDock

The Telerik docking platform is composed of the controls RadDockLayout, RadDockZone, and RadDock. With them, you can create an interface with movable parts (docks) that you can drag around the different zones (dock zones) defined inside a dock layout.

RadDock is Telerik's implementation of a technology similar to Microsoft's web parts only with more functionality. You can create dashboard or portal applications, where users can create their own layouts with the information that is relevant to them.

RadDocks can be dragged between different RadDockZones, and you can define custom commands for actions RadDocks can perform. RadDocks can also be defined as floating, meaning that they can be placed outside the boundaries of the defined RadDockZones. If that's not enough, for each RadDock, you can also define forbidden zones with the ForbiddenZones property, so in those zones, the RadDock can't be docked.

Creating a Working Dock Layout

Listing 8-16 shows one of the most common ways to create a working dock layout with some RadDocks that contain simple objects. Figure 8-20 shows the running sample.

Note that one of the docks has the floating feature enabled. When you take the dock outside the dock zones the pin/unpin command button appears and gives you the ability to pin the dock in the position where it is, so it becomes unmovable.

Listing 8-16. *Basic RadDockLayout Implementation*

ASPX Page

```
<telerik:RadDockLayout ID="RadDockLayout1" runat="server">
    <table style="width:600px" cellspacing="5" cellpadding="5">
        <tr>
            <td style="width:50%">
                <telerik:RadDockZone ID="RadDockZone1" runat="server"
                                Height="300px"
                                Width="100%">
                    <telerik:RadDock ID="RadDock1" runat="server"
                                Title="Calendar Dock"
                                EnableAnimation="true"
                                EnableRoundedCorners="true"
                                DockMode="Docked">
                    <ContentTemplate>
                        <telerik:RadCalendar ID="RadCalendar1" runat="server">
                        </telerik:RadCalendar>
                    </ContentTemplate>
                    </telerik:RadDock>
                    <telerik:RadDock ID="RadDock2" runat="server"
                                Title="Text Dock"
                                EnableAnimation="true"
                                EnableRoundedCorners="true"
                                DockMode="Docked">
                    <ContentTemplate>
                        This is a simple text.
                    </ContentTemplate>
                    </telerik:RadDock>
                </telerik:RadDockZone>
            </td>
            <td style="width:50%">
                <telerik:RadDockZone ID="RadDockZone2" runat="server"
                                    Height="300px"
                                    Width="100%">
                    <telerik:RadDock ID="RadDock3" runat="server"
                                    Title="Pin/UnPin Dock"
                                    EnableAnimation="true"
                                    EnableRoundedCorners="true"
                                    DefaultCommands="All">
                    <ContentTemplate>
                        This dock has floating enabled. Just dragg it outside any
                        area to enable the pin command.
                        <br /><br />
                        Pin the dock and verify that you can't move it.
                    </ContentTemplate>
                    </telerik:RadDock>
                </telerik:RadDockZone>
            </td>
        </tr>
    </table>
</telerik:RadDockLayout>
```

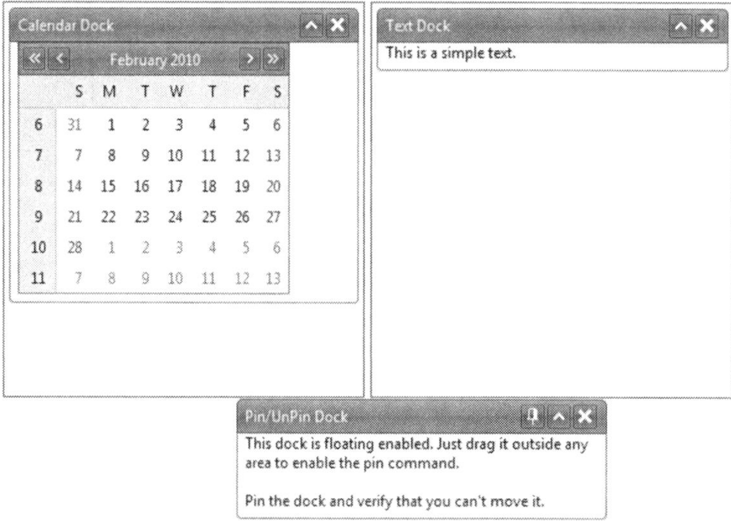

Figure 8-20. *RadDocks showing different content and functionality*

Writing Custom Commands

By default, RadDock has three basic commands: Close, ExpandCollapse, and PinUnpin. These commands are enabled depending on the current state or localization of the dock. You can create your own custom commands and even modify their properties to make them look like the built-in commands.

Each command has its corresponding ClientCommand event handler to handle the action on the client and Command event handler to handle the action on the server.

The example in Listing 8-17 demonstrates how to handle the command action on the client. You just need to define the command in the Commands section of the RadDock control and associate the handler to it. Figure 8-21 shows the running sample.

Listing 8-17. *RadDock Custom Commands*

ASPX Page

```
<telerik:RadDockLayout ID="RadDockLayout2" runat="server">
<table width="300px"
        cellspacing="5"
        cellpadding="5">
    <tr>
        <td style="width:100%">
            <telerik:RadDockZone ID="RadDockZone3" runat="server"
                                        Height="300px"
                                        Width="100%">
                <telerik:RadDock ID="RadDock4" runat="server"
                                        Title="Calendar Dock"
                                        EnableAnimation="true"
                                        EnableRoundedCorners="true"
                                        DockMode="Docked">
```

```
                <ContentTemplate>
                    <telerik:RadCalendar ID="RadCalendar2" runat="server">
                    </telerik:RadCalendar>
                </ContentTemplate>
                <Commands>
                    <telerik:DockCommand Text="Set Today's Date"
                                         OnClientCommand="SetToday"
                                         Name="SetTodayDate" />
                    <telerik:DockCloseCommand />
                    <telerik:DockExpandCollapseCommand />
                </Commands>
                </telerik:RadDock>
            </telerik:RadDockZone>
        </td>
    </tr>
</table>
</telerik:RadDockLayout>

<script type="text/javascript" language="javascript">
    function SetToday(sender, eventArgs) {
        var calendar = $find("<%=RadCalendar2.ClientID %>");
        var todaysDate = new Date();
        var todayTriplet = [todaysDate.getFullYear(),
                            todaysDate.getMonth() + 1,
                            todaysDate.getDate()];
        calendar.selectDate(todayTriplet, true);
    }
</script>
```

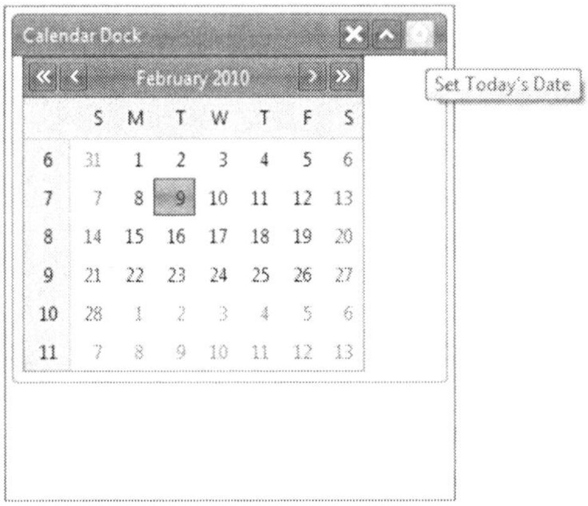

Figure 8-21. *The custom command is next to the default comands of the RadDock.*

Dynamically Creating RadDocks

One important feature in the docking platform is the ability to create RadDocks dynamically, not just declaratively. In addition, regardless on the way you create RadDocks, you can dynamically add the content to them. You need to perform certain actions to provide such functionality, but the one thing you must keep in mind is that you handle the `Init` event in the page for proper dock creation. That way, the newly created docks are available for registration in `ViewState`.

In Listing 8-18, I will create two web user controls that will provide the content for the `RadDocks`, and everything will be dynamically created. Additional information is in the comments on the code. The code for the user controls can be found in the samples application. Figure 8-22 shows this approach in action.

Listing 8-18. *Dynamically Created RadDocks*

ASPX Page

```
<telerik:RadComboBox ID="rcbContent" runat="server">
    <Items>
        <telerik:RadComboBoxItem Text="Login Box"
                                 Value="login.ascx"
                                 Selected="true" />
        <telerik:RadComboBoxItem Text="Sales Chart"
                                 Value="Chart.ascx" />
    </Items>
</telerik:RadComboBox>
<asp:Button ID="Button1" runat="server"
                Text="Add Dock"
                OnClick="Button1_Click" />
<br />
<asp:UpdatePanel runat="server" ID="UpdatePanel2"
                ChildrenAsTriggers="false"
                UpdateMode="Conditional">
     <ContentTemplate>
         <telerik:RadDockLayout ID="RadDockLayout3" runat="server"
                                 OnSaveDockLayout="RadDockLayout3_SaveDockLayout"
                                 OnLoadDockLayout="RadDockLayout3_LoadDockLayout">
          <table style="width:600px"
                cellspacing="5"
                cellpadding="5">
              <tr>
                  <td style="width:50%">
                    <telerik:RadDockZone ID="RadDockZone4" runat="server"
                                         Width="100%"
                                         Height="200px">
                    </telerik:RadDockZone>
               </td>
               <td style="width:50%">
                    <telerik:RadDockZone ID="RadDockZone5" runat="server"
                                         Width="100%"
                                         Height="200px">
                    </telerik:RadDockZone>
               </td>
            </tr>
        </table>
    </telerik:RadDockLayout>
</ContentTemplate>
```

```
<Triggers>
     <asp:AsyncPostBackTrigger ControlID="Button1"
                               EventName="Click" />
</Triggers>
</asp:UpdatePanel>

Code Behind

// Storage for the state of the docking platform
// I will store the state in a session variable and expose it as a generic
// list of type DockState.
private List<DockState> CurrentDockStates
{
    get
    {
        var _currentDockStates = (List<DockState>)Session["CurrentDockStates"];
        if (Object.Equals(_currentDockStates, null))
        {
            _currentDockStates = new List<DockState>();
            Session["CurrentDockStates"] = _currentDockStates;
        }
        return _currentDockStates;
    }
    set
    {
        Session["CurrentDockStates"] = value;
    }
}

// Handler for the click event of the button that will create the docks
protected void Button1_Click(object sender, EventArgs e)
{
    // create a default RadDock with basic properties, add it to the zone
    // and apply the default state
    var dock = CreateRadDock();
    RadDockZone4.Controls.Add(dock);
    CreateSaveStateTrigger(dock);


    // Load the dock content based on the user selection
    dock.Tag = rcbContent.SelectedValue;
    dock.Title = rcbContent.SelectedItem.Text;
    LoadDockContent(dock);
}

// Save the layout as needed by calling the GetRegisteredDockState() method
// to the dock state storage (session variable defined before)
protected void RadDockLayout3_SaveDockLayout(object sender, DockLayoutEventArgs e)
{
    CurrentDockStates = RadDockLayout3.GetRegisteredDocksState();
}
```

```
// Load the dock state as needed and refresh the layout
protected void RadDockLayout3_LoadDockLayout(object sender, DockLayoutEventArgs e)
{
    foreach (var state in CurrentDockStates)
    {
        e.Positions[state.UniqueName] = state.DockZoneID;
        e.Indices[state.UniqueName] = state.Index;
    }
}

// On Page_Init we do the re-recreation of docks. Note that we will
// only recreate those docks that are not closed.
protected void Page_Init(object sender, EventArgs e)
{
    foreach (var dock in from t in CurrentDockStates
                         where t.Closed == false
                        select CreateRadDockFromState(t))
    {
        RadDockLayout3.Controls.Add(dock);
        //Create a dock with state so on every action the app knows what to do
        CreateSaveStateTrigger(dock);
        //Load the dock content
        LoadDockContent(dock);
    }
}

// Create a new RadDock and apply the current state
private RadDock CreateRadDockFromState(DockState state)
{
    var dock = new RadDock
                   {
                       DockMode = DockMode.Docked,
                       ID = string.Format("RadDock{0}", state.UniqueName),
                       EnableAnimation = true,
                       EnableRoundedCorners = true
                   };
    dock.ApplyState(state);
    dock.Commands.Add(new DockCloseCommand());
    dock.Commands.Add(new DockExpandCollapseCommand());

    return dock;
}

// Create a new RadDock with default settings (no state)
private RadDock CreateRadDock()
{
    var dock = new RadDock
                   {
                       DockMode = DockMode.Docked,
                       UniqueName = Guid.NewGuid().ToString(),
                       EnableAnimation = true,
                       EnableRoundedCorners = true
                   };
```

```
    dock.ID = string.Format("RadDock{0}", dock.UniqueName);
    dock.Width = Unit.Pixel(300);

    dock.Commands.Add(new DockCloseCommand());
    dock.Commands.Add(new DockExpandCollapseCommand());

    return dock;
}

// enables the update panel to save the state for RadDocks by adding
// the command events to the async triggers
private void CreateSaveStateTrigger(RadDock dock)
{
    dock.AutoPostBack = true;
    dock.CommandsAutoPostBack = true;

    var saveStateTrigger = new AsyncPostBackTrigger
{
                                    ControlID = dock.ID,
                                    EventName = "DockPositionChanged"
                                };
    UpdatePanel2.Triggers.Add(saveStateTrigger);

    saveStateTrigger = new AsyncPostBackTrigger
                                {
                                    ControlID = dock.ID,
                                    EventName = "Command"
                                };
    UpdatePanel2.Triggers.Add(saveStateTrigger);
}

// Loads the content of the RadDock. It loads the user control
// defined in the Tag property
private void LoadDockContent(RadDock dock)
{
    if (string.IsNullOrEmpty(dock.Tag)) return;
    var content = LoadControl(dock.Tag);
    dock.ContentContainer.Controls.Add(content);
}
```

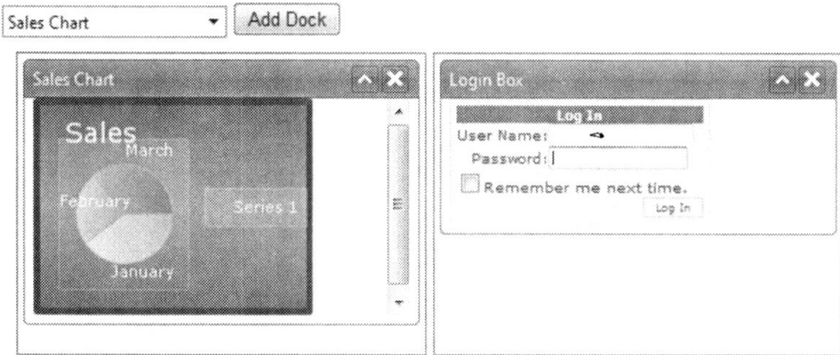

Figure 8-22. *The RadDocks shown were dynamically created, and their state is saved across postbacks.*

Using RadRotator

RadRotator is a UI component that enables you to have multiple, rotating content areas, like those huge ads you find in stores or the street where the current ad changes every few seconds.

The content areas are defined as RadRotatorItems. They can be populated from an external datasource if the RadRotator control is also bound to that datasource. The items appearance can be modified using ItemTemplates, where you can leverage your design skills with HTML, CSS, and other controls.

Another component related to RadRotator is RadTicker, which displays text by writing one letter at a time over a given interval, so it produces an effect like a typewriter. It consists of multiple RadTickerItems that may contain only text. Once the full text of the current item is displayed, the control switches to the next item, and when the last item is reached, it starts all over again.

RadTicker and RadRotator work very closely with one another, and you can include tickers inside rotator items for improved appearance and enhanced functionality.

Using Data Binding, Templates, and Rotations

The first example I want to show demonstrates how you can create a rotator bound to a database table that will populate all the items. Then, using a template, we'll create ID cards for employees based on the information in the datasource. You will also have the ability to choose the type of rotation. Listing 8-19 shows how to implement data binding with templates and adds the ability to choose the rotation type. Figure 8-23 shows the example running.

Listing 8-19. *Data Binding, Template, and Rotation Type*

ASPX Page

```
<asp:UpdatePanel ID="UpdatePanel1" runat="server">
<ContentTemplate>
    <h3>Rotation Type</h3>
    <asp:RadioButtonList ID="rblRotationType" runat="server"
        AutoPostBack="true"
        RepeatDirection="Horizontal"
        RepeatColumns="3"
        OnSelectedIndexChanged="rblRotationType_SelectedIndexChanged">
    </asp:RadioButtonList>
    <br />
```

```
    <telerik:RadRotator ID="RadRotator1" runat="server"
        DataSourceID="SqlDataSource1"
        Width="202px"
        Height="404px">
    <ItemTemplate>
        <div class="idcard">
            <div class="companyName">
                My Company
            </div>
            <div class="picture">
                <asp:Image ID="employeePhoto" runat="server"
                        Width="150"
                        Height="200"
                        ImageAlign="Middle"
                        ImageUrl='<%# "Images/employees/" +
                                        Eval("EmployeeID") + ".jpg" %>' />
            </div>
            <div class="employeeInfo">
                <div class="employeeName">
                <asp:Label ID="lblName" runat="server"
                                Text='<%# Eval("LastName") + ", " + Eval("FirstName") %>'>
                </asp:Label>
            </div>
                <div class="employeeTitle">
                <asp:Label ID="lblTitle" runat="server"
                                Text='<%# Eval("Title") %>'>
                </asp:Label>
                </div>
                <div class="employeeOffice">
                Works in our office located on:
                <asp:Label ID="lblOffice" runat="server"
                        Text='<%# Eval("City") + ", " + Eval("Country") %>'>
                </asp:Label>
                </div>
            </div>
        </div>
    </ItemTemplate>
    </telerik:RadRotator>
</ContentTemplate>
</asp:UpdatePanel>
<asp:SqlDataSource ID="SqlDataSource1" runat="server"
    ConnectionString="<%$ ConnectionStrings:NorthwindConnectionString %>"
    SelectCommand="SELECT [EmployeeID], [LastName],
                        [FirstName], [Title], [HireDate],
                        [ReportsTo], [City], [Country],
                        [Extension]
                   FROM [Employees]">
</asp:SqlDataSource>
```

Code Behind

```
protected void Page_Load(object sender, EventArgs e)
{
    if (Page.IsPostBack) return;
    LoadRotatorOptions();
}


private void LoadRotatorOptions()
{
    rblRotationType.Items.Clear();
    foreach (string type in Enum.GetNames(typeof(RotatorType)))
    {
        rblRotationType.Items.Add(type);
        if (RadRotator1.RotatorType == (RotatorType)Enum.Parse(typeof(RotatorType), type))
            rblRotationType.Items[rblRotationType.Items.Count - 1].Selected = true;
    }

}

protected void rblRotationType_SelectedIndexChanged(object sender, EventArgs e)
{
    RadRotator1.RotatorType = (RotatorType)Enum
                                              .Parse(typeof(RotatorType),
                                                     rblRotationType.SelectedValue);

    switch (RadRotator1.RotatorType)
    {
        case RotatorType.SlideShow:
            RadRotator1.Width = Unit.Pixel(202);
            break;
        case RotatorType.SlideShowButtons:
        case RotatorType.ButtonsOver:
        case RotatorType.Buttons:
            // 20px for every button
            RadRotator1.Width = Unit.Pixel(242);
            break;
        default:
            RadRotator1.Width = Unit.Pixel(202);
            break;
    }

}
```

```
CSS Classes

<style type="text/css">
    .idcard
    {
        width:200px;
        height:400px;
        border:1px solid #000000;
        text-align:center;
    }

    .companyName
    {
        font-family:Verdana;
        font-size:20px;
        text-align:center;
        height:35px;
    }

    .picture
    {
        width:150px;
        height:220px;
        text-align:center;
        margin-left:auto;
        margin-right:auto;
    }

    .employeeInfo
    {
        border:1px solid #000000;
        text-align:center;
        height:130px;
        width:150px;
        margin-left:auto;
        margin-right:auto;
    }

    .employeeName
    {
        font-family:Verdana;
        font-weight:bold;
        font-size:12px;
        height:30px;
    }

    .employeeTitle
    {
        font-family:Verdana;
        font-size:10px;
        height:30px;
    }
```

```
    .employeeOffice
    {
        font-family:Verdana;
        font-size:10px;
        height:30px;
        vertical-align:middle;
    }

</style>
```

Figure 8-23. *Rotator items are populated from the database and formated using templates. You can choose the rotation type and examine the different options.*

Working with RadTicker

The `RadTicker` is designed to display text one character at a time. The speed at which letters are revealed is configured using the `TickSpeed` property, which is defined in milliseconds. Listing 8-20 is an example of the implementation of `RadTicker`.

Listing 8-20. *A RadTicker Control*

ASPX Page

```
<telerik:RadTicker ID="RadTicker1" runat="server"
        AutoStart="true"
        Loop="true"
        Width="450px"
        Height="50px"
        CssClass="TickerClass"
        DataSourceID="SqlDataSource2"
        DataTextField="Name"
        AppendDataBoundItems="true">
<Items>
    <telerik:RadTickerItem Text="Do you like our company?"></telerik:RadTickerItem>
    <telerik:RadTickerItem Text="Meet our team!"></telerik:RadTickerItem>
</Items>
</telerik:RadTicker>
<asp:SqlDataSource ID="SqlDataSource2" runat="server"
    ConnectionString="<%$ ConnectionStrings:NorthwindConnectionString %>"
    SelectCommand="SELECT [LastName] + ', ' + [FirstName] as [Name] FROM [Employees]">
</asp:SqlDataSource>
```

Combining RadRotator and RadTicker

The combination of RadRotator and RadTicker enables you to create outstanding rotating content, and the best part is that combining them is as easy as adding the RadTicker to the item template and setting binding information that is shared between both controls.

Listing 8-21 shows how to improve the example from Listing 8-19 by displaying the employee information using not simple labels but nice-looking RadTickers. Figure 8-24 shows the end result (note that the text is incomplete, because the controls were still rendering when the screenshot was captured).

Listing 8-21. *Implementing RadRotator and RadTicker Together*

ASPX Page

```
<telerik:RadRotator ID="RadRotator2" runat="server"
                DataSourceID="SqlDataSource1"
                Width="202px"
                Height="404px">
<ItemTemplate>
    <div class="idcard">
        <div class="companyName">
            My Company
        </div>
```

```
        <div class="picture">
                <asp:Image ID="employeePhoto" runat="server"
                        Width="150"
                        Height="200"
                        ImageAlign="Middle"
                        ImageUrl='<%# "Images/employees/" +
                                        Eval("EmployeeID") + ".jpg" %>' />
        </div>
        <div class="employeeInfo">
            <div class="employeeName">
                <telerik:RadTicker ID="employeeNameTicker" runat="server">
                    <Items>
                        <telerik:RadTickerItem
                                        Text='<%# Eval("LastName") + ", " +
                                                Eval("FirstName") %>'>
                        </telerik:RadTickerItem>
                    </Items>
                </telerik:RadTicker>
            </div>
            <div class="employeeTitle">
                <telerik:RadTicker ID="employeeTitleTicker" runat="server">
                    <Items>
                        <telerik:RadTickerItem
                                        Text='<%# Eval("Title") %>'>
                        </telerik:RadTickerItem>
                    </Items>
                </telerik:RadTicker>
            </div>
            <div class="employeeOffice">
                <telerik:RadTicker ID="employeeOfficeTicker" runat="server">
                    <Items>
                        <telerik:RadTickerItem
                                Text='<%# "Works in our office located on: " +
                                Eval("City") + ", " + Eval("Country") %>'>
                        </telerik:RadTickerItem>
                    </Items>
                </telerik:RadTicker>
            </div>
        </div>
    </div>
</ItemTemplate>
</telerik:RadRotator>
```

Figure 8-24. *When implementing RadRotator and RadTicker, note that the rotator will not move to the next item until the ticker rendering is complete.*

Summary

In this chapter, you have seen various controls that help organize content in your pages in different ways. RadTabStrip is a powerful tab component that supports features such as data binding, hierarchical data representation, and simple navigation. Tabs can be customized with templates, and the integration with RadMultiPage greatly enhances the user experience.

RadWindow takes an application to a different level by providing a windowing platform that can host any type of content from within the application or an external source. Windows behave according to specifications in the Behaviors property, and with the help of RadWindowManager, you can even have replacement browser dialogs for alerts, confirmations, and prompts. Communication between windows is possible and so is the creation of MDI-style windows.

RadSplitter enables you to divide your page in different areas called panes that user can resize, collapse, or expand. With sliding panes, users have the ability to show and hide panes, so they can focus on the main area of a page. You can also use RadSplitter to make your content fill an entire page, so no space is wasted.

RadDock provides a wonderful platform for creating dashboard-style interfaces where different content areas can be moved around defined zones, thus allowing users a high level of personalization so they can organize content in the ways that they like.

RadRotator is a component for rotating content. You can have banner images or custom content from datasources showing one or many items at a time, either automatically or with the aid of buttons. When you combine RadRotator with RadTicker, you have a versatile presentation platform for your content.

CHAPTER 9

Chart and Image RadControls

When working with business applications, it is very important to present information this is not only accurate but easy to read and understand, so decision makers can take correct and on-time action in the modern competitive and globalized world.

With this principle in mind, Telerik has created powerful controls to create graphical representations of information depending on the needs of businesses. RadChart is one of the most advanced charting controls for ASP.NET. RadBinaryImage is a component designed to show images stored in databases as binary data. RadColorPicker enables your users to select colors from a palette. RadRating is a control that allows users to graphically assign a score or rating by selecting a number of predefined items in the list.

RadChart

RadChart allows you to build sophisticated business charts. You can build 17 different chart types including bar, line, area, and pie, and you can blend different types in one single chart. With new abilities for zooming and scrolling, the possibilities for analyzing graphical information are huge.

RadChart Structure

RadChart is a collection of Series that contain data that will be used to build the chart; additionally, RadChart as a Title and a Legend. The title appears on top of the chart identifying what the data represents. The Legend displays a description of each series of data.

Series refers to a collection of data points displayed in the chart. The number of series used depends on the type of chart. A Pie chart type only uses a single series. Stacked charts like the Stacked Area chart use several series.

Each ChartSeries object contains a collection of ChartSeriesItem objects that contain the actual data points displayed on the chart. You can add data to a series programmatically at run time, at design time in the Properties window of Visual Studio, declaratively in the ASP.NET HTML markup, or by binding to a data source. Each chart series item encapsulates a single data point.

For simple charts along a single axis, you need to use the YValue property. Use the XValue property to add a second data dimension. For example, the Y values might be Sales Volume, and the X values might be time periods or geographic regions.

The background of the chart is the outermost rectangle that encloses all other elements of the chart. It stretches for the whole width and length of the output image of the chart. The plot area is the working rectangular area between X and Y axes where data is displayed. The size of the plot depends on the chart background size and the chart margins, which define the distance between the border of the plot area and the border of the chart background. This area is represented by the PlotArea property.

X and Y axes are included in all chart types but the Pie chart. Typically, the YAxis displays values and the XAxis displays categories. Each axis has grid lines that display perpendicular to the axis covering the plot area, axis line, axis label, and axis marks along the axis line and item labels below the axis line. Axis ticks are the small marks that identify the position of items on the axes and the starting points of gridlines. Gridlines are auxiliary lines that form a grid for easier reading of the chart, and they can be horizontal or vertical.

Legends are symbols and text used to provide additional information about the chart. In a multiple series chart, the legend typically describes each series to improve readability. By default, RadChart includes the color and name of each chart series in the legend. You can also define your own legend and control the style for the legend or each item in the legend using the RadChart Legend property.

Chart margins are the distances from the outermost chart borders to the borders of the plot area. The title for the chart as a whole is controlled by the RadChart.ChartTitle object.

Examining Chart Types

Let's go over a brief description of the chart types so you can better understand what they are and see how they look.

Bar Charts

Bar charts graphically summarize and display categories of data and let the user easily compare amounts or values between different categories. Each category is displayed as a bar giving each category a unique color for easy identification. Other variations of bar charts are Stacked Bar, which display the categories of data in a single bar for each interval, and Stacked Bar 100%, which is similar to Stacked Bar but displays the category data as percentages. Figure 9-1 shows an example bar chart.

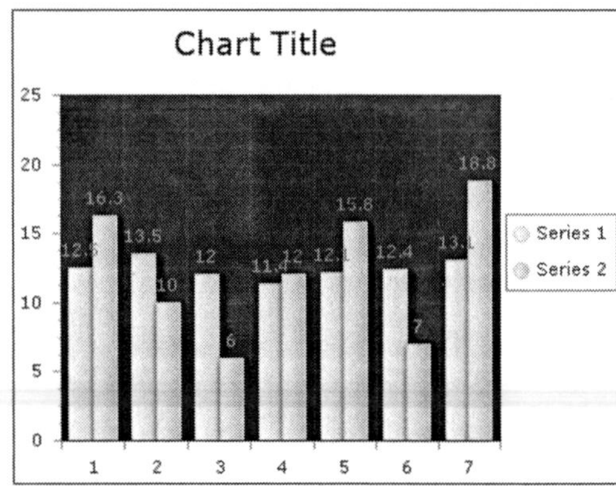

Figure 9-1. *Bar chart*

Line Chart

Line charts are used to display a series of data points, typically to show trends over a period of time and one or more series of data can be used in the same chart (see Figure 9-2).

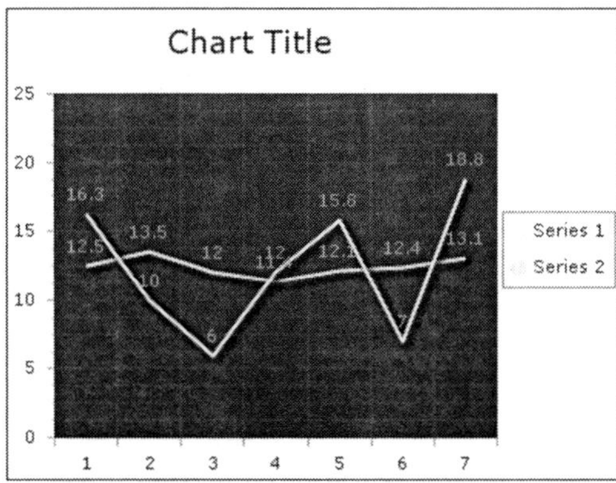

Figure 9-2. *Line chart*

Pie Charts

Pie charts are used to display the contribution of fractional parts to a whole. A Pie chart uses a single series of data. Multiple series of data can be defined and are each displayed in a separate pie chart. Figure 9-3 illustrates a pie chart.

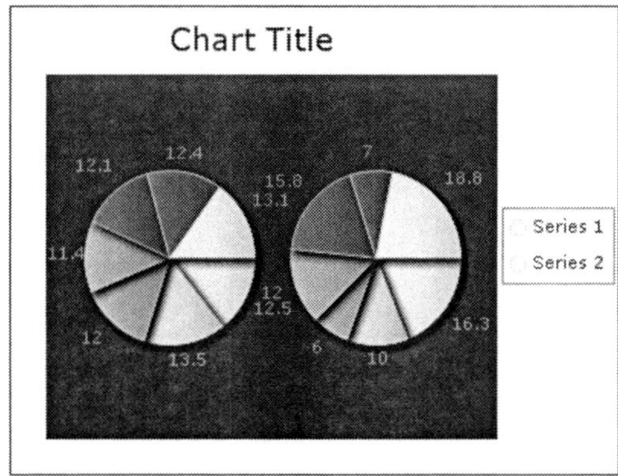

Figure 9-3. *Pie chart*

Area Charts

The Area chart consists of a series of data points joined by a line and where the area below the line is filled. Area charts are appropriate for visualizing data that fluctuates over a period of time and can be useful for emphasizing trends. Other area charts are stacked areas with similar functionality to stacked bars and spline area. Figure 9-4 illustrates the area and spline area charts.

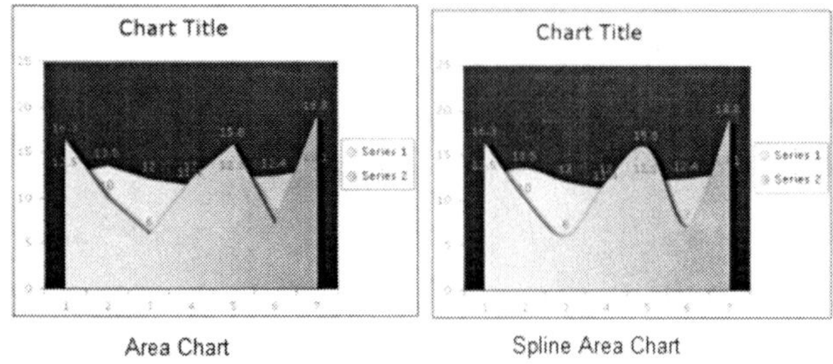

Figure 9-4. *An Area chart (left) and a Spline Area chart (right)*

Gantt Charts

Gantt charts help visualize time-based information. Gantt charts, also known as Time charts, display separate events, each with a beginning and an end. These charts are often used for project and time planning, where data can be plotted using a date-time scale or a numerical scale. `XValue2` and `YValue2` are used by the Gantt chart to indicate a period of time. Figure 9-5 illustrates a Gantt chart.

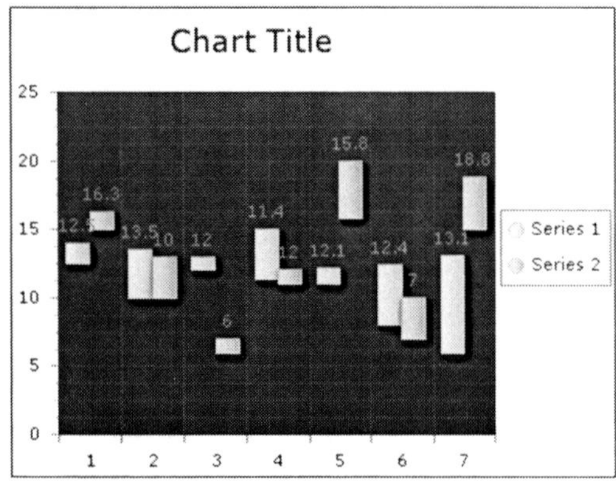

Figure 9-5. *Gantt chart*

Point and Bubble Charts

Point, or Scatter, charts are used to show correlations between two sets of values. The point chart lets you observe the dependence of one value to another and is often used for scientific data modeling. This chart is typically not used with time-dependent data where a Line chart is more suited.

The Bubble chart is an extension of the Point chart, but each point can be a circle or oval of any size or dimension. Instead of using just `XValue` and `YValue`, the Bubble chart uses `XValue` and `XValue2`, and `YValue` and `YValue2` pairs to define the dimensions of each bubble. Bubble charts are commonly used to display financial information where the size of the bubble can be proportionate to the data values. Figure 9-6 shows these two chart types.

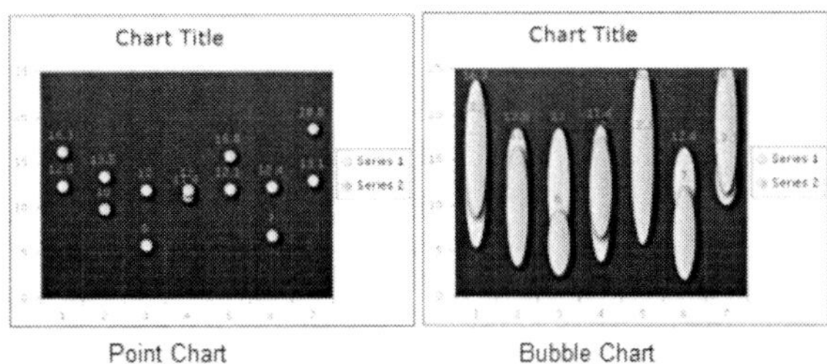

Figure 9-6. *A Point chart (left) and Bubble chart (right)*

Bezier Charts

The Bezier chart is often used for modeling data by interpolating data points through which curved lines pass. To draw a Bezier chart series you add (1 + 3 ~TMS N) items to a series. You can have 4 data points or 7, 10, 13, and so on. The simplest set of data would be four data points: two end points and two control points, which control the position and amount of curvature in the line between the two end points. See Figure 9-7 for an example of Bezier chart. Each of the data points must have an X and Y value.

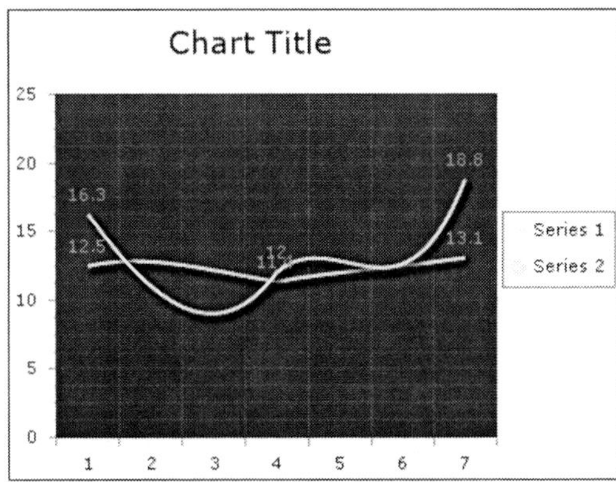

Figure 9-7. *Bezier chart*

CandleStick Charts

The CandleStick chart combines bar and line chart styles to show a range of value movement over time. A filled bar indicates the opening value was greater than the closing value. An empty bar indicates that the closing value was greater than the opening value. The line through the center (the wick) shows the extreme high and low values. The bar portion of each chart item is formed between the `YValue` and `YValue2` properties; `YValue` indicates the bar start point, and `YValue2` indicates the end. The wick portion of the chart is defined with the `YValue3` and `YValue4` chart item properties; `YValue3` is the start, and `YValue4` is the end.

The example in Listing 9-1 is designed so you can examine different chart types described before. It creates a chart with two series, and you can select the type of chart. It is important, though, to describe in detail certain elements and types of charts to fully understand its purpose and construction. Figure 9-8 illustrates the CandleStick chart.

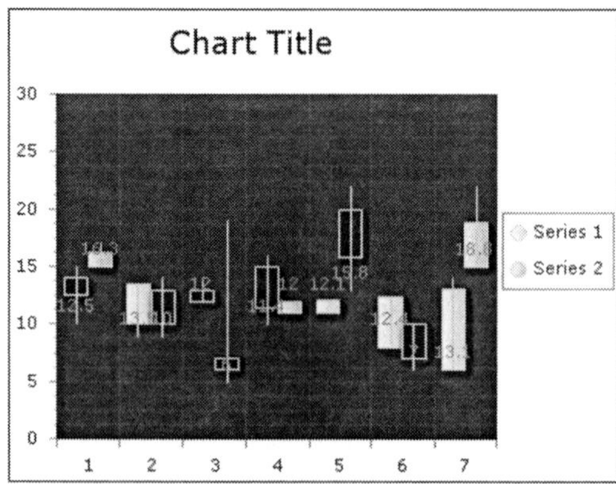

Figure 9-8. *CandleStick chart*

Listing 9-1. *Examining Chart Types*

```
ASPX Page

<asp:RadioButtonList ID="rbChartType" runat="server"
        RepeatDirection="Horizontal"
        AutoPostBack="true"
        OnSelectedIndexChanged="rbChartType_SelectedIndexChanged">
</asp:RadioButtonList>

<asp:RadioButtonList ID="rbChart" runat="server"
        RepeatDirection="Horizontal"
        AutoPostBack="true"
        OnSelectedIndexChanged="rbChart_SelectedIndexChanged">
    </asp:RadioButtonList>

<telerik:RadChart ID="RadChart1" runat="server"
        AutoLayout="True">
        <Series>
            <telerik:ChartSeries Name="Series 1">
                <Appearance Shadow-Blur="5"
                        Shadow-Distance="3">
                </Appearance>
                <Items>
                        <telerik:ChartSeriesItem Name="Item 1"
                                        YValue="12.5"
                                        YValue2="14"
                                        YValue3="10"
                                        YValue4="15">
                        </telerik:ChartSeriesItem>
```

```
                <telerik:ChartSeriesItem Name="Item 2"
                                YValue="13.5"
                                YValue2="10"
                                YValue3="9"
                                YValue4="10">
                </telerik:ChartSeriesItem>
                <telerik:ChartSeriesItem Name="Item 3"
                                YValue="12"
                                YValue2="13"
                                YValue3="12"
                                YValue4="14">
                </telerik:ChartSeriesItem>
                <telerik:ChartSeriesItem Name="Item 4"
                                YValue="11.4"
                                YValue2="15"
                                YValue3="10"
                                YValue4="16">
                </telerik:ChartSeriesItem>
                <telerik:ChartSeriesItem Name="Item 5"
                                YValue="12.1"
                                YValue2="11"
                                YValue3="12"
                                YValue4="11.5">
                </telerik:ChartSeriesItem>
                <telerik:ChartSeriesItem Name="Item 6"
                                YValue="12.4"
                                YValue2="8"
                                YValue3="9"
                                YValue4="10">
                </telerik:ChartSeriesItem>
                <telerik:ChartSeriesItem Name="Item 7"
                                YValue="13.1"
                                YValue2="6"
                                YValue3="6"
                                YValue4="14">
                </telerik:ChartSeriesItem>
        </Items>
    </telerik:ChartSeries>
    <telerik:ChartSeries Name="Series 2">
        <Appearance Shadow-Blur="5"
                Shadow-Distance="3">
        </Appearance>
        <Items>
                <telerik:ChartSeriesItem Name="Item 1"
                                YValue="16.3"
                                YValue2="15"
                                YValue3="15"
                                YValue4="17">
                </telerik:ChartSeriesItem>
```

```
                    <telerik:ChartSeriesItem Name="Item 2"
                                YValue="10"
                                YValue2="13"
                                YValue3="9"
                                YValue4="14">
                    </telerik:ChartSeriesItem>
                    <telerik:ChartSeriesItem Name="Item 3"
                                YValue="6"
                                YValue2="7"
                                YValue3="5"
                                YValue4="19">
                    </telerik:ChartSeriesItem>
                    <telerik:ChartSeriesItem Name="Item 4"
                                YValue="12"
                                YValue2="11"
                                YValue3="12"
                                YValue4="11">
                    </telerik:ChartSeriesItem>
                    <telerik:ChartSeriesItem Name="Item 5"
                                YValue="15.8"
                                YValue2="20"
                                YValue3="13"
                                YValue4="22">
                    </telerik:ChartSeriesItem>
                    <telerik:ChartSeriesItem Name="Item 6"
                                YValue="7"
                                YValue2="10"
                                YValue3="6"
                                YValue4="10">
                    </telerik:ChartSeriesItem>
                    <telerik:ChartSeriesItem Name="Item 7"
                                YValue="18.8"
                                YValue2="15"
                                YValue3="15"
                                YValue4="22">
                    </telerik:ChartSeriesItem>
                </Items>
            </telerik:ChartSeries>
        </Series>
        <PlotArea>
            <YAxis AxisMode="Extended"/>
        </PlotArea>
    </telerik:RadChart>
</ContentTemplate>
</asp:UpdatePanel>
```

Code Behind

```
public class mChartType
{
    public mChartType (string charttype, string chartname)
    {
        chartType = charttype;
        chartName = chartname;
    }

    public string chartType { get; set; }
    public string chartName { get; set; }
}

public class mChart
{
    public mChart(mChartType type, string code, string name)
    {
        chartType = type;
        chartCode = code;
        chartName = name;
    }
    public mChartType chartType { get; private set; }
    public string chartCode { get; set; }
    public string chartName { get; set; }
}

private readonly List<mChartType> ListOfChartTypes = new List<mChartType>();
private List<mChart> ListOfCharts = new List<mChart>();

protected void Page_Load(object sender, EventArgs e)
{
    if (Page.IsPostBack) return;
    LoadLists();
    SetDefaults();
}

private void SetDefaults()
{
    rbChartType.SelectedIndex = 0;
    var items = ListOfCharts.Where(x => x.chartType.chartType == rbChartType.SelectedValue);
    rbChart.DataSource = items;
    rbChart.DataTextField = "chartName";
    rbChart.DataValueField = "chartCode";
    rbChart.DataBind();
    rbChart.SelectedIndex = 0;
    UpdateChart(rbChart.SelectedValue);
}

private void LoadLists()
{
    var typeBars = new mChartType("Bars", "Bars");
    var typeLines = new mChartType("Lines", "Lines");
    var typePie = new mChartType("Pie", "Pie");
```

```
    var typeAreas = new mChartType("Areas", "Areas");
    var typeOther = new mChartType("Other", "Other");
    ListOfChartTypes.Add(typeBars);
    ListOfChartTypes.Add(typeLines);
    ListOfChartTypes.Add(typePie);
    ListOfChartTypes.Add(typeAreas);
    ListOfChartTypes.Add(typeOther);

    rbChartType.DataSource = ListOfChartTypes;
    rbChartType.DataTextField = "chartName";
    rbChartType.DataValueField = "chartType";
    rbChartType.DataBind();

    ListOfCharts.Add(new mChart(typeBars, "Bar", "Bar"));
    ListOfCharts.Add(new mChart(typeBars, "StackedBar", "Stacked Bar"));
    ListOfCharts.Add(new mChart(typeBars, "StackedBar100", "Stacked Bar 100"));
    ListOfCharts.Add(new mChart(typeLines, "Line", "Line"));
    ListOfCharts.Add(new mChart(typeLines, "BezierLine", "Bezier Line"));
    ListOfCharts.Add(new mChart(typeLines, "SplineLine", "Spline Line"));
    ListOfCharts.Add(new mChart(typeLines, "StackedLine", "Stacked Line"));
    ListOfCharts.Add(new mChart(typeLines, "StackedSplineLine", "Stacked Spline Line"));
    ListOfCharts.Add(new mChart(typeAreas, "Area", "Area"));
    ListOfCharts.Add(new mChart(typeAreas, "SplineArea", "Spline Area"));
    ListOfCharts.Add(new mChart(typeAreas, "StackedArea", "Stacked Area"));
    ListOfCharts.Add(new mChart(typeAreas, "StackedArea100", "Stacked Area 100"));
    ListOfCharts.Add(new mChart(typeAreas, "StackedSplineArea", "Stacked Splane Area"));
    ListOfCharts.Add(new
            mChart(typeAreas, "StackedSplineArea100", "Stacked Spline Area 100"));
    ListOfCharts.Add(new mChart(typePie, "Pie", "Pie"));
    ListOfCharts.Add(new mChart(typeOther, "Point", "Point"));
    ListOfCharts.Add(new mChart(typeOther, "Gantt", "Gantt"));
    ListOfCharts.Add(new mChart(typeOther, "Bubble", "Bubble"));
    ListOfCharts.Add(new mChart(typeOther, "CandleStick", "Candle Stick"));

    Session["charts"] = ListOfCharts;
}

protected void rbChartType_SelectedIndexChanged(object sender, EventArgs e)
{
    ListOfCharts = (List<mChart>) Session["charts"];
    var items = ListOfCharts.Where(x => x.chartType.chartType == rbChartType.SelectedValue);
    rbChart.DataSource = items;
    rbChart.DataTextField = "chartName";
    rbChart.DataValueField = "chartCode";
    rbChart.DataBind();
    rbChart.SelectedIndex = 0;
    UpdateChart(rbChart.SelectedValue);

}

protected void rbChart_SelectedIndexChanged(object sender, EventArgs e)
{
    UpdateChart(rbChart.SelectedValue);
}
```

```
private void UpdateChart(string chart)
{
    switch (chart)
    {
        case "Bar":
            foreach (var s in RadChart1.Series)
                s.Type = ChartSeriesType.Bar;
            break;
        case "StackedBar":
            foreach (var s in RadChart1.Series)
                s.Type = ChartSeriesType.StackedBar;
            break;
        case "StackedBar100":
            foreach (var s in RadChart1.Series)
                s.Type = ChartSeriesType.StackedBar100;
            break;
        case "Line":
            foreach (var s in RadChart1.Series)
                s.Type = ChartSeriesType.Line;
            break;
        case "BezierLine":
            foreach (var s in RadChart1.Series)
                s.Type = ChartSeriesType.Bezier;
            break;
        case "SplineLine":
            foreach (var s in RadChart1.Series)
                s.Type = ChartSeriesType.Spline;
            break;
        case "StackedLine":
            foreach (var s in RadChart1.Series)
                s.Type = ChartSeriesType.StackedLine;
            break;
        case "StackedSplineLine":
            foreach (var s in RadChart1.Series)
                s.Type = ChartSeriesType.StackedSpline;
            break;
        case "Area":
            foreach (var s in RadChart1.Series)
                s.Type = ChartSeriesType.Area;
            break;
        case "StackedArea":
            foreach (var s in RadChart1.Series)
                s.Type = ChartSeriesType.StackedArea;
            break;
        case "StackedArea100":
            foreach (var s in RadChart1.Series)
                s.Type = ChartSeriesType.StackedArea100;
            break;
        case "SplineArea":
            foreach (var s in RadChart1.Series)
                s.Type = ChartSeriesType.SplineArea;
            break;
```

```
        case "StackedSplineArea":
            foreach (var s in RadChart1.Series)
                s.Type = ChartSeriesType.StackedSplineArea;
            break;
        case "StackedSplineArea100":
            foreach (var s in RadChart1.Series)
                s.Type = ChartSeriesType.StackedSplineArea100;
            break;
        case "Pie":
            foreach (var s in RadChart1.Series)
                s.Type = ChartSeriesType.Pie;
            break;
        case "Point":
            foreach (var s in RadChart1.Series)
                s.Type = ChartSeriesType.Point;
            break;
        case "Bubble":
            foreach (var s in RadChart1.Series)
                s.Type = ChartSeriesType.Bubble;
            break;
        case "Gantt":
            foreach (var s in RadChart1.Series)
                s.Type = ChartSeriesType.Gantt;
            break;
        case "CandleStick":
            foreach (var s in RadChart1.Series)
                s.Type = ChartSeriesType.CandleStick;
            break;
    }
}
```

Zooming and Scrolling

The zooming and scrolling features enable the user to zoom into an area of the chart so the data is shown in greater detail. For performance reasons, only the visible image chunk is requested from the server. However, the user can scroll other parts of the chart data into view, and the requested image chunks are automatically loaded on the fly via ASP.NET 2.0 callback requests.

Zooming and scrolling are disabled by default. Enable them by setting the `RadChart.ClientSettings.EnableZoom` to `true` and `RadChart.ClientSettings.ScrollMode` property to a value other than `None`. The available `ScrollMode` values are `None`, `XOnly`, `YOnly`, and `Both`. Listing 9-2 shows how to implement these features; it creates a `RadChart` with zooming and scrolling capabilities. You can see the end result in Figure 9-9.

Listing 9-2. *Working with RadChart Zooming and Scrolling*

ASPX Page

```
<telerik:RadChart ID="RadChart2" runat="server"
        Skin="Default"
        AutoLayout="True">
        <ClientSettings
                EnableZoom="true"
                ScrollMode="Both" />
```

```
<Series>
    <telerik:ChartSeries Name="Series 1">
        <Appearance Shadow-Blur="5"
                Shadow-Distance="3">
        </Appearance>
        <Items>
                <telerik:ChartSeriesItem Name="Item 1"
                                YValue="12.5"
                                YValue2="14"
                                YValue3="10"
                                YValue4="15">
                </telerik:ChartSeriesItem>
                <telerik:ChartSeriesItem Name="Item 2"
                                YValue="13.5"
                                YValue2="10"
                                YValue3="9"
                                YValue4="10">
                </telerik:ChartSeriesItem>
                <telerik:ChartSeriesItem Name="Item 3"
                                YValue="12"
                                YValue2="13"
                                YValue3="12"
                                YValue4="14">
                </telerik:ChartSeriesItem>
                <telerik:ChartSeriesItem Name="Item 4"
                                YValue="11.4"
                                YValue2="15"
                                YValue3="10"
                                YValue4="16">
                </telerik:ChartSeriesItem>
                <telerik:ChartSeriesItem Name="Item 5"
                                YValue="12.1"
                                YValue2="11"
                                YValue3="12"
                                YValue4="11.5">
                </telerik:ChartSeriesItem>
                <telerik:ChartSeriesItem Name="Item 6"
                                YValue="12.4"
                                YValue2="8"
                                YValue3="9"
                                YValue4="10">
                </telerik:ChartSeriesItem>
                <telerik:ChartSeriesItem Name="Item 7"
                                YValue="13.1"
                                YValue2="6"
                                YValue3="6"
                                YValue4="14">
                </telerik:ChartSeriesItem>
        </Items>
    </telerik:ChartSeries>
    <telerik:ChartSeries Name="Series 2">
        <Appearance Shadow-Blur="5"
                Shadow-Distance="3">
        </Appearance>
```

```
                <Items>
                    <telerik:ChartSeriesItem Name="Item 1"
                                YValue="16.3"
                                YValue2="15"
                                YValue3="15"
                                YValue4="17">
                    </telerik:ChartSeriesItem>
                    <telerik:ChartSeriesItem Name="Item 2"
                                YValue="10"
                                YValue2="13"
                                YValue3="9"
                                YValue4="14">
                    </telerik:ChartSeriesItem>
                    <telerik:ChartSeriesItem Name="Item 3"
                                YValue="6"
                                YValue2="7"
                                YValue3="5"
                                YValue4="19">
                    </telerik:ChartSeriesItem>
                    <telerik:ChartSeriesItem Name="Item 4"
                                YValue="12"
                                YValue2="11"
                                YValue3="12"
                                YValue4="11">
                    </telerik:ChartSeriesItem>
                    <telerik:ChartSeriesItem Name="Item 5"
                                YValue="15.8"
                                YValue2="20"
                                YValue3="13"
                                YValue4="22">
                    </telerik:ChartSeriesItem>
                    <telerik:ChartSeriesItem Name="Item 6"
                                YValue="7"
                                YValue2="10"
                                YValue3="6"
                                YValue4="10">
                    </telerik:ChartSeriesItem>
                    <telerik:ChartSeriesItem Name="Item 7"
                                YValue="18.8"
                                YValue2="15"
                                YValue3="15"
                                YValue4="22">
                    </telerik:ChartSeriesItem>
                </Items>
            </telerik:ChartSeries>
        </Series>
        <PlotArea>
            <Appearance Dimensions-Margins="18%, 24%, 12%, 10%">
            </Appearance>
            <YAxis AxisMode="Extended"></YAxis>
        </PlotArea>
</telerik:RadChart>
```

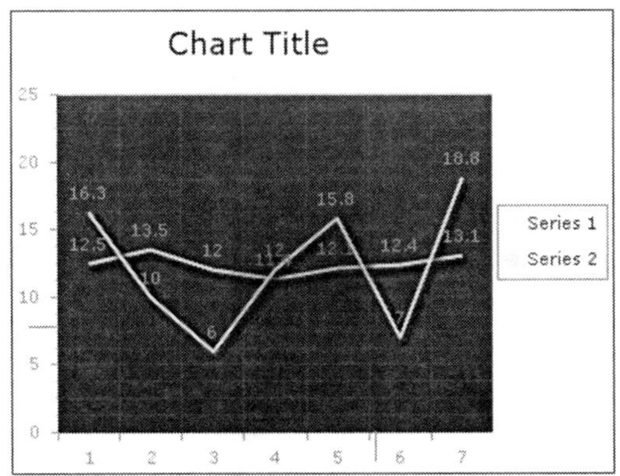

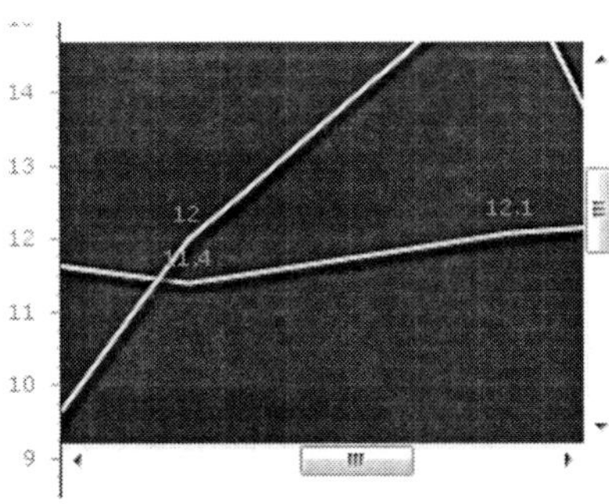

Figure 9-9. *When selecting an area in the RadChart (left), you automatically zoom in to see detailed information and scroll to move to other areas of the chart (right).*

Creating Marked Zones

When presenting business information in charts, sometimes it's important to highlight areas that indicate whether data is out of regular ranges. For example, in a temperature chart, you could define an area as too hot; in stock market charts, you could define an area for high-risk options.

For this purpose, RadChart includes a feature called marked zones. A *marked zone* is a data range in the chart that will be painted differently to highlight in the chart the special areas relevant to the business in question. Listing 9-3 describes how to build a RadChart that includes marked zones, and Figure 9-10 shows the end result.

Listing 9-3. *Marked Zones*

ASPX Page

```
<telerik:RadChart ID="RadChart3" runat="server"
        Skin="Default"
        AutoLayout="True">
        <Series>
            <telerik:ChartSeries Name="Series 1">
                <Appearance Shadow-Blur="5"
                        Shadow-Distance="3">
                </Appearance>
                <Items>
                        <telerik:ChartSeriesItem Name="Item 1"
                                        YValue="12.5"
                                        YValue2="14"
                                        YValue3="10"
                                        YValue4="15">
                        </telerik:ChartSeriesItem>
```

```
                    <telerik:ChartSeriesItem Name="Item 2"
                                    YValue="13.5"
                                    YValue2="10"
                                    YValue3="9"
                                    YValue4="10">
                    </telerik:ChartSeriesItem>
                    <telerik:ChartSeriesItem Name="Item 3"
                                    YValue="12"
                                    YValue2="13"
                                    YValue3="12"
                                    YValue4="14">
                    </telerik:ChartSeriesItem>
                    <telerik:ChartSeriesItem Name="Item 4"
                                    YValue="11.4"
                                    YValue2="15"
                                    YValue3="10"
                                    YValue4="16">
                    </telerik:ChartSeriesItem>
                    <telerik:ChartSeriesItem Name="Item 5"
                                    YValue="12.1"
                                    YValue2="11"
                                    YValue3="12"
                                    YValue4="11.5">
                    </telerik:ChartSeriesItem>
                    <telerik:ChartSeriesItem Name="Item 6"
                                    YValue="12.4"
                                    YValue2="8"
                                    YValue3="9"
                                    YValue4="10">
                    </telerik:ChartSeriesItem>
                    <telerik:ChartSeriesItem Name="Item 7"
                                    YValue="13.1"
                                    YValue2="6"
                                    YValue3="6"
                                    YValue4="14">
                    </telerik:ChartSeriesItem>
                </Items>
            </telerik:ChartSeries>
            <telerik:ChartSeries Name="Series 2">
                <Appearance Shadow-Blur="5"
                    Shadow-Distance="3">
                </Appearance>
                <Items>
                    <telerik:ChartSeriesItem Name="Item 1"
                                    YValue="16.3"
                                    YValue2="15"
                                    YValue3="15"
                                    YValue4="17">
                    </telerik:ChartSeriesItem>
```

```
                <telerik:ChartSeriesItem Name="Item 2"
                               YValue="10"
                               YValue2="13"
                               YValue3="9"
                               YValue4="14">
                </telerik:ChartSeriesItem>
                <telerik:ChartSeriesItem Name="Item 3"
                               YValue="6"
                               YValue2="7"
                               YValue3="5"
                               YValue4="19">
                </telerik:ChartSeriesItem>
                <telerik:ChartSeriesItem Name="Item 4"
                               YValue="12"
                               YValue2="11"
                               YValue3="12"
                               YValue4="11">
                </telerik:ChartSeriesItem>
                <telerik:ChartSeriesItem Name="Item 5"
                               YValue="15.8"
                               YValue2="20"
                               YValue3="13"
                               YValue4="22">
                </telerik:ChartSeriesItem>
                <telerik:ChartSeriesItem Name="Item 6"
                               YValue="7"
                               YValue2="10"
                               YValue3="6"
                               YValue4="10">
                </telerik:ChartSeriesItem>
                <telerik:ChartSeriesItem Name="Item 7"
                               YValue="18.8"
                               YValue2="15"
                               YValue3="15"
                               YValue4="22">
                </telerik:ChartSeriesItem>
        </Items>
    </telerik:ChartSeries>
</Series>
<legend>
    <appearance dimensions-margins="1%, 1%, 1%, 1%">
    </appearance>
</legend>
```

```
        <PlotArea>
            <markedzones>
                <telerik:ChartMarkedZone
                                Name="Danger - High"
                                ValueEndY="20"
                                ValueStartY="15">
                    <label>
                        <textblock text="Too High!">
                                <appearance
                                        textproperties-color="White"
                                        textproperties-font="Verdana, 8.25pt, style=Bold">
                                </appearance>
                        </textblock>
                    </label>
                    <appearance>
                        <fillstyle filltype="Gradient"
                                maincolor="Red"
                                secondcolor="White">
                        </fillstyle>
                    </appearance>
                </telerik:ChartMarkedZone>
                <telerik:ChartMarkedZone Name="Danger - Low"
                                ValueStartY="0"
                                ValueEndY="8">
                    <label>
                        <textblock text="Too Low!!">
                                <appearance
                                        textproperties-color="White"
                                        textproperties-font="Verdana, 8.25pt, style=Bold">
                                </appearance>
                        </textblock>
                    </label>
                    <appearance>
                        <fillstyle filltype="Gradient"
                                        maincolor="Green"
                                        secondcolor="Yellow">
                        </fillstyle>
                    </appearance>
                </telerik:ChartMarkedZone>
            </markedzones>
            <appearance dimensions-margins="18%, 24%, 12%, 10%">
            </appearance>
            <YAxis AxisMode="Extended"></YAxis>
        </PlotArea>
        <charttitle>
            <appearance dimensions-margins="1%, 1%, 1%, 1%"
                        position-alignedposition="Top">
            </appearance>
        </charttitle>
    </telerik:RadChart>
```

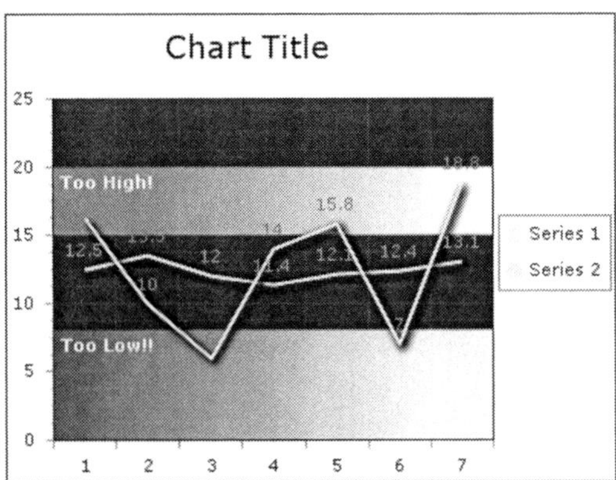

Figure 9-10. *Note the marked zones "Too High!" and "Too Low!".*

Adding Scale Breaks

The scale breaks feature was introduced to preserve the correct presentation of a chart when some of the values are far outside the current scale. The purpose of a scale break is to keep the chart readable by not allowing data considered as peaks to diminish the other data that is more even. Listing 9-4 creates a chart with a high value to illustrate how scale breaks work. See Figure 9-11 for the end result.

Listing 9-4. *Scale Breaks*

ASPX Page

```
<telerik:RadChart ID="RadChart4" runat="server"
        Skin="Default"
        AutoLayout="True">
    <Series>
            <telerik:ChartSeries Name="Series 1">
                <Appearance Shadow-Blur="5"
                        Shadow-Distance="3">
                </Appearance>
                <Items>
                        <telerik:ChartSeriesItem Name="Item 1"
                                        YValue="12.5"
                                        YValue2="14"
                                        YValue3="10"
                                        YValue4="15">
                        </telerik:ChartSeriesItem>
                        <telerik:ChartSeriesItem Name="Item 2"
                                        YValue="13.5"
                                        YValue2="10"
                                        YValue3="9"
                                        YValue4="10">
                        </telerik:ChartSeriesItem>
```

```
                <telerik:ChartSeriesItem Name="Item 3"
                                YValue="12"
                                YValue2="13"
                                YValue3="12"
                                YValue4="14">
                </telerik:ChartSeriesItem>
                <telerik:ChartSeriesItem Name="Item 4"
                                YValue="11.4"
                                YValue2="15"
                                YValue3="10"
                                YValue4="16">
                </telerik:ChartSeriesItem>
                <telerik:ChartSeriesItem Name="Item 5"
                                YValue="12.1"
                                YValue2="11"
                                YValue3="12"
                                YValue4="11.5">
                </telerik:ChartSeriesItem>
                <telerik:ChartSeriesItem Name="Item 6"
                                YValue="12.4"
                                YValue2="8"
                                YValue3="9"
                                YValue4="10">
                </telerik:ChartSeriesItem>
                <telerik:ChartSeriesItem Name="Item 7"
                                YValue="13.1"
                                YValue2="6"
                                YValue3="6"
                                YValue4="14">
                </telerik:ChartSeriesItem>
        </Items>
    </telerik:ChartSeries>
    <telerik:ChartSeries Name="Series 2">
        <Appearance Shadow-Blur="5"
                Shadow-Distance="3">
        </Appearance>
        <Items>
                <telerik:ChartSeriesItem Name="Item 1"
                                YValue="16.3"
                                YValue2="15"
                                YValue3="15"
                                YValue4="17">
                </telerik:ChartSeriesItem>
                <telerik:ChartSeriesItem Name="Item 2"
                                YValue="10"
                                YValue2="13"
                                YValue3="9"
                                YValue4="14">
                </telerik:ChartSeriesItem>
```

```
                    <telerik:ChartSeriesItem Name="Item 3"
                                YValue="6"
                                YValue2="7"
                                YValue3="5"
                                YValue4="19">
                    </telerik:ChartSeriesItem>
                    <telerik:ChartSeriesItem Name="Item 4"
                                YValue="200"
                                YValue2="11"
                                YValue3="12"
                                YValue4="11">
                    </telerik:ChartSeriesItem>
                    <telerik:ChartSeriesItem Name="Item 5"
                                YValue="15.8"
                                YValue2="20"
                                YValue3="13"
                                YValue4="22">
                    </telerik:ChartSeriesItem>
                    <telerik:ChartSeriesItem Name="Item 6"
                                YValue="7"
                                YValue2="10"
                                YValue3="6"
                                YValue4="10">
                    </telerik:ChartSeriesItem>
                    <telerik:ChartSeriesItem Name="Item 7"
                                YValue="18.8"
                                YValue2="15"
                                YValue3="15"
                                YValue4="22">
                    </telerik:ChartSeriesItem>
                </Items>
            </telerik:ChartSeries>
    </Series>
    <legend>
        <appearance dimensions-margins="1%, 1%, 1%, 1%">
        </appearance>
    </legend>
    <PlotArea>
        <appearance dimensions-margins="18%, 24%, 12%, 10%">
        </appearance>
                <YAxis ScaleBreaks-Enabled="true"
                       ScaleBreaks-MaxCount="2"
                       AxisMode="Extended">
                </YAxis>
    </PlotArea>
    <charttitle>
        <appearance dimensions-margins="1%, 1%, 1%, 1%"
                position-alignedposition="Top">
        </appearance>
    </charttitle>
</telerik:RadChart>
```

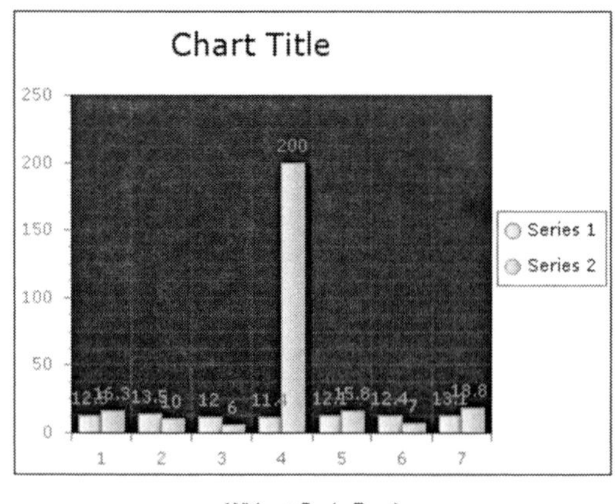

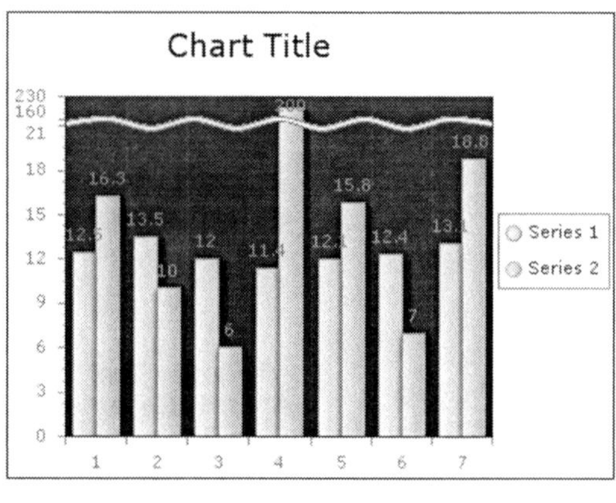

Figure 9-11. *You can help prevent distorted charts due off-scale values (left) by using scale breaks (right).*

Plotting Negative Values

RadChart can plot negative values as well as positive ones. See the example in Listing 9-5. Figure 9-12 illustrates how `RadChart` handle negative values.

Listing 9-5. *Negative Values*

ASPX Page

```
<telerik:RadChart ID="RadChart5" runat="server"
        Skin="Default"
        AutoLayout="True">
        <Series>
            <telerik:ChartSeries Name="Series 1">
                <Appearance Shadow-Blur="5"
                        Shadow-Distance="3">
                </Appearance>
                <Items>
                        <telerik:ChartSeriesItem Name="Item 1"
                                        YValue="12.5"
                                        YValue2="14"
                                        YValue3="10"
                                        YValue4="15">
                        </telerik:ChartSeriesItem>
                        <telerik:ChartSeriesItem Name="Item 2"
                                        YValue="13.5"
                                        YValue2="10"
                                        YValue3="9"
                                        YValue4="10">
                        </telerik:ChartSeriesItem>
```

```
                <telerik:ChartSeriesItem Name="Item 3"
                                YValue="12"
                                YValue2="13"
                                YValue3="12"
                                YValue4="14">
                </telerik:ChartSeriesItem>
                <telerik:ChartSeriesItem Name="Item 4"
                                YValue="11.4"
                                YValue2="15"
                                YValue3="10"
                                YValue4="16">
                </telerik:ChartSeriesItem>
                <telerik:ChartSeriesItem Name="Item 5"
                                YValue="12.1"
                                YValue2="11"
                                YValue3="12"
                                YValue4="11.5">
                </telerik:ChartSeriesItem>
                <telerik:ChartSeriesItem Name="Item 6"
                                YValue="12.4"
                                YValue2="8"
                                YValue3="9"
                                YValue4="10">
                </telerik:ChartSeriesItem>
                <telerik:ChartSeriesItem Name="Item 7"
                                YValue="13.1"
                                YValue2="6"
                                YValue3="6"
                                YValue4="14">
                </telerik:ChartSeriesItem>
        </Items>
    </telerik:ChartSeries>
    <telerik:ChartSeries Name="Series 2">
        <Appearance Shadow-Blur="5"
                Shadow-Distance="3">
        </Appearance>
        <Items>
                <telerik:ChartSeriesItem Name="Item 1"
                                YValue="-16.3"
                                YValue2="15"
                                YValue3="15"
                                YValue4="17">
                </telerik:ChartSeriesItem>
                <telerik:ChartSeriesItem Name="Item 2"
                                YValue="-10"
                                YValue2="13"
                                YValue3="9"
                                YValue4="14">
                </telerik:ChartSeriesItem>
```

```
                        <telerik:ChartSeriesItem Name="Item 3"
                                        YValue="-6"
                                        YValue2="7"
                                        YValue3="5"
                                        YValue4="19">
                        </telerik:ChartSeriesItem>
                        <telerik:ChartSeriesItem Name="Item 4"
                                        YValue="-17"
                                        YValue2="11"
                                        YValue3="12"
                                        YValue4="11">
                        </telerik:ChartSeriesItem>
                        <telerik:ChartSeriesItem Name="Item 5"
                                        YValue="-15.8"
                                        YValue2="20"
                                        YValue3="13"
                                        YValue4="22">
                        </telerik:ChartSeriesItem>
                        <telerik:ChartSeriesItem Name="Item 6"
                                        YValue="-7"
                                        YValue2="10"
                                        YValue3="6"
                                        YValue4="10">
                        </telerik:ChartSeriesItem>
                        <telerik:ChartSeriesItem Name="Item 7"
                                        YValue="-18.8"
                                        YValue2="15"
                                        YValue3="15"
                                        YValue4="22">
                        </telerik:ChartSeriesItem>
                </Items>
            </telerik:ChartSeries>
        </Series>
        <legend>
            <appearance dimensions-margins="1%, 1%, 1%, 1%">
            </appearance>
        </legend>
        <PlotArea>
            <appearance dimensions-margins="18%, 24%, 12%, 10%">
            </appearance>
            <YAxis AxisMode="Extended"></YAxis>
        </PlotArea>
        <charttitle>
            <appearance dimensions-margins="1%, 1%, 1%, 1%"
                        position-alignedposition="Top">
            </appearance>
        </charttitle>
    </telerik:RadChart>
```

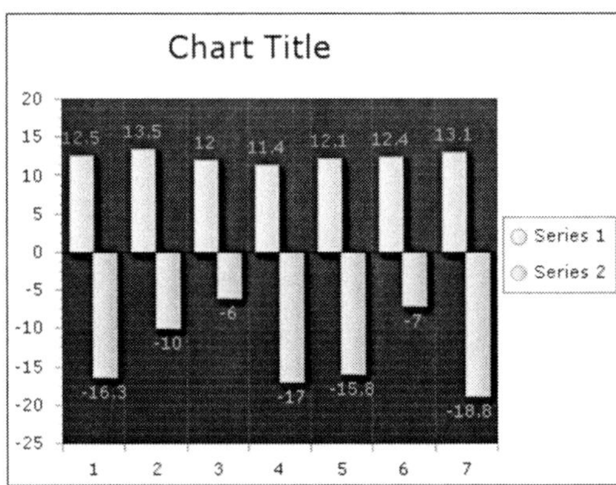

Figure 9-12. *RadChart correctly plots negative values as well as positive ones.*

Using Multiple Series Types in One Chart and Data Table

Because the type of chart is a per-series property, you can have multiple chart types in a single chart. Additionally, you can instruct RadChart to show the data table used to construct the chart. See Listing 9-6 for a sample on how to do this. Figure 9-13 illustrates these capabilities.

Listing 9-6. *Multiple Series Types in One Chart and Data Table*

ASPX Page

```
<telerik:RadChart ID="RadChart6" runat="server"
        Skin="Default"
        AutoLayout="True">
        <Series>
            <telerik:ChartSeries Name="Series 1"
                                    Type="Bar">
                <Items>
                        <telerik:ChartSeriesItem Name="Item 1"
                                        YValue="12.5"
                                        YValue2="14"
                                        YValue3="10"
                                        YValue4="15">
                        </telerik:ChartSeriesItem>
                        <telerik:ChartSeriesItem Name="Item 2"
                                        YValue="13.5"
                                        YValue2="10"
                                        YValue3="9"
                                        YValue4="10">
                        </telerik:ChartSeriesItem>
                        <telerik:ChartSeriesItem Name="Item 3"
                                        YValue="12"
                                        YValue2="13"
                                        YValue3="12"
                                        YValue4="14">
```

```
                </telerik:ChartSeriesItem>
                <telerik:ChartSeriesItem Name="Item 4"
                               YValue="11.4"
                               YValue2="15"
                               YValue3="10"
                               YValue4="16">
                </telerik:ChartSeriesItem>
                <telerik:ChartSeriesItem Name="Item 5"
                               YValue="12.1"
                               YValue2="11"
                               YValue3="12"
                               YValue4="11.5">
                </telerik:ChartSeriesItem>
                <telerik:ChartSeriesItem Name="Item 6"
                               YValue="12.4"
                               YValue2="8"
                               YValue3="9"
                               YValue4="10">
                </telerik:ChartSeriesItem>
                <telerik:ChartSeriesItem Name="Item 7"
                               YValue="13.1"
                               YValue2="6"
                               YValue3="6"
                               YValue4="14">
                </telerik:ChartSeriesItem>
        </Items>
    </telerik:ChartSeries>
    <telerik:ChartSeries Name="Series 2"
                    Type="Line">
        <Items>
                <telerik:ChartSeriesItem Name="Item 1"
                               YValue="16.3"
                               YValue2="15"
                               YValue3="15"
                               YValue4="17">
                </telerik:ChartSeriesItem>
                <telerik:ChartSeriesItem Name="Item 2"
                               YValue="10"
                               YValue2="13"
                               YValue3="9"
                               YValue4="14">
                </telerik:ChartSeriesItem>
                <telerik:ChartSeriesItem Name="Item 3"
                               YValue="6"
                               YValue2="7"
                               YValue3="5"
                               YValue4="19">
                </telerik:ChartSeriesItem>
                <telerik:ChartSeriesItem Name="Item 4"
                               YValue="200"
                               YValue2="11"
                               YValue3="12"
                               YValue4="11">
                </telerik:ChartSeriesItem>
```

```
                        <telerik:ChartSeriesItem Name="Item 5"
                                YValue="15.8"
                                YValue2="20"
                                YValue3="13"
                                YValue4="22">
                        </telerik:ChartSeriesItem>
                        <telerik:ChartSeriesItem Name="Item 6"
                                YValue="7"
                                YValue2="10"
                                YValue3="6"
                                YValue4="10">
                        </telerik:ChartSeriesItem>
                        <telerik:ChartSeriesItem Name="Item 7"
                                YValue="18.8"
                                YValue2="15"
                                YValue3="15"
                                YValue4="22">
                        </telerik:ChartSeriesItem>
                    </Items>
                </telerik:ChartSeries>
            </Series>
            <legend>
                <appearance>
                    <itemmarkerappearance figure="Circle">
                    </itemmarkerappearance>
                </appearance>
            </legend>
            <PlotArea>
                <datatable visible="True">
                </datatable>
                <YAxis AxisMode="Extended">
                    </YAxis>
            </PlotArea>
        </telerik:RadChart>
</ContentTemplate>
</asp:UpdatePanel>
```

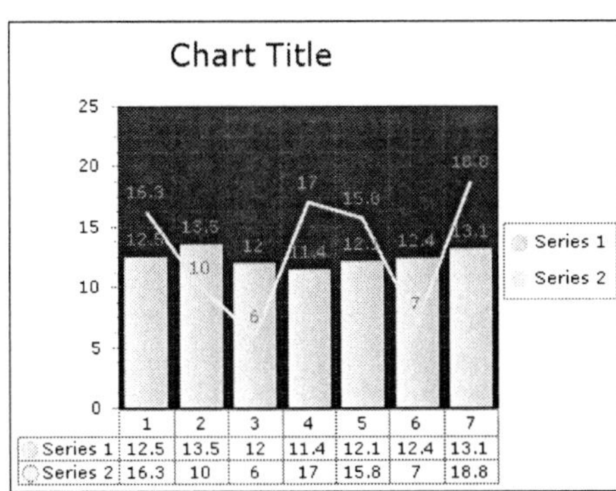

Figure 9-13. *Displaying multiple series types in one chart as well as the data table*

Working with Image Maps

Image maps are visual areas within a chart that display tool tips; the user can click them to navigate. Image map areas are represented by the ActiveRegion property. ActiveRegion appears for many of the UI elements in the chart including labels, chart series, chart series items, chart title, legend, axis items, and the empty series message. Image maps can be used to implement drill-down user interfaces.

The example in Listing 9-7 shows how to work with the ActiveRegion property to create and open a window with details regarding the clicked series item.

Listing 9-7. *Image Maps*

ASPX Page

```
<telerik:RadChart ID="RadChart8" runat="server"
        DataSourceID="SqlDataSource4"
        DefaultType="Pie"
        OnItemDataBound="RadChart8_ItemDataBound"
        AutoLayout="true">
    <Series>
        <telerik:ChartSeries Name="Orders"
                        DataLabelsColumn="Country"
                        DataYColumn="Orders"
                        Type="Pie">
        </telerik:ChartSeries>
    </Series>
    <PlotArea>
        <XAxis AutoScale="False"
                DataLabelsColumn="Country"
                MaxValue="7"
                MinValue="1"
                Step="1">
            <Items>
                <telerik:ChartAxisItem Value="1">
                </telerik:ChartAxisItem>
                <telerik:ChartAxisItem Value="2">
                </telerik:ChartAxisItem>
                <telerik:ChartAxisItem Value="3">
                </telerik:ChartAxisItem>
                <telerik:ChartAxisItem Value="4">
                </telerik:ChartAxisItem>
                <telerik:ChartAxisItem Value="5">
                </telerik:ChartAxisItem>
                <telerik:ChartAxisItem Value="6">
                </telerik:ChartAxisItem>
                <telerik:ChartAxisItem Value="7">
                </telerik:ChartAxisItem>
            </Items>
        </XAxis>
        <Appearance Dimensions-Margins="18%, 24%, 12%, 10%">
        </Appearance>
    </PlotArea>
```

```
        <ChartTitle>
            <TextBlock Text="Orders By Country">
            </TextBlock>
        </ChartTitle>
</telerik:RadChart>

<asp:SqlDataSource ID="SqlDataSource4" runat="server"
    ConnectionString="<%$ ConnectionStrings:NorthwindConnectionString %>"
    SelectCommand="SELECT Country, COUNT(*) Orders
                      FROM dbo.[Orders Qry]
                    GROUP BY Country
                    HAVING COUNT(*) > 30">
</asp:SqlDataSource>

<telerik:RadWindow ID="RadWindow1" runat="server"
                 Width="800px"
                 Height="600px"
                 Behaviors="Close, Move"
                 style="z-index:20000">
</telerik:RadWindow>

<script language="javascript" type="text/javascript">
    function ShowOrders(country) {
        var wnd = $find("<%=RadWindow1.ClientID %>");
        wnd.setUrl("radchart_ImageMaps.aspx?country=" + country);
        wnd.set_title("Orders in " + country);
        wnd.show();
    }
</script>

Code Behind

protected void RadChart8_ItemDataBound(object sender, ChartItemDataBoundEventArgs e)
{
    e.SeriesItem.ActiveRegion.Url = string.Format("javascript:ShowOrders('{0}');",
                                            e.SeriesItem.Label.TextBlock.Text);
}

Radchart_ImageMaps.aspx

<!DOCTYPE html PUBLIC "-//W3C//DTD XHTML 1.0 Transitional//EN"
        "http://www.w3.org/TR/xhtml1/DTD/xhtml1-transitional.dtd">
```

```
<html xmlns="http://www.w3.org/1999/xhtml">
<head runat="server">
    <title></title>
    <style type="text/css">
    html, body, form
    {
        height: 100%;
        margin: 0px;
        padding: 0px;
        overflow: hidden;
    }
    </style>
</head>
<body>
    <form id="form1" runat="server">
    <telerik:RadScriptManager ID="RadScriptManager1" runat="server">
    </telerik:RadScriptManager>
    <div style="width:100%; height:100%; overflow:hidden">
        <telerik:RadSplitter ID="RadSplitter1" runat="server"
                        Width="100%"
                        Height="100%"
                        FullScreenMode="True">

            <telerik:RadPane ID="RadPane3" runat="server"
                        Width="100%"
                        Height="100%"
                        Scrolling="None">

                <telerik:RadGrid ID="RadGrid1" runat="server"
                                DataSourceID="SqlDataSource1"
                                GridLines="None"
                                Width="100%"
                                Height="100%">
                    <ClientSettings>
                        <Scrolling AllowScroll="True"
                                UseStaticHeaders="True" />
                    </ClientSettings>
                        <MasterTableView AutoGenerateColumns="False"
                                DataKeyNames="OrderID"
                                DataSourceID="SqlDataSource1">
                        <RowIndicatorColumn>
                        <HeaderStyle Width="20px"></HeaderStyle>
                        </RowIndicatorColumn>

                        <ExpandCollapseColumn>
                        <HeaderStyle Width="20px"></HeaderStyle>
                        </ExpandCollapseColumn>
```

```
<Columns>
    <telerik:GridBoundColumn DataField="OrderID"
                        DataType="System.Int32"
                        HeaderText="OrderID"
                        ReadOnly="True"
                        SortExpression="OrderID"
        UniqueName="OrderID">
    </telerik:GridBoundColumn>
    <telerik:GridBoundColumn DataField="CustomerID"
                        HeaderText="CustomerID"
                        SortExpression="CustomerID"
                        UniqueName="CustomerID">
    </telerik:GridBoundColumn>
    <telerik:GridBoundColumn DataField="EmployeeID"
                        DataType="System.Int32"
                        HeaderText="EmployeeID"
                        SortExpression="EmployeeID"
                        UniqueName="EmployeeID">
    </telerik:GridBoundColumn>
    <telerik:GridBoundColumn DataField="OrderDate"
                        DataType="System.DateTime"
                        HeaderText="OrderDate"
                        SortExpression="OrderDate"
                        UniqueName="OrderDate">
    </telerik:GridBoundColumn>
    <telerik:GridBoundColumn DataField="RequiredDate"
                        DataType="System.DateTime"
                        HeaderText="RequiredDate"
                        SortExpression="RequiredDate"
                        UniqueName="RequiredDate">
    </telerik:GridBoundColumn>
    <telerik:GridBoundColumn DataField="ShippedDate"
                        DataType="System.DateTime"
                        HeaderText="ShippedDate"
                        SortExpression="ShippedDate"
                        UniqueName="ShippedDate">
    </telerik:GridBoundColumn>
    <telerik:GridBoundColumn DataField="ShipVia"
                        DataType="System.Int32"
                        HeaderText="ShipVia"
                        SortExpression="ShipVia"
                        UniqueName="ShipVia">
    </telerik:GridBoundColumn>
    <telerik:GridBoundColumn DataField="Freight"
                        DataType="System.Decimal"
                        HeaderText="Freight"
                        SortExpression="Freight"
                        UniqueName="Freight">
    </telerik:GridBoundColumn>
    <telerik:GridBoundColumn DataField="ShipName"
                        HeaderText="ShipName"
                        SortExpression="ShipName"
                        UniqueName="ShipName">
    </telerik:GridBoundColumn>
```

```
<telerik:GridBoundColumn DataField="ShipAddress"
                         HeaderText="ShipAddress"
                         SortExpression="ShipAddress"
                         UniqueName="ShipAddress">
</telerik:GridBoundColumn>
<telerik:GridBoundColumn DataField="ShipCity"
                         HeaderText="ShipCity"
                         SortExpression="ShipCity"
                         UniqueName="ShipCity">
</telerik:GridBoundColumn>
<telerik:GridBoundColumn DataField="ShipRegion"
                         HeaderText="ShipRegion"
                         SortExpression="ShipRegion"
                         UniqueName="ShipRegion">
</telerik:GridBoundColumn>
<telerik:GridBoundColumn DataField="ShipPostalCode"
                         HeaderText="ShipPostalCode"
                         SortExpression="ShipPostalCode"
                         UniqueName="ShipPostalCode">
</telerik:GridBoundColumn>
<telerik:GridBoundColumn DataField="ShipCountry"
                         HeaderText="ShipCountry"
                         SortExpression="ShipCountry"
                         UniqueName="ShipCountry">
</telerik:GridBoundColumn>
<telerik:GridBoundColumn DataField="CompanyName"
                         HeaderText="CompanyName"
                         SortExpression="CompanyName"
                         UniqueName="CompanyName">
</telerik:GridBoundColumn>
<telerik:GridBoundColumn DataField="Address"
                         HeaderText="Address"
                         SortExpression="Address"
                         UniqueName="Address">
</telerik:GridBoundColumn>
<telerik:GridBoundColumn DataField="City"
                         HeaderText="City"
                         SortExpression="City"
                         UniqueName="City">
</telerik:GridBoundColumn>
<telerik:GridBoundColumn DataField="Region"
                         HeaderText="Region"
                         SortExpression="Region"
                         UniqueName="Region">
</telerik:GridBoundColumn>
<telerik:GridBoundColumn DataField="PostalCode"
                         HeaderText="PostalCode"
                         SortExpression="PostalCode"
                         UniqueName="PostalCode">
</telerik:GridBoundColumn>
```

```
                        <telerik:GridBoundColumn DataField="Country"
                                                 HeaderText="Country"
                                                 SortExpression="Country"
                                                 UniqueName="Country">
                        </telerik:GridBoundColumn>
                    </Columns>
                </MasterTableView>
            </telerik:RadGrid>
            <asp:SqlDataSource ID="SqlDataSource1" runat="server"
                ConnectionString="<%$ ConnectionStrings:NorthwindConnectionString %>"
                SelectCommand="SELECT *
                                FROM dbo.[Orders Qry]
                                WHERE Country = @country">
                <SelectParameters>
                    <asp:QueryStringParameter Name="country"
                                              QueryStringField="country" />
                </SelectParameters>
            </asp:SqlDataSource>
        </telerik:RadPane>
    </telerik:RadSplitter>
    </div>
    </form>
</body>
</html>
```

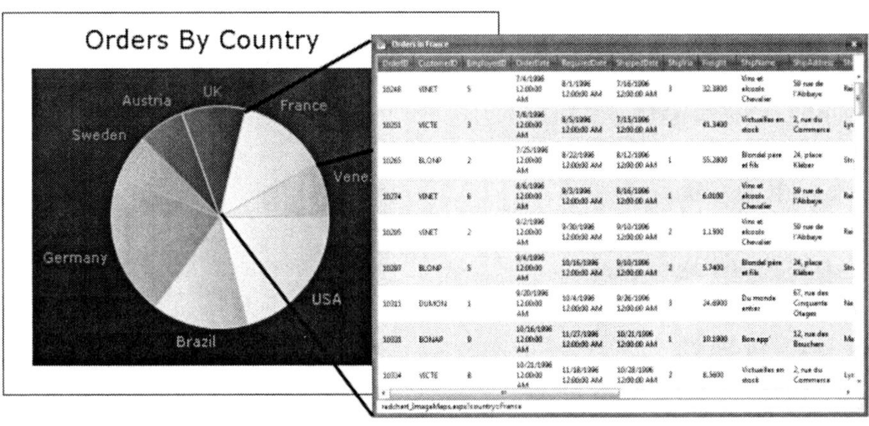

Figure 9-14. *When a user clicks in a RadChart ActiveRegion, a window is opened to show detailed information.*

Creating Drill-Down Charts

With the same principle as image maps, you can create the effect of drill-down charts by reloading data into the chart or navigating to another page by handling the `Click` event of `RadChart`.

For the following example, I'm using three `SqlDataSources`. The first one will be used as the first level of data, showing orders information per year. When the user clicks one of the years, the `Click` event handler recognizes which year was clicked and loads the monthly detail from the second data source.

During the monthly data view, if the user clicks one of the months, the Click event handler recognizes the month and loads from the third data source—the daily order information for that month and year. The example in Listing 9-8 shows how to implement this feature, and Figure 9-15 shows how it looks.

Listing 9-8. *Drill-Down Charts*

ASPX Page

```
<telerik:RadChart ID="RadChart7" runat="server"
                Skin="Default"
                AutoLayout="True"
                DataSourceID="SqlDataSource1"
                OnClick="RadChart7_Click"
                Width="500px">
        <series>
            <telerik:ChartSeries DataYColumn="Orders By Year"
                                DataXColumn="Year"
                                Name="Orders By Year">
            </telerik:ChartSeries>
        </series>
        <PlotArea>
            <xaxis autoscale="False"
                        datalabelscolumn="Year"
                        maxvalue="1998"
                        minvalue="1996"
                        step="1">
                <Items>
                    <telerik:ChartAxisItem Value="1996">
                    </telerik:ChartAxisItem>
                    <telerik:ChartAxisItem Value="1997">
                    </telerik:ChartAxisItem>
                    <telerik:ChartAxisItem Value="1998">
                    </telerik:ChartAxisItem>
                </Items>
            </xaxis>
            <YAxis AxisMode="Extended"></YAxis>
        </PlotArea>
        <charttitle>
            <textblock text="Orders">
            </textblock>
        </charttitle>
    </telerik:RadChart>

<asp:SqlDataSource ID="SqlDataSource1" runat="server"
        ConnectionString="<%$ ConnectionStrings:NorthwindConnectionString %>"
        SelectCommand="SELECT DATEPART(yyyy,OrderDate) [Year], COUNT(*) AS [Orders By Year]
                        FROM dbo.Orders
                        GROUP BY DATEPART(yyyy,OrderDate)
                        ORDER BY 1">
</asp:SqlDataSource>
```

```
<asp:SqlDataSource ID="SqlDataSource2" runat="server"
        ConnectionString="<%$ ConnectionStrings:NorthwindConnectionString %>"
        SelectCommand="SELECT DATEPART(mm,OrderDate) [Month],
                               DATENAME(month,
                                       CAST(CAST(DATEPART(yyyy,OrderDate) AS VARCHAR)
                                       + '/' + CAST(DATEPART(mm,OrderDate) AS VARCHAR)
                                       + '/01' AS DATETIME))
                                       AS [Month Name],
                        COUNT(*) AS [Orders By Month]
                        FROM dbo.Orders
                        WHERE DATEPART(yyyy,OrderDate) = @Year
                        GROUP BY DATEPART(mm,OrderDate),
                                DATEPART(yyyy,OrderDate)
                        ORDER BY 1">
        <SelectParameters>
                <asp:Parameter Name="Year" Type="Int32" />
        </SelectParameters>
</asp:SqlDataSource>

<asp:SqlDataSource ID="SqlDataSource3" runat="server"
        ConnectionString="<%$ ConnectionStrings:NorthwindConnectionString %>"
        SelectCommand="SELECT DATEPART(dd, OrderDate) AS [Day], COUNT(*) AS [Daily Orders]
                        FROM dbo.Orders
                        WHERE DATEPART(yyyy,OrderDate) = @Year
                           AND DATEPART(mm,OrderDate) = @Month
                        GROUP BY DATEPART(dd, OrderDate)
                        ORDER BY 1">
        <SelectParameters>
                <asp:Parameter Name="Year" Type="Int32" />
                <asp:Parameter Name="Month" Type="Int32" />
        </SelectParameters>
</asp:SqlDataSource>
```

Code Behind

```
protected void RadChart7_Click(object sender, ChartClickEventArgs args)
{
    if (args.SeriesItem != null)
        switch (args.SeriesItem.Parent.Name)
        {
            case "Orders By Year":
                {
                    var Year = int.Parse(args.SeriesItem.XValue.ToString());
                    Session["year"] = Year;
                    SqlDataSource2.SelectParameters[0].DefaultValue = Year.ToString();
                    RadChart7.PlotArea.XAxis.DataLabelsColumn = "Month";
                    RadChart7.Series[0].Clear();
                    RadChart7.Series[0].DataXColumn = "Month";
                    RadChart7.Series[0].PlotArea.XAxis.DataLabelsColumn = "Month Name";
                    RadChart7.Series[0].PlotArea.XAxis.Appearance
                                            .LabelAppearance
                                            .RotationAngle = 270;
                    RadChart7.Series[0].DataYColumn = "Orders By Month";
                    RadChart7.Series[0].Name = "Orders By Month";
```

```
                RadChart7.DataSourceID = "SqlDataSource2";
                RadChart7.ChartTitle.TextBlock.Text =
                                 string.Format("Monthly Orders in {0}", Year);
            }
            break;
        case "Orders By Month":
            {
                var Month = int.Parse(args.SeriesItem.XValue.ToString());
                var Year = int.Parse(Session["year"].ToString());
                SqlDataSource3.SelectParameters[0].DefaultValue = Year.ToString();
                SqlDataSource3.SelectParameters[1].DefaultValue = Month.ToString();
                RadChart7.Series[0].Clear();
                RadChart7.Series[0].DataXColumn = "Day";
                RadChart7.Series[0].DataYColumn = "Daily Orders";
                RadChart7.Series[0].Name = "Daily Orders";
                RadChart7.DataSourceID = "SqlDataSource3";
                RadChart7.ChartTitle.TextBlock.Text =
                           string.Format("Daily Orders in {0}-{1}", Year, Month);
            }
            break;
    }
}
```

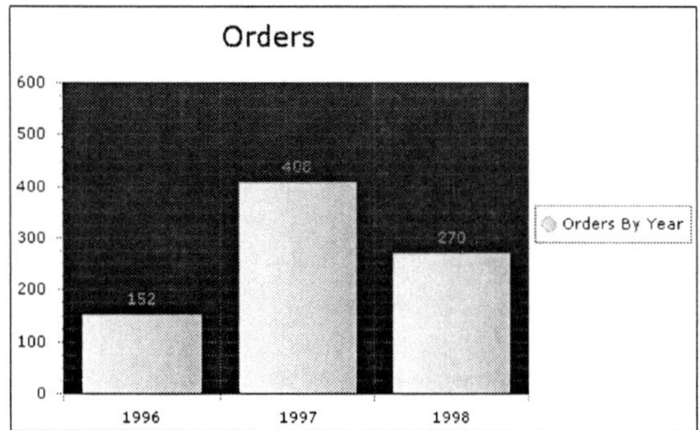

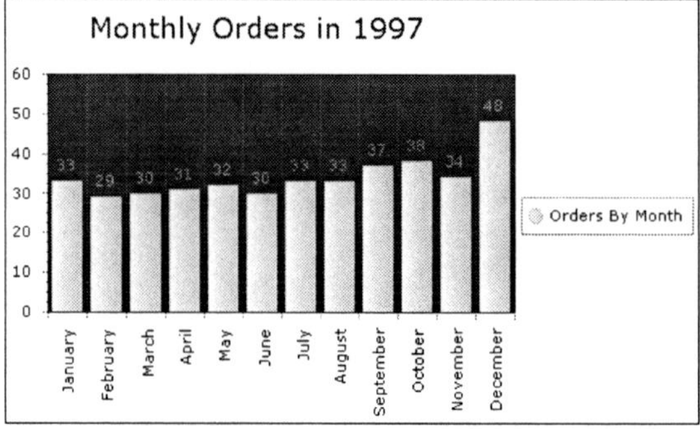

Figure 9-15. *Clicking in a bar in the chart on the left loads the detailed data shown on the right.*

RadBinaryImage

The `RadBinaryImage` control displays images stored in databases in binary format, so clearly, the control is designed for use in data-bound controls such as ASP.NET Repeater, DataList, and GridView, as well as with Telerik's `RadGrid`, `RadListView`, and so forth. The control uses an internal HTTP handler, which streams the image from the binary source to the page in which it has to be visualized.

It is important to understand that an image loaded to `RadBinaryImage` is cached in the browser for up to 2 hours, and if browser cache is disabled, the image is cached in the server for up to 2 minutes before the data is requested again to the database server. You can request the data from the server again when the control where `RadBinaryImage` is nested is re-bound or re-created. The HTTP handler can be overridden (and enhanced) by writing a custom HTTP handler that extends `RadBinaryImage`'s HTTP handler with different cache settings.

Using RadBinaryImage in ASP.NET Repeater

Since I started programming ASP.NET, one of my favorite controls has always been Repeater. It's very simple; it renders whatever you put in the templates without adding anything, and it allows you to generate clean HTML. Yes, it has its limitations, but it's a good basic control to present data from data sources.

So, in the following example (Listing 9-9), you'll see how to use `RadBinaryImage` inside an ASP.NET Repeater. Note the use of the `DataValue` property, which is the one used for the source field from which the binary data will be passed. Figure 9-16 illustrates the end result.

Listing 9-9. *Implementing RadBinaryImage Inside an ASP.NET Repeater*

ASPX Page

```
<asp:Repeater ID="Repeater1" runat="server"
        DataSourceID="SqlDataSource1">
<HeaderTemplate>
    <table width="100%"
                border="1"
                cellpadding="3"
                cellspacing="3">
        <tr>
            <th>ID</th>
            <th>Name</th>
            <th>Photo</th>
        </tr>
</HeaderTemplate>
<ItemTemplate>
        <tr>
                <td><asp:Label ID="lblID" runat="server"
                        Text='<%# Eval("EmployeeID") %>'></asp:Label>
                </td>
                <td><asp:Label ID="lblName" runat="server"
                        Text='<%# Eval("Name") %>'></asp:Label>
                </td>
                <td>
                    <telerik:RadBinaryImage ID="RadBinaryImage1" runat="server"
                             DataValue='<%# Eval("Photo") %>'
                             ToolTip='<%# "Photo of " + Eval("Name") %>'
                             AlternateText='<%# "Photo of " + Eval("Name") %>'
                             SavedImageName='<%# "Employee_" + Eval("EmployeeID") %>' />
                </td>
        </tr>
</ItemTemplate>
<FooterTemplate>
    </table>
</FooterTemplate>
</asp:Repeater>
```

```
<asp:SqlDataSource ID="SqlDataSource1" runat="server"
    ConnectionString="<%$ ConnectionStrings:NorthwindConnectionString %>"
    SelectCommand="SELECT [EmployeeID], [LastName], [FirstName], [Photo]
                     FROM [Employees]">
</asp:SqlDataSource>
```

Figure 9-16. *RadBinaryImage shows data stored in the database that was loaded in ASP.NET Repeater.*

Using RadBinaryImage in RadGrid

When used inside a RadGrid, `RadBinaryImage` is represented by a column of type `GridBinaryImageColumn`. An important benefit of using this control is that `RadGrid` automatically makes available for the user a `RadUpload` component when a record is added or edited, so an image is easily added or modified, and as a benefit for us developers, those additions and modifications are handled by the controls without having to write any code.

Listing 9-10. *RadBinaryImage in RadGrid*

ASPX Page

```
<telerik:RadGrid ID="RadGrid1" runat="server"
        AutoGenerateColumns="False"
        DataSourceID="SqlDataSource2"
        GridLines="None">
    <ClientSettings>
        <Scrolling AllowScroll="True"
                UseStaticHeaders="True" />
    </ClientSettings>
    <MasterTableView DataKeyNames="EmployeeID"
                DataSourceID="SqlDataSource2"
                EditMode="PopUp">
    <RowIndicatorColumn>
    <HeaderStyle Width="20px"></HeaderStyle>
    </RowIndicatorColumn>
    <ExpandCollapseColumn>
    <HeaderStyle Width="20px"></HeaderStyle>
    </ExpandCollapseColumn>
```

```
<Columns>
    <telerik:GridEditCommandColumn ButtonType="ImageButton">
        <HeaderStyle Width="10px" />
        <ItemStyle Width="10px" />
    </telerik:GridEditCommandColumn>
    <telerik:GridButtonColumn Text="Delete"
                CommandName="Delete" ButtonType="ImageButton">
        <HeaderStyle Width="10px" />
        <ItemStyle Width="10px" />
    </telerik:GridButtonColumn>
    <telerik:GridBoundColumn DataField="EmployeeID"
                             DataType="System.Int32"
                             HeaderText="ID"
                             ReadOnly="True"
                             SortExpression="EmployeeID"
        UniqueName="EmployeeID">
        <HeaderStyle HorizontalAlign="Center"
                     VerticalAlign="Middle"
                     Width="30px" />
        <ItemStyle HorizontalAlign="Center"
                     VerticalAlign="Middle"
                     Width="30px" />
    </telerik:GridBoundColumn>
    <telerik:GridBoundColumn DataField="LastName"
                             HeaderText="Last Name"
                             SortExpression="LastName"
                             UniqueName="LastName">
        <HeaderStyle HorizontalAlign="Left"
                     VerticalAlign="Middle"
                     Width="50px" />
        <ItemStyle HorizontalAlign="Left"
                     VerticalAlign="Middle"
                     Width="50px" />
    </telerik:GridBoundColumn>
    <telerik:GridBoundColumn DataField="FirstName"
                             HeaderText="First Name"
                             SortExpression="FirstName"
                             UniqueName="FirstName">
        <HeaderStyle HorizontalAlign="Left"
                     VerticalAlign="Middle"
                     Width="50px" />
        <ItemStyle HorizontalAlign="Left"
                     VerticalAlign="Middle"
                     Width="50px" />
    </telerik:GridBoundColumn>
```

```
            <telerik:GridBinaryImageColumn DataField="Photo"
                                           HeaderText="Photo"
                                           ImageHeight=""
                                           ImageWidth=""
                                           SortExpression="Photo"
                                           UniqueName="Photo">
                <HeaderStyle Width="100px" />
                <ItemStyle Width="100px" />
            </telerik:GridBinaryImageColumn>
        </Columns>
        <EditFormSettings>
                <EditColumn ButtonType="ImageButton" />
        </EditFormSettings>
    </MasterTableView>
</telerik:RadGrid>

<asp:SqlDataSource ID="SqlDataSource2" runat="server"
        ConnectionString="<%$ ConnectionStrings:NorthwindConnectionString %>"
        SelectCommand="SELECT [EmployeeID], [LastName], [FirstName], [Photo]
                        FROM [Employees]">
</asp:SqlDataSource>
```

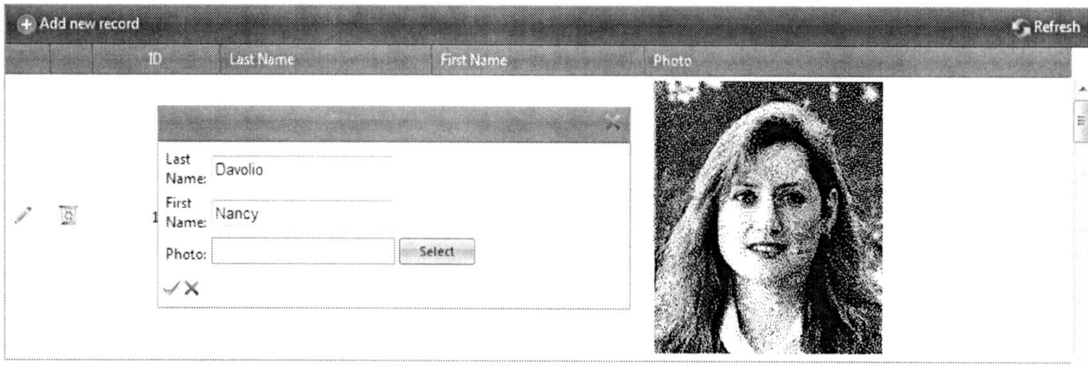

Figure 9-17. *When used in RadGrid, RadBinaryImage supports a default editor with built-in upload functionality.*

RadRating

The RadRating control will enable you to add rating capabilities to your application; it offers a graphical way to let your users rate things, such as product quality or level of customer service.

You can configure several settings of the rating control. For example, using the Orientation property, you can display the control horizontally (the default) or vertically. The ItemCount property specifies how many items (stars for example) to be displayed for rating. The Precision property determines the type of value for the rating; you can rate by selecting a precise part of the star (Exact), half a star (Half) or the whole star (Item). The SelectionMode property indicates whether a single item is selected (single-selection mode) or all the items from the first one are selected (continuous selection mode). Finally, the IsDirectionReversed property will dictate if the control will be shown in reverse mode or not; reverse mode controls display from right to left or bottom to top, depending on the orientation (the default is left to right or top to bottom). Figure 9-18 illustrates the precision and selection modes.

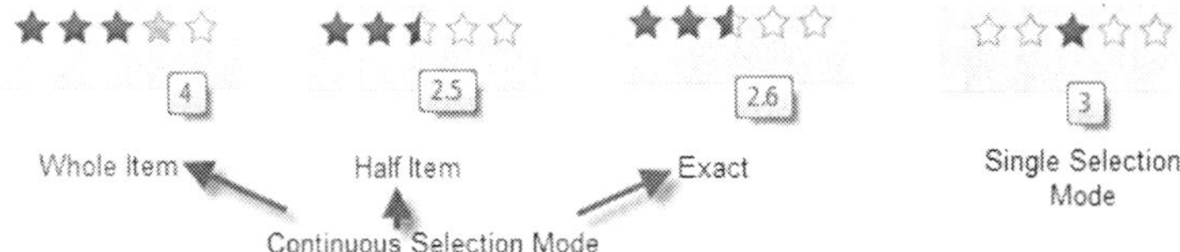

Figure 9-18. *Precision and selection modes in RadRating*

Using RadRating to Collect Feedback

The example in Listing 9-11 uses the `RadRating` control nested inside an ASP.NET `Repeater` similar to the example in Listing 9-9. When the user rates the employee, a pop-up window appears to let the user add additional feedback. Once the feedback is entered and the window closed, the information is passed back to the previous page where the feedback is shown. Once feedback is entered, the rating control is made read-only. Figures 8-19 and 8-20 show the sample working.

Listing 9-11. *Implementing RadRating in an ASP.NET Repeater*

ASPX Page

```
<asp:Repeater ID="Repeater1" runat="server"
                DataSourceID="SqlDataSource1">
<HeaderTemplate>
    <table width="100%"
        border="1"
        cellpadding="3"
        cellspacing="3">
        <tr>
            <th>ID</th>
            <th>Name</th>
            <th>Photo</th>
            <th>Rate Our Service</th>
        </tr>
</HeaderTemplate>
<ItemTemplate>
        <tr>
            <td><asp:Label ID="lblID" runat="server"
                        Text='<%# Eval("EmployeeID") %>'></asp:Label>
        </td>
        <td><asp:Label ID="lblName" runat="server"
                        Text='<%# Eval("Name") %>'></asp:Label>
        </td>
```

```
        <td>
            <telerik:RadBinaryImage ID="RadBinaryImage1" runat="server"
                        DataValue='<%# Eval("Photo") %>'
                        ToolTip='<%# "Photo of " + Eval("Name") %>'
                        AlternateText='<%# "Photo of " + Eval("Name") %>'
                        SavedImageName='<%# "Employee_" + Eval("EmployeeID") %>' />
        </td>
        <td>
                <telerik:RadRating ID="RadRating1" runat="server"
                        ItemCount="5"
                        Precision="Half"
                        OnClientRated="EmployeeRated" />
                <br /><br />
                <div id="feedback" runat="server"></div>
            </td>
        </tr>
</ItemTemplate>
<FooterTemplate>
    </table>
</FooterTemplate>
</asp:Repeater>

<asp:SqlDataSource ID="SqlDataSource1" runat="server"
    ConnectionString="<%$ ConnectionStrings:NorthwindConnectionString %>"
    SelectCommand="SELECT [EmployeeID], [LastName] + ' ' + [FirstName] AS [Name], [Photo]
                 FROM [Employees]">
</asp:SqlDataSource>

<telerik:RadWindow ID="FeedbackRadWindow" runat="server"
                        Width="400px"
                        Height="400px"
                        Title="Feedback"
                        OnClientClose="GetFeedback"
                        Modal="true"
                        style="z-index:20000">
</telerik:RadWindow>

<script type="text/javascript">
    function EmployeeRated(sender, eventArgs) {
        var empId = $get(sender.get_id().replace("RadRating1", "lblID"));
        var empName = $get(sender.get_id().replace("RadRating1", "lblName"));
        var fb = sender.get_id().replace("RadRating1", "feedback");
        var rating = sender.get_value();

        var wnd = $find("<%=FeedbackRadWindow.ClientID %>");
        wnd.setUrl("radrating_feedback.aspx?Id=" + empId.innerHTML
                                + "&Name=" + empName.innerHTML
                                + "&Rating=" + rating
                                + "&fb=" + fb);
        wnd.show();
    }
```

```
    function GetFeedback(sender, eventArgs) {
        var arg = eventArgs.get_argument();

        if (arg) {
            var fbField = arg.fb;
            $get(fbField).innerHTML = "Rating: " + arg.rating
                                    + "<br /><br />Your feedback:<br /><br /><strong>"
                                    + arg.comments + "</strong><br /><br />Thank you!!";
            var rt = $find(fbField.replace("feedback", "RadRating1"));
            rt.set_readOnly(true);
        }

    }
</script>
```

radrating_feedback.aspx

```
<!DOCTYPE html PUBLIC "-//W3C//DTD XHTML 1.0 Transitional//EN"
        "http://www.w3.org/TR/xhtml1/DTD/xhtml1-transitional.dtd">

<html xmlns="http://www.w3.org/1999/xhtml">
<head runat="server">
    <title></title>
</head>
<body>
    <form id="form1" runat="server">
    <div>
        <table>
            <tr>
                <td>Employee ID:</td>
                <td><%=Request.QueryString["Id"] %></td>
            </tr>
            <tr>
                <td>Employee Name:</td>
                <td><%=Request.QueryString["Name"] %></td>
            </tr>
            <tr>
                <td>Rating:</td>
                <td><%=Request.QueryString["Rating"] %></td>
            </tr>
            <tr>
                <td>Comments:</td>
                <td>
                    <asp:TextBox ID="txtComments" runat="server"
                                TextMode="MultiLine" Columns="30" Rows="10">
                    </asp:TextBox>
                </td>
            </tr>
            <tr>
                <td colspan="2"> </td>
            </tr>
```

```
            <tr>
                <td colspan="2" align="center">
                <asp:Button ID="btnClose" runat="server"
                        OnClientClick="javascript:CloseWindow();return false;"
                        Text="Close" />
                </td>
            </tr>
        </table>
    </div>
    <script language="javascript" type="text/javascript">
        function GetRadWindow() {
            var oWindow = null;
            if (window.radWindow) oWindow = window.radWindow;
            else if (window.frameElement.radWindow) oWindow = window.frameElement.radWindow;
            return oWindow;
        }

        function CloseWindow() {
            var arg = new Object();
            var txt = document.getElementById("<%=txtComments.ClientID %>");
            var fb = '<%=Request.QueryString["fb"] %>';
            var r = '<%=Request.QueryString["Rating"] %>';
            arg.comments = txt.value;
            arg.fb = fb;
            arg.rating = r;
            var wnd = GetRadWindow();
            wnd.close(arg);
        }
    </script>

    </form>
</body>
</html>
```

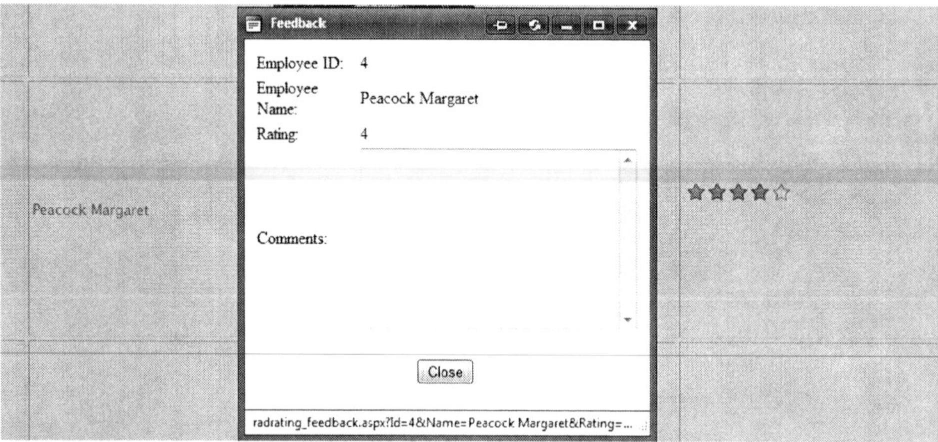

Figure 9-19. *Requesting feedback after rating has been entered*

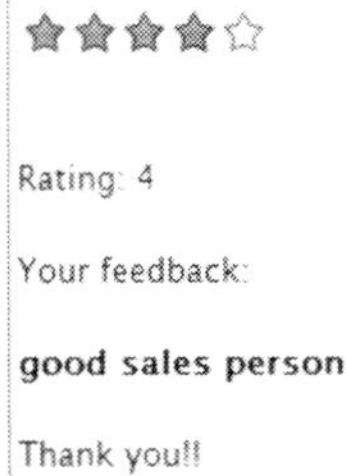

Rating: 4
Your feedback:
good sales person
Thank you!!

Figure 9-20. *Feedback has been entered.*

Using RadRating in RadGrid

The functionality of RadRating is available in controls such as RadGrid. For example, RadRating allows users to rate multiple items inside lists. Let's examine Listing 9-12 where RadRating is implemented by the GridRatingColumn; the example is illustrated in Figure 9-21.

Listing 9-12. *RadRating in RadGrid*

ASPX Page

```
<telerik:RadGrid ID="RadGrid1" runat="server"
        AllowPaging="True"
        AutoGenerateColumns="False"
        DataSourceID="SqlDataSource2"
        GridLines="None"
        ShowGroupPanel="True">
    <ClientSettings AllowDragToGroup="True">
        <Scrolling AllowScroll="True"
                UseStaticHeaders="True" />
    </ClientSettings>
    <MasterTableView DataKeyNames="ProductID"
                DataSourceID="SqlDataSource2">
      <GroupByExpressions>
         <telerik:GridGroupByExpression>
           <SelectFields>
              <telerik:GridGroupByField
                        FieldName="CategoryName"
                        HeaderText="Category"/>
           </SelectFields>
           <GroupByFields>
              <telerik:GridGroupByField
                        FieldName="CategoryName"
                        SortOrder="Ascending" />
           </GroupByFields>
         </telerik:GridGroupByExpression>
       </GroupByExpressions>
    <RowIndicatorColumn>
    <HeaderStyle Width="20px"></HeaderStyle>
    </RowIndicatorColumn>
```

```
    <ExpandCollapseColumn>
    <HeaderStyle Width="20px"></HeaderStyle>
    </ExpandCollapseColumn>
        <Columns>
            <telerik:GridBoundColumn DataField="ProductID"
                                    DataType="System.Int32"
                                    HeaderText="ProductID"
                                    ReadOnly="True"
                                    SortExpression="Product"
                UniqueName="ProductID">
            </telerik:GridBoundColumn>
            <telerik:GridBoundColumn DataField="ProductName"
                                    HeaderText="Name"
                                    SortExpression="ProductName"
                                    UniqueName="ProductName">
            </telerik:GridBoundColumn>
            <telerik:GridBoundColumn DataField="CategoryName"
                                    HeaderText="Category"
                                    SortExpression="CategoryName"
                                    UniqueName="CategoryName">
            </telerik:GridBoundColumn>
                <telerik:GridRatingColumn HeaderText="Rating"
                                    UniqueName="ratingColumn"
                                    Precision="Exact"
                                    AllowRatingInViewMode="true">
                </telerik:GridRatingColumn>
        </Columns>
    </MasterTableView>
</telerik:RadGrid>

<asp:SqlDataSource ID="SqlDataSource2" runat="server"
    ConnectionString="<%$ ConnectionStrings:NorthwindConnectionString %>"
    SelectCommand="SELECT [ProductID], [ProductName], [CategoryName], 0 as [AverageRating]
                 FROM [Alphabetical list of products]">
</asp:SqlDataSource>
```

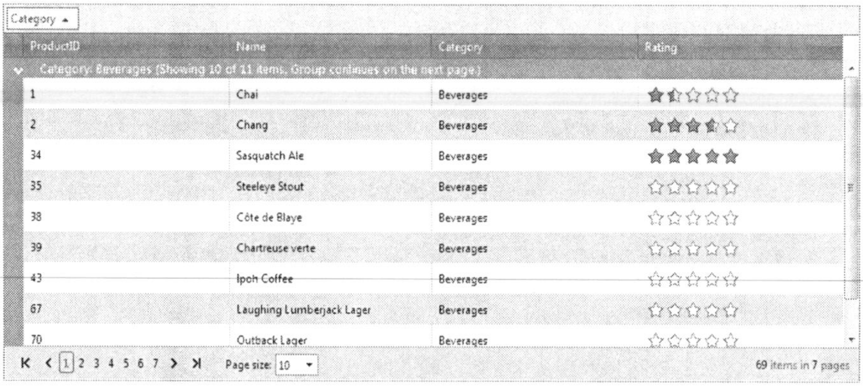

Figure 9-21. *RadRating can be used inside RadGrid with GridRatingColumn*

RadColorPicker

The `RadColorPicker` control allows users to select a color in the Red, Green, Blue (RGB) or hexadecimal (HEX) color spaces in a very easy way. You can configure it to show different types of color selectors using the property `PaletteMode`, and you can specify one of the many built-in color palettes or build your own.

`RadColorPicker` can be configured appear when a page is loaded or as a drop-down. It features an empty color button that will erase the previous color selection and a preview mode of the color before selecting it.

The example in Listing 9-13 shows how to configure `RadColorPicker`, and Figure 9-22 shows the example running.

Listing 9-13. *Configuring RadColorPicker*

```
ASPX Page

<table>
    <tr>
        <td>Show As DropDown:</td>
        <td>
            <asp:CheckBox ID="chkIcon" runat="server"
                        AutoPostBack="true"
                        OnCheckedChanged="chkIcon_CheckedChanged">
            </asp:CheckBox>
        </td>
    </tr>
    <tr>
        <td>Preview Color:</td>
        <td>
            <asp:CheckBox ID="chkPreview" runat="server"
                        AutoPostBack="true"
                        Checked="true"
                        OnCheckedChanged="chkPreview_CheckedChanged">
            </asp:CheckBox>
        </td>
    </tr>
    <tr>
        <td>Show No Empty Color:</td>
        <td>
            <asp:CheckBox ID="chkNoColor" runat="server"
                        AutoPostBack="true"
                        Checked="true"
                        OnCheckedChanged="chkNoColor_CheckedChanged">
            </asp:CheckBox>
        </td>
    </tr>
```

```
    <tr>
        <td>Palette Mode:</td>
        <td>
            <asp:CheckBoxList ID="chkPaletteMode" runat="server"
                        RepeatDirection="Horizontal"
                        AutoPostBack="true"
                        OnSelectedIndexChanged="chkPaletteMode_SelectedIndexChanged">
                 <asp:ListItem Value="WebPalette"
                                Selected="True">WebPalette</asp:ListItem>
                 <asp:ListItem Value="RGBSliders"
                                Selected="True">RGBSliders</asp:ListItem>
                 <asp:ListItem Value="HSB"
                                Selected="True">HSB</asp:ListItem>
                 <asp:ListItem Value="HSV"
                                Selected="True">HSV</asp:ListItem>
            </asp:CheckBoxList>
        </td>
    </tr>
    <tr>
        <td>Select the palette: </td>
        <td>
            <telerik:RadComboBox ID="rcbPalette" runat="server"
                                AutoPostBack="true"
                                OnSelectedIndexChanged="rcbPalette_SelectedIndexChanged">
            </telerik:RadComboBox>
        </td>
    </tr>
    <tr>
        <td colspan="2">
            <telerik:RadColorPicker ID="RadColorPicker1" runat="server"
                                PaletteModes="All">
            </telerik:RadColorPicker>
        </td>
    </tr>
</table>
```

Code Behind

```
protected void Page_Load(object sender, EventArgs e)
{
        if (Page.IsPostBack) return;
        LoadColorPalettes();
}

private void LoadColorPalettes()
{
    foreach (ColorPreset preset in Enum.GetValues(typeof(ColorPreset)))
    {
        rcbPalette.Items.Add(new RadComboBoxItem(preset.ToString()));
    }
    rcbPalette.SelectedIndex = 0;
    SelectPalette(rcbPalette.SelectedValue);
}
```

```
protected void rcbPalette_SelectedIndexChanged(
                                        object o,
                                        RadComboBoxSelectedIndexChangedEventArgs e)
{
    SelectPalette(e.Text);
}

private void SelectPalette(string palette)
{
    ColorPreset preset;
    if (Enum.TryParse(palette, true, out preset))
        RadColorPicker1.Preset = preset;
}

protected void chkIcon_CheckedChanged(object sender, EventArgs e)
{
    RadColorPicker1.ShowIcon = chkIcon.Checked;
}

protected void chkPreview_CheckedChanged(object sender, EventArgs e)
{
    RadColorPicker1.PreviewColor = chkPreview.Checked;
}

protected void chkNoColor_CheckedChanged(object sender, EventArgs e)
{
    RadColorPicker1.ShowEmptyColor = chkNoColor.Checked;
}

protected void chkPaletteMode_SelectedIndexChanged(object sender, EventArgs e)
{
    var firstSelectedItem = chkPaletteMode.SelectedItem;
    RadColorPicker1.PaletteModes =
                    (PaletteModes)Enum.Parse(typeof(PaletteModes),
                                             firstSelectedItem.Value);
    foreach (ListItem box in chkPaletteMode.Items)
    {
        if (box.Value == firstSelectedItem.Value) continue;

        if (box.Selected)
        {
            RadColorPicker1.PaletteModes |= (PaletteModes)Enum
                                            .Parse(typeof(PaletteModes), box.Value);
        }
    }

}
```

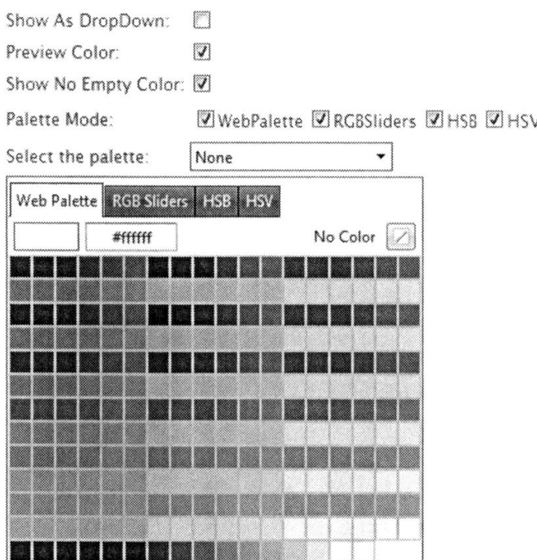

Figure 9-22. *RadColorPicker can be easily configured to display any type of colors.*

Building a Custom Palette

With `RadColorPicker`, you can build your own palette of colors by any of the four available methods:

- Using the `Preset` property to use one of the built-in palettes
- Using the `Items` collection
- Using the `Preset` property and `Items` collection
- Combining palettes programmatically in code behind

The example in Listing 9-14 uses the `Items` collection to create a fixed list of colors to show in `RadColorPicker`. I have also added a client-side event handler to change the background color of a div element when a color selection is made. Figure 9-23 shows how it looks.

Listing 9-14. *Creating a Custom Palette for RadColorPicker*

```
ASPX Page

<table>
    <tr>
        <td valign="top">
            <telerik:RadColorPicker ID="RadColorPicker2" runat="server"
                                    OnClientColorChange="ChangeColor"
                                    ShowEmptyColor="false"
                                    PreviewColor="false">
            </telerik:RadColorPicker>
        </td>
```

```
        <td valign="top">
            <div id="divColor" style="width:100px;height:100px;
                                        border:1px solid #000000">
            </div>
        </td>
    </tr>
</table>
<script language="javascript" type="text/javascript">
    function ChangeColor(sender, eventArgs) {
        var picker = $find("<%=RadColorPicker2.ClientID %>");
        var color = picker.get_selectedColor();
        $get("divColor").style.backgroundColor = color;
    }
</script>
```

Code Behind

```
protected void Page_Load(object sender, EventArgs e)
{
    if (Page.IsPostBack) return;
    LoadCustomPalette();
}

private void LoadCustomPalette()
{
    RadColorPicker2.Preset = ColorPreset.None;
    RadColorPicker2.Items.Add(new ColorPickerItem(Color.White, "White"));
    RadColorPicker2.Items.Add(new ColorPickerItem(Color.Black, "Black"));
    RadColorPicker2.Items.Add(new ColorPickerItem(Color.Green, "Green"));
    RadColorPicker2.Items.Add(new ColorPickerItem(Color.Yellow, "Yellow"));
    RadColorPicker2.Items.Add(new ColorPickerItem(Color.Silver, "Silver"));
    RadColorPicker2.Items.Add(new ColorPickerItem(Color.Red, "Red"));
    RadColorPicker2.Items.Add(new ColorPickerItem(Color.Navy, "Navy"));
    RadColorPicker2.Items.Add(new ColorPickerItem(Color.RoyalBlue, "Royal Blue"));
    RadColorPicker2.Items.Add(new ColorPickerItem(Color.Plum, "Plum"));
    RadColorPicker2.Items.Add(new ColorPickerItem(Color.LightBlue, "Light Blue"));
    RadColorPicker2.Items.Add(new ColorPickerItem(Color.Indigo, "Indigo"));
    RadColorPicker2.Items.Add(new ColorPickerItem(Color.Gray, "Gray"));

}
```

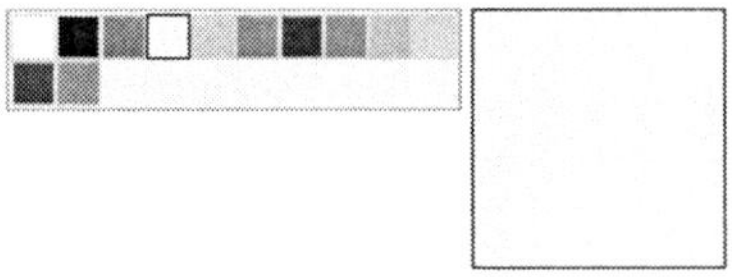

Figure 9-23. *A RadColorPicker custom palette*

Summary

RadChart is a powerful charting component that can help you create the most demanding graphical representations of information. With lots of built-in chart types, you can create very interesting charts in a very efficient way. RadCharts can be bound to a data source, and with minimal effort, they can be configured to allow zooming and scrolling for detailed analysis of certain areas of a chart.

You can add marked zones to highlight areas of a chart and scale breaks to avoid disfiguration of a chart when points are way off the scale. A RadChart can easily present negative values and different types of series (bar and line for example) in a single chart, and you can enable it to display the data table used to build the chart.

With image maps, you can recognize when a user clicks a specific portion of the chart and take action based on that click; for example, you could open a pop-up window to display relevant information regarding the area clicked, or you can use it to create a drill-down chart.

RadBinaryImage is a control specifically designed to understand images stored as binary data in databases. Its main purpose is to show those images in a very efficient way by enabling caching on the client and the server, and it can be used within data objects such as ASP.NET Repeaters or RadGrids.

RadRating allows you to give users a graphical way to rate elements on your web site. You can configure the look and feel and the type of rating, and you can work with it in either client-side code or code behind.

RadColorPicker enables your users to select colors from different types of color palettes and in several different modes. You can use one of the built-in palettes, or you can build your own.

CHAPTER 10

■ ■ ■

Additional RadControls

Some controls developed by Telerik with functionality that don't fall into a defined set, and we'll cover those RadControls in this chapter.

The controls are RadFormDecorator, RadToolTip, RadUpload, RadCaptcha, RadSlider, and RadFileExplorer. We'll tour these controls, highlighting their main functionality along with some tips in implementing them.

RadFormDecorator

RadFormDecorator is a control designed to provide skinning capabilities to regular ASP.NET and HTML controls. The idea is simple—make the controls look as good as Telerik's own.

RadFormDecorator can be configured in different ways, targeting specific controls or specific areas called *decorated zones*. RadFormDecorator works with buttons, check boxes, fieldsets (including legend tags), headings (H4, H5, and H6), labels, radio buttons, scroll bars, text areas, text boxes, and SELECT elements (drop-downs and list boxes). The styling mechanism involves a combination of CSS and images, so it is a lightweight implementation.

There are also some limitations in its usage. For example, RadFormDecorator can't decorate the ASP.NET Label control, as this is rendered as a SPAN element and therefore can't be accurately recognized. However, the Label element can be decorated. Another limitation (this one is by design) is that RadFormDecorator only decorates H4, H5, and H6 headings; this is because normally, within a project, the H1, H2, and H3 elements are already handled by designers.

Decorating Controls

The example in Listing 10-1 demonstrates how RadFormDecorator can apply a consistent style to controls and elements in a page. Note that you can use the property DecoratedControls to specify which types of controls will be decorated.

The valid values for the DecoratedControls property are All, Buttons, CheckBoxes, Default, Fieldset, H4H5H6, Label, None, GridFormDetailsViews, RadioButtons, Select, Scrollbars, Textarea, and Textbox. The value Default includes only CheckBoxes, Buttons, RadioButtons, and ScrollBars.

Figure 10-1 shows how the controls look after applying a style using RadFormDecorator.

Listing 10-1. *Decorating Controls Using the DecoratedControls Property*

ASPX Page

```
<telerik:RadFormDecorator ID="RadFormDecorator1" runat="server"
                          DecoratedControls="Default">
</telerik:RadFormDecorator>
```

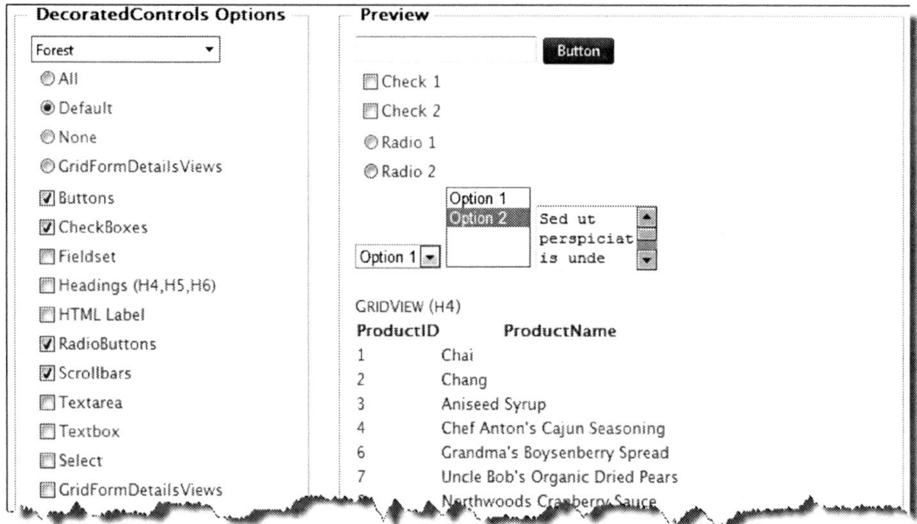

Figure 10-1. *Note that only the default controls are decorated. For example, Select, List, and Textbox were not included.*

Using the DecoratedZoneID Property

One thing to note in the previous example is that `RadFormDecorator` styled all the controls of the specified type, and sometimes, that's not the desired behavior. For this reason, `RadFormDecorator` implements the property `DecoratedZoneID`, which is used to decorate the controls only in a certain area of the page by taking as its value the ID of the element surrounding the desired controls, for example, a `div` or `fieldset` element. If you're using a server control, such as an ASP.NET `Panel`, `DecoratedZoneID` must use the value of the `ClientID` property for the panel control.

The example in Listing 10-2 is a modification of the example in Listing 10-1. This time, it will apply the style only to the fieldset named Preview. See the result in Figure 10-2.

Listing 10-2. *Decorating a Specific Area of the Page Using the DecoratedZoneID Property*

```
<telerik:RadFormDecorator ID="RadFormDecorator1" runat="server"
                          DecoratedControls="Default"
                          DecoratedZoneID="panelDecoratedControls">
</telerik:RadFormDecorator>
```

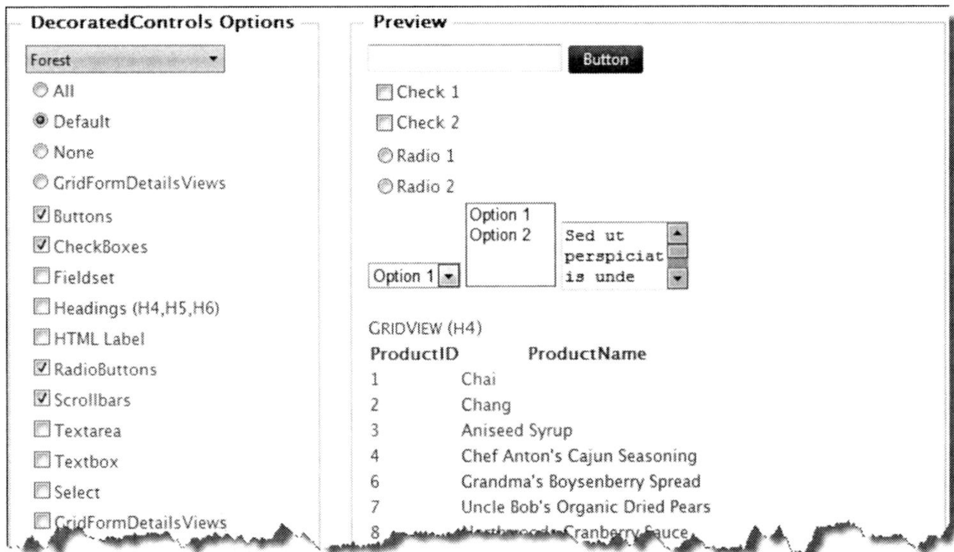

Figure 10-2. *Note that only the Preview fieldset is decorated; the DecoratedControls Options fieldset was not.*

Note While `RadFormDecorator` is part of the suite Telerik RadControls for ASP.NET AJAX, Telerik has released it for the community free of charge. You can download it from the Free Products page in Telerik's Community web site at `http://www.telerik.com/community/free-products.aspx`.

RadCaptcha

Completely Automated Public Touring test to tell Computers and Humans Apart (CAPTCHA) was developed by a team of researchers in Carnegie Mellon University composed of Luis von Ahn, Manuel Blum, Nicholas Hopper, and John Langford, who were asked by Yahoo for a way to stop automated bots that were creating thousands of accounts for malicious uses.

The solution was to present a set of characters that are impossible for a computer program to read but are somewhat easy for humans. In compliance with accessibility standards, an audio file describing the set of characters is also provided. If the set of characters is correctly confirmed by the user, the system allows that user to enter the site or perform whatever task the CAPTCHA protects.

Telerik's `RadCaptcha` is a control aimed to help developers implement the CAPTCHA mechanism to protect web sites from automated bots. In the latest release at the time of this writing (early 2010), `RadCaptcha` also includes audio (for .NET 3.5 and above only).

The control provides two protection strategies:

- *CAPTCHA image*: An image with distorted symbols (letters and numbers) is presented in a form for the user, who must identify the symbols by typing them in a text box. If the characters entered in the text box perfectly match those presented, `RadCaptcha` validates the page and allows the user to proceed. Some properties can be set to control the behavior of `RadCaptcha` in this mode:

  Text length, font, font color, and background color.

  Image noise, such as the background noise level, line noise level, and font warp factor. These properties make the CAPTCHA image more difficult to read by including dots, lines, and other figures (noise). The font warp factor defines how distorted the set of characters will be.

  Session expiration time.

  Error message to display to the user when a wrong entry has been submitted.

- *Automatic robot discovery*: In this mode, `RadCaptcha` can be configured to require that a minimum amount of time pass before accepting form entries or to inject an invisible text box (sometimes called a honey pot) into the page.

  Submission time: With the first approach, the presumption is that a human cannot input the fields in a form correctly for a time less than a few seconds. If the form is submitted in less time than that, the control assumes a robot is submitting the form.

  Invisible text box: The idea here is that a human could not see an invisible text box; therefore if a value is entered, a robot is submitting the form and trying to fill all the fields available.

`RadCaptcha` doesn't have a client-side API, and it doesn't support client-side validation for security reasons. Client-side validation is insecure because users have the option to disable client-side scripts. If they opt to disable the client-side functionality, the validation simply won't work.

■ **Note** Even though `RadCaptcha` doesn't have a client-side API, you can have access to the CAPTCHA text box using the technique described in the community forum thread at `http://www.telerik.com/community/forums/aspnet-ajax/captcha/client-side-support-needed-for-radcaptcha.aspx`.

`RadCaptcha` allows you to define the type and set of characters to use when using the CAPTCHA image strategy. You can set the property `CaptchaImage.TextChars` to any of `Letters`, `Numbers`, `LettersAndNumbers`, or `CustomCharSet`. If you select `CustomCharSet`, you can define the set of allowed characters with the property `CharSet`.

Implementing RadCaptcha Image Mode

Listing 10-3 shows how to work with the CAPTCHA image mode. The example shows a simple form that asks for a name, e-mail address, and the CAPTCHA characters. I added some ASP.NET validators that will perform the validation of the entries in the name and e-mail text boxes, but I have disabled the text boxes' ability to validate on the client side with the property `EnableClientScript="False"`. This approach was taken to have only one validation point on the server side, so the two text boxes and RadCaptcha are validated in the same place. Figure 10-3 shows the example in action.

Listing 10-3. *RadCaptcha in CAPTCHA Image Mode*

ASPX Page

```
<table width="350px">
    <tr>
        <td width="150px">Name:</td>
        <td wdith="200px">
            <telerik:RadTextBox ID="txtName" runat="server"></telerik:RadTextBox>
            <asp:RequiredFieldValidator ID="RequiredfieldValidator1" runat="server"
                                        ControlToValidate="txtName"
                                        Display="Dynamic"
                                        ValidationGroup="Captcha1"
                                        Text="*"
                                        ErrorMessage="Name is required"
                                        EnableClientScript="False">
            </asp:RequiredFieldValidator>
        </td>
    </tr>
    <tr>
        <td width="150px">Email:</td>
        <td width="200px">
            <telerik:RadTextBox ID="txtEmail" runat="server"></telerik:RadTextBox>
            <asp:RequiredFieldValidator ID="RequiredfieldValidator2" runat="server"
                                        ControlToValidate="txtEmail"
                                        Display="Dynamic"
                                        EnableClientScript="false"
                                        ValidationGroup="Captcha1"
                                        Text="*"
                                        ErrorMessage="Email is required">
            </asp:RequiredFieldValidator>
            <asp:RegularExpressionValidator ID="RegularExpressionValidator1" runat="server"
                 Display="Dynamic"
                 Text="Invalid Email"
                 ErrorMessage="Email should be like: foo@bar.com"
                 ControlToValidate="txtEmail"
                 EnableClientScript="false"
                 ValidationExpression="\w+([-+.']\w+)*@\w+([-.]\w+)*\.\w+([-.]\w+)*"
                 ValidationGroup="Captcha1">
            </asp:RegularExpressionValidator>
        </td>
    </tr>
```

```
    <tr>
        <td width="150px" valign="top">Validation Code:</td>
        <td width="200px">
            <telerik:RadCaptcha ID="RadCaptcha1" runat="server"
                EnableRefreshImage="True"
                ErrorMessage="Invalid validation code"
                ValidationGroup="Captcha1"
                CaptchaTextBoxLabel="&lt;br /&gt;Type the code from the image">
                <CaptchaImage BackgroundNoise="Medium"
                              LineNoise="Low"
                              FontWarp="High"
                              EnableCaptchaAudio="true"
                              TextChars="LettersAndNumbers" />
            </telerik:RadCaptcha>
        </td>
    </tr>
    <tr>
        <td colspan="2">
            <asp:Button ID="btnSubmit" runat="server"
                        Text="Submit"
                        CausesValidation="true"
                        ValidationGroup="Captcha1" />
        </td>
    </tr>
    <tr>
        <td colspan="2">
            <asp:ValidationSummary ID="ValidationSummary1" runat="server"
                                   ValidationGroup="Captcha1" />
        </td>
    </tr>
</table>
```

Figure 10-3. *The validation happened on the server for the TextBox controls and RadCaptcha.*

Implementing RadCaptcha's Invisible Text Box Mode

Now, let's implement the invisible text box mode. Listing 10-4 is similar to the last one but uses RadCaptcha's ProtectionMode property set to InvisibleTextBox. In this mode, the control creates a hidden text box with ID InvisibleTextBox that is used to trick the robots. In the example, the check box labeled Fill Invisible Textbox simulates a robot filling the invisible text box; only the modifications to the code in Listing 10-3 are shown in Listing 10-4. The results can be seen in Figure 10-4.

Listing 10-4. *Using RadCaptcha in Invisible Text Box Mode*

ASPX Page

```
<asp:CheckBox ID="chkFill" runat="server"
                Text="Fill Invisible Textbox"
                onclick="FillInvisible(this);" />

<telerik:RadCaptcha ID="RadCaptcha2" runat="server"
                EnableRefreshImage="True"
                ErrorMessage="Oops! Robot detected"
                ValidationGroup="Captcha2"
                CaptchaTextBoxLabel="&lt;br /&gt;Type the code from the image"
                ProtectionMode="InvisibleTextBox">
</telerik:RadCaptcha>

<script type="text/javascript">
     function FillInvisible(chk) {
               var invisibleTextBox =
                   $get("ctl00_MainContent_RadCaptcha2_InvisibleTextBox");
               if (chk.checked) {
                   invisibleTextBox.value = "something";
                   }
                   else {
                        invisibleTextBox.value = "";
                   }
         }
</script>
```

Name: *
Email: *
☑ Fill Invisible Textbox   Oops! Robot detected
Submit

- Name is required
- Email is required
- Oops! Robot detected

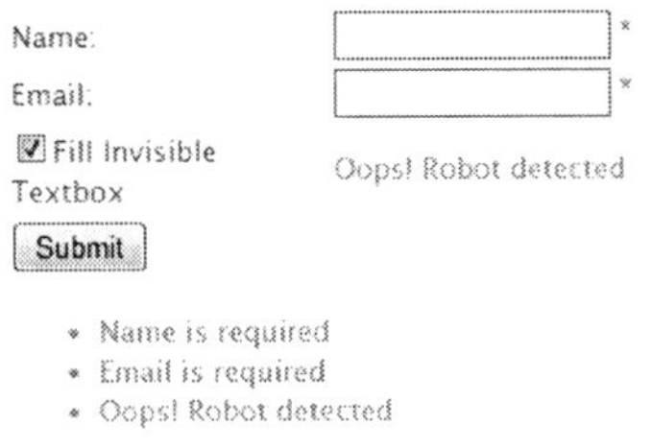

Figure 10-4. *RadCaptcha can detect if a robot program is trying to fill all the fields in the form with an invisible text box.*

Implementing RadCaptcha Minimum Submission Time

Next, we'll implement RadCaptcha's minimum submission time mode. You can configure the minimum submission time with the property MinTimeout and set the number of seconds before a submission is considered valid. Then, change the property ProtectionMode to MinimumTimeout (see Listing 10-5). Figure 10-5 illustrates the example.

Listing 10-5. *RadCaptcha in Minimum Submission Time Mode*

ASPX Page

```
<telerik:RadCaptcha ID="RadCaptcha3" runat="server"
                EnableRefreshImage="True"
                ErrorMessage="Form submitted too fast!"
                ValidationGroup="Captcha3"
                CaptchaTextBoxLabel="&lt;br /&gt;Type the code from the image"
                MinTimeout="5"
                ProtectionMode="MinimumTimeout">
</telerik:RadCaptcha>
```

Name: *
Email: *
Form submitted too fast!
Submit

- Name is required
- Email is required
- Form submitted too fast!

Figure 10-5. *If the form is submitted in less than 5 seconds, RadCaptcha validation will fail.*

RadToolTip

RadToolTip is a control that enables you to build enhanced tooltips in different ways. You can configure it to display simple text or rich content, including complex scenarios with other server controls. You can load dynamic tooltip content asynchronously with AJAX requests. In addition to RadToolTip, there is also a RadToolTipManager control. Both controls share much functionality, and the main difference between them is that RadToolTip is designed to add a tooltip for one element, and RadToolTipManager can add tool tips for many.

When working with RadToolTip, you need to configure, at minimum, the TargetControlID property with the ID of the control you want to add a tooltip for. Additionally, you can use the IsClientID property to indicate whether or not the ID defined is a client ID.

Now, you might be wondering what's so cool about RadToolTip. Why is so important? Why should you care? Well, it's all about making your application look good, and I mean really look good!

The real power behind RadToolTip is in making your tooltips look more professional and behave better than native browser tooltips. With this goal in mind, Telerik created a rich set of properties and functionality that enables you to do a lot of things. For example, you have the property Animation that makes your tooltip appear and disappear with style; you can choose one animation from Fade, Slide,

Resize, FlyIn, and None. You can position the tooltip anywhere with the Position property in conjunction with the RelativeTo property that accepts the values Mouse, Element, and BrowserWindow. Position accepts one of the following values: BottomCenter, BottomLeft, BottomRight, TopCenter, TopLeft, TopRight, Center, MiddleLeft and MiddleRight, and these positions are shown in Figure 10-6.

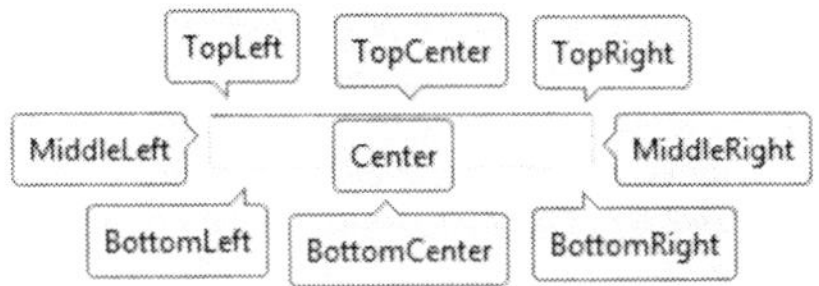

Figure 10-6. *The Position property can place the tooltip in one of nine different locations.*

You can also define a Skin for RadToolTip from the set of built-in skins, or you can create your own. The control can also be assigned a title with the Title property (see Figure 10-7), and you can control how much time the tooltip will be shown, as well as how long it will take to appear and disappear, with the AutoCloseDelay, ShowDelay, and HideDelay properties (these are set in milliseconds).

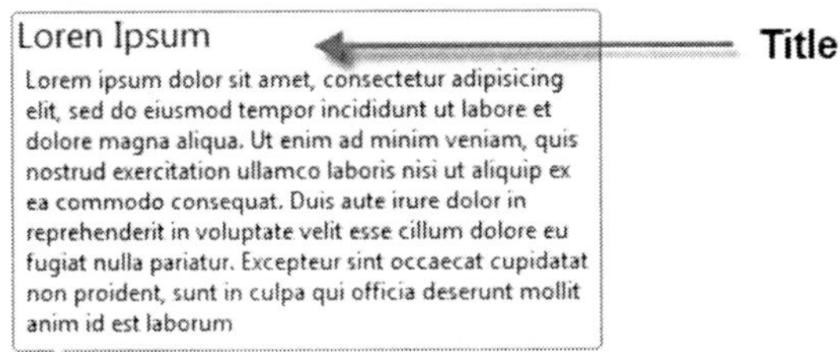

Figure 10-7. *RadToolTip supports the Title property, so your tooltips look more professional.*

If that is not enough, you can enable the MouseTrailing property, so the tooltip moves as the mouse does while you hover over the tooltip's element. You can also make the tooltip Modal.

You can control when and how the tooltip is shown and hidden too, by setting the properties ShowEvent and HideEvent.

ShowEvent accepts FromCode, OnClick, OnRightClick, OnFocus, or OnMouseOver (the default). The FromCode option in both properties causes RadToolTip to be shows and hidden only in response to calls to the client side functions show() and hide() respectively. The OnClick and OnRightClick events tell a RadToolTip to show whenever the user clicks or right-clicks the target control, and OnFocus tells it to show when the target control receives focus. The OnMouseOver event instructs RadToolTip to show when the mouse hovers over the target control.

The HideEvent property accepts Default, FromCode, LeaveTargetAndToolTip, LeaveToolTip, or ManualClose. The Default hide event hides RadToolTip when the mouse is out of the target control. The LeaveToolTip event hides RadToolTip when the mouse hovers over the tooltip and then leaves. The LeaveTargetAndToolTip event hides RadToolTip when the mouse hovers and leaves from the target control and the tooltip. The ManualClose event instructs RadToolTip to hide when the user clicks the close button in the upper right corner of the tooltip (see Figure 10-8).

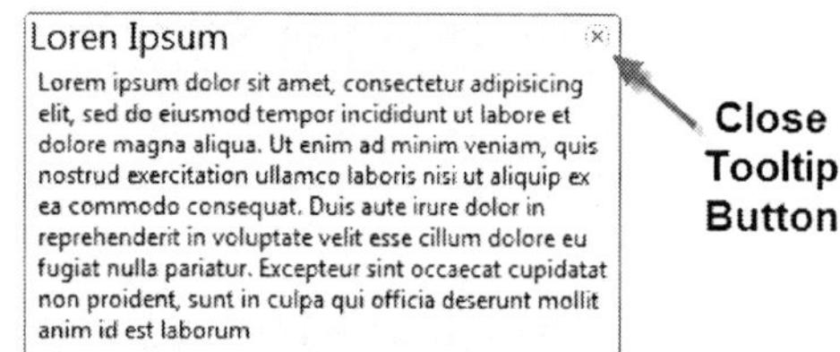

Figure 10-8. *When set to ManualClose, RadToolTip can be hidden by clicking the close button in the upper right corner of the tooltip.*

The example in Listing 10-6 demonstrates the differences between `RadToolTip` and the built-in `ToolTip` property, and Figure 10-9 illustrates those big differences.

Listing 10-6. *RadToolTip Vs. Built-In ToolTip*

ASPX Page

```
<table width="350px">
    <tr>
        <td width="150px">Traditional ToolTip:</td>
        <td width="200px">
            <telerik:RadTextBox ID="txtName" runat="server"
                                ClientIDMode="Static"
                                Width="200px"
                                ToolTip="Please enter your full name">
            </telerik:RadTextBox>
        </td>
    </tr>
    <tr>
        <td width="150px">RadToolTip:</td>
        <td width="200px">
            <telerik:RadTextBox ID="txtEmail" runat="server"
                     Width="200px"
                     ToolTip="Please enter your email in the form: foo@bar.com">
            </telerik:RadTextBox>
            <telerik:RadToolTip ID="tooltipEmail" runat="server"
                                TargetControlID="txtEmail"
                                IsClientID="false"
                                Animation="Fade"
                                AutoCloseDelay="10000"
                                RelativeTo="Element"
                                Position="MiddleRight">
            </telerik:RadToolTip>
        </td>
    </tr>
</table>
```

Traditional ToolTip:

Please enter your full name

RadToolTip:

Please enter your email in the form: foo@bar.com

Figure 10-9. *Note the huge differences in design between ToolTip and RadToolTip*

There are other properties you can configure in `RadToolTip`. The `Animation` property defines the animation that will be played when `RadToolTip` appears. Valid values are `Slide`, `FlyIn`, `Resize`, `Fade`, and `None`.

One property that is very important is `RelativeTo`. This property, in conjunction with `Position`, defines where exactly your `RadToolTip` will be shown. `RelativeTo` can be set to `BrowserWindow`, `Element`, or `Mouse`. If the value is `BrowserWindow`, `RadToolTip` will be shown based on the browser window, as shown in Figure 10-10. If the value is `Element`, `RadToolTip` will be shown next to the element based on the defined position (see Figure 10-11). If set to `Mouse`, it will be shown next to the mouse cursor (see Figure 10-12).

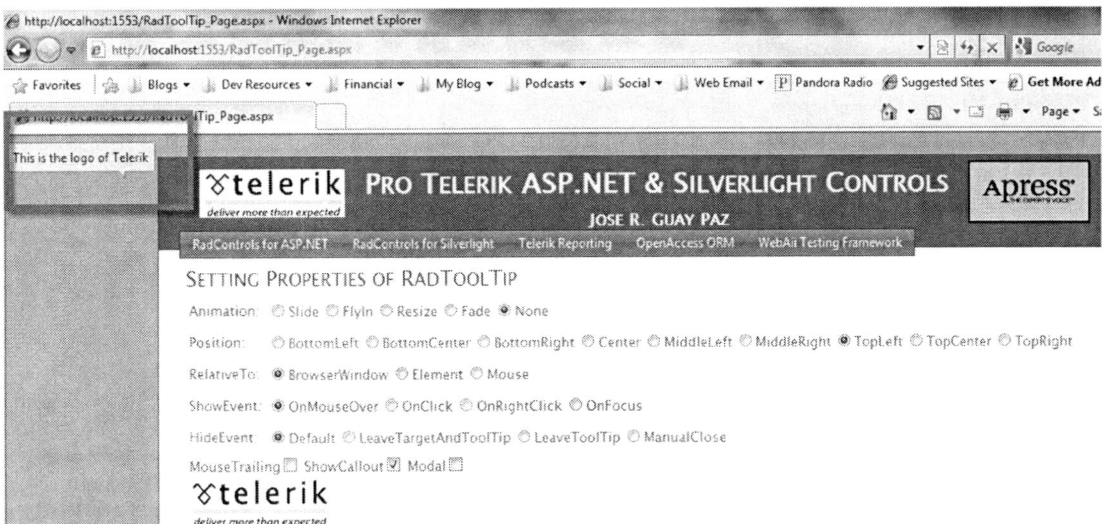

Figure 10-10. *The RelativeTo property is set to BrowserWindow, and the Position property to TopLeft. The box shows where the RadToolTip is located.*

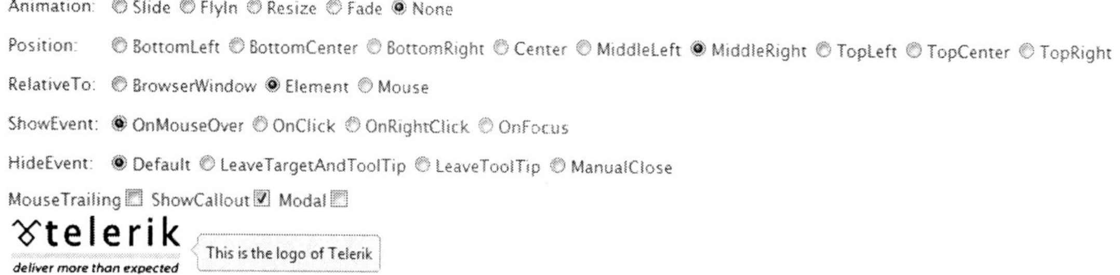

Figure 10-11. *The RelativeTo property is set to Element and the Position property to MiddleRight. The RadToolTip is shown next to the Telerik logo.*

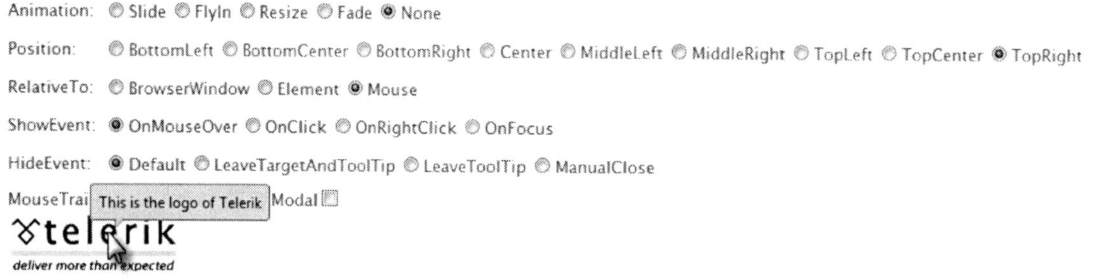

Figure 10-12. *The RelativeTo property is set to Mouse and the Position property to TopRight. The RadToolTip is shown next to the mouse cursor.*

Implementing RadToolTipManager's AutoTooltipify and ToolTipZoneID

`RadToolTipManager` is used primarily when you need a standard way to add tooltips for more than one element within the page. In Listing 10-7, I implement `RadToolTipManager` with the `AutoTooltipify` property to add `RadToolTips` to elements in a `RadGrid`. Note that I didn't have to specify which controls will have a `RadToolTip`—with `AutoTooltipify` set to `true`, all elements that have a tooltip defined will be automatically added to the `TargetControls` collection.

To use the `AutoTooltipify` property in a proper way and to prevent that all the controls in the page from being added to the `TargetControls` collection, you can use the `ToolTipZoneID` property to define only a part of the page to for adding tooltips. This zone can be a panel so all the controls in the panel will be tooltipified, or it can be a complex control such as `RadGrid` or `RadScheduler`.

Note in Figure 10-13 how easy is to create a more complex tooltip with just a few HTML elements and the `ContentScrolling` property. In this case, scroll bars are enabled to read all the content in a tooltip because it won't fit into the defined tooltip size.

Listing 10-7. *Implementing RadToolTipManager AutoTooltipify and ToolTipZoneID*

ASPX Page

```
<telerik:RadGrid ID="RadGrid1" runat="server"
                AutoGenerateColumns="False"
                DataSourceID="EmployeesDataSource"
                GridLines="None">
    <MasterTableView DataKeyNames="EmployeeID"
                    DataSourceID="EmployeesDataSource">
    <RowIndicatorColumn>
    <HeaderStyle Width="20px"></HeaderStyle>
    </RowIndicatorColumn>

    <ExpandCollapseColumn>
    <HeaderStyle Width="20px"></HeaderStyle>
    </ExpandCollapseColumn>
        <Columns>
            <telerik:GridTemplateColumn HeaderText="ID"
                DataField="EmployeeID"
                DataType="System.Int32"
                SortExpression="EmployeeID"
                UniqueName="EmployeeID">
                <ItemTemplate>
                    <asp:Label ID="lblID" runat="server"
                               Text='<%# Eval("EmployeeID") %>'
                               ToolTip='<%#
                                Eval("TitleOfCourtesy") + " "
                                + Eval("FirstName") + " " + Eval("LastName")
                                + "<br />"
                                + "Hire on " + DateTime
                                             .Parse(Eval("HireDate")
                                             .ToString())
                                             .ToShortDateString() + "<br />"
                                + Eval("Address") + "<br />"
                                + Eval("City") + " " + Eval("Region") + ", "
                                + Eval("PostalCode") + "<br />"
                                + Eval("Country") + "<br />"
                                + "Home Phone " + Eval("HomePhone") + "<hr>"
                                + Eval("Notes")
                                %>'>
                    </asp:Label>
                </ItemTemplate>
            </telerik:GridTemplateColumn>
            <telerik:GridBoundColumn DataField="LastName"
                HeaderText="LastName"
                SortExpression="LastName"
                UniqueName="LastName">
            </telerik:GridBoundColumn>
```

```
            <telerik:GridBoundColumn DataField="FirstName"
                HeaderText="FirstName"
                SortExpression="FirstName"
                UniqueName="FirstName">
            </telerik:GridBoundColumn>
            <telerik:GridBoundColumn DataField="Title"
                HeaderText="Title"
                SortExpression="Title"
                UniqueName="Title">
            </telerik:GridBoundColumn>
        </Columns>
    </MasterTableView>
</telerik:RadGrid>

<asp:SqlDataSource ID="EmployeesDataSource" runat="server"
    ConnectionString="<%$ ConnectionStrings:NorthwindConnectionString %>"
    SelectCommand="SELECT * FROM [Employees]">
</asp:SqlDataSource>

<telerik:RadToolTipManager ID="RadToolTipManager1" runat="server"
                           AutoTooltipify="true"
                           ToolTipZoneID="RadGrid1"
                           Position="TopCenter"
                           Animation="Resize"
                           RelativeTo="Element"
                           Title="Employee Details"
                           HideEvent="ManualClose"
                           ShowCallout="false"
                           ContentScrolling="Auto"
                           Width="300px"
                           Height="200px">
</telerik:RadToolTipManager>
```

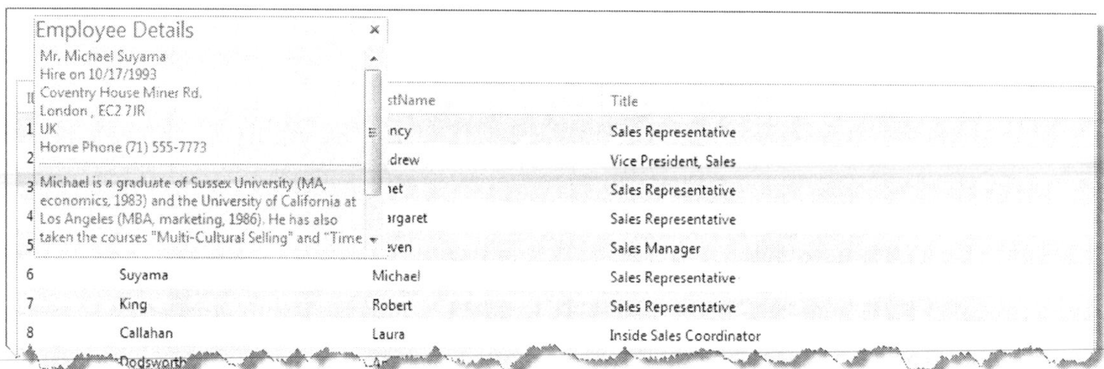

Figure 10-13. *RadToolTipManager is used to automatically create nice tooltips to targeted areas with the AutoTooltipify and ToolTipZoneID properties.*

Loading RadToolTip Information on Demand

RadToolTip is capable of loading information on demand through various mechanisms, but one that is very important is that you can display a web user control in a RadToolTip and pass information so the tool tip will show specific information.

The example in Listing 10-8 uses a RadGrid showing a list of orders made by customers. When you hover over an order ID, a RadToolTip is displayed showing a web user control that implements a second RadGrid listing the products in the order. This second RadGrid in the web user control is loaded based on the order ID passed to the web user control when the OnAjaxUpdate event is raised. The TargetControls collection is filled in the ItemDataBound event of the orders grid, and that's why, in this case, the AutoTooltipify property is not used. See Figure 10-14 for the end result.

Listing 10-8. *Implementing the RadToolTipManager Load-on-Demand Functionality*

ASPX Page

```
<telerik:RadGrid ID="RadGrid2" runat="server"
        AllowFilteringByColumn="True"
        AllowPaging="True"
        AllowSorting="True"
        AutoGenerateColumns="False"
        DataSourceID="OrdersDataSource"
        GridLines="None"
        OnItemDataBound="RadGrid2_ItemDataBound">
<MasterTableView CellSpacing="-1"
                 DataKeyNames="OrderID"
                 DataSourceID="OrdersDataSource">
<RowIndicatorColumn>
<HeaderStyle Width="20px"></HeaderStyle>
</RowIndicatorColumn>

<ExpandCollapseColumn>
<HeaderStyle Width="20px"></HeaderStyle>
</ExpandCollapseColumn>
    <Columns>
        <telerik:GridTemplateColumn HeaderText="Order ID"
                                    UniqueName="TemplateColumn">
            <ItemTemplate>
                <asp:Label ID="lblOrderID" runat="server"
                           Text='<%# Eval("OrderID") %>'>
                </asp:Label>
            </ItemTemplate>
        </telerik:GridTemplateColumn>
        <telerik:GridBoundColumn DataField="CustomerID"
            HeaderText="Customer ID"
            SortExpression="CustomerID"
            UniqueName="CustomerID">
        </telerik:GridBoundColumn>
```

```
        <telerik:GridBoundColumn DataField="OrderDate"
            DataType="System.DateTime"
            HeaderText="Order Date"
            SortExpression="OrderDate"
            UniqueName="OrderDate">
        </telerik:GridBoundColumn>
        <telerik:GridBoundColumn DataField="ShipName"
            HeaderText="Ship Name"
            SortExpression="ShipName"
            UniqueName="ShipName">
        </telerik:GridBoundColumn>
        <telerik:GridBoundColumn DataField="ShipCountry"
            HeaderText="Ship Country"
            SortExpression="ShipCountry"
            UniqueName="ShipCountry">
        </telerik:GridBoundColumn>
    </Columns>
</MasterTableView>
<ClientSettings>
    <Selecting AllowRowSelect="True" />
    <Scrolling AllowScroll="True" UseStaticHeaders="True" />
</ClientSettings>
</telerik:RadGrid>

<telerik:RadAjaxLoadingPanel ID="RadAjaxLoadingPanel1" Runat="server">
</telerik:RadAjaxLoadingPanel>

<asp:SqlDataSource ID="OrdersDataSource" runat="server"
ConnectionString="<%$ ConnectionStrings:NorthwindConnectionString %>"
SelectCommand="SELECT * FROM [Orders]">
</asp:SqlDataSource>

<telerik:RadToolTipManager ID="RadToolTipManager2" runat="server"
                HideEvent="ManualClose"
                Animation="Resize"
                Position="TopRight"
                Width="600px"
                Height="250px"
                ToolTipZoneID="RadGrid2"
                OnAjaxUpdate="RadToolTipManager2_AjaxUpdate"
                Title="Order Details">
</telerik:RadToolTipManager>

<telerik:RadAjaxManager ID="RadAjaxManager1" runat="server">
    <AjaxSettings>
        <telerik:AjaxSetting AjaxControlID="RadGrid2">
            <UpdatedControls>
                <telerik:AjaxUpdatedControl ControlID="RadGrid2"
                                            LoadingPanelID="RadAjaxLoadingPanel1" />
                <telerik:AjaxUpdatedControl ControlID="RadToolTipManager2" />
            </UpdatedControls>
        </telerik:AjaxSetting>
    </AjaxSettings>
</telerik:RadAjaxManager>
```

Code Behind

```
bool IsTooltify(string ClientId)
{
    return RadToolTipManager2.TargetControls
                .Cast<ToolTipTargetControl>()
                .Any(item => item.TargetControlID == ClientId);
}

protected void RadGrid2_ItemDataBound(object sender, GridItemEventArgs e)
{
    if ((e.Item.ItemType != GridItemType.Item
                && e.Item.ItemType != GridItemType.AlternatingItem)
                || !e.Item.Visible || IsTooltify(e.Item.ClientID)) return;
    Label l = (Label)e.Item.FindControl("lblOrderID");
    RadToolTipManager2.TargetControls.Add(l.ClientID, l.Text, true);

}

protected void RadToolTipManager2_AjaxUpdate(object sender, ToolTipUpdateEventArgs e)
{
    int value;
    if (!int.TryParse(e.Value, out value)) return;
    OrderDetails control = (OrderDetails)LoadControl("OrderDetails.ascx");
    control.OrderID = value;
    e.UpdatePanel.ContentTemplateContainer.Controls.Add(control);
}
```

OrderDetails.ascx

```
<%@ Control Language="C#"
        AutoEventWireup="true"
        CodeBehind="OrderDetails.ascx.cs"
        Inherits="WebApplication1.OrderDetails" %>

<telerik:RadGrid ID="RadGrid1" runat="server"
                DataSourceID="OrderDetailsDataSource"
                GridLines="None">
    <MasterTableView autogeneratecolumns="False"
            cellspacing="-1"
            datakeynames="OrderID,ProductID"
            datasourceid="OrderDetailsDataSource">
    <RowIndicatorColumn>
    <HeaderStyle Width="20px"></HeaderStyle>
    </RowIndicatorColumn>
```

```
    <ExpandCollapseColumn>
    <HeaderStyle Width="20px"></HeaderStyle>
    </ExpandCollapseColumn>
        <Columns>
            <telerik:GridBoundColumn DataField="OrderID"
                DataType="System.Int32"
                HeaderText="OrderID"
                ReadOnly="True"
                SortExpression="OrderID"
                UniqueName="OrderID">
            </telerik:GridBoundColumn>
            <telerik:GridBoundColumn DataField="ProductID"
                DataType="System.Int32"
                HeaderText="ProductID"
                ReadOnly="True"
                SortExpression="ProductID"
                UniqueName="ProductID">
            </telerik:GridBoundColumn>
            <telerik:GridBoundColumn DataField="ProductName"
                HeaderText="ProductName"
                SortExpression="ProductName"
                UniqueName="ProductName">
            </telerik:GridBoundColumn>
            <telerik:GridBoundColumn DataField="UnitPrice"
                DataType="System.Decimal"
                HeaderText="UnitPrice"
                SortExpression="UnitPrice"
                UniqueName="UnitPrice">
            </telerik:GridBoundColumn>
            <telerik:GridBoundColumn DataField="Quantity"
                DataType="System.Int16"
                HeaderText="Quantity"
                SortExpression="Quantity"
                UniqueName="Quantity">
            </telerik:GridBoundColumn>
            <telerik:GridBoundColumn DataField="Discount"
                DataType="System.Single"
                HeaderText="Discount"
                SortExpression="Discount"
                UniqueName="Discount">
            </telerik:GridBoundColumn>
            <telerik:GridBoundColumn DataField="ExtendedPrice"
                DataType="System.Decimal"
                HeaderText="ExtendedPrice"
                ReadOnly="True"
                SortExpression="ExtendedPrice"
                UniqueName="ExtendedPrice">
            </telerik:GridBoundColumn>
        </Columns>
    </MasterTableView>
</telerik:RadGrid>
```

```
<asp:SqlDataSource ID="OrderDetailsDataSource" runat="server"
    ConnectionString="<%$ ConnectionStrings:NorthwindConnectionString %>"
    SelectCommand="SELECT * FROM [Order Details Extended] WHERE ([OrderID] = @OrderID)">
    <SelectParameters>
        <asp:Parameter Name="OrderID" Type="Int32" />
    </SelectParameters>
</asp:SqlDataSource>
```

OrderDetails.ascx.cs

```
using System;
using System.Web.UI;

namespace WebApplication1
{
    public partial class OrderDetails : UserControl
    {
        public int OrderID { get; set; }

        protected void Page_Load(object sender, EventArgs e)
        {
            OrderDetailsDataSource.SelectParameters[0]
                .DefaultValue = OrderID.ToString();
            RadGrid1.DataBind();
        }
    }
}
```

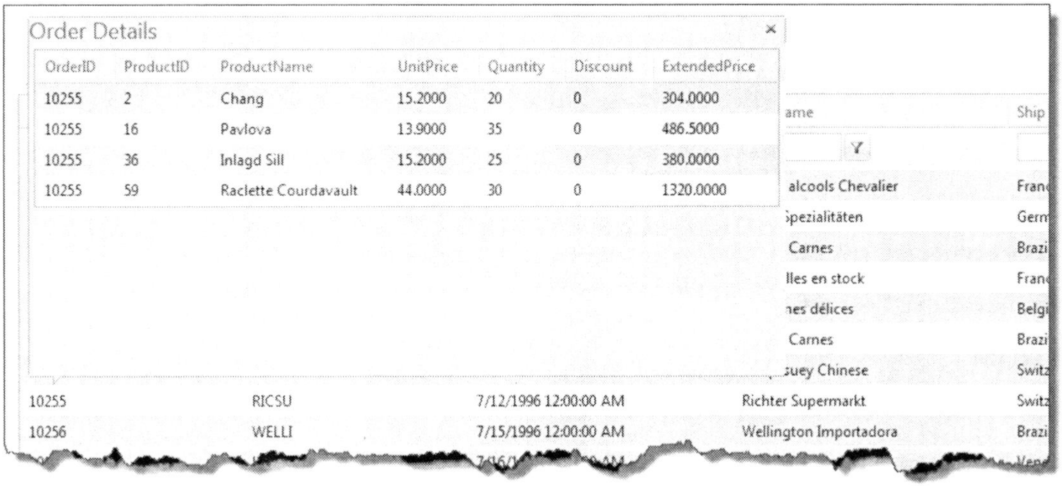

Figure 10-14. *When hovering over an order ID in RadGrid, a RadToolTip showing the order details is shown loading the information on demand.*

Loading RadToolTip on Demand from a Web Service

RadToolTip can also load information on demand from a web service. This ability is an extension of the technique illustrated in Listing 10-8. In Listing 10-9, I created a web service that loads information related to appointments that are shown in a RadScheduler. Once each appointment is created in the scheduler, it is added to the TargetControls collection in RadToolTipManager, which is bound to a web service. Note, in Figure 10-15, that when you hover over an appointment, a RadToolTip is shown with information fetched from a call to the web service method.

Listing 10-9. *Implementing RadToolTipManager Load-On-Demand Functionality from a Web Service*

ASPX Page

```
<telerik:RadScheduler ID="RadScheduler1" runat="server"
    DataDescriptionField="Description"
    DataEndField="End"
    DataKeyField="ID"
    DataRecurrenceField="RecurrenceRule"
    DataRecurrenceParentKeyField="RecurrenceParentID"
    DataSourceID="SqlDataSource1"
    DataStartField="Start"
    DataSubjectField="Subject"
    OnAppointmentCreated="RadScheduler1_ApplintmentCreated"
    SelectedDate="2/1/2010">
</telerik:RadScheduler>

<asp:SqlDataSource ID="SqlDataSource1" runat="server"
    ConnectionString="<%$ ConnectionStrings:NorthwindConnectionString %>"
    SelectCommand="SELECT * FROM [Appointments]">
</asp:SqlDataSource>

<telerik:RadToolTipManager ID="RadToolTipManager3" runat="server"
                           HideEvent="ManualClose"
                           Animation="Resize"
                           Position="TopCenter"
                           Width="300px"
                           Height="100px"
                           Title="Appointment Details">
    <WebServiceSettings Path="WebServices/RadToolTip_Service.asmx"
                        Method="GetAppointmentData" />
</telerik:RadToolTipManager>
```

Code Behind

```
protected void RadScheduler1_ApplintmentCreated(
                                        object sender,
                                        AppointmentCreatedEventArgs e)
{
    if (!IsTooltify(RadToolTipManager3, e.Appointment.ClientID))
        RadToolTipManager3.TargetControls
                        .Add(e.Appointment.ClientID,
                             e.Appointment.ID.ToString(), true);
}
```

```
bool IsTooltify(RadToolTipManager manager, string ClientId)
{
    return manager.TargetControls
            .Cast<ToolTipTargetControl>()
            .Any(item => item.TargetControlID == ClientId);
}
```

RadToolTip_Service.asmx.cs

```
namespace WebApplication1.WebServices
{
    /// <summary>
    /// Summary description for RadToolTip_Service
    /// </summary>
    [WebService(Namespace = "http://tempuri.org/")]
    [WebServiceBinding(ConformsTo = WsiProfiles.BasicProfile1_1)]
    [System.ComponentModel.ToolboxItem(false)]
    [ScriptService]
    public class RadToolTip_Service : WebService
    {

        [WebMethod]
        public string GetAppointmentData(object context)
        {
            IDictionary<string, object> contextDictionary =
                                        (IDictionary<string, object>)context;
            string elementID = ((string)contextDictionary["Value"]);

            if (elementID == string.Empty)
            {
                throw new Exception("No argument specified.");
            }

            DataTable information = new DataTable();

            using (SqlConnection conn = new SqlConnection(WebConfigurationManager
                                        .ConnectionStrings["NorthwindConnectionString"]
                                        .ConnectionString))
            {

try
                {
                    conn.Open();

                    SqlDataAdapter adapter = new SqlDataAdapter();

                    string Sql = "SELECT [Description], [Start], [End] ";
                    Sql += " FROM [Appointments] WHERE ID = @id";
                    adapter.SelectCommand = new SqlCommand(Sql, conn);
                    adapter.SelectCommand.Parameters.AddWithValue("@id", elementID);
                    adapter.Fill(information);
                }
```

```
                catch (Exception ex)
                {

                }
            }

            Page pageHolder = new Page();
            UserControl viewControl =
                        (UserControl)pageHolder.LoadControl("~/AppointmentInfo.ascx");

            Type viewControlType = viewControl.GetType();
            FieldInfo field = viewControlType.GetField("Data");

            if (field != null)
            {
                field.SetValue(viewControl, information);
            }

            pageHolder.Controls.Add(viewControl);
            StringWriter output = new StringWriter();
            HttpContext.Current.Server.Execute(pageHolder, output, false);

            return output.ToString();
        }
    }
}
```

AppointmentInfo.ascx

```
<%@ Control Language="C#"
            AutoEventWireup="true"
            CodeBehind="AppointmentInfo.ascx.cs"
            Inherits="WebApplication1.AppointmentInfo" %>

<table>
    <tr>
        <td>About: </td>
        <td>
            <asp:Label ID="lblDesc" runat="server"></asp:Label>
        </td>
    </tr>
    <tr>
        <td>Start: </td>
        <td>
            <asp:Label ID="lblStart" runat="server"></asp:Label>
        </td>
    </tr>
```

```
    <tr>
        <td>End: </td>
        <td>
            <asp:Label ID="lblEnd" runat="server"></asp:Label>
        </td>
    </tr>

</table>
```

AppointmentInfo.ascx.cs

```
namespace WebApplication1
{
    public partial class AppointmentInfo : UserControl
    {
        public object Data;

        protected void Page_Load(object sender, EventArgs e)
        {
            DataTable table = (DataTable) Data;
            lblDesc.Text = table.Rows[0]["Description"].ToString();
            lblStart.Text = DateTime.Parse(table.Rows[0]["Start"].ToString()).ToString();
            lblEnd.Text = DateTime.Parse(table.Rows[0]["End"].ToString()).ToString();
        }
    }
}
```

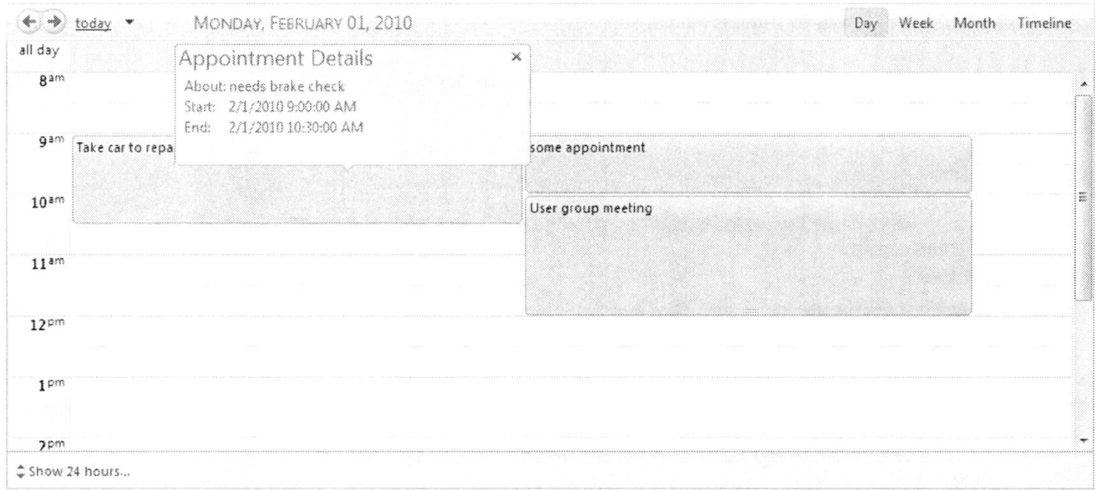

Figure 10-15. *Hovering over an appointment makes RadToolTipManager invoke the web method in the web service and displays a RadToolTip with the web method reponse.*

RadUpload

The next control doesn't need too much introduction. RadUpload is a control designed to upload files from the client computer to the server. It has a lot of optional configuration options that make it not only easy to use but also a powerful alternative to traditional input controls.

Among others, RadUpload has the following capabilities:

- Uploading multiple files
- Codeless uploading
- Asynchronous uploading with RadAsyncUpload
- Upload progress monitoring with RadProgressArea
- Integrated validation
- Client-side and server-side APIs

The configuration of RadUpload was described in detail in Chapter 2. What was not said there is that, to process large files, you need to adjust the maxRequestLength property of the httpRuntime tag in the system.web section from the web.config file. The default value (in kilobytes) for this parameter is 4096, meaning that, at the most, you can upload up to 4MB in a single postback. If your combined upload size is above the amount specified in this property, you'll get a Page Not Found error from the server.

Additionally, RadUpload has the MaxFileSize property (measured in bytes), which defines the maximum file size for each file uploaded with the control. When uploading large files, you can also have problems with the execution timeout, since those files might take a while to process, so you should increase this value (also in the web.config file) from its default of 110 seconds.

The example in Listing 10-10 shows the configuration sections needed in the web.config file for uploading files of up to 50MB in 1 hour. You can also configure these values using Telerik's Visual Studio Extensions (VSX), as shown in Figure 10-16.

Listing 10-10. *RadUpload Configuration Sections in web.config*

```
Web.Config

<configuration>
        <system. web>
                <httpRuntime maxRequestLength="51200" executionTimeout= "3600" />
        </system .web>
</configuration>
```

If using IIS7

```
<system.webServer>
<security>
        <requestFiltering>
                <requestLimits maxAllowedContentLength="52428800" />
        </requestFiltering>
</security>
</system.webServer>
```

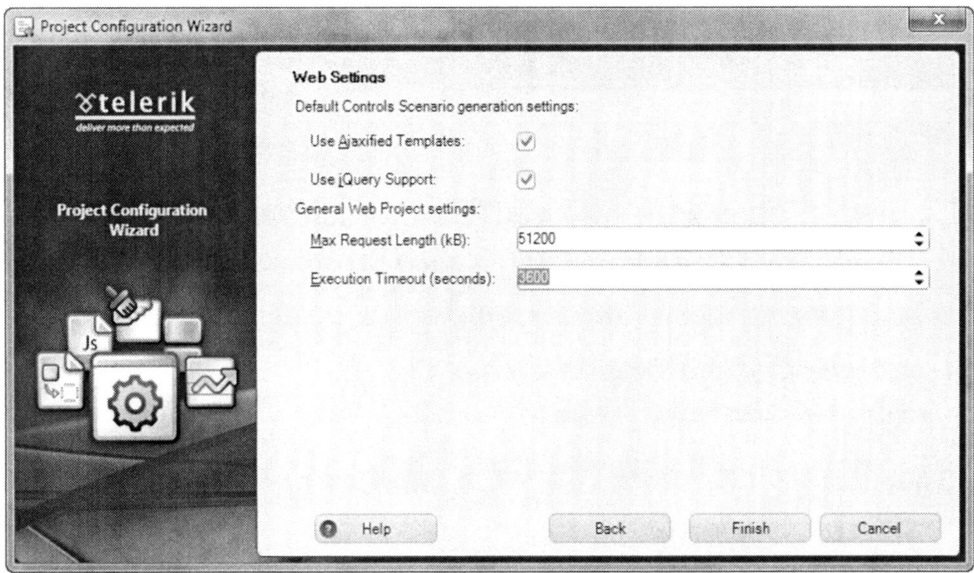

Figure 10-16. *Configuring RadUpload for large files using Visual Studio Extensions*

Implementing RadUpload

To implement RadUpload's default functionality, you only need to define the TargetFolder or TargetPhysicalFolder properties, so RadUpload knows the folder to save the files once they are uploaded to the server (see Listing 10-11). The first property defines the virtual path and the second a physical path, but you have to implement just one of them.

Figure 10-17 shows the default implementation of RadUpload. Note the Add and Delete buttons in the figure. They are used to dynamically add or delete upload fields to the control, so users can upload more files in a single operation. You control how many files users can upload with the properties InitialFileInputsCount, which defines how many upload fields will be shown when the page first loads, and MaxFileInputsCount, which defines the maximum upload fields that can be added. The check box next to each upload field is used to select the field so it can be selectively deleted; the idea is to select all the upload fields that won't be needed and remove them.

All the buttons and options are controlled by the property ControlObjectsVisibility, which is a comma-separated list of values that can take any of the following: Default, All, CheckBoxes, ClearButtons, AddButtons, RemoveButtons, DeleteSelectedButtons, and None. The Default value indicates to include all the buttons except ClearButtons.

Listing 10-11. *Implementing RadUpload*

```
<telerik:RadUpload ID="RadUpload1" runat="server"
                   TargetFolder="~/Files" >
</telerik:RadUpload>
```

Figure 10-17. *Default RadUpload*

Filtering Uploaded Files with AllowedFileExtensions

The property `AllowedFileExtensions` helps you filter the type of files that can be uploaded. In Listing 10-12, `RadUpload` limits the allowed files to only Adobe PDF and Microsoft Word and Excel files. Note in Figure 10-18 how the definition `InputSize` enlarged the control.

Listing 10-12. *Implementing the AllowedFileExtensions property*

```
<telerik:RadUpload ID="RadUpload1" runat="server"
    TargetFolder="~/Files"
    AllowedFileExtensions=".pdf,.doc,.docx,.xls,.xlsx"
    InputSize="40">
</telerik:RadUpload>
```

Figure 10-18. *RadUpload with a modified input size; this control allows only certain types of files.*

Implementing Asynchronous Uploads

A new addition to the RadControls for ASP.NET AJAX is `RadAsyncUpload`, which is designed to allow users to upload files asynchronously. The control works by immediately starting the upload asynchronously when a file is selected, and it displays a progress indicator and another indicator when the upload finishes.

What happens with the file? It is stored in a temporary location managed by the `TemporaryFolder` property with a default location in `~/App_Data/RadUploadTemp`. After that, a postback is required to move the file to the target folder. Additionally, you need to define the `TemporaryFileExpiration` property, which determines the amount of time the file will remain in the temporary folder after it has been uploaded if a postback has not yet occurred to move it to its final location.

Listing 10-13 implements `RadAsynUpload` and a button that actually doesn't do anything but provoke a postback. Figure 10-19 shows the example running. In Figure 10-20, you can see the temporary folder where files are stored in a controlled manner before they are moved to their final locations.

Listing 10-13. *Implementing RadAsyncUpload*

ASPX Page

```
<telerik:RadAsyncUpload ID="RadAsyncUpload1" runat="server"
    TargetFolder="~/UploadedFiles"
    AllowedFileExtensions=".pdf,.docx,.xlsx"
    InputSize="40"
    OverwriteExistingFiles="True"
    ControlObjectsVisibility="Default"
    Width="500px">
</telerik:RadAsyncUpload>

<asp:Button ID="btnUpload2" runat="server" Text="Upload" />
```

Figure 10-19. *Note that RadAsyncUpload works asynchronously, and when the asynchronous operation ends, a check mark is shown.*

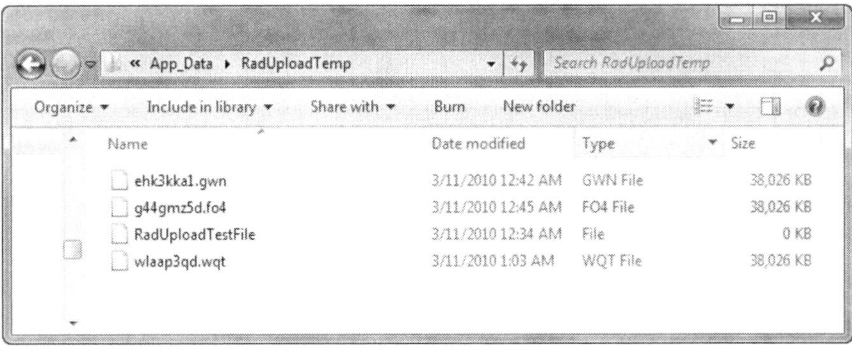

Figure 10-20. *A RadAsynchUpload temporary folder*

Monitoring the Upload Progress

Before asynchronous uploads came onto the scene, it was very difficult to tell what the actual progress of an upload was, so Telerik created the RadProgressArea control to do exactly that—inform users what was happening with the files while they were uploading. And the best part is that you really don't need to do anything; just drop the control in the page along with RadUpload or any regular FileUpload control, and it will automatically monitor uploads.

There are some properties you can set to have more control over the monitoring process. You can use the DisplayCancelButton property to display a button that will cancel the upload. There are also a number of indicators that are controlled by the ProgressIndicators property; it can take one or more of the following values (separated by commas):

- TotalProgressBar: Instructs the control to show the overall progress bar
- TotalProgress: Displays the total file size that has been uploaded
- TotalProgressPercent: Displays the percentage of the upload operation
- RequestSize: Displays the total size requested for upload
- FilesCountBar: Displays a progress bar that counts the uploaded files
- FilesCount: Displays the number of uploaded files
- FilesCountPercent: Displays the percentage of uploaded files
- SelectedFilesCount: Displays the number of files to be uploaded
- CurrentFileName: Displays the name of the file being uploaded
- TimeElapsed: Shows how much time the whole upload operation has taken
- TimeEstimated: Shows the estimated remaining time
- TransferSpeed: Displays the current transfer rate

An important note here is that RadProgressArea requires a RadProgressManager control in the page, which provides the AJAX mechanism to obtain the progress information.

Listing 10-14. *Implementing RadProgressArea*

ASPX Page

```
<telerik:RadProgressManager ID="RadProgressManager1" runat="server" />

<telerik:RadUpload ID="RadUpload2" runat="server"
    TargetFolder="~/UploadedFiles"
    InputSize="40"
    OverwriteExistingFiles="True"
    Width="500px">
</telerik:RadUpload>
```

```
<asp:Button ID="btnUpload3" runat="server" Text="Upload" />

<telerik:RadProgressArea ID="RadProgressArea1" runat="server"
    DisplayCancelButton="True">
</telerik:RadProgressArea>
```

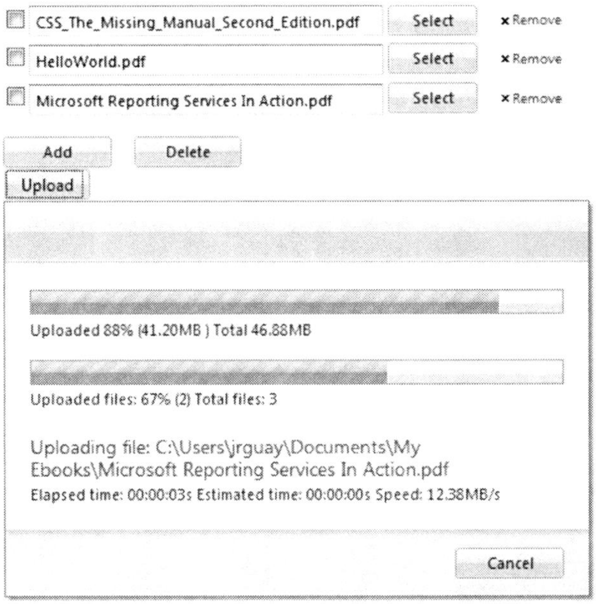

Figure 10-21. *RadProgressArea monitoring the upload progress*

Using RadProgressArea to Monitor Custom Processes

One of the most interesting aspects of RadProgressArea is that you can use it not just for uploads but for any process that takes time and for which you want to provide feedback to your users on the state of the process.

The technique is to intercept the progress area context in your process and use it to display feedback relevant to that process. In Listing 10-15, I have defined a RadProgressArea with specific indicators using the property ProgressIndicators. I have used a button-click event handler to simulate the running process with 100 steps, and I put the process to sleep for 2 seconds just to simulate that each of the steps in the process take some time.

Note, in the code, that I use the progress area context. The SecondaryTotal indicates total steps my process will run. The SecondaryValue and SecondaryPercent properties display the value and percentage of the completed steps. The CurrentOperationText displays information about the current step in the process. Figure 10-22 illustrates how everything works.

Listing 10-15. *Monitoring a Custom Process Using RadProgressArea*

```
<asp:Button ID="btnCustomProcess" runat="server"
                Text="Run Custom Process"
                OnClick="btnCustomProcess_Click" />

<telerik:RadProgressArea ID="RadProgressArea2" runat="server"
        ProgressIndicators="FilesCountBar,
                            FilesCountPercent,
                            CurrentFileName,
                            TimeElapsed">
    <Localization UploadedFiles="Completed: "
                  CurrentFileName=""
                  TotalFiles="">
    </Localization>
</telerik:RadProgressArea>

Code Behind

protected void btnCustomProcess_Click(object sender, EventArgs e)
{
    RadProgressContext context = RadProgressContext.Current;

    context.SecondaryTotal = 100;

    for (int i = 0; i < 100; i++)
    {
        context.SecondaryValue = i;
        context.SecondaryPercent = (Convert.ToDecimal(i)).ToString("##0.00");
        context.CurrentOperationText = string.Format("Processing step #{0}", i + 1);

        // Do some work here

        // simulates a delay
        System.Threading.Thread.Sleep(2000);
    }
}
```

Run Custom Process

Completed: 8.00%

Processing step #9

Elapsed time: 00:00:18s

Figure 10-22. *The process feeds information to RadProgressArea to display to users.*

Note RadUpload and RadProgressArea have certain limitations that are worth considering before using them. You can find the information in the product documentation at http://www.telerik.com/help/aspnet-ajax/upload_uploadinglimitations.html and http://www.telerik.com/help/aspnet-ajax/progressarea-known-limitations.html.

RadFileExplorer

RadFileExplorer provides user with a Windows Explorer–like window for files and folders in a web application. It enables users to upload files, create folders, and delete and rename files and folders. It also supports drag-and-drop functionality for moving files and load-on-demand capabilities for directory loading using callbacks. Then too, it allows you to create context menus to perform actions on files and folders, sorting files and folders, and much more.

RadFileExplorer is based on the FileBrowserContentProvider model of RadEditor, so you can create your own file content provider abstraction that can be integrated with whatever server or backend system such as CMSs and databases.

The main property to enable RadFileExplorer is InitialPath, which indicates the (relative) path that will be used as a root folder. Then, the other properties are Configuration.DeletePaths, Configuration.UploadPaths, and Configuration.ViewPaths, and these represent paths to the places the control can perform the indicated operations.

The example in Listing 10-16 shows you how to configure RadFileExplorer, and the control is illustrated in Figure 10-23.

Listing 10-16. *Implementing RadFileExplorer*

ASPX Page

```
<telerik:RadFileExplorer ID="RadFileExplorer1" runat="server"
    InitialPath="~/Images">
    <Configuration SearchPatterns="*.*"
                   DeletePaths="~/Images"
                   UploadPaths="~/Images"
                   ViewPaths="~/Images">
    </Configuration>
</telerik:RadFileExplorer>
```

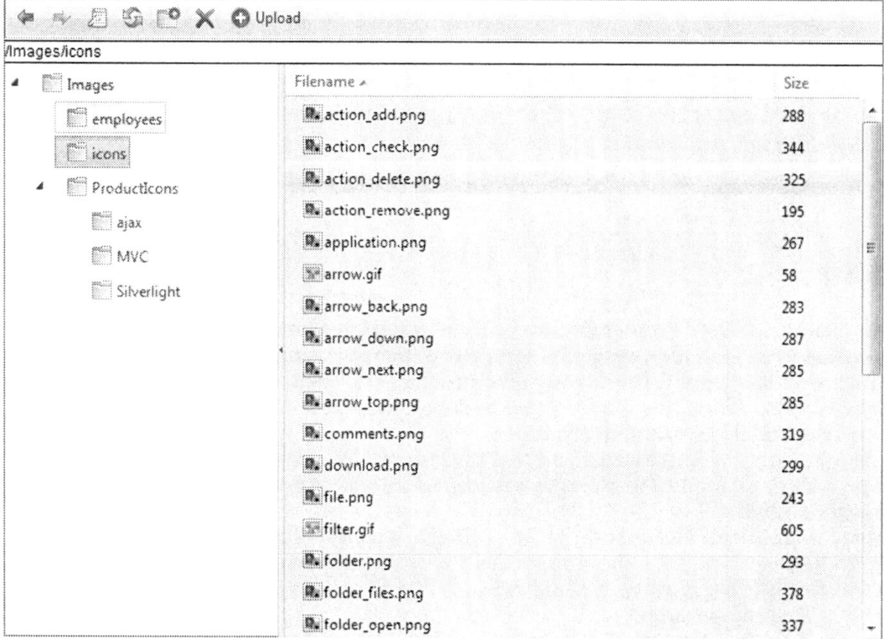

Figure 10-23. *Basic implementation of RadFileExplorer*

RadSlider

RadSlider is a control that enables users to select a value from within a defined range. This control exposes a huge client-side API along with a rich set of features that will help you with almost any needs you have.

When configuring RadSlider, you have to first define if you will use a numeric range or a set of items. For this purpose, you need to set the property ItemType to either Tick (for a numeric range of values) or Items (for a set of items). If you set up RadSlider to use a numeric range (ticks), use the MaximumValue and MinimunValue properties to create the desired range of allowed values. Also, set the optional LargeChange and SmallChange properties to the values used to present track lines that RadSlider will show. If you set LargeChange, the slider will use this value as the step for which it will change the selected value. If you set SmallChange and LargeChange, the step value will be the one defined in SmallChange, but track lines will be shown for both values.

In Listing 10-17, you can see how to create a RadSlider with a numeric range. Figure 10-24 illustrates the example.

Listing 10-17. *Implementing RadSlider*

ASPX Page

```
<telerik:RadSlider ID="RadSlider1" runat="server"
                   Orientation="Horizontal"
                   MinimumValue="-50"
                   MaximumValue="50"
                   Value="0"
                   SmallChange="5"
                   LargeChange="10"
                   ItemType="tick">
</telerik:RadSlider>
```

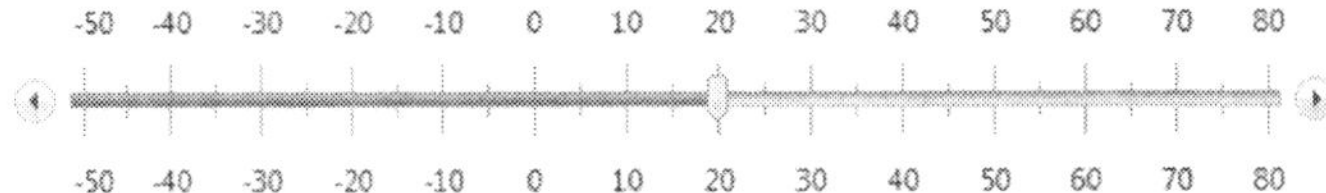

Figure 10-24. *RadSlider with a numeric range of allowed values*

The track lines can be shown centered, on the top, or the bottom of the slider using the `TrackPosition` property. You also can change the direction of the values range with the `IsDirectionReversed` property, so the minimum and maximum values will swap. Of course, you can customize `RadSlider` further by enabling or disabling the increase, decrease, and drag handles using the `ShowIncreaseHandle`, `ShowDecreaseHandle`, and `ShowDragHandle` properties.

You can also use `RadSlider` to enable users to define a selected range. For this to work, you need to set the `IsSelectionRangeEnabled` property to `true`, as shown in Listing 10-18; `RadSlider` will show two drag handlers. Then, use the `SelectionStart` and `SelectionEnd` properties to get or set the range selection. Figure 10-25 illustrates these properties in action.

Listing 10-18. *Implementing a Range Selection with RadSlider*

```
<telerik:RadSlider ID="RadSlider1" runat="server"
                   Orientation="Horizontal"
                   MinimumValue="-50"
                   MaximumValue="50"
                   SmallChange="5"
                   LargeChange="10"
                   IsSelectionRangeEnabled="true"
                   SelectionStart="-10"
                   SelectionEnd="25"
                   ItemType="tick">
</telerik:RadSlider>
```

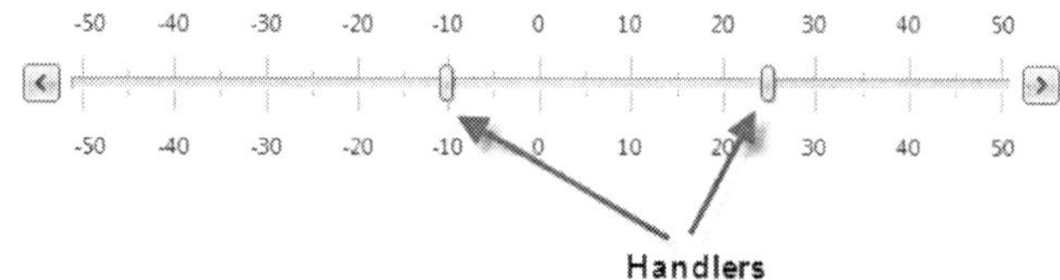

Figure 10-25. *two handlers are shown when implementing a selection range.*

Implementing RadSlider Items

As I described before, you can use RadSlider to display a range of items instead of a range of allowed numeric values. You need here to set the property ItemType to Item and define the set of items to choose from in the Items collection. Listing 10-19 shows this approach, and it's illustrated in Figure 10-26. Note the differences in the implementation in Figures 10-24 and 10-25.

Listing 10-19. *Implementing RadSlider Items*

ASPX Page

```
<telerik:RadSlider ID="RadSlider2" runat="server"
                   Orientation="Horizontal"
                   Value="0"
                   SmallChange="5"
                   LargeChange="10"
                   ItemType="Item"
                   Width="500px"
                   Height="70px">
    <Items>
        <telerik:RadSliderItem Text="Poor" Value="1" />
        <telerik:RadSliderItem Text="Needs Improvement" Value="2" />
        <telerik:RadSliderItem Text="Fair" Value="3" />
        <telerik:RadSliderItem Text="Good" Value="4" />
        <telerik:RadSliderItem Text="Excellent" Value="5" />
    </Items>
</telerik:RadSlider>
```

Poor Needs Improvement Fair Good Excellent

Figure 10-26. *When implemented for Items, RadSlider looks a little different, but the idea is the same.*

Using the RadSlider Client-Side API

A common characteristic of all of the controls (RadSlider included) is the ability to access the huge client-side API. The example in Listing 10-20 is a little long, but it illustrates many of the functions found in that API.

Listing 10-20. *Implementing RadSlider Client-Side API*

ASPX Page

```
<table>
    <tr>
        <td>Range of values</td>
        <td>
            <table>
                <tr>
                    <td>
                        <telerik:RadNumericTextBox ID="txtClientMinValue"
                                  runat="server"
                                  Value="-50"
                                  Width="100px"
                                  Label="Min">
                            <NumberFormat DecimalDigits="0" />
                            <EnabledStyle HorizontalAlign="Center" />
                        </telerik:RadNumericTextBox>
                    </td>
                    <td>
                        <telerik:RadNumericTextBox ID="txtClientMaxValue"
                                  runat="server"
                                  Value="50"
                                  Width="100px"
                                  Label="Max">
                            <NumberFormat DecimalDigits="0" />
                            <EnabledStyle HorizontalAlign="Center" />
                        </telerik:RadNumericTextBox>
                    </td>
                    <td>
                        <asp:Button ID="btnSetClientValueRange"
                                  runat="server"
                                  Text="Apply"
                                  OnClientClick="SetValueRange();return false;" />
                    </td>
                </tr>
            </table>
        </td>
    </tr>
    <tr>
        <td>Orientation</td>
        <td>
            <telerik:RadSlider ID="sldOrientation" runat="server"
                                   ItemType="Item"
                                   Value="0"
```

```
OnClientValueChanged="sldOrientation_ClientValueChanged"
                              Height="70px">
                <Items>
                    <telerik:RadSliderItem Text="Horizontal" Value="0" />
                    <telerik:RadSliderItem Text="Vertical" Value="1" />
                </Items>
            </telerik:RadSlider>
        </td>
    </tr>
    <tr>
        <td>Track Position</td>
        <td>
            <telerik:RadSlider ID="sldTrackPosition" runat="server"
                              ItemType="Item"
                              Value="0"
                              OnClientValueChanged="sldTrackPosition_ClientValueChanged"
                              Height="70px"
                              Width="300px">
                <Items>
                    <telerik:RadSliderItem Text="Center" Value="0" />
                    <telerik:RadSliderItem Text="TopLeft" Value="1" />
                    <telerik:RadSliderItem Text="BottomRight" Value="2" />
                </Items>
            </telerik:RadSlider>
        </td>
    </tr>
</table>
<table>
    <tr>
        <td>Reverse Direction</td>
        <td>
            <asp:CheckBox ID="chkClientReverseDirection" runat="server"
                          onclick="ChangeDirection();" />
        </td>
        <td> </td>
        <td>Make it a Range RadSlider</td>
        <td>
            <asp:CheckBox ID="chkClientRange" runat="server"
                          onclick="ChangeRange();" />
        </td>
        <td> </td>
        <td>Track MouseWheel</td>
        <td>
            <asp:CheckBox ID="chkClientMouseWheel" runat="server"
                          Checked="true"
                          onclick="TrackMouseWheel();" />
        </td>
    </tr>
```

```
    <tr>
       <td>Enable Drag Handle</td>
       <td>
           <asp:CheckBox ID="CheckBox4" runat="server"
                         Checked="true"
                         onclick="EnableDragHandle();" />
       </td>
       <td> </td>
       <td>Show Increase Handle</td>
       <td>
           <asp:CheckBox ID="CheckBox5" runat="server"
                         Checked="true"
                         onclick="ShowIncreaseHandle();" />
       </td>
       <td> </td>
       <td>Show Decrease Handle</td>
       <td>
           <asp:CheckBox ID="CheckBox6" runat="server"
                         Checked="true"
                         onclick="ShowDecreaseHandle();" />
       </td>
    </tr>
</table>
<br />
<telerik:RadSlider ID="RadSlider3" runat="server"
                   Orientation="Horizontal"
                   MinimumValue="-50"
                   MaximumValue="50"
                   Value="0"
                   SmallChange="5"
                   LargeChange="10"
                   ItemType="tick"
                   OnClientValueChanged="RadSlider3_ClientValueChanged"
                   Width="500px"
                   Height="70px">
</telerik:RadSlider>
<telerik:RadNumericTextBox ID="txtClientValue" runat="server"
                           Label="Selected Value"
                           Value="0">
    <NumberFormat DecimalDigits="0" />
</telerik:RadNumericTextBox>
<br /><br /><br /><br /><br /><br /><br /><br /><br />
<telerik:RadCodeBlock ID="RadCodeBlock1" runat="server">
<script type="text/javascript">
    function SetValueRange() {
        var slider = $telerik.findSlider("<%=RadSlider3.ClientID %>", null);
        var txtMin = $telerik.findNumericTextBox("<%=txtClientMinValue.ClientID %>", null);
        var txtMax = $telerik.findNumericTextBox("<%=txtClientMaxValue.ClientID %>", null);
        slider.set_minimumValue(txtMin.get_value());
        slider.set_maximumValue(txtMax.get_value());
    }
```

```
    function sldOrientation_ClientValueChanged(sender, eventArgs) {
        var sldOrientation = $telerik.toSlider(sender);
        var slider = $telerik.findSlider("<%=RadSlider3.ClientID %>", null);
        if (sldOrientation.get_selectedItem().get_value() == "0") {
            slider.set_orientation(Telerik.Web.UI.Orientation.Horizontal);
            slider.set_width(500);
            slider.set_height(70);
        }
        else {
            slider.set_orientation(Telerik.Web.UI.Orientation.Vertical);
            slider.set_width(70);
            slider.set_height(500);
        }
    }

    function sldTrackPosition_ClientValueChanged(sender, eventArgs) {
        var sldTrackPosition = $telerik.toSlider(sender);
        var slider = $telerik.findSlider("<%=RadSlider3.ClientID %>", null);
        if (sldTrackPosition.get_selectedItem().get_value() == "0") {
            slider.set_trackPosition(Telerik.Web.UI.SliderTrackPosition.Center);
        }
        else {
            if (sldTrackPosition.get_selectedItem().get_value() == "1") {
                slider.set_trackPosition(Telerik.Web.UI.SliderTrackPosition.TopLeft);
            }
            else {

slider.set_trackPosition(Telerik.Web.UI.SliderTrackPosition.BottomRight);
            }
        }
    }

    function ChangeDirection() {
        var slider = $telerik.findSlider("<%=RadSlider3.ClientID %>", null);
        slider.set_isDirectionReversed(!slider.get_isDirectionReversed());
    }

    function ChangeRange() {
        var slider = $telerik.findSlider("<%=RadSlider3.ClientID %>", null);
        slider.set_isSelectionRangeEnabled(!slider.get_isSelectionRangeEnabled());
        var txtMin = $telerik.findNumericTextBox("<%=txtClientMinValue.ClientID %>", null);
        var txtMax = $telerik.findNumericTextBox("<%=txtClientMaxValue.ClientID %>", null);
        if (slider.get_isSelectionRangeEnabled()) {
            slider.set_selectionStart(txtMin.get_value() + 10);
            slider.set_selectionEnd(txtMax.get_value() - 10);
        }
        else {
            slider.set_selectionStart(0);
            slider.set_selectionEnd(0);
            slider.set_value(0);
        }
    }
```

```
    function TrackMouseWheel() {
        var slider = $telerik.findSlider("<%=RadSlider3.ClientID %>", null);
        slider.set_trackMouseWheel(!slider.get_trackMouseWheel());
    }

    function EnableDragHandle() {
        var slider = $telerik.findSlider("<%=RadSlider3.ClientID %>", null);
        slider.set_showDragHandle(!slider.get_showDragHandle());
    }

    function ShowIncreaseHandle() {
        var slider = $telerik.findSlider("<%=RadSlider3.ClientID %>", null);
        slider.set_showIncreaseHandle(!slider.get_showIncreaseHandle());
    }

    function ShowDecreaseHandle() {
        var slider = $telerik.findSlider("<%=RadSlider3.ClientID %>", null);
        slider.set_showDecreaseHandle(!slider.get_showDecreaseHandle());
    }

    function RadSlider3_ClientValueChanged(sender, eventArgs) {
        var slider = $telerik.toSlider(sender);
        var txt = $telerik.findNumericTextBox("<%=txtClientValue.ClientID %>", null);
        txt.set_value(slider.get_value());
    }

</script>
</telerik:RadCodeBlock>
```

Summary

In this chapter, you have seen a set of controls that have a unique application for different scenarios. First, we examined RadFormDecorator, a free control that brings all the skinning goodies to HTML elements to give your application a consistent look and feel.

RadCaptcha provides CAPTCHA functionality that helps prevent automated programs (bots) from posting content or creating accounts in your applications.

RadToolTip is a control for creating enhanced tooltips across an entire page, and it can provide all types of information. A RadToolTip can even render web user controls full of information on demand. It automatically adds tooltip elements in the page and can target specific areas such as panels or complex controls like RadGrid or RadScheduler.

You saw how RadUpload minimizes the effort in handling file upload operations and now includes a control to perform asynchronous uploads (RadAsyncUpload). You can monitor the upload progress with RadProgressArea, and it is so powerful you can use it to monitor other processes.

RadFileExplorer provides users with a Windows Explorer–like window for files and folders in a web application. Users can easily upload, move, rename, and delete files as well as create and modify folders in a familiar interface.

RadSlider is a control for value selection in a specific range of values. It can be configured to either have a numeric range of values or a set of items from which a value can be chosen. It exposes a huge client-side API and different properties to allow lots of configurations. You can also allow users to select a range of values, change the display orientation, and reverse the allowed range, and much more.

CHAPTER 11

RadAjax

Working with AJAX is all about making an application communicate asynchronously with the server so it remains responsive to end users while still doing all the required work.

Telerik's RadAjax is a set of components created for the developer and the end user; this means that developers can now add AJAX functionality to their applications in an easy and powerful way so all the client-side code to make it work is already done, and if that's not enough, RadAjax provides a graphical user interface to "AJAXify" what's needed. For end users, this means more responsive applications with all the required functionality.

RadAjax is composed of four controls: `RadAjaxManager`, `RadAjaxManagerProxy`, `RadAjaxPanel`, and `RadAjaxLoadingPanel`. `RadAjaxManager` is the main control designed to translate postbacks into AJAX calls. `RadAjaxManagerProxy` is a proxy control created for complex scenarios in which you have web user controls and master pages. `RadAjaxPanel` is Telerik's version of the ASP.NET `UpdatePanel` designed to contain all the controls that need to be AJAXified. `RadAjaxLoadingPanel` is the control used to provide a progress indicator to the end user regarding the current AJAX call.

We'll also take a look at the `RadCodeBlock` and `RadScriptBlock` components that allow you to have a seamless interaction between client-side scripts and server-side code. Finally, we'll review the `RadXmlHttpPanel` control for handling asynchronous callbacks or web service calls.

RadAjaxManager and RadAjaxManagerProxy

One of the two main controls in RadAjax is `RadAjaxManager`. It was created with the goal of having a component that is easily configurable and capable to provide RadAjax functionality to the pages in which it is created.

`RadAjaxManager` uses a graphical user interface for its configuration, which generates the markup necessary for the components to work; this markup can be manually edited. The idea is to take the controls that normally perform postback operations and translate them into AJAX requests. You do this by selecting the controls that will initiate the AJAX request. Then, for each of those controls, you define which other controls in the page will get modified by the request so that each will behave like an `UpdatePanel` region without the boundaries. Optionally, you can define some other properties such as `RadAjaxLoadingPanel` that will be used to provide a progress indicator to the user and to specify whether you will use AJAX history (for the Back and Forward browser buttons).

You don't need to write any client-side code to make AJAX requests; `RadAjaxManager` will do it for you. What's important is that the program logic doesn't have to change, because even though the page will be processed normally, only the markup for the regions of the page that need to be updated will be sent back from the server.

Figure 11-1 shows the design-time support of `RadAjaxManager` through its smart tag. These are the properties that can be set:

- *Enable AJAX*: With this property, you control whether AJAX functionality is turned on or off. When turned off, the page executes a full postback.
- *Enable AJAX history*: This option is to allow the Back and Forward browser buttons to work with AJAX requests.
- *Enable update of Page <head> element*: With this option, you enable or disable modifications to the page header element during AJAX requests such as updates to styles, title information, or script elements.
- *Choose LoadingPanelID*: Here you can select a `RadAjaxLoadingPanel` instance to provide a progress indicator to all AJAX requests handled by `RadAjaxManager` (except for those that already have defined a specific `RadAjaxLoadingPanel`). We'll review `RadAjaxLoadingPanel` later in this chapter.

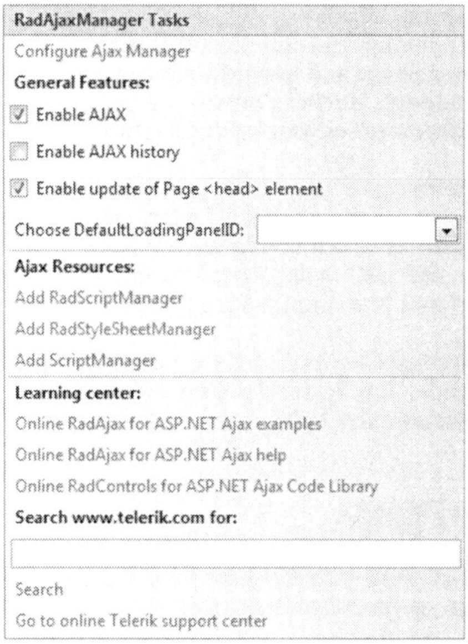

Figure 11-1. *RadAjaxManager smart tag*

The link Configure Ajax Manager opens the RadAjaxManager Property Builder window (shown in Figure 11-2), which is probably the most efficient place to define the controls to be AJAXified.

In the first panel, you define the controls that will initiate the AJAX requests. Then, for each of these controls, you define the set of controls that will be updated by the AJAX request. This causes each control to be wrapped in an HTML element (controlled by the Render Mode property) and adds the control to an internal collection that is used to track and intercept postback events so that they can be AJAXified instead of allowing them to continue as normal postbacks. Finally, in the third panel, you define for each of the updated controls the `RadAjaxLoadingPanel` for that specific control and the render mode, which can be `Block` (the default) or `Inline`. For block elements, the target controls are surrounded by a `DIV` and rendered in "block" format; for inline elements, the target controls are surrounded by a `SPAN` and rendered in "inline" format.

Regardless of the RadAjaxLoadingPanel instance used and the AJAXified controls, RadAjax always shows the RadAjaxLoadingPanel in a separate HTML DIV tag that will display as a block or inline element.

■ **Note** You can define only one RadAjaxManager instance per page, but you can define multiple RadAjaxLoadingPanel instances and have them configured differently for personalized loading indications. Nevertheless, use multiple RadAjaxLoadingPanel instances only if the contents of the loading panel are different for each. If they all look the same, then only one should be used to minimize the size of the page markup and client script. The reason is that the RadAjaxManager makes a copy of itself and overlays that copy on top of the target controls every time it is triggered (except when its Sticky property is set to true).

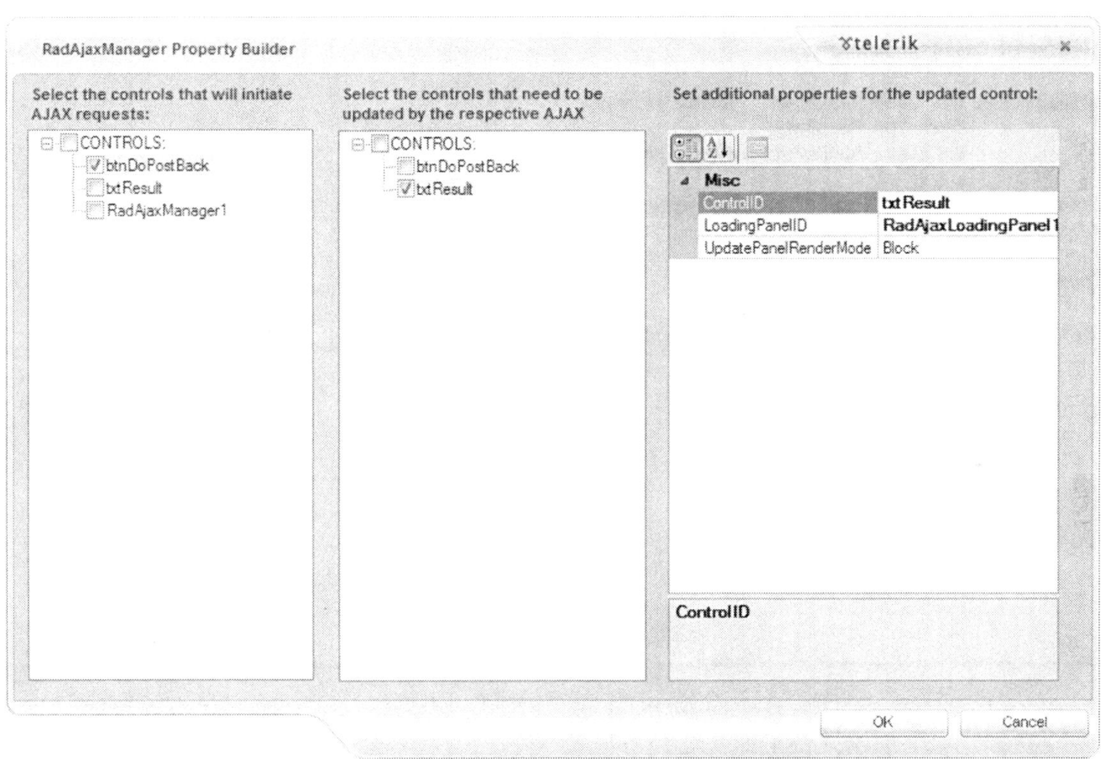

Figure 11-2. *RadAjaxManager Property Builder window*

Listing 11-1 represents what gets generated by the Property Builder window when you AJAXify a button initiating the AJAX request to update a text box (see Figure 11-3).

Listing 11-1. *RadAjaxManager in Action with RadAjaxLoadingPanel*

ASPX Page

```
<telerik:RadAjaxManager ID="RadAjaxManager1" runat="server">
    <AjaxSettings>
        <telerik:AjaxSetting AjaxControlID="btnDoPostBack">
            <UpdatedControls>
                <telerik:AjaxUpdatedControl ControlID="txtResult"
                                LoadingPanelID="RadAjaxLoadingPanel1" />
            </UpdatedControls>
        </telerik:AjaxSetting>
    </AjaxSettings>
</telerik:RadAjaxManager>

<telerik:RadAjaxLoadingPanel ID="RadAjaxLoadingPanel1" runat="server">
</telerik:RadAjaxLoadingPanel>

<asp:Button ID="btnDoPostBack" runat="server"
            Text="Do PostBack"
            OnClick="btnDoPostBack_Click" />

<asp:TextBox ID="txtResult" runat="server">
</asp:TextBox>
```

Code Behind

```
protected void btnDoPostBack_Click(object sender, EventArgs e)
{
    txtResult.Text = "Hooray!";
}
```

Figure 11-3. *RadAjaxManager intercepted the postback initiated by the button, showed the RadAjaxLoadingPanel, and then hid it when the operation was complete.*

Implementing Client-Side Events

`RadAjaxManager` provides two client-side event handlers that, if defined, are called whenever a request starts or a response ends, and they are appropriately called `OnRequestStart` and `OnResponseEnd`.

The argument parameter in both event handlers has access to the control that originates the request via its `get_eventTargetElement()` method. To define it, use the `set_eventTargetElement()` method; if you want the `UniqueID` of the element that raised the request, you can use the `get_eventTarget()` method or, to define it, the `set_eventTarget()` method.

In the OnRequestStart event handler, you can control the request at different levels. First, you can modify the request behavior with the set_enableAjax() method. If called with a Boolean parameter that has the value of false, then the request is performed as a regular postback. Second, you can completely cancel the request using the set_cancel() method by sending a Boolean parameter with the value of true. You can also get the RadAjaxManager configuration settings as an Array with the get_ajaxSettings() method.

In Listing 11-2, the OnRequestStart event handlers is implemented for a RadGrid that has data exporting enabled. This feature of RadGrid relies on a full postback to perform the data export and won't work with AJAX requests. Note how RadAjaxManager identifies the exact object that initiates the request, and only when the export button is clicked does it perform a regular postback. On all other operations, it uses AJAX requests. Note in Figure 11-4 how a normal operation is performed with an AJAX request, and in Figure 11-5 the data export is done with a full postback.

Listing 11-2. *Implementing RadAjaxManager OnRequestStart Event*

ASPX Page

```
<telerik:RadAjaxManager ID="RadAjaxManager1" runat="server">
    <ClientEvents OnRequestStart="onRequestStart" />
    <AjaxSettings>
        <telerik:AjaxSetting AjaxControlID="RadGrid1">
            <UpdatedControls>
                <telerik:AjaxUpdatedControl ControlID="RadGrid1"
                                LoadingPanelID="RadAjaxLoadingPanel1" />
            </UpdatedControls>
        </telerik:AjaxSetting>
    </AjaxSettings>
</telerik:RadAjaxManager>

<telerik:RadAjaxLoadingPanel ID="RadAjaxLoadingPanel1" runat="server">
</telerik:RadAjaxLoadingPanel>

<telerik:RadGrid ID="RadGrid1" runat="server"
                AllowFilteringByColumn="True"
                AutoGenerateColumns="true"
                AllowPaging="True"
                AllowSorting="True"
                DataSourceID="ProductsSqlDataSource"
                GridLines="None" >
    <ExportSettings ExportOnlyData="True"
                    IgnorePaging="True"
                    OpenInNewWindow="True">
        <Csv RowDelimiter="Comma" />
    </ExportSettings>
    <ClientSettings AllowDragToGroup="True">
        <Selecting AllowRowSelect="True" />
        <Scrolling AllowScroll="True" UseStaticHeaders="True" />
    </ClientSettings>
    <MasterTableView AutoGenerateColumns="False"
                    DataKeyNames="ProductID"
                    DataSourceID="ProductsSqlDataSource"
                    CommandItemDisplay="Top">
```

```
    <RowIndicatorColumn>
    <HeaderStyle Width="20px"></HeaderStyle>
    </RowIndicatorColumn>
    <CommandItemSettings ShowExportToPdfButton="true"
                         ShowAddNewRecordButton="False"
                         ShowExportToCsvButton="True"
                         ShowExportToExcelButton="True"
                         ShowExportToWordButton="True"
                         ShowRefreshButton="False" />

    <ExpandCollapseColumn>
    <HeaderStyle Width="20px"></HeaderStyle>
    </ExpandCollapseColumn>
        <Columns>
            <telerik:GridBoundColumn DataField="ProductID"
                                     DataType="System.Int32"
                                     HeaderText="ID"
                                     ReadOnly="True"
                                     SortExpression="ProductID"
                                     UniqueName="ProductID">
                <ItemStyle Width="120px" HorizontalAlign="Center" />
                <HeaderStyle Width="120px" HorizontalAlign="Center" />
            </telerik:GridBoundColumn>
            <telerik:GridBoundColumn DataField="ProductName"
                                     HeaderText="Name"
                                     SortExpression="ProductName"
                                     UniqueName="ProductName">
            </telerik:GridBoundColumn>
        </Columns>
    </MasterTableView>
</telerik:RadGrid>

<asp:SqlDataSource ID="ProductsSqlDataSource" runat="server"
    ConnectionString="<%$ ConnectionStrings:NorthwindConnectionString %>"
    SelectCommand="SELECT ProductID, ProductName FROM [Products]">
</asp:SqlDataSource>

<script type="text/javascript">
     function onRequestStart(sender, eventArgs) {
         // get the control's UniqueID that initiated the
         // request.
         var target = eventArgs.get_eventTarget();

         if (target.indexOf("ExportToExcelButton") >= 0 ||
             target.indexOf("ExportToWordButton") >= 0 ||
             target.indexOf("ExportToPdfButton") >= 0 ||
             target.indexOf("ExportToCsvButton") >= 0) {

             // if any of the export buttons is clicked,
             // perform a regular postback
             eventArgs.set_enableAjax(false);
         }
     }
</script>
```

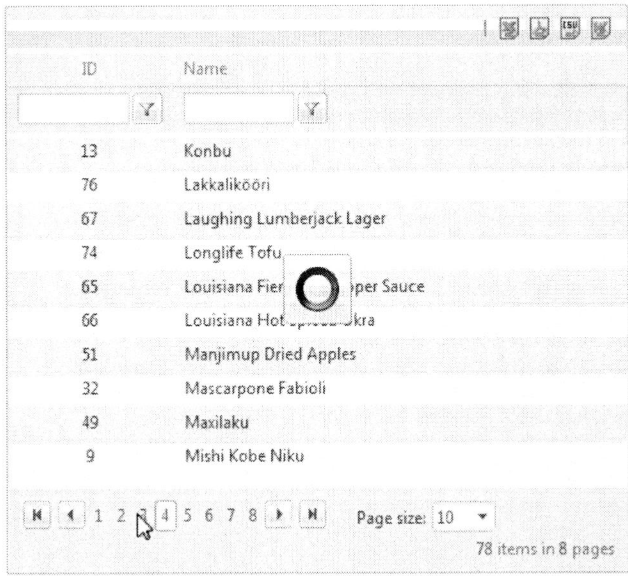

Figure 11-4. *AJAXified RadGrid performing an AJAX request (paging)*

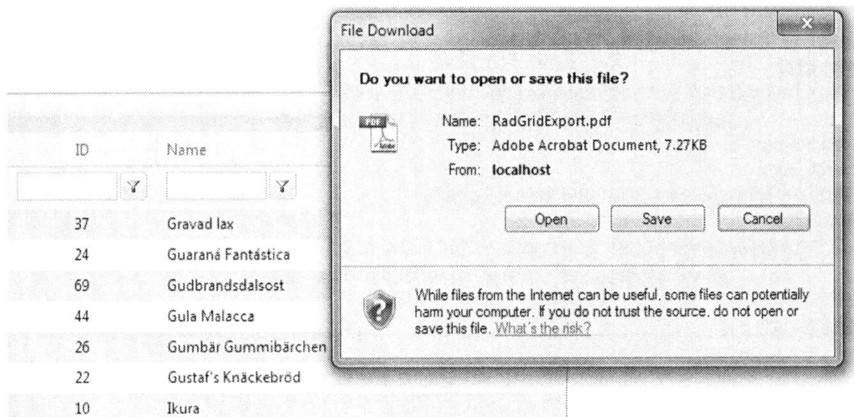

Figure 11-5. *AJAXified RadGrid performing a regular postback (export to PDF)*

■ **Note** It is considered good practice to define the `RadAjaxManager` (or proxy) at the top of the page, just beneath the `ScriptManager` control. The largest benefit of the `RadAjaxManager` is that it provides a single place to configure AJAX settings, and this benefit is best realized when the control is defined in a common and easy-to-find location (at the top of the page).

Working with the Client-Side API

RadAjaxManager supports two client-side methods that are very important when performing AJAX requests:

- ajaxRequest(arguments): Initiates a generic AJAX request and passes the arguments parameter to the manager so it makes it available on the server side for the AjaxRequest server method. In this case, the control initiating the AJAX request is the RadAjaxManager instance; however, an AjaxSetting must be defined with the RadAjaxManager as the initiating control and one or more control in the UpdatedControls collection that it should update; otherwise, the AJAX request will not occur. (The server-side AjaxRequest event handler is fired only when the RadAjaxManager is the initiating control.)
- ajaxRequestWithTarget(eventTarget, eventArgument): Initiates a specific AJAX request as if it were initiated by the control with the UniqueID specified in the eventTarget parameter, and optionally you can add an argument for the event. This method is designed to substitute the __doPostBack() function, so in order to access the argument in server-side code, you need to override the RaisePostBackEvent method, or you can grab the value in the Request.Params collection (Request.Params["__EVENTARGUMENT"]).

Listing 11-3 (which is simple enough) will show you how these two methods work.

Listing 11-3. *RadAjaxManager Client-Side API*

ASPX Page

```
<telerik:RadAjaxManager ID="RadAjaxManager1" runat="server"
                        OnAjaxRequest="RadAjaxManager1_AjaxRequest">
    <AjaxSettings>
        <telerik:AjaxSetting AjaxControlID="RadAjaxManager1">
            <UpdatedControls>
                <telerik:AjaxUpdatedControl ControlID="txtClientAPI"
                                            LoadingPanelID="RadAjaxLoadingPanel1" />
            </UpdatedControls>
        </telerik:AjaxSetting>
        <telerik:AjaxSetting AjaxControlID="btnServerCode">
            <UpdatedControls>
                <telerik:AjaxUpdatedControl ControlID="txtClientAPI"
                                            LoadingPanelID="RadAjaxLoadingPanel1" />
            </UpdatedControls>
        </telerik:AjaxSetting>
    </AjaxSettings>
</telerik:RadAjaxManager>

<telerik:RadAjaxLoadingPanel ID="RadAjaxLoadingPanel1" runat="server">
</telerik:RadAjaxLoadingPanel>

<table>
    <tr>
        <td>
            <asp:Button ID="btnAjaxRequest" runat="server"
                        Text="ajaxRequest"
                        OnClientClick="RunGenericAjaxRequest();return false;" />
        </td>
```

```
        <td>
            <asp:Button ID="btnAjaxRequestWithTarget" runat="server"
                        Text="ajaxRequest"
                        OnClientClick="RunAjaxRequestWithTarget();return false;" />
        </td>
        <td>
            <asp:Button ID="btnServerCode" runat="server"
                        Text="execute Server Code"
                        OnClick="btnServerCode_Click" />
        </td>
    </tr>
    <tr>
        <td colspan="3">
            <asp:TextBox ID="txtClientAPI" runat="server"  Width="200px"></asp:TextBox>
        </td>
    </tr>
</table>

<telerik:RadCodeBlock ID="RadCodeBlock1" runat="server">
<script type="text/javascript">
    function RunGenericAjaxRequest() {
        var ajaxManager = $find("<%=RadAjaxManager1.ClientID %>");
        ajaxManager.ajaxRequest("goAjaxRequest");
    }
    function RunAjaxRequestWithTarget() {
        var ajaxManager = $find("<%=RadAjaxManager1.ClientID %>");
        var targetUniqueID = "<%=btnServerCode.UniqueID %>";
        ajaxManager.ajaxRequestWithTarget(targetUniqueID, '');
    }
</script>
</telerik:RadCodeBlock>

Code Behind

protected void btnServerCode_Click(object sender, EventArgs e)
{
    txtClientAPI.Text = "From ajaxRequestWithTarget()";
}

protected void RadAjaxManager1_AjaxRequest(object sender, AjaxRequestEventArgs e)
{
    if (e.Argument != "goAjaxRequest") return;
    txtClientAPI.Text = "From ajaxRequest()";
}
```

Implementing RadAjaxManager in Web User Controls and Master Pages

When dealing with more complex scenarios such as having master pages and loading web user controls in applications, it becomes necessary to add `RadAjaxManager` instances to them in order to AJAXify the controls in content pages and web user controls. However, RadAjax allows for only one instance of

RadAjaxManager in each page, so this is why Telerik introduced the RadAjaxManagerProxy object specifically designed for this scenario.

The idea is to have the RadAjaxManager instance in the master page and create this proxy object in content pages and web user controls. You define a structured mechanism to collect the AJAXified settings for controls in each content page and web user control and pass them to the RadAjaxManager instance to build the full set of settings at runtime.

With RadAjaxManagerProxy, you have the design-time support for AJAXifying controls in master pages or web user controls, but it doesn't provide any client-side object or events. To access these features, you must use the RadAjaxManager object in the master page. You can obtain a reference to this object at any time by calling the static method RadAjaxManager.GetCurrent(Page), passing in a reference to the current page.

Listing 11-4 shows you how this works with a web user control in a content page. The controls get AJAXified with the help of RadAjaxManagerProxy.

Listing 11-4. *RadAjaxManager Client-Side API*

```
ASPX Page

<%@ Register Src="~/AjaxWebUserControl.ascx" TagPrefix="uc1" TagName="AjaxUserControl" %>

...

<uc1:AjaxUserControl ID="UC1" runat="server" />

<telerik:RadAjaxManager ID="RadAjaxManager1" runat="server"
                        DefaultLoadingPanelID="RadAjaxLoadingPanel1">
</telerik:RadAjaxManager>
<telerik:RadAjaxLoadingPanel ID="RadAjaxLoadingPanel1" runat="server">
</telerik:RadAjaxLoadingPanel>


AjaxWebUserControl.ascx

<%@ Control Language="C#"
            AutoEventWireup="true"
            CodeBehind="AjaxWebUserControl.ascx.cs"
            Inherits="WebApplication1.AjaxWebUserControl" %>

<telerik:RadAjaxManagerProxy ID="RadAjaxManagerProxy1" runat="server">
    <AjaxSettings>
        <telerik:AjaxSetting AjaxControlID="btnDoPostBack">
            <UpdatedControls>
                <telerik:AjaxUpdatedControl ControlID="txtResult" />
            </UpdatedControls>
        </telerik:AjaxSetting>
    </AjaxSettings>
</telerik:RadAjaxManagerProxy>

<asp:Button ID="btnDoPostBack" runat="server"
            Text="Do PostBack"
            OnClick="btnDoPostBack_Click" />
<asp:TextBox ID="txtResult" runat="server">
</asp:TextBox>
```

```
AjaxWebUserControl.ascx.cs

using System;
using System.Web.UI;

namespace WebApplication1
{
    public partial class AjaxWebUserControl : UserControl
    {
        protected void Page_Load(object sender, EventArgs e)
        {
            if (Page.IsPostBack) return;
        }

        protected void btnDoPostBack_Click(object sender, EventArgs e)
        {
            txtResult.Text = "Go RadAjax!";
        }
    }
}
```

RadAjaxPanel

The other main control in RadAjax is the `RadAjaxPanel`. It provides the easiest AJAXification for the pages in your application. It works like an ASP.NET `UpdatePanel`, but there are no `Triggers` or `UpdateMode` property. Simply add a `RadAjaxPanel` to the page, and then add to it all the controls that should be updated as part of an AJAX request.

You have to carefully consider the controls you want in `RadAjaxPanel` because *all* the controls inside it will be updated with the AJAX update every time one of them initiates the request. If you have too many controls or all the controls in the page are inside `RadAjaxPanel`, you may actually reduce the performance of your page.

The smart tag for design-time support in `RadAjaxPanel` has all the features found in `RadAjaxManager` except for the Property Builder window. Also, `RadAjaxPanel` supports the `OnRequestStart` and `OnResponseEnd` client-side event handlers and the `OnAjaxRequest` server-side event.

Working with RadAjaxPanel

Listing 11-5 shows how `RadAjaxPanel` works when having a `RadGrid` in the page performing some of its operations such as paging and sorting. Note that there is no `RadAjaxManager` or ASP.NET `UpdatePanel` controls in the implementation. Also, note how you didn't have to code anything for page updates to be performed asynchronously instead of with a full-page postback. Figure 11-6 illustrates the example.

Listing 11-5. *RadAjaxPanel in Action*

ASPX Page

```
<telerik:RadAjaxPanel ID="RadAjaxPanel1" runat="server"
                    LoadingPanelID="RadAjaxLoadingPanel1">
    <telerik:RadGrid ID="RadGrid1" runat="server"
                    AllowFilteringByColumn="True"
                    AutoGenerateColumns="true"
                    AllowPaging="True"
                    AllowSorting="True"
                    DataSourceID="ProductsSqlDataSource"
                    GridLines="None"
                    Width="450px" Height="400px">
        <ClientSettings>
            <Selecting AllowRowSelect="True" />
            <Scrolling AllowScroll="True" UseStaticHeaders="True" />
        </ClientSettings>
        <MasterTableView AutoGenerateColumns="False"
                        DataKeyNames="ProductID"
                        DataSourceID="ProductsSqlDataSource">
        <RowIndicatorColumn>
        <HeaderStyle Width="20px"></HeaderStyle>
        </RowIndicatorColumn>
        <ExpandCollapseColumn>
        <HeaderStyle Width="20px"></HeaderStyle>
        </ExpandCollapseColumn>

            <Columns>
                <telerik:GridBoundColumn DataField="ProductID"
                                        DataType="System.Int32"
                                        HeaderText="ID"
                                        ReadOnly="True"
                                        SortExpression="ProductID"
                                        UniqueName="ProductID">
                    <ItemStyle Width="120px" HorizontalAlign="Center" />
                    <HeaderStyle Width="120px" HorizontalAlign="Center" />
                </telerik:GridBoundColumn>
                <telerik:GridBoundColumn DataField="ProductName"
                                        HeaderText="Name"
                                        SortExpression="ProductName"
                                        UniqueName="ProductName">
                </telerik:GridBoundColumn>

            </Columns>

        </MasterTableView>
    </telerik:RadGrid>
```

```
    <asp:SqlDataSource ID="ProductsSqlDataSource" runat="server"
        ConnectionString="<%$ ConnectionStrings:NorthwindConnectionString %>"
        SelectCommand="SELECT ProductID, ProductName FROM [Products]">
    </asp:SqlDataSource>
</telerik:RadAjaxPanel>
<telerik:RadAjaxLoadingPanel ID="RadAjaxLoadingPanel1" Runat="server">
</telerik:RadAjaxLoadingPanel>
```

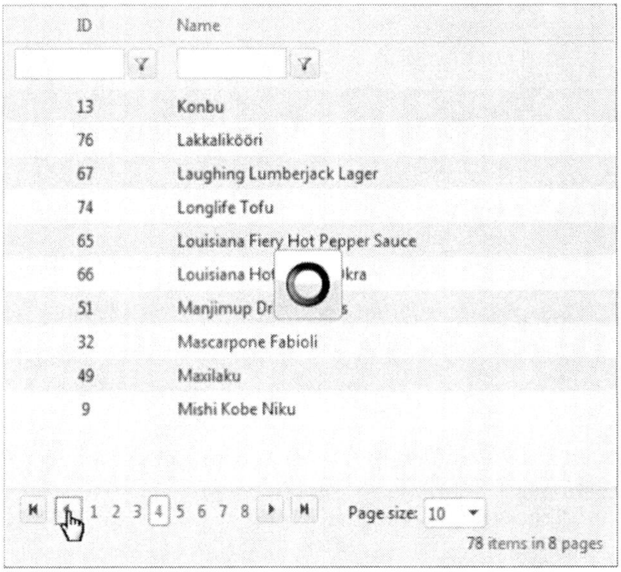

Figure 11-6. *A RadGrid was placed inside a RadAjaxPanel, and it performs an AJAX request for its operations.*

■ **Note** `RadAjaxPanel` is not designed to handle scenarios where controls outside of it become the initiators of the AJAX update. For such scenarios, use `RadAjaxManager`.

Forcing an AJAX Update

Now that you have been warned about not to do this, you can use this little trick to force `RadAjaxPanel` to perform an AJAX update initiated by a control outside of it. Note that what I said was that `RadAjaxPanel` is not designed for this; I didn't say it can't be done.

What you do is override the `RaisePostBackEvent` method (as shown in Listing 11-6) to handle the request made via the `ajaxRequest()` or `ajaxRequestWithTarget()` method call; then check for the argument sent and perform the appropriate action. Figure 11-7 shows the end result.

Listing 11-6. *Forcing an AJAX Update*

ASPX Page

```
<asp:Button ID="btnForceAJAX" runat="server"
        Text="Force an AJAX Update"
        OnClientClick="DoForceAJAXUpdate();return false;" />

<telerik:RadAjaxPanel ID="RadAjaxPanel2" runat="server"
                    LoadingPanelID="RadAjaxLoadingPanel1">

    <telerik:RadTextBox ID="txtTest" runat="server"
                        Label="Now is:">
    </telerik:RadTextBox>
</telerik:RadAjaxPanel>

<telerik:RadCodeBlock ID="RadCodeBlock1" runat="server">
<script type="text/javascript">
        function DoForceAJAXUpdate() {
                $find("<%=RadAjaxPanel2.ClientID %>")
                        .ajaxRequestWithTarget("<%=RadAjaxPanel2.UniqueID %>", "ForceAJAXUpdate");
    }
</script>
</telerik:RadCodeBlock>
```

Code Behind

```
protected override void RaisePostBackEvent(IPostBackEventHandler sourceControl,
                                           string eventArgument)
{
    base.RaisePostBackEvent(sourceControl, eventArgument);
    if (eventArgument == "ForceAJAXUpdate")
    {
        txtTest.Text = DateTime.Now.ToString();
    }
}
```

Force an AJAX Update

Now is: 3/4/2010 10:45:57 PM

Figure 11-7. *Note how the button initiated the AJAX update even though it is outside the RadAjaxPanel.*

RadAjaxLoadingPanel

This control was created to provide a visual indicator during AJAX requests. It has a smart tag window for design-time support in which you can set the four main properties (shown in Figure 11-8):

- *Is sticky*: This property defines where the loading panel will appear. By default this property is set to `false`, meaning it will appear over the updated control. When set to `true`, it will appear where it was defined in the page. Another important distinction is that the `RadAjaxLoadingPanel` HTML element is cloned and placed on top of the updated control when it is triggered if this property is set to `false`. When this property is set to `true`, the element is not cloned and is instead displayed at the location it is defined in the page.
- *Initial delay time*: Defines the time in milliseconds that will take the loading panel to appear. If the request finishes before this time, then the loading panel will not be shown.
- *Min display time*: Defines the minimum time in milliseconds that the loading panel will be shown. If the request finished before this time, then the loading panel will remain visible until this time has elapsed.
- *Transparency*: This property defines how transparent the loading panel will be. A value of 0 means the panel is completely visible, and a value of 100 means it is invisible. Increasing transparency makes the controls beneath the loading panel more visible underneath.

`RadAjaxLoadingPanel` supports animation for when it shows and hides. This is handled by a simple extender that uses jQuery.

Out of the box, `RadAjaxLoadingPanel` supports fade-in and fade-out animations that are enabled using the property `AnimationDuration`. Here you set the time in milliseconds it will take the fade to complete. However, for customized animations, you can use the `OnClientShowing` and `OnClientHiding` client events.

When handling these events, you need to cancel the default show/hide by calling the `set_cancelNativeDisplay()` method of the `eventArgs` argument and passing to it a value of `true`. Then you have to use the `eventArgs.get_updatedElement()` method to obtain the reference of the updated element (a DOM reference) so you can properly show/hide the loading panel.

Figure 11-8. *Main properties of RadAjaxLoadingPanel shown in its smart tag window*

Configuring RadAjaxLoadingPanel Properties

Listing 11-7 is designed to show you how to set up some of the properties and creates a custom animation for a `RadAjaxLoadingPanel` instance (see Figure 11-9).

Listing 11-7. *Configuring RadAjaxLoadingPanel Properties*

ASPX Page

```
<table>
    <tr>
        <td>Enable 30% Transparency</td>
        <td>
            <asp:CheckBox ID="chkTransparency" runat="server"
                          AutoPostBack="true"
                          OnCheckedChanged="chkTransparency_CheckedChanged" />
        </td>
    </tr>
    <tr>
        <td>Enable Custom Animation</td>
        <td>
            <asp:CheckBox ID="chkAnimation" runat="server"
                          AutoPostBack="true"
                          OnCheckedChanged="chkAnimation_CheckedChanged" />
        </td>
    </tr>
    <tr>
        <td>Change Skin</td>
        <td>
            <telerik:RadComboBox ID="rcbSkin" runat="server"
                                 AutoPostBack="true"

OnSelectedIndexChanged="rcbSkin_SelectedIndexChanged">
                <Items>
                    <telerik:RadComboBoxItem Text="Default" />
                    <telerik:RadComboBoxItem Text="Black" />
                    <telerik:RadComboBoxItem Text="Forest" />
                    <telerik:RadComboBoxItem Text="Hay" />
                    <telerik:RadComboBoxItem Text="Office2007" />
                    <telerik:RadComboBoxItem Text="Outlook" />
                    <telerik:RadComboBoxItem Text="Simple" />
                    <telerik:RadComboBoxItem Text="Sitefinity" />
                    <telerik:RadComboBoxItem Text="Sunset" />
                    <telerik:RadComboBoxItem Text="Telerik" />
                    <telerik:RadComboBoxItem Text="Vista" />
                    <telerik:RadComboBoxItem Text="Web20" />
                    <telerik:RadComboBoxItem Text="WebBlue" />
                    <telerik:RadComboBoxItem Text="Windows7" />
                </Items>
            </telerik:RadComboBox>
        </td>
    </tr>
</table>
<telerik:RadAjaxManager ID="RadAjaxManager1" runat="server">
    <AjaxSettings>
        <telerik:AjaxSetting AjaxControlID="chkTransparency">
            <UpdatedControls>
                <telerik:AjaxUpdatedControl ControlID="RadAjaxLoadingPanel1" />
            </UpdatedControls>
```

```
        </telerik:AjaxSetting>
        <telerik:AjaxSetting AjaxControlID="Button1">
            <UpdatedControls>
                <telerik:AjaxUpdatedControl ControlID="Panel1"
                                        LoadingPanelID="RadAjaxLoadingPanel1" />
            </UpdatedControls>
        </telerik:AjaxSetting>
    </AjaxSettings>
</telerik:RadAjaxManager>

<telerik:RadAjaxLoadingPanel ID="RadAjaxLoadingPanel1" runat="server">
</telerik:RadAjaxLoadingPanel>

<asp:Button ID="Button1" runat="server"
                         Text="Show RadAjaxLoadingPanel"
                         OnClick="Button1_Click" />
<asp:Panel id="Panel1" runat="server" style="width:300px; height: 200px">
</asp:Panel>

<telerik:RadCodeBlock ID="RadCodeBlock2" runat="server">
<script type="text/javascript">
    function CustomShowing(sender, args) {
        args.set_cancelNativeDisplay(true);
        $telerik.$(args.get_loadingElement()).slideToggle("slow");
    }

    function CustomHiding(sender, args) {
        args.set_cancelNativeDisplay(true);
        $telerik.$(args.get_loadingElement()).slideToggle("slow");
    }
</script>
</telerik:RadCodeBlock>
```

Code Behind

```
protected void rcbSkin_SelectedIndexChanged(object o, ➥
RadComboBoxSelectedIndexChangedEventArgs e)
{
    RadAjaxLoadingPanel1.Skin = e.Text;
}

protected void chkTransparency_CheckedChanged(object sender, EventArgs e)
{
    RadAjaxLoadingPanel1.Transparency = chkTransparency.Checked ? 30 : 0;
}
```

```
protected void Button1_Click(object sender, EventArgs e)
{
    System.Threading.Thread.Sleep(2000);
}

protected void chkAnimation_CheckedChanged(object sender, EventArgs e)
{
    if (chkAnimation.Checked)
    {
        RadAjaxLoadingPanel1.OnClientShowing = "CustomShowing";
        RadAjaxLoadingPanel1.OnClientHiding = "CustomtHiding";
    }
    else
    {
        RadAjaxLoadingPanel1.OnClientShowing = "";
        RadAjaxLoadingPanel1.OnClientHiding = "";
    }
}
```

Enable 30% Transparency

Enable Custom Animation

Change Skin Default

Show RadAjaxLoadingPanel

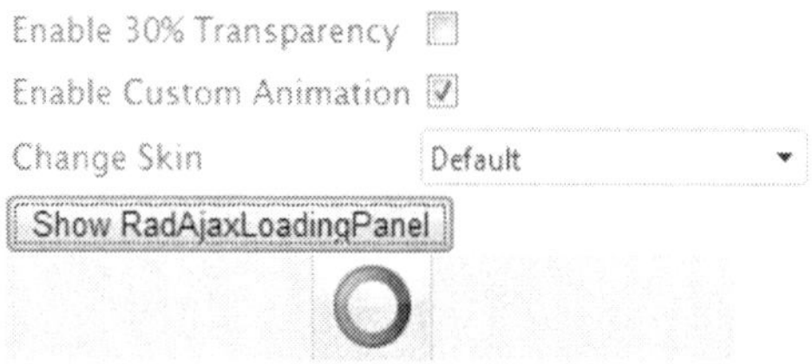

Figure 11-9. *Note how the RadAjaxLoadingPanel is partially showing because of the animation that is in progress.*

Implementing Explicit Show/Hide

Have you ever needed to display a loading indicator for a long-running operation? How many times have you built the same functionality? Or copied it from application to application? Well, with RadAjaxLoadingPanel, you can have an easy-to-use, good-looking loading indicator that just happens to have the ability to be shown and hidden at will (your will actually).

You just need to call the show() and hide() methods as described in Listing 11-8 from the RadAjaxLoadingPanel client object and pass to it the client ID of the target element over which the loading panel will appear. Figure 11-10 illustrates the example.

Listing 11-8. *Explicit Show/Hide of RadAjaxLoadingPanel*

ASPX Page

```
<telerik:RadAjaxLoadingPanel ID="RadAjaxLoadingPanel2" runat="server">
</telerik:RadAjaxLoadingPanel>

<div id="showLoadingPanel" style="width:300px; height: 200px">
</div>
```

```
<asp:Button ID="btnShow" runat="server"
                        Text="Show RadAjaxLoadingPanel"
                        OnClientClick="ExplicitShow();return false;" />
<asp:Button ID="btnHide" runat="server"
                        Text="Hide RadAjaxLoadingPanel"
                        OnClientClick="ExplicitHide();return false;" />
<telerik:RadCodeBlock ID="RadCodeBlock1" runat="server">
<script type="text/javascript">
    function ExplicitShow() {
        var loadingPanel = $find("<%= RadAjaxLoadingPanel2.ClientID%>");
        var targetObject = "showLoadingPanel";
        loadingPanel.show(targetObject);
    }
    function ExplicitHide() {
        var loadingPanel = $find("<%= RadAjaxLoadingPanel2.ClientID%>");
        var targetObject = "showLoadingPanel";
        loadingPanel.hide(targetObject);
    }
</script>
</telerik:RadCodeBlock>
```

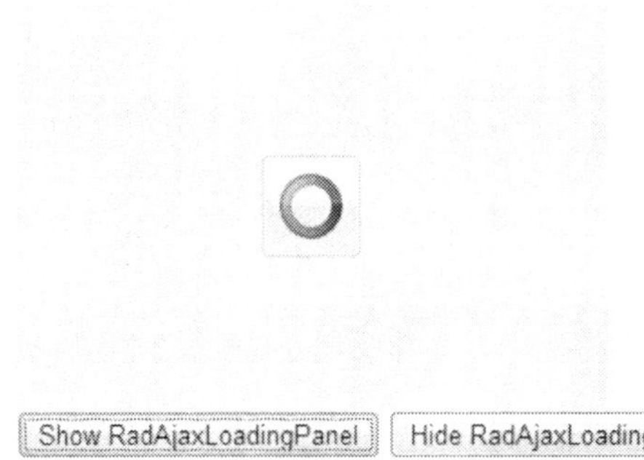

Figure 11-10. *RadAjaxLoadingPanel was explicitly shown using the show() method.*

RadCodeBlock and RadScriptBlock

In RadAjax are RadCodeBlock and RadScriptBlock, which are objects created to close the gap of interoperability between server and client scripts.

Figure 11-11 shows a typical error found when you have server code blocks inside your client-side scripts. RadCodeBlock prevents this error by isolating the code blocks, executing them, and rendering the final results along with the client scripts.

Server Error in '/' Application.

The Controls collection cannot be modified because the control contains code blocks (i.e. <% ... %>).

Figure 11-11. *Error when having server code blocks in client-side scripts*

RadScriptBlock is used to wrap client-side scripts that are inside updating areas in your web form such as a RadAjaxPanel. They are executed after the AJAX request. Listing 11-9 is an extract of Listing 11-8 to show how these controls work.

Listing 11-9. *Implementing RadCodeBlock*

```
ASPX Page

<telerik:RadCodeBlock ID="RadCodeBlock1" runat="server">
<script type="text/javascript">
    function ExplicitShow() {
        var loadingPanel = $find("<%= RadAjaxLoadingPanel2.ClientID%>");
        var targetObject = "showLoadingPanel";
        loadingPanel.show(targetObject);
    }
    function ExplicitHide() {
        var loadingPanel = $find("<%= RadAjaxLoadingPanel2.ClientID%>");
        var targetObject = "showLoadingPanel";
        loadingPanel.hide(targetObject);
    }
</script>
</telerik:RadCodeBlock>


// When the page is rendered, the RadCodeBlock executing will produce a
// script block similar to the following as it will evaluate all code blocks
// defined

<script type="text/javascript">
    function ExplicitShow() {
        var loadingPanel = $find("ctl00_ContentPlaceHolder1_RadAjaxLoadingPanel2");
        var targetObject = "showLoadingPanel";
        loadingPanel.show(targetObject);
    }
    function ExplicitHide() {
        var loadingPanel = $find("ctl00_ContentPlaceHolder1_RadAjaxLoadingPanel2");
        var targetObject = "showLoadingPanel";
        loadingPanel.hide(targetObject);
    }
</script>
```

RadXmlHttpPanel

The final control in this category is not actually part of RadAjax but a complementary control that works by updating its content through a callback or a web method call to a web service. The whole idea behind the design of this control is to use something that doesn't require the passing of state (in view state) between server and client and avoids all or part of the page life cycle.

In this sense, RadXmlHttpPanel is more lightweight and doesn't generate the level of overhead for the update process that you get with RadAjaxPanel and RadAjaxManager. Going further, you can avoid having to handle and process complex page events. If you use a web service to update the RadXmlHttpPanel content, you can avoid the page life cycle altogether.

So, that being said, RadXmlHttpPanel is not designed to directly replace the RadAjax controls. Sometimes you need the full page life cycle, and sometimes don't. Then the question is, "When should I use RadXmlHttpPanel vs. a RadAjax control?" The answer is simpler than you might expect. If your panel content includes controls that must respond to server-side events or track state between requests, then use RadAjaxPanel or RadAjaxManager. If you are just presenting data and operations results and do not need to keep track of state across requests, then use RadXmlHttpPanel.

■ **Note** You can combine both controls by having a RadAjaxPanel around a RadXmlHttpPanel and having the inner RadXmlHttpPanel execute callbacks to load data and having the RadAjaxPanel perform server-side event handlers. You can find a sample scenario of doing this on the documentation site for RadXmlHttpPanel; see www.telerik.com/help/aspnet-ajax/radxmlhttppanel-vs-radajaxpanel.html.

Implementing RadXmlHttpPanel with Callback

Let's see now how RadXmlHttpPanel works with the callback mechanism (see Listing 11-10). You need to wire up the OnServiceRequest event with an event handler that will perform the necessary logic to update the panel's content. The panel will execute a callback by executing its client-side method set_value() and passing as a parameter the argument that will be used to perform the action. The OnServiceRequest event handler has a parameter of type RadXmlHttpPanelEventArgs that will have access to the argument value via the Value property, which is of type String. With the callback mechanism, only a small part of the page is processed. Client state is not updated, and no changes in state are sent back to the client (see Figure 11-12).

Listing 11-10. *Implementing RadXmlHttpPanel with Callback*

ASPX Page

```
<telerik:RadComboBox ID="rcbEmployee" runat="server"
                     OnClientSelectedIndexChanged="LoadEmployee"
                     AppendDataBoundItems="true">
    <Items>
        <telerik:RadComboBoxItem Text="-- Select Employee --" Value="-1" />
    </Items>
</telerik:RadComboBox>
<telerik:RadXmlHttpPanel ID="RadXmlHttpPanel1" runat="server"
                         ClientIDMode="Static"
                         OnServiceRequest="RadXmlHttpPanel1_ServiceRequest">

    <asp:Panel ID="panelData" runat="server" Visible="false">
        <fieldset>
        <legend>Employee Details</legend>
        <table>
            <tr>
                <td>
                    <asp:Image ID="employeePic" runat="server"
                               width="100px">
                    </asp:Image>
                    <br />
                </td>
```

```
                <td>
                    <asp:Label ID="lblEmployeeName" runat="server"
                               Font-Bold="true" Font-Size="14px">
                    </asp:Label>
                    <br />
                    <asp:Label ID="lblTitle" runat="server">
                    </asp:Label>
                    <hr />
                    <asp:Label ID="lblNotes" runat="server">
                    </asp:Label>
                </td>
            </tr>
        </table>
    </fieldset>
    </asp:Panel>
</telerik:RadXmlHttpPanel>
<script type="text/javascript">
    function LoadEmployee(sender, eventArgs) {
        var item = eventArgs.get_item();
        var value = item.get_value();
        var panel = $find("RadXmlHttpPanel1");

        panel.set_value(value);
    }
</script>

Code Behind

protected void Page_Load(object sender, EventArgs e)
{
    if (Page.IsPostBack || Page.IsCallback) return;
    Initialize();
}

private void Initialize()
{
    rcbEmployee.DataSource = GetEmployeeSimpleDataTable();
    rcbEmployee.DataTextField = "Name";
    rcbEmployee.DataValueField = "EmployeeID";
    rcbEmployee.DataBind();
}

private DataTable GetEmployeeSimpleDataTable()
{
    string ConnString = WebConfigurationManager
                                .ConnectionStrings["NorthwindConnectionString"]
                                .ConnectionString;
    string query = "SELECT [EmployeeID], [FirstName] + ' ' + [LastName] As [Name]";
    query += "         FROM [Employees]";
    DataTable myDataTable = new DataTable();
    using (SqlConnection conn = new SqlConnection(ConnString))
    {
        using (SqlDataAdapter adapter = new SqlDataAdapter())
        {
```

```
            try
            {
                adapter.SelectCommand = new SqlCommand(query, conn);
                conn.Open();
                adapter.Fill(myDataTable);
            }
            finally
            {
                conn.Close();
            }
        }
    }
    return myDataTable;
}

private DataTable GetEmployeeDataTable(string id)
{
    string ConnString = WebConfigurationManager
                            .ConnectionStrings["NorthwindConnectionString"]
                            .ConnectionString;
    string query = "SELECT [EmployeeID], [FirstName] + ' ' + [LastName] As [Name], ";
    query += "              [Title], [Notes]";
    query += "        FROM [Employees]";
    query += "       WHERE [EmployeeID] = @id";
    DataTable myDataTable = new DataTable();
    using (SqlConnection conn = new SqlConnection(ConnString))
    {
        using (SqlDataAdapter adapter = new SqlDataAdapter())
        {
            try
            {
                var cmd = new SqlCommand(query, conn);
                var param = new SqlParameter("id", id);
                cmd.Parameters.Add(param);
                adapter.SelectCommand = cmd;
                conn.Open();
                adapter.Fill(myDataTable);
            }
            finally
            {
                conn.Close();
            }
        }
    }
    return myDataTable;
}


protected void RadXmlHttpPanel1_ServiceRequest(object sender, RadXmlHttpPanelEventArgs e)
{
    LoadEmployeeData(e.Value);
}
```

```
private void LoadEmployeeData(string strId)
{
    var employeeDT = GetEmployeeDataTable(strId);
    if (employeeDT.Rows.Count == 0)
    {
        panelData.Visible = false;
        employeePic.ImageUrl = string.Empty;
        lblEmployeeName.Text = string.Empty;
        lblTitle.Text = string.Empty;
        lblNotes.Text = string.Empty;
    }
    else
    {
        panelData.Visible = true;
        string photo = string.Format("~/Images/employees/{0}.jpg", strId);
        employeePic.ImageUrl = Page.ResolveUrl(photo);
        lblEmployeeName.Text = employeeDT.Rows[0]["Name"].ToString();
        lblTitle.Text = employeeDT.Rows[0]["Title"].ToString();
        lblNotes.Text = employeeDT.Rows[0]["Notes"].ToString();
    }
}
```

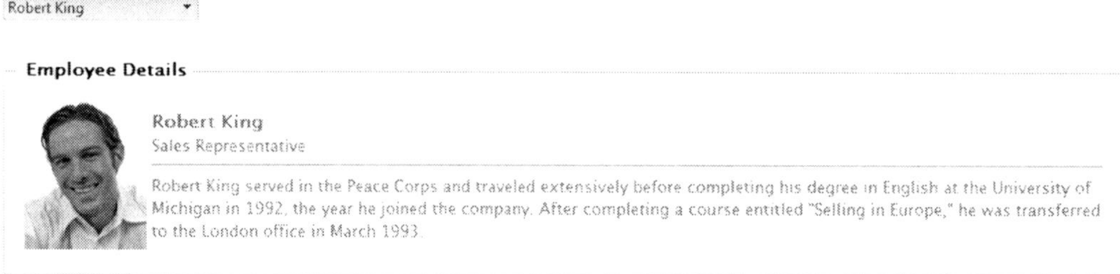

Figure 11-12. *When an employee is selected from the RadComboBox, a callback will be made, and the content of RadXmlHttpPanel will be updated.*

Implementing RadXmlHttpPanel with WebService

When working with web services, there are two main differences from working with callbacks:

- The first one is that the web method will receive an object parameter that is an instance of, and should be cast to, an `IDictionary<string, string>` object. In the object you can obtain a reference to the value being passed from the client.
- The content of the panel is generated by the web method. This means that the method return value is of type `string` and will fill the entire HTML content unless you catch it with the `OnClientRequestEnding` event, calling the `get_content()` method of the `arguments` parameter, and then process it in client-side code.

Listing 11-11 shows the same functionality I showed before for a callback but implemented for a web service that generates the HTML content for the `RadXmlHttpPanel`.

Listing 11-11. *RadXmlHttpPanel with Web Service*

ASPX Page

```
<telerik:RadComboBox ID="rcbEmployee1" runat="server"
                     OnClientSelectedIndexChanged="LoadEmployee1"
                     AppendDataBoundItems="true">
    <Items>
        <telerik:RadComboBoxItem Text="-- Select Employee --" Value="-1" />
    </Items>
</telerik:RadComboBox>
<telerik:RadXmlHttpPanel ID="RadXmlHttpPanel2" runat="server"
                         ClientIDMode="Static"
                         WebMethodPath="RadXmlHttpPanel_Employee.asmx"
                         WebMethodName="LoadEmployeeData"
                         RegisterWithScriptManager="true">
</telerik:RadXmlHttpPanel>
<script type="text/javascript">
    function LoadEmployee1(sender, eventArgs) {
        var item = eventArgs.get_item();
        var value = item.get_value();
        var panel = $find("RadXmlHttpPanel2");

        panel.set_value(value);
    }
</script>
```

Code Behind

```
protected void Page_Load(object sender, EventArgs e)
{
    if (Page.IsPostBack || Page.IsCallback) return;
    Initialize();
}

private void Initialize()
{
    rcbEmployee1.DataSource = GetEmployeeSimpleDataTable();
    rcbEmployee1.DataTextField = "Name";
    rcbEmployee1.DataValueField = "EmployeeID";
    rcbEmployee1.DataBind();
}
```

RadXmlHttpPanel_Employee.asmx.cs

```
namespace WebApplication1
{
    /// <summary>
    /// Summary description for RadXmlHttpPanel_Employee
    /// </summary>
    [WebService(Namespace = "http://tempuri.org/")]
    [WebServiceBinding(ConformsTo = WsiProfiles.BasicProfile1_1)]
    [System.ComponentModel.ToolboxItem(false)]
    [ScriptService]
    public class RadXmlHttpPanel_Employee : WebService
    {

        [WebMethod]
        public string LoadEmployeeData(object context)
        {
            IDictionary<string, object> contextDictionary =
                                        (IDictionary<string, object>)context;
            string id = ((string)contextDictionary["Value"]);
            var employeeDT = GetEmployeeDataTable(id);
            string photo = string.Format("Images/employees/{0}.jpg", id);
            string Img = string.Format("<img src=\"{0}\" width=\"100px\">", photo);
            string name = employeeDT.Rows[0]["Name"].ToString();
            string nameDiv =
                  string.Format("<div style=\"font-weight:bold;font-size:14px\">{0}</div>",
                              name);
            string title = employeeDT.Rows[0]["Title"].ToString();
            string titleDiv = string.Format("<div>{0}</div>", title);
            string notes = employeeDT.Rows[0]["Notes"].ToString();
            string notesDiv = string.Format("<div>{0}</div>", notes);

            StringBuilder sb = new StringBuilder();
            sb.AppendLine("<fieldset>");
            sb.AppendLine(" <legend>Employee Details</legend>");
            sb.AppendLine("<table>");
            sb.AppendLine("    <tr>");
            sb.AppendLine("<td>");
            sb.AppendLine(Img);
            sb.AppendLine("<br />");
            sb.AppendLine("</td>");
            sb.AppendLine("<td>");
            sb.AppendLine(nameDiv);
            sb.AppendLine("<br />");
            sb.AppendLine(titleDiv);
            sb.AppendLine("<hr />");
            sb.AppendLine(notesDiv);
            sb.AppendLine("</td>");
            sb.AppendLine("</tr>");
            sb.AppendLine("</table>");
            sb.AppendLine("</fieldset>");

            return sb.ToString();
        }
```

```
        private DataTable GetEmployeeDataTable(string id)
        {
            string ConnString = WebConfigurationManager
                                .ConnectionStrings["NorthwindConnectionString"]
                                .ConnectionString;
            string query = "SELECT [EmployeeID], [FirstName] + ' ' + [LastName] As [Name],";
            query += "               [Title], [Notes]";
            query += "          FROM [Employees]";
            query += "         WHERE [EmployeeID] = @id";
            DataTable myDataTable = new DataTable();
            using (SqlConnection conn = new SqlConnection(ConnString))
            {
                using (SqlDataAdapter adapter = new SqlDataAdapter())
                {
                    try
                    {
                        var cmd = new SqlCommand(query, conn);
                        var param = new SqlParameter("id", id);
                        cmd.Parameters.Add(param);
                        adapter.SelectCommand = cmd;
                        conn.Open();
                        adapter.Fill(myDataTable);
                    }
                    finally
                    {
                        conn.Close();
                    }
                }
            }
            return myDataTable;
        }
    }
}
```

Summary

RadAjax is the implementation of the AJAX framework based on two main controls, RadAjaxManager and RadAjaxPanel.

RadAjaxManager works by transforming regular postbacks into AJAX requests that define the controls in the page that will be updated asynchronously and the controls that will initiate the request.

RadAjaxManagerProxy is a control created to overcome the limitation of having only one RadAjaxManager in the page. When you have master/content pages, you define a RadAjaxManager instance in the master page, and in the content pages you have RadAjaxManagerProxy instances that work all in conjunction to create a unified collection of AJAXified areas on the page with a single RadAjaxManager coordinating their interactions. In another scenario, you can have a RadAjaxManager in a content page and RadAjaxManagerProxy in web user controls.

`RadAjaxPanel` works like the regular ASP.NET `UpdatePanel` in the sense that it surrounds a markup area in the page, and all the controls defined within the RadAjaxPanel are updated in each AJAX request. `RadAjaxLoadingPanel` provides visual loading indicators to provide feedback about the current request.

`RadXmlHttpPanel` is a control that's not part of RadAjax, but it complements it by adding a mechanism for loading items asynchronously while avoiding all or part of the page life cycle. It offers a lightweight alternative to the RadAjax controls at the cost of having the ability to maintain state across requests.

CHAPTER 12

Telerik Extensions for ASP.NET MVC

It's time now to examine the Telerik Extensions for ASP.NET MVC. This is a framework that provides an extension to Microsoft's ASP.NET MVC framework to seamlessly integrate with your application in order to create rich user interfaces.

The framework relies heavily upon jQuery, and the controls are extensions of the `HtmlHelper` object for UI render. It supports natively the view engine from Microsoft, but it also can work with other view engines such as Spark or NHaml.

It also has a complete asset management system (JavaScript and CSS), which allows you to compress the scripts and CSS files using GZIP compression and reduce web calls by combining resources in a single request and CDN support.

Telerik Extensions currently has eight controls that you can use in your applications, with additional controls planned for future releases. They are `Calendar`, `DatePicker`, `PanelBar`, `Menu`, `TabStrip`, `NumericTextBox`, `TreeView`, and `Grid`.

It is recommended that you have some experience with jQuery and ASP.NET MVC before diving into this chapter because it will improve your learning experience.

Note Telerik Extensions for ASP.NET MVC has a very special licensing model. Basically, Telerik Extensions for ASP.NET MVC is a free and open source product, but there are also commercial licenses. Please check the latest information regarding licensing at `www.telerik.com/help/aspnet-mvc/licensing.html`.

Quick Recap on Configuration

Chapter 2 has a complete guide for installing and configuring Telerik Extensions for ASP.NET MVC, but the following is a quick, step-by-step configuration guide:

1. In your ASP.NET MVC application, add a reference to the `Telerik.Web.Mvc.dll` file. This file is located in the `Binaries` folder of the Telerik Extensions for ASP.NET MVC installation directory. You will find two folders inside: one called `MVC1` for applications targeting ASP.NET MVC 1.0 and one called `MVC2` for applications using version 2.0. Select the one that targets the version of ASP.NET MVC you are using.

2. Register Telerik Extensions for ASP.NET MVC within your application. Open your `web.config` file, and find the `<namespaces>` tag located under the `<pages>` tag. You will need to add the namespace `Telerik.Web.Mvc.UI` using the following definition: `<add namespace="Telerik.Web.Mvc.UI">`.

3. Add the JavaScript files to your application. These scripts are in a folder under the `Scripts` folder of the Telerik Extensions for ASP.NET MVC installation directory, which is named after the extension version (for example: `Scripts\2010.1.309`). If you haven't done so, create a `Scripts` folder in your application, and copy the folder named after the extension version to `Scripts` (this will make upgrades easier).

   Alternatively, you can enable Telerik CDN support so you don't have to manage the scripts locally. You do so either programmatically in the `Global.asax` file:

```
protected void Application_Start()
{
  RegisterRoutes(RouteTable.Routes);
  WebAssetDefaultSettings
        .UseTelerikContentDeliveryNetwork = true;
}
```

   or by adding an entry in the web.config file:

```
<telerik useTelerikContentDeliveryNetwork="true">
...
</telerik>
```

4. Register your scripts in the application using the `ScriptRegistar()` component. You normally do this by adding it at the end of your master page so all content pages use it. Add the following to the end of your master page:

```
<% Html.Telerik().ScriptRegistar() %>.
```

5. Add the CSS files to the `Content` folder in your application. Following the same pattern in step 3, locate the folder with the version of the extensions under the `Content` folder of your installation directory (for example `Content\2010.1.309`). Copy this folder into the `Content` folder in your application.

6. To use the CSS files, you need to register them using the `StyleSheetRegistar()` component in the same way as for the script files. The following example sets the application to use the Windows7 skin:

```
<% Html.Teleriko.css"))
```

That's all there is to start using the Telerik Extensions for ASP.NET MVC.

Calendar

The `Calendar` control renders a calendar in the default month view mode. You can choose the view from four choices: Month view (default) showing all the days in the month; Year view, showing all the months in the selected year; Decade view, showing all the years in the selected decade; and Century view, showing the years in the selected century.

You only need to define a name for the calendar using the `Name` property to make it work; other properties allow you to define different behaviors. The following examples will show you how to work with them.

Defining the Date Range

Calendar has the MinDate and MaxDate properties that define the range of allowed dates that can be selected (and shown) in the control. Listing 11-1 shows how the range is defined starting three days before today and ending three days after today. Use the Value property to set the selected date. Figure 12-1 illustrates the example.

Listing 12-1. *Calendar Date Range*

```
Controller

public ActionResult MinMaxDates()
{
    return View();
}

View

<% Html.Telerik().Calendar()
       .Name("Calendar1")
       .MinDate(DateTime.Today.AddDays(-3))
       .MaxDate(DateTime.Today.AddDays(3))
       .Value(DateTime.Today)
       .Render();
%>
```

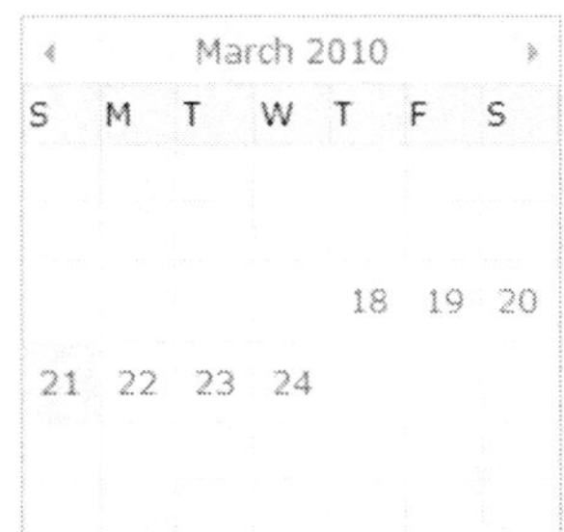

Figure 12-1. *Calendar date range*

Implementing a Select Action

Calendar is capable of attaching an action to a date, a set of dates, or all dates, so that when it's selected, it performs the action. Listing 12-2 demonstrates this capability, and Figure 12-2 shows the end result.

Listing 12-2. *Calendar Select Action*

```
Controller

public ActionResult SelectAction(CalModel model)
{
    model.selectedDate = model.selectedDate ?? DateTime.Today;
    return View(model);
}

public class CalModel
{
    public CalModel()
    {
        selectedDate = DateTime.Today;
    }
    public DateTime? selectedDate { get; set; }
}

View

<%@ Page Title=""
        Language="C#"
        MasterPageFile="~/Views/Shared/Site.Master"
        Inherits="System.Web.Mvc.ViewPage<TelerikMvcApplication.Controllers.CalModel>" %>

<%@ Import Namespace="Telerik.Web.Mvc.UI" %>

<% Html.Telerik()
        .Calendar()
        .Name("Calendar2")
        .Selection(s=>
                s.Action("SelectAction", new { selectedDate = "{0}" })
                    .Dates(new List<DateTime>
                            {
                                DateTime.Today.AddDays(-5),
                                DateTime.Today.AddDays(-1),
                                DateTime.Today.AddDays(4),
                                DateTime.Today.AddDays(10)
                            })
                    )
            .Value(Model.selectedDate.Value == null
                                ? DateTime.Today
                                : Model.selectedDate.Value)
            .Render();
%>
```

```
<%  Html.Telerik()
        .Calendar()
        .Name("Calendar3")
        .Selection(s=> s.Action("SelectAction", new { selectedDate = "{0}" }))
        .Value(Model.selectedDate.Value == null
                    ? DateTime.Today : Model.selectedDate.Value)
                    .Render();
%>

<% if (Model.selectedDate != null)
  {
  %>
            <p>
                The selected date was: <%= Model.selectedDate.Value.ToShortDateString() %>
            </p>
 <%
  }
%>
```

Figure 12-2. *When a date is clicked in the calendar, the selected action will be executed.*

Implementing Globalization

`Calendar` supports rendering in different culture configurations. By changing the current culture definition of the running thread, you can set the specific culture for which to render the calendar. To create this thread change, it is necessary to define a custom attribute that decorates the action result method that will render the view. Listing 12-3 shows this in action. Note in Figure 12-3 the new globalized calendar.

Listing 12-3. *Implementing Globalization*

```
Controller

[CultureAction]
public ActionResult Globalization()
{
    return View();
}

View

<% Html.BeginForm("Globalization", "Calendar", FormMethod.Get); %>
    <select id="culture" name="culture">
         <option value="en-US">English</option>
         <option value="fr-FR">Francais</option>
         <option value="de-DE">Deutsch</option>
         <option value="bg-BG">Български</option>
    </select>

    <input type="submit" value="Submit" />

<%= Html.Telerik().Calendar()
        .Name("CalendarGlobalization")
        .HtmlAttributes(new { style = "width: 294px;" })
%>

<% Html.EndForm(); %>

<% Html.Telerik().ScriptRegistrar().Globalization(true); %>

CultureActionAttribute.cs

namespace TelerikMvcApplication.Filters
{
    using System.Globalization;
    using System.Threading;
    using System.Web.Mvc;

    public class CultureActionAttribute : ActionFilterAttribute
    {
        public override void OnActionExecuting(ActionExecutingContext filterContext)
        {
            base.OnActionExecuting(filterContext);
```

```
                if (!string.IsNullOrEmpty(filterContext.HttpContext.Request["culture"]))
                {
                    string newCulture = filterContext.HttpContext.Request["culture"];
                    CultureInfo newCI = new CultureInfo(newCulture);
                    Thread.CurrentThread.CurrentCulture = newCI;
                    Thread.CurrentThread.CurrentUICulture = newCI;
                }
            }
        }
    }
```

Figure 12-3. *When a new language is selected, the calendar changes accordingly.*

Working with Calendar's Client API

With `Calendar`'s client API, you can handle the `Load` and `Change` events that occur when the calendar is first loaded and on every change of a date, respectively. You can also get the currently selected date and programmatically change that selected date using the `Value()` method of the `tCalendar` object after finding the calendar with the jQuery selector `$("selector").data("tCalendar")`. Listing 12-4 shows you how to work with the client API. Figure 12-4 shows the end result.

Listing 12-4. *Calendar Client API*

```
Controller

public ActionResult ClientAPI()
{
    return View();
}
```

View

```
<%= Html.Telerik().DatePicker()
        .Name("pickDate")
        .Value(DateTime.Today) %>

<input  type="button"
value="Set New Date"
onclick="setNewDate();" />

<%= Html.Telerik().Calendar()
        .Name("MyCalendar")
        .ClientEvents(e=>e
                .OnChange("onChange")
                .OnLoad("onLoad"))
%>

<div id="logChanges"></div>

<script type="text/javascript">
    function onLoad(sender) {
        var lbl = document.getElementById("logChanges");
        lbl.innerHTML = "Event: onLoad [Calendar loaded succesfully]";
    }

    function onChange(sender) {
        var lbl = document.getElementById("logChanges");
        var newDate = $.telerik.formatString('{0:MM/dd/yyyy}', sender.date);
        var prevDate = $.telerik.formatString('{0:MM/dd/yyyy}', sender.previousDate);
        lbl.innerHTML = lbl.innerHTML + "<br />";
        lbl.innerHTML = lbl.innerHTML +
                        "Event: onChange [New Date: " + newDate +
                        "] [Previous Date: " + prevDate + "]";
    }

    function setNewDate() {
        var picker = $("#pickDate").data("tDatePicker");
        var newDate = picker.value();
        var calendar = $("#MyCalendar").data("tCalendar");
        calendar.value(newDate);
        var newDateFormated = $.telerik.formatString('{0:MM/dd/yyyy}', newDate);
        var lbl = document.getElementById("logChanges");
        lbl.innerHTML = lbl.innerHTML + "<br />";
        lbl.innerHTML = lbl.innerHTML + "Changed Date To: " + newDateFormated;
    }

</script>
```

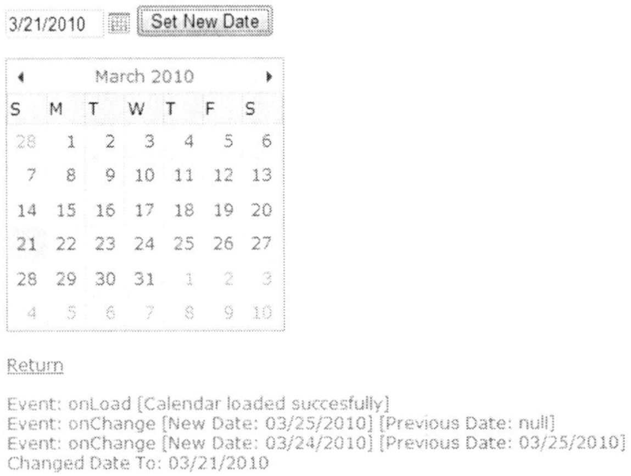

3/21/2010 Set New Date

◂			March 2010			▸
S	M	T	W	T	F	S
28	1	2	3	4	5	6
7	8	9	10	11	12	13
14	15	16	17	18	19	20
21	22	23	24	25	26	27
28	29	30	31	1	2	3
4	5	6	7	8	9	10

Return

Event: onLoad [Calendar loaded succesfully]
Event: onChange [New Date: 03/25/2010] [Previous Date: null]
Event: onChange [New Date: 03/24/2010] [Previous Date: 03/25/2010]
Changed Date To: 03/21/2010

Figure 12-4. *Calendar client API*

Date Picker

The DatePicker control renders a text box where users can enter the selected date and a button that shows a calendar for a visual date selection (this calendar is created on the client). The following examples will show you the functionality of DatePicker.

Implementing Date Ranges and the ShowButton Property

The properties MinDate and MaxDate are exposed for the DatePicker in the same way they are for the Calendar. They provide a means to define a range of allowed dates. The ShowButton property defines whether the calendar button will be shown. Listing 12-5 shows you how to implement a date range and to display or hide the ShowButton. See the end result in Figure 12-5.

Listing 12-5. *DatePicker Date Range and Show Button*

```
Controller

public ActionResult MinMaxDate(DPModel model)
{
    model.showDropDown = model.showDropDown ?? true;
    return View(model);
}

public class DPModel
{
    public DPModel()
    {
        showDropDown = true;
    }
```

```
    public bool? showDropDown { get; set; }
}
```

View

```
<%@ Page Title=""
        Language="C#"
        MasterPageFile="~/Views/Shared/Site.Master"
        Inherits="System.Web.Mvc.ViewPage<TelerikMvcApplication.Controllers.DPModel>" %>

<%@ Import Namespace="Telerik.Web.Mvc.UI" %>


<% Html.BeginForm("MinMaxDate", "DatePicker"); %>
        <%= Html.CheckBox("showDropDown", Model.showDropDown.Value) %>
            <label for="showDropDown">Show the dropdown button</label>
            <button type="submit">Apply</button>

    <%= Html.Telerik().DatePicker()
            .Name("pickDate")
            .MinDate(DateTime.Today.AddDays(-3))
            .MaxDate(DateTime.Today.AddDays(3))
            .Value(DateTime.Today)
            .ShowButton(Model.showDropDown.Value)%>

    <% Html.EndForm(); %>
```

Figure 12-5. *DatePicker date range and show button*

Parsing Dates

DatePicker supports predefined words that translate into dates for easy selection. These predefined words can be entered into the DatePicker text box in order to select a date. Also, as part of the parsing procedure, any input is validated, and the immediate feedback is provided to the user if an error occurs.

The words that can be used for parsing are *today*, *tomorrow*, *yesterday*, and the name of the month. Also, the words *next* and *last* can be used in conjunction with the words *day*, *week*, *month*, or *year*.

This works for the English language. If you work with different languages in your application, then you need to provide the definition of the `cultureinfo` object in the `telerik.calendar.js` script file.

Listing 12-6 will help you examine this capability. See how it works in Figure 12-6.

Listing 12-6. *DatePicker Date Parsing*

```
Controller

public ActionResult DateParsing()
{
    return View();
}

View

    <%= Html.Telerik().DatePicker()
            .Name("pickDate")
            .Value(DateTime.Today)
    %>
```

Figure 12-6. *Just type in the DatePicker which date to parse.*

Implementing Globalization

The globalization of the `DatePicker` works the same way as with the `Calendar`. You need to change the culture in the working thread. See this in Listing 12-7 and the end result in Figure 12-7.

Listing 12-7. *DatePicker Globalization*

```
Controller

[CultureAction]
public ActionResult Globalization()
{
    return View();
}

View

<% Html.BeginForm("Globalization", "DatePicker", FormMethod.Get); %>

<select id="culture" name="culture">
     <option value="en-US">English</option>
     <option value="fr-FR">Francais</option>
     <option value="de-DE">Deutsch</option>
     <option value="bg-BG">Български</option>
</select>

<input type="submit" value="Submit" />

<%= Html.Telerik().DatePicker()
        .Name("pickDateGlobalization")
        .Value(DateTime.Today)
        .HtmlAttributes(new { style = "width: 294px;" })
%>

<% Html.EndForm(); %>

<% Html.Telerik().ScriptRegistrar().Globalization(true); %>
```

Figure 12-7. *The language of DatePicker changes based on the user selection.*

Working with DatePicker's Client API

The client API of the DatePicker is similar to the one of Calendar, but it exposes two more events, Open and Close, that are raised when the calendar is opened and closed, respectively, using the ShowButton. You can also open and close the calendar programmatically. The object that exposes this API is tDatePicker.

Listing 12-8 demonstrates the client API. Figure 12-8 shows the example running.

Listing 12-8. *DatePicker Client API*

```
Controller

public ActionResult ClientAPI()
{
    return View();
}
View

<input type="button" value="Show Selected Date" onclick="showDate();" />
<input type="button" value="Set Date to Tomorrow" onclick="setTomorrow();" />
<input type="button" value="Open DatePicker" onclick="showDatePicker(event);" />
<input type="button" value="Close DatePicker" onclick="hideDatePicker(event);" />

<%= Html.Telerik().DatePicker()
        .Name("pickDate")
            .Value(DateTime.Today)
            .ClientEvents(e=>e
                .OnChange("onChange")
                .OnLoad("onLoad")
                .OnOpen("onOpen")
                .OnClose("onClose"))
        %>

<div id="logChanges"></div>

<script type="text/javascript">

    function showDate() {
        var picker = $("#pickDate").data("tDatePicker");
        var date = picker.value();
        var lbl = document.getElementById("logChanges");
        lbl.innerHTML = lbl.innerHTML + "<br />";
        lbl.innerHTML = lbl.innerHTML + "Selected Date: " + date;

        alert("Selected Date: " + date);
    }
```

```
function setTomorrow() {
    var picker = $("#pickDate").data("tDatePicker");
    picker.value("tomorrow");
    var date = picker.value();
    var lbl = document.getElementById("logChanges");
    lbl.innerHTML = lbl.innerHTML + "<br />";
    lbl.innerHTML = lbl.innerHTML + "Changed Date to: " + date;

    alert("Changed Date to: " + date);
}

function showDatePicker(e) {
    var picker = $("#pickDate").data("tDatePicker");
    picker.showPopup();
    if (e.stopPropagation)
        e.stopPropagation();
    e.cancelBubble = true;

    var lbl = document.getElementById("logChanges");
    lbl.innerHTML = lbl.innerHTML + "<br />";
    lbl.innerHTML = lbl.innerHTML + "DatePicker opened progrmamatically";
}

function hideDatePicker(e) {
    var picker = $("#pickDate").data("tDatePicker");
    picker.hidePopup();
    if (e.stopPropagation)
        e.stopPropagation();
    e.cancelBubble = true;
    var lbl = document.getElementById("logChanges");
    lbl.innerHTML = lbl.innerHTML + "<br />";
    lbl.innerHTML = lbl.innerHTML + "DatePicker closed programmatically";
}

function onLoad(sender) {
    var lbl = document.getElementById("logChanges");
    lbl.innerHTML = "Event: onLoad [DatePicker loaded succesfully]";
}

function onChange(sender) {
    var lbl = document.getElementById("logChanges");
    var newDate = $.telerik.formatString('{0:MM/dd/yyyy}', sender.date);
    var prevDate = $.telerik.formatString('{0:MM/dd/yyyy}', sender.previousDate);
    lbl.innerHTML = lbl.innerHTML + "<br />";
    lbl.innerHTML = lbl.innerHTML +
                            "Event: onChange [New Date: " + newDate +
                            "] [Previous Date: " + prevDate + "]";
}
function onOpen(sender) {
    var lbl = document.getElementById("logChanges");
    lbl.innerHTML = lbl.innerHTML + "<br />";
    lbl.innerHTML = lbl.innerHTML + "Event: onOpen [DatePicker opened]";
}
```

```
    function onClose(sender) {
        var lbl = document.getElementById("logChanges");
        lbl.innerHTML = lbl.innerHTML + "<br />";
        lbl.innerHTML = lbl.innerHTML + "Event: onClose [DatePicker closed]";
    }

</script>
```

Figure 12-8. *You can take advantage of DatePicker's client API in many ways, as shown in the figure.*

NumericTextBox

`NumericTextBox` is a control designed to render a text box but allows only numeric input (digits, the decimal point, and the minus, percentage, or dollar signs). If defined, it also renders spin buttons that enable users to increase and decrease the value entered by predefined increments, or *steps*.

You can define your `NumericTextBox` to render for general numbering, percentage, and currency.

Implementing Value Range and Spin Buttons

The following example shows how to define a range of allowed values and also how to enable or disable the spin buttons in a `NumericTextBox`. Listing 12-9 demonstrates how to implement a range of values and to work with the spin buttons. Figure 12-9 shows the example running.

Listing 12-9. *NumericTextBox Value Range and Spin Buttons*

```
Controller

public ActionResult MinMaxValues(NTBModel model)
{
    model.showSpinner = model.showSpinner ?? true;
    return View(model);
}
```

```
public class NTBModel
{
    public bool? showSpinner { get; set; }
    public double? value { get; set; }
}
```

View

```
<%@ Page Title=""
        Language="C#"
        MasterPageFile="~/Views/Shared/Site.Master"
        Inherits="System.Web.Mvc.ViewPage<TelerikMvcApplication.Controllers.NTBModel>" %>

<%@ Import Namespace="Telerik.Web.Mvc.UI" %>

<asp:Content ID="Content2" ContentPlaceHolderID="MainContent" runat="server">

    <% Html.BeginForm("MinMaxValues", "NumericTextBox"); %>

        <%= Html.CheckBox("showSpinner", Model.showSpinner.Value) %>
        <label for="showSpinner">Show Spin Buttons</label>
        <button type="submit">Apply</button>

    <%= Html.Telerik().NumericTextBox()
            .Name("NumericTextBox1")
            .MinValue(0)
            .MaxValue(10)
            .Value(3)
            .Spinners(Model.showSpinner.Value)
        %>

    <% Html.EndForm(); %>

</asp:Content>
```

Min Value: 0 / Max Value: 10

☑ Show Spin Buttons Apply

3

Figure 12-9. *Implementing spin buttons and a value range in NumericTextBox*

Validating User Input with Server Validation

NumericTextBox can be validated on the server using the built-in validation mechanism in ASP.NET MVC. The idea is to run the validation procedure in the controller and, if an error is found, then return that to the view using the AddModelError method of the ModelState object.

Listing 12-10 shows you how to implement server validation. Figure 12-10 illustrates the example.

Listing 12-10. *NumericTextBox Server Validation*

```
Controller

public ActionResult ServerValidation(NTBModel model)
{
    model.value = model.value ?? 0;
    return View(model);
}

[AcceptVerbs(HttpVerbs.Post)]
public ActionResult ServerValidation(double? numericTextBox, NTBModel model)
{
    if (!numericTextBox.HasValue)
    {
        ModelState.AddModelError("numericTextBox", "Required");
    }
    else
    {
        if (numericTextBox.Value < 0 || numericTextBox.Value > 10)
        {
            ModelState.AddModelError("numericTextBox", "Value out of range");
        }
    }

    return View(model);
}


View

<% Html.BeginForm("ServerValidation", "NumericTextBox"); %>

<%= Html.Telerik().NumericTextBox()
   .Name("numericTextBox")
   .Value(Model.value)
    %>
<%= Html.ValidationMessage("numericTextBox") %>

<input type="submit" value="Make Post" />

<% Html.EndForm(); %>
```

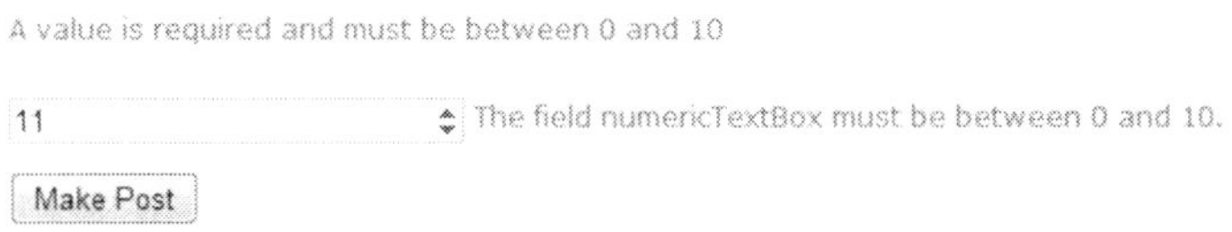

A value is required and must be between 0 and 10

11 The field numericTextBox must be between 0 and 10.

Make Post

Figure 12-10. *The value in the NumericTextBox was validated in the server.*

Validating User Input with Model-Based Validation

Using data annotations in ASP.NET MVC 2.0, you can validate the data entered in a NumericTextBox using the model definition. Listing 12-11 shows how the validation is not made in any part of the code; it is only defined in the model using the RangeAttribute class. Figure 12-11 shows how this works.

Listing 12-11. *NumericTextBox Model-Based Validation*

```
Controller

public ActionResult ClientValidation()
{
    var model = new NTBModel();
    model.numericTextBox = model.numericTextBox ?? 0;
    return View(model);
}

[AcceptVerbs(HttpVerbs.Post)]
public ActionResult ClientValidation(NTBModel model)
{
    return View(model);
}

public class NTBModel
{
    public bool? showSpinner { get; set; }
    public double? value { get; set; }

    [Range(0, 10)]
    public double? numericTextBox { get; set; }
}

View

<% Html.BeginForm("ClientValidation", "NumericTextBox"); %>

<%= Html.Telerik().NumericTextBox()
        .Name("numericTextBox")
        .Value(Model.numericTextBox)
    %>

    <div class="error"><%= Html.ValidationMessageFor(x=>x.numericTextBox) %></div>

    <input type="submit" value="Make Post" />

<% Html.EndForm(); %>
```

11

The field numericTextBox must be between 0 and 10.

Make Post

Figure 12-11. *NumericTextBox model–based validation*

Implementing Globalization

Using the same mechanism explained in Calendar and DatePicker, you can make NumericTextBox to display localized information by changing the culture information of the working thread. The technique is in Listing 12-12, and the end result is shown in Figure 12-12.

Listing 12-12. *NumericTextBox Globalization*

```
Controller

[CultureAction]
public ActionResult Globalization()
{
    return View();
}

View

<% Html.BeginForm("Globalization", "NumericTextBox", FormMethod.Get); %>

<select id="culture" name="culture">
        <option value="en-US">English</option>
        <option value="fr-FR">Francais</option>
        <option value="de-DE">Deutsch</option>
        <option value="bg-BG">Български</option>
</select>

<%= Html.Telerik().NumericTextBox()
        .Name("numericNumber")
        .Value(11)
%>

<%= Html.Telerik().CurrencyTextBox()
        .Name("numericCurrency")
        .Value(10)
%>

<%= Html.Telerik().PercentTextBox()
        .Name("numericPercentage")
        .Value(74.5)
%>

<input type="submit" value="Submit" />

<% Html.EndForm(); %>

<% Html.Telerik().ScriptRegistrar().Globalization(true); %>
```

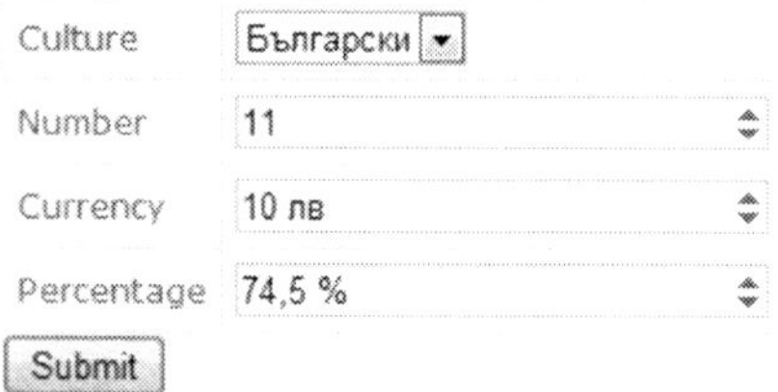

Figure 12-12. *Globalization in NumericTextBox is applied in all types of numeric text boxes.*

Working with NumericTextBox's Client API

NumericTextBox exposes two client events, Load and Change, that are raised when the control first loads and when the value changes, respectively; also, with the Value() method of the tTextBox object, you can get and set the control's value. Listing 12-13 shows how to interact with the client API. See how it looks in Figure 12-13.

Listing 12-13. *NumericTextBox Client API*

```
Controller

public ActionResult ClientAPI()
{
    return View();
}

View

<%= Html.TextBox("txtValue") %>

<input type="button" value="Change Value" onclick="setValue();" />
<input type="button" value="Get Value" onclick="getValue();" />

<%=
    Html.Telerik().NumericTextBox()
        .Name("numericTextBox")
        .ClientEvents(e=>e
                .OnLoad("onLoad")
                .OnChange("onChange")
            )
     %>

<div id="logChanges"></div>

<script type="text/javascript">
     function onLoad(sender) {
         var log = document.getElementById("logChanges");
         log.innerHTML = "Event: onLoad [NumericTextBox loaded succesfully]";
     }
```

```
    function onChange(sender) {
        var log = document.getElementById("logChanges");
        var newValue = sender.newValue;
        var oldValue = sender.oldValue;
        log.innerHTML = log.innerHTML + "<br />";
        log.innerHTML = log.innerHTML +
                              "Event: onChange [New Value: " + newValue +
                              "] [Previous Value: " + oldValue + "]";
    }

    function setValue() {
        var log = document.getElementById("logChanges");
        var txt = $("#txtValue");
        var newValue = txt.val();
        var nTxt = $("#numericTextBox").data("tTextBox");
        nTxt.value(newValue);
        log.innerHTML = log.innerHTML + "<br />";
        log.innerHTML = log.innerHTML + "Changed value to: " + newValue;
    }

    function getValue() {
        var log = document.getElementById("logChanges");
        var nTxt = $("#numericTextBox").data("tTextBox");
        var currentValue = nTxt.value();
        alert(currentValue);
        log.innerHTML = log.innerHTML + "<br />";
        log.innerHTML = log.innerHTML + "Get current value: " + currentValue;
    }
</script>
```

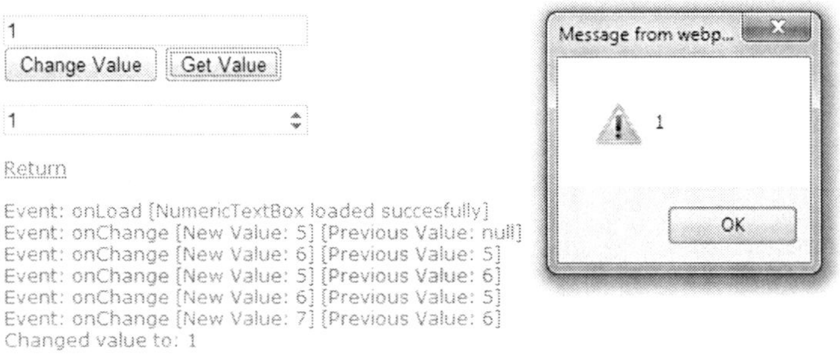

1
Change Value Get Value
1
Return
Event: onLoad [NumericTextBox loaded succesfully]
Event: onChange [New Value: 5] [Previous Value: null]
Event: onChange [New Value: 6] [Previous Value: 5]
Event: onChange [New Value: 5] [Previous Value: 6]
Event: onChange [New Value: 6] [Previous Value: 5]
Event: onChange [New Value: 7] [Previous Value: 6]
Changed value to: 1

Message from webp...
1
OK

Figure 12-13. *The NumericTextBox's client API is very easy to work with and provides a lot of functionality.*

Menu

The Menu control is the ASP.NET MVC equivalent to RadMenu in Telerik RadControls for ASP.NET AJAX. It is composed of root items that can have nested child items. You can define whether the menu is displayed horizontally or vertically with the Orientation property; also, it can have animations for when the menu items are shown and hidden, and it can be bound to a model data source.

Creating a Menu Declarative and Defining the Menu Orientation

Listing 12-14 shows you how to create a menu declaratively (manually), and it also shows how to use the Orientation property. Figure 12-14 shows it in action.

Listing 12-14. *Menu Creation and Orientation Declaratively*

```
Controller

public ActionResult DeclarativeItems()
{
    var model = new MModel
                    {
                        menuOrientation = MenuOrientation.Horizontal,
                        checkedHorizontal = "checked",
                        checkedVertical = string.Empty
                    };
    return View(model);
}

[AcceptVerbs(HttpVerbs.Post)]
public ActionResult DeclarativeItems(MModel model)
{

    model.checkedHorizontal = model.radioOrientation == "Horizontal"
                                ? "checked"
                                : string.Empty;
    model.checkedVertical = model.radioOrientation == "Vertical"
                                ? "checked"
                                : string.Empty;
    model.menuOrientation = model.radioOrientation == "Horizontal"
                                ? MenuOrientation.Horizontal
                                : MenuOrientation.Vertical;
    return View(model);
}

public class MModel
{
    public MenuOrientation menuOrientation { get; set; }
    public string radioOrientation { get; set; }
    public string checkedHorizontal { get; set; }
    public string checkedVertical { get; set; }
}
```

View

```
<% Html.BeginForm("DeclarativeItems", "Menu"); %>

<input type="submit" value="Change" />

<%=
    Html.Telerik().Menu()
        .Name("myMenu")
        .Orientation(Model.menuOrientation)
        .Items(menu =>
                   {
                       menu.Add()
                           .Text("File")
                           .Items(i =>
                                      {
                                          i.Add().Text("New");
                                          i.Add().Text("Open");
                                          i.Add().Text("Save");
                                      });
                       menu.Add()
                           .Text("Edit")
                           .Items(i =>
                                      {
                                          i.Add().Text("Cut");
                                          i.Add().Text("Copy");
                                          i.Add().Text("Paste");
                                      });
                   })
     %>

<% Html.EndForm(); %>
```

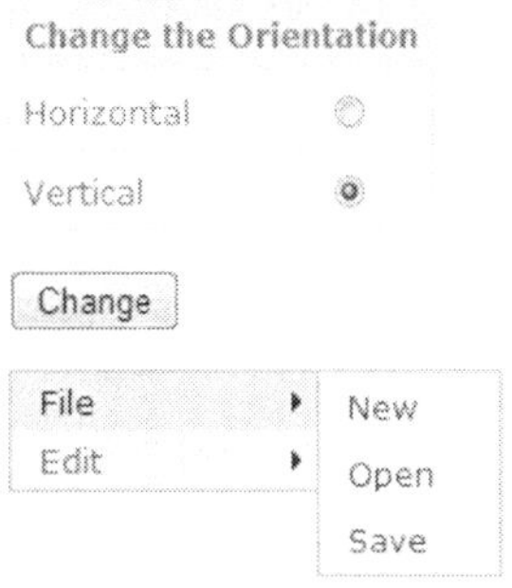

Figure 12-14. *You can change the orientation of Menu using the Orientation property.*

Binding to an Object Model

Menu supports data binding to an object view model. It can build the hierarchy automatically based on the definition of the relations between the objects.

In Listing 12-15, note how the view is strongly typed to an object model that represents the Regions table in the Northwind database. Then the Model is bound to the control in the BindTo section of the menu declaration, which in turn uses the model to create the mappings between the fields containing the data from the database and the menu items. The first mapping traverses the Regions table and binds the menu item's Text property to the RegionDescription field from the Model. Then for each menu item bound to a region, a second mapping occurs for the territories in each region doing the same procedure binding the child menu item's Text property to the TerritoryDescription field in the Model. Figure 12-15 displays the resulting menu.

Listing 12-15. *Menu Bound to Model*

```
Controller

public ActionResult BindToModel()
{
    NorthwindDataContext nwd = new NorthwindDataContext();
    return View(nwd.Regions);
}


View

<%@ Page Title=""
        Language="C#"
        MasterPageFile="~/Views/Shared/Site.Master"
        Inherits="System.Web.Mvc.ViewPage<IEnumerable<TelerikMvcApplication.Models.➥
Region>>" %>
<%@ Import Namespace="Telerik.Web.Mvc.UI" %>
<%@ Import Namespace="TelerikMvcApplication.Models" %>

<asp:Content ID="Content2" ContentPlaceHolderID="MainContent" runat="server">
    <%= Html.Telerik().Menu()
        .Name("RegionsMenu")
            .Orientation(MenuOrientation.Vertical)
            .BindTo(Model, mappings =>
                            {
                                mappings.For<Region>(binding => binding
                                     .ItemDataBound((item, region) =>
                                         {
                                            item.Text = region.RegionDescription;
                                         })
                                     .Children(region=>region.Territories));
                                mappings.For<Territory>(binding => binding
                                     .ItemDataBound((item, territory) =>
                                        {
                                            item.Text = territory.TerritoryDescription;
                                        }));
                            })
        %>
</asp:Content>
```

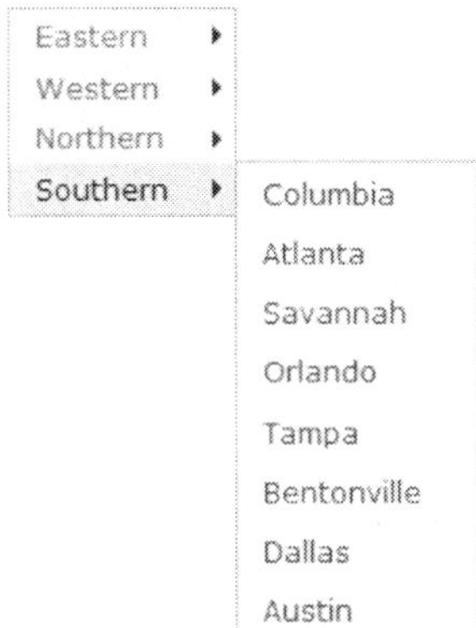

Figure 12-15. *Menu bound to model*

Creating Menu Templates

You can create templates for your menu items so they display richer content than just a hyperlink. Listing 12-16 shows you how to create templates displaying a login box and a Google search box. These templates are fully functional, and users can interact with them. Figure 12-16 shows the end result.

Listing 12-16. *Menu Templates*

```
Controller

public ActionResult Templates()
{
    return View();
}

View

<%
Html.Telerik().Menu()
    .Name("myMenu")
    .Items(menu =>
                {
                    menu.Add()
                        .Text("Login")
                        .Content(() =>
                                    {
                                %>
                                    <table>
                                    <tr>
                                        <th colspan="2">Credentials</th>
                                    </tr>
```

```
                                            <tr>
                                            <td>Username:</td>
                                                <td>
                                                    <%=Html.TextBox("Username")%>
                                                </td>
                                            </tr>
                                            <tr>
                                                <td>Password:</td>
                                                <td>
                                                    <%=Html.Password("Password")%>
                                                </td>
                                            </tr>
                                            <tr>
                                                <td colspan="2" align="center">
                                                   <input type="button" value="Login" />
                                                </td>
                                            </tr>
                                        </table>
                                    <%
                                        });
                    menu.Add()
                        .Text("Google Search")
                        .Content(() =>
                                        {
                                    %>
                                    <div id="cse" style="width: 100%;">Loading</div>
                                    <script src="http://www.google.com/jsapi"
                                            type="text/javascript">
                                    </script>
                                    <script type="text/javascript">
                                      google.load('search', '1', {language : 'en'});
                                      google.setOnLoadCallback(function() {
                                      var customSearchControl =
                                            new google
                                                    .search
                                                    .CustomSearchControl(
                                                       '013497957494942316161:q9_vrpus8gk');
                                            customSearchControl
                                                    .setResultSetSize(google
                                                    .search
                                                    .Search
                                                    .LARGE_RESULTSET);
                                            customSearchControl.draw('cse');
                                       }, true);
                                    </script>
                                    <link rel="stylesheet"
                                    href="http://www.google.com/cse/style/look/default.css"
                                    type="text/css" />
                                        <%
                                        });
                }).Render();
%>
```

Figure 12-16. *Implementing Menu templates to display a Google search box*

Working with Menu's Client API

Menu's client API exposes the Load, Open, Close, and Select events, which are fired when the menu loads and when an item is opened, closed, and selected, respectively. You can also open or close menu items programmatically and enable and disable items. Listing 12-17 shows this functionality, and Figure 12-17 shows the end result.

Listing 12-17. *Menu Client API*

```
Controller

public ActionResult ClientAPI()
{
    return View();
}

View

<input type="button" value="Open Menu: File" onclick="openFile();" />
<input type="button" value="Close Menu: File" onclick="closeFile();" />
<input type="button" value="Disable Menu: Edit" onclick="disableEdit();" />
<input type="button" value="Enable Menu: Edit" onclick="enableEdit();" />

<%=
    Html.Telerik().Menu()
        .Name("myMenu")
        .ClientEvents(e=>e
            .OnLoad("onLoad")
            .OnOpen("onOpen")
            .OnClose("onClose")
            .OnSelect("onSelect"))
        .Items(menu =>
                    {
                        menu.Add()
                            .Text("File")
                            .Items(i =>
                                        {
                                            i.Add().Text("New");
                                            i.Add().Text("Open");
                                            i.Add().Text("Save");
                                        });
```

```
                    menu.Add()
                        .Text("Edit")
                        .Items(i =>
                                   {
                                       i.Add().Text("Cut");
                                       i.Add().Text("Copy");
                                       i.Add().Text("Paste");
                                   });
                })
    %>

<div id="logChanges"></div>

<script type="text/javascript">
    function onLoad(sender) {
        var log = document.getElementById("logChanges");
        log.innerHTML = "Event: onLoad [Menu loaded succesfully]";
    }

    function onOpen(sender) {
        var item = $(sender.item);
        var log = document.getElementById("logChanges");
        log.innerHTML = log.innerHTML + "<br />";
        log.innerHTML = log.innerHTML + "Event: onOpen [Menu item " +
                        item.find("> .t-link").text() + " opened]";
    }

    function onClose(sender) {
        var item = $(sender.item);
        var log = document.getElementById("logChanges");
        log.innerHTML = log.innerHTML + "<br />";
        log.innerHTML = log.innerHTML + "Event: onClose [Menu item " +
                        item.find("> .t-link").text() + " closed]";
    }

    function onSelect(sender) {
        var item = $(sender.item);
        var log = document.getElementById("logChanges");
        log.innerHTML = log.innerHTML + "<br />";
        log.innerHTML = log.innerHTML + "Event: onSelect [Item " +
                        item.find("> .t-link").text() + " selected]";
    }

    function openFile() {
        var menu = $("#myMenu").data("tMenu");
        var item = $("> li", menu.element)[0];

        menu.open(item);
        var log = document.getElementById("logChanges");
        log.innerHTML = log.innerHTML + "<br />";
        log.innerHTML = log.innerHTML + "Opened menu item File from client API";
    }
```

```
    function closeFile() {
        var menu = $("#myMenu").data("tMenu");
        var item = $("> li", menu.element)[0];

        menu.close(item);
        var log = document.getElementById("logChanges");
        log.innerHTML = log.innerHTML + "<br />";
        log.innerHTML = log.innerHTML + "Closed menu item File from client API";
    }

    function disableEdit() {
        var menu = $("#myMenu").data("tMenu");
        var item = $("> li", menu.element)[1];

        menu.disable(item);
        var log = document.getElementById("logChanges");
        log.innerHTML = log.innerHTML + "<br />";
        log.innerHTML = log.innerHTML + "Disabled menu item Edit from client API";
    }

    function enableEdit() {
        var menu = $("#myMenu").data("tMenu");
        var item = $("> li", menu.element)[1];

        menu.enable(item);
        var log = document.getElementById("logChanges");
        log.innerHTML = log.innerHTML + "<br />";
        log.innerHTML = log.innerHTML + "Enabled menu item Edit from client API";
    }
</script>
```

Open Menu: File | Close Menu: File | Disable Menu: Edit | Enable Menu: Edit

File ▾ | Edit ▾

Event: onLoad [Menu loaded succesfully]
Event: onOpen [Menu item File opened]
Event: onClose [Menu item File closed]
Disabled menu item Edit from client API
Enabled menu item Edit from client API
Opened menu item File from client API
Closed menu item File from client API
Event: onOpen [Menu item Edit opened]
Event: onClose [Menu item Edit closed]
Event: onOpen [Menu item Edit opened]
Event: onClose [Menu item Edit closed]

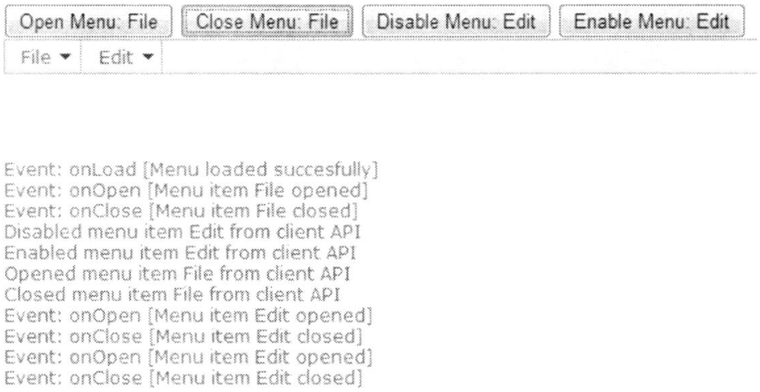

Figure 12-17. *Menu's client API exposes a lot of functionality.*

PanelBar

The PanelBar is a control similar to the RadPanelBar in the ASP.NET AJAX suite. It is composed of PanelBarItem objects, each of which contains a title and a content area. When displayed in the page, the title is used to collapse and expand the content area. The content area can be loaded on the server or on demand. Listing 12-18 shows you how to create a PanelBar object declaratively, and Figure 12-18 shows how it looks.

Listing 12-18. *Creating a PanelBar Declaratively*

```
Controller

public ActionResult DeclarativeItems()
{
    PBModel model = new PBModel
                        {
                            ExpandMode = PanelBarExpandMode.Single,
                            radioExpandMode = "OnePanel",
                            checkedOnePanel = "checked",
                            checkedMultiplePanels = ""
                        };

    return View(model);
}

[AcceptVerbs(HttpVerbs.Post)]
public ActionResult DeclarativeItems(PBModel model)
{

    model.checkedOnePanel = model.radioExpandMode == "OnePanel"
                                ? "checked"
                                : string.Empty;
    model.checkedMultiplePanels = model.radioExpandMode == "MultiplePanels"
                                ? "checked"
                                : string.Empty;
    model.ExpandMode = model.radioExpandMode == "OnePanel"
                                ? PanelBarExpandMode.Single
                                : PanelBarExpandMode.Multiple;
    return View(model);
}

public class PBModel
{
    public PanelBarExpandMode ExpandMode { get; set; }
    public string radioExpandMode { get; set; }
    public string checkedOnePanel { get; set; }
    public string checkedMultiplePanels { get; set; }
}
```

View

```
<% Html.BeginForm("DeclarativeItems", "PanelBar"); %>

<%
    Html.Telerik().PanelBar()
        .Name("myPanelBar")
        .ExpandMode(Model.ExpandMode)
        .Items(i =>
                  {
                      i.Add()
                          .Text("File")
                          .Items(subItem =>
                                     {
                                         subItem.Add().Text("New");
                                         subItem.Add().Text("Open");
                                         subItem.Add().Text("Save");
                                     });
                      i.Add()
                          .Text("Edit")
                          .Items(subItem =>
                                     {
                                         subItem.Add().Text("Cut");
                                         subItem.Add().Text("Copy");
                                         subItem.Add().Text("Past");
                                     });
                  }

        ).Render();

     %>
```

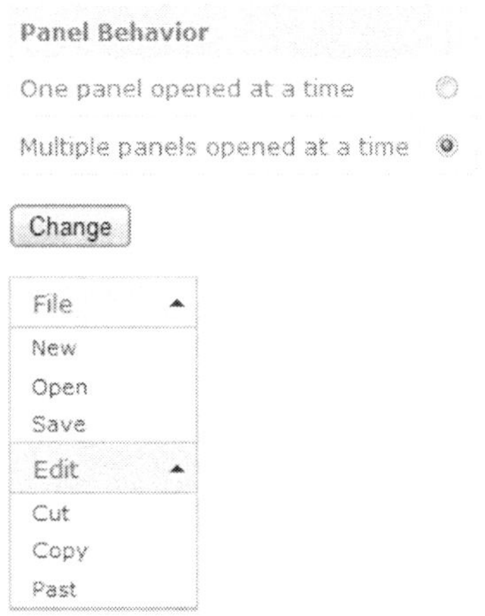

Figure 12-18. *PanelBar created declaratively*

Binding to an Object Model

PanelBar can be bound to a view model object in the same way as Menu. In this scenario, you can create content based on the information retrieved from the model and place it on the content area.

In Listing 12-19, the view is strongly typed, as you have seen before, to an object model that represents the Regions table in the Northwind database. The BindTo section defines how the control is bound to the model and creates the mappings between the fields containing the data from the database and the PanelBar items. The first mapping traverses the Regions table and binds the panel bar item's Text property to the RegionDescription field from the Model. Then for each panel bar item bound to a region, a second mapping occurs for the territories in each region doing the same process of binding the child menu item's Text property to the TerritoryDescription field in the Model. In Figure 12-19 the resulting PanelBar is displayed.

Listing 12-19. *PanelBar Bound to Model*

```
Controller

public ActionResult BindToModel()
{
    NorthwindDataContext nwd = new NorthwindDataContext();
    return View(nwd.Regions);
}


View

<%@ Page Title=""
        Language="C#"
        MasterPageFile="~/Views/Shared/Site.Master"
        Inherits="System.Web.Mvc.ViewPage<IEnumerable<TelerikMvcApplication.Models.➥
Region>>" %>
<%@ Import Namespace="Telerik.Web.Mvc.UI" %>
<%@ Import Namespace="TelerikMvcApplication.Models" %>

<asp:Content ID="Content2" ContentPlaceHolderID="MainContent" runat="server">

    <%= Html.Telerik().PanelBar()
        .Name("MyPanelBar")
            .ExpandMode(PanelBarExpandMode.Single)
            .BindTo(Model, mappings =>
                      {
                            mappings.For<Region>(binding => binding
                                    .ItemDataBound((item, region) =>
                                          {
                                                item.Text = region.RegionDescription;
                                          })
                                    .Children(region=>region.Territories));
```

```
                    mappings.For<Territory>(binding => binding
                            .ItemDataBound((item, territory) =>
                                {
                                    item.Text = territory.TerritoryDescription;
                                }));
                      })
    %>

</asp:Content>
```

Figure 12-19. *PanelBar bound to an object model view*

Creating Templates

As with Menu, you can create templates for the content area for each PanelBar item. In Listing 12-20, note how the syntax is much like the one used in Menu. Figure 12-20 shows the example running.

Listing 12-20. *PanelBar Templates*

```
Controller

public ActionResult Templates()
{
    return View();
}
```

View

```
    <div style="width:400px">
            <%
            Html.Telerik().PanelBar()
                .Name("myPanelBar")
                .ExpandMode(PanelBarExpandMode.Single)
                .Items(p =>
                           {
                               p.Add()
                                   .Text("Login")
                                   .Content(() =>
                                                {
                                            %>
                                               <table>
                                                <tr>
                                                    <th colspan="2">Credentials</th>
                                                </tr>
                                                <tr>
                                                    <td>Username:</td>
                                                        <td>
                                                            <%=Html.TextBox("Username")%>
                                                    </td>
                                                </tr>
                                                    <tr>
                                                        <td>Password:</td>
                                                        <td>
                                                            <%=Html.Password("Password")%>
                                                        </td>
                                                </tr>
                                                <tr>
                                                        <td colspan="2" align="center">
                                                           <input type="button"
                                                                   value="Login" />
                                                        </td>
                                                </tr>
                                               </table>
                                            <%
                                                });
                               p.Add()
                                   .Text("Google Search")
                                   .Content(() =>
                                                {
                                            %>
                                                // Code omitted for clarity of the example
                                           <%
                                                });
                           }).Render();
        %>
```

Figure 12-20. *Creating PanelBarItem templates*

Loading Content on Demand

The content for the PanelBar items can be created on demand, and not when the page loads, to increase the responsiveness of the application. The approach is to create a partial view (equivalent to a web user control) for each PanelBar item, and the content for the PanelBar item is added to the content area when it is expanded the first time. All subsequent item expansions happen faster because the content is not created again. Listing 12-21 implements this concept. The end result is similar to the one in Figure 12-20.

Listing 12-21. *Loading Content on Demand*

```
Controller

public ActionResult LoadOnDemand()
{
    return View();
}

public ActionResult AjaxLogin()
{
    // Added to create the effect of a long-running process
    Thread.Sleep(2000);

    return PartialView();
}

public ActionResult AjaxGoogle()
{
    // Added to create the effect of a long-running process
    Thread.Sleep(2000);

    return PartialView();
}
```

```
View

<%
        Html.Telerik().PanelBar()
            .Name("myPanelBar")
            .ExpandMode(PanelBarExpandMode.Single)
            .Items(p =>
                       {
                           p.Add()
                               .Text("Login")
                               .LoadContentFrom("AjaxLogin", "PanelBar");
                           p.Add()
                               .Text("Weather")
                               .LoadContentFrom("AjaxGoogle", "PanelBar");
                       }).Render();
    %>
</div>

AjaxLogin.ascx

<%@ Control Language="C#" Inherits="System.Web.Mvc.ViewUserControl" %>

<table>
<tr>
    <th colspan="2">Credentials</th>
</tr>
    <tr>
        <td>Username:</td>
        <td>
            <%=Html.TextBox("Username")%>
        </td>
    </tr>
    <tr>
        <td>Password:</td>
        <td>
            <%=Html.Password("Password")%>
        </td>
    </tr>
    <tr>
        <td colspan="2" align="center">
                <input type="button" value="Login" />
        </td>
    </tr>
</table>

AjaxGoogle.ascx

<%@ Control Language="C#" Inherits="System.Web.Mvc.ViewUserControl" %>

    <div id="cse" style="width: 100%;">Loading</div>
    <script src="http://www.google.com/jsapi"
    type="text/javascript">
    </script>
```

```
<script type="text/javascript">
    google.load('search', '1', { language: 'en' });
    google.setOnLoadCallback(function () {
        var customSearchControl =
new google
.search
.CustomSearchControl(
    '013497957494942316161:q9_vrpus8gk');
        customSearchControl
.setResultSetSize(google
.search
.Search
.LARGE_RESULTSET);
        customSearchControl.draw('cse');
    }, true);
</script>
<link rel="stylesheet"
href="http://www.google.com/cse/style/look/default.css"
type="text/css" />
```

Working with PanelBar's Client API

PanelBar exposes events and methods similar to those from Menu, but the Open and Close events are replaced here for the Expand and Collapse events. You can also expand, collapse, disable, and enable PanelBar items programmatically, as shown in Listing 12-22. Figure 12-21 shows the example running.

Listing 12-22. *PanelBar Client API*

Controller

```
public ActionResult ClientAPI()
{
    return View();
}
```

View

```
<input type="button" value="Open PanelBar: File" onclick="openFile();" />
<input type="button" value="Close PanelBar: File" onclick="closeFile();" />
<input type="button" value="Disable PanelBar: Edit" onclick="disableEdit();" />
<input type="button" value="Enable PanelBar: Edit" onclick="enableEdit();" />
```

```
<%=
    Html.Telerik().PanelBar()
        .Name("myPanelBar")
        .ClientEvents(e=>e
            .OnLoad("onLoad")
            .OnExpand("onExpand")
            .OnCollapse("onCollapse")
            .OnSelect("onSelect"))
        .Items(p =>
                   {
                       p.Add()
                           .Text("File")
                           .Items(i =>
                                      {
                                          i.Add().Text("New");
                                           i.Add().Text("Open");
                                          i.Add().Text("Save");
                                      });
                       p.Add()
                           .Text("Edit")
                           .Items(i =>
                                      {
                                          i.Add().Text("Cut");
                                          i.Add().Text("Copy");
                                          i.Add().Text("Paste");
                                      });
                   })
%>

<div id="logChanges"></div>

<script type="text/javascript">
     function onLoad(sender) {
         var log = document.getElementById("logChanges");
         log.innerHTML = "Event: onLoad [PanelBar loaded succesfully]";
     }

     function onExpand(sender) {
         var item = $(sender.item);
         var log = document.getElementById("logChanges");
         log.innerHTML = log.innerHTML + "<br />";
         log.innerHTML = log.innerHTML + "Event: onExpand [PanelBar item " +
                               item.find("> .t-link").text() + " expanded]";
     }

     function onCollapse(sender) {
         var item = $(sender.item);
         var log = document.getElementById("logChanges");
         log.innerHTML = log.innerHTML + "<br />";
         log.innerHTML = log.innerHTML + "Event: onCollapse [PanelBar item " +
                               item.find("> .t-link").text() + " collapsed]";
     }
```

```
    function onSelect(sender) {
        var item = $(sender.item);
        var log = document.getElementById("logChanges");
        log.innerHTML = log.innerHTML + "<br />";
        log.innerHTML = log.innerHTML + "Event: onSelect [PanelBar " +
                                item.find("> .t-link").text() + " selected]";
    }

    function openFile() {
        var pb = $("#myPanelBar").data("tPanelBar");
        var item = $("> li", pb.element)[0];

        pb.expand(item);
        var log = document.getElementById("logChanges");
        log.innerHTML = log.innerHTML + "<br />";
        log.innerHTML = log.innerHTML + "Opened PanelBar item File from client API";
    }

    function closeFile() {
        var pb = $("#myPanelBar").data("tPanelBar");
        var item = $("> li", pb.element)[0];

        pb.collapse(item);
        var log = document.getElementById("logChanges");
        log.innerHTML = log.innerHTML + "<br />";
        log.innerHTML = log.innerHTML + "Closed PanelBar item File from client API";
    }

    function disableEdit() {
        var pb = $("#myPanelBar").data("tPanelBar");
        var item = $("> li", pb.element)[1];

        pb.disable(item);
        var log = document.getElementById("logChanges");
        log.innerHTML = log.innerHTML + "<br />";
        log.innerHTML = log.innerHTML + "Disabled PanelBar item Edit from client API";
    }

    function enableEdit() {
        var pb = $("#myPanelBar").data("tPanelBar");
        var item = $("> li", pb.element)[1];

        pb.enable(item);
        var log = document.getElementById("logChanges");
        log.innerHTML = log.innerHTML + "<br />";
        log.innerHTML = log.innerHTML + "Enabled PanelBar item Edit from client API";
    }

</script>
```

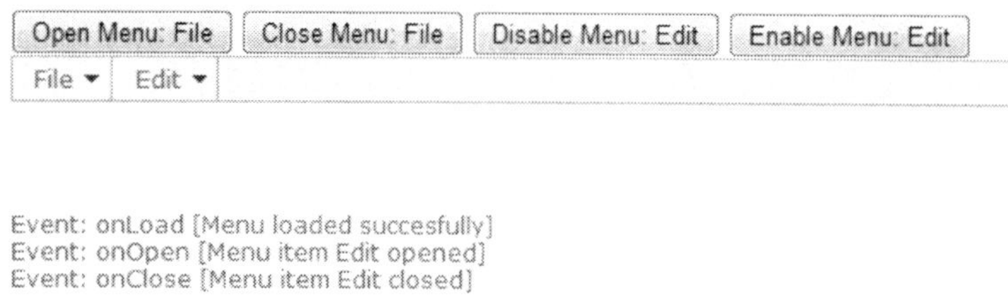

Event: onLoad [Menu loaded succesfully]
Event: onOpen [Menu item Edit opened]
Event: onClose [Menu item Edit closed]

Figure 12-21. *PanelBar client API*

TabStrip

The TabStrip control is designed to have a tab navigation style in the same way as RadTabStrip for ASP.NET AJAX. It is composed of a set of TabStripItem objects, each with its own content that is shown when the tab item is selected.

You can add TabStripItem objects declaratively, or they can be created by binding TabStrip to a view model object. You need to at least set the Name property and add one TabStripItem to the Items collection.

Creating a TabStrip Declaratively

Listing 12-23 shows you how to declaratively create a TabStrip. See how it looks in Figure 12-22.

Listing 12-23. *TabStrip Declarative Creation*

```
Controller

public ActionResult DeclarativeItems()
{
    return View();
}

View

<%
    Html.Telerik().TabStrip()
        .Name("myTab")
        .Items(t =>
                   {
                       t.Add().Text("File")
                           .Selected(true)
                           .Content(() =>
                                        {
                                        %>
                                            File content...
                                        <%
                                        });
```

```
                    t.Add().Text("Edit")
                        .Content(() =>
                                    {
                                    %>
                                        Edit content...
                                    <%
                                    });
                    t.Add().Text("Window")
                        .Content(() =>
                                    {
                                    %>
                                        Window content...
                                    <%
                                    });
                    t.Add().Text("View")
                        .Content(() =>
                                    {
                                    %>
                                        View content...
                                    <%
                                    });
                    t.Add().Text("Help")
                        .Content(() =>
                                    {
                                    %>
                                        Help content...
                                    <%
                                    });
                }).Render();
%>
```

File Edit Window View Help
Edit content...

Figure 12-22. *TabStrip declarative creation*

Binding TabStrip to an Object Model

Using the same binding technique shown in previous controls, you can bound `TabStrip` to an object model, and `TabStripItem` objects are created as a result of a mapping operation. Listing 12-24 shows the binding approach, and Figure 12-23 illustrates the result.

Listing 12-24. *Binding TabStrip to an Object Model*

```
Controller

public ActionResult BindToModel()
{
    NorthwindDataContext nwd = new NorthwindDataContext();
    return View(nwd.Regions);
}

View

<%@ Page Title=""
        Language="C#"
        MasterPageFile="~/Views/Shared/Site.Master"
        Inherits="System.Web.Mvc.ViewPage<IEnumerable<TelerikMvcApplication.Models.Region>>"
%>

<%@ Import Namespace="Telerik.Web.Mvc.UI" %>

<asp:Content ID="Content2" ContentPlaceHolderID="MainContent" runat="server">

    <% Html.Telerik().TabStrip()
        .Name("myTabs")
            .BindTo(Model,
                (item, region)=>
                    {
                        item.Text = region.RegionDescription;
                    })
            .Render();
     %>

</asp:Content>
```

Eastern	Western	Northern	Southern

Figure 12-23. *TabStripItems are created automatically with information from the object model.*

Creating TabStripItem's Content

Each `TabStripItem` exposes a `Content` method that is used to define what to show when the tab is selected. This content can be any HTML you need. Listing 12-25 shows you how to define this content. You can see how it looks in Figure 12-24.

Listing 12-25. *TabStrip Item Content*

```
Controller

public ActionResult Content()
{
    return View();
}

View

<%
    Html.Telerik().TabStrip()
        .Name("myTabs")
        .Items(t =>
                   {
                       t.Add()
                           .Text("Login")
                           .Selected(true)
                           .Content(() =>
                                        {
                                    %>
                                       <table>
                                        <tr>
                                            <th colspan="2">Credentials</th>
                                        </tr>
                                            <tr>
                                                <td>Username:</td>
                                                <td>
                                                    <%=Html.TextBox("Username")%>
                                                </td>
                                            </tr>
                                            <tr>
                                                <td>Password:</td>
                                                <td>
                                                    <%=Html.Password("Password")%>
                                                </td>
                                            </tr>
                                            <tr>
                                                <td colspan="2" align="center">
                                                    <input type="button" value="Login" />
                                                </td>
                                            </tr>
                                       </table>
```

```
                                    <%
                                        });
                        t.Add()
                            .Text("Google Search")
                            .Content(() =>
                                        {
                                    %>
                                        // Code omitted for clarity of the example
                                   <%
                                        });
                    }).Render();
%>
```

Figure 12-24. *The content in TabStripItems can be created with any combination of HTML and server controls.*

Loading Content on Demand

The content of an item can also be loaded on demand using the `LoadContentFrom` method and AJAX requests. The source of the content is based on partial views, so you create an action result method in your controller that is responsible for rendering the partial view back to the main view via AJAX. While this operation executes, the `TabStripItem` shows a loading icon next to the tab title. In the following example (Listing 12-26), I'm using a delay to simulate wait time. Figure 12-25 shows the end result.

Listing 12-26. *TabStrip Load Content on Demand*

```
Controller

public ActionResult LoadOnDemand()
{
    return View();
}

public ActionResult AjaxLogin()
{
    Thread.Sleep(2000);
    return PartialView();
}
```

```
public ActionResult AjaxGoogle()
{
    Thread.Sleep(2000);
    return PartialView();
}
```

View

```
<%    Html.Telerik().TabStrip()
        .Name("myTabs")
        .Items(p =>
                   {
                       p.Add()
                           .Text("Login")
                           .LoadContentFrom("AjaxLogin", "TabStrip");
                       p.Add()
                           .Text("Google Search")
                           .LoadContentFrom("AjaxWeather", "TabStrip");
                   }).Render();
 %>
```

Figure 12-25. *TabStrip loads the item's content on demand.*

Working with TabStrip's Client API

TabStrip exposes the `Load` and `Select` client events. They are raised when the control is first loaded and when a tab is selected, respectively. You can also enable or disable a tab with the `enable()` and `disable()` methods.

When `TabStrip` is rendered in the page, the `TabStripItem` objects are represented within an HTML unordered list of items (`<ul>`), and you have access to this code using the `tTabStrip` client object. The items are accessible using jQuery, as shown in Listing 12-27. Figure 12-26 illustrates the example.

Listing 12-27. *Working with TabStrip's Client API*

Controller

```
public ActionResult ClientAPI()
{
    return View();
}
```

View

```
<input type="button" value="Select Tab: File" onclick="openFile();" />
<input type="button" value="Disable Tab: Edit" onclick="disableEdit();" />
<input type="button" value="Enable Tab: Edit" onclick="enableEdit();" />

<%
    Html.Telerik().TabStrip()
        .Name("myTabs")
        .ClientEvents(e => e
                          .OnLoad("onLoad")
                          .OnSelect("onSelect"))
        .Items(t =>
                     {
                         t.Add().Text("File")
                             .Selected(true)
                             .Content(() =>
                                          {

                                          %>
                                              File content...
                                          <%
                                          });
                         t.Add().Text("Edit")
                             .Content(() =>
                                          {
                                          %>
                                              Edit content...
                                          <%
                                          });
                         t.Add().Text("Window")
                             .Content(() =>
                                          {
                                          %>
                                              Window content...
                                          <%
                                          });
                         t.Add().Text("View")
                             .Content(() =>
                                          {
                                          %>
                                              View content...
                                          <%
                                          });
```

```
                    t.Add().Text("Help")
                        .Content(() =>
                                        {
                                        %>
                                            Help content...
                                        <%
                                        });
                }).Render();
    %>

<div id="logChanges"></div>

<script type="text/javascript">
    function onLoad(sender) {
        var log = document.getElementById("logChanges");
        log.innerHTML = "Event: onLoad [TabStrip loaded succesfully]";
    }

    function onSelect(sender) {
        var item = $(sender.item);
        var log = document.getElementById("logChanges");
        log.innerHTML = log.innerHTML + "<br />";
        log.innerHTML = log.innerHTML +
                             "Event: onSelect [Tab " +
                             item.find("> .t-link").text() + " selected]";
    }

    function openFile() {
        var tab = $("#myTabs").data("tTabStrip");
        var item = $("li", tab.element)[0];

        tab.select(item);
        var log = document.getElementById("logChanges");
        log.innerHTML = log.innerHTML + "<br />";
        log.innerHTML = log.innerHTML + "Selected Tab File from client API";
    }

    function disableEdit() {
        var tab = $("#myTabs").data("tTabStrip");
        var item = $("li", tab.element)[1];

        tab.disable(item);
        var log = document.getElementById("logChanges");
        log.innerHTML = log.innerHTML + "<br />";
        log.innerHTML = log.innerHTML + "Disabled Tab Edit from client API";
    }
```

```
    function enableEdit() {
        var pb = $("#myTabs").data("tTabStrip");
        var item = $("li", pb.element)[1];

        pb.enable(item);
        var log = document.getElementById("logChanges");
        log.innerHTML = log.innerHTML + "<br />";
        log.innerHTML = log.innerHTML + "Enabled Tab Edit from client API";
    }

</script>
```

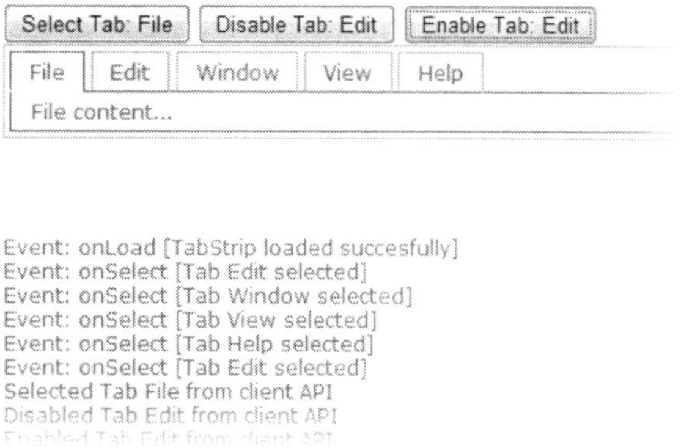

Figure 12-26. *TabStrip properties and items can be modified using its client API.*

TreeView

TreeView is a component that displays hierarchical information in a visual tree. It has many of the features of the RadTreeView for ASP.NET AJAX. A TreeView is composed of TreeViewItem objects, and these items have properties that enable specific functionality such as drag-and-drop, check boxes, and so forth.

TreeView can be created and populated with nodes declaratively or bound to a view model object or site map. It supports load on demand of items and animation effects and provides a client API.

Creating a TreeView Declaratively and Enabling Check Boxes

Let's examine how to populate a TreeView declaratively and how to enable the check boxes functionality with the ShowCheckBox property.

Listing 12-28 shows a TreeView created declaratively, and the check boxes functionality is enabled based on the selection made by the user, which is stored in an object model. See Figure 12-27.

Listing 12-28. *Creating a TreeView Declaratively and Enabling Check Boxes*

```
Controller

public ActionResult DeclarativeItems()
{
    TVModel model = new TVModel();
    return View(model);
}

public class TVModel
{
    public TVModel()
    {
        showCheckboxes = false;
    }
    public bool? showCheckboxes { get; set; }
    public string showChecked { get; set; }
}

View

<% Html.BeginForm("DeclarativeItems", "TreeView"); %>

<%= Html.CheckBox("showCheckboxes", Model.showCheckboxes) %>

<input type="submit" value="Change" />

<%
    Html.Telerik().TreeView()
        .Name("myTreeView")
        .ShowCheckBox(Model.showCheckboxes.Value)
        .Items(t =>
                   {
                       t.Add()
                           .Text("File")
                           .Items(i =>
                                      {
                                          i.Add().Text("New");
                                          i.Add().Text("Open");
                                          i.Add().Text("Save");
                                      });
                       t.Add()
                           .Text("Edit")
                           .Items(i =>
                                      {
                                          i.Add().Text("Cut");
                                          i.Add().Text("Copy");
                                          i.Add().Text("Paste");
                                      });
```

```
                        t.Add()
                            .Text("Window")
                            .Items(i =>
                                       {
                                           i.Add().Text("Tile");
                                           i.Add().Text("Floating");
                                           i.Add().Text("Cascade");
                                       });
                    }).Render();
    %>

<% Html.EndForm(); %>
```

Figure 12-27. *The check boxes functionality is enabled in TreeView.*

Working with Drag-and-Drop

Out of the box, TreeView supports drag-and-drop between nodes, and with minimal effort it can drop items on other parts of the page. To enable drag-and-drop between nodes, you use the DragAndDrop property with a call to the Enable(true) method. Then, to enable drag-and-drop to other elements, you need to define the drop areas with the DropTargets method and handle the client event OnNodeDrop.

Listing 12-29 shows you how to work with drag-and-drop. Figure 12-28 illustrates the functionality.

Listing 12-29. *Working with TreeView Drag-and-Drop*

```
Controller
public ActionResult DragAndDrop()
{
    return View();
}
```

View

```
<style type="text/css">
        .dropArea
        {
                border-width: 1px;
                border-style: solid;
                border-color:Navy;
                width: 24em;
                height: 8em;
                overflow: auto;
                margin-bottom: 1em;
                padding: .70em;
        }

        fieldset
        {
                width:26em;
                height:12em;
        }

</style>

<%
    Html.Telerik().TreeView()
        .Name("myTreeView")
        .DragAndDrop(d=>d
                .Enabled(true)
                .DropTargets(".dropArea"))
        .ClientEvents(e=>e
            .OnNodeDrop("onNodeDrop"))
        .Items(t =>
                    {
                        t.Add()
                            .Text("File")
                            .Items(i =>
                                        {
                                            i.Add().Text("New");
                                            i.Add().Text("Open");
                                            i.Add().Text("Save");
                                        });
                        t.Add()
                            .Text("Edit")
                            .Items(i =>
                                        {
                                            i.Add().Text("Cut");
                                            i.Add().Text("Copy");
                                            i.Add().Text("Paste");
                                        });
```

```
                        t.Add()
                            .Text("Window")
                            .Items(i =>
                                        {
                                            i.Add().Text("Tile");
                                            i.Add().Text("Floating");
                                            i.Add().Text("Cascade");
                                        });
                    }).Render();
    %>

<script type="text/javascript">
    function onNodeDrop(e) {
        var dropContainer = $(e.dropTarget).closest('.dropArea');
        if (dropContainer.length > 0) {
            $('<div><strong>' + $(e.item).text() + '</strong></div>')
                        .hide()
                        .appendTo(dropContainer)
                        .slideDown('fast');

            e.preventDefault();
        }
    }
</script>

<fieldset>
    <legend>Drop items here</legend>
    <div class="dropArea">
    </div>
</fieldset>
```

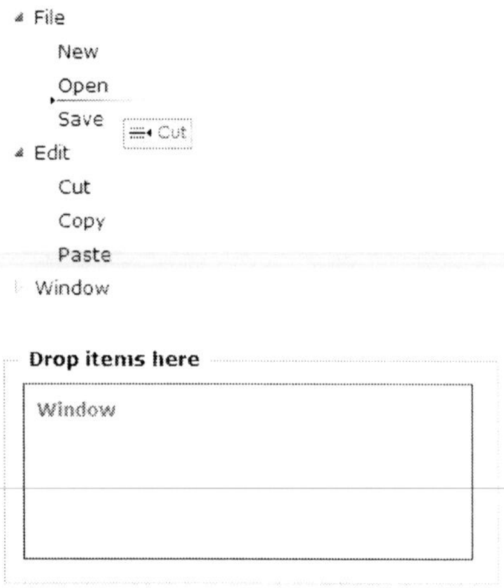

Figure 12-28. *TreeView supports drag-and-drop between nodes and to other areas.*

Binding TreeView to an Object Model

TreeView can also be populated with items by binding it to a view model object, as you've seen before. The methodology is the same. All the items are created based on the information in the model and the relations it defined by the data. Listing 12-30 shows you how to bind a TreeView to an object model. Figure 12-29 shows you the end result.

Listing 12-30. *Binding TreeView to an Object Model*

```
Controller

public ActionResult BindToModel()
{
    NorthwindDataContext nwd = new NorthwindDataContext();
    return View(nwd.Regions);
}

View

<%=
    Html.Telerik().TreeView()
        .Name("myTreeView")
        .BindTo(Model, mappings =>
                           {
                               mappings.For<Region>(binding => binding
                                   .ItemDataBound((item, region) =>
                                          {
                                              item.Text = region.RegionDescription;
                                          })
                                        .Children(region=>region.Territories));
                                mappings.For<Territory>(binding => binding
                                    .ItemDataBound((item, territory) =>
                                         {
                                             item.Text = territory.TerritoryDescription;
                                         }));
                           })


%>
```

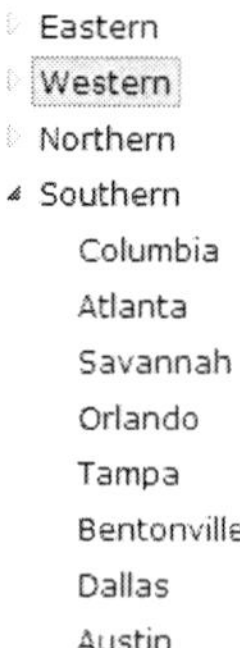

Figure 12-29. *TreeViewItems were created automatically because of the binding operation.*

Creating Templates

In the same way you created templates for other components, `TreeViewItem` objects support templates that are rendered using the `Content` property. Listing 12-31 shows you how to implement templates. Figure 12-30 displays the resulting `TreeView`.

Listing 12-31. *TreeViewItem Templates*

```
Controller

public ActionResult Templates()
{
    return View();
}

View

<%
Html.Telerik().TreeView()
    .Name("myTreeView")
    .Items(p =>
                {
                    p.Add()
                        .Text("Login")
                        .Content(() =>
                                    {
                            %>
                                <table>
                                 <tr>
                                     <th colspan="2">Credentials</th>
                                 </tr>
                                     <tr>
                                         <td>Username:</td>
                                         <td>
                                             <%=Html.TextBox("Username")%>
                                         </td>
```

```
                                        </tr>
                                            <tr>
                                                <td>Password:</td>
                                                <td>
                                                    <%=Html.Password("Password")%>
                                                </td>
                                        </tr>
                                        <tr>
                                                <td colspan="2" align="center">
                                                    <input type="button" value="Login" />
                                                </td>
                                        </tr>
                                        </table>
                                    <%
                                        });
                         p.Add()
                             .Text("Weather")
                             .Content(() =>
                                        {
                                    %>
                                    // Code omitted for clarity of the example
                                        <%
                                        });
                     }).Render();
%>
```

Login
Google Search

Google™ Custom Search

Figure 12-30. *TreeView templates*

Loading Content on Demand

Loading content on demand is supported via AJAX or web service requests that return the items as JSON objects. Listing 12-32 shows you how to use both approaches.

Listing 12-32. *TreeView Load on Demand*

```
Controller

public ActionResult LoadOnDemand()
{
    NorthwindDataContext nwd = new NorthwindDataContext();
    return View(nwd.Regions);
}
```

```
[AcceptVerbs(HttpVerbs.Post)]
public ActionResult LoadTerritories_Ajax(TreeViewItemModel node)
{
    NorthwindDataContext nwd = new NorthwindDataContext();
    int? parentId = !string.IsNullOrEmpty(node.Value)
                            ? (int?)Convert.ToInt32(node.Value)
                            : null;

    IEnumerable nodes = from item in nwd.Territories
                        where item.RegionID == parentId || parentId == null
                        select
                            new TreeViewItemModel
                                {
                                    Text = item.TerritoryDescription,
                                    Value = item.TerritoryID,
                                    Enabled = true
                                };

    return new JsonResult {Data = nodes};
}
```

View

```
<%= Html.Telerik().TreeView()
        .Name("treeView_LOD_Ajax")
        .BindTo(Model, (item, region) =>
                    {
                          item.Text = region.RegionDescription;
                          item.Value = region.RegionID.ToString();
                          item.LoadOnDemand = region.Territories.Count > 0;
                     })
        .DataBinding(db => db.Ajax().Select("LoadTerritories_Ajax", "TreeView"))
%>

<%= Html.Telerik().TreeView()
        .Name("treeView_LOD_Ajax")
        .BindTo(Model, (item, region) =>
                    {
                          item.Text = region.RegionDescription;
                          item.Value = region.RegionID.ToString();
                          item.LoadOnDemand = region.Territories.Count > 0;
                     })
        .DataBinding(db =>
                        db.WebService().Select("~/Models/WS_Regions.asmx/LoadTerritories"))
%>
```

WS_Regions.asmx

```
namespace TelerikMvcApplication.Models
{
    [WebService(Namespace = "http://tempuri.org/")]
    [WebServiceBinding(ConformsTo = WsiProfiles.BasicProfile1_1)]
```

```
    [ToolboxItem(false)]
    [ScriptService]
    public class WS_Regions : WebService
    {

        [WebMethod]
        public IEnumerable LoadTerritories(TreeViewItemModel node)
        {
            NorthwindDataContext nwd = new NorthwindDataContext();
            int? parentId = !string.IsNullOrEmpty(node.Value)
                                        ? (int?)Convert.ToInt32(node.Value)
                                        : null;

            IEnumerable nodes = from item in nwd.Territories
                                where item.RegionID == parentId || parentId == null
                                select
                                    new TreeViewItemModel
                                    {
                                        Text = item.TerritoryDescription,
                                        Value = item.TerritoryID,
                                        Enabled = true
                                    };

            return nodes;
        }
    }
}
```

Working with the Client API

The client API of TreeView exposes client events and even the possibility to bind an object on the client. The Load event is raised when the control first loads. The Expand and Collapse events are raised when an item is expanded and collapsed, respectively. When an item is selected, then the Select event is raised.

For drag-and-drop operations, the OnNodeDragStart, OnNodeDrop, OnNodeDropped, and OnNodeDragCancelled events are raised.

When binding TreeView in the client, then the DataBinding event is raised, and the DataBound event is raised after the binding operation. Listing 12-33 shows you the client events. See how the example works in Figure 12-31.

Listing 12-33. *TreeView Client API*

Controller

```
public ActionResult ClientAPI()
{
    return View();
}
```

View

```
<%
    Html.Telerik().TreeView()
        .Name("myTreeView")
        .DragAndDrop(d=>d
                .Enabled(true))
        .ClientEvents(e=>e
                    .OnLoad("onLoad")
                    .OnSelect("onSelect")
                    .OnCollapse("onCollapse")
                    .OnExpand("onExpand")
                    .OnNodeDragStart("onNodeDragStart")
                    .OnNodeDrop("onNodeDrop")
                    .OnNodeDropped("onNodeDropped")
                    .OnNodeDragCancelled("onNodeDragCancelled")
                    )
        .Items(t =>
                    {
                        t.Add()
                            .Text("File")
                            .Items(i =>
                                    {
                                        i.Add().Text("New");
                                        i.Add().Text("Open");
                                        i.Add().Text("Save");
                                    });
                        t.Add()
                            .Text("Edit")
                            .Items(i =>
                                    {
                                        i.Add().Text("Cut");
                                        i.Add().Text("Copy");
                                        i.Add().Text("Paste");
                                    });
                        t.Add()
                            .Text("Window")
                            .Items(i =>
                                    {
                                        i.Add().Text("Tile");
                                        i.Add().Text("Floating");
                                        i.Add().Text("Cascade");
                                    });
                    }).Render();
     %>

<br /><br />

<div id="logChanges"></div>
```

```
<script type="text/javascript">
    function onLoad(sender) {
        var log = document.getElementById("logChanges");
        log.innerHTML = "Event: onLoad [TreeView loaded succesfully]";
    }
    function onExpand(sender) {
        var item = $(sender.item);
        var log = document.getElementById("logChanges");
        log.innerHTML = log.innerHTML + "<br />";
        log.innerHTML = log.innerHTML + "Event: onExpand [TreeView node " +
                                item.text() + " expanded]";
    }

    function onCollapse(sender) {
        var item = $(sender.item);
        var log = document.getElementById("logChanges");
        log.innerHTML = log.innerHTML + "<br />";
        log.innerHTML = log.innerHTML + "Event: onCollapse [TreeView node " +
                                item.text() + " collapsed]";
    }

    function onSelect(sender) {
        var item = $(sender.item);
        var log = document.getElementById("logChanges");
        log.innerHTML = log.innerHTML + "<br />";
        log.innerHTML = log.innerHTML + "Event: onSelect [TreeView node " +
                                item.text() + " selected]";
    }

    function onNodeDragStart(sender) {
        var item = $(sender.item);
        var log = document.getElementById("logChanges");
        log.innerHTML = log.innerHTML + "<br />";
        log.innerHTML = log.innerHTML + "Event: onNodeDragStart [TreeView node " +
                                item.text() + "]";
    }

    function onNodeDragCancelled(sender) {
        var item = $(sender.item);
        var log = document.getElementById("logChanges");
        log.innerHTML = log.innerHTML + "<br />";
        log.innerHTML = log.innerHTML + "Event: onNodeDragCancelled [TreeView node " +
                                item.text() + "]";
    }

    function onNodeDrop(sender) {
        var item = $(sender.item);
        var log = document.getElementById("logChanges");
        log.innerHTML = log.innerHTML + "<br />";
        log.innerHTML = log.innerHTML + "Event: onNodeDrop [TreeView node " +
                                item.text() + "]";
    }
```

```
    function onNodeDropped(sender) {
        var item = $(sender.item);
        var log = document.getElementById("logChanges");
        log.innerHTML = log.innerHTML + "<br />";
        log.innerHTML = log.innerHTML + "Event: onNodeDropped [TreeView node " +
                                 item.text() + "]";
    }
</script>
```

File
Edit
Cut
Copy
Paste
Floating
Window
Tile
Cascade

Event: onLoad [TreeView loaded succesfully]
Event: onExpand [TreeView node Edit expanded]
Event: onCollapse [TreeView node Edit collapsed]
Event: onExpand [TreeView node Window expanded]
Event: onCollapse [TreeView node Window collapsed]
Event: onExpand [TreeView node Window expanded]
Event: onNodeDragStart [TreeView node Floating]
Event: onNodeDrop [TreeView node Floating]
Event: onExpand [TreeView node Edit expanded]
Event: onNodeDropped [TreeView node Floating]

Figure 12-31. *TreeView client API*

Grid

The Grid UI component delivers many of the same features found in its counterpart for WebForms, the RadGrid for ASP.NET AJAX, and new features continue to be added with each new release. You can create a grid that has features such as scrolling, paging, grouping, sorting, and filtering. In addition, it can be bound using server-side methods with a view model object or with the results of AJAX or web service requests. Automatic editing operations are supported in all binding methods, and different column types make it possible to display almost all kinds of information.

Implementing Grid Operations

To implement grouping, you need to enable it using the Groupable method. You can also call the Add method from the grouping configuration to define a grouped column declaratively.

Paging is enabled using the Pageable method. You can also define some properties such as PageSize to define how many rows will be in each page and the position of the pager with the Position property, which can be Top, Bottom, or Both. The style of the pager is defined with the Style property, which can take values such as NextPrevious, NextPreviousAndNumeric, NextPreviousAndInput, PageInput, Status, and Numeric, as well as combinations of these values.

Sorting is enabled with the Sorteable method. You can define if you want the grid to enable single-column or multiple-column sorting with the SortMode property. Individual columns can be disabled for sorting with the Sorteable property set to false in each column.

Filtering is achieved with the Filterable method, and you can also add initial filters using the Filters collection. Individual columns can have this feature disabled by setting its Filterable property to false.

To enable scrolling, you use the Scrollable method. You can define the height of the scrollable area with the Height property, which accepts a number (in pixels).

Listing 12-34 shows how to enable the scrolling, paging, grouping, sorting, and filtering features of the Grid control. The view model object is the products table from the Northwind database. Because LINQ to SQL uses lazy loading by default, you need to instruct it to preload data from referenced tables, so in order to show the category to which each product belongs to, you have to load that information because it is not automatically populated. Figure 12-32 shows the example running.

Listing 12-34. *Implementing Grid Operations*

```
Controller

public ActionResult GridOperations()
{
    NorthwindDataContext nwd = new NorthwindDataContext();
    DataLoadOptions loadOptions = new DataLoadOptions();
    loadOptions.LoadWith<Product>(p => p.Category);
    nwd.LoadOptions = loadOptions;
    return View(nwd.Products);
}

View

<%
    Html.Telerik().Grid(Model)
        .Name("gridOperations")
        .Columns(c =>
                    {
                        c.Bound(p => p.ProductID);
                        c.Bound(p => p.ProductName);
                        c.Bound(p => p.Category.CategoryName);
                        c.Bound(p => p.UnitPrice).Format("{0:c}");
                        c.Bound(p => p.Discontinued);
                    })
        .Groupable(g=>g.Enabled(true))
        .Pageable(p=>p.Enabled(true)
                        .PageSize(10)
                        .Position(GridPagerPosition.Both)
                        .Style(GridPagerStyles.NextPreviousAndNumeric
                                | GridPagerStyles.PageInput))
```

```
        .Sortable(s=>s.Enabled(true)
                    .SortMode(GridSortMode.MultipleColumn))
        .Filterable(f=>f.Enabled(true))
        .Scrollable(s=>s.Enabled(true)
                    .Height(200))
        .Render();
    %>
```

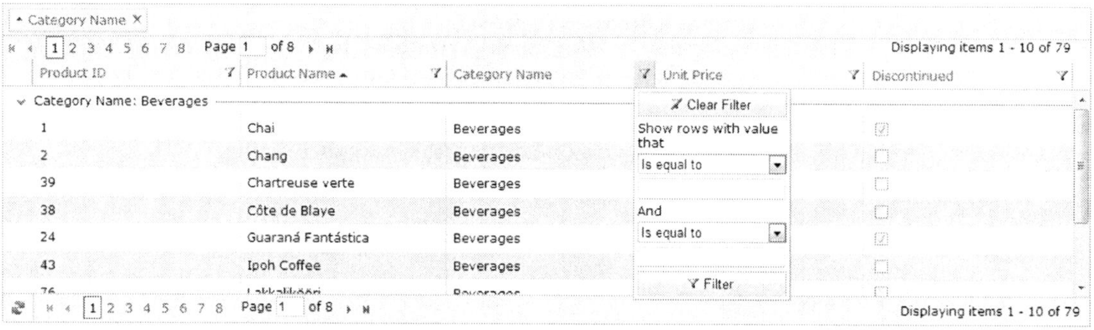

Figure 12-32. *Grid with filtering, sorting, grouping, paging, and scrolling enabled*

Binding to Data

As mentioned before, Grid can be bound directly on the server or via AJAX or web service calls.

It is important to understand that although all the methods are fairly easy to set up, using AJAX or web services will result in the best performance and a more responsive application.

Server binding is a common way to bind to data. It involves the same mechanism you have seen in previous examples, which is passing an object as the model for the view in strongly typed views, as shown in Listing 12-35.

Listing 12-35. *Grid Server Data Binding*

```
Controller

public ActionResult ServerBinding()
{
    NorthwindDataContext nwd = new NorthwindDataContext();
    DataLoadOptions loadOptions = new DataLoadOptions();
    loadOptions.LoadWith<Product>(p => p.Category);
    nwd.LoadOptions = loadOptions;
    return View(nwd.Products);
}
```

```
View

<%
    Html.Telerik().Grid(Model)
        .Name("serverBindedGrid")
        .Columns(c =>
                    {
                        c.Bound(p => p.ProductID);
                        c.Bound(p => p.ProductName);
                        c.Bound(p => p.Category.CategoryName);
                        c.Bound(p => p.UnitPrice).Format("{0:c}");
                        c.Bound(p => p.Discontinued);
                    })
        .Groupable()
        .Pageable()
        .Sortable()
        .Filterable()
        .Render();
 %>
```

When implementing AJAX data binding, the method is a little different. The controller has two action result methods. This first is for when the page first loads and binds the grid using the same server method (don't worry it happens only in the first load). The second action result method is to respond to the grid operations, and it's decorated with the `GridAction` property. This method will be used for all AJAX requests, such as when paging and sorting occurs. When your action result methods are created, you use the `DataBinding` method and set the Ajax property to the action result method with the `GridAction` property. See Listing 12-36 for an implementation of AJAX binding.

Listing 12-36. *Grid AJAX Data Binding*

```
Controller

public ActionResult AjaxBinding()
{
    NorthwindDataContext nwd = new NorthwindDataContext();
    var model = from regs in nwd.Regions
                select new RegionViewModel
                           {
                               RegionID = regs.RegionID,
                               RegionDescription = regs.RegionDescription
                           };
    return View(model);
}

[GridAction]
public ActionResult _AjaxBinding()
{
    NorthwindDataContext nwd = new NorthwindDataContext();
    var model = from regs in nwd.Regions
                select new RegionViewModel
```

```
                {
                    RegionID = regs.RegionID,
                    RegionDescription = regs.RegionDescription
                };
    return View(new GridModel
                    {
                        Data = model
                    });
}

Models/RegionViewModel.cs

namespace TelerikMvcApplication.Models
{
    public class RegionViewModel
    {
        public int RegionID { get; set; }
        public string RegionDescription { get; set; }
    }
}

View

<%
    Html.Telerik().Grid<RegionViewModel>()
        .Name("ajaxBindedGrid")
        .Columns(c =>
                    {
                        c.Bound(p => p.RegionID);
                        c.Bound(p => p.RegionDescription);
                    })
        .DataBinding(b => b.Ajax()
                        .Select("_AjaxBinding", "Grid"))
        .Groupable()
        .Pageable()
        .Sortable()
        .Filterable()
        .Render();
%>
```

When binding `Grid` to a web service, the web method results a `GridModel` object with the data and fields definition. The controller's action result won't load any information because all the loads, even the initial one, are through calls to the web service. See Listing 12-37 for the full implementation of web services data binding. Note that the binding definition includes the path to the web service and the web method that implements the operation.

Listing 12-37. *Grid Web Service Data Binding*

```
Controller

public ActionResult WebServiceBinding()
{
    return View();
}

WS_Regions.asmx

[WebService(Namespace = "http://tempuri.org/")]
[WebServiceBinding(ConformsTo = WsiProfiles.BasicProfile1_1)]
[ToolboxItem(false)]
[ScriptService]
public class WS_Regions : WebService
{
        [WebMethod]
        public GridModel GetRegions(GridState state)
        {
            NorthwindDataContext nwd = new NorthwindDataContext();
            var model = from regs in nwd.Regions
                        select new RegionViewModel
                        {
                            RegionID = regs.RegionID,
                            RegionDescription = regs.RegionDescription
                        };

            return model.ToGridModel(state);
        }
}

View

<%
    Html.Telerik().Grid<RegionViewModel>()
        .Name("wsBindedGrid")
        .Columns(c =>
                    {
                        c.Bound(p => p.RegionID);
                        c.Bound(p => p.RegionDescription);
                    })
        .DataBinding(b => b.WebService()
                            .Select("~/Models/WS_Regions.asmx/GetRegions"))
        .Groupable()
        .Pageable()
        .Sortable()
        .Filterable()
        .Render();
     %>
```

Editing Operations

Editing operations allow users to insert, update, and delete records displayed in the grid. `Grid` supports editing in all three binding scenarios: server binding, AJAX binding, and web services binding.

Implementing server binding with editing is quite simple. What you need to create is a strongly typed view and the action result methods to support each operation. In Listing 12-38, our read action result is called `ServerEditing()`, and our strongly typed view is bound to the `Categories` object model. To create new records, you need to enable the `ToolBar` in which there will be a button that will allow users to have a blank new row to save new information. The button is activated with the toolbar's `Insert()` method. To support the creation operation, the action result method `ServerInsert()` was created, and it allows only `Post` requests. This action result method is in charge of the actual interaction with the model to create the new record; if the process is successful, then it rebinds the grid with the new information. Otherwise, it will keep the grid in edit mode.

The action result methods `ServerUpdate()` and `ServerDelete()` support the update and delete operations, respectively. They work in the same way as `ServerInsert()`.

In the grid declaration, all the operations are enabled using the `Binding` methods `Select()`, `Insert()`, `Update()`, and `Delete()` that map to the action result methods in the controller.

The buttons that enable the actions to edit and delete records are created as `Commands` in the `Columns` section of the grid definition. Figure 12-33 illustrates the example.

Listing 12-38. *Grid Server Editing*

```
Controller

public ActionResult ServerEditing()
{
    NorthwindDataContext nwd = new NorthwindDataContext();
    return View(nwd.Categories);
}

[AcceptVerbs(HttpVerbs.Post)]
public ActionResult ServerInsert()
{
    NorthwindDataContext nwd = new NorthwindDataContext();
    Category cat = new Category();
    if (TryUpdateModel(cat))
    {
        nwd.Categories.InsertOnSubmit(cat);
        nwd.SubmitChanges();
        return RedirectToAction("ServerEditing", this.GridRouteValues());
    }
    return View("ServerEditing", nwd.Categories);
}

[AcceptVerbs(HttpVerbs.Post)]
public ActionResult ServerUpdate(int id)
{
    NorthwindDataContext nwd = new NorthwindDataContext();
    Category cat = nwd.Categories.Single(p => p.CategoryID == id);
```

```
    if (TryUpdateModel(cat))
    {
        nwd.SubmitChanges();
        return RedirectToAction("ServerEditing", this.GridRouteValues());
    }

    return View("ServerEditing", nwd.Categories);
}

[AcceptVerbs(HttpVerbs.Post)]
public ActionResult ServerDelete(int id)
{
    NorthwindDataContext nwd = new NorthwindDataContext();
    Category cat = nwd.Categories.Single(p => p.CategoryID == id);
    if (TryUpdateModel(cat))
    {
        nwd.Categories.DeleteOnSubmit(cat);
        nwd.SubmitChanges();
        return RedirectToAction("ServerEditing", this.GridRouteValues());
    }
    return View("ServerEditing", nwd.Categories);
}
```

View

```
<%@ Page
      Title=""
      Language="C#"
      MasterPageFile="~/Views/Shared/Site.Master"
      Inherits="System.Web.Mvc.ViewPage<IEnumerable<TelerikMvcApplication.Models.Category>>"
%>

<%@ Import Namespace="Telerik.Web.Mvc.UI" %>

<asp:Content ID="Content2" ContentPlaceHolderID="MainContent" runat="server">

    <%
        Html.Telerik().Grid(Model)
            .Name("serverEditingGrid")
            .DataKeys(k=>k.Add(p=>p.CategoryID))
            .ToolBar(t=>t.Insert())
            .Columns(c =>
                        {
                            c.Bound(p => p.CategoryID).ReadOnly(true).Width(100);
                            c.Bound(p => p.CategoryName).Width(200);
                            c.Bound(p => p.Description).Width(300);
                            c.Bound(p => p.DisplayOrder).Width(100);
                            c.Command(cmd =>
                                          {
                                              cmd.Edit();
                                              cmd.Delete();
                                          });
                        })
```

```
            .DataBinding(b=>b.Server()
                               .Select("ServerEditing", "Grid")
                               .Insert("ServerInsert", "Grid")
                               .Update("ServerUpdate", "Grid")
                               .Delete("ServerDelete", "Grid"))
            .Pageable()
            .Sortable()
            .Render();
        %>

</asp:Content>
```

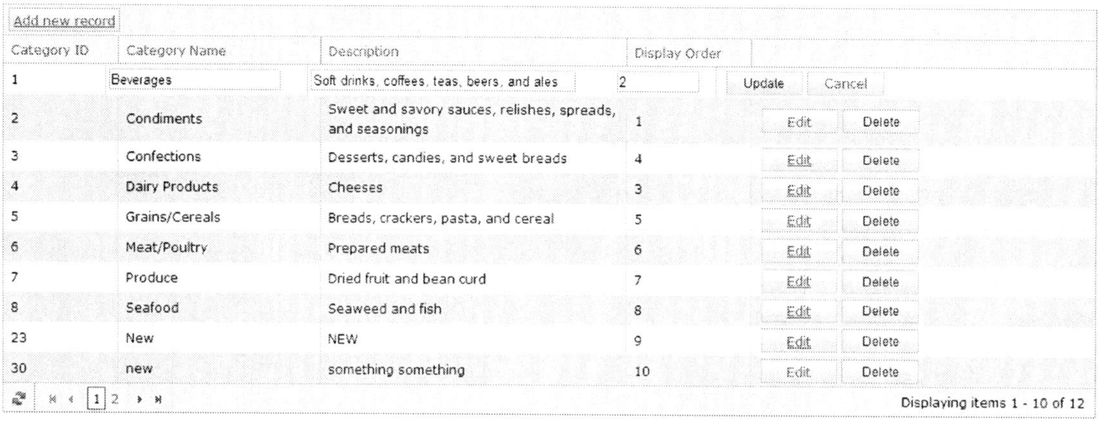

Add new record

Category ID	Category Name	Description	Display Order		
1	Beverages	Soft drinks, coffees, teas, beers, and ales	2	Update	Cancel
2	Condiments	Sweet and savory sauces, relishes, spreads, and seasonings	1	Edit	Delete
3	Confections	Desserts, candies, and sweet breads	4	Edit	Delete
4	Dairy Products	Cheeses	3	Edit	Delete
5	Grains/Cereals	Breads, crackers, pasta, and cereal	5	Edit	Delete
6	Meat/Poultry	Prepared meats	6	Edit	Delete
7	Produce	Dried fruit and bean curd	7	Edit	Delete
8	Seafood	Seaweed and fish	8	Edit	Delete
23	New	NEW	9	Edit	Delete
30	new	something something	10	Edit	Delete

1 2 Displaying items 1 - 10 of 12

Figure 12-33. *Grid supporting editing operations. A record is being updated.*

Editing with AJAX is similar to server editing. There must be action result methods in the controller that support the operations, and you have to map those action result methods to the operations in the grid definition.

In Listing 12-39, the action result methods are decorated with the `GridAction` property and accept only `Post` requests. Here I'm implementing a `ViewModel` class that represents the actual object in the model and a repository class that will do the interaction with the `ViewModel`; this is the recommended approach to avoid circular references when using ORM tools to create the model (for example LINQ to SQL or Entity Framework).

The `Grid` definition is the same as in Listing 12-38; the only change is that now the `Binding` indicates the AJAX binding instead of server binding. Figure 12-34 shows how the grid looks when editing a record using AJAX.

Listing 12-39. *Implementing AJAX Editing*

`ViewModel Class (RegionViewModel.cs)`

```
public class RegionViewModel
{
    public int RegionID { get; set; }
    public string RegionDescription { get; set; }
}
```

Region Repository Class (RegionRepository.cs)

```
public static class RegionRepository
{
    public static List<RegionViewModel> GetAll()
    {
        NorthwindDataContext nwd = new NorthwindDataContext();
        var model = from regs in nwd.Regions
                    select new RegionViewModel
                    {
                        RegionID = regs.RegionID,
                        RegionDescription = regs.RegionDescription
                    };
        return model.ToList();
    }

    public static void Insert(RegionViewModel region)
    {
        var regions = from regs in GetAll()
                      orderby regs.RegionID descending
                      select regs;
        if (regions.Count() > 0)
        {
            var id = regions.First().RegionID + 1;
            region.RegionID = id;
        }
        else
        {
            region.RegionID = 1;
        }

        NorthwindDataContext nwd = new NorthwindDataContext();
        Region r = new Region();
        r.RegionID = region.RegionID;
        r.RegionDescription = region.RegionDescription;
        nwd.Regions.InsertOnSubmit(r);
        nwd.SubmitChanges();
    }

    public static void Update(RegionViewModel region)
    {
        NorthwindDataContext nwd = new NorthwindDataContext();
        Region r = nwd.Regions.Single(reg => reg.RegionID == region.RegionID);
        r.RegionDescription = region.RegionDescription;
        nwd.SubmitChanges();
    }
```

```
    public static void Delete(RegionViewModel region)
    {
        NorthwindDataContext nwd = new NorthwindDataContext();
        Region r = nwd.Regions.Single(reg => reg.RegionID == region.RegionID);
        nwd.Regions.DeleteOnSubmit(r);
        nwd.SubmitChanges();
    }

}

Controller

[GridAction]
public ActionResult AjaxEditing()
{
    return View(new GridModel
    {
        Data = RegionRepository.GetAll()
    });
}

[GridAction]
public ActionResult _AjaxSelect()
{
    return View(new GridModel
    {
        Data = RegionRepository.GetAll()
    });
}

[AcceptVerbs(HttpVerbs.Post)]
[GridAction]
public ActionResult _AjaxInsert()
{
    RegionViewModel reg = new RegionViewModel();
    if (TryUpdateModel(reg))
    {
        RegionRepository.Insert(reg);
    }

    return View(new GridModel(RegionRepository.GetAll()));
}
```

```
[AcceptVerbs(HttpVerbs.Post)]
[GridAction]
public ActionResult _AjaxUpdate(int id)
{
    RegionViewModel reg = new RegionViewModel();
    if (TryUpdateModel(reg))
    {
        RegionRepository.Update(reg);
    }

    return View(new GridModel(RegionRepository.GetAll()));
}

[AcceptVerbs(HttpVerbs.Post)]
[GridAction]
public ActionResult _AjaxDelete(int id)
{
    RegionViewModel reg = new RegionViewModel();
    if (TryUpdateModel(reg))
    {
        RegionRepository.Delete(reg);
    }

    return View(new GridModel(RegionRepository.GetAll()));
}
```

RegionRepository.cs

```
public static class RegionRepository
{
    public static List<RegionViewModel> GetAll()
    {
        NorthwindDataContext nwd = new NorthwindDataContext();
        var model = from regs in nwd.Regions
                    select new RegionViewModel
                    {
                        RegionID = regs.RegionID,
                        RegionDescription = regs.RegionDescription
                    };

        return model.ToList();
    }

    public static void Insert(RegionViewModel region)
    {
        var regions = from regs in GetAll()
                      orderby regs.RegionID descending
                      select regs;
        if (regions.Count() > 0)
        {
            var id = regions.First().RegionID + 1;
            region.RegionID = id;
        }
```

```
        else
        {
            region.RegionID = 1;
        }

        NorthwindDataContext nwd = new NorthwindDataContext();
        Region r = new Region();
        r.RegionID = region.RegionID;
        r.RegionDescription = region.RegionDescription;
        nwd.Regions.InsertOnSubmit(r);
        nwd.SubmitChanges();
    }

    public static void Update(RegionViewModel region)
    {
        NorthwindDataContext nwd = new NorthwindDataContext();
        Region r = nwd.Regions.Single(reg => reg.RegionID == region.RegionID);
        r.RegionDescription = region.RegionDescription;
        nwd.SubmitChanges();
    }

    public static void Delete(RegionViewModel region)
    {
        NorthwindDataContext nwd = new NorthwindDataContext();
        Region r = nwd.Regions.Single(reg => reg.RegionID == region.RegionID);
        nwd.Regions.DeleteOnSubmit(r);
        nwd.SubmitChanges();
    }

}
```

View

```
<%
    Html.Telerik().Grid<RegionViewModel>()
        .Name("ajaxEditingGrid")
        .DataKeys(k => k.Add(p => p.RegionID))
        .ToolBar(t => t.Insert())
        .Columns(c =>
                    {
                        c.Bound(p => p.RegionID);
                        c.Bound(p => p.RegionDescription);
                        c.Command(cmd =>
                                    {
                                        cmd.Edit();
                                        cmd.Delete();
                                    });
                    })
        .DataBinding(b => b.Ajax()
                            .Select("AjaxEditing", "Grid")
                            .Insert("_AjaxInsert", "Grid")
                            .Update("_AjaxUpdate", "Grid")
                            .Delete("_AjaxDelete", "Grid"))
```

```
        .Pageable()
        .Sortable()
        .Render();
    %>
```

Figure 12-34. *The record in the Grid is being edited using AJAX.*

Editing with web services is similar to AJAX editing, but instead of having a repository class that handles the interaction with the ViewModel, there is a web service doing exactly that.

Listing 12-40 shows how to create the web service to handle the editing operations. Always remember to decorate the methods with the WebMethod property, and all the methods return a GridModel object and accept a GridState parameter, so they are aware of the current state of the grid. Figure 12-35 shows it in action.

Listing 12-40. *Grid Web Services Editing*

```
Controller

public ActionResult WebServiceEditing()
{
    return View(new GridModel
    {
        Data = RegionRepository.GetAll()
    });
}

WS_Regions.asmx

[WebService(Namespace = "http://tempuri.org/")]
[WebServiceBinding(ConformsTo = WsiProfiles.BasicProfile1_1)]
[ToolboxItem(false)]
[ScriptService]
ublic class WS_Regions : WebService
{
        [WebMethod]
        public GridModel Select(GridState state)
        {
            return RegionRepository.GetAll().AsQueryable().ToGridModel(state);
        }
```

```
        [WebMethod]
        public GridModel Insert(RegionViewModel region, GridState state)
        {
            RegionRepository.Insert(region);

            return RegionRepository.GetAll().AsQueryable().ToGridModel(state);
        }

        [WebMethod]
        public GridModel Update(RegionViewModel region, GridState state)
        {
            RegionRepository.Update(region);

            return RegionRepository.GetAll().AsQueryable().ToGridModel(state);
        }

        [WebMethod]
        public GridModel Delete(RegionViewModel region, GridState state)
        {
            RegionRepository.Delete(region);

            return RegionRepository.GetAll().AsQueryable().ToGridModel(state);
        }
}
```

View

```
<%
    Html.Telerik().Grid<RegionViewModel>()
        .Name("wsEditingGrid")
        .DataKeys(k => k.Add(p => p.RegionID))
        .ToolBar(t => t.Insert())
        .Columns(c =>
                     {
                         c.Bound(p => p.RegionID).ReadOnly(true);
                         c.Bound(p => p.RegionDescription);
                         c.Command(cmd =>
                                       {
                                           cmd.Edit();
                                           cmd.Delete();
                                       });
                     })
        .DataBinding(b => b.WebService()
                              .Select("~/Models/WS_Regions.asmx/Select")
                              .Insert("~/Models/WS_Regions.asmx/Insert")
                              .Update("~/Models/WS_Regions.asmx/Update")
                              .Delete("~/Models/WS_Regions.asmx/Delete"))
        .Pageable()
        .Sortable()
        .Render();
%>
```

Add new record

Region ID	Region Description	
0		Insert Cancel
1	Eastern	Edit Delete
2	Western	Edit Delete
3	Northern	Edit Delete
4	Southern	Edit Delete

1 — Displaying items 1 - 4 of 4

Figure 12-35. *Creating a new record in the Grid using weba services editing*

Implementing Templates

Following the a templating tradition, `Grid` also supports templates. They are based on the `Content` property of each individual column, so you are free to leverage your imagination with anything you can do with HTML.

In Listing 12-41, a template is created to display employee information supporting an image that is not in the standard set of column types. Figure 12-36 shows the resulting grid.

Listing 12-41. *Implementing Grid Templates*

```
Controller

public ActionResult Templates()
{
    NorthwindDataContext nwd = new NorthwindDataContext();
    return View(nwd.Employees);
}

View

<%
    Html.Telerik().Grid(Model)
        .Name("serverBindedGrid")
        .Columns(c =>
            {
            c.Bound(p => p.EmployeeID);
            c.Template(x =>
                        {
                        %>
                        <table>
                            <tr>
                                <td align="center">
                                    <%=x.FirstName + " " + x.LastName%>
                                </td>
                            </tr>
```

```
                                <tr>
                                    <td align="center">
                                        <img src="<%=Url.Content("~/Images/Employees/"
                                                    + x.EmployeeID + ".jpg")%>"
                                             alt="<%=x.EmployeeID%>"
                                             width="100px" />
                                    </td>
                                </tr>
                            </table>
                            <%
                            }).Title("Picture");
                c.Bound(p => p.Title);
                c.Template(x =>
                            {
                                %>
                                    <%=x.Region + ", " + x.Country%>
                                <%
                            }).Title("Location");
                c.Bound(p => p.HireDate).Format("{0:d}");
                })
        .Pageable(x=>x.PageSize(2))
        .Sortable()
        .Render();
%>
```

Employee ID	Picture	Title	Location	Hire Date
1	Nancy Davolio	Sales Representative	WA, USA	5/1/1992
2	Andrew Fuller	Vice President, Sales	WA, USA	8/14/1992

1 2 3 4 5 Displaying items 1 - 2 of 9

Figure 12-36. *Employees Grid that implements a template that loads an image of each employee*

Working with Grid's Client API

The client API created for Grid has many interesting operations and events. The supported events are Load, which is raised when the grid first loads; and DataBinding and DataBound, which are raised every time the grid is bound to data and when the binding operation is finished, respectively. The RowDataBound is raised for every row in the grid once it's bound to the data. The Select event is raised when a row is selected, and there is an Error event that is raised whenever an error has occurred.

The ajaxRequest() method causes Grid to request data during AJAX and web services binding scenarios. dataBind() binds the grid to an array of JavaScript objects. The rebind() method rebinds the grid when bound with AJAX or web services. The pageTo() method displays in the grid the rows in the specified page number.

To implement all these methods and operations, you need to get access to the Grid client object tGrid after finding the grid with the jQuery selector $("selector").data("tGrid").

You can also sort the grid using the sort() method and passing a sort expression as a parameter. A sort expression is a pair of values composed by the column name and the sort order separated by a dash. For example, if you are sorting the Regions grid by RegionID in ascendant order, you would use it like sort(RegionID-asc).

Filtering is also supported by the client API using the filter() method and passing a filter expression as a parameter. You can build filter expressions in the form of member~operator~value or filterFunction(member, value). The member represents the column by which you want to filter the grid. The following are supported operators:

- eq: Is equal to
- ne: Is not equal to
- gt: Is greater than
- ge: Is greater or equal than
- lt: Is lower than
- le: Is lower or equal than

If you want to filter the Regions grid by a specific RegionID, you could use a filter expression like filter('RegionID~eq~123').

Filter functions are supported only for string members; the available ones are as follows:

- endswith: Ends with
- startswith: Starts with
- substringof: Contains

A filter expression with a function could be substringof(RegionName, 'North'). Also, complex expressions can be composed by joining simple expressions. Here's an example:

```
substringof(RegionName, 'North')~and~RegionID~ge~5
```

Listing 12-42 shows you how to implement some of the many functions in Grid's client API. Figure 12-37 shows the example running.

Listing 12-42. *Implementing Grid's Client API*

```
Controller

public ActionResult ClientAPI()
{
    return View();
}
ViewModel class (ProductViewModel.cs)

public class ProductViewModel
{
    public int ProductID { get; set; }
    public string ProductName { get; set; }
}

Web service for binding (WS_Products.asmx.cs)

[WebService(Namespace = "http://tempuri.org/")]
[WebServiceBinding(ConformsTo = WsiProfiles.BasicProfile1_1)]
[ToolboxItem(false)]
[ScriptService]
public class WS_Products : WebService
{
    [WebMethod]
    public GridModel ListProducts(GridState state)
    {
        NorthwindDataContext nwd = new NorthwindDataContext();
        var model = from prds in nwd.Products
                    select new ProductViewModel
                    {
                        ProductID = prds.ProductID,
                        ProductName = prds.ProductName
                    };
        return model.ToGridModel(state);
    }

}

View

<%@ Page Title=""
        Language="C#"
        MasterPageFile="~/Views/Shared/Site.Master"
        Inherits="System.Web.Mvc.ViewPage" %>

<%@ Import Namespace="Telerik.Web.Mvc.UI" %>
<%@ Import Namespace="TelerikMvcApplication.Models" %>
<input type="button"
        value="Go to Page 3"
        onclick="gotoPage(3);" />
```

```
<input type="button"
       value="Sort by Product ID ASC"
       onclick="sortAsc();" />



<input type="button"
       value="Show only products with ID lower than 10"
       onclick="filter10();" />

<input type="button"
       value="Reset Grid"
       onclick="reset();" />

<%
    Html.Telerik().Grid<ProductViewModel>()
        .Name("wsBindedGrid")
        .Columns(c =>
                        {
                            c.Bound(p => p.ProductID);
                            c.Bound(p => p.ProductName);
                        })
        .DataBinding(b => b.WebService()
                           .Select("~/Models/WS_Products.asmx/ListProducts")
                        )
        .ClientEvents(e=>e
            .OnLoad("onLoad")
            .OnDataBinding("onDataBinding")
            .OnRowDataBound("onRowDataBound")
            .OnRowSelected("onRowSelected")
            .OnDataBound("onDataBound")
            )
        .Pageable()
        .Sortable()
        .Selectable()
        .Filterable()
        .Render();
        %>

<div id="logChanges"></div>

<script type="text/javascript">

        function gotoPage(page) {
            var grid = $('#wsBindedGrid').data('tGrid');
            grid.pageTo(page);
            var lbl = document.getElementById("logChanges");
            lbl.innerHTML = lbl.innerHTML + "<br />";
            lbl.innerHTML = lbl.innerHTML + "Navigated to page 3";
        }
```

```
function sortAsc() {
    var grid = $('#wsBindedGrid').data('tGrid');
    grid.sort('ProductID-asc');
    var lbl = document.getElementById("logChanges");
    lbl.innerHTML = lbl.innerHTML + "<br />";
    lbl.innerHTML = lbl.innerHTML + "Sorted grid by ProductID ASC";
}

function filter10() {
    var grid = $('#wsBindedGrid').data('tGrid');
    grid.filter('ProductID~lt~10');
    var lbl = document.getElementById("logChanges");
    lbl.innerHTML = lbl.innerHTML + "<br />";
    lbl.innerHTML = lbl.innerHTML +
                   "Filtered products with ProductID lower than 10";
}

function reset() {
    var grid = $('#wsBindedGrid').data('tGrid');
    grid.rebind();
    var lbl = document.getElementById("logChanges");
    lbl.innerHTML = lbl.innerHTML + "<br />";
    lbl.innerHTML = lbl.innerHTML + "Grid rebinded";
}

function onLoad(sender) {
    var lbl = document.getElementById("logChanges");
    lbl.innerHTML = "Event: onLoad [Grid loaded succesfully]";
}

function onDataBinding(sender) {
    var lbl = document.getElementById("logChanges");
    lbl.innerHTML = lbl.innerHTML + "<br />";
    lbl.innerHTML = lbl.innerHTML + "Event: onDataBinding [Grid binding]";
}

function onDataBound(sender) {
    var lbl = document.getElementById("logChanges");
    lbl.innerHTML = lbl.innerHTML + "<br />";
    lbl.innerHTML = lbl.innerHTML + "Event: onDataBound [Grid bound succesfully]";
}

function onRowDataBound(sender) {
    var lbl = document.getElementById("logChanges");
    var dataItem = sender.dataItem;
    lbl.innerHTML = lbl.innerHTML + "<br />";
    lbl.innerHTML = lbl.innerHTML + "Event: onRowDataBound [Product ID: "
                         + dataItem.ProductID + "]";
}
```

```
        function onRowSelected(sender) {
            var lbl = document.getElementById("logChanges");
            var row = sender.row;
            lbl.innerHTML = lbl.innerHTML + "<br />";
            lbl.innerHTML = lbl.innerHTML + "Event: onRowSelected [Product ID: "
                                          + row.cells[0].innerHTML + "]";
        }
</script>
```

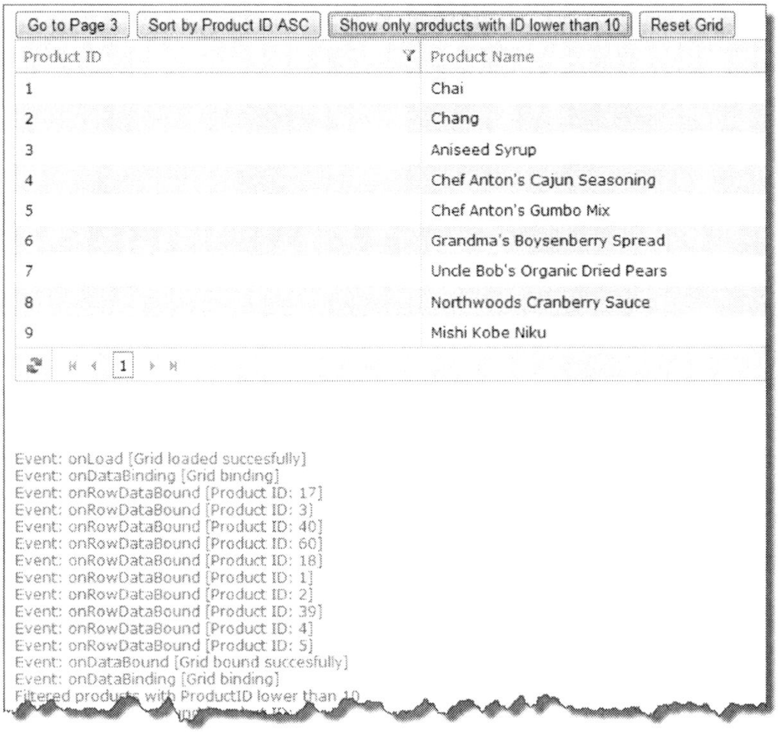

Figure 12-37. *Working with Grid and its client API*

Summary

You have seen how to work with Telerik Extensions for ASP.NET MVC. The controls exposed by the extensions are `Calendar`, `DatePicker`, `PanelBar`, `Menu`, `TabStrip`, `NumericTextBox`, `TreeView`, and `Grid`.

All the controls provide a lot of the functionality found in their counterparts in the WebForms world. All the controls rely heavily on jQuery and are extensions of the `HtmlHelper` object for UI render. They are superfast and support a wide range of functionality not easily found in the MVC framework.

With `Calendar` and `DatePicker`, you can define the range of allowed dates; also, they recognize automatically the culture in the working thread for globalization support and expose a client API.

Calendar also has select actions, which are triggered whenever a specific date is selected, and DatePicker incorporates a wide selection of words for easy date parsing.

NumericTextBox supports minimum and maximum values, globalization, and a client API. But that's not all; it can also be validated on the server using ASP.NET MVC's built-in validation support or by applying the new DataAnnotationsAttribute class to your ViewModel properties.

Menu, TabStrip, and PanelBar are highly customizable controls for navigation and content display that can be populated with items declaratively or by data binding to a view model object. They all expose a client API and offer support for content templates. PanelBar and TabStrip can even load content on demand, thus improving performance on first load.

TreeView is a full-featured tree control. It supports item check boxes and templates, drag-and-drop between nodes and to other elements in the view, load on demand, and a client API.

Grid is probably the most complete control in the suite. It can be bound on the server or via AJAX or web service calls. Editing operations are also supported with each of those approaches. Grid operations such as paging, scrolling, sorting, filtering, and grouping are also supported along with a rich client API.

CHAPTER 13

■ ■ ■

RadControls for Silverlight

This chapter introduces Telerik's support for Microsoft Silverlight with the Telerik RadControls suite for Silverlight. Telerik is the first third-party software vendor that has Silverlight native controls, and it has been on the top of the game since the first Silverlight release.

The suite provides more than 30 controls, including its flagship products RadGridView and RadScheduler, as well as others new to the platform, such as RadTileView, RadGauge, RadBook, and RadTransition. Other controls like RadChart and RadUpload have significant improvements, especially in UI and asynchronous operations.

The approach in this chapter is a little different than that taken in the previous chapters. I will walk through building a Silverlight application that incorporates Telerik's controls to improve it. I will show you how to make these controls work seamlessly in the application, focusing on those controls that don't have an ASP.NET counterpart or have improvements that can't be simply ignored. Also, Silverlight 4 and Visual Studio 2010 will be used for the development.

The application is built using WCF RIA Services, which greatly improves the information exchange between the server and the presentation layer. In WCF RIA Services, you expose data from the server project to the client project by adding domain services. The WCF RIA Services framework implements each domain service as a WCF service; therefore, you can apply the concepts you know from WCF services to domain services when customizing the configuration.

Note For more information on installation of Silverlight 4 and WCF RIA Services, visit www.silverlight.net/getstarted/ and www.silverlight.net/getstarted/riaservices/.

Configuring Telerik RadControls for Silverlight

To begin, create a new Silverlight Business Application with the name ProTelerikDemo, as shown in Figure 13-1. The Visual Studio 2010 template will create a Silverlight 4 application and a web site that will host the application.

The next step is to configure Telerik RadControls for Silverlight. The installation is a simple "click Next" procedure, as explained in the "Installing the Controls and Tools" section in Chapter 2.

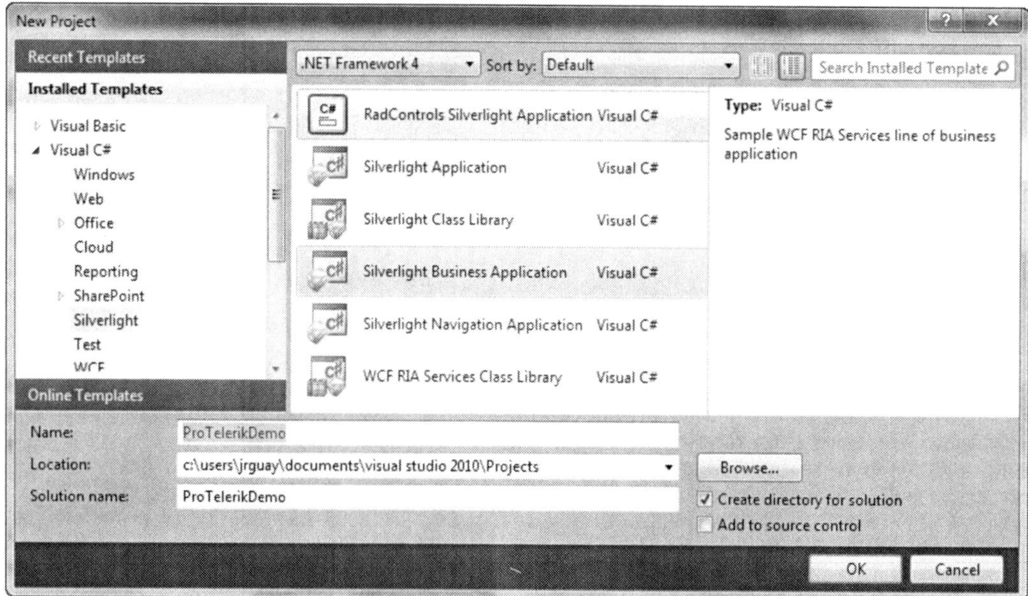

Figure 13-1. *Creating a Silverlight Business Application in Visual Studio 2010*

You can configure the Silverlight application simply by dragging the desired control onto the XAML page, and Visual Studio will add the necessary assembly references to the project. The other option is to use Visual Studio Extensions for Silverlight. Select the menu option Telerik ➤ RadControls for Silverlight ➤ Convert to Telerik Silverlight Application, as shown in Figure 13-2.

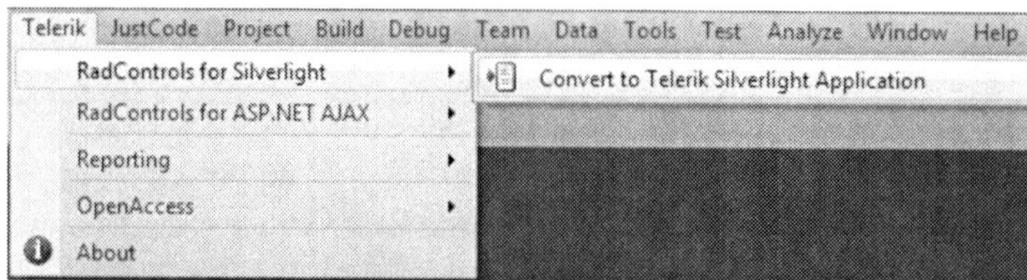

Figure 13-2. *Using Visual Studio Extensions to configure RadControls for Silverlight*

The option will open the Project Configuration Wizard, shown in Figure 13-3. Here, you can select the version of Telerik controls to use, the assemblies that can be added to the project, and the themes for the controls. I strongly suggest you add only those references you need; you want to keep the application small and not bloated with unused libraries. Assembly references can be added or removed at a later time if the needs of the application change.

Figure 13-3. *Using the Project Configuration Wizard*

Now it's time to configure the data access in the web application. Create an ADO.NET Entity Data Model (which is part of Entity Framework), which will be the interface to the Northwind database. Name the data model `Northwind.edmx` and add all the tables from the database, keeping all the default settings.

Next, you need to add the WCF service that will expose the data to the Silverlight application. At this point, you need to compile the project before adding the service so the data model will be visible to the service. After the project compilation, create a domain service class in the `Services` folder and name it `NorthwindDomainService.cs`, as shown in Figure 13-4. The service configuration window will be displayed. Select all the objects in the list to generate associated classes for metadata, as shown in Figure 13-5.

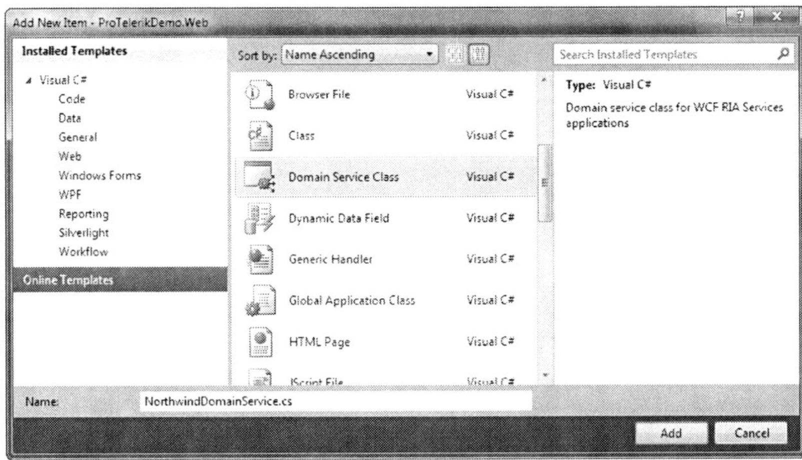

Figure 13-4. *Adding a new domain service class named NorthwindDataService.cs*

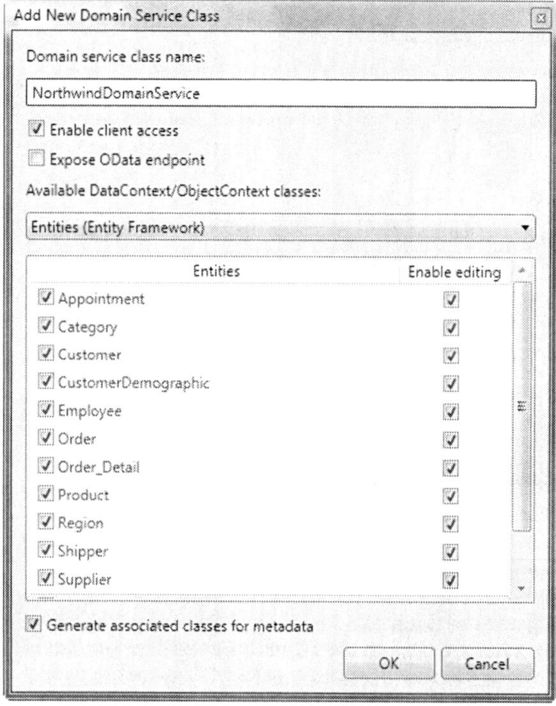

Figure 13-5. *Configuring the domain service class*

When you run the application, you will see something similar to Figure 13-6. The window includes a logo, an application name, and links for the navigation between pages.

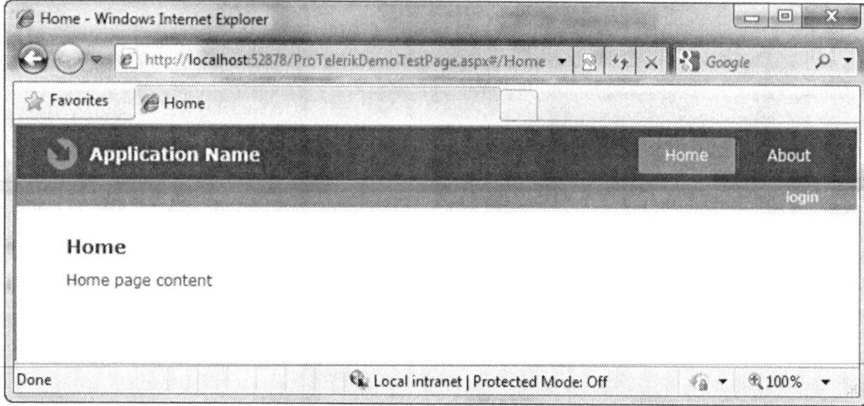

Figure 13-6. *Application running with default settings*

Enhancing the Navigation

The first task to improve the application is to modify the navigation. Let's replace the current hyperlink-based menu structure with RadMenu so we have a better experience. Open the file MainPage.xaml in the Silverlight application. Add the namespaces shown in Listing 13-1 to gain access to the navigation controls.

Listing 13-1. *Telerik Namespaces to Have Access to the Navigation Controls*

```
xmlns:telerik="clr-namespace:Telerik.Windows.Controls;
                assembly=Telerik.Windows.Controls"
xmlns:telerikNavigation= "clr-namespace:Telerik.Windows.Controls;
                        assembly=Telerik.Windows.Controls.Navigation"
```

Now find the navigation links shown in Listing 13-2 and replace them with the RadMenu declaration in Listing 13-3.

Listing 13-2. *Current Hyperlinks for Navigation in the Silverlight Application*

```
<HyperlinkButton x:Name="Link1"
                Style="{StaticResource LinkStyle}"
                NavigateUri="/Home"
                TargetName="ContentFrame"
                Content="{Binding Path=ApplicationStrings.HomePageTitle,
                Source={StaticResource ResourceWrapper}}"/>

<Rectangle x:Name="Divider1" Style="{StaticResource DividerStyle}"/>

<HyperlinkButton x:Name="Link2"
                Style="{StaticResource LinkStyle}"
                NavigateUri="/About"
                TargetName="ContentFrame"
                Content="{Binding Path=ApplicationStrings.AboutPageTitle,
                Source={StaticResource ResourceWrapper}}"/>
```

Listing 13-3. *New Navigation Using Telerik RadMenu*

```
<telerikNavigation:RadMenu x:Name="BusinessMenu"
                           VerticalAlignment="Center"
                           ItemClick="BusinessMenu_ItemClick" >

    <telerikNavigation:RadMenuItem Header="Home" />

    <telerikNavigation:RadMenuItem Header="Inventory">
        <telerikNavigation:RadMenuItem Header="Categories" />
        <telerikNavigation:RadMenuItem Header="Products" />
    </telerikNavigation:RadMenuItem>
```

```
    <telerikNavigation:RadMenuItem Header="Sales">
        <telerikNavigation:RadMenuItem Header="Employees and Orders" />
    </telerikNavigation:RadMenuItem>

    <telerikNavigation:RadMenuItem Header="About" />
</telerikNavigation:RadMenu>
```

Listing 13-4 shows the event handler for the ItemClick event defined in RadMenu. This event will intercept user selections and execute the appropriate navigation action.

Listing 13-4. *RadMenu ItemClick Event Handler*

```
private void BusinessMenu_ItemClick(object sender, Telerik.Windows.RadRoutedEventArgs e)
{
    RadMenuItem item = e.OriginalSource as RadMenuItem;
    if (item != null)
    {
        switch (item.Header.ToString())
        {
            case "Categories":
                this.ContentFrame
                    .Navigate(new
                        System.Uri("/Categories", System.UriKind.Relative));
                break;

            case "Products":
                this.ContentFrame
                    .Navigate(new
                        System.Uri("/Products", System.UriKind.Relative));
                break;

            case "Employees and Orders":
                this.ContentFrame
                    .Navigate(new
                        System.Uri("/Employees", System.UriKind.Relative));
                break;

            case "About":
                this.ContentFrame
                    .Navigate(new
                        System.Uri("/About", System.UriKind.Relative));
                break;

            default:
                this.ContentFrame
                    .Navigate(new
                        System.Uri("/Home", System.UriKind.Relative));
                break;
        }
    }
}
```

The result of this change is shown in Figure 13-7. Notice how we have a fully working menu that resembles the one in ASP.NET applications.

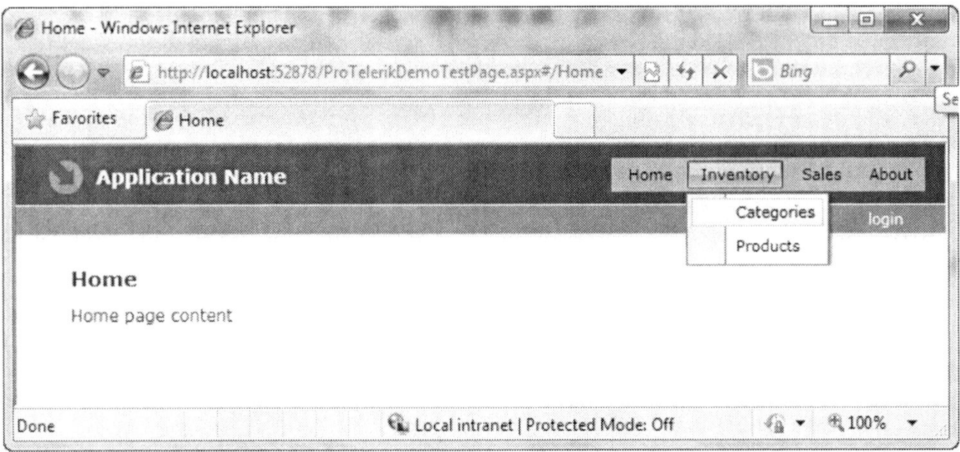

Figure 13-7. *Silverlight RadMenu working in the application*

Now let's create the categories, products, and employees XAML pages so the navigation won't get broken. Don't worry about the content—we will create that as we progress through the application development. Figure 13-8 shows how to create a XAML page. Also, remember to create the pages in the `Views` folder to keep the same application structure.

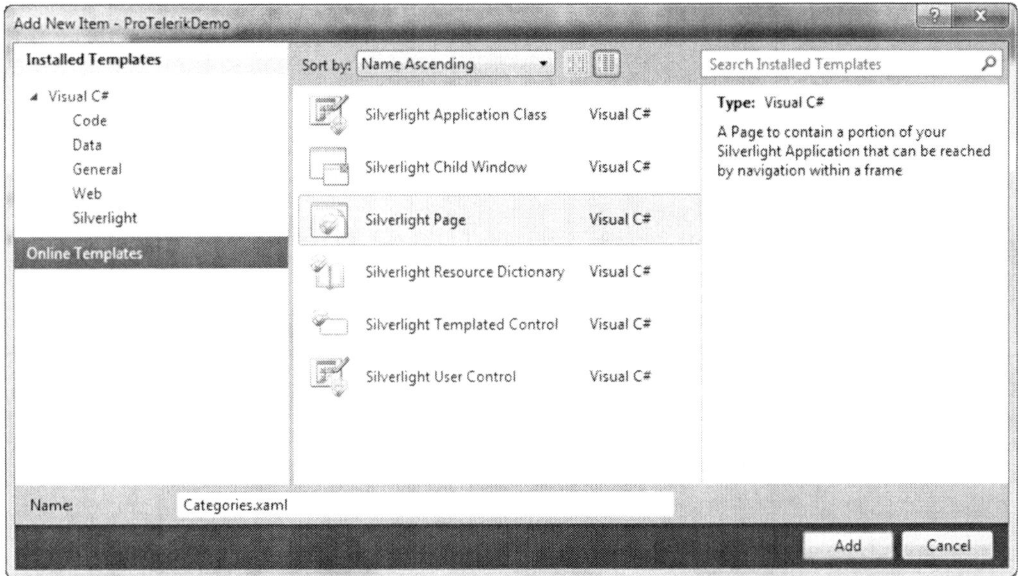

Figure 13-8. *Creating a XAML page*

The next navigation enhancement is to improve the transition from one page to another when selected in the menu. Telerik has a specific control to manage transitions between elements: the

RadTransition control. This control handles the transition animation between two elements, such as list items, navigation pages, and so forth. The configuration is very simple. All you need to do is add a RadTransition control to the page and bind the Content property to the element for which you want to provide transition animations. Then you define the type of animation with the effects in the TransitionEffects namespace.

To have a nice animation when navigating to another page in the application, you need to add a reference to the TransitionEffects namespace, and then create the RadTransition control in the definition of the navigation frame, as shown in Listing 13-5.

Listing 13-5. *Configuring RadTransition to Provide Transition Animations When Navigating from Page to Page in the Silverlight Application*

```
Add the TransitionEffects namespace

xmlns:effects="clr-namespace:Telerik.Windows.Controls.TransitionEffects;
assembly=Telerik.Windows.Controls"

Modify the navigation frame to include the transition control

<navigation:Frame x:Name="ContentFrame"
                  Style="{StaticResource ContentFrameStyle}"
                  Source="/Home"
                  Navigated="ContentFrame_Navigated"
                  NavigationFailed="ContentFrame_NavigationFailed">
    <navigation:Frame.UriMapper>
        <uriMapper:UriMapper>
        <uriMapper:UriMapping Uri=""
                              MappedUri="/Views/Home.xaml"/>
        <uriMapper:UriMapping Uri="/{pageName}"
                              MappedUri="/Views/{pageName}.xaml"/>
        </uriMapper:UriMapper>
    </navigation:Frame.UriMapper>

    <navigation:Frame.Template>
        <ControlTemplate TargetType="navigation:Frame">
            <telerik:RadTransitionControl Content="{TemplateBinding Content}"
                                          ContentTemplate="{TemplateBinding Content}">
                <telerik:RadTransitionControl.Transition>
                    <effects:SlideAndZoomTransition />
                </telerik:RadTransitionControl.Transition>
            </telerik:RadTransitionControl>
        </ControlTemplate>
    </navigation:Frame.Template>

</navigation:Frame>
```

In Listing 13-5, notice how RadTransition is defined inside the navigation frame template and is bound to the template content (meaning, the navigation pages). The transition animation is determined by the Transition property that is defined as a SlideAndZoomTransition. This animation zooms out the current frame, making it look farther and smaller (about 15%), and then it slides that frame out to the right while sliding in the new frame, which then is zoomed in to fill the available space.

Other animations include FadeTransition, LinearFadeTransition, MotionBlurredZoom, WaveTransition, FlipWarpTransition, and RollTransition.

Adding the Product Catalog

The next feature of the application is the product catalog. RadBook is a control that shows content in a way that resembles a traditional book. You can see information in the left and right pages, with a transition animation that simulates turning the book's page, as shown in Figure 13-9.

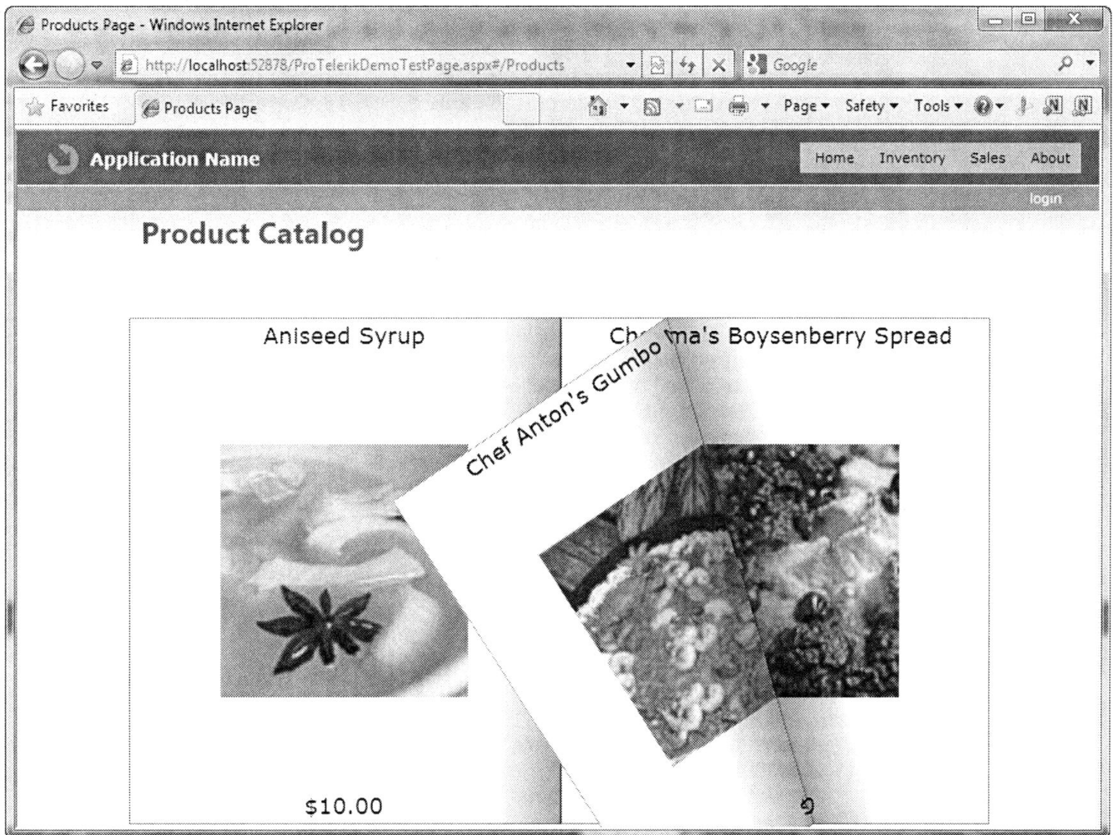

Figure 13-9. *The product catalog is shown as if it were an actual book.*

In the products.xaml page, add the references to the namespace Telerik.Windows.Controls in the Telerik.Windows.Controls.Navigation assembly where RadBook is defined. Then add two DataTemplate definitions to build the layout of the left and right pages of RadBook. The layout has one TextBlock for the product name, then an Image for the product image, and finally another TextBlock for the price. The layout is built with a Grid with three rows. In order to show the picture of the product, we use the new StringFormat property of the Binding syntax introduced in Silverlight 4. Notice in Listing 13-6 how data is brought from the WCF service we added earlier.

Listing 13-6. *Using RadBook to Present the Product Catalog Bound to a WCF RIA Service*

```
<navigation:Page x:Class="ProTelerikDemo.Views.Products"
                 xmlns="http://schemas.microsoft.com/winfx/2006/xaml/presentation"
                 xmlns:x="http://schemas.microsoft.com/winfx/2006/xaml"
                 xmlns:d="http://schemas.microsoft.com/expression/blend/2008"
                 xmlns:mc="http://schemas.openxmlformats.org/markup-compatibility/2006"
                 mc:Ignorable="d"
                 xmlns:navigation="clr-namespace:System.Windows.Controls;
                                   assembly=System.Windows.Controls.Navigation"
                 xmlns:telerikNavigation="clr-namespace:Telerik.Windows.Controls;
                                          assembly=Telerik.Windows.Controls.Navigation"
                 d:DesignWidth="640"
                 d:DesignHeight="480"
                 Title="Products Page">
    <navigation:Page.Resources>

        <!-- Style definition for the page title -->
        <Style TargetType="TextBlock" x:Key="PageTitle">
            <Setter Property="Foreground" Value="#0b4366" />
            <Setter Property="FontSize" Value="24" />
            <Setter Property="FontWeight" Value="Bold" />
            <Setter Property="FontFamily" Value="Segoe UI" />
            <Setter Property="VerticalAlignment" Value="Center" />
            <Setter Property="HorizontalAlignment" Value="Center" />
            <Setter Property="Padding" Value="10 0" />
            <Setter Property="Margin" Value="0 0 0 50" />
        </Style>

        <!-- Style definition for the book pages (left and right) -->
        <DataTemplate x:Key="LeftPageTemplate">
            <Border BorderBrush="Gray" BorderThickness="1">
                <Grid Background="White">
                    <Grid.RowDefinitions>
                        <RowDefinition Height="Auto" />
                        <RowDefinition Height="*" />
                        <RowDefinition Height="Auto" />
                    </Grid.RowDefinitions>
                    <TextBlock Text="{Binding ProductName}"
                               HorizontalAlignment="Center"
                               VerticalAlignment="Center"
                               FontSize="18"
                               TextWrapping="Wrap" />
                    <Image Source="{Binding ProductID,
                               StringFormat=../Images/Products/Thumbs/\{0\}.jpg}"
                           HorizontalAlignment="Center"
                           VerticalAlignment="Center"
                           Width="200"
                           Height="200"
                           Grid.Row="1" />
```

```
                <TextBlock Text="{Binding UnitPrice, StringFormat=\{0:c\}}"
                                HorizontalAlignment="Center"
                                Grid.Row="2"
                                VerticalAlignment="Center"
                                FontSize="18"
                                TextWrapping="Wrap" />
            </Grid>
        </Border>
    </DataTemplate>
    <DataTemplate x:Key="RightPageTemplate">
        <Border BorderBrush="Gray" BorderThickness="1">
            <Grid Background="White">
                <Grid.RowDefinitions>
                    <RowDefinition Height="Auto" />
                    <RowDefinition Height="*" />
                    <RowDefinition Height="Auto" />
                </Grid.RowDefinitions>
                <TextBlock Text="{Binding ProductName}"
                                HorizontalAlignment="Center"
                                VerticalAlignment="Center"
                                FontSize="18"
                                TextWrapping="Wrap" />
                <Image Source="{Binding ProductID,
                                StringFormat=../Images/Products/Thumbs/\{0\}.jpg}
                            HorizontalAlignment="Center"
                            Width="200"
                            Height="200"
                            VerticalAlignment="Center"
                            Grid.Row="1" />
                <TextBlock Text="{Binding UnitPrice, StringFormat=\{0:c\}}"
                                HorizontalAlignment="Center"
                                Grid.Row="2"
                                VerticalAlignment="Center"
                                FontSize="18"
                                TextWrapping="Wrap" />
            </Grid>
        </Border>
    </DataTemplate>
</navigation:Page.Resources>

<Grid x:Name="LayoutRoot">
    <Grid.RowDefinitions>
        <RowDefinition Height="Auto" />
        <RowDefinition Height="*" />
    </Grid.RowDefinitions>

    <TextBlock Text="Product Catalog"
               Style="{StaticResource PageTitle}"
               Width="700"
               HorizontalAlignment="Center" />
```

```
        <!-- RadBook definition -->
        <telerikNavigation:RadBook x:Name="Products_RadBook"
                                   IsKeyboardNavigationEnabled="True"
                                   LeftPageTemplate="{StaticResource LeftPageTemplate}"
                                   RightPageTemplate="{StaticResource RightPageTemplate}"
                                   Grid.Row="1"
                                   Width="700"
                                   Height="400" />

    </Grid>

</navigation:Page>
```

```
Code Behind

using ProTelerikDemo.Web.Services;
using System.Windows.Controls;
using System.Windows.Navigation;

namespace ProTelerikDemo.Views
{
    public partial class Products : Page
    {
        public Products()
        {
            InitializeComponent();
            LoadProducts();
        }

        public void LoadProducts()
        {
            // Create the domain context to connect to the service
            NorthwindDomainContext nwd = new NorthwindDomainContext();
            // Bind RadBook to the products table
            Products_RadBook.ItemsSource = nwd.Products;
            // Get the data
            nwd.Load(nwd.GetProductsQuery());
        }

        // Executes when the user navigates to this page
        protected override void OnNavigatedTo(NavigationEventArgs e)
        {
        }

    }
}
```

Improving the Home Page with a Dashboard

Visitors like to see a home page that displays some information, not just an empty page with a bunch of menu options. Many applications implement some kind of dashboard for the landing page, with relevant summary information. Let's add a dashboard to the sample application.

Implementing RadTileView

For the dashboard, we will implement a RadTileView control. This control is a container for objects of type RadTileViewItem, although it can also be classified as a layout control like Grid and StackPanel. Items are displayed in the form of boxes that can be dragged with the mouse to a new location, and only one item at a time can be maximized.

Each RadTileViewItem is capable of implementing a RadFluidContentControl, which provides three content areas for displaying information; each of these areas is shown according to the current state of the RadTileViewItem (Maximized, Minimized, or Restored). If the RadTileViewItem doesn't implement a RadFluidContentControl, then it is capable of displaying only one content area of information, regardless of its state.

The names of the content areas in a RadFluidContentControl are Large, Normal, and Small, which indicate the relation to the RadTileViewItem state. If the item state is Maximized, it will show the Large content area; if it is Minimized, it will show the Small content area; and if it is Restored, it will show the Normal content area.

When implemented, each RadFluidContentControl manages its state either automatically or manually based on the value of the property ContentChangeMode. If you choose to manage the state automatically, you need to work with the four threshold properties: LargeToNormalThreshold, NormalToLargeThreshold, SmallToNormalThreshold, and NormalToSmallThreshold. These let RadTileView know which threshold it must reach in order to change the state of the fluid control. On the other hand, should you choose to manage the state manually, you must instruct the control when to change the fluid control's state and to which state, because the threshold properties will be ignored. The easiest way to manually manage the state of the fluid controls is by implementing the OnTileStateChange server event.

The first thing to do is add the namespaces to the Home.xaml page, as shown in Listing 13-7.

Listing 13-7. *Namespaces Needed to Implement RadTileView*

```
xmlns:telerik="http://schemas.telerik.com/2008/xaml/presentation"
xmlns:telerikNavigation="clr-namespace:Telerik.Windows.Controls;
                         assembly=Telerik.Windows.Controls.Navigation"
```

Now you can create the RadTileView object, as shown in Listing 13-8.

Listing 13-8. *Dashboard Definition with RadTileView and FourRadTileViewItems*

```
<Grid x:Name="LayoutRoot">
      <telerikNavigation:RadTileView x:Name="RadTileView1"
                                     Width="835"
                                     Height="500"
                                     MinimizedColumnWidth="197"
                                     HorizontalAlignment="Center"
                                     VerticalAlignment="Center">
          <telerikNavigation:RadTileViewItem>
              One
          </telerikNavigation:RadTileViewItem>
          <telerikNavigation:RadTileViewItem>
              Two
          </telerikNavigation:RadTileViewItem>
          <telerikNavigation:RadTileViewItem>
              Three
          </telerikNavigation:RadTileViewItem>
```

```
            <telerikNavigation:RadTileViewItem>
                Four
            </telerikNavigation:RadTileViewItem>
        </telerikNavigation:RadTileView>
</Grid>
```

This sets up some important properties. `Width` and `Height` determine the space available for the tile items, as the control will size them accordingly. The `MinimizedColumnWidth` property indicates the width of the column for the minimized tiles. The `TileStateChangeTrigger` property defines how tiles change the state, with `DoubleClick` (the default), `SingleClick`, or `None`. If you choose `None`, the state of the tiles will always be `Restored`. The `HorizontalAlignment` and `VerticalAlignment` properties control the positioning of the `RadTileView` object in the page. Setting them to `Center` means that the control will be centered in the page.

Listing 13-8 defines four tile items with no fluid controls. This is to create a basic layout as a starting point and show you how it looks (see Figure 13-10). Figure 13-11 shows a maximized item. Notice how the other items give their space on the screen to the maximized one.

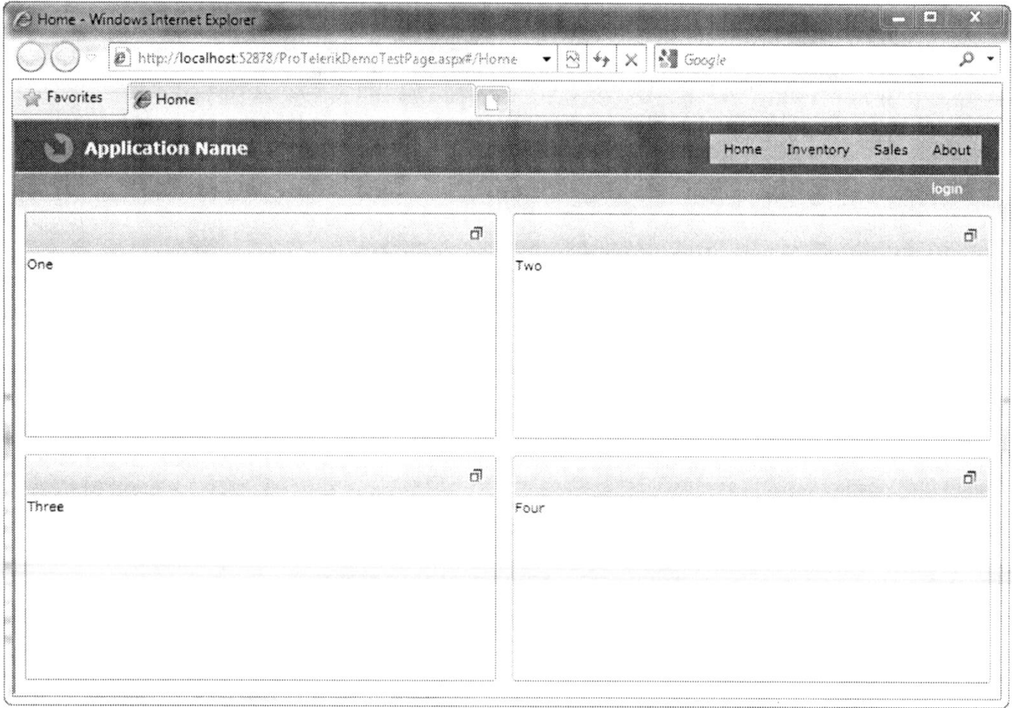

Figure 13-10. *Basic layout for the dashboard*

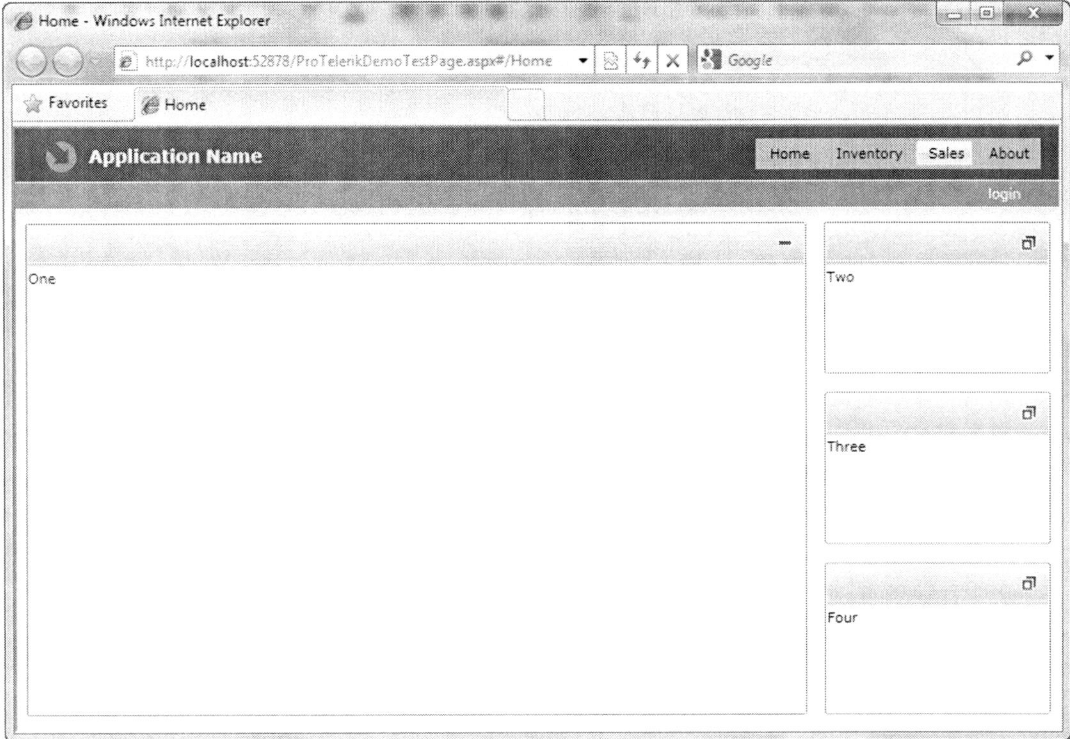

Figure 13-11. *Maximized RadTileViewItem*

Now let's add the fluid content controls to have more flexibility in showing information in our tile items. What's important at this point is to define if you want to control the content change of the fluid content controls automatically or manually. As noted earlier, if you choose the automatic option, you need to define the threshold properties. Listing 13-9 shows an implementation of a fluid content control using automatic content change and the threshold properties.

Listing 13-9. *RadTileViewItem Implementing a RadFluidContentControl with Automatic State Control and Threshold Properties*

```
<telerikNavigation:RadTileViewItem Header="Item Title">
   <telerik:RadFluidContentControl SmallToNormalThreshold="200 200"
                                   NormalToSmallThreshold="200 200"
                                   NormalToLargeThreshold="300 300"
                                   LargeToNormalThreshold="300 300">

        <telerik:RadFluidContentControl.SmallContent>
                <Border idth="100" Height="100">
                        <TextBlock Text="100 x 100" />
                </Border>
        </telerik:RadFluidContentControl.SmallContent>
```

```
        <telerik:RadFluidContentControl.Content>
                <Border Width="200" Height="200">
                        <TextBlock Text="200 x 200" />
                </Border>
        </telerik:RadFluidContentControl.Content>

        <telerik:RadFluidContentControl.LargeContent>
                <Border Width="300" Height="300">
                        <TextBlock Text="300 x 300" />
                </Border>
        </telerik:RadFluidContentControl.LargeContent>
   </telerik:RadFluidContentControl>
</telerikNavigation:RadTileViewItem>
```

■ **Note** For more information about the threshold properties, visit www.telerik.com/help/silverlight/radtileview-fluid-content-control.html.

Personally, I like to have full control with a programmatic approach to manage the content change of the fluid content controls, which requires an event handler for the TileStateChanged event. Listing 13-10 shows how to instruct the fluid content controls to use manual content change mode. Listing 13-11 shows the full implementation with the event handler and the whole RadTileView definition.

Listing 13-10. *Implementing Manual Content Change for RadFluidContentControls*

```
<telerikNavigation:RadTileViewItem>
    <telerik:RadFluidContentControl ContentChangeMode="Manual">
        <telerik:RadFluidContentControl.SmallContent>
            <Border Width="100" Height="100">
                <TextBlock Text="100 x 100" />
            </Border>
        </telerik:RadFluidContentControl.SmallContent>
        <telerik:RadFluidContentControl.Content>
            <Border Width="200" Height="200">
                <TextBlock Text="200 x 200" />
            </Border>
        </telerik:RadFluidContentControl.Content>
        <telerik:RadFluidContentControl.LargeContent>
            <Border Width="300" Height="300">
                <TextBlock Text="300 x 300" />
            </Border>
        </telerik:RadFluidContentControl.LargeContent>
    </telerik:RadFluidContentControl>
</telerikNavigation:RadTileViewItem>
```

Listing 13-11. *Full Implementation of Manual Content Change*

```
<Grid x:Name="LayoutRoot">
      <telerikNavigation:RadTileView x:Name="DashboardRadTileView"
              Width="835"
              Height="500"
              MinimizedColumnWidth="197"
              TileStateChangeTrigger="DoubleClick"
              HorizontalAlignment="Center"
              VerticalAlignment="Center"
              TileStateChanged="DashboardRadTileView_TileStateChanged">
          <telerikNavigation:RadTileViewItem>
              <telerik:RadFluidContentControl ContentChangeMode="Manual"
                                                      State="Normal">
                  <telerik:RadFluidContentControl.SmallContent>
                      <Border Width="100" Height="100">
                          <TextBlock Text="100 x 100" />
                      </Border>
                  </telerik:RadFluidContentControl.SmallContent>
                  <telerik:RadFluidContentControl.Content>
                      <Border Width="200" Height="200">
                          <TextBlock Text="200 x 200" />
                      </Border>
                  </telerik:RadFluidContentControl.Content>
                  <telerik:RadFluidContentControl.LargeContent>
                      <Border Width="300" Height="300">
                          <TextBlock Text="300 x 300" />
                      </Border>
                  </telerik:RadFluidContentControl.LargeContent>
              </telerik:RadFluidContentControl>
          </telerikNavigation:RadTileViewItem>
          <telerikNavigation:RadTileViewItem>
              <telerik:RadFluidContentControl ContentChangeMode="Manual"
                                                      State="Normal">
                  <telerik:RadFluidContentControl.SmallContent>
                      <Border Width="100" Height="100">
                          <TextBlock Text="100 x 100" />
                      </Border>
                  </telerik:RadFluidContentControl.SmallContent>
                  <telerik:RadFluidContentControl.Content>
                      <Border Width="200" Height="200">
                          <TextBlock Text="200 x 200" />
                      </Border>
                  </telerik:RadFluidContentControl.Content>
                  <telerik:RadFluidContentControl.LargeContent>
                      <Border Width="300" Height="300">
                          <TextBlock Text="300 x 300" />
                      </Border>
                  </telerik:RadFluidContentControl.LargeContent>
              </telerik:RadFluidContentControl>
          </telerikNavigation:RadTileViewItem>
```

```
        <telerikNavigation:RadTileViewItem>
            <telerik:RadFluidContentControl ContentChangeMode="Manual"
                                                    State="Normal">
                <telerik:RadFluidContentControl.SmallContent>
                    <Border Width="100" Height="100">
                        <TextBlock Text="100 x 100" />
                    </Border>
                </telerik:RadFluidContentControl.SmallContent>
                <telerik:RadFluidContentControl.Content>
                    <Border Width="200" Height="200">
                        <TextBlock Text="200 x 200" />
                    </Border>
                </telerik:RadFluidContentControl.Content>
                <telerik:RadFluidContentControl.LargeContent>
                    <Border Width="300" Height="300">
                        <TextBlock Text="300 x 300" />
                    </Border>
                </telerik:RadFluidContentControl.LargeContent>
            </telerik:RadFluidContentControl>
        </telerikNavigation:RadTileViewItem>
        <telerikNavigation:RadTileViewItem>
            <telerik:RadFluidContentControl ContentChangeMode="Manual"
                                                    State="Normal">
                <telerik:RadFluidContentControl.SmallContent>
                    <Border Width="100" Height="100">
                        <TextBlock Text="100 x 100" />
                    </Border>
                </telerik:RadFluidContentControl.SmallContent>
                <telerik:RadFluidContentControl.Content>
                    <Border Width="200" Height="200">
                        <TextBlock Text="200 x 200" />
                    </Border>
                </telerik:RadFluidContentControl.Content>
                <telerik:RadFluidContentControl.LargeContent>
                    <Border Width="300" Height="300">
                        <TextBlock Text="300 x 300" />
                    </Border>
                </telerik:RadFluidContentControl.LargeContent>
            </telerik:RadFluidContentControl>
        </telerikNavigation:RadTileViewItem>
    </telerikNavigation:RadTileView>
</Grid>
```

Code

```
private void DashboardRadTileView_TileStateChanged(object sender,
                                                   Telerik.Windows.RadRoutedEventArgs e)
{
    RadTileViewItem item = e.Source as RadTileViewItem;
    if (item != null)
    {
        RadFluidContentControl fluidControl = item.Content as RadFluidContentControl;
                          if (fluidControl != null)
                             {
                                 switch (item.TileState)
                                    {
                                       case TileViewItemState.Maximized:
                                          fluidControl.State = FluidContentControlState.Large;
                                          break;
                                       case TileViewItemState.Minimized:
                                          fluidControl.State = FluidContentControlState.Small;
                                          break;
                                       case TileViewItemState.Restored:
                                          fluidControl.State = FluidContentControlState.Normal;
                                          break;
                                    }
                             }
    }
}
```

Implementing RadTileViewItem

First, let's implement a tile item with just simple text and images. This will give you an idea of the possibilities of showing information. The idea here is to show a featured sales representative, with just some information about that sales rep. Listing 13-12 shows the implementation of this item.

Listing 13-12. *Implementing a Simple Fluid Content Control with Text and Images*

```
<telerikNavigation:RadTileViewItem Header="Featured Sales Rep">
    <telerik:RadFluidContentControl ContentChange Mode="Manual"
                                                  State="Normal">
            <telerik:RadFluidContentControl.SmallContent>
                <Border Width="193"
                        Height="100">
                    <TextBlock Text="Nancy Davolio"
                               Style="{StaticResource SmallBox}" />
                </Border>
            </telerik:RadFluidContentControl.SmallContent>
            <telerik:RadFluidContentControl.Content>
                <Grid Width="250"
                      Height="250">
                    <Grid.ColumnDefinitions>
                        <ColumnDefinition Width="Auto" />
                        <ColumnDefinition Width="*" />
                    </Grid.ColumnDefinitions>
```

```
            <Image Source="../Images/Customers/Thumbs/ALFKI.jpg"
                   Width="90"
                   Height="110"
                   Grid.Column="1"
                   HorizontalAlignment="Left"
                   Margin="13 13 0 0"
                   VerticalAlignment="Top" />

            <TextBlock Text="Sales representative in Seattle, WA.
                            Hired on 01/05/1992"
                       Grid.Column="1"
                       Style="{StaticResource SmallBox}"
                       Margin="109,13,16,116"
                       Height="70"
                       TextWrapping="Wrap" />
        </Grid>
    </telerik:RadFluidContentControl.Content>
    <telerik:RadFluidContentControl.LargeContent>
        <Grid Width="425"
              Height="350">
            <Grid.RowDefinitions>
                <RowDefinition Height="Auto" />
                <RowDefinition Height="*" />
            </Grid.RowDefinitions>
            <Image Source="../Images/Customers/ALFKI.jpg"
                   VerticalAlignment="Top"
                   Width="104"
                   Height="156"
                   Grid.ColumnSpan="3"
                   Margin="11 11 16 0" />
            <Border BorderBrush="#c9cdd2"
                   Margin="10 190 10 20"
                   VerticalAlignment="Top"
                   BorderThickness="0 1 0 0"
                   Grid.ColumnSpan="3">
                <Border BorderBrush="#ffffff"
                       BorderThickness="0 1 0 0" />
            </Border>
            <StackPanel Grid.Row="1">
                <TextBlock Text="Nancy Davolio"
                           Style="{StaticResource Title}"
                           VerticalAlignment="Top"
                           HorizontalAlignment="Center"
                           TextWrapping="Wrap" />
```

```
                    <TextBlock Text="Education includes a BA in psychology from
                                Colorado State University in 1970. She also
                                completed The Art of the Cold Call. Nancy is
                                a member of Toastmasters International."
                            Style="{StaticResource SmallBox}"
                            VerticalAlignment="Top"
                            HorizontalAlignment="Center"
                            TextWrapping="Wrap" />
                </StackPanel>
            </Grid>
        </telerik:RadFluidContentControl.LargeContent>
    </telerik:RadFluidContentControl>
</telerikNavigation:RadTileViewItem>
```

Figure 13-12 shows the normal and large content displayed for the first tile item.

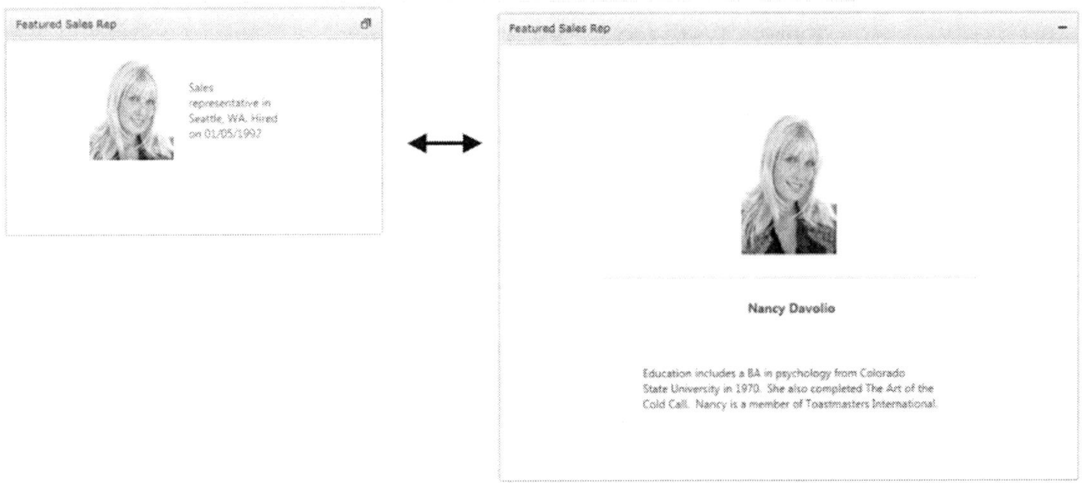

Figure 13-12. *The normal and large content for the first tile item*

Implementing RadChart

The next dashboard item uses RadChart. In Silverlight, RadChart has been taken to the next level with support for 3D chart types, animations, interactivity, and much more.

We will implement a bar chart for the normal content and a 3D pie chart for the large content. For the small content, we will show only the sales total in a TextBlock. The data will be returned from the orders in the database using the WCF RIA Service that we set up earlier, but this time we'll query the data from the MonthlySales entity. You need to add a new namespace to the XAML page, as shown in Listing 13-13.

Listing 13-13. *RadChart Implemented for a RadTileViewItem*

```
Namespace

xmlns:telerikChart="clr-namespace:Telerik.Windows.Controls;
     assembly=Telerik.Windows.Controls.Charting"

RadTileViewItem

<telerikNavigation:RadTileViewItem Header="Monthly Sales">
    <telerikNavigation:RadTileViewItem.Content>
        <telerik:RadFluidContentControl ContentChangeMode="Manual"
                                        State="Normal">
            <telerik:RadFluidContentControl.SmallContent>
                <Border Width="193"
                        Height="100">
                    <TextBlock
                        x:Name="totalSales"
                        Text=""
                        Style="{StaticResource SmallBox}" />
                </Border>
            </telerik:RadFluidContentControl.SmallContent>
            <telerik:RadFluidContentControl.Content>
                 <telerikChart:RadChart x:Name="SalesByCountryNormal">
                 </telerikChart:RadChart>
            </telerik:RadFluidContentControl.Content>
            <telerik:RadFluidContentControl.LargeContent>
                 <telerikChart:RadChart x:Name="SalesByCountryLarge">
                 </telerikChart:RadChart>
            </telerik:RadFluidContentControl.LargeContent>
        </telerik:RadFluidContentControl>
    </telerikNavigation:RadTileViewItem.Content>
</telerikNavigation:RadTileViewItem>
```

In order to correctly show the chart, we need to configure some properties. For this purpose, there are two methods: SetBarMappings and SetPieMappings. Both take a RadChart parameter. The idea is that each method will configure the charts with specific information for the type of chart it's displaying. Listing 13-14 shows the mapping methods.

Listing 13-14. *Configuration Methods for the Bar and Pie Charts*

```
private void SetPieMappings(RadChart chart)
{
    SeriesMapping seriesMapping = new SeriesMapping();
    seriesMapping.SeriesDefinition = new Pie3DSeriesDefinition();
    seriesMapping.SeriesDefinition.ItemLabelFormat = "#Y{C0}";
    ItemMapping itemMapping = new ItemMapping();
    itemMapping.DataPointMember = DataPointMember.YValue;
```

```
    itemMapping.FieldName = "Sales";
    seriesMapping.ItemMappings.Add(itemMapping);
    itemMapping = new ItemMapping();
    itemMapping.DataPointMember = DataPointMember.LegendLabel;
    itemMapping.FieldName = "MonthName";
    seriesMapping.ItemMappings.Add(itemMapping);
    chart.SeriesMappings.Add(seriesMapping);
    chart.DefaultView.ChartArea.Extensions.Add(new CameraExtension());
}

private void SetBarMappings(RadChart chart)
{
    SeriesMapping seriesMapping = new SeriesMapping();
    seriesMapping.SeriesDefinition = new BarSeriesDefinition();
    seriesMapping.LegendLabel = "Sales";
    seriesMapping.SeriesDefinition.ItemLabelFormat = "#Y{C0}";
    ItemMapping itemMapping = new ItemMapping();
    itemMapping.DataPointMember = DataPointMember.YValue;
    itemMapping.FieldName = "Sales";
    seriesMapping.ItemMappings.Add(itemMapping);
    itemMapping = new ItemMapping();
    itemMapping.DataPointMember = DataPointMember.XCategory;
    itemMapping.FieldName = "MonthName";
    seriesMapping.ItemMappings.Add(itemMapping);
    chart.SeriesMappings.Add(seriesMapping);
}
```

The methods define an object of type `SeriesMapping`. This object is in charge of defining the entire configuration for the chart. At the end of both methods, the `SeriesMapping` object is added to the `SeriesMappings` collection of each chart.

The type of chart is defined by the `SeriesDefinition` property of the `SeriesMapping` object. For the bar mapping, the chart type is defined by the `BarSeriesDefinition` class; for the pie mapping, the type is defined by the `Pie3DSeriesDefinition` class. The label for the legend is defined by the `LegendLabel` property. The `ItemLabelFormat` property defines how the value of the chart item will be formatted—in this case, as a currency value.

Then we need to create two `ItemMapping` objects: one for the actual value of the chart item and one for the label associated with the value. For the bar chart, the label property is of type `DataPointMember.XCategory`; for the pie chart, it is of type `DataPointMember.LegendLabel`. The `FieldName` property defines which field from the datasource has its value. Once those item mapping objects are created , we must add them to the `ItemMappings` collection of the `SeriesMapping` object.

For the 3D pie chart, we add a `CameraExtension` to the `ChartArea.Extensions` collection so users have the ability to rotate the 3D chart.

Listing 13-15 shows how data is loaded into the charts and the sales total is loaded to the `TextBlock`. Note here that, since all communications with the service are asynchronous, the only way to calculate the sales total is when all the records are retrieved. For that, the load method of the context object provides a callback implementation that is executed when all the data has been loaded.

Listing 13-15. *Loading the Data Asynchronously and Calculating the Sales Total Using the Callback Method*

```
private void LoadChartData()
{
    // Create the context object
    NorthwindDomainContext nwd = new NorthwindDomainContext();

    // Set the mappings for the charts
    SetBarMappings(this.SalesByCountryNormal);
    SetPieMappings(this.SalesByCountryLarge);

    // Get the sales data
    this.SalesByCountryNormal.ItemsSource = nwd.MonthlySales;
    this.SalesByCountryLarge.ItemsSource = nwd.MonthlySales;
    nwd.Load(nwd.GetMonthlySalesQuery(), result =>
            {
                decimal total = 0;
                result.Entities.ToList().ForEach(e =>
                                                {
                                                    total += e.Sales;
                                                });
                totalSales.Text = string.Format("Total Sales: {0:c}", total);
            }, null);
}
```

Figure 13-13 shows how these charts look in the application.

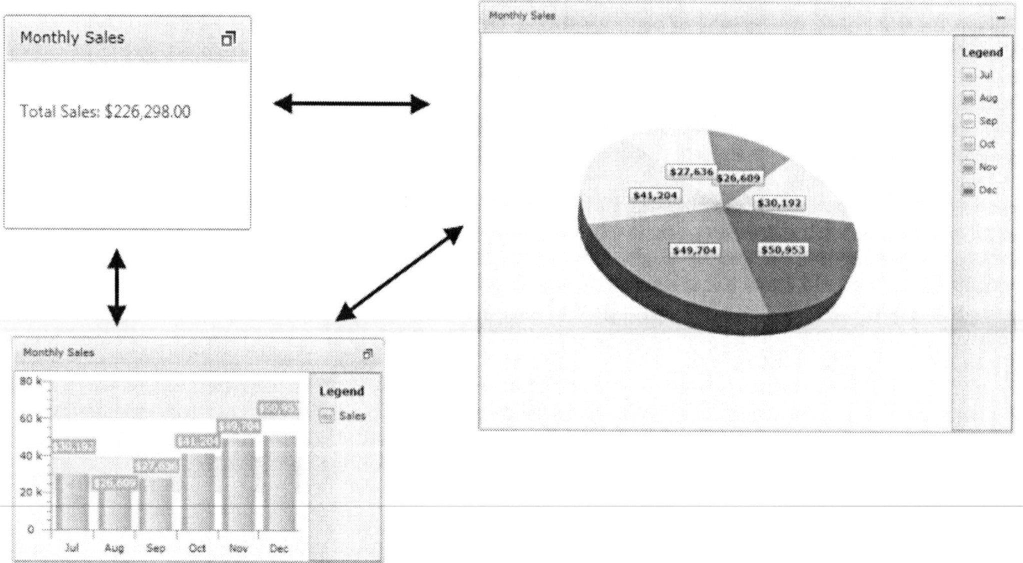

Figure 13-13. *Implementation of RadChart*

Implementing RadGridView

RadGridView is another Telerik control that has been enhanced for working with Silverlight. It supports many of the capabilities of its counterpart in ASP.NET, including sorting, grouping, filtering, editing, aggregate and frozen columns, and asynchronous data binding. It also supports some Silverlight-specific features like integration with Microsoft Expression Blend and shared base code with WPF. The feature list is long, but for now, the implementation for the dashboard will be very simple, just displaying the list of the most expensive products in the catalog.

For the normal content, the RadGridView will display the name and unit price of the products sorted by unit price. In the large content, there will be another RadGridView, which will contain all the columns of information from the table in the database. In the small content, there will be only the name of the most expensive product.

Listing 13-16 shows the definition of the RadTileViewItem with the two RadGridView objects. They are both the same, except that the one for the large content has more columns. In the code that loads the data, notice the use of the IsBusy property. This property shows a built-in loading indicator if it's set to true. Figure 13-14 shows how both RadGridView controls look.

Listing 13-16. *Displaying Information in RadGridView*

```
<telerikNavigation:RadTileViewItem Header="Most Expensive Products">
    <telerik:RadFluidContentControl ContentChange Mode="Manual"
                                                State="Normal">
        <telerik:RadFluidContentControl.SmallContent>
            <Border Width="100" Height="100">
                <TextBlock x:Name="mostExpensiveProduct"
                           Style="{StaticResource SmallBox}" />
            </Border>
        </telerik:RadFluidContentControl.SmallContent>
        <telerik:RadFluidContentControl.Content>
            <telerik:RadGridView
                    x:Name="gridExpensiveProducts"
                    IsReadOnly="True"
                    AutoGenerateColumns="False"
                    ShowGroupPanel="False">
                <telerik:RadGridView.Columns>
                    <telerik:GridViewDataColumn Header="Product"
                                DataMemberBinding="{Binding ProductName}"
                                IsFilterable="False"
                                Width="250"
                                IsSortable="False" />
                    <telerik:GridViewDataColumn Header="Unit Price"
                                DataMemberBinding="{Binding UnitPrice}"
                                DataFormatString="{}{0:c}"
                                IsFilterable="False"
                                Width="100"
                                IsSortable="False" />
                </telerik:RadGridView.Columns>
            </telerik:RadGridView>
        </telerik:RadFluidContentControl.Content>
```

```
        <telerik:RadFluidContentControl.LargeContent>
            <telerik:RadGridView
                    x:Name="largeGridExpensiveProducts"
                    IsReadOnly="True"
                    AutoGenerateColumns="False"
                    ShowGroupPanel="False"
                <telerik:RadGridView.Columns>
                    <telerik:GridViewDataColumn Header="ID"
                                        DataMemberBinding="{Binding ProductID}"
                                        IsFilterable="False"
                                        Width="50"
                                        IsSortable="False" />
                    <telerik:GridViewDataColumn Header="Product"
                                        DataMemberBinding="{Binding ProductName}"
                                        IsFilterable="False"
                                        Width="250"
                                        IsSortable="False" />
                    <telerik:GridViewDataColumn Header="Unit Price"
                                        DataMemberBinding="{Binding UnitPrice}"
                                        DataFormatString="{}{0:c}"
                                        IsFilterable="False"
                                        Width="100"
                                        IsSortable="False" />
                    <telerik:GridViewDataColumn Header="Qth Per Unit"
                                        DataMemberBinding="{Binding QuantityPerUnit}"
                                        IsFilterable="False"
                                        Width="150"
                                        IsSortable="False" />
                    <telerik:GridViewDataColumn Header="Reorder Level"
                                        DataMemberBinding="{Binding ReorderLevel}"
                                        IsFilterable="False"
                                        Width="100"
                                        IsSortable="False" />
                    <telerik:GridViewDataColumn Header="In Stock"
                                        DataMemberBinding="{Binding UnitsInStock}"
                                        IsFilterable="False"
                                        Width="100"
                                        IsSortable="False" />
                    <telerik:GridViewDataColumn Header="On Order"
                                        DataMemberBinding="{Binding UnitsOnOrder}"
                                        IsFilterable="False"
                                        Width="100"
                                        IsSortable="False" />
                </telerik:RadGridView.Columns>
            </telerik:RadGridView>
        </telerik:RadFluidContentControl.LargeContent>
    </telerik:RadFluidContentControl>
</telerikNavigation:RadTileViewItem>
```

Code

```
private void LoadGridData()
{
    // Create the context object
    NorthwindDomainContext nwd = new NorthwindDomainContext();

    // Load the data
    this.gridExpensiveProducts.IsBusy = true;
    this.largeGridExpensiveProducts.IsBusy = true;
    this.gridExpensiveProducts.ItemsSource = nwd.Products;
    this.largeGridExpensiveProducts.ItemsSource = nwd.Products;
    nwd.Load(nwd.GetMostExpensiveProductsQuery(), result => {
        this.gridExpensiveProducts.IsBusy = false;
        this.largeGridExpensiveProducts.IsBusy = false;
        if (result.Entities.Count() > 0)
                    {
                        this.mostExpensiveProduct.Text =
                              result.Entities.First().ProductName;
                    }
    }, null);
}
```

Figure 13-14. *Simple RadGrid implementation*

Implementing RadGauge

Gauges provide a different visual representation of data that lets users monitor and regulate the level, state, and dimensions or forms of what it represents. RadGauge includes a full set of circular, linear, and numeric gauges for you to use. A few of its features include scale multiplier, reverse and logarithmic scales, multiple gauges in a single container, multiple scales in a single gauge, and multiple indicators of different types in a single scale.

The final RadTileViewItem will include a RadGauge control that will indicate the level of the sales based on the goal set for the year. In the normal and large content, there will be a RadGauge control with a radial scale. The normal content will have a half radial gauge, and the large content will have a full radial gauge. Listing 13-17 shows the definition of RadGauge. Figure 13-15 shows how RadGauge looks.

Listing 13-17. *Implementation of RadGauge*

```
<telerikNavigation:RadTileViewItem>
    <telerik:RadFluidContentControl ContentChange Mode="Manual"
                                    State="Normal">
        <telerik:RadFluidContentControl.SmallContent>
            <Border Width="230" Height="130">
                <TextBlock Text="YTD Sales Goal: 65%"
                        Style="{StaticResource SmallBox}" />
            </Border>
        </telerik:RadFluidContentControl.SmallContent>

        <telerik:RadFluidContentControl.Content>
            <telerik:RadGauge x:Name="performanceNormal" Margin="20 20 20 20">
                <telerik:RadialGauge x:Name="radialGauge"
                            Style="{StaticResource RadialGaugeHalfCircleNStyle}">
                    <telerik:RadialScale x:Name="radialScale"
                            Style="{StaticResource RadialScaleHalfCircleNStyle}">
                        <telerik:RadialScale.MajorTick>
                            <telerik:MajorTickProperties />
                        </telerik:RadialScale.MajorTick>
                        <telerik:RadialScale.MiddleTick>
                            <telerik:MiddleTickProperties
                                    Length="0.05"
                                    TickWidth="0.2" />
                        </telerik:RadialScale.MiddleTick>
                        <telerik:RadialScale.MinorTick>
                            <telerik:MinorTickProperties
                                    Length="0.03"
                                    TickWidth="0.3" />
                        </telerik:RadialScale.MinorTick>
                        <telerik:IndicatorList>
                            <telerik:Needle x:Name="needle"
                                    IsAnimated="True"
                                    Value="65"/>
                        </telerik:IndicatorList>
                    </telerik:RadialScale>
                </telerik:RadialGauge>
            </telerik:RadGauge>
        </telerik:RadFluidContentControl.Content>
```

```
        <telerik:RadFluidContentControl.LargeContent>
            <telerik:RadGauge x:Name="performanceLarge"
                              Margin="20 20 20 20">
                <telerik:RadialGauge x:Name="radialGaugeLarge">
                    <telerik:RadialScale x:Name="radialScaleLarge">
                        <telerik:RadialScale.MajorTick>
                            <telerik:MajorTickProperties />
                        </telerik:RadialScale.MajorTick>
                        <telerik:RadialScale.MiddleTick>
                            <telerik:MiddleTickProperties
                                Length="0.05"
                                TickWidth="0.2" />
                        </telerik:RadialScale.MiddleTick>
                        <telerik:RadialScale.MinorTick>
                            <telerik:MinorTickProperties Length="0.03" TickWidth="0.3" />
                        </telerik:RadialScale.MinorTick>
                        <telerik:IndicatorList>
                            <telerik:Needle x:Name="needleLarge"
                                        IsAnimated="True"
                                        Value="65"/>
                        </telerik:IndicatorList>
                    </telerik:RadialScale>
                </telerik:RadialGauge>
            </telerik:RadGauge>
        </telerik:RadFluidContentControl.LargeContent>
    </telerik:RadFluidContentControl>
</telerikNavigation:RadTileViewItem>
```

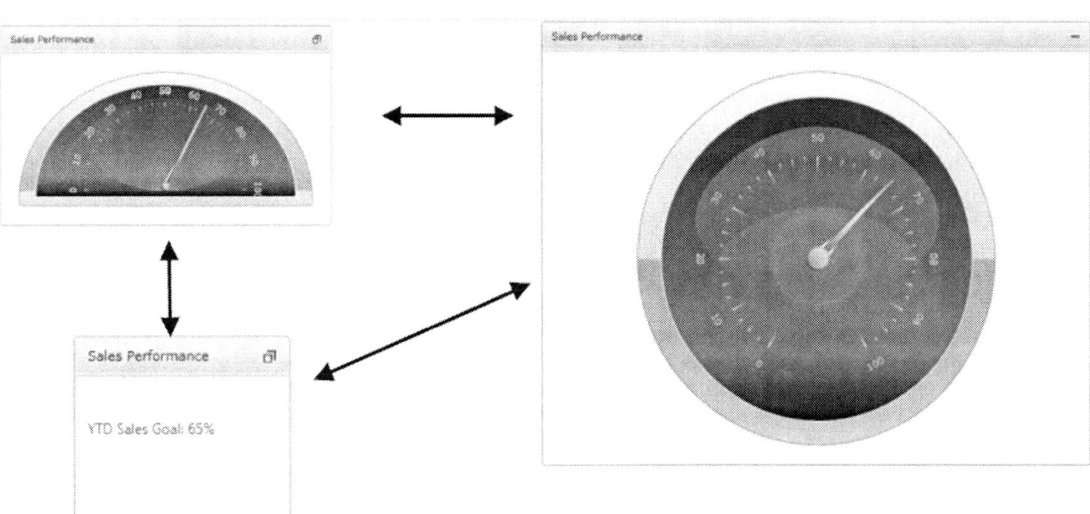

Figure 13-15. *RadGauge inside a RadTileViewItem*

Figure 13-16 shows what the dashboard looks like at this point.

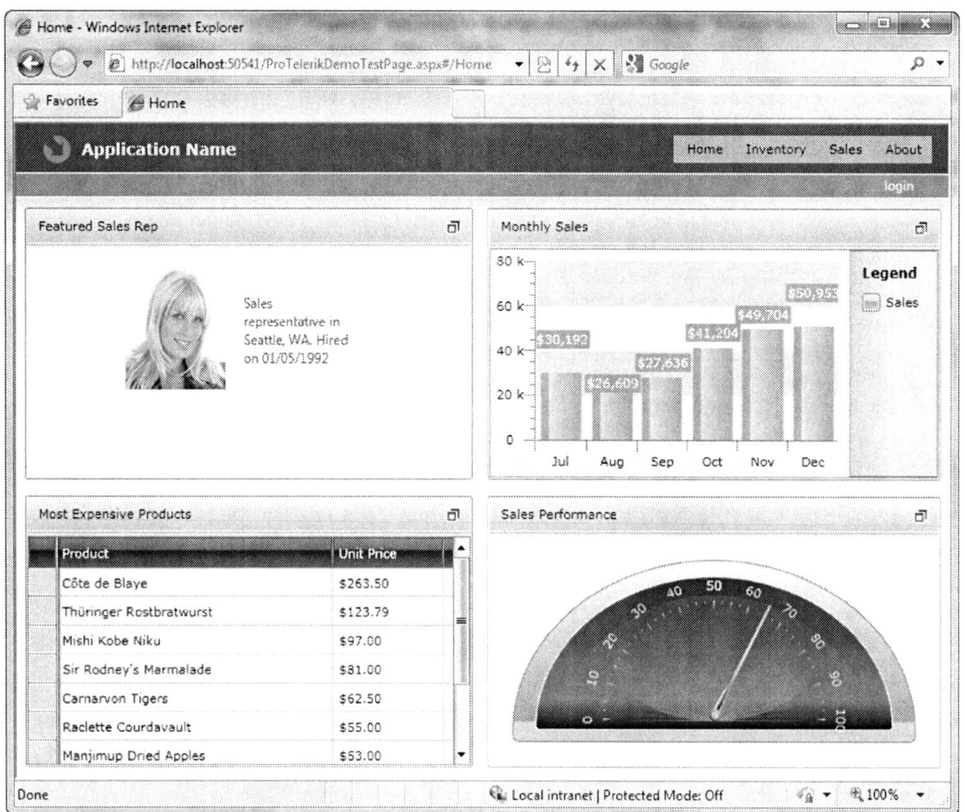

Figure 13-16. *The complete dashboard implemented with RadTileView*

Creating the Categories Page

Next up is the categories page. The first step is to load the data the same way as for the expensive products in the dashboard, as shown in Listing 13-18. Figure 13-17 shows how the grid looks. Notice how grouping, sorting, filtering, and editing are enabled by default. Figure 13-18 shows the powerful filtering menu, which displays filtering options depending on the column data type.

Listing 13-18. *Loading Data into RadGridView*

```
<telerik:RadGridView x:Name="categoriesGridView"
                        AutoGenerateColumns="False">
    <telerik:RadGridView.Columns>
        <telerik:GridViewDataColumn Header="Category ID"
                                    DataMemberBinding="{Binding CategoryID}" />
        <telerik:GridViewDataColumn Header="Category Name"
                                    DataMemberBinding="{Binding CategoryName}" />
        <telerik:GridViewDataColumn Header="Description"
                                    DataMemberBinding="{Binding Description}" />
    </telerik:RadGridView.Columns>
</telerik:RadGridView>

Code

private NorthwindDomainContext nwd = null;

public Categories()
{
    InitializeComponent();
    nwd = new NorthwindDomainContext();
    LoadGridData();
}

private void LoadGridData()
{
    categoriesGridView.ItemsSource = nwd.Categories;
    categoriesGridView.IsBusy = true;
    nwd.Load(nwd.GetCategoriesQuery(),
        result =>
            {
                    categoriesGridView.IsBusy = false;
            }, null);
}
```

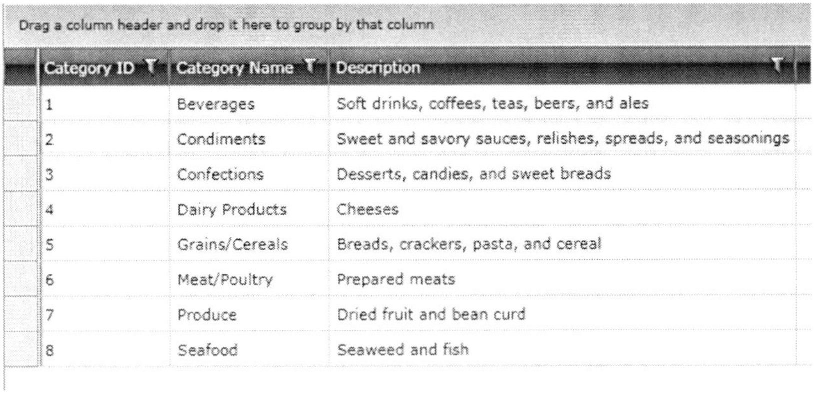

Drag a column header and drop it here to group by that column

Category ID	Category Name	Description
1	Beverages	Soft drinks, coffees, teas, beers, and ales
2	Condiments	Sweet and savory sauces, relishes, spreads, and seasonings
3	Confections	Desserts, candies, and sweet breads
4	Dairy Products	Cheeses
5	Grains/Cereals	Breads, crackers, pasta, and cereal
6	Meat/Poultry	Prepared meats
7	Produce	Dried fruit and bean curd
8	Seafood	Seaweed and fish

Figure 13-17. *RadGridView with grouping, sorting and filtering enabled by default*

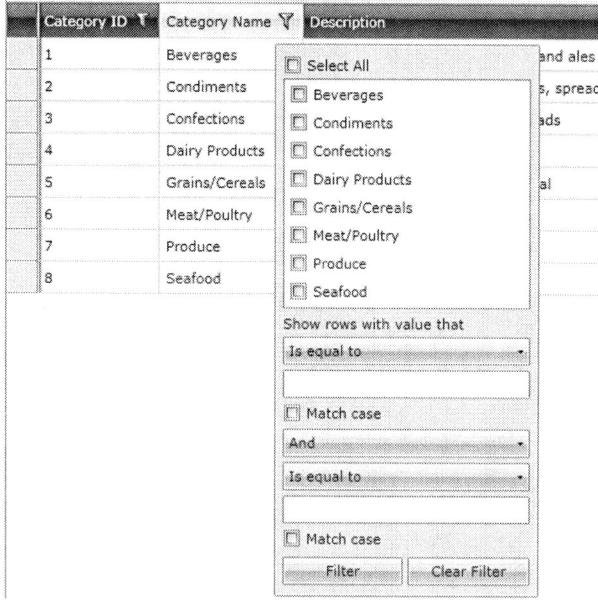

Figure 13-18. *RadGridView filtering menu*

If you don't want to use the default RadGridView features, you need to turn them off explicitly, as follows:

- To disable grouping, set the property ShowGroupPanel to false. To prevent a particular column from being grouped, set in the column definition the property IsGroupable to false.
- To disable filtering, set the property IsFilteringAllowed to false. For a particular column, set the column property IsFilterable to false.
- To disable sorting, set the property CanUserSortColumns to false. For a particular column, set the column property IsSortable to false.
- To disable row editing, set the IsReadOnly property to false at the grid or column level.

To perform editing operations, you need to handle several events in order to correctly implement the editing behavior:

- BeginningEdit occurs when the cell is about to enter into EditMode (can be canceled).
- RowValidating occurs when a row is about to commit new content (can stop commit process of the row).
- RowValidated occurs when a row has validated the new content.
- CellValidating occurs when a cell is about to commit new content (can stop the commit process of the cell).
- CellValidated occurs when a cell has validated the new content.

- CellEditEnded occurs when a cell validation is passed successfully and new data is committed to the RadGridView.ItemsSource.
- RowEditEnded occurs when a row validation has passed successfully and new data is committed to the RadGridView.ItemsSource.

To add a category, you need to tell RadGridView that you want to enable the edit mode using the BeginInsert() method or by pressing the Insert key in the keyboard. This adds a new, empty row for users to type the new information. To save the new category, call the method CommitEdit() or just navigate to another row. To cancel the operation, press the Esc key or call the method CancelEdit(). RadGridView raises the AddingNewDataItem event just before displaying the new empty row; in this event, you add a new instance of the class to which the grid is bound.

An important aspect regarding editing operations is that the column binding must be set to TwoWay binding using the Mode property. Saving the changes back to the database using WCF RIA Services is made by calling the method SubmitChanges() of the DomainContext object. Note here that you can call this method once for all the modifications in the grid, or you can invoke it on a per-modification basis.

Modifying and deleting a category is quite simple. Since RadGridView is already bound, you just need to call the SubmitChanges() method to save the changes back to the database.

Regardless of the operation performed, upon accepting it, RadGridView will raise the RowEditEnded event, which will serve to perform the appropriate final steps in saving the information. Listing 13-19 shows how to enable all the editing operations and how to use the integrated context menus in RadGridView. Figures 12-19 and 12-20 show the adding and modifying operations in action. Figure 13-21 shows the contextual menus defined for RadGridView.

Listing 13-19. *Implementing CRUD Operations in RadGridView using WCF RIA Services*

```
<navigation:Page x:Class="ProTelerikDemo.Views.Categories"
                 xmlns="http://schemas.microsoft.com/winfx/2006/xaml/presentation"
                 xmlns:x="http://schemas.microsoft.com/winfx/2006/xaml"
                 xmlns:d="http://schemas.microsoft.com/expression/blend/2008"
                 xmlns:mc="http://schemas.openxmlformats.org/markup-compatibility/2006"
                 mc:Ignorable="d"
                 xmlns:navigation="clr-namespace:System.Windows.Controls;
                                 assembly=System.Windows.Controls.Navigation"
                 xmlns:telerikNavigation="clr-namespace:Telerik.Windows.Controls;
                                 assembly=Telerik.Windows.Controls.Navigation"
                 xmlns:telerik="http://schemas.telerik.com/2008/xaml/presentation"
                 d:DesignWidth="640"
                 d:DesignHeight="480"
                 Title="Categories Page">

    <Grid x:Name="LayoutRoot" Width="700">

        <telerik:RadGridView x:Name="categoriesGridView"
                             AutoGenerateColumns="False"
                             CanUserInsertRows="True"
                             IsReadOnly="False"
                             AddingNewDataItem="categoriesGridView_AddingNewDataItem"
                             RowEditEnded="categoriesGridView_RowEditEnded">
            <telerik:RadGridView.Columns>
                <telerik:GridViewDataColumn Header="Category ID"
                                            DataMemberBinding="{Binding CategoryID}"
                                            IsReadOnly="True" />
```

```
                <telerik:GridViewDataColumn Header="Category Name"
                                            DataMemberBinding="{Binding CategoryName,
                                                                Mode=TwoWay}" />
                <telerik:GridViewDataColumn Header="Description"
                                            DataMemberBinding="{Binding Description,
                                                                Mode=TwoWay}" />
            </telerik:RadGridView.Columns>

            <telerikNavigation:RadContextMenu.ContextMenu>
                <telerikNavigation:RadContextMenu x:Name="gridContextMenu"
                                                  Opened="gridContextMenu_Opened"
                                                  ItemClick="gridContextMenu_ItemClick">
                    <telerikNavigation:RadContextMenu.Items>
                        <telerikNavigation:RadMenuItem Header="Add" />
                        <telerikNavigation:RadMenuItem Header="Delete" />
                    </telerikNavigation:RadContextMenu.Items>
                </telerikNavigation:RadContextMenu>
            </telerikNavigation:RadContextMenu.ContextMenu>

        </telerik:RadGridView>

    </Grid>
</navigation:Page>
```

Code

```
namespace ProTelerikDemo.Views
{
    public partial class Categories : Page
    {
        private NorthwindDomainContext nwd = null;

        public Categories()
        {
            InitializeComponent();
            nwd = new NorthwindDomainContext();
            LoadGridData();
        }

        private void LoadGridData()
        {
            // Load the data
            this.categoriesGridView.ItemsSource = nwd.Categories;
            this.categoriesGridView.IsBusy = true;
            nwd.Load(nwd.GetCategoriesQuery(),
                result =>
                    {
                        this.categoriesGridView.IsBusy = false;
                    }, null);
        }
```

```
// Executes when the user navigates to this page
protected override void OnNavigatedTo(NavigationEventArgs e)
{
}

private void categoriesGridView_AddingNewDataItem(
                        object sender,
                        GridViewAddingNewEventArgs e)
{
    e.NewObject = new ProTelerikDemo.Web.Category();
}

private void categoriesGridView_RowEditEnded(
                        object sender,
                        GridViewRowEditEndedEventArgs e)
{
    switch (e.EditOperationType)
    {
        case GridViewEditOperationType.Edit:
            nwd.SubmitChanges();
            break;
        case GridViewEditOperationType.Insert:
            ProTelerikDemo.Web.Category cat =
                                    e.NewData as
                                            ProTelerikDemo.Web.Category;
            if (cat != null)
            {
                nwd.Categories.Add(cat);
                nwd.SubmitChanges();
            }
            break;
        default:
            break;
    }
    this.categoriesGridView.CancelEdit();
    nwd.Load(nwd.GetCategoriesQuery());
}

private void gridContextMenu_Opened(object sender, RoutedEventArgs e)
{
    RadContextMenu menu = (RadContextMenu)sender;
    GridViewRow row = menu.GetClickedElement<GridViewRow>();

    if (row != null)
    {
        row.IsSelected = row.IsCurrent = true;
    }

}
```

```
        private void gridContextMenu_ItemClick(
                                object sender,
                                Telerik.Windows.RadRoutedEventArgs e)
        {
            RadContextMenu menu = (RadContextMenu)sender;
            RadMenuItem clickedItem = e.OriginalSource as RadMenuItem;

            if (clickedItem != null)
            {
                string header = Convert.ToString(clickedItem.Header);

                switch (header)
                {
                    case "Add":
                        this.categoriesGridView.BeginInsert();
                        break;
                    case "Delete":
                        GridViewRow row = menu.GetClickedElement<GridViewRow>();
                        if (row != null)
                        {
                            ProTelerikDemo.Web.Category cat =
                                                row.DataContext as
                                                        ProTelerikDemo.Web.Category;
                            if (cat != null)
                            {
                                nwd.Categories.Remove(cat);
                                nwd.SubmitChanges();
                                categoriesGridView.Rebind();
                            }
                        }
                        break;
                    default:
                        break;
                }
            }

        }

    }
}
```

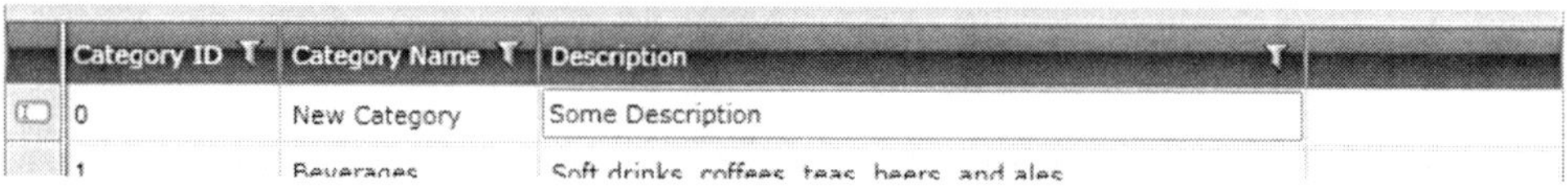

Figure 13-19. *Adding a new category*

Figure 13-20. *Modifying an existing category*

Figure 13-21. *RadGridView custom context menu*

Validation is also integrated based on the rules provided by the domain context object for the category class. For example, when adding or modifying a category and leaving the name empty, a visual clue will be shown, as in the example in Figure 13-22.

Figure 13-22. *Integrated validation*

Creating the Employees Page

The final page for the sample application is the employee's page. For this page, we'll use a few controls that I think are great.

The employee page will display the employee regions in `RadTreeView`, and then show the employees in each region and territory in `RadGridView`. When an employee is selected from the list, another `RadGridView` will show the orders made by that employee. Finally, when an order is selected, `RadMap` will show the shipped address using the integrated Bing Maps provider. So there is quite a bit of information in the page, and we need a nice way to organize it. That's where the `RadDocking` control comes into the picture.

Implementing RadDocking

The `RadDocking` control is a layout control that provides a docking experience for your windows, like that found in Visual Studio. You get the dockable `ToolWindows`, a hidden `DockingManager` control, and a designer to make the creation of attractive layouts easy.

At its core, RadDocking is composed of RadPane objects. You need at least one RadPane inside RadDocking to make it work. Different types of panes can be used in RadDocking. RadPane is the most basic. RadDocumentPane, a derivate class of RadPane, is designed to host documents (actually, any kind of content) that will be used by the application. Normally, you will use RadPane to present utilities or services that will open documents in RadDocumentPane, much like Visual Studio has the Solution Explorer (RadPane) opening files into the editor window (RadDocumentPane). RadPaneGroup enables the grouping of panes within the same docking area. RadSplitContainer is a special pane that enables users to resize the panes within it.

Panes have properties that enable them to be docked, floating, pinned, and unpinned. To manage the pane state, you use the InitialPosition property. There are five possible locations for a docked pane: left, right, top, bottom, and tabbed document. The property InitialPosition takes a value that defines whether it is docked or floating. If it is docked, the possible values are DockedTop, DockedBottom, DockedLeft, and DockedRight. If it is floating, the values are FloatingDockable and FloatingOnly. The docked values determine the position where the pane is docked, and the floating values determine whether or not the pane can be docked.

The built-in pin/unpin functionality in RadPane allows the pane to stay at its position or to be hidden. If it is unpinned, the pane is not visible; hovering the mouse over it will make it visible. Again, Visual Studio is a great example of this functionality.

Listing 13-20 shows how to implement RadDocking with the layout needed for presenting information for the application. Figure 13-23 shows the end result.

Listing 13-20. *Layout Created with RadDocking*

```
<!-- Namespaces -->
xmlns:telerik="http://schemas.telerik.com/2008/xaml/presentation"
xmlns:radDock="clr-namespace:Telerik.Windows.Controls;
                assembly=Telerik.Windows.Controls.Docking"


<!-- RadDocking definition -->
<radDock:RadDocking x:Name="radDocking1">
    <radDock:RadDocking.DocumentHost>

        <radDock:RadSplitContainer>
            <radDock:RadPaneGroup>
                <radDock:RadDocumentPane Title="Employees">
                    <radDock:RadDocumentPane.Content>
                        Employees Grid
                    </radDock:RadDocumentPane.Content>
                </radDock:RadDocumentPane>
            </radDock:RadPaneGroup>
        </radDock:RadSplitContainer>

    </radDock:RadDocking.DocumentHost>
```

```
    <radDock:RadSplitContainer
            radDock:DockingPanel.InitialSize="150,150"
            MaxWidth="600"
            Name="LeftContainer"
            InitialPosition="DockedLeft">
        <radDock:RadPaneGroup x:Name="Group1">
            <radDock:RadPane x:Name="Pane1"
                            Header="Locations">
                Regions and territories
            </radDock:RadPane>
        </radDock:RadPaneGroup>
    </radDock:RadSplitContainer>

    <radDock:RadSplitContainer
            radDock:DockingPanel.InitialSize="600,200"
            x:Name="RightContainer"
            InitialPosition="DockedRight">
        <radDock:RadPaneGroup x:Name="Group2">
            <radDock:RadPane x:Name="Pane3"
                            Header="Destination Map">
                Map
            </radDock:RadPane>
        </radDock:RadPaneGroup>
    </radDock:RadSplitContainer>

    <radDock:RadSplitContainer
            radDock:DockingPanel.InitialSize="200,350"
            x:Name="BottomContainer"
            InitialPosition="DockedBottom">
        <radDock:RadPaneGroup x:Name="Group3">
            <radDock:RadPane x:Name="Pane5" Header="Orders">
                Orders grid
            </radDock:RadPane>
        </radDock:RadPaneGroup>
    </radDock:RadSplitContainer>

</radDock:RadDocking>
```

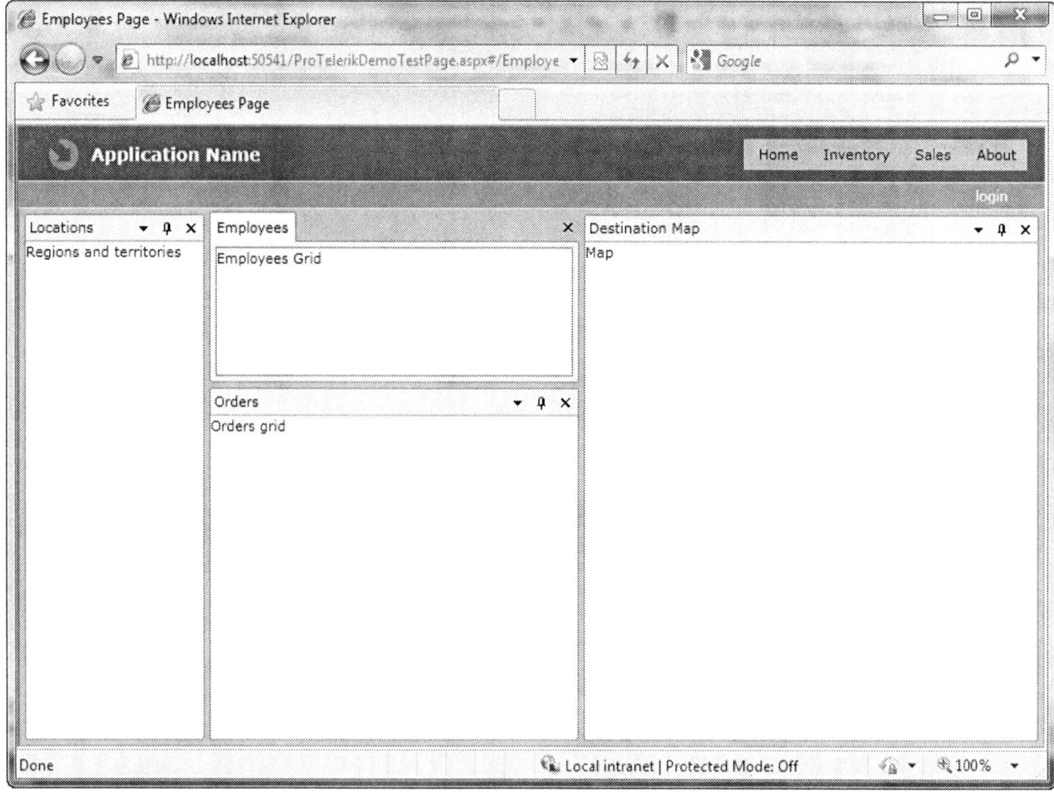

Figure 13-23. *RadDocking in action*

Adding the Regions and Territories

We will implement a `RadTreeView` control to show the regions and territories. For `RadTreeView` to work. we need to set up a hierarchical data template. This template will instruct the tree items how the hierarchy is built and where to look for the items for child items.

The first step is to create the hierarchical data template for the regions and the template for the territories. Listing 13-21 shows the data templates declaration in the `Employees.xaml` page.

Listing 13-21. *Data Templates*

```
<navigation:Page.Resources>

    <DataTemplate x:Key="TerritoryTemplate">
        <TextBlock Text="{Binding TerritoryDescription}" />
    </DataTemplate>
```

```
    <telerik:HierarchicalDataTemplate x:Key="RegionTemplate"
                                      ItemsSource="{Binding Territories}"
                                      ItemTemplate="{StaticResource TerritoryTemplate}">
        <TextBlock Text="{Binding RegionDescription}" />
    </telerik:HierarchicalDataTemplate>

</navigation:Page.Resources>
```

Now let's create the RadTreeView and the event handlers for the LoadOnDemand and ItemPrepared events. LoadOnDemand is raised whenever data is retrieved on demand, and ItemPrepared is raised when the bind operation is complete for each item. Listing 13-22 shows the complete code. Figure 13-24 shows the tree view in action.

Listing 13-22. *Implementation of RadTreeView with Load-on-Demand Capabilities*

```
<telerikNavigation:RadTreeView x:Name="treeLocations"
                               IsLoadOnDemandEnabled="True"
                               LoadOnDemand="treeLocations_LoadOnDemand"
                               ItemPrepared="treeLocations_ItemPrepared"
                               ItemTemplate="{StaticResource RegionTemplate}">
</telerikNavigation:RadTreeView>

Code

public Employees()
{
    InitializeComponent();
    LoadRegions();
}

private void LoadRegions()
{
    NorthwindDomainContext nwd = new NorthwindDomainContext();
    treeLocations.ItemsSource = nwd.Regions;
    nwd.Load(nwd.GetRegionsQuery());
}

// Executes when the user navigates to this page
protected override void OnNavigatedTo(NavigationEventArgs e)
{
}

private void treeLocations_LoadOnDemand(object sender, RadRoutedEventArgs e)
{
    RadTreeViewItem item = e.OriginalSource as RadTreeViewItem;

    Region r = item.Item as Region;
    if (r != null)
    {
        NorthwindDomainContext nwd = new NorthwindDomainContext();
        item.ItemsSource = nwd.Territories;
        nwd.Load(nwd.GetTerritoriesByRegionQuery(r.RegionID), TerritoriesLoaded, item);
    }
```

```
        else
        {
            item.IsLoadOnDemandEnabled = false;
        }
}

private void TerritoriesLoaded(LoadOperation operation)
{
    if (!operation.HasError)
        ((RadTreeViewItem)operation.UserState).IsExpanded = true;
}

private void treeLocations_ItemPrepared(object sender, RadTreeViewItemPreparedEventArgs e)
{
    RadTreeViewItem item = e.PreparedItem;
    if (item.Item is Territory)
    {
        item.IsLoadOnDemandEnabled = false;
    }
}
```

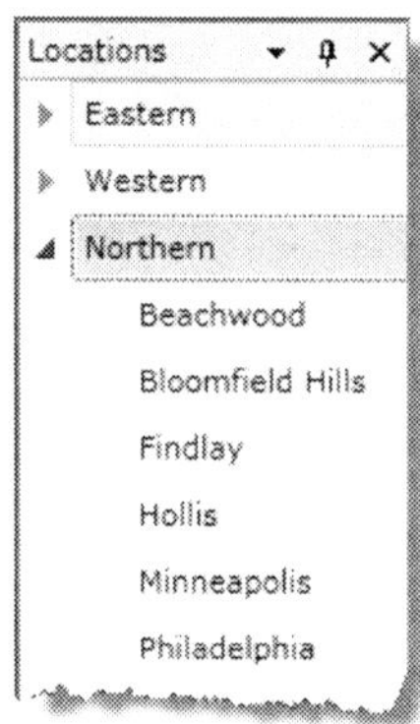

Figure 13-24. *RadTreeView implemented with load on demand and hierarchical data templates*

The next step is to load the employees when a territory is selected in the tree view. The employees and orders are created using RadGridView, which we've already used for the other pages. The important aspect here is the implementation of the Selected event for the tree view, which will recognize the type of item. If it is a territory, then it will populate the employee's grid. Both grids implement the SelectionChanged event, so whenever an employee is selected, it will load its orders in the second grid, which in turn will map the order address in RadMap. Listing 13-23 shows the implementation. Figure 13-25 shows how the grids look.

Listing 13-23. *Populating a RadGrid Based on the Selection of a Tree Item*

```
<radDock:RadDocking x:Name="radDocking1">
    <radDock:RadDocking.DocumentHost>

        <radDock:RadSplitContainer>
            <radDock:RadPaneGroup>
                <radDock:RadDocumentPane Title="Employees">
                    <radDock:RadDocumentPane.Content>
                        <telerik:RadGridView
                                x:Name="gridEmployees"
                                IsReadOnly="True"
                                AutoGenerateColumns="False"
                                ShowGroupPanel="False"
                                CanUserSortColumns="False"
                                IsFilteringAllowed="False"
                                SelectionChanged="gridEmployees_SelectionChanged">
                            <telerik:RadGridView.Columns>
                                <telerik:GridViewDataColumn Header="ID"
                                                DataMemberBinding="{Binding EmployeeID}" />
                                <telerik:GridViewDataColumn Header="First Name"
                                                DataMemberBinding="{Binding FirstName}" />
                                <telerik:GridViewDataColumn Header="Last Name"
                                                DataMemberBinding="{Binding LastName}" />
                                <telerik:GridViewDataColumn Header="City"
                                                DataMemberBinding="{Binding City}" />
                                <telerik:GridViewDataColumn Header="Country"
                                                DataMemberBinding="{Binding Country}" />
                            </telerik:RadGridView.Columns>
                        </telerik:RadGridView>
                    </radDock:RadDocumentPane.Content>
                </radDock:RadDocumentPane>
            </radDock:RadPaneGroup>
        </radDock:RadSplitContainer>

    </radDock:RadDocking.DocumentHost>

    <radDock:RadSplitContainer radDock:DockingPanel.InitialSize="150,150" MaxWidth="600"
            Name="LeftContainer" InitialPosition="DockedLeft">
        <radDock:RadPaneGroup x:Name="Group1">
            <radDock:RadPane x:Name="Pane1" Header="Locations">
                <telerikNavigation:RadTreeView x:Name="treeLocations"
                                IsLoadOnDemandEnabled="True"
                                LoadOnDemand="treeLocations_LoadOnDemand"
                                ItemPrepared="treeLocations_ItemPrepared"
                                Selected="treeLocations_Selected"
                                ItemTemplate="{StaticResource RegionTemplate}">
                </telerikNavigation:RadTreeView>
            </radDock:RadPane>
        </radDock:RadPaneGroup>
    </radDock:RadSplitContainer>
```

```
    <radDock:RadSplitContainer radDock:DockingPanel.InitialSize="600,200"
            x:Name="RightContainer" InitialPosition="DockedRight">
        <radDock:RadPaneGroup x:Name="Group2">
            <radDock:RadPane x:Name="Pane3" Header="Destination Map">
                Map
            </radDock:RadPane>
        </radDock:RadPaneGroup>
    </radDock:RadSplitContainer>

    <radDock:RadSplitContainer radDock:DockingPanel.InitialSize="200,350"
            x:Name="BottomContainer" InitialPosition="DockedBottom">
        <radDock:RadPaneGroup x:Name="Group3">
            <radDock:RadPane x:Name="Pane5" Header="Orders">
                <telerik:RadGridView x:Name="gridOrders"
                                     IsReadOnly="True"
                                     AutoGenerateColumns="False"
                                     ShowGroupPanel="False"
                                     CanUserSortColumns="False"
                                     IsFilteringAllowed="False"
                                     SelectionChanged="gridOrders_SelectionChanged">
                    <telerik:RadGridView.Columns>
                        <telerik:GridViewDataColumn Header="ID"
                                     DataMemberBinding="{Binding OrderID}" />
                        <telerik:GridViewDataColumn Header="Date"
                                     DataMemberBinding="{Binding Path=OrderDate,
                                                    StringFormat='MM-dd-yyyy'}" />
                        <telerik:GridViewDataColumn Header="Address"
                                     DataMemberBinding="{Binding ShipAddress}" />
                        <telerik:GridViewDataColumn Header="City"
                                     DataMemberBinding="{Binding ShipCity}" />
                        <telerik:GridViewDataColumn Header="Region"
                                     DataMemberBinding="{Binding ShipRegion}" />
                        <telerik:GridViewDataColumn Header="Country"
                                     DataMemberBinding="{Binding ShipCountry}" />
                    </telerik:RadGridView.Columns>
                </telerik:RadGridView>
            </radDock:RadPane>
        </radDock:RadPaneGroup>
    </radDock:RadSplitContainer>

</radDock:RadDocking>
```

Code

```
private void treeLocations_Selected(object sender, Telerik.Windows.RadRoutedEventArgs e)
{
    RadTreeViewItem item = e.OriginalSource as RadTreeViewItem;
    Territory t = item.Item as Territory;
    if (t != null)
    {
        NorthwindDomainContext nwd = new NorthwindDomainContext();
        gridEmployees.IsBusy = true;
        gridEmployees.ItemsSource = nwd.Employees;
        nwd.Load(nwd.GetEmployeesByTerritoryQuery(t.TerritoryID), result =>
```

```
            {
                gridEmployees.IsBusy = false;
            }, null);
        }
    }

    private void gridEmployees_SelectionChanged(object sender, SelectionChangeEventArgs e)
    {
        Employee employee = gridEmployees.SelectedItem as Employee;
        if (employee != null)
        {
            NorthwindDomainContext nwd = new NorthwindDomainContext();
            gridOrders.IsBusy = true;
            gridOrders.ItemsSource = nwd.Orders;
            nwd.Load(nwd.GetEmployeeOrdersQuery(employee.EmployeeID), result =>
            {
                gridOrders.IsBusy = false;
            }, null);
        }
    }

    private void gridOrders_SelectionChanged(object sender, SelectionChangeEventArgs e)
    {
        Order order = gridOrders.SelectedItem as Order;
        if (order != null)
        {
            // Add the code for RadMap here
        }

    }
```

Figure 13-25. *Population of RadGridView started from the selection of a tree item*

Implementing RadMap

RadMap allows you to display rich geographical information from different sources, including Microsoft Bing Maps, which is already implemented and available for you to use.

RadMap supports zooming, panning, and mapping between screen and geographical coordinates. It also supports layers that allow you to overlay elements on the maps. Layers allow you to visualize standard framework elements as well as custom shapes (e.g., lines or polygons) on the map by specifying their geographic position in latitude/longitude coordinates.

■ **Note** For the Bing Maps provider to work, you need an access key. During the development phase, a developer account is used, but after that, a purchased access key is needed. Instructions for getting your Bing Maps developer account can be found at `http://msdn.microsoft.com/en-us/library/ee681900.aspx`.

There are two types of layers in RadMap: information and dynamic layers. The information layer uses a standard ItemsControl approach (Items and ItemSource properties). The dynamic layer issues requests whether it should display new items every time when the map view is changed.

RadMap also supports shapes, pin points, and hot spots, along with any type of CLR information that can be layered on top of the map. In the application, we're going to use pin points to display the exact location of the order based on the ship address. Since the addresses are not exact and RadMap requires a latitude and longitude to accurately locate a point in the map, the geocoding service needs to be used. Geocoding will transform a descriptive address into latitude and longitude coordinates. A caveat is that geocoding is not an exact science, so there is the possibility of having a collection of nearby locations based on an address. For the sake of simplicity, we will use only the first location returned by the geocoding service (hoping it will be exact or close enough to the real location).

Listing 13-24 shows the implementation of RadMap and geocoding service. Figure 13-26 shows the entire page, now fully functional. Notice in the code that the first step to make RadMap work is to initialize it with the Bing Maps provider. The initialization sets the view mode (MapMode.Aerial), and also indicates if it is to show the map labels and the access key. The zoom level is set to 12, which is very close to the ground. Then we create the geocoding service object to fetch the latitude and longitude for the address provided. The geocoding service works asynchronously, which is why we need a callback function to ensure the pin point is created at that time, and not before the coordinates are known. There is also the possibility of not having any response, meaning that the address was not found. That's why it is important to test whether there is at least one location in the results collection.

Listing 13-24. *Implementation of RadMap and Geocoding Service*

```
<!-- Namespaces -->
xmlns:layer="clr-namespace:Telerik.Windows.Controls.Map;
              assembly=Telerik.Windows.Controls.DataVisualization"
xmlns:core="clr-namespace:Telerik.Windows.Controls;
              assembly=Telerik.Windows.Controls"

<!-- Declaration -->
<telerik:RadMap x:Name="RadMap1">
    <layer:InformationLayer Name="InformationLayer"/>
</telerik:RadMap>
```

Code

```
// This Bing Key is for use with the address
// http://localhost:12345/. Please make sure
// you use this specific port when running
// this sample application
private string BingMapKey =
        "Aoz1sqSFDj6wtUjgGGH7PLsc09W8nL81Fexx_lPK7_W4mq3k9WYkxpoqWIXqkH6p";

private void gridOrders_SelectionChanged(object sender, SelectionChangeEventArgs e)
{
    Order order = gridOrders.SelectedItem as Order;
    if (order != null)
    {
        // Initialize RadMap
        RadMap1.Provider = new BingMapProvider(MapMode.Aerial, true, BingMapKey);
        RadMap1.ZoomLevel = 12;

        // Create the geocoding object
        BingGeocodeProvider geocodeProvider = new BingGeocodeProvider();
        geocodeProvider.ApplicationId = BingMapKey;
        geocodeProvider.MapControl = RadMap1;
        // Create a new address object to feed the geocoding service
        Address adr = new Address();
        adr.AddressLine = order.ShipAddress;
        adr.PostalCode = order.ShipPostalCode;
        adr.PostalTown = order.ShipCity;
        adr.AdminDistrict = order.ShipRegion;
        adr.CountryRegion = order.ShipCountry;
        // Create the request object
        GeocodeRequest request = new GeocodeRequest { Address = adr };
        geocodeProvider.GeocodeCompleted += geocodeProvider_GeocodeCompleted;
        // Request the address translation
        geocodeProvider.GeocodeAsync(request);
    }

}

private void geocodeProvider_GeocodeCompleted(object sender, GeocodeCompletedEventArgs e)
{
    // Grab the response from the geocoding service
    GeocodeResponse response = e.Response;
    InformationLayer.Items.Clear();
    // Verify that there were results and take the
    // first one
    if (response.Results.Count == 0) return;
    var result = response.Results.First();
    // Now verify that there are actual locations (lat, long)
    // to work with and then take the first one
    if (result.Locations.Count == 0) return;
    Location l = result.Locations.First();
```

```
    // Create the pin point for the first location
    MapPinPoint pinPoint = new MapPinPoint()
    {
        Background = new SolidColorBrush(Colors.White),
        Foreground = new SolidColorBrush(Colors.Red),
        FontSize = 10,
        ImageSource = new BitmapImage(new
                Uri("/Telerik.Silverlight.RadMap;component/Resources/PinPoint.png",
                UriKind.Relative)),
        Text = result.Address.FormattedAddress
    };
    Location loc = new Location(l.Latitude, l.Longitude);
    RadMap1.Center = loc;
    MapLayer.SetLocation(pinPoint, loc);
    // Add the pin point to the information layer
    InformationLayer.Items.Add(pinPoint);
}
```

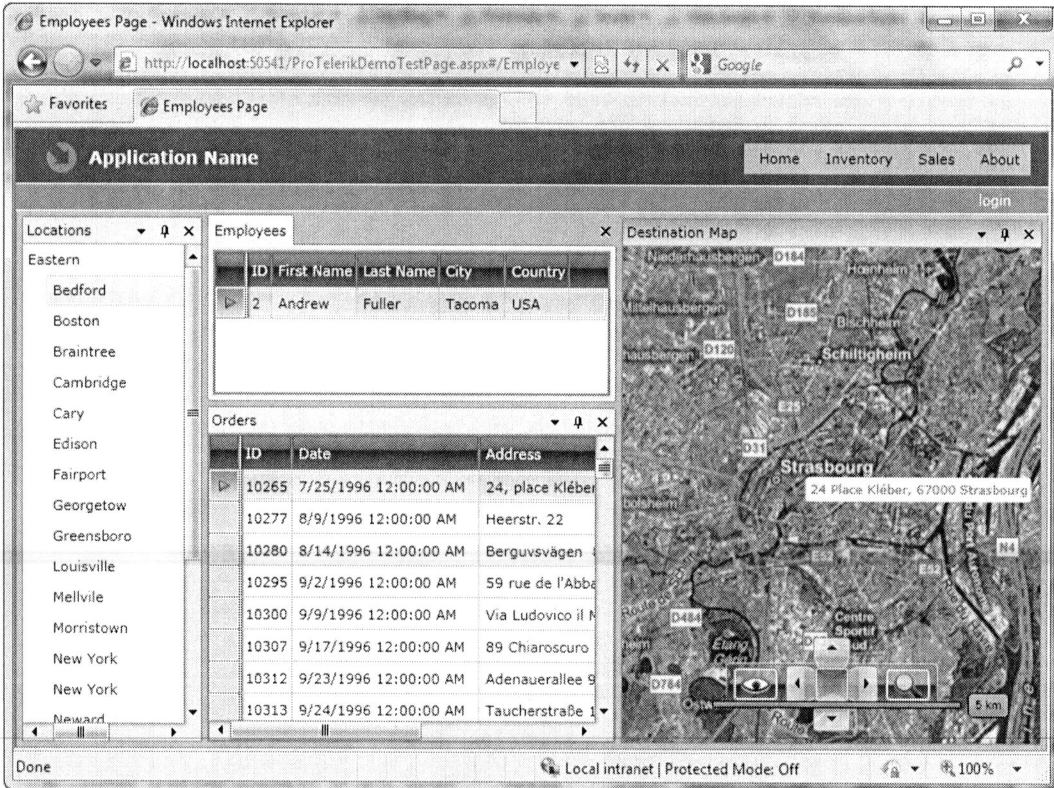

Figure 13-26. *RadMap implemented using Bing Maps as the information provider*

More Interesting Controls

Telerik RadControls for Silverlight is a huge collection of controls. We used some of them in the sample application, but certainly there are more that you should know about. Some are very much like those in ASP.NET. `RadMediaPlayer` and `RadRibbonBar` are available only in the Silverlight world. `RadUpload` delivers some interesting capabilities in this environment. Here, I will provide a brief overview of some of the interesting RadControls that you may want to investigate.

RadScheduler

Telerik `RadScheduler` for Silverlight delivers all the functionality found in its ASP.NET counterpart. However, it has some unique capabilities that you can use, such as theme customizations with Microsoft Expression Blend and code sharing between Silverlight and WPF. Figure 13-27 shows how `RadScheduler` for Silverlight looks. The following are some of its features:

- *Day, week, month, and timeline views:* You can choose between four different views to easily navigate through the appointments.
- *Edit forms*: You can easily create and edit appointments using the edit forms the control provides.
- *Rich user experience*: The control allows you to perform various operations in an interactive manner. You can drag tasks to new time slots or days, resize tasks to change their length, create all-day appointments, and modify your appointments through in-line editing.
- *Flexible recurring appointments support*: The control features the ability to configure repeating appointments with ultimate flexibility.
- *Customizable appointments*: The `AppointmentTemplateSelector` property provides different templates for the appointments according to your custom conditions.
- *Resource grouping.*: `RadScheduler` allows you to assign each appointment to a certain resource or assign several appointments to the same resources.
- *Style and appearance*: `RadScheduler` comes with several predefined themes, which will help you deliver a consistent look and feel in your application.
- *Culture awareness*: The localization mechanism of `RadScheduler` lets you adjust the control to any culture.
- *Enhanced Routed Events Framework*: The Enhanced Routed Events Framework for RadControls for Silverlight is implemented to help your code become even more elegant and concise.
- *Microsoft Expression Blend support*: All RadControls for Silverlight can be easily customized using Microsoft Expression Blend.
- *WPF/Silverlight code compatibility*: RadScheduler for Silverlight shares a single code base with its WPF counterpart. This means that you can achieve close to 100% code reuse for your scheduling logic if you have parallel Silverlight/WPF development.
- *Codeless test automation for scheduler*: You can record, execute, and debug functional tests for `RadScheduler` with Telerik WebUI Test Studio.

Figure 13-27. *RadScheduler for Silverlight*

RadCoverFlow

`RadCoverFlow` is a useful tool that can be used to navigate through a collection of horizontally aligned images. It gives you the flexibility to change the camera position and reflection opacity so you have full control over the appearance of the images. Figure 13-28 shows `RadCoverFlow`.

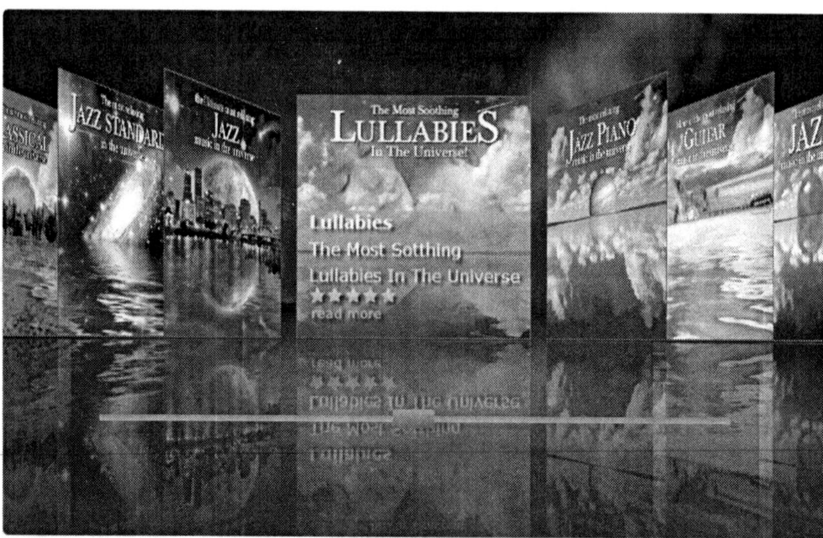

Figure 13-28. *RadCoverFlow*

RadMediaPlayer

RadMediaPlayer allows you to easily deliver audio and video content to your web site. You can create and load playlists, set chapters, watch the video in a full-screen mode, and completely customize the appearance of the control. Figure 13-29 shows a RadMediaPlayer control.

Figure 13-29. *RadMediaPlayer*

RadRibbonBar

RadRibbonBar is an easy-to-use implementation of the Microsoft Office 2007 "ribbon" UI, which allows you to codelessly organize the navigation functionality of your application into a single compact toolbar control. Figure 13-20 shows a RadRibbonBar. Its key features include the following:

- Microsoft Office 2007 interface
- Automatic resizing and minimization
- Galleries and pop-ups
- Application menu and recent documents menu
- Quick access toolbar
- Nested controls
- Screen tips
- Styling and appearance
- Commands support

- Localization support
- Enhanced Routed Events Framework
- Styling with Microsoft Expression Blend
- WPF/Silverlight code compatibility

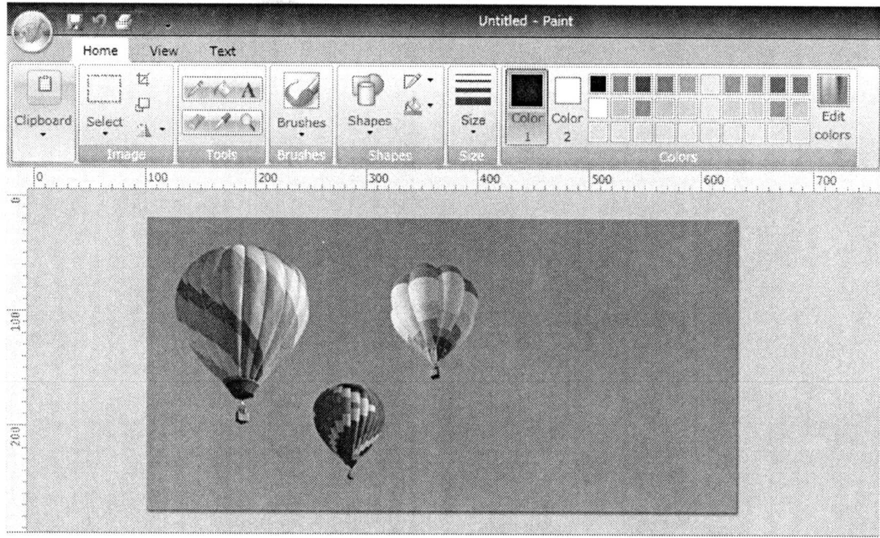

Figure 13-30. *RadRibbonBar*

RadUpload

`RadUpload` is a file-upload control specifically implemented for Silverlight. It allocates a minimum amount of server memory, while enabling optimized and fully configurable file uploads. Figure 13-31 shows a `RadUpload` control. Some of its features include the following:

- Multiple file upload
- Styling and appearance
- Extension filters
- Automatic upload
- Files size and count limitation
- Codeless test automation

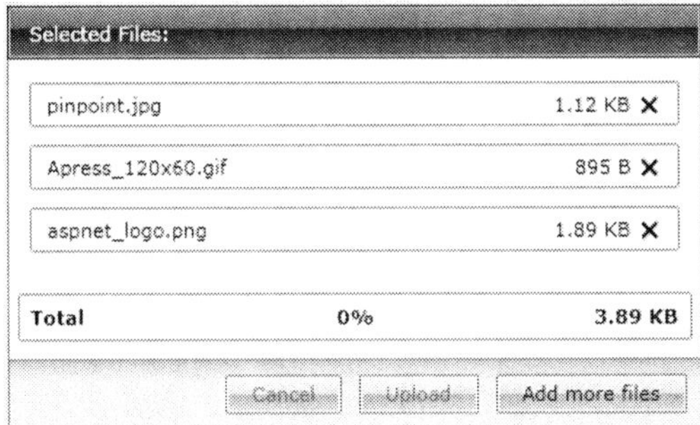

Figure 13-31. *RadUpload*

RadDragAndDropManager

The `RadDragAndDropManager` control allows users to drag any element and drop it on to any other element. The associated events allow users to completely handle the drag-and-drop process, thus easily building complex and flexible business logic. Furthermore, the framework provides visual cues that guide the user. Figure 13-32 shows the drag-and-drop framework in action. The following are some of this control's features :

- *Rich event handling*: The control provides a wide set of events that can be used to handle the actions happening upon a drag-and-drop operation.
- *Visual arrow cues*: You can set visual cues while dragging elements.
- *Visual drag cues*: The control uses a drag cue to follow the mouse while the user performs drag-and-drop operations. The drag cue appears on the top of the other objects.
- *Scroll viewers*: The control automatically uses scroll viewers to reveal content when the destination of the drag-and-drop operation is not visible.
- *Drag threshold*: You can choose the minimum distance that a user needs to move the mouse to start a drag operation.
- *Enhanced Routed Events Framework*: The Enhanced Routed Events Framework is implemented.
- *Silverlight/WPF code compatibility*: `RadDragAndDropManager` shares a single code base with its WPF counterpart.

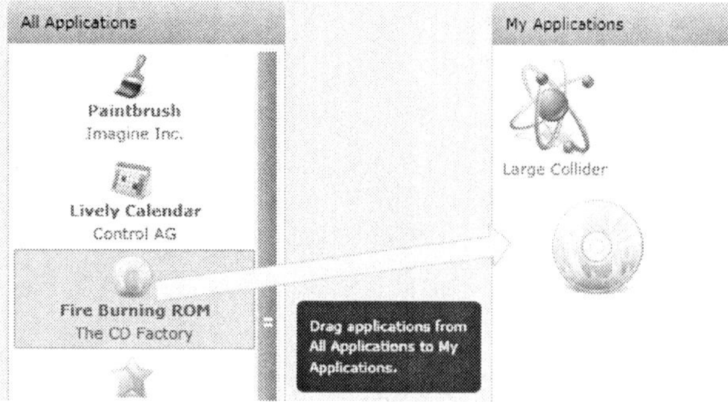

Figure 13-32. *Drag- and-drop framework*

Summary

This chapter demonstrated how the Silverlight controls work through a sample application. This application used WCF RIA Services for data access, and the full implementation was through Visual Studio 2010 and Silverlight 4.

The beginning of the chapter covered how to configure the Silverlight application to run Telerik's components. The suggested approach is using Telerik Visual Studio Extensions for Silverlight to prevent possible configuration mistakes that are introduced when doing manual configurations.

The first steps in building the application were to improve the navigation between pages. For that, we used RadMenu to replace the links based menu of the application template. Then we used RadTransition to have an animation when navigating to another page. RadTransition can be used not only for page navigation scenarios, but also when changing the control's content—for example, when changing from one list item selection to another.

The home page was improved creating a dashboard using RadTileView. RadTileView created a layout where content areas were provided to display information regarding the sales personel, performance, levels, and general information.

The first dashboard item displayed simple information regarding the featured salesperson. The next dashboard item was implemented using RadChart, which in Silverlight has been greatly improved to have 3D charts, animations, and other features. In the RadTileViewItem, there was two charts. One was a 2D bar chart that was shown when the fluid content control was in normal state, but changed to a 3D pie chart when its state changed to large.

The last two items in the dashboard included RadGridView and RadGauge. RadGauge provides a different visual representation of data that let users monitor and regulate the level, state, and dimensions or forms of what it represents.

RadGridView was used in several parts of the application. It exposes similar functionality to RadGrid in ASP.NET. You can filter, sort, group, and edit grid rows. Validation is implemented automatically based on the information provided for the entity that the grid displays.

For layout, RadDocking is a complete framework that enables the division of the screen in several ways for viewing information. In the application, we used RadDocking to create a layout based on four panes in which we implemented a RadTreeView, two RadGridView, and RadMap controls.

RadMap displays the location of the shipped orders implemented with the Bing Maps provider. This built-in provider also has geocoding functionality, so you can translate an address-based location into a latitude/longitude-based location.

Finally, you had a brief introduction to some other interesting controls for the Silverlight platform. They were included as a reference so you get an idea of their capabilities.

CHAPTER 14

Introducing Telerik Reporting

Telerik Reporting is a full-featured reporting solution with a unified code base for Windows Forms, WPF, ASP.NET, and Silverlight. Telerik Reporting features include a Report Wizard that walks you through the process of creating a report, a powerful data-processing model that provides a flexible approach to expression evaluation, the ability to apply conditional formatting, and a rich set of measurement units.

The design-time experience is also very rich. It includes a visual report designer; preview modes for Windows and web reports; a Report Explorer window with a hierarchical representation; expression and style editors; a format builder with integrated preview functionality; and different dialogs for tasks like editing groups, filters, and sorting.

In this chapter, I will introduce you to Telerik Reporting. By the end, you will be able to create reports that can be easily integrated into any type of application.

Installing and Configuring Telerik Reporting

Based on the same pattern as other Telerik products, Telerik Reporting installation program uses a "click Next" approach. There is no actual configuration when installing the product, other than selecting a Microsoft SQL Server database instance for the samples database, and if a custom installation is selected, the path where the files will be installed.

The system requirements are the same as those for RadControls for ASP.NET AJAX (see the "Installing the Controls and Tools" in Chapter 2 for system requirements).

Configuring Your Application

Configuring your web application to run Telerik Reporting is as simple as adding two references to your project; well, actually it depends on how you structure your application. The recommended pattern of implementation is to place your reports in a separate class library project so other applications can reuse them, and then add a reference to `Telerik.Reporting.dll` to this new project to start creating reports. Finally, add a reference to `Telerik.ReportViewer.WebForms.dll` and `Telerik.Reporting.dll` to the web application project where users will use the reports using Telerik's ASP.NET `ReportViewer` component, along with a reference to the reports project.

If the reports are going to be created within the same web application, then the references to `Telerik.Reporting.dll` and `Telerik.ReportViewer.WebForms.dll` must be added to the web application.

If you have a Silverlight application, in your project, you need to add references to `Telerik.Reporting.Service.dll`, `Telerik.Reporting.XamlRendering.dll`, and `Telerik.ReportViewer.Silverlight.dll`.

Another approach to configure your application is to create a new report (see Figure 14-1), and the reference to `Telerik.Reporting.dll` will be added to the project automatically. The same technique can be applied to the report viewer; if you add a `ReportViewer` control to a page, the reference to `Telerik.ReportViewer.WebForms.dll` will be added to the project.

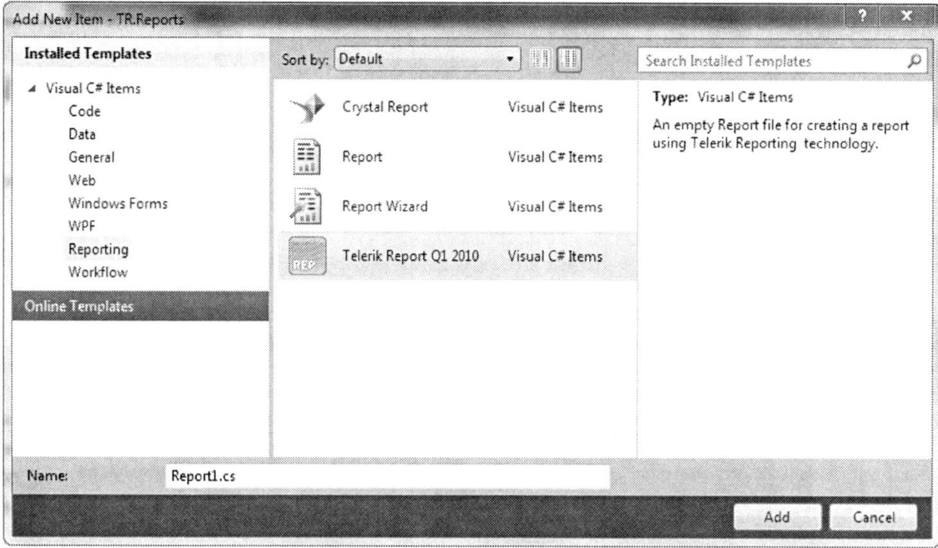

Figure 14-1. *Creating a new report using the Add New Item option in Visual Studio*

If you are migrating from a previous version of Telerik Reporting to a newer one, you can use Visual Studio Extensions for Telerik Reporting and select the Upgrade Wizard option, as shown in Figure 14-2. The wizard will ask you which projects in your solution to upgrade and to which installed version of Telerik Reporting you want to migrate, as shown in Figure 14-3. If your application hasn't been configured to use Telerik Reporting, the Upgrade Wizard will add that configuration for you.

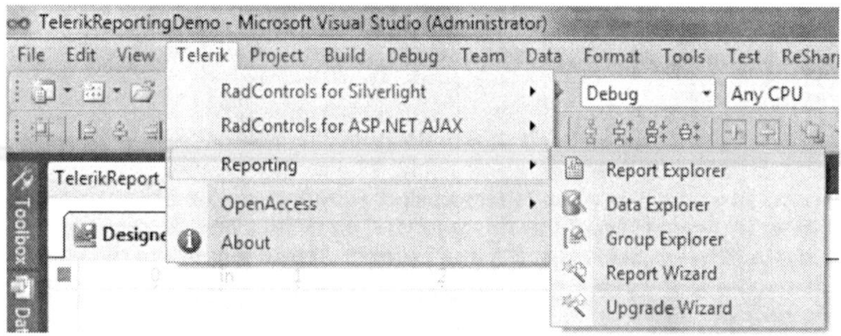

Figure 14-2. *Using Visual Studio Extensions for Telerik Reporting*

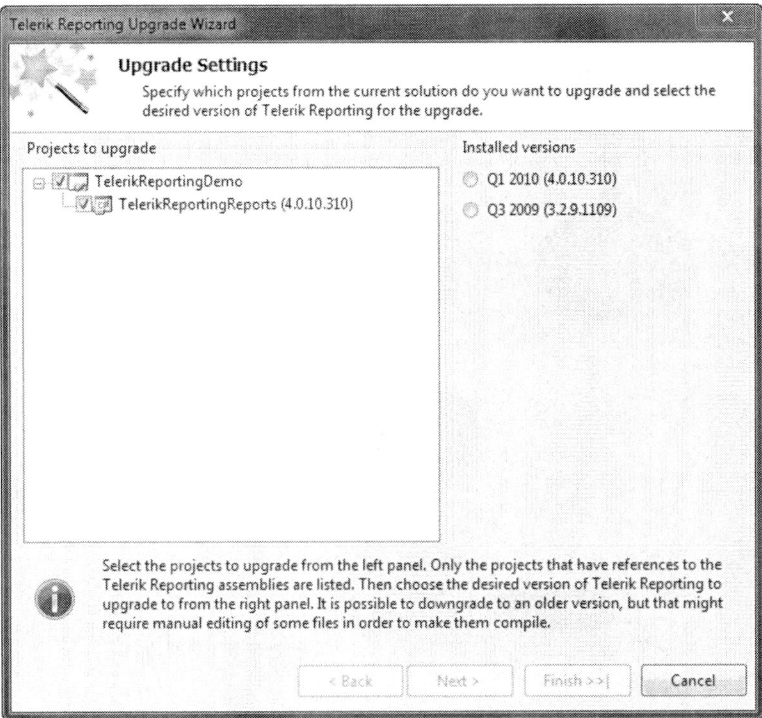

Figure 14-3. *Using the Telerik Reporting Upgrade Wizard*

Knowing the Players

I like to make a distinction between the actual elements that are involved when working with Telerik Reporting because they play very specific roles. There are three basic elements:

- *Reports* are the elements that collect data from the datasource and transform the data into information with the format and layout defined for it.
- *Viewers* are the elements that allow users to view and manipulate the reports.
- *Designers* help developers create the reports.

Reports

Reports are classes that define the presentation layout and format for data you want to display. Reports have a well-defined life cycle that is critical to understand because it explains how and when to use data-bound items, aggregate functions, and page information. The report life cycle is shown in Figure 14-4.

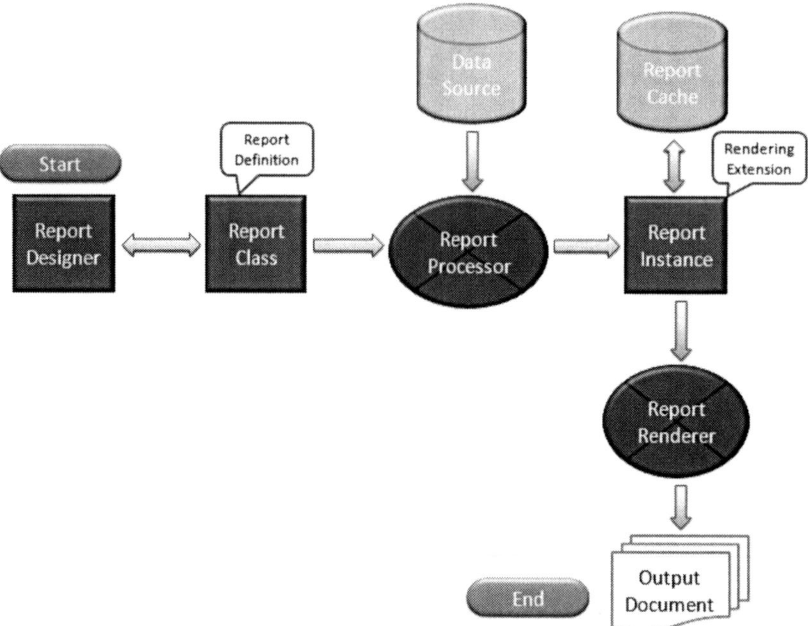

Figure 14-4. *Report life cycle events*

You start in Visual Studio with the report designer, which will generate a report class that includes all the information for the layout, format, and data. That class, along with the data from the datasource, is passed to the report processor, which produces a report instance that is ready to be consumed by the report renderer based on a rendering extension (which determines the report output format, such as PDF or Excel). This produces the final document that is sent to the viewer.

The report layout is divided into the following sections:

- *Page header*: This section is printed at the top of every page. You can use this section to include a report title on every page. This section and its items are processed by the corresponding rendering extension after the report data has been processed, so the report's datasource is no longer available. This means that you cannot use item-binding expressions for data fields and aggregate functions; however, you can use the built-in `PageNumber` and `PageCount` objects. It's possible to suppress the printing of this section on the first and last pages of the report.
- *Report header*: This section is printed just once at the beginning of the report. You might use the report header for a logo, title, or date. Data-binding expressions can be used in this section, but only for aggregated functions. If the datasource returns only one row, a data-bound item that uses an aggregate function is calculated for the entire report data.
- *Group header*: This section is printed at the beginning of each new group of records. In this section, you commonly add a group name and specific information regarding the group. For example, in a report that is grouped by category, the group header would include the category name. As with the report header section, you can use data-binding expressions, but only for aggregated functions; such functions will be calculated for the data in the whole group.

- *Detail*: This section is printed once for every row in the datasource. This is where you place the report items that make up the main body of the report.
- *Group footer*: This section is printed at the end of each group of records. A common use of this section is to print summary information for a group, such as group totals. Similar to the group header section, you should always use aggregate functions for the data-bound items that are calculated for the group data.
- *Report footer*: This section is printed just once, at the end of the report. Use the report footer to print report totals or other summary information for the entire report. Similar to the report header section, you should always use aggregate functions for the data-bound items that are calculated for the entire report data.
- *Page footer*: This section is printed at the end of every page and is commonly used to print page numbers or per-page information. Similar to the page header section, you cannot use data-bound items, but can access the `PageNumber` and `PageCount` objects.

Figure 14-5 shows a report with its sections.

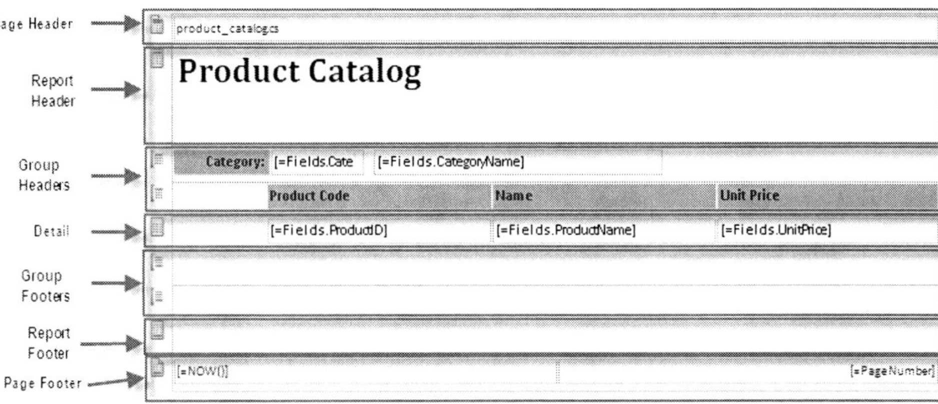

Figure 14-5. *A simplified view of the report designer. Report sections are identified by distinctive icons to their left.*

The following report items are available items in the Visual Studio Toolbox:

- `TextBox`: This item is used to display text in the report, and it can also be bound to a field from the datasource. It can have its own style, be configured to grow/shrink, be formatted for specific data types (for example, `DateTime`), and be multiline.
- `HtmlTextBox`: This item allows developers to insert HTML-formatted text into a report. You can specify the HTML value at design time or retrieve it from a field in the datasource that contains correctly formatted HTML.
- `PictureBox`: This item allows you to place images in the report using image files from different formats (for example, `.bmp`, `.gif`, `.jpg`, `.png`, or `.ico`).
- `Panel`: This item is used to group other items together and to quickly apply a style to a group of items. A single style can be given to the panel, and it will apply to all items inside the panel.

- `SubReport`: This very important item lets you display one report within another report. This allows you to create complex reports from different datasources using multiple layouts and formatting.
- `Table`: This item is used to display fields either as detail data or as grouped data in a grid or free-form layout. Telerik Reporting provides three items that can be used as templates, and you can add them directly from the Toolbox: `Table`, `Crosstab`, and `List`.
- `CheckBox`: This item displays a check mark (small picture) and a text field, which can be styled in the same way as a `TextBox`. The check mark and text can be aligned vertically and horizontally. There are three predefined check mark images, but they can be replaced with your own images.
- `Chart`: This item lets you display data in a visually compelling way. The chart can be bound to data. You can choose from many chart types, such as bar, pie, Gantt, line, area, and bubble.
- `Barcode`: This item is used for automatic bar-code generation directly from numeric or character data, without requiring a bar-code font to be installed on the end user's PC.
- `Shape`: This item displays different shapes in the report, including ellipses, stars, squares, lines, and triangles.

Figure 14-6 shows the items in Visual Studio's Toolbox. You can see that the Toolbox also includes the Table Wizard and Crosstab Wizard items, which are used to load those wizards, as well as the datasource items `SqlDataSource` and `ObjectDataSource`, which are used to create datasources for the report.

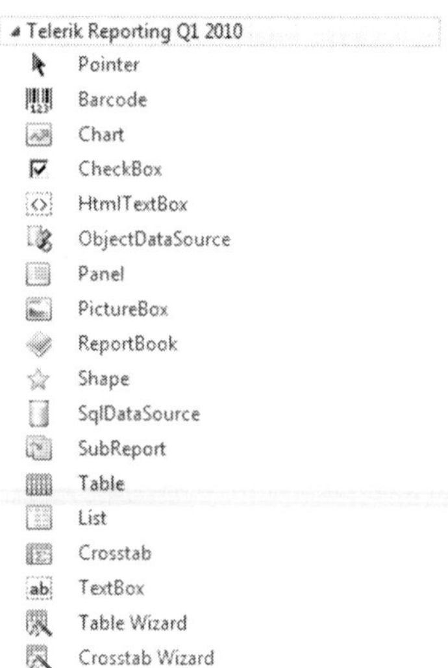

Figure 14-6. *Report items in Visual Studio's Toolbox*

Viewers

The viewers allow users to interact with the reports in different ways. Users can navigate between report pages, zoom in and out, print the report, and export the report using various file formats (such as Adobe

PDF and Excel). If the report has parameters, users can interact with them using the parameter form button. Figure 14-7 shows the web report viewer, and Figure 14-8 shows the Silverlight report viewer. There are also viewers for other platforms, such as Windows Forms and WPF.

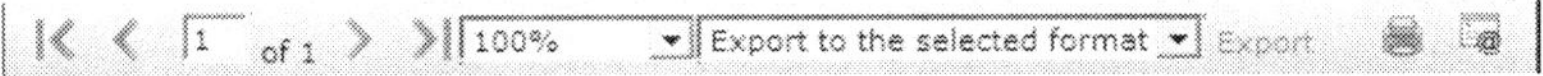

Figure 14-7. *Web report viewer*

Figure 14-8. *Silverlight report viewer*

Designers

The Telerik Reporting report designer allows you to easily create and maintain reports for your users. Additional explorers and wizards are available with Visual Studio Extensions for Telerik Reporting, as shown earlier in Figure 14-2. These include the Report Explorer, Data Explorer, Group Explorer, and Report Wizard.

Report Designer

The report designer is a visual editor for the report layout. You can create, modify, and delete sections and items. Figure 14-9 shows the report designer and its parts.

The design views allow you to switch between the designer and previews. The preview views show an approximation of how the report will look like when rendered with the corresponding viewer (Preview for the Windows viewer and Html Preview for the web viewer).

Clicking the report selector button makes the report active in the Properties window. Rulers are helpers for aligning elements in the report. Report sections allow you to define items that will present data from the datasource, data transformations using functions, and static text. You can add or remove sections using the context menu.

The component tray is where items like datasets and datasources will be created. The zoom element allows you zoom in and out on the report using percentages or specific sizes. Clicking the report map icon will open a small map window with a scheme of the report (useful for reports with a large layout), allowing you to quickly navigate to a specific portion of the report.

The snap grid options provide functions for aligment and visual aids so you can apply automatic aligment operations to the items in the report.

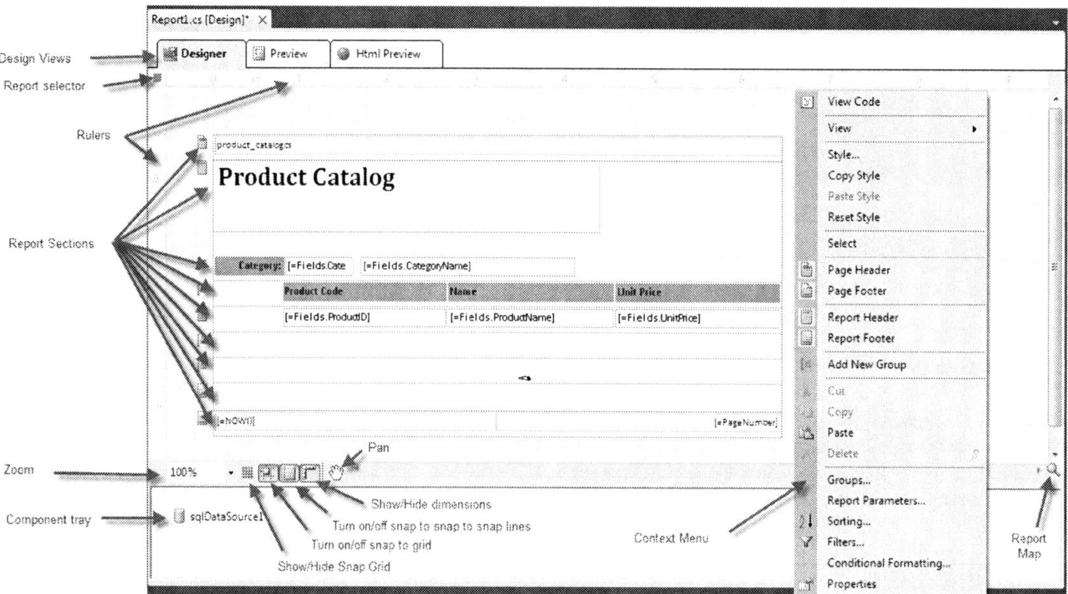

Figure 14-9. *Parts of the report designer*

Report Explorer

The Report Explorer lets you view the report structure and select any item to modify its properties. This tool is especially helpful with large and complex reports. Figure 14-10 shows the Report Explorer window.

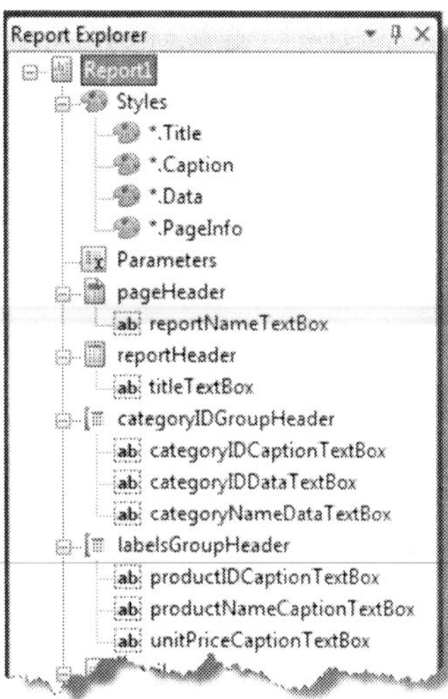

Figure 14-10. *Report Explorer*

Data Explorer

The Data Explorer displays the report datasources and fields available so you can bind report items to these fields. Here, you can also create calculated fields, which are fields created at the report level (not datasource fields) to perform operations in the client, rather than the server. Figure 14-11 shows the Data Explorer window.

Figure 14-11. *Data Explorer*

Group Explorer

The Group Explorer displays information regarding the report groups. You can create, modify, and delete groups. It allows you to define group fields and sorting and filtering criteria. Figure 14-12 shows the Group Explorer window.

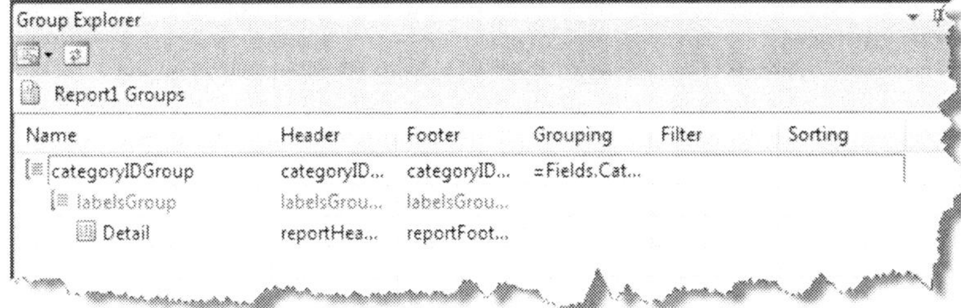

Figure 14-12. *Group Explorer*

Report Wizard

With the Report Wizard, you can build your report step by step. It will provide you with all the options to create your report easily. After the initial Welcome page, the steps are as follows:

- Choose if you want to create a new report or to convert a report from a different format to Telerik Reporting. Telerik offers built-in converters that work with reports from competing reporting products and transform them into Telerik reports.
- Select a datasource from those that have been previously created or create a new one. If you select to create a new one, the New Datasource Wizard starts.

- Select the type of report you want to create. The options are Standard (general purpose) Report, and Label Report. A label report is a specialized type of report normally used to create labels, such as those used for mailing envelopes or bar codes.
- Select which fields will go into the report header, group, and detail sections. For each field you add to the group list, a new group section is created.
- Select a layout that will structure your report. The options are Stepped, Outline, and Left Aligned. You can see a preview of the layout, add subtotals, and modify the page dimensions. The stepped layout arranges items in columns so they don't overlap vertically. The outline layout arranges items from left to right, with each group's items going further to the right by a fixed offset. A left-aligned layout places items in each section starting from the section's beginning.
- Select one of the built-in style sheets to apply to the report.
- Complete the wizard. In the final step, you will see a summary of what operations will be done in the report. After clicking Finish, your selections will be applied to create the report.

■ **Note** For more information about the Report Wizard, visit `www.telerik.com/help/reporting/ui-report-wizard.html`.

Loading Data

Reports can obtain data from different sources. The supported datasources are `DataTable`, `DataView`, `DataSet`, `DataViewManager`, and any component that implements the `IListSource`, `IEnumerable`, or `IDataAdapter` interface.

Telerik Reporting supports two datasource components:

- `SqlDataSource` to load data from a Microsoft SQL Server, Oracle, OLE DB, or ODBC database
- `ObjectDataSource` to load data from a business object, such as a Telerik OpenAccess ORM mapped entity

Both of these components are in the `Telerik.Reporting` namespace, so don't confuse them with Microsoft's controls.

Using the Datasource Components in the Report Designer

In the report designer, you just drop the datasource component of your choice from Visual Studio's Toolbox onto the report surface so it will be made available to you from the component tray at the bottom of the designer (see Figure 14-13). As soon as you drop the component, the Datasource Wizard launches so you can configure it.

To enable the `SqlDataSource` component, you define the provider name, connection string, and select either a command or a stored procedure. The `ObjectDataSource` component needs the type of object that is returning and the method that will be called.

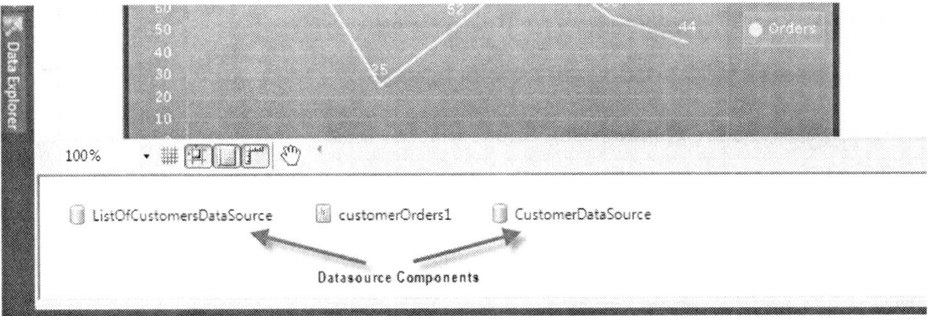

Figure 14-13. *The component tray in the report designer*

Using Expressions and the Expression Dialog

In the context of reports, expressions are used throughout the report definition to specify or calculate values for parameters, filters, report item properties, group and sort definitions, and so forth. The report item's properties are strongly typed, and you can use expressions as values for some of them. To specify that the value of a property is an expression, the value should be a string starting with an equal sign (=). If the equal sign is not present, the value will be interpreted as a simple string.

The Edit Expression dialog, shown in Figure 14-14, helps you create expressions. It loads all predefined functions plus the datasource's fields so you can build your expressions. The Edit Expression dialog allows you to create complex expressions that involve not only datasource fields, but also aggregate functions, built-in functions, constants, operators, parameters, and other user-defined functions.

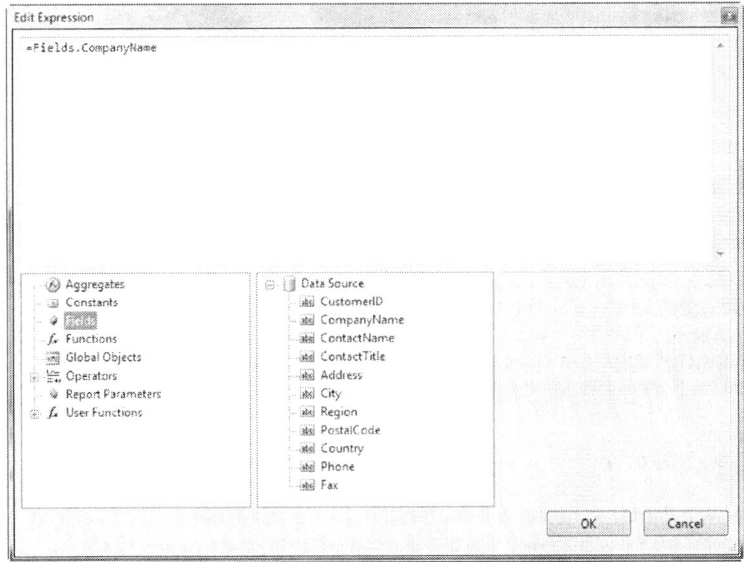

Figure 14-14. *The Edit Expression dialog*

Using the Datasource Components Programmatically

Listing 14-1 shows how to create a SqlDataSource component in code.

Listing 14-1. *Creating a SqlDataSource Component*

```
Telerik.Reporting.SqlDataSource CustomersDataSource = new Telerik.Reporting.SqlDataSource();
CustomersDataSource.ProviderName = "System.Data.SqlClient";
CustomersDataSource.ConnectionString =
   "Datasource=(local)\\SQLEXPRESS;Initial Catalog=Northwind;Integrated Security=True";
CustomersDataSource. SelectCommand = "SELECT * FROM Customers";
```

Listing 14-2 shows the creation of an ObjectDataSource component.

Listing 14-2. *Creating an ObjectDataSource Component*

```
Telerik.Reporting.ObjectDataSource CustomersDataSource =
                                new Telerik.Reporting.ObjectDataSource()
CustomersDataSource.DataMember = "GetCustomers";
CustomersDataSource.DataSource = typeof(TRData.Customers);
```

Adding parameters to any datasource component is very easy—use the Parameters property calling its Add method. Listing 14-3 shows how to create a parameter in code.

Listing 14-3. *Creating a Report Parameter*

```
Telerik.Reporting.Parameter pYear = new Telerik.Reporting.Parameter();
pYear.Name = "Year";
pYear.Value = 2010;
CustomersDataSource.Parameters.Add(pYear);
```

Data Binding

You can perform data-binding operations in two ways:

- *Using the report properties*: With this method, you create the datasource object and assign this object to the DataSource property in the Properties window. This will ensure that all the design-time tools will have access to the list of fields, providing a richer experience when developing reports.
- *In the event handler of the* NeedDataSource *event*: With this method, the design-time tools won't have the field's information, limiting your visibility into the datasource. On the bright side, you gain more control over how data is loaded. You can even choose from different datasources based on parameter selections.

Adding Calculated Fields

Both datasource components support calculated fields. A calculated field is a field that doesn't exist in the datasource but will be created based on its expression during the data-loading operation of the component. For example, you could create a field relating the city and country of an address to form a piece of data that looks like "Chicago, United States." Listing 14-4 shows an example of creating a calculated field.

Listing 14-4. *Creating a Calculated Field*

```
ObjectDataSource ods = new ObjectDataSource();
CalculatedField cf = new CalculatedField();
cf.Name = "CityCountry";
cf.DataType = Type.GetType("System.String");
cf.Expression = "City + ', ' + Country";
ods.CalculatedFields.Add(cf);
```

Filtering with Report Parameters

Report parameters provide the means for users to tell the report the values by which to filter the data. You can add report parameters by using the `ReportParameters` property of the `Report` class or by using the Properties window in Visual Studio (see Figure 14-15).

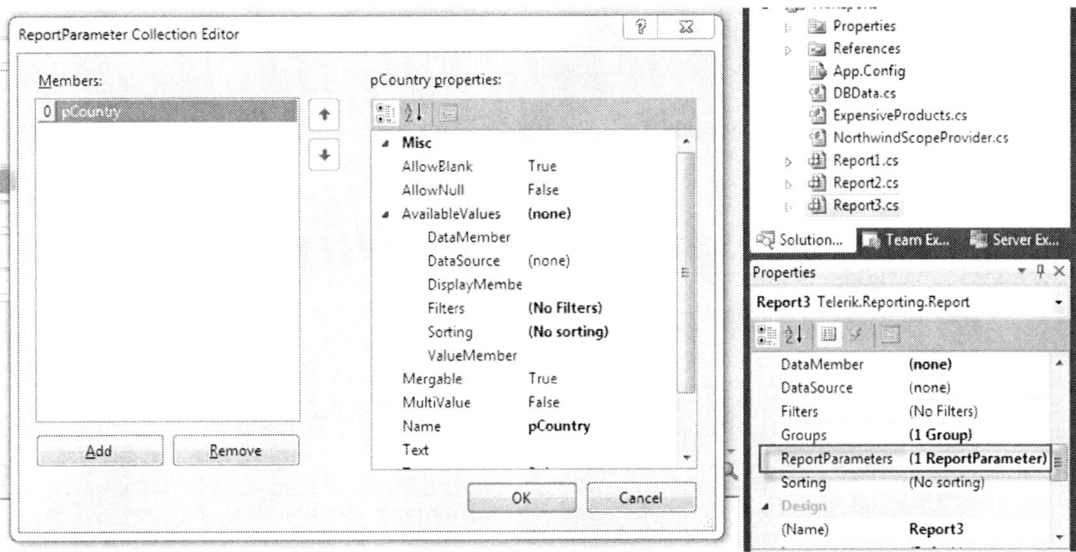

Figure 14-15. *Choosing ReportParameters in the Properties window*

Once you have defined the report parameters, they are available for you to filter the reports data. You can apply the filter in two ways, depending on the approach used to load the data:

- If you are using the design-time tools, you can use the `Filters` property. Choosing this property will open the window shown in Figure 14-16. Here, you select the datasource field by which you want to filter and relate it to the parameter using an operator. Operators vary depending on the data type of the field.
- If you are using the `NeedDataSource` event handler to load the report data, you must take care of passing the parameter values to the datasource component so the data gets filtered. Normally, this is done using the `Parameters` collection of the datasource component.

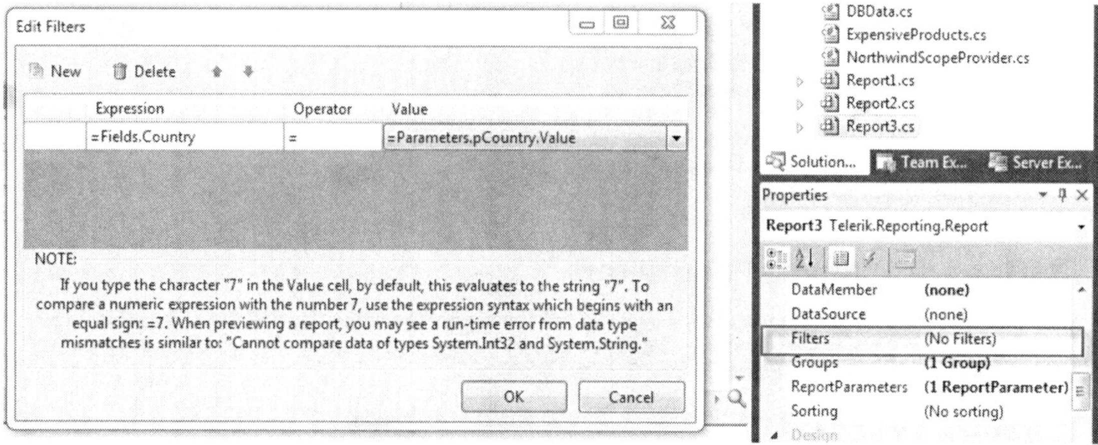

Figure 14-16. *Filtering data with the Edit Filters dialog*

Filtering can also be done by creating the filters in code. Listing 14-5 creates the same filter as shown in Figure 14-16.

Listing 14-5. *Creating a New Filter*

```
Telerik.Reporting.Data.Filter f = new Telerik.Reporting.Data.Filter();
f.Expression = "=Fields.Country";
f.Operator = FilterOperator.Equal;
f.Value = this.ReportParameters["pCountry"].Value.ToString();
this.Filters.Add(f);
```

Grouping and Sorting Data

Two of the most common operations with data are grouping and sorting. When you define a group in your report, you define a field (or set of fields) for which the grouping operation will be performed. For example, let's say you have a report that displays products and you want to show them grouped by category. You create a group in your report and move the category field from the detail section to the new group section. This is the equivalent to saying `GROUP BY Category` in a SQL `SELECT` statement.

Groups are created by adding new `Group` objects to the report's `Groups` collection. This can be done in code, as shown in Listing 14-6, or by using the `Groups` property in the Properties window (see Figure 14-17). Groups are evaluated in the order they are defined in the `Groups` collection, so you need to carefully design the ordering of the groups when you create them.

Listing 14-6. *Grouping the Report's Data*

```
Telerik.Reporting.Group g = new Telerik.Reporting.Group();
g.Name = "CategoryGroup";
Telerik.Reporting.Data.Grouping gping = new Telerik.Reporting.Data.Grouping();
gping.Expression = "=Fields.Category";
g.Grouping.Add(gping);
this.Groups.Add(g);
```

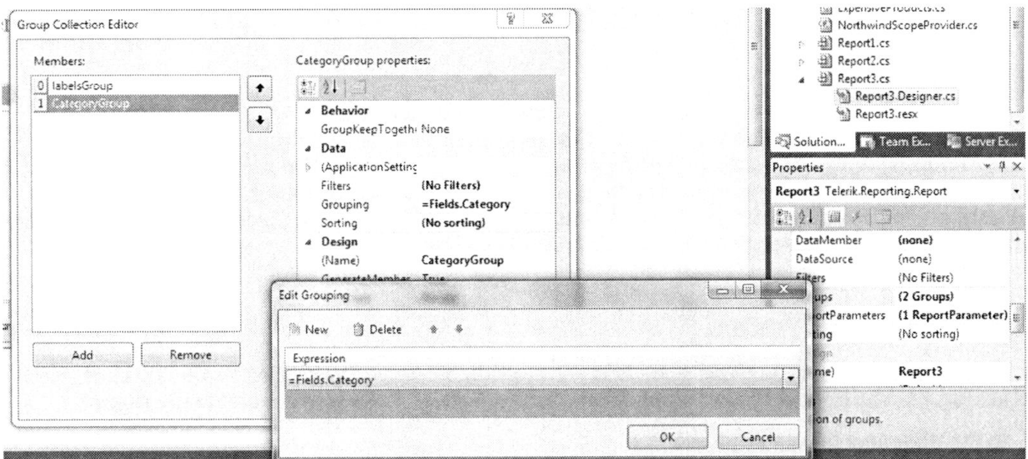

Figure 14-17. *Adding a group using the Properties window and Group Collection Editor*

Sorting is as easy as grouping. You can create the sort criteria by adding sort expressions to the `Sorting` collection. Figure 14-18 shows you how to set up sorting from the Properties window, and Listing 14-7 shows how to do it in code.

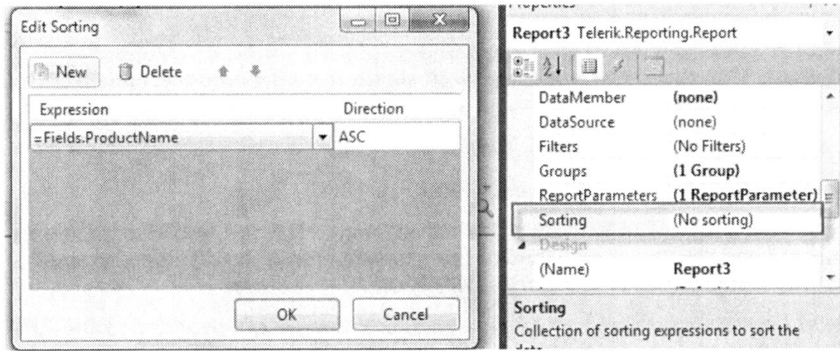

Figure 14-18. *Adding a sorting expression to the Sorting collection using the Properties window*

Listing 14-7. *Adding a Sorting Expression*

```
Telerik.Reporting.Data.Sorting s = new Telerik.Reporting.Data.Sorting();
s.Expression = "=Fields.ProductName";
s.Direction = SortDirection.Asc;
this.Sorting.Add(s);
```

Creating Reports

Now it's time to start creating some reports. The first report we'll create will simply list products. Then we'll change it to add more elements, including grouping and filtering. We'll also explore some of the item types to create a nicer presentation. The next report will be a crosstab report. Then I'll show you how to combine reports using subreports. We'll finish by using the new `ReportBook` control to present an easier interface to navigate through a collection of reports.

Using the Report Wizard

Let's start by creating a new report using the Add New option in Visual Studio (see Figure 14-1). Name it `ProductCatalog.cs`. The Report Wizard starts immediately. Follow these steps to create the report:

1. In the Welcome page, click Next.
2. In the Report Choice step, choose to create a new report, and then click Next.
3. In the Choose Data Source step, create a `SqlDataSource` component with the SQL Data Source Wizard. Name the `SqlDataSource` object `ProductsDataSource`, and then click Next. (If you don't have a data connection, you can create one by clicking the New Connection button in the first step and selecting the Northwind database.)
4. If you want to save the connection string, select the check box in the Save Connection step.
5. In the Data Source Command step, select to create a new statement and type the following: `SELECT * FROM Products`. This statement will select all the fields from the Products table from the Northwind database. Click Next.
6. Test the query using the Execute Query button. Then click Finish.
7. In the Report Type step, select Standard. Then click Next.
8. In the Design Layout step, add the fields `ProductID`, `ProductName`, `UnitPrice`, and `Discontinued` to the detail section and add the `CategoryID` field to the group section (this will create a report group to show the products grouped by category). Click Next.
9. In the Choose Report Layout step, select Left Aligned and leave the rest of the options with their default values. Click Next.
10. In the Choose Report Style step, select the style named Civic, and then click Next.
11. In the final step, review all the selected options, and then click Finish.

Your report should look like the one shown in Figure 14-19.

Figure 14-19. *Report created with the Report Wizard*

Figure 14-20 shows the report preview. Notice how the project was compiled to accurately reflect all the steps performed by the wizard.

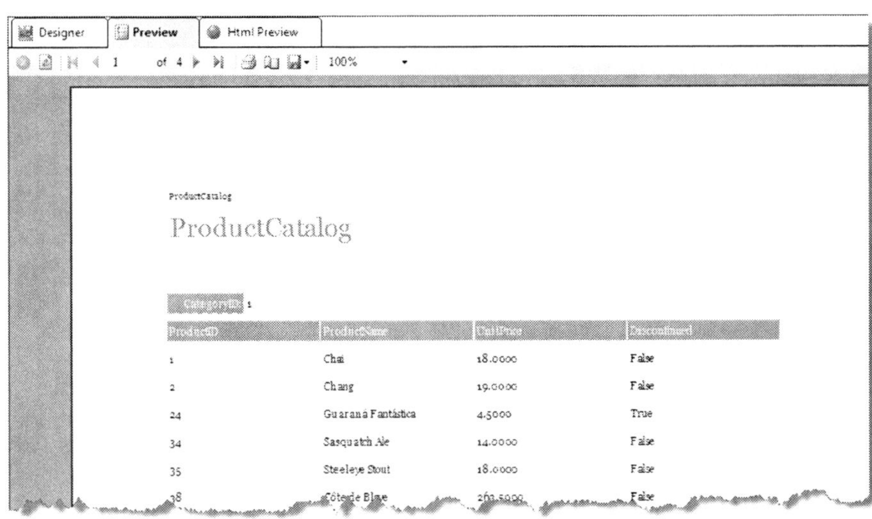

Figure 14-20. *The report in the Preview window*

Sorting

The report looks good, but notice that the products are not ordered in any way. Let's sort them by product name. After selecting the report (by clicking in any empty part of it), choose the `Sorting` property in the Properties window and click New to add a new sorting. Then select the `CategoryID` field from the expressions list. The direction should be ASC to first order by category. Now add a second sorting for the `ProductName` field with the same direction, as shown in Figure 14-21.

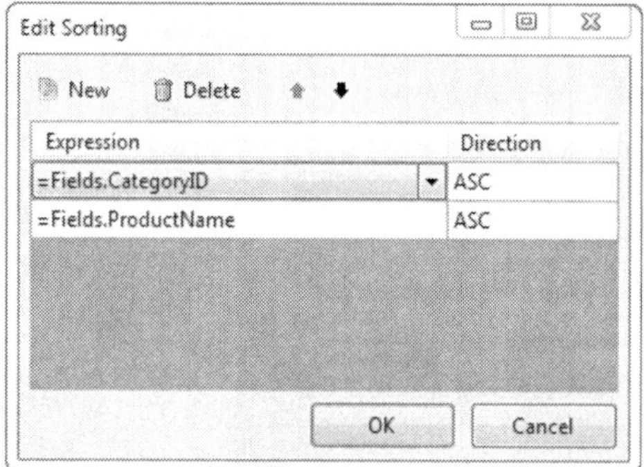

Figure 14-21. *Sorting the report by category and product name*

As shown in Figure 14-22, the products are now listed in alphabetic order by product name, and all the product categories are ordered, too.

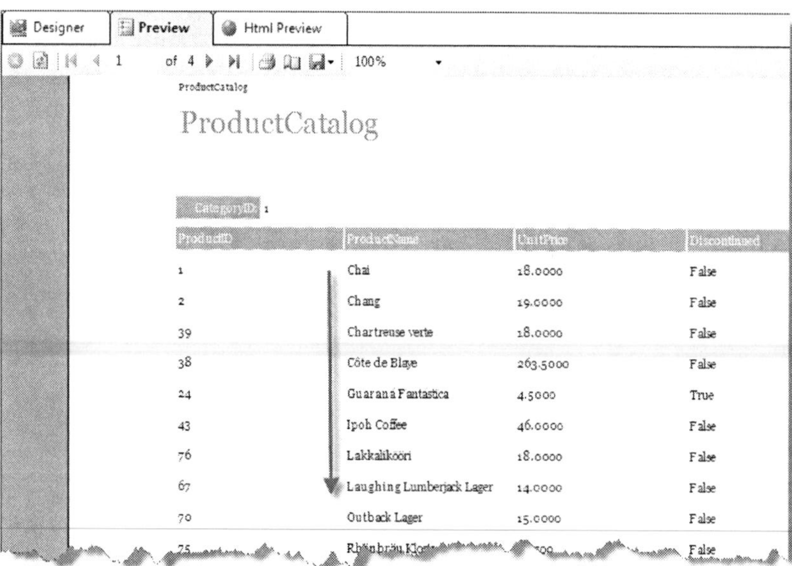

Figure 14-22. *Report showing the products sorted alphabetically*

Filtering

Now let's add the ability to filter the products to show those that are discontinued or active. This is a two-step process:

1. Add a report parameter using the `ReportParameters` property from the Properties window. Add a parameter and name it `pDiscontinued`. Make it of type `Boolean`. Give the `Text` property the text **Discontinued?**. Finally, select `True` for the `Visible` property, which will show the parameter in the parameters area so users can select a value. Figure 14-23 shows these settings.

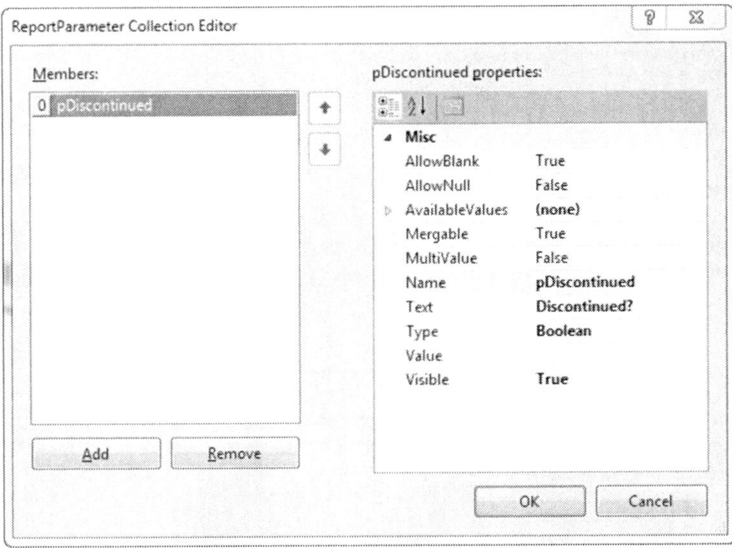

Figure 14-23. *Adding a report parameter to filter the report data*

2. Make the report parameter filter the data. Choose the `Filters` property from the Properties window and add a new filter using the New button. In the expression list, select the `Discontinued` field. The operand should be an equal sign (`=`). For the value, select the value of the parameter `pDiscontinued`, as shown in Figure 14-24.

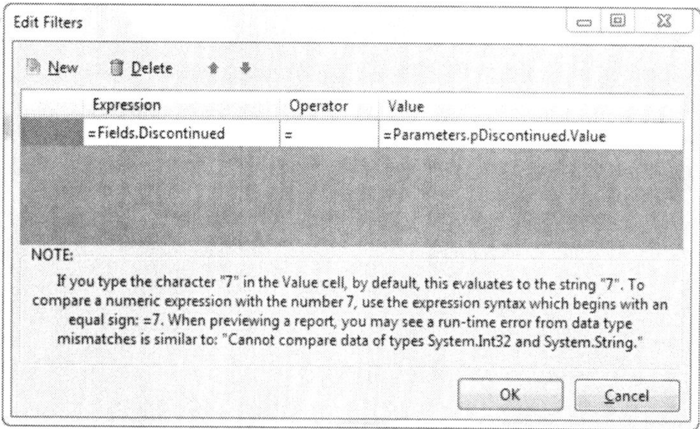

Figure 14-24. *Adding a filter using the report parameter*

After recompiling the project, you will see in the report preview that you now have the option to select either True or False for the parameter, and a Preview button appears in the upper-right corner of the previewer, as shown in Figure 14-25.

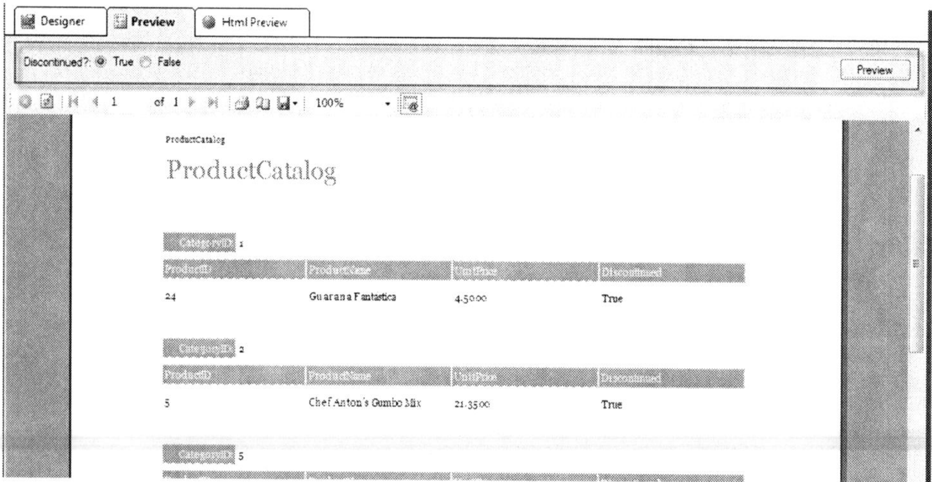

Figure 14-25. *The report now filters the information based on the pDiscontinued parameter*

Creating a Crosstab Report

Now we are going to create a crosstab report. A crosstab is a table of data that has the ability to display information that grows not only vertically, but also horizontally. These types of tables are heavily used in business intelligence (BI) systems because they allow users to manipulate and present summarized information. For example, you might present product sales by year and quarter, with the rows representing the products and the columns showing the information grouped by year and quarter.

Follow these steps to create the crosstab report using the Crosstab Wizard:

1. Create a new report as you did in the previous example.
2. Close the Report Wizard, as we are not going to use it for this example.
3. Add two report parameters called `pStartDate` and `pEndDate`. They both are of type `DateTime`. They will be used to filter the information from the datasource.
4. Remove the page header and footer.
5. Drag a the Crosstab Wizard item to the report section where you want the crosstab to appear. For this example, drag it to the detail section.
6. In the Welcome page, click Next.
7. In the Choose Data Source step, create a `SqlDataSource` component with the SQL Data Source Wizard. Name the `SqlDataSource` object `SalesDataSource`, and then click Next. (If you don't have a data connection, you can create one by clicking the New Connection button in the first step and selecting the Northwind database.)
8. If you want to save the connection string, select the check box in the Save Connection step.
9. In the Data Source Command step, select to use a stored procedure and select Employee Sales by Country from the list. Then click Next.
10. Now you need to configure the stored procedure parameters. In the `Value` list, select the report parameters you created in step 3. For the parameter `@Beginning_Date`, select `=Parameters.pStartDate.Value`. For the parameter `@Ending_Date`, select `=Parameters.pEndDate.Value`.
11. Test the query by clicking the Execute Query button and entering some dates for the parameters. Then click Finish.
12. Click Next after the selecting the newly created datasource.
13. The Arrange Fields step is very important. Here is where you define the field's arrangement for the crosstab. For the Row Groups section, add the `LastName` field. For the Column Groups, add the `Country` and `ShippedDate` fields. Finally, add the `SaleAmount` field to the detail section. (This field was created with the aggregate function `SUM` by default, but you can change it to another function later.) Click Next.
14. In the Choose Layout step, select the second option (Blocked layout, subtotals below) so the wizard will create totals automatically. Click Next.
15. In the Choose Style step, select the Corporate option. Click Next.
16. In the final step, click Finish to generate the crosstab report.

Your report should look similar to the one shown in Figure 14-26.

■ **Note** If your report is data-bound, then adding the crosstab to the detail section is not a good idea, because it will repeat the crosstab once for every row returned from the datasource. If this is the case for your report, it is better to create the crosstab in the report header or footer.

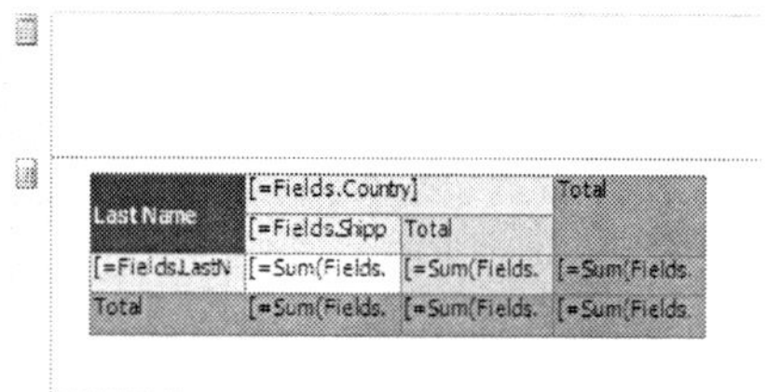

Figure 14-26. *Crosstab report created with the Crosstab Wizard*

When you preview the report using 1/1/1996 and 12/31/1996 for the report parameters `pStartDate` and `pEndDate`, respectively, you will see the result shown in Figure 14-27.

Designer | Preview | Html Preview

From: 1/ 1/1996 To: 12/31/1996

1 of 3 100%

Last Name	UK 7/10/1996 12:00:00 AM	7/15/1996 12:00:00 AM	7/16/1996 12:00:00 AM	7/23/1996 12:00:00 AM	7/31/1996 12:00:00 AM	8/6/1996 12:00:00 AM	8/9/1996 12:00:00 AM	8/16/1996 12:00:00
Buchanan			440	556.62			642.2	
Callahan								
Davolio								
Dodsworth		2490.5			1873.8			
Fuller								
King								
Leverling								
Peacock								
Suyama	1863.4					1456		538.6
Total	1863.4	2490.5	440	556.62	1873.8	1456	642.2	538.6

Figure 14-27. *Previewing the newly created crosstab report*

Grouping

Notice in Figure 14-27 how the data was supposed to be grouped, but because we added the whole shipped date, the report shows each date in one column. This is fine for smaller date ranges such as in a weekly report. However, for this example, we want to show this crosstab grouping the sales by country and monthly, which will require some tweaks.

Follow these steps to configure the crosstab report to display a better layout:

1. Return to the designer view.
2. Right-click an empty area of the report and select the View Code option from the context menu. This will open the report file in the code editor.
3. To format the date to show the month and year (i.e., Jun'10), add the following method to the report class:

```
public static string MonthName(DateTime date)
{
  return string.Format("{0}'{1}",
                date.ToString("MMM"),
                date.ToString("yy"));
}
```

4. Right-click the shipped date text box and select the Expression option to open the expression editor. Replace the `=Fields.ShippedDate` expression with `=MonthName(Fields.ShippedDate)`.

5. Right-click the shipped date text box again and select the Column Group ➤ Group Properties option to open the group properties window. It now shows the `Grouping` property with the value of `=Fields.ShippedDate`. Change this to the value `=Fields.ShippedDate.Month`.

Preview the report. It should look similar to the one shown in Figure 14-28.

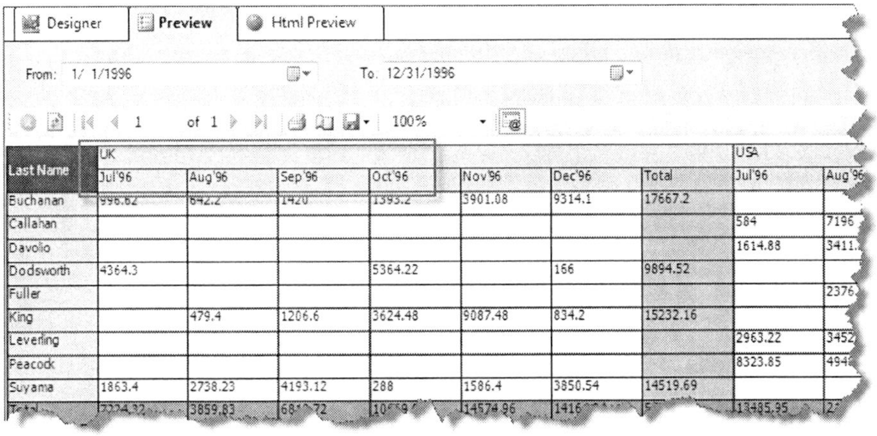

Figure 14-28. *Grouping by month and formatting the date*

Formatting

We can improve the report by formatting the fields to show the sales with the currency format and right-aligned. We will also center the country and month, and show the totals in bold. The tools for applying such formats are available to all report types.

Follow these steps to apply a better format to the crosstab report:

1. Right-click the country text box and select Style to open the style editor. In the Text section, change the alignment to Center. Click OK.

2. Repeat the previous step for the Total headers. (You can select both text boxes and edit their style at the same time.)

3. For each summarized field, right-click and select Format to open the format builder window. Select Currency, and then click OK. (This option is not available when multiple fields are selected.)

4. Select all the summarized fields and open the style editor. Change the alignment to Right.

5. Right-click the Last Name text box and select Expression. Replace the current expression with `=Fields.FirstName + ' ' + Fields.LastName` so the employees' full names are shown.

6. Change the column title from Last Name to **Employee**.

7. Make the Employee column wider by dragging the right column border to the right. This operation must be performed from the top column marker, as shown in Figure 14-29.

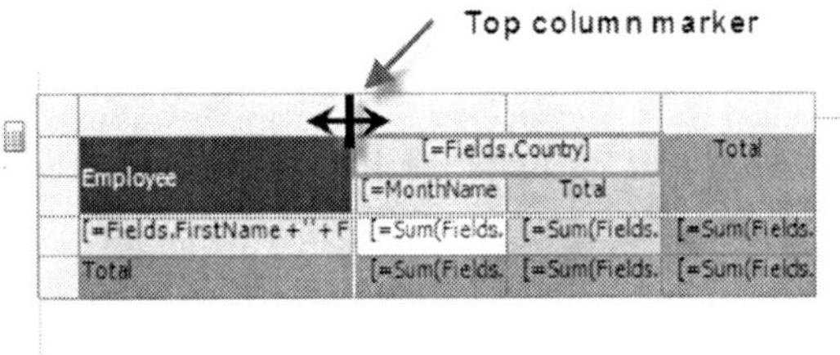

Figure 14-29. *The top column marker is shown when selecting the column border at the top of the crosstab.*

Now when you preview the report, it should look like the one shown in Figure 14-30.

Designer | Preview | Html Preview

From: 1/ 1/1996 To: 12/31/1996

1 of 1 100%

Employee	UK								
	Jul'96	Aug'96	Sep'96	Oct'96	Nov'96	Dec'96	Total	Jul'96	Aug'96
Steven Buchanan	$996.62	$642.20	$1,420.00	$1,393.20	$3,901.08	$9,314.10	$17,667.20		
Laura Callahan								$584.00	$7,196.0
Nancy Davolio								$1,614.88	$3,411.2
Anne Dodsworth	$4,364.30			$5,364.22		$166.00	$9,894.52		
Andrew Fuller									$2,376.80
Robert King		$479.40	$1,206.60	$3,624.48	$9,087.48	$834.20	$15,232.16		
Janet Leverling								$2,963.22	$3,452.0
Margaret Peacock								$8,323.85	$4,948.88
Michael Suyama	$1,863.40	$2,738.23	$4,193.12	$288.00	$1,586.40	$3,850.54	$14,519.69		
Total	$7,224.32	$3,859.83	$6,819.72	$10,659.90	$14,574.96	$14,164.84	$57,313.57	$13,485.95	$21,384.9

Figure 14-30. *After modifying the format and expressions of some of the fields, the crosstab report looks much better*

Using Subreports

Some reports cannot be generated just by using a wizard because the data representation is simply impossible to create in one layout. This is where subreports can help. Subreports allow the creation of isolated reports that can then be combined into a single report.

Each subreport is a complete report, although it is recommended that you use only the detail section. Once all subreports are created, you link them into a single report using the `SubReport` control and passing the parameters to the subreport to filter the appropriate data relevant to the full report.

As an example, we will create a report that displays a customer's information and orders in a date range. Additionally, we'll add a chart to see the customer's purchasing history. The following steps guide you through creating the report for the order detail information, the main report that will display the customer information, the chart, and the subreport.

1. Create a new report as you did in the previous examples. Name the report `CustomerOrders.cs`.

2. Cancel the Report Wizard and remove the report footer (leave the report header).

3. Create a new report parameter and name it `Customer`.

4. Create a new `SqlDataSource` component from the `DataSource` property in the Properties window and name it `OrdersDataSource`. Connect it to the Northwind database. In the command text area, enter the following statement:

```
SELECT  O.OrderID,
        O.OrderDate,
        O.ShippedDate,
        COUNT(D.ProductID) AS Products,
        SUM(D.Quantity * D.UnitPrice) AS Total
FROM    Orders O
        INNER JOIN [Order Details] D ON O.OrderID = D.OrderID
WHERE   CustomerID = @CustomerID
GROUP BY O.OrderID,
        O.OrderDate,
        O.ShippedDate
```

5. In the Configure Data Source Parameters step, select the value of the report parameter for the value of the `@CustomerID` parameter.

6. Using the Data Explorer tool, drag all the fields in the `OrdersDataSource` to the detail section of the report, forming a line (adjust the size of the detail section accordingly).

7. In the report header, add text boxes for the titles of the fields: **Order No.**, **Date**, **Shipped**, **Products**, and **Total**.

8. You can make some format modifications; for example, define the format for the Total field as Currency, and define the format for the Date and Shipped fields as Date. Formatting can also be applied to the header labels.

9. Create the main report. Name the report `CustomerInformation.cs`.

10. Cancel the Report Wizard and remove the report footer. Keep only the report header and detail sections.

11. Create a report parameter using the `ReportParameters` property. Name the parameter `Customer`.

12. Expand the `AvailableValues` property. In the `DataSource` subproperty, select Add New Data Source to create a new `SqlDataSource` component for the parameter. Name the new datasource `ListOfCustomersDataSource`.

13. Connect to the Northwind database and in the command text area, type the following statement:

```
SELECT CustomerID, CompanyName
FROM Customers
ORDER BY CompanyName
```

14. Save the new `SqlDataSource` and return to the parameter properties.

15. In the DisplayMember property, select CompanyName.
16. In the ValueMember property, select CustomerID.
17. In the Visible property, select True. Click OK and return to the report.
18. In the report header, add a text box for the report title. In the text box, enter the title **Customer Information**. Change the style of the text box to highlight it—change the font color, type, and size as you wish.
19. From the Data Explorer, add to the report header the fields CustomerID, CompanyName, ContactName, Phone, and Country.
20. Drag a Chart control from the Toolbox to the detail section. Enlarge the control enough to display the information. For example, you can make it the same width as the detail section and about 250 pixels high.
21. In the Properties window, change the chart type using the DefaultType property and set it to Line.
22. Change the title of the chart by selecting the Chart Title property, then TextBlock, then Text property. Give it the title **Monthly Purchases History**.
23. Create an event handler for the chart's NeedDataSource event. Switch to code view and add the following lines to the event handler:

```
private void chart1_NeedDataSource(object sender, EventArgs e)
{
    var chart = sender as Telerik.Reporting.Processing.Chart;
    string sql = @"SELECT SUBSTRING(CONVERT(VARCHAR, OrderDate, 101),1,3) +
                          SUBSTRING(CONVERT(VARCHAR, OrderDate, 101),9,2) AS
                          OrderDate, COUNT(*) AS OrdersCount
                     FROM dbo.Orders
                   WHERE CustomerID='" + this.ReportParameters["Customer"] .Value + "'" +
                   "GROUP BY SUBSTRING(CONVERT(VARCHAR, OrderDate, 101),1,3) +
                   "SUBSTRING(CONVERT(VARCHAR, OrderDate, 101),9,2)";

    string connectionString = "Data Source=(local)\\SQLEXPRESS; " +
                              "Initial Catalog=NorthWind; " +
                              "Integrated Security=True";
    SqlDataAdapter adapter = new SqlDataAdapter(sql, connectionString);
    DataSet dataSet = new DataSet();
    adapter.Fill(dataSet);
    chart.DataSource = dataSet;
    chart1.Series[0].DataYColumn = "OrdersCount";
    chart1.PlotArea.XAxis.DataLabelsColumn = "OrderDate";
}
```

24. Right-click the Chart control and select Properties to open a configuration window. Switch to the Skin tab and select a skin that you like. Then close the window.
25. From the Toolbox, drag a SubReport control to the detail section below the Chart control.
26. Make the SubReport control width the same as the detail section.
27. Select the SubReport control. From the Properties window, select the CustomerOrders report you created for the ReportSource property.

28. In the Parameters property, select the Customer property defined for the subreport and link it to the CustomerID field from the datasource.

We are finished! You should have a report definition like the one shown in Figure 14-31.

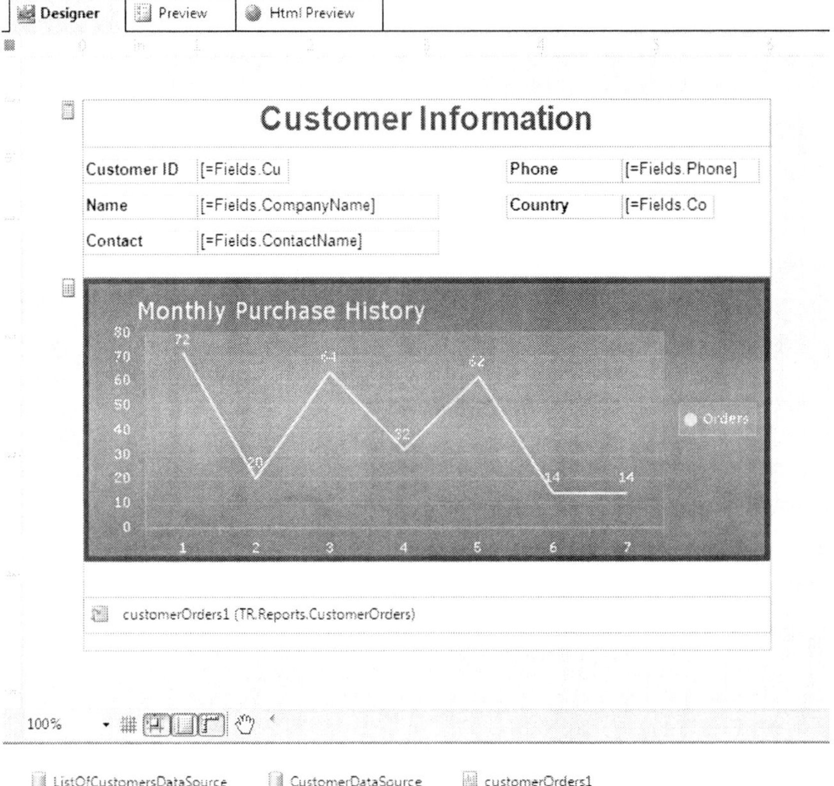

Figure 14-31. *The layout of the report with a chart and a subreport*

When you preview the report, it will look like the one shown in Figure 14-32. Notice the drop-down menu to select the customer for the report parameter (this is created automatically from the ListOfCustomersDataSource datasource). Also notice how all of the report elements are shown when you select one of them.

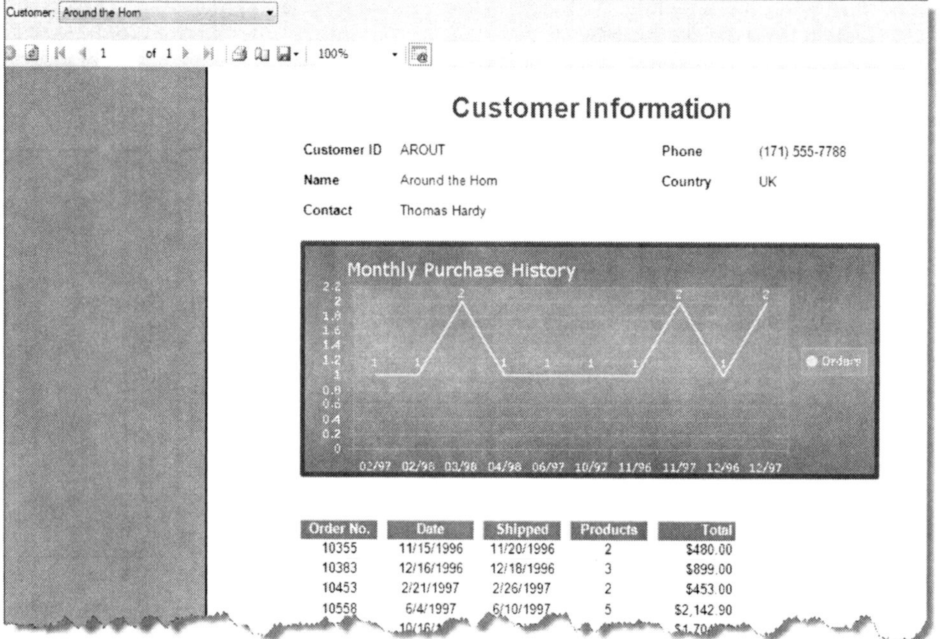

Figure 14-32. *Previewing the report with the chart and subreport*

Displaying Reports in the Application

It is time to return to your application and make use of the reports you created. For this, you need only three things:

- To create a reference in your application to the reports project to gain access to the reports.
- To have a report viewer in your web page or Silverlight application. Just drag the `ReportViewer` component from Visual Studio's Toolbox onto the web page or XAML page.
- To define the report you want to display in the viewer. You can do this either by selecting it from the report viewer's `Report` property in the Properties window or by programmatically creating an instance of the report class and assigning it to the `Report` property of the viewer.

Using the Web Report Viewer

The use of the ASP.NET `ReportViewer` component is actually very simple—just drag the component onto the page, and it's ready. You can select the report to display from the `Report` property in the Properties window when the report viewer is selected. To programmatically select the report to display, you can use the `Page_Load` event handler to create an instance of the report class and assign it to the `Report` property of the viewer, as shown in Listing 14-8. Figure 14-33 shows the result.

Listing 14-8. *Adding the Report Viewer to the Page and Loading a Report*

ASPX Page

```
<%@ Page Language="C#"
        AutoEventWireup="true"
        CodeBehind="Default.aspx.cs"
        Inherits="TR.Demo._Default" %>


<%@ Register Assembly="Telerik.ReportViewer.WebForms,
                        Version=4.0.10.421,
                        Culture=neutral,
                        PublicKeyToken=a9d7983dfcc261be"
                Namespace="Telerik.ReportViewer.WebForms"
                TagPrefix="telerik" %>

<!DOCTYPE html PUBLIC "-//W3C//DTD XHTML 1.0 Transitional//EN"
"http://www.w3.org/TR/xhtml1/DTD/xhtml1-transitional.dtd">

<html xmlns="http://www.w3.org/1999/xhtml">
<head runat="server">
    <title></title>
</head>
<body>
    <form id="form1" runat="server">
    <div>
        <telerik:ReportViewer ID="ReportViewer1" runat="server"
                Width="100%"
                Height="500px">
        </telerik:ReportViewer>
    </div>
    </form>
</body>
</html>
```

Code Behind

```
protected void Page_Load(object sender, EventArgs e)
{
    if (Page.IsPostBack) return;
    ReportViewer1.Report = new TR.Reports.ProductCatalog();
}
```

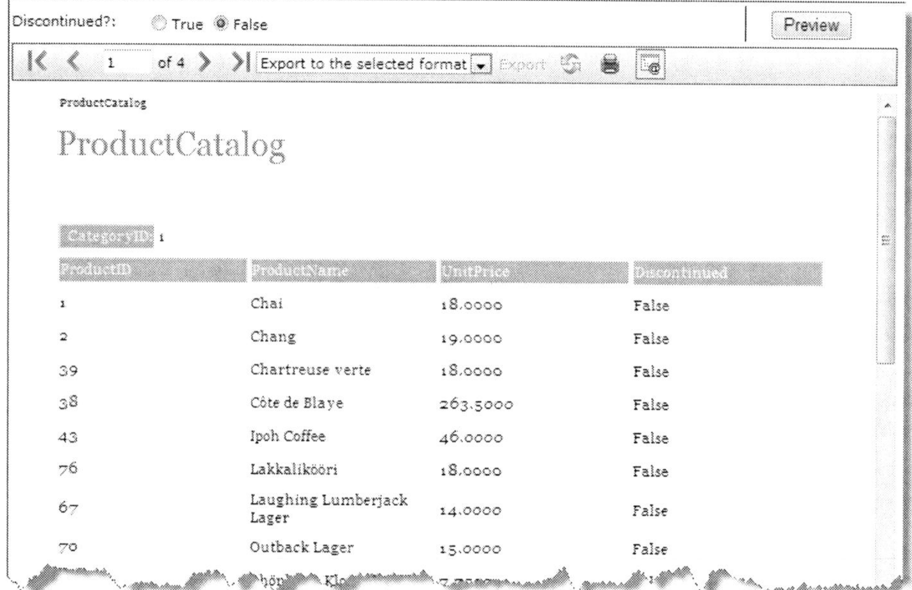

Figure 14-33. *The web report viewer showing a report*

Using the Silverlight Report Viewer

To use the Silverlight report viewer in your application takes a few more configuration steps than are required for the web report viewer, but rest assured, they are quite simple.

Configuring the Web Application

In your web application, you need to add the references to the assemblies `Telerik.Reporting.dll`, `Telerik.Reporting.Service.dll`, and `Telerik.Reporting.XamlRendering.dll`. Additionally, you need to add a reference to your project for the Silverlight project hosting the application and the class library project hosting the reports.

The Silverlight report viewer relies on a WCF service to stream the report information from the source to the viewer. Therefore, you need a WCF service in the web application hosting the Silverlight application that only creates an interface to the `Telerik.Reporting.Service` assembly. To create this service, create an empty text file in the web application project, and then rename it to a name with the extension `.svc`, such as `ReportService.svc`. Then add the following line to the file:

```
<%@ServiceHost Service="Telerik.Reporting.Service.ReportService,
                   Telerik.Reporting.Service" %>
```

Now you need to make your application aware of the WCF service. Add the following configuration to your `web.config` file at the end of the file, just before the `</configuration>` tag:

```
<system.serviceModel>
    <serviceHostingEnvironment aspNetCompatibilityEnabled="true" />
    <services>
        <service
                name="Telerik.Reporting.Service.ReportService"
                behaviorConfiguration="ReportServiceBehavior">
            <endpoint
                    address=""
                    binding="basicHttpBinding"
                    contract="Telerik.Reporting.Service.IReportService">
                <identity>
                    <dns value="localhost" />
                </identity>
            </endpoint>
            <endpoint
                    address="resources"
                    binding="webHttpBinding"
                    behaviorConfiguration="WebBehavior"
                    contract="Telerik.Reporting.Service.IResourceService"/>
            <endpoint
                    address="mex"
                    binding="mexHttpBinding"
                    contract="IMetadataExchange" />
        </service>
    </services>
    <behaviors>
        <serviceBehaviors>
            <behavior name="ReportServiceBehavior">
                <serviceMetadata httpGetEnabled="true" />
                <serviceDebug includeExceptionDetailInFaults="false" />
            </behavior>
        </serviceBehaviors>
        <endpointBehaviors>
            <behavior name="WebBehavior">
                <webHttp />
            </behavior>
        </endpointBehaviors>
    </behaviors>
</system.serviceModel>
```

■ **Note** For more information about Telerik Reporting and WCF, visit `www.telerik.com/help/reporting/silverlight-hosting-in-iis.html`.

Now you are ready to configure the web page that will host the Silverlight application. You need a page configured similar to the one shown in Listing 14-9. Remember that normally the compiled Silverlight application (XAP file) will be located in the `ClientBin` directory of your application, so if your configuration hasn't changed, then it should be there.

Listing 14-9. *Web Page Hosting the Silverlight Application*

```
<%@ Page Language="C#" AutoEventWireup="true" %>
<!DOCTYPE html PUBLIC "-//W3C//DTD XHTML 1.0 Transitional//EN"
        "http://www.w3.org/TR/xhtml1/DTD/xhtml1-transitional.dtd">
<html xmlns="http://www.w3.org/1999/xhtml" >
<head runat="server">
    <title>TR.Silverlight</title>
    <script type="text/javascript" src="Silverlight.js"></script>
</head>
<body>
    <form id="form1" runat="server" style="height:100%">
    <div id="silverlightControlHost">
        <object data="data:application/x-silverlight-2,"
                type="application/x-silverlight-2"
                width="100%"
                height="100%">
                <param name="source" value="ClientBin/TR.Silverlight.xap"/>
                <param name="background" value="white" />
                <param name="minRuntimeVersion" value="3.0.40818.0" />
                <param name="autoUpgrade" value="true" />
                <a href="http://go.microsoft.com/fwlink/?LinkID=149156&v=3.0.40818.0"
                   style="text-decoration:none">
                        <img src="http://go.microsoft.com/fwlink/?LinkId=161376"
                                alt="Get Microsoft Silverlight"
                                style="border-style:none"/>
                </a>
            </object>
        <iframe id="_sl_historyFrame"
                style="visibility:hidden;height:0px;width:0px;border:0px">
        </iframe>
    </div>
    </form>
</body>
</html>
```

Configuring the Silverlight Application

In the Silverlight application, you need to add references to the assemblies Telerik.ReportViewer.Silverlight, Telerik.Windows.Controls, Telerik.Windows.Controls.Input, and Telerik.Window.Controls.Navigation.

In your XAML page, you need to add a namespace for the viewer. Here's an example:

```
xmlns:my="clr-namespace:Telerik.ReportViewer.Silverlight;
assembly=Telerik.ReportViewer.Silverlight"
```

Add the declaration of the report viewer to the XAML page:

```
<my:ReportViewer x:Name="Reportviewer1" />
```

The report viewer needs two important properties in order to display the report. The first one is a reference to the WCF service. The property is `ReportServerUri="../ReportService.svc"`. The property requires the exact location of the WCF service file, so you need to keep in mind that the XAP file will be in the `ClientBin` directory and the service file is in the root directory—that's why you need the `../` part.

The other property is the actual report you want to display, and it is properly named `Report`. The `Report` property needs the fully qualified name of the report. Basically, if the assembly containing the report is not signed or has any specific configuration, it should be something similar to this:

```
Report="TR.Reports.ProductCatalog,
        TR.Reports,
        Version=1.0.0.0,
        Culture=neutral,
        PublicKeyToken=null"
```

The final XAML of the page should be similar to that shown in Listing 14-10.

Listing 14-10. *XAML Page with the Report Viewer Definition*

```
<UserControl
    x:Class="TR.Silverlight.MainPage"
    xmlns="http://schemas.microsoft.com/winfx/2006/xaml/presentation"
    xmlns:x="http://schemas.microsoft.com/winfx/2006/xaml"
    xmlns:d="http://schemas.microsoft.com/expression/blend/2008"
    xmlns:mc="http://schemas.openxmlformats.org/markup-compatibility/2006"
    xmlns:my="clr-namespace:Telerik.ReportViewer.Silverlight;
              assembly=Telerik.ReportViewer.Silverlight"
    mc:Ignorable="d" d:DesignWidth="640" d:DesignHeight="480">
  <Grid x:Name="LayoutRoot">
        <my:ReportViewer x:Name="Reportviewer1"
                         ReportServerUri="../ReportService.svc"
                         Report="TR.Reports.ProductCatalog,
                                 TR.Reports,
                                 Version=1.0.0.0,
                                 Culture=neutral,
                                 PublicKeyToken=null" />
    </Grid>
</UserControl>
```

After this configuration, you are ready to see your report within the Silverlight report viewer, as shown in Figure 14-34.

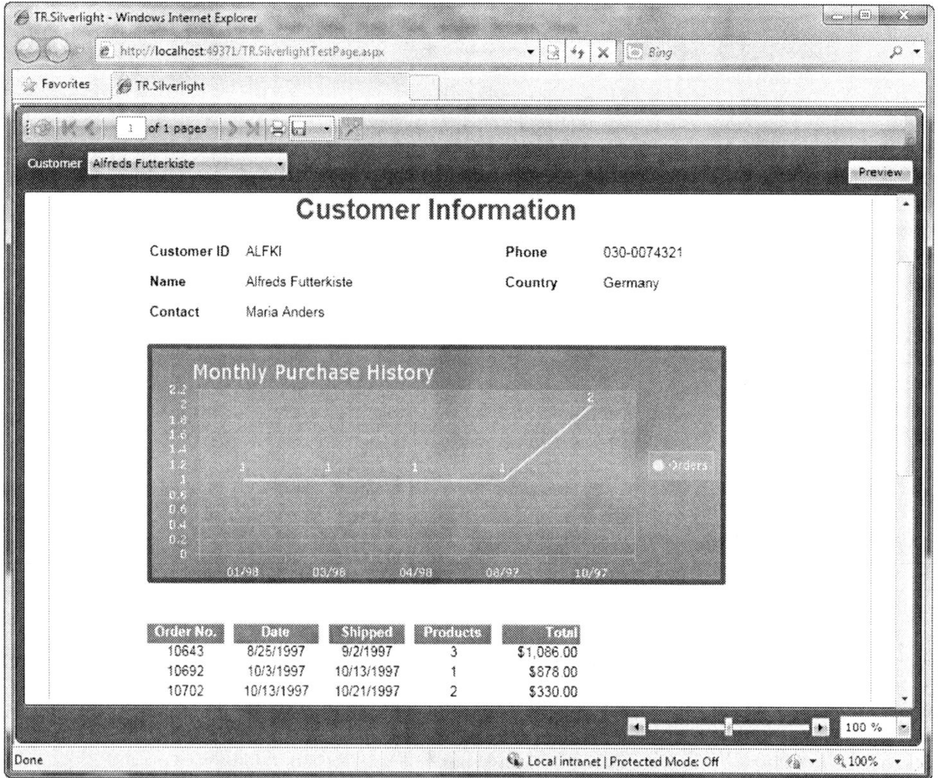

Figure 14-34. *The Silverlight report viewer in action*

Using the ReportBook Control

The ReportBook control is a new addition to Telerik Reporting. Its main purpose is to combine reports in order to print all of them in a single operation. As of this writing, this control exists only for Windows and web applications.

The control configuration is actually quite simple. You just need to list the reports you want to combine, and then let the report viewer know you want to use ReportBook. Listing 14-11 shows how to configure the control. Figure 14-35 shows the ReportBook control in action.

Listing 14-11. *Configuring ReportBook*

```
<telerik:ReportViewer ID="ReportViewer1" runat="server"
                      ReportBookID="ReportBookControl1">
</telerik:ReportViewer>
```

```
<telerik:ReportBookControl ID="ReportBookControl1" runat="server">
    <Reports>
        <telerik:ReportInfo Report="TR.Reports.CustomerInformation,
                                    TR.Reports" />
        <telerik:ReportInfo Report="TR.Reports.ProductCatalog,
                                    TR.Reports" />
    </Reports>
</telerik:ReportBookControl>
```

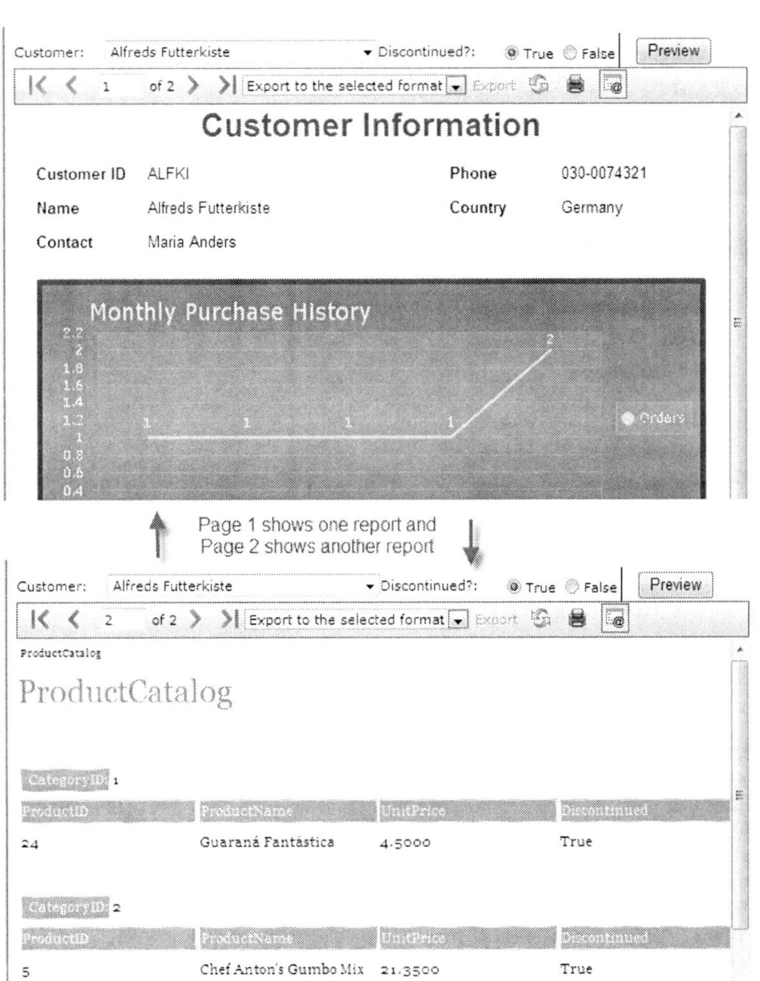

Figure 14-35. *ReportBook working with two reports*

Adding a Document Map

A document map is a set of links defined for a report that works much like a table of contents for a book. When you click a link, it will take you to a specific part of the report.

The document map is generated based on the `Bookmark` property for items and groups in your reports. The `Bookmark` property accepts static text, expressions, or text with expressions. The resulting text will be displayed in the document map tree.

Let's modify the product catalog report so it includes a document map. Open the report and select the categories group. In the Properties window, select the `Bookmark` property and open the expression editor. Type `="Category " + Fields.CategoryID`, and then close the editor. Now compile the project for the changes to take effect. Figure 14-36 shows the result of this small change.

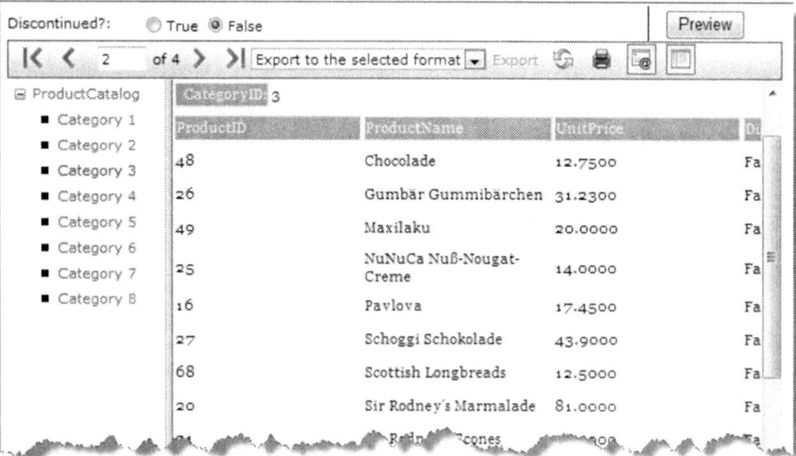

Figure 14-36. *The product catalog report using a document map for quick navigation*

Summary

Telerik Reporting is a powerful reporting solution. It generates reports that can be used in Windows Forms, ASP.NET Web Forms, Silverlight, and WPF applications, without requiring any modifications.

The product includes a full set of wizards, flexible expression and style editors, and a visual editor for creating reports. The Report Wizard takes you step by step through the creation of the report. Other wizards are available for complex tasks such as table and crosstab report creation.

Configuring an application to run reports is very easy and can be done using Visual Studio Extensions for Telerik Reporting. Reports can be laid out for simple lists of data, tables, and crosstabs. Report parameters help filter data and provide the means of passing information to subreports.

Reports are composed of different sections that each serve a special purpose. You can add different types of items to reports, including text boxes, shapes, panels, bar codes, and charts. Reports also can be combined to into a single viewer for easy printing using the `ReportBook` control.

CHAPTER 15

■ ■ ■

Telerik OpenAccess ORM

In October 2008, Telerik announced that it had acquired the German company Vanatec, which specialized in object relational mapping (ORM) software. Their flagship product, Vanatec OpenAccess, was then rebranded to Telerik OpenAccess ORM.

Since then, Telerik has been able to offer its customers an enterprise-class ORM solution that provides reverse and forward mapping; support for various databases such as Microsoft SQL Server, Oracle, MySQL, Sybase, VistaDB; and more. It is also the first ORM to support SQL Azure, Microsoft's version of SQL Server in the cloud.

In this chapter, I will introduce you to Telerik OpenAccess ORM and will show you some of its most powerful capabilities including forward and reverse mapping, fetch plans, inheritance and transactions.

System Requirements

Telerik OpenAccess ORM requires the following to work properly:

- Microsoft .NET Framework 2.0 and above
- Microsoft .NET Framework 3.5 (the minimum required version for the new visual data model designer and LINQ provider)
- Microsoft Visual Studio 2005 and above
- Access to a supported database

    Microsoft SQL Server 2000 and above

    Microsoft SQL Azure

    Microsoft SQL Server CE

    Microsoft SQL Server 2005/2008 Express

    Oracle Server 9.2 and above

    Oracle Database XE

    MySQL 5.0 and above

    Sybase iAnywhere Advantage Database Server 8.1

    Sybase iAnywhere SQL Anywhere Server 10 (only with Visual Studio 2005)

    Firebird Server version 2.0 (only with Visual Studio 2005)

    VistaDB

Installing Telerik OpenAccess ORM

Installing Telerik OpenAccess ORM is a very simple process; the setup program takes care of installing the required assemblies and integrating with Visual Studio with the click of a few buttons.

The file you download from Telerik's web site is a compressed zip file that contains all the files necessary to install the product. You first have to decompress it to a folder and then run the `setup.exe` file. There are only two questions you have to answer during the installation process after accepting the license agreement.

The first question is the location of a local instance of Microsoft SQL Server (version 2005 at least); the installer deploys a special version of the Northwind database to use with the OpenAccess ORM samples. If you leave this field blank, no database will be installed.

The second question is the destination folder where all the files will be copied. The default folder is `C:\Program Files\Telerik\OpenAccess ORM`. If you are in a 64-bit platform, the default folder is `C:\Program Files(x86)\Telerik\OpenAccess ORM`. Figure 15-1 shows the destination folder created by the installer.

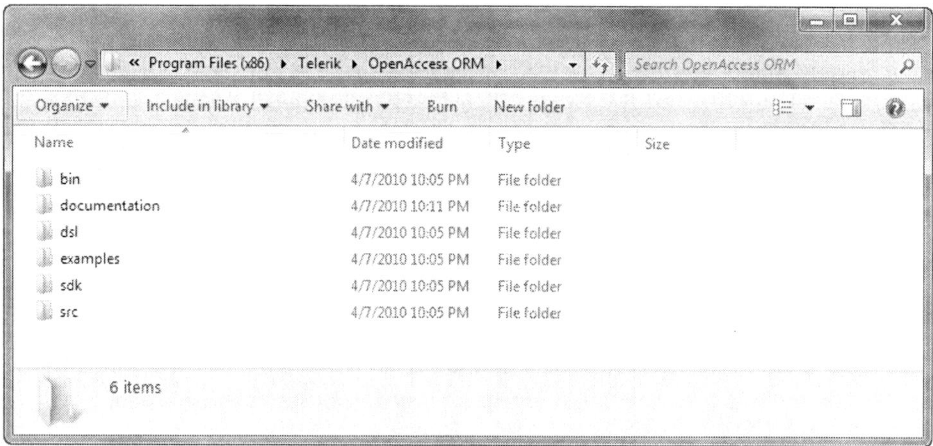

Figure 15-1. *Telerik OpenAccess ORM destination folder*

The folders contain the following:

- The `bin` folder contains all the binaries for redistribution of the product with your applications.
- The `documentation` folder contains all the documentation files in CHM format and in the format for Microsoft's Document Explorer.
- The `dsl` folder contains the Visual Studio templates for the new visual data model designer.
- The `examples` folder contains all the Visual Studio projects to run the examples.
- The `sdk` folder contains all the files and tools in the software development kit.
- The `src` contains the product's source code.

Configuring Your Application

Your application can be configured to run Telerik OpenAccess ORM by using either the Enable Project wizard or the Visual Entity Model Designer. These two approaches cannot be used at the same time in the same solution; you have to choose one or another.

- When using the Enable Project Wizard with your application, OpenAccess will generate persistent classes and a scope provider. *Persistent classes* are classes that represent objects in the database; for example, a class maps to a table and properties of the class map to fields of the table. The scope provider is a helper class that provides the means to interact with the database through the persistent classes.
- The other option for using OpenAccess is with the Visual Domain Entity Designer. With this option, a special class file is created that supports a visual representation of the database objects (tables, views, and stored procedures). The extension of this special file is RLINQ, which stands for "relational LINQ." Each object in the designer is created in a separate code-behind class file, which contains all the necessary information for usage within the designer. It is recommended that you do not modify these files, as they are automatically generated by the designer and will be overwritten when any changes are made to the designer file.

Regardless of the approach taken, a best practice is to place the persistent classes or entity model in a separate project and the scope provider in the project containing your data access code. This will provide better support for scalability and future changes, and on top of that, you may reuse the project for data access in other applications. While it is possible (and supported) to have everything in the same project, I strongly advise against it.

This best practice is actually mandatory if you used the Visual Studio Web Site Project template to create your project, because OpenAccess enhances the application assembly during compilation, and a Web Site Project does not generate a static assembly. The enhancement process is used to avoid using reflection in your code, thus allowing for a greater level of performance.

Figure 15-2 shows a web application that uses Telerik OpenAccess ORM Visual Entity Model Designer within the same application project.

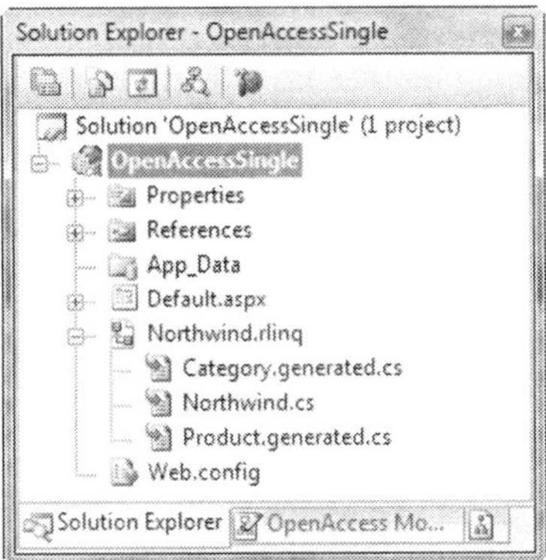

Figure 15-2. *Web application configure to use Telerik OpenAccess ORM Visual Domain Model Designer*

Figure 15-3 shows a web application after the configuration of Telerik OpenAccess ORM. Note that there are two projects in the solution: OpenAccessData contains the persistent classes, and OpenAccessDemo is the actual web application.

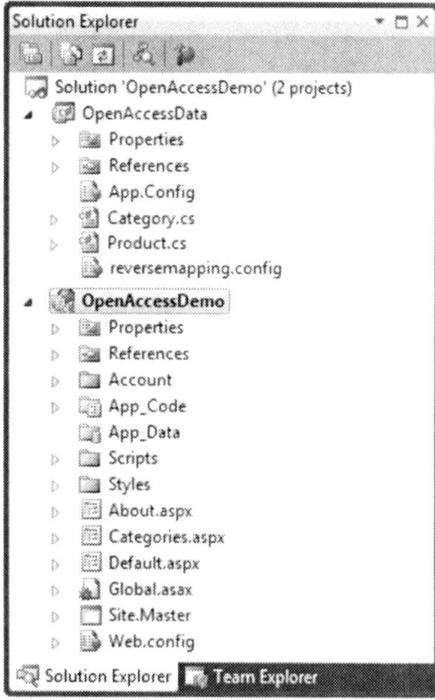

Figure 15-3. *A web application configured to use Telerik OpenAccess ORM and the recommended pattern*

Deploying Your Application

When you finish your application and are ready to deploy it, you are entitled to use and redistribute the Telerik OpenAccess ORM assemblies with it. There is no need for your clients to purchase a license to use these assemblies. In certain cases, you may be required to obtain written authorization from Telerik, such as when exposing some design time functionality or for open source projects.

When you compile and publish your project using Visual Studio, normally all assemblies required to run the application are either created or copied for you in the target folder, so you can copy the whole application to the destination server.

Several assemblies are needed for OpenAccess to run; make sure you have the following files in your bin folder:

- `Telerik.OpenAccess.dll`: This is the core library that contains all the API classes.
- `Telerik.OpenAccess.Adonet2.dll`: This assembly contains the database-specific classes used for accessing all supported databases. It uses the `SqlClient` when connecting against SQL Server 2005 or SqlExpress or the `OracleClient` when connecting against an Oracle server.
- `Telerik.OpenAccess.Query.dll`: This assembly contains the LINQ implementation for Telerik OpenAccess ORM.
- `MySql.Data.dll`: This assembly contains the backend-specific implementation for MySQL.

- `Telerik.OpenAccess.Web.dll`: This one is required when implementing `OpenAccessDataSource`, `ObjectView`, and `ObjectProvider` in Visual Studio 2010 because of profile requirements. In Windows Forms applications, you will need `Telerik.OpenAccess.Windows.dll` instead.
- `Telerik.OpenAccess.35.Extensions.dll`: This assembly is required when using LINQ and .NET Framework 3.5.
- `Telerik.OpenAccess.40.Extensions.dll`: This one is required when using LINQ and .NET Framework 4.0.

■ **Note** For information on licensing and redistributing Telerik OpenAccess ORM, please visit the documentation pages at `http://www.telerik.com/help/openaccess-orm/deploying-openaccess-redistribution.html` and `http://www.telerik.com/help/openaccess-orm/deploying-openaccess-licensing.html`, or contact Telerik at `http://www.telerik.com/company/contact-us.aspx`.

Creating the Data Model

The first step to use Telerik OpenAccess ORM is to create the data model. In the data model, you will have all the classes that will map to tables, views and stored procedures from the database.

You can build your data model inside your application, but as mentioned before, the recommended pattern is to have the data model in its own project; doing so has these advantages:

- *Maintainability*: Your data model will be easily maintainable, because you won't have modify and recompile your application after an update. Also, if you ever have to switch database engines, all you need to do is target the new engine (for example, from Oracle to MySQL) and recompile it.
- *Scalability*: If your data model is separate from the application, it will be easier to scale it up. As your application moves from a single web server to a web farm, your data model can also take advantage of this growth.
- *Testability*: This approach isolates the data model in a separate unit that can be tested using different test frameworks.
- *Code reuse*: Your data model can be use by other applications targeting the same databases it maps to.

To create the data model in a separate project, you need to create a new Class Library project in your solution (right click on the solution name in the solution explorer, then select Add ➤ New Project).

Once you have the new project you need to choose one of the two approaches described before, enabling your project or using the visual domain model designer.

Using the Enable Project Wizard

When you enable your project using the Enable Project Wizard, you will be creating classes that will map to objects in the database. To start, go to the Telerik Visual Studio Extensions menu option inside Visual Studio and select Open Access ➤ Enable Project to use ORM. See Figure 15-4. This option is also available when you right-click the project and select OpenAccess ➤ Enable Project from the context menu.

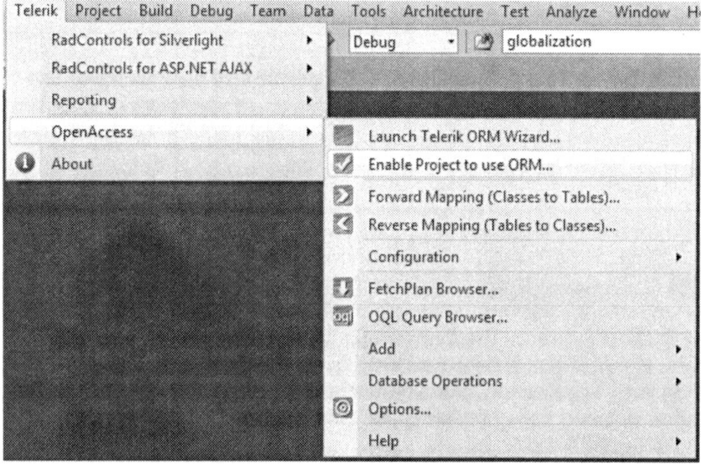

Figure 15-4. *Enable Project to use ORM.*

The first step in the Enable Project Wizard explains the actions it will execute. After you click Next, the wizard will ask you a very important question, "Does your project contain the following?" And it provides two possible answers: "Persistent classes?" and "Data access code (DAL)?". Figure 15-5 shows this wizard step.

The two answers are presented with check boxes, so you choose the one you want your project be enabled with. If you choose persistent classes, you will create the classes that represent the data model in the project. If you choose data access code, you will be creating the scope provider, which is a class that interacts with the persistent classes to perform operations with the database.

You should choose persistent classes for your newly created class library project and data access code for your web application project. If you want to create the data model inside your application, you enable your web application project with both options selected.

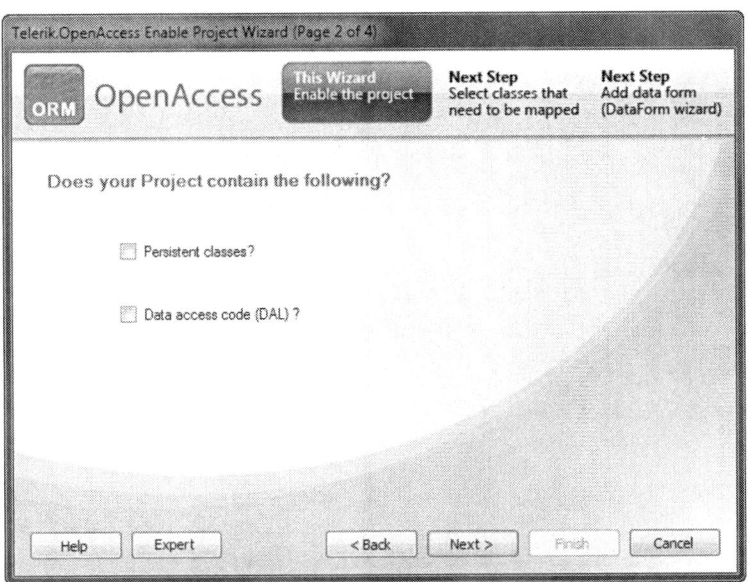

Figure 15-5. *Enabling the project to work with OpenAccess*

In your new class library project, you then select "Persistent classes" and click next. The next step is the database connection configuration. You are required to type the connection ID, select the correct database management system, and define the connection settings. See Figure 15-6. In the connection settings section, you can select if you want your connection information to be stored using standard connection strings in the `web.config` and `app.config` files or if you want to use OpenAccess connection settings. If you select OpenAccess connection settings, the connection information will be created using XML in the OpenAccess section of the project configuration file.

The final step in the Enable Project Wizard is a summary of the actions it will make to enable the project:

- Add or update a configuration file with the database connection information.
- Add the assemblies needed by OpenAccess to the project references if needed.
- Set or update the project properties used by OpenAccess which will be used by the enhancer and other tools.

When you click the Finish button, the wizard will perform all the actions described in the final step.

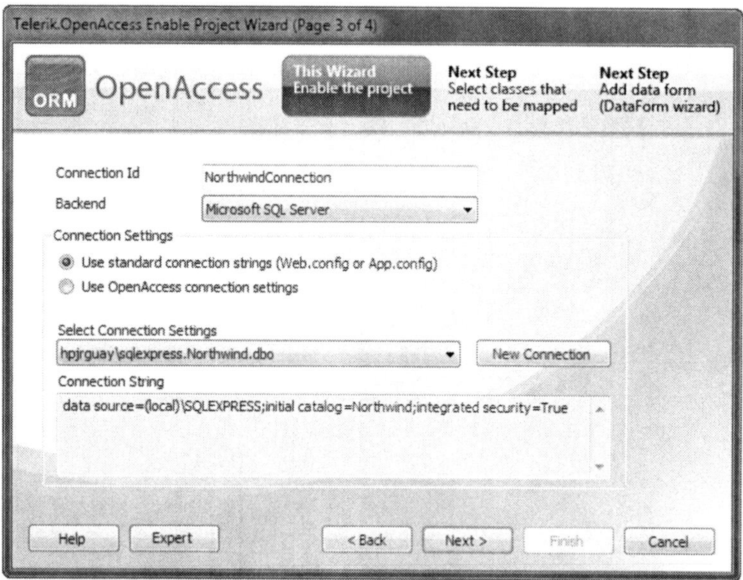

Figure 15-6. *Database connection configuration*

In your web application project, you have to perform the same steps I just described for the Enable Project Wizard; the difference is that, in the second step, you will select "Data access code (DAL)?". Then you will add the database connection information with the same information and options we used before.

In this case, the Enable Project Wizard will perform a slightly different process which includes

- Adding or updating a scope provider class to the project
- Adding or updating the configuration file to include the database connection information
- Adding the assemblies needed by OpenAccess to the project references if needed
- Setting or updating the project properties used by OpenAccess that will be used by the enhancer and other tools

Listing 15-1 shows the code that is generated for the scope provider class.

Listing 15-1. *Scope Provider Class*

```
using Telerik.OpenAccess;
using Telerik.OpenAccess.Util;
using System.Web;
using System.Threading;
```

```
namespace OpenAccessDemo
{
        /// <summary>
        /// This class provides an object context for connected database access.
        /// </summary>
        /// <remarks>
        /// This class can be used to obtain an IObjectScope instance
        /// required for a connected database
        /// access.
        /// </remarks>
        public class ObjectScopeProvider1 : IObjectScopeProvider
        {
                private Database myDatabase;
                private IObjectScope myScope;

                static private ObjectScopeProvider1 theObjectScopeProvider1;

                /// <summary>
                /// Constructor.
                /// </summary>
                /// <remarks></remarks>
                public ObjectScopeProvider1()
                {
                }

        /// <summary>
        /// Adjusts for dynamic loading when no entry assembly
        /// is available/configurable.
        /// </summary>
        /// <remarks>
        /// When dynamic loading is used, the configuration path from the
        /// applications entry assembly to the connection setting might be broken.
        /// This method makes up the necessary configuration entries.
        /// </remarks>
        static public void AdjustForDynamicLoad()
        {
            if( theObjectScopeProvider1 == null )
                theObjectScopeProvider1 = new ObjectScopeProvider1();

            if( theObjectScopeProvider1.myDatabase == null )
            {
                string assumedInitialConfiguration =
                           "<openaccess>" +
                               "<references>" +
                                   "<reference assemblyname='PLACEHOLDER'
                                                configrequired='True'/>" +
                               "</references>" +
                           "</openaccess>";
                System.Reflection.Assembly dll = theObjectScopeProvider1.GetType()
                                                         .Assembly;
                assumedInitialConfiguration = assumedInitialConfiguration
                                                .Replace("PLACEHOLDER",
                                                        dll.GetName().Name);
```

```
                System.Xml.XmlDocument xmlDoc = new System.Xml.XmlDocument();
                xmlDoc.LoadXml(assumedInitialConfiguration);
                Database db = Telerik.OpenAccess.Database.Get("NorthwindConnection",
                                              xmlDoc.DocumentElement,
                                              new System.Reflection.Assembly[] { dll } );

                theObjectScopeProvider1.myDatabase = db;
            }
        }

                /// <summary>
                /// Returns the instance of Database for the connectionId
                /// specified in the Enable Project Wizard.
                /// </summary>
                /// <returns>Instance of Database.</returns>
                /// <remarks></remarks>
                static public Database Database()
                {
                        if( theObjectScopeProvider1 == null )
                                theObjectScopeProvider1 = new ObjectScopeProvider1();

                        if( theObjectScopeProvider1.myDatabase == null )
                                theObjectScopeProvider1.myDatabase =
                                                Telerik.OpenAccess
                                                        .Database
                                                        .Get( "NorthwindConnection" );

                        return theObjectScopeProvider1.myDatabase;
                }

                /// <summary>
                /// Returns the instance of ObjectScope for the application.
                /// </summary>
                /// <returns>Instance of IObjectScope.</returns>
                /// <remarks></remarks>
                static public IObjectScope ObjectScope()
                {
                        Database();

                        if( theObjectScopeProvider1.myScope == null )
                                theObjectScopeProvider1.myScope = GetNewObjectScope();

                        return theObjectScopeProvider1.myScope;
                }

                /// <summary>
                /// Returns the new instance of ObjectScope for the application.
                /// </summary>
                /// <returns>Instance of IObjectScope.</returns>
                /// <remarks></remarks>
```

```
        static public IObjectScope GetNewObjectScope()
        {
                Database db = Database();

                IObjectScope newScope = db.GetObjectScope();
                return newScope;
        }
    /// <summary>
    /// Returns the new instance of the ObjectScope using the HttpContext
    /// aproach described in the best practices articles.
    /// </summary>
    /// <returns>Instance of IObjectScope.</returns>
    /// <remarks></remarks>
    public static IObjectScope GetPerRequestScope(HttpContext context)
    {
        string key = HttpContext.Current.GetHashCode().ToString("x") +
                         Thread.CurrentContext.ContextID.ToString();
        IObjectScope scope;
        if (context == null)
        {
            scope = ObjectScopeProvider1.GetNewObjectScope();
        }
        else
        {
            scope = (IObjectScope)context.Items[key];
            if (scope == null)
            {
                scope = ObjectScopeProvider1.GetNewObjectScope();
                context.Items[key] = scope;
            }
        }
        return scope;
    }
    }
}
```

Adding the Mapping Classes

Now, you have to create the classes that will map to database objects. You can use two different approaches here. If you already have a database that your application will use, you use reverse mapping, meaning you will create classes based on preexisting database tables. If, on the other hand, you will start by creating your persistent classes, you have to use forward mapping, which will take the classes and generate database tables from them. Note that with forward mapping the database must already exist.

Using Reverse Mapping (Tables to Classes)

To use reverse mapping, you use the Reverse Mapping tool located in the Telerik menu; select Open Access ➤ Reverse Mapping (Tables to Classes). See Figure 15-7.

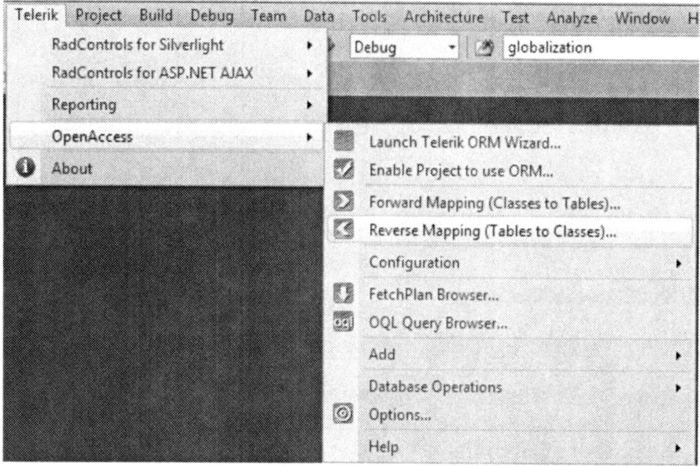

Figure 15-7. *Reverse mapping option*

Selecting this option will open the Reverse Mapping Wizard window shown in Figure 15-8. The window has two tabs; the first one is Simple View (Classes) and contains a grid with the information about the objects it found in the database and what is about to generate (see Figure 15-8). The second tab is the Advanced View (Treeview); it has a tree view with the same information but with more options to configure how the classes will be generated (see Figure 15-9).

In the Simple View grid, the first two columns present the type and name of the object found in the database, and you will only find tables and views in this grid. The next columns are the class name and namespace that will contain the class (you can modify these columns). Then, you have the maps to column that indicates what type of object will be generated for the database object. Here, you have four options, Ignore (nothing is generated), Class (a class is generated), Collection (the object is a join table and only a collection is generated in the referenced classes), and Map (the object is a join table but defines key/value pairs). The Lock column indicates whether or not the class can be modified later. The Generate column indicates whether the database object will be included in the generation process. The Status column indicates if there is a problem with the object or if it is ready to be processed. If there is a problem, the status will be in red, and you can click it to see the details of the errors found. Other options in the Simple View tab are general mapping options like those in the grid for specific objects.

The Advanced View tab has a few more options than Simple View and is shown in a tree view. The main difference is that it provides the options to generate code for stored procedures and for all objects it shows a preview of the code that will get generated.

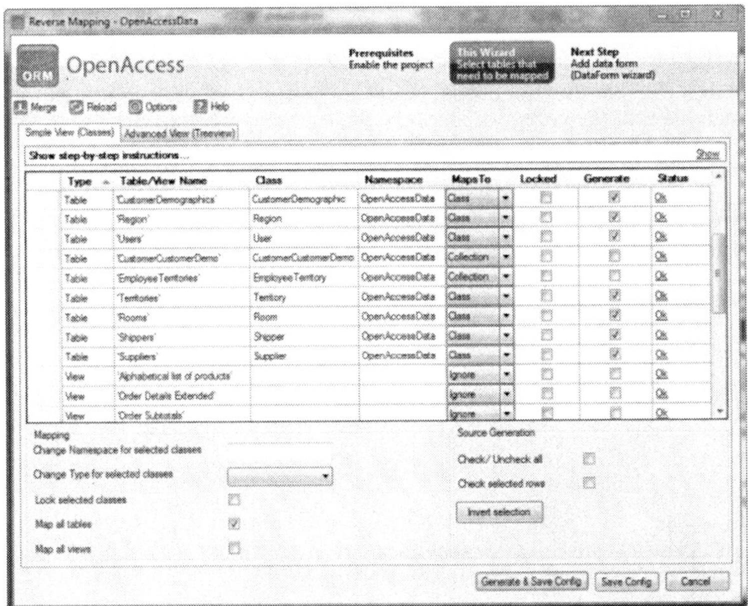

Figure 15-8. *Reverse Mapping Wizard's Simple View tab*

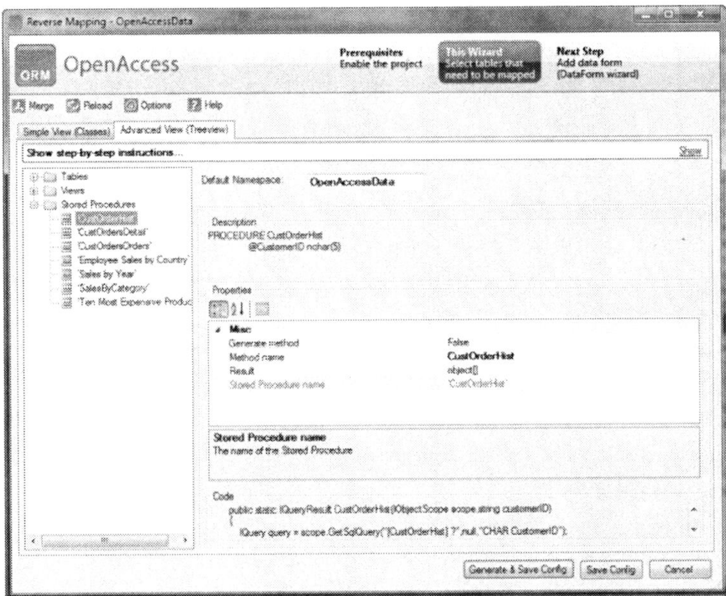

Figure 15-9. *Reverse Mapping Wizard's Advanced View tab*

After you click the Generate & Save Config button, the mapping classes are generated in the project, and an XML configuration file called `reversemapping.config` is created with the information regarding the configuration of each object mapping.

For each class, two files are created. The first one is a partial class that presents all the properties that are exposed and the fields in the table that they map to. The second file is another partial class with private fields for the public properties; this file is regenerated every time the reverse mapping wizard is run. If you want to add your own properties or any other code to the class, it must be added in the first file along with the other properties, so it is not overwritten by the reverse mapping wizard. Listing 15-2 show the classes created for the Category table in the Northwind database.

Listing 15-3 shows the StoredProcedure class created to support calling database stored procedures.

Listing 15-2. *OpenAccess Classes Created for the Category Table in the Northwind Database*

```
Category.cs

using System;
using System.Collections.Generic;

namespace OpenAccessData
{
    // Generated by Telerik OpenAccess
    // Used template: c:\program files (x86)\telerik\openaccess
    // orm\sdk\IDEIntegrations\templates\PCClassGeneration\cs\templates\
    // classgen\class\partialuserdefault.vm
    // NOTE: Field declarations and 'Object ID' class implementation are added
    // to the 'designer' file.
    //       Changes made to the 'designer' file will be overwritten by the wizard.
    public partial class Category
    {
        //The 'no-args' constructor required by OpenAccess.
        public Category()
        {
        }

        [Telerik.OpenAccess.FieldAlias("categoryID")]
        public int CategoryID
        {
            get { return categoryID; }
            set { this.categoryID = value; }
        }

        [Telerik.OpenAccess.FieldAlias("categoryName")]
        public string CategoryName
        {
            get { return categoryName; }
            set { this.categoryName = value; }
        }
```

```
        [Telerik.OpenAccess.FieldAlias("description")]
        public string Description
        {
            get { return description; }
            set { this.description = value; }
        }

        [Telerik.OpenAccess.FieldAlias("displayOrder")]
        public int? DisplayOrder
        {
            get { return displayOrder; }
            set { this.displayOrder = value; }
        }

        [Telerik.OpenAccess.FieldAlias("picture")]
        public byte[] Picture
        {
            get { return picture; }
            set { this.picture = value; }
        }


    }
}
```

Category.Telerik.OpenAccess.cs

```
using System;
using System.Collections.Generic;

namespace OpenAccessData
{
    // Generated by Telerik OpenAccess
    // Used template: c:\program files (x86)\telerik\openaccess
    // orm\sdk\IDEIntegrations\templates\PCClassGeneration\cs\templates\
    // classgen\class\partialdesignerdefault.vm
    [Telerik.OpenAccess.Persistent(IdentityField = "categoryID")]
    public partial class Category
    {
        private int categoryID; // pk

        private string categoryName;

        private string description;

        private int? displayOrder;

        private byte[] picture;


    }
}
```

Listing 15-3. *Stored Procedures Generated with the Reverse Mapping Wizard*

```
//Copyright (c) Telerik.  All rights reserved.

using System;
using System.Collections.Generic;
using Telerik.OpenAccess;

namespace OpenAccessData
{
    /// <summary>
    /// This class holds static methods defined to invoke user defined stored procedures
    /// </summary>
    /// <remarks>
    /// <para>
    /// It is generated by the Reverse Engineering wizard.
    /// </para>
    /// </remarks>

   public static class StoredProcedure
   {
        public static IQueryResult SalesByYear(
                                IObjectScope scope,
                                DateTime? beginning_Date,
                                DateTime? ending_Date)
        {
            IQuery query = scope.GetSqlQuery("[Sales by Year] ?,?",
                                        null,
                                        "TIMESTAMP Beginning_Date,
                                        TIMESTAMP Ending_Date");

            IQueryResult res = query.Execute(new object[] {beginning_Date,ending_Date});
            int a = res.Count;//Actually executes the query

            return res;
        }
   }
 }
```

Forward Mapping

With forward mapping, you start by creating your classes and then launch the Forward Mapping Wizard to generate the database and tables based on what you have created.

Figure 15-10 shows the forward mapping wizard window. It takes the information in your classes and infers the data types, table, and field names as well as all the information for database object generation, which, of course, you can modify.

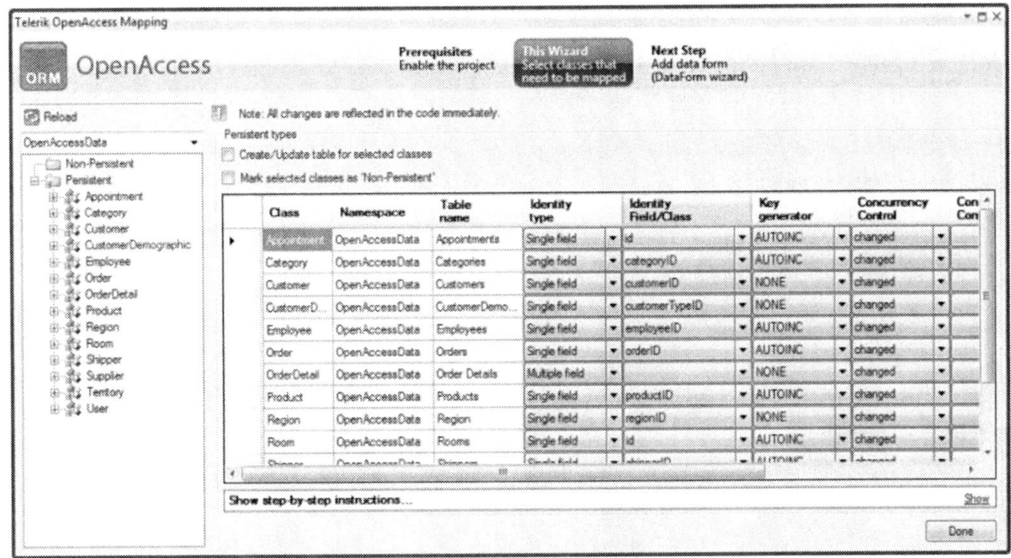

Figure 15-10. *Forward mapping wizard*

Using the Visual Domain Model Designer

If you opt to use the new Visual Entity Model Designer, you don't enable your projects like you did in the previous section. All you need to do is add a Telerik OpenAccess Domain Model to the class library project. The template for this file is under the Data section in the Project ➤ Add New Item menu option (see Figure 15-11).

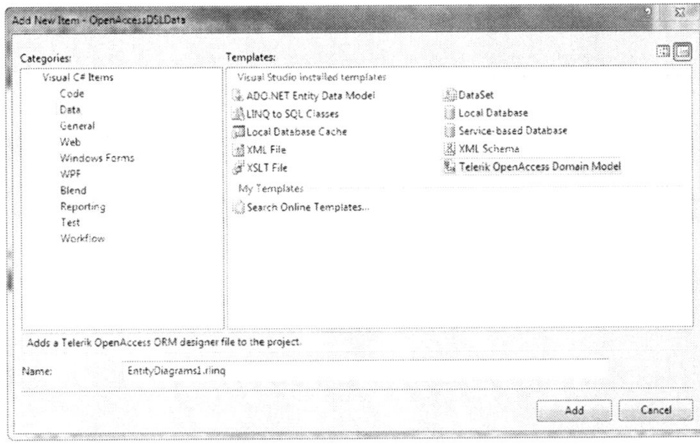

Figure 15-11. *Creating the visual domain model designer file*

After you add the file, the Data Wizard starts, so you can add entities to the designer; see Figure 15-12. Entities represent tables, views, and stored procedures from the database. The first step in the

Data Wizard is creating the database connection. You have to select the database management system from the options in the Backend list and then select an available connection from the Connections list. If the connection to the database does not exist, you can create it with the "New connection" button. The last piece of information is the connection string name.

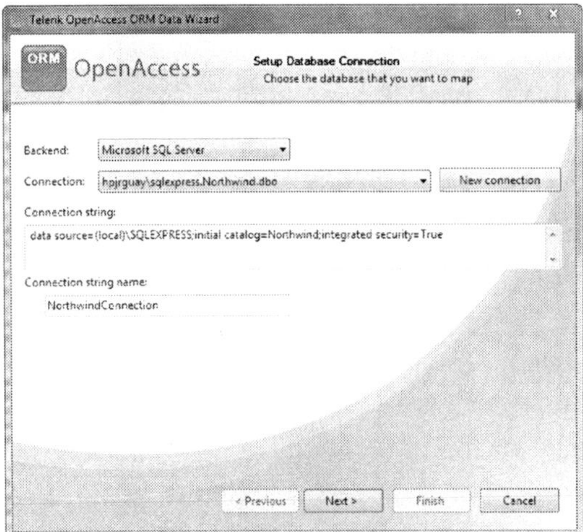

Figure 15-12. *Data Wizard database connection settings*

The next step of the wizard is selecting which objects from the database you want in the designer and adding a name to the data model. The data model name is important, because this is the name of the underlying class that is generated to access the entities in the designer. See Figure 15-13.

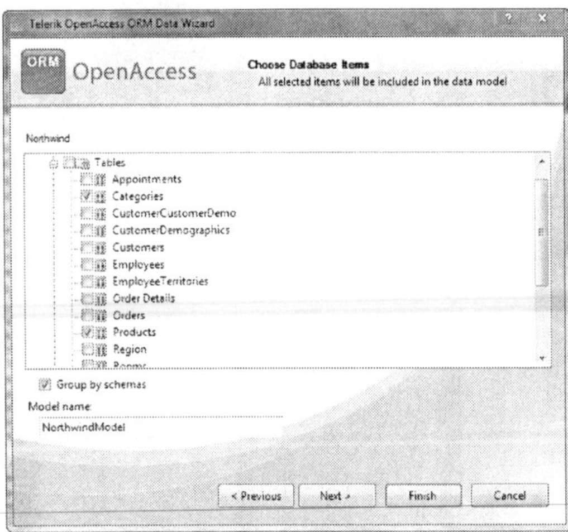

Figure 15-13. *Database object selection in the Data Wizard*

The next step is for naming rules. You have options to add and remove suffixes or prefixes, remove underscores, and apply casing rules. These options can be applied for classes, fields, and properties. See Figure 15-14.

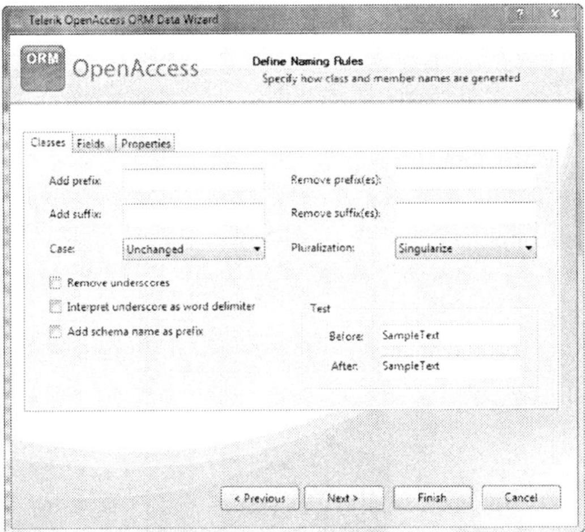

Figure 15-14. *Setting naming rules for the entities*

In the last step, you provide the model and code generation settings, and you have the option to use your own templates in the generation. You will also have the option to generate one or multiple files for the classes, because even though you are using a single designer file for all the entities, every single entity has its own implementation in a separate class. These entity classes are generated with the `.generated.cs` (or `.generated.vb`) file extension. See Figures 14-15 and 14-16 for the last step and resulting designer and entities files.

Figure 15-15. *Model and code generation settings*

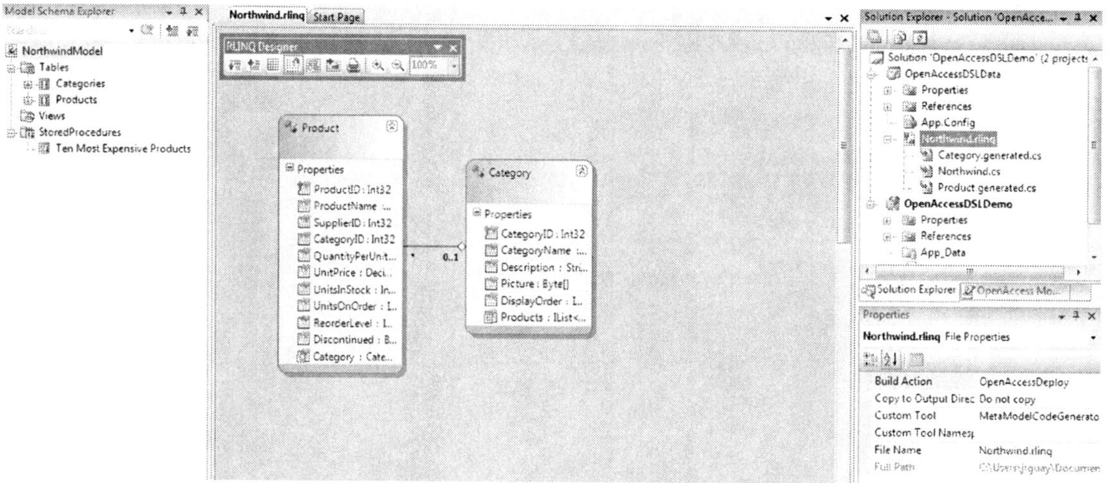

Figure 15-16. *Visual data model designer*

Querying the Data Model

To query objects in the data model, there are a few approaches you can take depending on your application's needs. The first one is using Language Integrated Query (LINQ), which most of the time is just what you need. The second one is using Object Query Language (OQL), and that is used mostly when queries are dynamically created at runtime. However, since you can also create runtime queries with LINQ, this option is rarely used. The final approach is to use SQL queries created using strings.

Using LINQ

Using LINQ to query the data model is no different than using other LINQ implementations, such as LINQ to Entities, LINQ to SQL, or LINQ to Objects. Telerik OpenAccess ORM provides support for most LINQ operations and continues to add more support with each release.

Another option for querying the data model is with the `Extent<T>()` extension method to the `IObjectScope` classes. This method returns an `ExtentQuery<T>` object that inherits from `IQueryable<T>` and can be bound to controls in the page. To have access to it, you must include the `Telerik.OpenAccess` namespace in the code file where is being used. The example in Listing 15-4 shows this implementation.

Listing 15-4. *Querying the Data Model with LINQ*

```
IObjectScope nwd = NorthwindScopeProvider.ObjectScope();
var q = from c in nwd.Extent<Categories>()
        select c;
```

If you built your data model using the Visual Entity Model Designer, the previous example changes quite a bit, and you don't need the methods discussed before. You may recognize this as similar to querying Entity Framework or LINQ to SQL entities. Listing 15-5 implements the new scenario.

Listing 15-5. *Querying the Data Model Created with the Visual Entity Model Designer*

```
NorthwindModel nwd = new NorthwindModel();
var categories = from c in nwd.Categories
                 where c.CategoryID < 10
                 select c;
```

or

```
NorthwindModel nwd = new NorthwindModel();
var q = nwd.Categories.ToList();
```

Using OQL

OQL is a language similar to SQL; the difference resides in that you are not actually querying tables in the database but objects called extents that exist in your data model. An *extent* contains all objects in a database that belong to a specific persistence capable class; and they must be called with the class name plus `Extent`.

For this, we use the `GetOqlQuery(querystring)` method of scope provider. Listing 15-6 shows how to query the categories table in the `Northwind` database. Here, a `Category` class is created in the data model, and the query string uses `CategoryExtent` in the `FROM` clause.

Listing 15-6. *Using OQL to Query the Data Model*

```
IObjectScope nwd = ObjectScopeProvider1.ObjectScope();
string oql = "SELECT * FROM CategoryExtent";
var result = nwd.GetOqlQuery(oql).Execute();
```

Using SQL Statements

Using SQL directly is more familiar to most developers and actually is a very simple process. All you need to do is create a query string with the SQL syntax of the database backend you are programming against and call the `GetSqlQuery(querystring, return type, parameters)` method. Listing 15-7 implements the execution of a simple SQL statement. Note that OpenAccess helps you prevent SQL injection attacks by protecting your code using parameters in your queries, as shown in Listing 15-8.

Listing 15-7. *Implementing SQL Statements with No Parameters*

```
IObjectScope nwd = ObjectScopeProvider1.ObjectScope();
string sql = "SELECT * FROM Categories";
var result = nwd.GetSqlQuery(sql, typeof(Category), "").Execute();
```

Listing 15-8. *Implementign Parameters in SQL Statements*

```
IObjectScope nwd = ObjectScopeProvider1.ObjectScope();
string sql = "SELECT * FROM Categories WHERE CategoryID < ?";
var result = nwd.GetSqlQuery(sql, typeof(Category), "Integer id").Execute(10);
```

Executing Stored Procedures

When working with stored procedures, there is a very important situation you must take into consideration. Since there is no way of knowing the output of the stored procedure execution, Telerik OpenAccess ORM does its best to create a multidimensional array of objects where results are stored. You then need to cast the results to the appropriate data types using anonymous types or your own predefined type (`class` or `struct`).

The example in Listing 15-9 shows you how to execute stored procedures using the scope provider, and the one in Listing 15-10 uses the visual designer.

Listing 15-9. *Executing Stored Procedures Using the Scope Provider*

```
IObjectScope nwd = NorthwindScopeProvider.ObjectScope();
var sp_result = StoredProcedure.TenMostExpensiveProducts(nwd).Cast<object[]>;
var result = new ArrayList();
foreach (object[] o in sp_result)
{
    result.Add(new
                   {
                       ProductName = Convert.ToString(o.ElementAt(0)),
                       UnitPrice = Convert.ToDecimal(o.ElementAt(1))
                   });
}
```

Listing 15-10. *Executing Stored Procedures Using the Visual Data Model Designer*

```
var nwd = new NorthwindModel();
var sp_result = nwd.TenMostExpensiveProducts();
var result = new ArrayList();
foreach (object[] o in sp_result)
{
    result.Add(new
                   {
                       ProductName = Convert.ToString(o.ElementAt(0)),
                       UnitPrice = Convert.ToDecimal(o.ElementAt(1))
                   });
}
```

If the stored procedure accepts parameters, you need to include them, just as you would for any method that takes parameters. Listing 15-11 illustrates the execution of a stored procedure with parameters.

Listing 15-11. *Executing a Stored Procedure with Parameters*

```
// Using the scope provider

IObjectScope nwd = NorthwindScopeProvider.ObjectScope();
DateTime? startDate = DateTime.Today.AddDays(-30);
DateTime? endDate = DateTime.Today;
var sp_result = StoredProcedure.SalesByYear(nwd, startDate, endDate);
```

```
// Using the visual data model designer

var nwd = new NorthwindModel();
DateTime startDate = DateTime.Today.AddDays(-30);
DateTime endDate = DateTime.Today;
var sp_result = nwd.SalesByYear(startDate, endDate);
```

Working Within Transactions

Any operation (with the exception of read data) in Telerik OpenAccess ORM must be performed within the context of a transaction. A *transaction* is a unit of operation that is executed under the principals of atomicity, consistency, isolation, and durability (ACID).

- *Atomicity*: Within the context of a transaction, the property of *atomicity* guarantees that all the operations performed must succeed for the whole transaction to be considered successful. If any of the operations fail, the whole transaction fails.
- *Consistency*: A *consistent* transaction doesn't violate any integrity constraint during its execution, and in the event of a failure during an operation, all previous operations that were successful must be undone to leave the database in the same state that was before the transaction started.
- *Isolation*: The property of *isolation* defines how and when the result of a transaction becomes visible to other concurrent operations. The level of isolation depends on the implementation provided by the database system, but there are standards that mandate what levels should exist. For example, the ANSI/ISO SQL standard defines four basic isolation levels: serializable, repeatable read, read committed, and read uncommitted. Microsoft SQL Server and Oracle use "read committed" by default.
- *Durability*: The *durability* property states that, once the transaction has succeeded and enters the commit state, it will be persisted permanently.

Setting the Transaction Scope

All transactions have a well-defined scope. They all start at some point, and they are marked as finished with one of two possible results, success or failure.

In Telerik OpenAccess ORM, a transaction is started with the `Transaction.Begin()` method of the of the scope provider. Once the transaction finishes successfully, it must be committed with the `Transaction.Commit()` method. If an error occurs, a call to `Transaction.Rollback()` must be performed to assure that all previous operations will be undone.

Listing 15-12 shows how to start a transaction, verify the success of the operations, and either commit or roll back the transaction.

Listing 15-12. *Implementing Transactions*

```
IObjectScope nwd = NorthwindScopeProvider.ObjectScope();
nwd.Transaction.Begin();
try
{
    var cat = (from c in nwd.Extent<Category>()
               where c.CategoryID == 1
               select c).First();
```

```
    cat.DisplayOrder = 1;

    // more modifications and/or operations

    nwd.Transaction.Commit();
}
catch (Exception)
{
    nwd.Transaction.Rollback();
}
```

Telerik OpenAccess ORM supports multithreading. If your application is using multiple threads for execution, the only modification needed in your code is to have an independent scope provider for each thread. Basically, the technique is to create the scope provider instance in the method that starts the thread rather than reusing the one in the application thread. Behind the scenes, the Telerik OpenAccess ORM runtime engine will handle the concurrency issues.

One last thing regarding transactions is that, whenever you close the connection to the database by calling the scope provider's `Dispose()` method, you will get an error if a transaction is still active, so you have to verify that all transactions are either committed or rolled back before closing the database connection. The code example in Listing 15-13 shows you how to check this.

Listing 15-13. *Verifying If a Transaction Is Open Before Closing the Connection*

```
If (nwd.Transaction.IsActive)
    nwd.Transaction.Commit();

nwd.Dispose();
```

Adding, Updating, and Deleting Objects

The processes of adding, updating, and deleting objects is simple; you just have to keep in mind that these actions must be performed within the scope of a transaction.

To add an object, you need to create a new instance of a class that represents the object, add it to the scope provider, and call the `Commit()` method. See Listing 15-14.

Listing 15-14. *Adding a New Object*

```
IObjectScope nwd = NorthwindScopeProvider.ObjectScope();
nwd.Transaction.Begin();
try
{
    var cat = new Category();
    cat.CategoryName = "Oriental Imports";
    cat.Description = "Food imported from Asia";
    cat.DisplayOrder = 100;
    nwd.Add(cat);
    nwd.Transaction.Commit();
}
catch (Exception)
{
    nwd.Transaction.Rollback();
}
```

For updating records, you use the same algorithm. However, this time, you first must load the object from the database to perform the modifications. Also, you don't add the object to the scope provider; you only commit the changes, and OpenAccess ORM will take care of the rest. Listing 15-15 illustrates an update.

Listing 15-15. *Updating Objects*

```
IObjectScope nwd = NorthwindScopeProvider.ObjectScope();
nwd.Transaction.Begin();
try
{
    var cat = (from c in nwd.Extent<Category>()
               where c.CategoryID == 10
               select c).First();
    cat.DisplayOrder = 10;
    nwd.Transaction.Commit();
}
catch (Exception)
{
    nwd.Transaction.Rollback();
}
```

To delete an object, you have to load it and pass it as parameter of the scope provider's `Remove()` method, as shown in Listing 15-16. Then, commit the transaction.

Listing 15-16. *Deleting an Object*

```
IObjectScope nwd = NorthwindScopeProvider.ObjectScope();
nwd.Transaction.Begin();
try
{
    var cat = (from c in nwd.Extent<Category>()
               where c.CategoryID == 1
               select c).First();
    nwd.Remove(cat);
    nwd.Transaction.Commit();
}
catch (Exception)
{
    nwd.Transaction.Rollback();
}
```

Using Fetch Plans and Fetch Groups

When you create your data model, by default, it's configured to use *lazy loading*. Lazy loading is a data loading technique that works by loading only the information that is needed at any precise moment. This works well most of the time, but when loading data from different tables, it queries all the tables independently whenever is needed. This fact can lead to excessive round trips to the database server, which can saturate the network and eventually reduce performance.

To solve this problem, Telerik OpenAccess ORM uses fetch plans and fetch groups. The idea is to instruct OpenAccess on what fields it must load, and it will build the right SQL queries to minimize the impact of query execution. This will greatly improve the performance of the application.

OpenAccess includes some built-in Fetch Plans, so you can start using them right away. `FetchPlan.Default` is the default used in most scenarios. `FetchPlan.All` will retrieve all the fields of the object including referenced objects, up to one level deep. `FetchPlan.DefaultLimit` sets the number of objects that can be retrieved in one fetch operation and this is the initial value of the `Limit` property. `FetchPlan.DefaultMaxDepth` sets the default maximum tree depth that is fetched together, with a default value set to 3. `FetchPlan.NoLimit` sets no restriction on the number of objects that can be fetched together.

The `FetchPlan.Limit` property defines the maximum number of objects that can be fetched together. The `FetchPlan.MaxDepth` property helps in controlling the amount of data retrieved from the database; this property defines the maximum tree depth that is fetched together.

Listing 15-17 shows a simple `RadGrid` that will show information from the `products` table. Telerik OpenAccess ORM already created the classes for it, and if you look closely at the definition of the `Product` class, you will see that, because of its definition in the database, it has a property called `CategoryID`. This property is an integer, but because this column is defined as a foreign key related to the categories table, it also has a property named `Category`. The `Category` property is of the `Category` class, which in turn maps to the categories table. This structure allows you to automatically query the categories table, for example, to know the category name of a product.

Now, a similar situation exists for the supplier information in the `Product` class, as you again have two properties: `SupplierID`, which is an integer, and the `Supplier` property of type `Supplier`, which maps to the suppliers table.

See Figure 15-17 for an example. In the page load event handler, I query the `products` table normally using the scope provider.

Listing 15-17. *RadGrid Executing One Query But the Data Is Not Clear*

ASPX Page

```
<telerik:RadGrid ID="RadGrid1" runat="server"
    AutoGenerateColumns="false">
    <MasterTableView
        DataKeyNames="ProductID"
        ShowFooter="true">
        <Columns>
            <telerik:GridBoundColumn DataField="ProductID"
                                     HeaderText="ID"
                                     SortExpression="ProductID"
                                     UniqueName="ProductID">
            </telerik:GridBoundColumn>
            <telerik:GridBoundColumn DataField="ProductName"
                                     HeaderText="Name"
                                     SortExpression="ProductName"
                                     UniqueName="ProductName">
            </telerik:GridBoundColumn>
            <telerik:GridBoundColumn DataField="CategoryID"
                                     HeaderText="Category"
                                     SortExpression="CategoryID"
                                     UniqueName="CategoryID">
            </telerik:GridBoundColumn>
```

```
            <telerik:GridBoundColumn DataField="SupplierID"
                                     HeaderText="Supplier"
                                     SortExpression="SupplierID"
                                     UniqueName="SupplierID">
            </telerik:GridBoundColumn>
        </Columns>
    </MasterTableView>
</telerik:RadGrid>

Code Behind

public partial class _Default : System.Web.UI.Page
{
    private IObjectScope nwd = null;
    protected override void OnInit(EventArgs e)
    {
        base.OnInit(e);
        nwd = ObjectScopeProvider1.GetNewObjectScope();
    }

    protected void Page_Load(object sender, EventArgs e)
    {
        RadGrid1.DataSource = from p in nwd.Extent<Product>()
                              select p;
        RadGrid1.DataBind();

    }
}
```

ID	Name	Category	Supplier
1	Chai	1	1
2	Chang	1	1
3	Aniseed Syrup	2	1
4	Chef Anton's Cajun Seasoning	2	2
5	Chef Anton's Gumbo Mix	2	2
6	Grandma's Boysenberry Spread	2	3
7	Uncle Bob's Organic Dried Pears	7	3
8	Northwoods Cranberry Sauce	2	3
9	Mishi Kobe Niku		4

Figure 15-17. *Querying the* products *table*

A close examination reveals that the example actually generated one query to the database, and that it was based only on the products table:

```
SELECT  a.[ProductID] AS COL1,
        a.[CategoryID] AS COL2,
        a.[CategoryID] AS COL3,
        a.[Discontinued] AS COL4,
        a.[ProductName] AS COL5,
        a.[QuantityPerUnit] AS COL6,
        a.[ReorderLevel] AS COL7,
```

```
        a.[SupplierID] AS COL8,
        a.[SupplierID] AS COL9,
        a.[UnitPrice] AS COL10,
        a.[UnitsInStock] AS COL11,
        a.[UnitsOnOrder] AS COL12
FROM    [Products] a
```

The example was simple in terms of querying the products table. In fact, it was so simple that the information is not clear enough. If users do not have a complete categories and suppliers catalog, the category Id of 1 and supplier ID of 2 are meaningless. By changing the grid definition just a little bit, as shown in Listing 15-18, we have a different situation.

Listing 15-18. *Modifying the RadGrid to Show More Information, Thus Executing a Lot More Queries*

ASPX Page

```
<telerik:RadGrid ID="RadGrid1" runat="server"
    AutoGenerateColumns="false">
    <MasterTableView
        DataKeyNames="ProductID"
        ShowFooter="true">
        <Columns>
            <telerik:GridBoundColumn DataField="ProductID"
                                    HeaderText="ID"
                                    SortExpression="ProductID"
                                    UniqueName="ProductID">
            </telerik:GridBoundColumn>
            <telerik:GridBoundColumn DataField="ProductName"
                                    HeaderText="Name"
                                    SortExpression="ProductName"
                                    UniqueName="ProductName">
            </telerik:GridBoundColumn>
            <telerik:GridBoundColumn DataField="Category.CategoryName"
                                    HeaderText="Category"
                                    SortExpression="CategoryID"
                                    UniqueName="CategoryID">
            </telerik:GridBoundColumn>
            <telerik:GridBoundColumn DataField="Supplier.CompanyName"
                                    HeaderText="Supplier"
                                    SortExpression="SupplierID"
                                    UniqueName="SupplierID">
            </telerik:GridBoundColumn>
        </Columns>
    </MasterTableView>
</telerik:RadGrid>
```

Now, we are telling RadGrid to show the category name instead of the category ID and the supplier's company name instead of its ID. The result is shown in Figure 15-18.

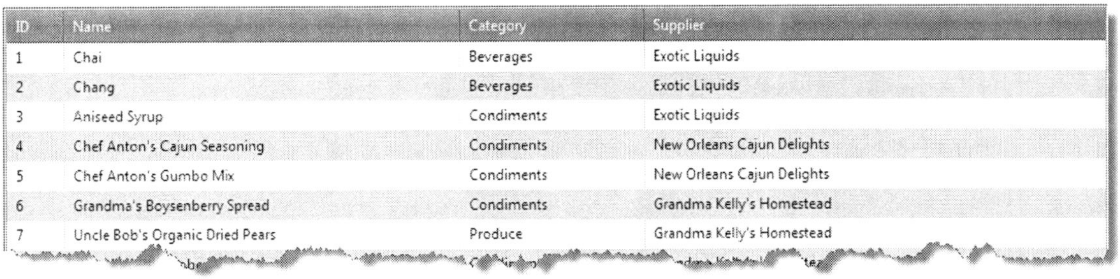

ID	Name	Category	Supplier
1	Chai	Beverages	Exotic Liquids
2	Chang	Beverages	Exotic Liquids
3	Aniseed Syrup	Condiments	Exotic Liquids
4	Chef Anton's Cajun Seasoning	Condiments	New Orleans Cajun Delights
5	Chef Anton's Gumbo Mix	Condiments	New Orleans Cajun Delights
6	Grandma's Boysenberry Spread	Condiments	Grandma Kelly's Homestead
7	Uncle Bob's Organic Dried Pears	Produce	Grandma Kelly's Homestead

Figure 15-18. *Improving the query to show meaningful information.*

Everything is going fine, until we realize that with lazy loading, we are not executing one query to the database—we are executing 38 queries. The reason for that is that OpenAccess loads the products information just as before, but because we requested the category name instead of the ID, it must query the categories table. However, it doesn't know that from the beginning. Once OpenAccess realizes that it has only the category ID (from the `products` table), it then queries the categories table—eight times more, one for each value of the `CategoryID` property. If you are counting, we have executed nine queries (one for the products and eight for the categories). Now, the same happens for the supplier, but there are 29 suppliers, all of which have been referenced in the `products` table through the `SupplierID` field; so in total, 38 queries are executed. The queries are as follows:

```
--This query was executed once

SELECT  a.[ProductID] AS COL1,
        a.[CategoryID] AS COL2,
        a.[CategoryID] AS COL3,
        a.[Discontinued] AS COL4,
        a.[ProductName] AS COL5,
        a.[QuantityPerUnit] AS COL6,
        a.[ReorderLevel] AS COL7,
        a.[SupplierID] AS COL8,
        a.[SupplierID] AS COL9,
        a.[UnitPrice] AS COL10,
        a.[UnitsInStock] AS COL11,
        a.[UnitsOnOrder] AS COL12
FROM    [Products] a

--This query was executed 8 times
SELECT  [CategoryName],
        [Description],
        [DisplayOrder]
FROM    [Categories]
WHERE   [CategoryID] = ?
```

```
--This query was executed 29 times
SELECT  [Address],
        [City],
        [CompanyName],
        [ContactName],
        [ContactTitle],
        [Country],
        [Fax],
        [HomePage],
        [Phone],
        [PostalCode],
        [Region]
FROM    [Suppliers]
WHERE   [SupplierID] = ?
```

You might be thinking that this scenario isn't so bad; actually, if you run the example code, it's very fast. But let's think of a real scenario for a second. Consider a few hundred users running queries to tables with thousands (or hundreds of thousands) of records related to other tables all day long—that is not a pretty scenario.

Now the question arises, "How do we fix it?" We use Fetch Plans. A *Fetch Plan* consists of a set of Fetch Groups that are additively combined for each affected class. *Fetch Groups* are used to identify the list of fields and the recursion depth that will be retrieved together if the Fetch Group name is part of the actual Fetch Plan in use at the time of execution. You can create multiple Fetch Plans with different settings.

Fetch Groups can be defined either programmatically or using the forward mapping wizard. You use the Fetch Plan Browser to visually create fetch plans. Fetch groups can be configured programmatically by having the `FetchField` attribute decorate the fields it will load and passing, as a parameter, the name of the fetch group. Alternatively, you can add the definition to the configuration file. In the previous example, the `Product` class would be modified as shown in Listing 15-19.

Listing 15-19. *Defining a Fetch Group for the Class Product*

```
public partial class Product
{
    [Telerik.OpenAccess.FetchField("CategoryFetch")]
    private int productID; // pk

    [Telerik.OpenAccess.FetchField("CategoryFetch")]
    private int? categoryID;

    [Telerik.OpenAccess.FetchField("CategoryFetch")]
    private bool discontinued;

    [Telerik.OpenAccess.FetchField("CategoryFetch")]
    private string productName;

    [Telerik.OpenAccess.FetchField("CategoryFetch")]
    private string quantityPerUnit;

    [Telerik.OpenAccess.FetchField("CategoryFetch")]
    private short? reorderLevel;
```

```
    [Telerik.OpenAccess.FetchField("CategoryFetch")]
    private int? supplierID;

    [Telerik.OpenAccess.FetchField("CategoryFetch")]
    private Decimal? unitPrice;

    [Telerik.OpenAccess.FetchField("CategoryFetch")]
    private short? unitsInStock;

    [Telerik.OpenAccess.FetchField("CategoryFetch")]
    private short? unitsOnOrder;

    [Telerik.OpenAccess.FetchField("CategoryFetch")]
    private Category category;

    [Telerik.OpenAccess.FetchField("CategoryFetch")]
    private Supplier supplier;

}
```

If you want to add the definition to the configuration file, you can do so as shown in Listing 15-20.

Listing 15-20. *Implementing a Fetch Group in the XML Configuration File*

```
<class name="Product">
        <fetch-group name="CategoryFetch">
                <field name="productID">
                <field name="categoryID">
                <field name="discontinued">
                <field name="productName">
                <field name=" quantityPerUnit">
                <field name=" reorderLevel">
                <field name=" supplierID">
                <field name=" unitPrice">
                <field name=" unitsInStock">
                <field name=" unitsOnOrder">
                <field name=" category">
                <field name=" supplier">
        </fetch-group>
</class>
```

This definition can also be created using the forward mapping wizard in the Fetch Group tab of each class. See Figure 15-19.

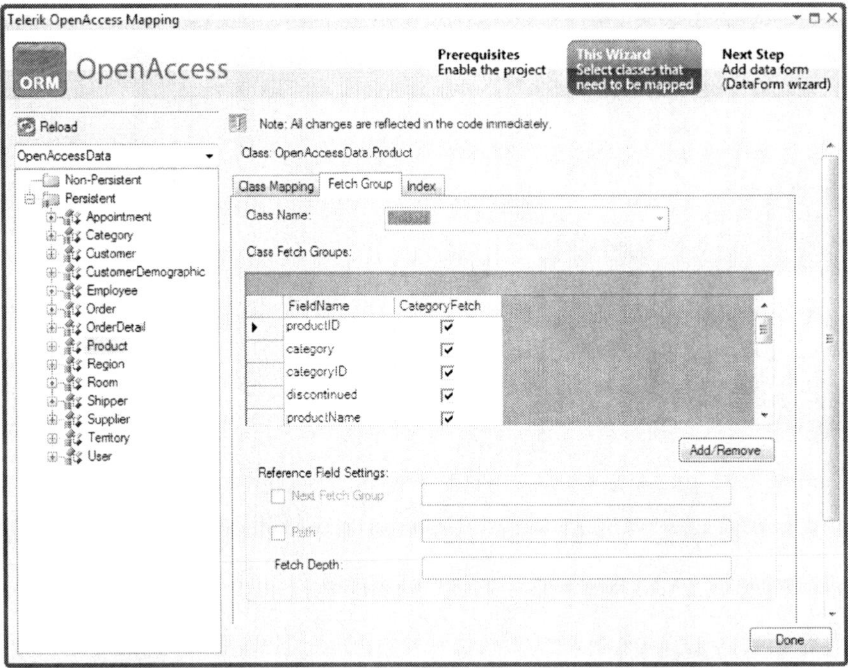

Figure 15-19. *Defining Fetch Groups using the forward mapping wizard*

Once all the fields that will be loaded have been included in the fetch group, only those fields will be loaded from the database in as few calls as possible.

A default fetch group is created for each class, and it will retrieve all the fields that are of a basic type or single reference type (int, string, decimal, etc.), and only the ID of the referenced object will be retrieved as a result of a query or while resolving a reference. The default fetch group is accessible through the `FetchPlan` enumeration.

There is only one more step to do in our web application to make the fetch groups work. We have to tell the scope provider to actually use the fetch plan by removing all previous fetch groups, adding the default fetch group, and adding the fetch groups that you want to work with. This must be done explicitly with every instance of `IObjectScope` (see Listing 15-21).

Listing 15-21. *Adding the Fetch Plan to the Scope Provider*

```
protected override void OnInit(EventArgs e)
{
    base.OnInit(e);
    IObjectScope nwd = ObjectScopeProvider1.GetNewObjectScope();

    nwd.FetchPlan.Clear();
    nwd.FetchPlan.Add(FetchPlan.Default);
    nwd.FetchPlan.Add("CategoryFetch");

}
```

This time, when we run the application, only the following query will be executed:

```
SELECT  a.[ProductID] AS COL1,
        a.[CategoryID] AS COL2,
        a.[CategoryID] AS COL3,
        a.[Discontinued] AS COL4,
        a.[ProductName] AS COL5,
        a.[QuantityPerUnit] AS COL6,
        a.[ReorderLevel] AS COL7,
        a.[SupplierID] AS COL8,
        a.[SupplierID] AS COL9,
        a.[UnitPrice] AS COL10,
        a.[UnitsInStock] AS COL11,
        a.[UnitsOnOrder] AS COL12,
        b.[CategoryID] AS COL13,
        c.[SupplierID] AS COL14,
        b.[CategoryName] AS COL15,
        b.[Description] AS COL16,
        b.[DisplayOrder] AS COL17,
        c.[Address] AS COL18,
        c.[City] AS COL19,
        c.[CompanyName] AS COL20,
        c.[ContactName] AS COL21,
        c.[ContactTitle] AS COL22,
        c.[Country] AS COL23,
        c.[Fax] AS COL24,
        c.[HomePage] AS COL25,
        c.[Phone] AS COL26,
        c.[PostalCode] AS COL27,
        c.[Region] AS COL28
FROM    [Products] a
        LEFT JOIN [Categories] AS b ON ( a.[CategoryID] = b.[CategoryID] )
        LEFT JOIN [Suppliers] AS c ON ( a.[SupplierID] = c.[SupplierID] )
```

Telerik OpenAccess ORM generates an enhanced version of the query to eliminate redundant or unneeded queries. Note, however, that in our particular example application that was the result, but in real applications, a single query may not do the work, and more queries may be needed. In any case, with fetch plans, you can control how OpenAccess accesses your data to fine-tune the performance of your application's interactions with the database.

Implementing Inheritance

Telerik OpenAccess ORM supports different inheritance scenarios for persistent classes. You can define your classes' inheritance, and OpenAccess will generate the backend database code to support them. Inheritance is only supported in forward mapping scenarios though.

There are four supported mapping strategies: flat, vertical, mixed (flat and vertical), and horizontal. In all four strategies, a discriminator column is used to determine which type each record represents.

To show how these strategies are supported, I created the classes and inheritance strategy shown in Figure 15-20.

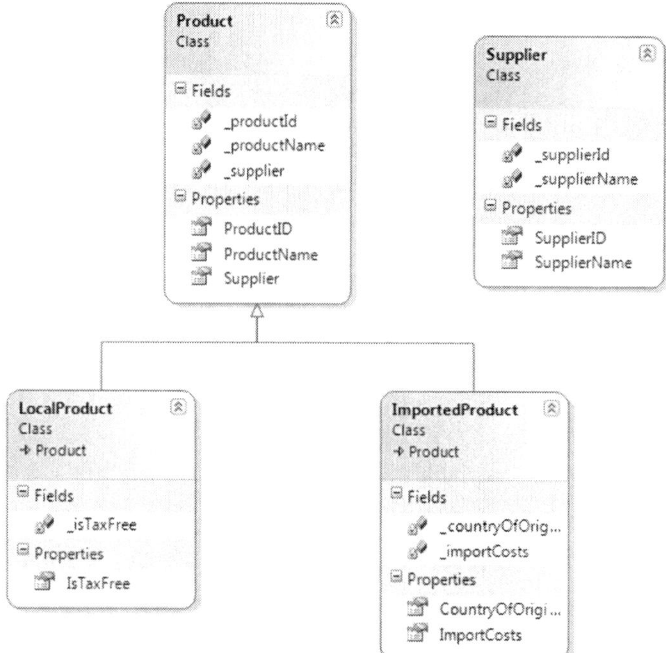

Figure 15-20. *Classes inheritance*

Flat Mapping

The default mapping strategy is flat mapping. *Flat mapping* means that all the classes in the inheritance tree will map to a single table that will contain all the fields for all the classes.

In the forward mapping wizard, which you can access by selecting menu Telerik ➤ OpenAccess ➤ Forward Mapping (Classes to Tables), you define the inheritance strategy OpenAccess should use when your persistent classes are mapped. See Figure 15-21.

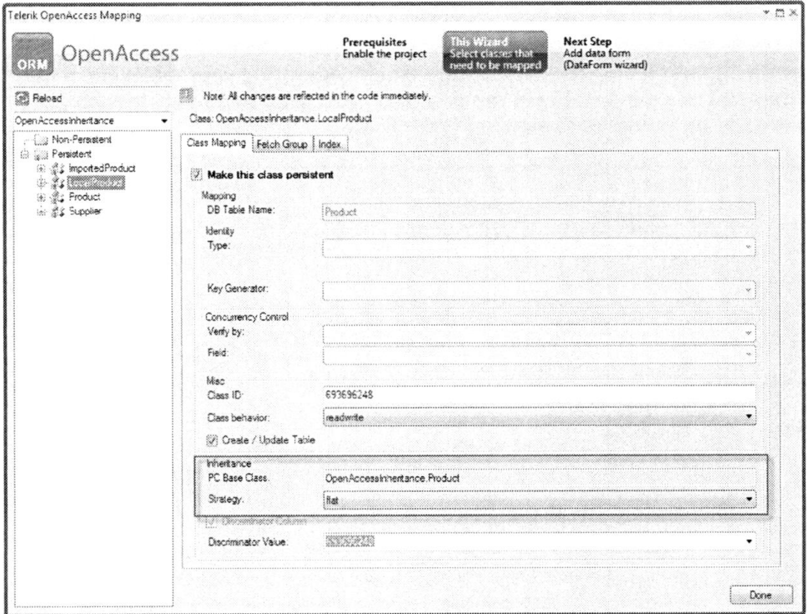

Figure 15-21. *Defining the inheratence strategy*

After you click the Done button and build the data model, the database is created with the tables shown in Figure 15-22.

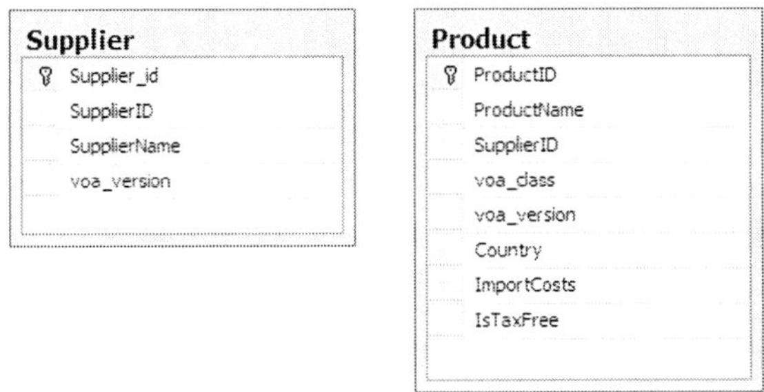

Figure 15-22. *Database generated with flat inheritance*

Note that all the fields from all three classes (`Product`, `LocalProduct`, and `ImportedProduct`) were generated in a single table. Also note the discriminator column, `voa_class`, used to determine which class each record represents.

There are some advantages in using this strategy. For example, a single query is required to load all the information in the hierarchy; no joins are needed; and only a single insert, update, or delete statement is required to perform an operation on the table.

There are some disadvantages as well, the table will contain a large number of columns, some of them are never to be used and it will be a waste of space.

Vertical Mapping

With *vertical mapping*, you get the highest level of normalization when generating your tables from the classes, because each class is mapped to a single table in the database. You need to configure each class in the mapping wizard to use vertical mapping, as shown in Figure 15-23.

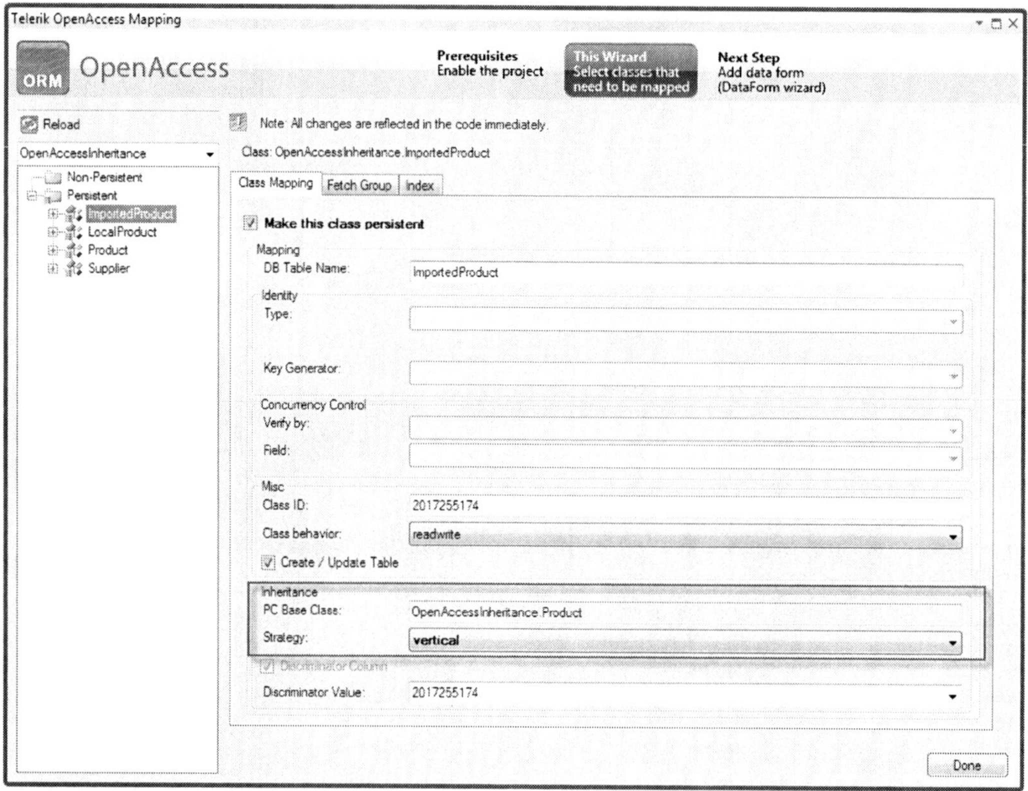

Figure 15-23. *Configuring vertical mapping*

When you build the data model project now, a different set of tables will be generated. See Figure 15-24.

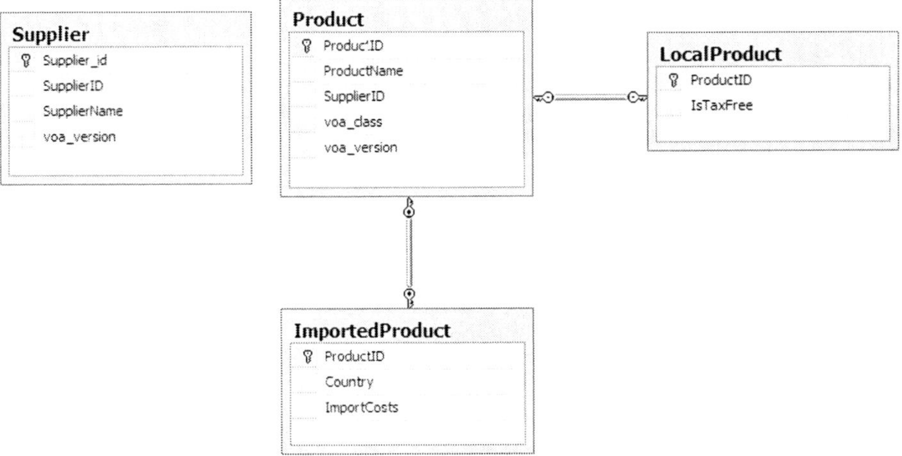

Figure 15-24. *Database generated with vertical mapping*

The advantages of vertical mapping are that the generated tables are highly normalized and new classes in the hierarchy can be mapped to new tables without modifying the actual structure.

The disadvantages are that we are now required to use joins to query the data and multiple SQL statements will be required to perform insert, update, and delete operations.

Mixed Mapping

Support for *mixed (vertical and flat) mapping* is achieved by selecting at least one of each of the previous strategies for the classes in the hierarchy. In our example, we can select flat mapping for the `LocalProduct` class and vertical mapping for the `ImportedProduct` class. See Figure 15-25 for the resulting tables.

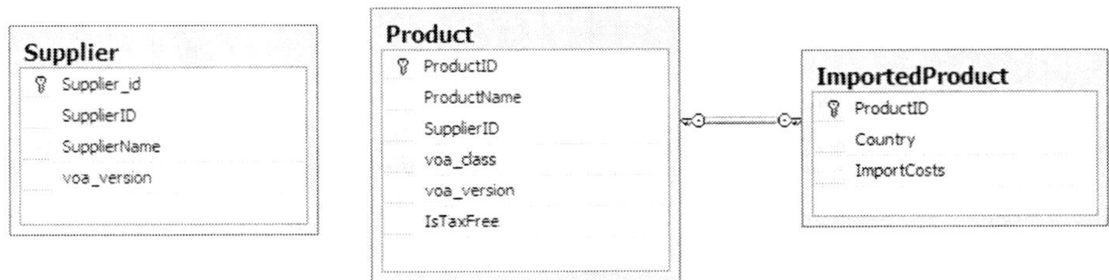

Figure 15-25. *Database generated with mixed mapping*

Note that the `Product` table now contains the `IsTaxFree` column that was defined for the `LocalProduct` class, but the `ImportedProduct` class has its own table.

Horizontal Mapping

Horizontal mapping can be achieved through the configuration of the topmost class in the hierarchy. The idea behind this strategy is that each individual sub classes will be mapped to its own single table in the database with a copy of the fields from the parent class. In this approach it is suggested although not required that the horizontal class should be made abstract because after all it is not directly persisted; only the sub classes can be persisted.

Figure 15-26 shows the resulting database tables.

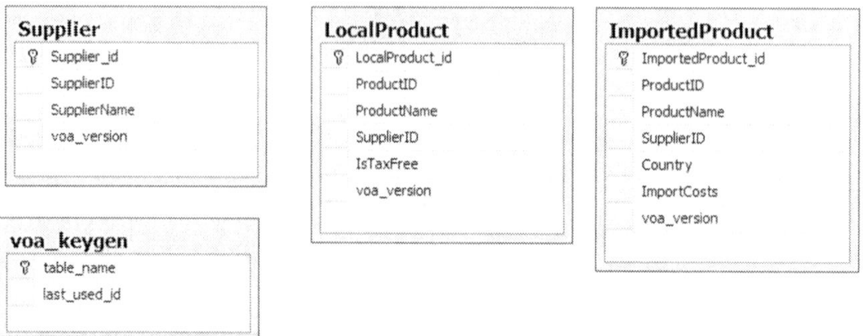

Figure 15-26. *Database generated with horizontal mapping*

Advantages of this approach are that normally a single SQL statement will be generated for each insert, delete, and update operation; fetching data will not require joins; and attributes that are common can be defined in base classes.

One disadvantage is that each class derived from the horizontally mapped base class starts a new hierarchy, which creates a problem when dealing with identity keys because they should be implemented in the derived classes and not the base class. Querying the class at the top of the hierarchy requires multiple select statements and references to collections, and maps in this class are not supported. Finally, this approach generates tables that are not normalized and could potentially create limitations in querying data.

Summary

Telerik OpenAccess ORM is a powerful ORM solution that offers great flexibility and a large amount of features.

With the launch of the new Visual Entity Model Designer, the process of creating the data model has become even easier, but the Enable Project Wizard is still available and continues to be a common way to work with OpenAccess.

The configuration process is fairly simple, and the suggested approach is to create the data model in a separate project to allow the application to be more scalable and easier to test and to enable other applications to work with the target database. You also gain the benefit of allowing your application to migrate from one database system to another without changing your code.

Every data operation in OpenAccess is executed within the scope of a transaction. Transactions guarantee that either all operations executed will succeed or none of them will. If all operations succeed, the transaction can be committed. However, if any of them fail, all operations are rolled back to protect the integrity of data.

Fetch plans enhance the performance of the application by reducing the number of queries that are sent back to the database for execution. Fetch plans are created from one or more fetch groups, which, in turn, list all the fields of a class that will be retrieved from the database with each call. By default, OpenAccess uses lazy loading to fetch data. With fetch plans, you can instead direct OpenAccess to behave more eagerly when retrieving data from the database.

OpenAccess supports forward and reverse mapping for all the supported databases. With forward mapping, you can define how your persistent classes will be generated into tables using strategies that take advantage of the inheritance hierarchy. Four mapping strategies are supported, flat (the default), vertical, mixed (flat and vertical), and horizontal.

Index

A

B

C

D

E

F

G

H

I

J

L

M

N

O

P

R

S

T

Breinigsville, PA USA
09 July 2010
241457BV00005B/1/P
9 781430 229407